The Stone Circles of the British Isles

The Stone Circles
of the
British Isles

AUBREY BURL

Yale University Press
New Haven and London

Library of Congress catalog card number: 75-43311

International standard book number: 0-300-01972-6 (cloth)
0-300-02398-7 (paper)

Designed by John Nicoll and set in Monophoto Times

Filmset and printed in Great Britain by
BAS Printers Limited, Over Wallop, Hampshire

Published in Great Britain, Europe, Africa, India and South East Asia by
Yale University Press, Ltd., London.
Distributed in Australia and New Zealand
by Book & Film Services, Artarmon, N.S.W., Australia;
in Japan by Harper & Row, Publishers, Tokyo.

To The Memory Of

JOHN AUBREY
1626–1697
of Easton Pierse, Wiltshire

'The Father of British Archaeology'

Whose work made 'those walke and appeare that have layen in their graves many hundreds of yeares: and to represent as it were to the eie, the places, Customes and Fashions, that were of old Times.'

Contents

4 The Stone Circles of Cumbria and their Function

5 Other Early Open Stone Circles

List of Plates

ACKNOWLEDGEMENTS FOR THE PLATES
Permission to reproduce plates has kindly been given by the following who
retain the copyright: nos 25, 33, Aerofilms Ltd.; 35, B. T. Batsford Ltd.;
5, 8, 10, 14, Crown Copyright, National Monuments Record, London; 7, 9,
30, 34, Crown Copyright, reproduced with the permission of the Controller
of Her Majesty's Stationery Office; 3, 16, 17, 18, Crown Copyright, repro-
duced by permission of the Department of the Environment; 11, 20, 31,
Crown Copyright, Royal Commission for Ancient & Historical Monuments,
Scotland; 27, 28, Crown Copyright, Historic Monuments Branch, Dept. of
Finance, Belfast; 24, 26, Commissioners of Public Works in Ireland; 29, Dr
J. Pilcher; 12, 36, West Air Photography, Weston-super-Mare; 4, Reece
Winstone; 1, 6, 13, Charles Woolf.

List of Text Figures

NOTE ON MAPS AND PLANS

Wherever possible True North rather than Magnetic North has been indicated, pointing to the top of the plan. Standing stones are shown in black, fallen as outlines.

With diameters of some rings in the British Isles being ninety times greater than others it was not feasible to keep a constant scale throughout the book; but wherever necessary each diagram has a common scale for the plans of all its stone circles.

Land-heights are shown in feet, the relevant contours being selected for the height at which steep inclines become significant in that area.

List of Tables

Abbreviations in Text

AOC	All-Over-Corded (Bell) beaker (Steps 1–2), *c*.2100–1900 bc.
bc	Radio-carbon years before 0 AD.
BC	Astronomical or 'real' years before 0 AD.
B/W	'Barbed-Wire' beaker (Steps 3–4), *c*.1900–1750 bc.
C-14	Dates based on radio-carbon analysis.
E	European (Bell) beaker (Steps 1–2), *c*.2100–1850 bc.
E.C.	Egyptian Cubit of 52.4 cm.
ECC	Enclosed Cremation Cemetery.
M.Y.	The Megalithic Yard of 0.829 m (2.72 ft).
N/2	Developed Northern (short-necked) beaker (Steps 4–5), *c*.1850–1700 bc.
N/3	Late Northern (short-necked) beaker (Step 5), *c*.1800–1650 bc.
N/MR	Northern/Middle Rhine beaker (Step 3), *c*.1900–1800 bc.
N/NR	Northern/North Rhine beaker (Steps 2–4), *c*.1950–1750 bc.
O.D.	Ordnance Datum.
OHR	Overhanging-Rim Urn.
RSC	Recumbent Stone Circle.
s1	Primary Southern (long-necked) beaker (Step 5), *c*.1800–1600 bc.
s2/w	Developed Southern/Western (funnel-necked) beaker (Steps 5–6), *c*.1750–1550 bc.
s3/w	Late Southern/Western (long-necked) beaker (Step 6), *c*.1700–1550 bc.
W/MR	Wessex/Middle Rhine beaker (Steps 2–3), *c*. 1900–1800 bc.

N.B. For beakers the nomenclature follows Clarke (1970). The chronological Steps are from Lanting and van der Waals (1972).

Preface

In his evocative book, *Song of a Falling World*, Jack Lindsay wrote of the despairing lines of poets as the Roman empire shifted and crumbled. From Maximian's Fifth Elegy he quoted:

'O, you don't know, it's clear . . . don't know.
Not private grief, but the world's chaos I mourn.

The author of the present work, written during a comparable cultural maelstrom, has the same sentiment, for this book was prepared not on the expected rock of civilization but in a marshland of change. During the writing the old imperial units of length were sneakingly replaced by metrication so that the 42 ft diameter of Rhos y Beddau stone circle became an alarming 12.8016 metres. And the metre itself was shaken by a prehistoric poltergeist, the Megalithic Yard (=2.72 ft or 0.829 m), dismissed as a statistical illusion by some archaeologists but accepted genuflectionally by others as the rediscovered key to the decoding of stone circles. Worse came when the circles, with diameters oscillating between the three systems of measurement, ceased to be circular and were pressed into flattened rings, ovals and egg-shapes.

While the diameters were being recalculated the dates of the rings, apparently secure in a radiocarbon chronology, suddenly shot backwards into deep prehistory as the bristlecone pines of California's White Mountains disgorged annular growth-rings sometimes a thousand years older than the C-14 method had indicated.

Buttressed with metrication and C-14 recalibration tables the writer found he was still buffeted by swirling winds. Names of British counties, safe since the Norman Conquest, were by a parliamentary whim altered unrecognisably, so that Gloucestershire became Avon, Flintshire became Clwyd, and Argyll became Strathclyde, titles perhaps familiar to King Arthur and the Gododdin but not to Victorian antiquaries whose field-notes must be consulted by the student of stone circles (or ovals, egg-shapes *et al*). Although the old names have been retained in the text because they are so well known, yet the new have been recognised by being added in parentheses in the gazetteer at the end of the book.

Thus the study desk had now to support not merely archaeological files containing the data from fieldwork and excavations but also records of mathematical, chronological and geographical transmutations. As a gloss, the Ordnance Survey decided to issue new 1:50,000 maps in place of the beloved 1 in Series so that even sheet-numbers lost their usefulness as references—but for only half the country! (Because the majority of stone circles are in those areas where the 1 in O.S. maps are still current, contour heights have been expressed in imperial feet.) There remained, however, the ultimate consolation, that the megalithic rings stayed where their builders had put them.

As I write this I learn that the circle at Moncrieffe, Perthshire (now Tayside), once 29 ft 10 in in diameter but now 9.1 m (or 11 M.Y.) has been moved from its original position at NO 133193 and re-erected near Moncrieffe House to make room for the improved road. That it remains circular is a matter for gratitude.

This searching after Antiquities is a wearisome Taske.

John Aubrey

Acknowledgements

During the preparation of this book I had much help from many archaeologists. In particular I must thank Dr Colin Burgess, Dr Graham Ritchie, Mr Derek Simpson and Dr John Waddell for reading some chapters. They corrected many errors and the blame for idiosyncratic opinion is mine alone. The generosity of Mr John Barber and Mr James Kenworthy in permitting me to read their unpublished researches on the recumbent stone circles of Ireland and Scotland respectively is something for which I shall always be in their debt as I am to Dr Ronald Hicks for sending me his dissertation about the Irish henges. I am also grateful to other scholars for discussions on the problems of stone circles: Mr William Griffiths; Miss Audrey Henshall; Miss Frances Lynch, Dr Isla McInnes and Mr Jon Patrick.

Many people were so kind as to send me plans and information: Mr. Michael Ansell; Mr Andrew Davidson and his nephew, Lt. Colin Davidson, R.N.; Mr Christopher Dunn; Mr Laurence Flanagan; Mr Andrew Fleming; Professor P-R Giot; Mr. Christopher Houlder; Mr Ian Keillar; Mr A. C. MacCarthy and his daughter, Cliona, who unwearyingly tramped the hills of Cork collecting data on the hitherto neglected Munster circles that they could send me. Other information came from Dr Euan MacKie; Mr Lionel Masters; Mr Roger Mercer about the location of Hautville's Quoit; Mrs Henrietta Miles; Mr Leslie Myatt; Professor Michael O'Kelly who snatched time from his New Grange excavations to clarify some of the enigmas of Cork prehistory; Mr Sean O'Nuallain; Mrs Sheila Pollard; Dr Margaret Stewart; and Professor Alexander Thom who, as he always is, was most helpful in his explanations of complex astronomical matters, and who provided me with much reference material. Mr Alfred Truckell of Dumfries Museum sent me details of forgotten circles. To these, and to all those with whom I have corresponded so greatly to my benefit, my sincere thanks for a graciousness I cannot repay.

From Kingston upon Hull College of Education came several grants that enabled me to visit and plan circles in distant parts, helped by my students who gallantly concealed their fatigue whether on Dartmoor, South-west Scotland, Cumbria, Derbyshire or elsewhere.

I must also express my appreciation of the staffs of several departments: to the gentlemen of the Archaeology Division, Ordnance Survey, Southampton, and to the equally helpful and courteous Scottish Ordnance Survey, at both of whose offices I explored the reference cards; to the National Museum of Antiquities of Edinburgh; to the National Museum of Ireland, Dublin, for information about Leinster sites; and to the Archaeological Survey of Eire, especially to Mr Peter Danaher, for similar services. The library staffs of both Leicester University and, in particular, of my own College were always ready to help with advice, and obtained elusive literature, usually at the shortest notice. The editors of *American Scientist* kindly permitted me to use excerpts from my paper on the dating of British stone circles.

I can only marvel at the patience and kindness of my late colleague, Miss Jean Warwick, who typed and amended the whole of a cross-annotated manuscript, and to whose assistance this book owes so much. Many improvements were made upon the advice of my editor, Mr John Nicoll whose guidance and interest I deeply appreciated.

And what my wife, Margaret, underwent while a decade of stone circles revolved around her cannot be imagined. Six hundred years ago Chaucer understood:

> What is bettre than wisdom? Womman. And
> What is bettre than a good womman? No-thing.

A Note on Dating Conventions

Because of past fluctuations in the level of atmospheric radio-activity, Carbon-14 determinations do not provide the precise dates once expected from them, and by the second and third millennia bc are too low. Such 'dates' can sometimes be tested against historical records and tree-ring dating, particularly the long-lived bristlecone pine, and a perceptible widening between C-14 and 'real' dates has been realized from about 1000 bc backwards. A calibration table correlating these differences (McKerrell, 1971) enables corrections to be made wherever necessary, although there are still considerable doubts (Switsur, 1973) about the accuracy of such corrections. So that readers may know which type of date is being used in this book all dates based on C-14 determinations are followed by bc, real years by BC. It will be appreciated that astronomical dates, which are calculated from exact celestial events, are 'real' and so followed by BC. All radiocarbon determinations are followed in brackets by their laboratory references.

Introduction

This Inquiry, I must confess, is a gropeing in the Dark; but although I have not brought it into a clear light; yet I can affirm that I have brought it from an utter darkness to a thin mist.

John Aubrey

To begin a book about stone circles by mentioning Stonehenge is like starting a discussion on birds by talking about the Dodo. Neither is a typical example of its class. Both are above average in size, of peculiar construction, and both represent a dead-end in development.

Yet if one were to ask what stone circles were many people would think of Stonehenge, a vague image coming to their minds of cumbrous pillars raised in antiquity by druids and their followers, stones arranged in a dark and dramatic ring where sacrifices of the most repelling and fascinating nature took place. Further questioning might evoke impressions of astronomy or astrology and midsummer sunrise. A few people might recall associations with witch-craft and black magic. But all this would be connected with Stonehenge. Asked if they could remember the name of any other stone circle the answers, hesitantly given, might include Avebury enquiringly, the Rollright Stones uncertainly, and after that, if there was an after that, probably only the names of circles that happened to be in the neighbourhood of their homes.

Ignorance, however, is not to be equated with indifference. Stone circles all over the British Isles attract scores of visitors each year. Marked on the Ordnance Survey maps are hundreds of sites labelled 'stone circle' in Gothic lettering, rings of standing stones, the circles often being big enough to fit comfortably around a modern home, the stones shoulder-high, whitened by centuries of rain. Every year thousands of people trudge to these lonely rings hoping to sense something of their atmosphere for these are some of the surviving memorials to prehistoric people who raised such pillars only with much effort for reasons that few books ever attempt to explain. And stirred by the mystery of these silent circles on the hillsides and moorlands of Britain visitors today come to them, wander around the stones, ask each other what the circles were for, and leave disappointed because nowhere is there an explanation. There is only emptiness. For miles there is heather, sometimes burned black and twiggy, or patches of wiry grass near peat-bogs, low-growing bilberry and lichen, an occasional flicker of a butterfly, the soaring and swooping of curlews and whinchats against the clouds, but alone in the silence of the circle of stones the visitor receives no answers to his questions. There

1

Pl. 1. *Tregeseal, Cornwall*. The east circle from the south-west, with Carn Kenidjack in the background. The tallest stone, at the WSW., is on the left.

are, perhaps, twelve stones around him, some erect or leaning, some fallen and three-quarters covered with peat and turf. Worn, deep patches show where sheep have grazed or cattle have come to rub themselves against the uprights. There may be something of a hollow within the circle. But nothing else. The persistent enquirer may discover in the County museum a dull-brown pot labelled with the name of the stone circle. But nothing else.

Elsewhere he may have seen tall stones standing by themselves, sometimes seen round mounds like little hills clustering together that the maps call 'tumuli', and which he remembers are prehistoric burial-places. Sometimes, more fortunately, he has come upon a tomb whose chambers are built of huge stones, a megalithic monument, and alongside is a cast-metal sign stating briefly that the tomb was built in the New Stone Age around 2500 bc. But only rarely is there such a sign for any stone circle so that many visits end in frustration. In 1773 Dr Samuel Johnson reacted irritably to the sight of a stone circle near Inverness. 'To go and see one druidical temple is only to see that it is nothing for there is neither art nor power in it, and seeing one is quite enough.' It is hoped that the reader of this book will disagree.

In the centuries after Britain became an island around 6000 bc, prehistoric societies slowly changed their ways of life from hunting to farming. As far as is known, stock-breeding and agriculture were being practised in these islands as early as 3500 bc by people of the Neolithic or New Stone Age who still relied on flint and stone for their hardest, sharpest tools, and who settled on the easily-worked chalk uplands of southern and eastern Britain and of north-east Ireland. Gradually these early farmers cleared wide areas of woodland in the primordial forests, ring-barking the largest trees, cutting down others, burning and raking away the undergrowth to make open stretches where their crops could be planted. Sometimes the people built huge mounds containing timber- or stone-built chambers to which, over the years, many dead bodies were brought and from which, periodically, bones were removed for religious ceremonies. Many of these tombs, timber-lined in the east and south of Britain, stone-constructed in the west, still exist: passage-graves like New Grange in Ireland with its fantastically carved stones, and Maes Howe in the Orkneys; long mounds like West Kennet in Wiltshire or Stoney Littleton in Somerset with the impression of a huge fossil ammonite on one of its entrance slabs, chosen perhaps for its magical symbolism.

Early in the second millennium bc the immigration of new people from the continent and the spreading knowledge of metallurgy in copper and bronze caused changes not only in technology but also in society as people began acquiring valuable objects made of bronze or amber or gold. It is in the Early Bronze Age from about 1800 bc that archaeologists find evidence in the single graves of the time of rich possessions such as great bronze daggers buried with the dead, often under the increasingly popular round barrows. During a thousand years of warmer, drier weather farming methods slowly improved, field-systems took in ever wider areas, populations grew and extended onto the high lands where moors stretch today, the new settlers eking out a living from the stony soils until, around 1000 bc, in the Late Bronze Age, a deterioration in the climate forced changes in farming, in land-ownership and in social patterns that ultimately blended into the aggressions of the Iron Age during the first millennium when, for the first time, the class of priests and law-givers known as druids appear in history.

It is within the period between the middle of the Neolithic and the Late Bronze Age from approximately 2500 to 1000 bc that stone circles flourished. It is only within the middle of this time that the great stones of Stonehenge belong. And the monument was still being modified late in the second millennium when many of the simpler stone rings had already fallen into disuse or had been deliberately wrecked by people in the Middle Bronze Age who had no need for such circular stone settings, preferring in some cases to heap small stones over them to make a round cairn into which urned cremations could be inserted.

It is the archaeological misfortune of most stone circles that so much attention has been paid to Stonehenge, its date, the way in which it was erected, and the controversy over its possible astronomical function, that the other rings have been largely neglected. In most recent accounts of British prehistory, the others, more than nine hundred megalithic rings, are entirely ignored. Yet their mysteries are no less than those at Stonehenge.

It was years ago on a Sunday morning during the war that I first visited Stonehenge, walking in those bus-less days from Amesbury through the country and hardly seeing a car on the sunlit road. It is the only time I have known Stonehenge deserted but I was too ignorant of such luxury to appreciate it. But I do remember staring at the incredible lintels, tons of stone that had been raised onto the tops of other, obviously smoothed pillars and wondering how it had been possible for people before the mechanical Romans to have achieved such engineering, how, even, the standing stones themselves had been put up. To help me there was just one little guide-book with line-drawings by Heywood Sumner, which told me the stones had been lifted by Megalithic builders from the west who had mingled with vigorous incomers from the east known as Beaker Folk. It said something about how the stones were put up, and it did make one very important point. 'Stonehenge may come to be regarded not as an isolated monument but rather as the climax of a long chain of stone circles . . .' (Stevens, 1938, 4). But it hardly mentioned astronomy, and certainly had nothing to say about the reasons for designing such an amazing edifice and what it was used for by those remote people on Salisbury Plain.

How different thirty years later. In 1973, 703,000 people visited Stonehenge, and to accommodate the crowds the Department of the Environment has laid out a carpark with lavatories, refreshment stall and gift-shop on the other side of the A344 and has moled a tunnel beneath that holiday highway so that people may approach the monument safely. Ropes and railings protect the bank and ditch from obliteration. Attendants lurk around the stones. The ticket-office sells not only Stonehenge wine-mats and tea-towels, colour slides and photographs but also guide-books in English, French and German about the various phases of the site, about its purpose and about its astro-nomical design. Laden with camera and compass the visitor can inspect stone after stone at his leisure, perhaps disappointed at how small Stonehenge is because photographs always seem to exaggerate its Cyclopean nature, but at least provided with a deal of information about its history.

Regrettably, elsewhere the position is much as it was for Stonehenge thirty years ago. At Avebury, eighteen miles north of Stonehenge, a gigantic circle within a bank and ditch and with an avenue of stones leading up to it, there is, it is true, a small, pleasant museum, and a smaller shop run by the Department of the Environment, that sells pictures but the information about Avebury itself is contained within just a few pages of a booklet about the prehistoric sites in the district. If, undespairing, the seeker of stone circles should travel thirty-eight miles to the north he will arrive at another of the most famous rings in the British Isles, the Rollright Stones in Oxfordshire, long known in folk-stories for its associations with witchcraft, standing alongside a lane in the lovely Cotswold countryside.

Over six hundred years ago a Cambridge clerk wrote: *In Oxenefordensi pago sunt magni lapides* . . . '(In the Oxford country there are great stones, arranged as it were in some connection by the hand of man. But at what time this was done, or by what people, or for what memorial or significance, is unknown. Though by the inhabitants that place is called Rollendrith)'.

But at what time . . . by what people . . . is unknown. For the casual visitor this is still true. At Rollright there is now a small hut where one may buy postcards. Even today, however, there is no information to satisfy the questioner, just the stones, half-surrounded by trees and separated from the lane by iron railings. And as Stonehenge, Avebury and the Rollright Stones are among the very few stone circles in the British Isles where material is sold on the site the visitor might understandably believe that there was nothing else to be learned about the other rings, that a stone circle was simply that, a ring of worn, standing stones put up long ago for reasons lost to our knowledge, and that for a visitor to go to other sites would be a waste of time. That this is often not true can be shown by looking at just one such ring with rather more care.

Sloping down to the sandy shallows of Morecambe Bay in north-west England is Birkrigg Common, and on the gentle eastern slope of the common is a ring of stones. Here in a clearing amongst the summer bracken are ten little stones on the circumference of a perfect circle. The ring is easily visited. Along the coast the main road runs south from Ulverston and just beyond Bardsea a minor road leads westwards over the common. Beyond a wood the road is unfenced and a short stroll brings one to the circle. Predictably it is called the Druids Temple.

The ring has bracken all around it but the limestone blocks stand whitely against the grass in a ring only a few metres across, some stones hip-high, others almost covered by turf. A critical observer will notice that two of the tallest are at the south-west flanking the lowest. The biggest of all is at the north. Not far away up the rise an outcrop shows the probable source of the stones, suggesting that prehistoric people chose the site partly because of such a convenient quarry, partly because here there was a level terrace on which to erect their stones. All this the visitor may work out for himself. But there is little more that he could learn without reference to old journals that are not easily located.

The fact is that the Druids Temple is not merely one circle but two concentric rings of which only the inner is apparent, the low and tumbled stones of the outer circle, about 26 m across, being concealed by the bracken. And where the visitor stood near the centre, Bronze Age people four thousand years before had dug little pits into which they placed cremated human bone, maybe in leather bags, one cremation in an urn, barely 14 cm high and decorated with fine cross-hatching where the unfired clay had been impressed with twisted cord or animal-gut. When the stone circle was excavated in 1911 and again in 1921 the archaeologists discovered several big patches of blackened earth and charcoal where the pyres may have burned. They found the pits, some stone tools, and a piece of red ochre that may have been used for body-painting much as the British Iron Age warriors are said to have patterned their bodies with blue woad before facing Caesar's invading Romans.

After the last pit had been dug, quite possibly many years after the first, the Bronze Age community had covered the entire central area with a rough paving of ice-borne cobbles, sealing the burials within the precincts of their stone circle. Such information enables the visitor in his imagination to reinhabit the ring with people who had aligned the south-western stones on the setting moon, for this is their direction, and at a particular time of the year had prepared for their ceremonies by decorating their bodies, had lit the great pyres, and finally had solemnly deposited the raked-up bones in a pit at the ring's centre.

Why they should do this and how such customs varied in different parts of the British Isles it is one of the purposes of this book to explain or, at the least, to indicate how the archaeological evidence may be interpreted, the point being that very little relevant information is available either at the sites themselves or even in the accessible literature. For the Druids Temple the guide-book says: 'Bardsea, Lancs. Situated on Morecambe Bay, with a sandy beach. One mile west are prehistoric stone circles.' There is nothing much more helpful elsewhere, for this or for the other nine hundred or more stone circles of the British Isles.

Today, like the dead fingers of Time, the stones jut from the ground, stark and unyielding to the enquiries of men who for centuries have asked why stone circles were built. Are they the wrecks of temples? Or astronomical observatories? Or is it that:

> 'Ever since the time of Stukeley archaeologists, ever more concerned with the accumulation of factual detail and less with the wider significance of the sites they investigate, have distracted attention from the possibility of an alternative approach to the problems of the past. Excavation can only test existing theories; and scientists, suspicious of the means by which they are reached, often fail to appreciate the views of poets and visionaries.' (Michell, 1973, 22.)

This may be so. Though it must be added that these visionaries customarily ignore the factual details in the construction of their own models of the past. Yet it is understandable that visitors to the rings of standing stones, often remote on moorlands far from cars and roads, will wonder why they were erected, the largest by rivers or in valleys, some of the smallest with low boulders half-hidden in long, wiry grass high in the hills. Few sites have explanatory notices. The lovely little ring of Altarnun on Bodmin, or the ruined, dark stones at Raedykes, Kincardine, stand in a perpetuated silence that the most careful inspection does not change.

The purpose of this book is to provide an introduction to the problems of stone circles in the British Isles. Despite many local studies there has never been a comprehensive survey of these monuments. In 1849, Herbert wrote in *Cyclops Christianus*: 'Few things have interested antiquarians more than the remarkable systems of unhewn stone erected with prodigious labour in these islands. Many conjectures have been expended [on them] . . . with singular ill success.' Here there is more conjecture, but, at least, based on that very accumulation of detail that is archaeologically necessary for any understanding of these prehistoric sites. The text, moreover, contains the first comprehensive set of references for the many excavations, good and bad, which have taken place in these rings since the eighteenth century.

Although three centuries have passed since John Aubrey's survey of Avebury and nearly 250 years since William Stukeley made his plans and drawings of it, stone circles remain enigmas. They are still unclassified while chambered tombs, hill-forts, barrows, henges, causewayed enclosures and settlements have been excavated, catalogued and analysed. There are two important reasons. The first is the lack of associated material. Charcoal is often present but has rarely, as yet, been used for dating. Pottery is scarce, other artefacts scarcer. This paucity of evidence has both deterred the archaeologist and attracted the fantast to whom the stones offered visions untrammelled by facts.

William Blake wrote of 'stony Druid temples' in *Jerusalem* and of how men 'reared mighty stones, danced naked around them', but there is no need to search as far back as the eighteenth century for exceptional notions of the functions of these circles. In the last few years there has been a book about Stonehenge as one of the five great cities of Britain (Crampton, 1967); another asserting that the architect of Stonehenge was Gwlyddin, a name to be translated as, 'Hero, foremost expert man of the Grey Stones' (Peach, 1961); and yet another stating that Stonehenge was built by Egyptian colonists and redesigned by Delian Greeks who insisted it should be dedicated to the god, Hyperborean Apollo (Ivimy, 1974). Modern Druids continue to visit Stonehenge. It has been supposed that stone circles were built in situations chosen by prehistoric water-divining (Underwood, 1969); that Canterbury Cathedral stands on the site of an earlier stone circle aligned on Betelgeuse (Borst, 1969); and that stone circles formed a gigantic telepathic network whose purpose remains obscure (W. G. Williams, 1968). It has even been suggested that beaker people, the first British metalusers, were Martians (Lethbridge, 1973, 110).

There may be obliquities of truth in some of this but such a mélange has not been conducive to more objective studies, and many archaeologists have been reluctant to tread far in the lush, lunatic pastures at the edges of their own well-tilled fields. Sober material on stone circles is today in much the same state as that on chambered tombs fifty years ago. There has been no corpus, only much fragmented work of variable quality. This book is an attempt to offer a distillation of the data from excavations, from field-studies and, sometimes, from the visionary, to indicate something of the present understanding of these sites.

A stone circle may be defined as an approximately circular setting of spaced standing stones which do not act as a kerb and which flourished from the Late Neolithic into the late stages of the Bronze Age, or from the mid-third millennium bc to the end of the second. Integrated with the structure may be banks, ditches, single stones, avenues, or other auxiliary settings which vary from locality to locality. The definition excludes cairn or barrow kerbs even when their height is considerably greater than the adjacent part of the mound they enclose, but it does include settings of detached stones around some chambered tombs like New Grange, Meath, and the Clava cairns, Inverness.

Over 900 stone circles are known in the British Isles (Fig. 1), either still preserved, or ruined, or as sites where the former existence of a circle is well attested. They are distributed all over the highland areas with concentrations in north-east Scotland, in the outer Hebrides, around the Sperrin Mountains in Ulster, in south-west Ireland, in Cornwall and the Lake District. There are lesser groups in Wiltshire and Somerset, in Wales, Dartmoor, the Peak District, Westmorland, Caithness and the Orkneys, and in Northumberland.

The number is arbitrary for it is impossible to establish how many circles have been destroyed and forgotten. The extension of agriculture into marginal lands in the late eighteenth and nineteenth centuries AD gave an incentive to farmers to bury, to blast or to haul away the stones of an obstructive circle, though, fortunately, superstition sometimes caused them to leave a few stones standing. This happened at Fortingall, Perthshire, where three neighbouring circles were deliberately buried deep in the ground in accidental conjunction with a century-old beer bottle. In each case, three stones were left erect. Folklore has it that when one of the Devil's Quoits, Oxfordshire, was removed to make a bridge over a nearby stream it invariably slipped into the water however carefully it was bedded in the banks, and, finally, it was returned to its place in the circle. Similarly, the capstone was taken from the Whispering Knights portal dolmen near the Rollright Stones circle by 'a farmer for his outhouse. In taking it downhill his waggon is broken and the horses killed. Next his crops failed, cattle died &c. His only remaining horse is put into a cart, and takes it up with ease. Then all goes well with him.'. (A. Evans 1895, 27.) There are many stories like this of the supernatural dangers attending the moving of old stones and it is probable that many megalithic monuments survived only because of country superstition. Others were preserved because of the dangers inherent in toppling the heavy pillars. A mediaeval barber was crushed to death at Avebury. And John Aubrey reports that, 'one Daniel

Fig. 1. The Distribution of Stone Circles in the British Isles. Important sites are named. Numbers and letters refer to Chapters and Sections in the text.

Healy, of Donaghmore, in Ireland, having three times dreamed that Money lay concealed under a large Stone in a field near where he lived, procured some Workmen to assist him in removing it, and when they had dug as far as the foundation, it fell suddenly and killed Healy on the spot'.

But often economics overcame fear. At Annaside, Cumberland, of a twelve-stone circle, 18.3 m in diameter, standing in 1803, one stone remains today. Carbalintober, Londonderry, was destroyed in 1833. At Grey Croft, Cumberland, a complete circle was buried in 1820. At Newbigging, Angus, a circle stood on an immense cairn. Four hundred cartloads of stones were removed from it. What was left of the circle was scheduled for protection in 1955. Within three years it was destroyed.

On many occasions destruction was caused by ignorance but even archaeological awareness was not always an adequate safeguard.

'In a western parish of Cornwall, some labourers were employed in enclosing waste land, when they came across a stone circle, and suspecting it to be akin to others popularly held in veneration, they hesitated to destroy it, and appealed for advice to a mine captain, who decided if noticed in Borlase (1754) it should be preserved, if not, it should be demolished. The doctor's *Antiquities* being referred to, and no mention of the circle found, it was at once cleared away.' (Blight, 1865.)

Even the indignation of landowners at the vandalism of their tenants was sometimes ineffective. At Strichen House, Aberdeenshire, a recumbent stone circle was pulled down in 1830; Lord Lovat, in whose grounds the circle had stood, ordered it to be restored. It was. But not all the stones were replaced, and those that were were re-erected in wrong positions so that the recumbent stone was set at the north instead of the SSW. (F. R. Coles, 1904; Thom, 1967, 142). Saddest of all, this abused site was finally destroyed in 1965 in the course of tree-felling with no preliminary excavation and no protest. Another site on a lovely mountainside at Pen y Beacon, Brecknockshire is now partly covered by a car-park.

The stone circles that have survived are often to be found in unpopulated areas. Other sites may be protected by the Department of the Environment as scheduled monuments. But it has not been only modern man that affected stone circles. Some like Cavancarragh, Fermanagh, were until recently lost under peat and there must be many still concealed. At Er Lannic, Brittany, an entire circle is submerged beneath the sea. Some stone circles in remote or overgrown areas are still being discovered (Keillar, 1972). Some like Bryn Celli Ddu, Anglesey, were incorporated into later prehistoric monuments (Lynch, 1969, 111; C. O'Kelly, 1969), or re-arranged (R. J. C. Atkinson, 1960, 77, 80).

To compound confusion there are also fakes and follies like those put up for modern Welsh Eisteddfods; or 'Gothick' romances like the Druid Temple near Ilton, Yorkshire, built by William Danby in the early nineteenth century; or Auldgirth, Dumfries, a circle and centre stone erected about 1827; or Ravensdale Park, Louth, almost certainly a bogus monument. To these spurious imitations can be added sites wrongly identified as the remains of stone circles. This was frequent in the nineteenth century when the ruins of passage-graves were often confused with circles. The remark of Westropp (1893) about Tountinna, Tipperary, 'a fine stone circle which still bears the name of "The Graves of the Leinster Men"', is typical. The site is a chambered tomb. Comparable errors occurred at monuments like the Wren's Egg, Wigtown, which the Royal Commission called the surviving elements of a huge concentric circle with central stone, whereas inspection shows it to be an erratic boulder and a pair of standing stones a little to its south, the pair being similar to several others in the vicinity. To these cases of mistaken identity can be added the stone circles that never were, sites where outcrops and scree have been misinterpreted. It happened often on mountainsides where the masses of tumbled stone could be descried as the wreckage of a stone circle (Bushell, 1911), and it happened at Summerhouse Hill, Lancashire, where the collapsing of a tor caused a clutter of stones about the top of the hill. Nearly all the smaller stones were removed for the building of a summerhouse on the site leaving only a few of the larger blocks forming the south-west arc of an apparently toppled circle 140 m in diameter with an outlying stone (North and Spence, 1936).

It can be seen that to put even an approximate figure to the original number of stone circles in the British Isles is an impossibility. All that can be said, with some caution, is that over 900 sites are recorded, and it is from this information that this book comes.

The earliest date yet recorded for a stone circle is the average of the series of C-14 determinations from New Grange, Meath, of 2465 bc ± 40 (GrN-5463); 2475 bc ± 45 (GrN-5462); and 2585 bc ± 105 (UB-361), averaging 2508 bc. The latest is from Sandy Road, Scone, Perthshire, of 1200 bc ± 150 (GaK-787). If these radiocarbon dates are converted into real years the chronological span is from about 3300–1500 BC, a period of 1800 years which must be considered the shortest time over which stone circles were being built.

Even if it is assumed that for each known circle two others were destroyed this would make an original total of about 2,700. If it is also proposed that two-thirds of them were constructed during the major period of circle-building between 2500 and 1600 BC this still would mean that 1,800 circles were erected in the whole of Britain over a span of 900 years, a rate of only two circles a year. It is likely that within specific localities there was a concentration of building over shorter periods but, notwithstanding, there is no need to seek for zealots and proselytizing missionaries advocating a crash-programme of building in order to observe the next lunar eclipse. Instead, one may believe in the slow dissemination of ideas amongst conservative societies more accustomed to perpetuation than innovation.

But slow as the spread may have been there is reason to think that the cult

Pl. 2. *Midmar Kirk*, *Aberdeenshire*. A recumbent stone circle seen from the north. The recumbent stone is flanked by tall pillars. The graded heights of the other stones is apparent. The site now stands in a churchyard as the gravestones show, a good example of the 'christianisation' of a pagan monument.

was a compelling one. One has only to consider the transportation of two different types of rock to Stonehenge to realize the strength of the tradition. Moreover, in a muted form it endured into the Christian era when bishops, alarmed at the survival of pagan beliefs, ordered churches to be built alongside or even within some circles and henges. Today one may still see Britain's tallest monolith standing in Rudston churchyard, Yorkshire; or a stone circle in the cemetery at Midmar, Aberdeenshire; or a church inside the henge of Knowlton, Dorset. In AD 452 the Lateran Council forbade the worship of stones 'in ruinosis locis et sylvestribus', and in 658 a council at Nantes decreed: 'As in remote places and in woodlands there stand certain stones which the people often worship, and at which vows are made, and to which oblations are presented—we decree that they all be cast down and concealed in such a place that their worshippers may not be able to find them.' But at Carnac, Brittany, the old customs continued up to the last century when barren wives still visited the stones whose power to create fertility was affirmed by generations of mothers. In AD 1560 the Synod of Argyll found it necessary to destroy a stone circle on Iona under whose twelve stones 'men had been buried alive' because people continued to worship in it (Swire, 1966, 4). In Ireland some standing stones were still painted white at Easter this century for reasons long forgotten (E. E. Evans, 1966, 21). Witches visited Rollright in 1949 for a May sabbat. It seems that some flickers of the past continue to illuminate stone circles. Myths of the Merry Maidens; the Pipers; the witch and her daughters are occasionally recorded. When such a fragment of folklore appears to help in the understanding of a circle it will be included alongside the known archaeology in the sense of the material remains.

CHAPTER ONE

The Earlier Work on Stone Circles

By my meanes many Antiquities have been reskued and preserved (I myself now inclining to be Ancient)—or else utterly lost and forgotten.

John Aubrey

Although there are so many stone circles in the British Isles there has been little systematic investigation of them. Here only a brief account of the development of field-archaeology can be given and readers interested are referred to Daniel, (1967) and Ashbee, (1972).

In his *History of the Kings of Britain*, c. AD 1136, Geoffrey of Monmouth wrote of Merlin moving the Giants Ring from Mount Killaurus in Ireland to Salisbury Plain where it became known as Stonehenge, and he seems to have confused Avebury with Amesbury (Mount Ambrius). It is remarkable that he should claim the stones to be Irish when they did indeed come from a source on the Irish–Wessex trade-route (R. J. C. Atkinson, 1960, 185),[1] and even more remarkable that Mount Killaurus may be a mediaeval name for the mountains around Kildare and Wicklow where there are several stone circles of a form related to those in Wessex (Thorpe, 1966, 339). Nevertheless, mediaeval references to prehistoric sites are rare, and observations on stone circles tended to be factual: courts were held there (F. R. Coles, 1903) or a farmer's land lay near a stone circle (Stout, 1961). Interference with the stones was unusual, speculation about them even rarer so that although the Church may have looked upon them with suspicion, scholars looked on them not at all. Attitudes changed only slowly.

'This Monumente seemeth to importe an intention of the memoriall of some mater . . . though Time haue worne out the maner.' John Norden's comment on the Hurlers stone circles, Cornwall, in 1584, almost perfectly reflected the uncaring beliefs of past centuries and it was only towards the end of Elizabeth I's reign that visitations and itineraries were being written that would make Englishmen more aware of the antiquities of their country. Even so, Norden's work did include novelties like an account and drawing of the Nine Maidens circle. William Camden published his *Britannia* in 1586 and its first English version appeared in 1610. John Speed's fifty-four maps 'Maps of England &

---

[1]See Kellaway, (1971), for a discussion of the area from which the bluestones may have been brought to Stonehenge and whether men were involved.

Wales' came out between 1608 and 1610. Sir William Dugdale wrote the *Antiquities of Warwickshire*, 1656, and visited many other parts of the country. It was parts of his work that John Aubrey (1626–97) incorporated into his own unpublished 'Monumenta Britannica' (Bodleian MS. Top. Gen. c. 24–5).

This increase in curiosity about the ancient remains of the countryside provided the seedbed not only for Aubrey's work (A. Powell, 1948; 1949) but for his less well-known contemporaries like James Garden of Aberdeen who, although he had seen several local recumbent stone circles like Old Keig (Garden, 1766) could find 'nothing in the names of the monuments or in the tradition that goes about them, which doth particularly relate to the Druids'. Aubrey himself was realistic about the standards of contemporary archaeology: 'It is said of Antiquaries, they wipe off the mouldinesse they digge and remove the rubbish,' but was hopeful that his own work had been useful. 'Some of their temples I pretend to have restored, as Avebury, Stonehenge etc., as also British sepulchres.'

John Toland (1670–1721) discussed the problems of stone circles with Aubrey and wrote that the latter was 'the only person I ever met who had the right notion of the temples of the Druids, or indeed any notion that the circles so often mentioned were such temples at all', but it was he himself who was most responsible for the myth of an association between stone circles and Druids in his *History of the Druids*, 1726. The early eighteenth century was an age of neo-classicism and developing science. Into an atmosphere of reason in which Dr Johnson could kick a stone to prove its philosophical existence came a reactionary passion for unspoiled wilderness and the unknown, romantic past. There were Grand Tours and lesser tours on which people visited Wales and Scotland instead of merely reading about them. And as more and more stone circles became known it was apparent that they could satisfy all sorts of needs from the scientifically astronomical to the Gothic demand for mystery. Even the associated Druids could be projected, according to taste, either as primitive but pure theologians or as barbarous and bloodstained necromancers.

From Martin Martin's *Description of the Western Isles* Toland read that Stenness and Brodgar in the Orkneys were believed by the natives to be places of pagan sacrifice with the sun being worshipped in the larger stone circle, the moon in the smaller. Toland wishfully deduced the same dichotomy for Callanish in the Hebrides. When one adds to this Smith's theory in 1771 that Stonehenge's Heel Stone was aligned on the midsummer sunrise it is clear that William Stukeley (1687–1765) with his certainty that Druids were the principal architects of stone circles was very much a creature of his time. Of Stukeley's own work there is no need to write for it has been described (Piggott, 1950). It is sufficient that he, despite his Druidical errors, more than anyone before him placed stone circles in a prehistoric context. Others were more vague in their dating:

> I will not forget these stones that are set
> In a round, on Salisbury Plaines,
> Though who brought 'em there, 'tis hard to declare,
> The Romans, or Merlin, or Danes.
>
> Walter Pope, 1676

And Bonney (1866) confirmed this tendency towards eccentricity: 'In England everything of unknown origin is instinctively assigned to one of four—Julius Caesar, King Arthur, the Druids, or the Devil.' Inigo Jones had argued that the circles were Roman; Charleton that they were Danish; Bolton that they were Ancient British, one being Boadicea's tomb; and Keysler that they were not Druidical but Anglo-Saxon monuments akin to those in his native Holstein. In contrast, Stukeley tried to demonstrate that Stonehenge and Avebury were larger representatives of many smaller sites. Unfortunately, he lost his objectivity in his search for snakelike avenues, suns and moons at Avebury, and Druids.

With the increasing knowledge of the past in the nineteenth century, the Druids slowly faded from the circles but little advance was made on any other front except for the persistent depredations of mid-nineteenth-century diggers in the centres of stone circles, achieving little but redeposited chaos for later excavators. Then, in the late 1870s, there was an explosion of fieldwork following the formation of many local archaeological societies. During a golden period of some thirty years between approximately 1880 and 1910 circles were visited, measured, planned and described all over Britain, though the writers seldom looked outside their county boundaries for related sites. It was in this time that areas were catalogued in: Cornwall (A. L. Lewis, 1896, 1898, 1899, 1905; Lukis and Borlase, 1885; C. F. Tregelles, 1906); Cumberland (J. C. Ward, 1876; C. W. Dymond, 1878, 1881); Derbyshire (J. Ward, 1905; A. L. Lewis, 1903; W. J. Andrew, 1907); Scotland (F. R. Coles, 1894–1911); and Ireland (J. P. Condon, 1916–18.) There were many other short reports of small groups and single sites. More recent, comprehensive surveys have been made: Dorset (S. and C. M. Piggott, 1939); Ulster (O. Davies, 1939a); Wales (Grimes, 1963); and Kerry (O'Nuallain, 1971.)

The late nineteenth century was the second great stage of stone-circle study after the work of Aubrey and Stukeley, but even this thirty-year Augustan Age was not without its problematical side. It was then that the advocates of an astronomical function for stone circles attracted the public's awareness. From A. L. Lewis (1883 et seq.) came many papers which were followed by N. Lockyer's *Stonehenge and Other British Stone Monuments Astronomically Considered* (1906b), a volume that was read with respect because it was by the Director of the Solar Physics Laboratory. The publication of a star-chronology (P. V. Neugebauer, 1929) made matters properly scientific. Somerville (1909 et seq.) continued beyond Lockyer with the examination of Irish and other sites. But because much peripheral work by other casual surveyors was careless it was of little value although its impact was great. One of its few opponents was Allcroft (1927) whose books were intended to show that stone circles were not observatories but moot-places of the early historical period.

Perhaps the scholarly archaeological climate of the 1930s was not conducive to travels across such troubled waters and, except for eddies in small local journals, stone circles submerged as a subject. The dubiety of the claims put forward for their more esoteric uses caused these monuments to be banished to the archaeological doldrums already occupied by Atlantis and the Old Straight Track, and the scholars themselves preferred to remain on the proper foundations of their subject rather than visit the astronomical quicksands into which circles appeared to be sinking. 'So much time and ingenuity has been spent on this matter in the past that it deserves some attention here if only to demonstrate the inadequacy of the arguments upon which it is based,' as R. J. C. Atkinson (1960, 93) wrote of Stonehenge's Heel Stone and sunrise.

The period since 1945 has been the time of the third progress. After the field-surveys of the beginning of the century which themselves were augmented by the work of the Ordnance Survey and the Royal Commissions for Ancient and Historical Monuments there is now more attention being paid to the establishment of the age of the sites and, more tentatively, of their function. Since 1964 at least a dozen stone circles have been acceptably excavated. Allied monuments like henges have been discussed by Atkinson, Piggott and Sandars (1951); Tratman (1967); Burl (1969) and Wainwright (1969–71). It has also been the time when different methods of investigation have been developed. Sometimes called the 'New Archaeology' and often expressed in tortuous, obfuscating word-patterns, its practitioners employ recently devised scientific techniques to compute and analyse the patterns of the past. 'Although their roots are old we suddenly have a number of vigorous, productive and competitive new paradigms which have condensed around the morphological, anthropological, ecological and geographical aspects of archaeological data.' (Clarke, 1973.)

Allied to these novel examples but more succinctly expressed is the work of Alexander Thom (1955 et seq.) whose studies of megalithic settings have resulted in claims that the builders of stone circles and rows had a standard unit of measurement, the Megalithic Yard (M.Y.); were capable of designing complex geometrical shapes; and had an erudite comprehension of the movements of sun, moon and stars. These views have been summarized by Hutchinson (1972) and Heggie (1972). Current thinking about archaeo-astronomy has been reviewed by Baity (1973).

'Every age has the Stonehenge it deserves—or desires,' wrote Jacquetta Hawkes, and this may explain the technological over-emphasis sometimes placed today on the functions of stone circles in the British Isles, which except where based on firm data are essentially little different from the Druidic fantasies of the eighteenth century.

Perhaps the greatest difficulty is to assess the societies that built and used the circles. If Late Neolithic and Bronze Age Britain was no more than a country of dispersed peasant-holdings, of skilful farmers knowledgeable about sources of stone and flint, combining at Autumntide for the building of chambered tombs and henges then the circles need be no more than megalithic rings used for communal ceremonies, each regional culture being doctrinally separate from the others. What is known of the primitive technology of the time does not contradict this aboriginal interpretation.

But more and more, some researchers speak of a unified Britain, of different regions it is true, but dominated by an intellectual élite of astronomer-priests whose influence extended north and south even into the farthest, quietest valleys. What archaeological evidence there is points to a time of peaceful existence and drier weather, a time when arcane knowledge of the movements of the moon and sun might be developed without interruption, a period very necessary if observations sometimes had to extend over a hundred years to delineate a particular alignment. During such an age the religious ceremonies which at first were simple and communal supposedly became increasingly complex as did society itself, evolving from egalitarian bands into a tighter, hierarchical structure of chiefs and concomitant priests who would organize and conduct the codified rituals. It is claimed that such rites were rooted in astronomy.

Once the existence of a nationally-used Megalithic Yard is accepted the idea of a unity across Britain must also be accepted, however modified locally. The similarities in architecture and function of many stone circles suggest the same thing. Yet there is a caveat. At least one major group of sites in north-east Scotland does not appear to conform to this national pattern and may have an origin different from the majority. So may others in Ireland. Another difficulty is the entire absence of written records that could confirm the astronomical theories, although some incised grooves on a bed-slab at Skara Brae, on a chalk plaque found near Stonehenge, and on antlers from Maxey, Northamptonshire, have been seen as lunations to mark calendrical phases of the moon. Whether they are or not, other than these if astronomical data was recorded the equipment has perished. Or it may simply have been memorized much as the Iron Age Druids remembered the thousands of bardic verses of their laws, needing, according to Caesar, some twenty years to assimilate the entire corpus.

Perhaps the monuments are their own record, containing within their stones the measurements, the geometrical designs, the remains of ceremonies, the astronomical orientations whose rediscovery could recreate today some of the activities that once took place within them. Possibly such science is an illusion evoked by a modern reaction from the belief in a noble savage and similarly prejudiced. The intention in this book is to gather together the data from excavation reports, from field-studies and astronomical surveys. Some material comes from written descriptions, and much from visits to nearly 400 megalithic rings. As John Aubrey wrote: 'These Antiquities are so exceedingly old that no Bookes doe reach them, so there is no Way to retrive them but by comparative antiquitie, which I have writt upon the spott, from the Monuments themselves.'

CHAPTER TWO

The Origins Of Stone Circles

Let us imagine then what kind of Countrie this was in the time of the ancient Britons.
John Aubrey

1. INTRODUCTION

Six thousand years ago families were entering Britain from western and northern Europe, crossing the sea in timber-framed skin boats, bringing with them a knowledge of farming. They also brought with them concepts of religious belief different from those of the Mesolithic natives. Semi-nomadic groups of these first farmers roamed the hill-ridges above the forested wildernesses of the British Isles, searching for good soil, clearing the trees, cultivating patches of land, struggling against the untouched countryside (A. G. Smith, 1970, 90). Their beliefs gradually changed, blended, were occasionally manifested in stone monuments, themselves sometimes copies of wooden or earthen prototypes. Across a thousand years the mixing and change continued until at some time, perhaps in the mid-third millennium bc, a stone circle was built. Where it was built, when, and from what impulse it came are unanswerable questions. The people who built it are gone and our own judgements, lacking an assemblage of dates and artefacts, are no more than speculative.

It is impossible today to indicate with certainty a single source from which the custom of erecting megalithic rings developed. It is possible to say that the great, open stone circles are indigenous to the British Isles and that their beginnings probably lie within the third millennium bc. Beyond that one can consider several sources, always with the reservation that a variety of circles possibly had a variety of origins which may now be impossible to define with assurance. A starting point is still needed. It has been argued elsewhere (Burl, 1973) that the very large circular settings may be amongst the earliest in the series, but this must remain a hypothesis in the absence of positive dating. The problem is further complicated by the probability that there are several types of stone circle in the British Isles, each with an ancestry different from the others. Thus it becomes necessary to examine earlier and disparate monuments in the hope that within them may be detected elements that could have developed into stone circles. In 1927 Callander proposed the evolution of the circles from the kerbstones that revetted the mounds of

19

megalithic tombs, a belief repeated by the surveyors of Hebridean tombs, '. . . nearly every one of the Hebridean round cairns . . . has had a fringe of large stones or boulders set either on edge or on end in a manner that suggests the stone circle in process of evolution.' (RCAHM-S, 1928.) These cairns, however, are almost certainly too late to provide such an ancestry. The reverse seems likely, that the existence of stone circles elsewhere impelled people to place tall stones around the bases of their own round cairns, a fusion of traditions resulting in monuments like spiky coronets. Such cairns may be seen on North and South Uist, and in Wales at Carn Llechart, Glamorgan, and Bryn Cader Faner, Merioneth.

Other writers believed the megalithic circle was a counterpart in stone of the earth or timber circles of lowland Britain. The paucity of dating material prevented them from constructing any typological sequence to substantiate this. Still others looked to those passage-graves of western Britain with surrounding stones or banks or ditches for a possible source. 'A low mound in Ballyanny townland near Nenagh appears to have a kerb and also a concentric ring of stones outside it. This phenomenon of a ring of stones encircling a burial mound is of interest in relation to the origin of the stone circle.' (S. P. O'Riordain, 1964, 90.)

But it has to be admitted that any typology of stone circles is, at present, innately unreliable because there are so few dates on which to construct it. Artefactual material is sparse and unevenly distributed. In the search for beginnings one can look only at various possibilities: that the British stone circles had a foreign origin; that they developed from ritual enclosures; or from passage-graves; or from timber circles; or from the circular embanked areas known as henges.

2. FOREIGN ORIGINS

It has sometimes been claimed that stone circles are to be found exclusively in the British Isles. This is true only for the great open circles of western Britain and even for these there are a few continental counterparts. Yet although forms of stone circle are known in many areas of Europe, those remote sites in Gambia or in India being of no relevance, they are usually later, smaller than the circles in Britain, and almost invariably they surround burial mounds.

In Italy there are *tomba a circulo*, tombs dating from the Neolithic to the Iron Age, with small stone circles around them. In Czechoslovakia burials of the Middle/Late Bronze Age Podoli culture are sometimes surrounded by a circle of stones. In western Europe, in the Iberian peninsula, there are some very small circles in the Alter Pedroso, Alentejo, Portugal (G. and V. Leisner, 1956) which may be connected with early prospectors for copper; and others in the Medonas da Mourela, Galicia, surrounding burial mounds of the mid-second millennium bc. Some of the passage-graves at Los Millares 9, notably gr. 1, and S601 (G. and V. Leisner, 1943) are encircled by standing stones. At Odilienberg, Alsace, there was a circle which Kendrick (1927) likened to Stonehenge but which was in fact a folly of the fourth century AD (Piggott, 1968, 71). Perhaps akin to this was the Cuvelée du Diable at Forrières, Luxembourg, which even a century ago consisted of six small trilithons (de Laet, 1958, 111) but which is now a ruin. Excavations early in this century produced no evidence of its date.

Further north, in Denmark, single or multiple settings of stones may encircle the oak coffin burials of the Early Bronze Age and boulder circles are fairly common in Scandinavia although belonging to periods as late as the Iron Age. Even later are the Viking dom-rings like that at Blomshulm, Bohuslan, where ten standing stones enclose a large area with a huge central stone (W. C. Borlase, 1897, II, 505). The same writer mentions many circles in Germany, and other continental references may be found in J. Anderson (1886) and Fergusson (1872).

It is noticeable that nearly all these monuments encircle burials and the concept of encompassing a grave mound with standing stones is so simple that it is not surprising to find it widespread. But with the exception of some French examples these continental circles are too far away or too late or too dissimilar to be the progenitors of the circles in Britain.

Some circles in France, however, near the Channel coast are very like others in the south-west peninsula of England and may belong to the same cultural group. They are not to be confused with the 'cromlechs' listed by the *Monuments Historiques* as stone circles. These are probably the remains of chambered tombs or groups of standing stones (Gilbert, 1962, 215–61). Among the proper stone circles is La Gorgue in the Pas de Calais, where ten large boulders were set in a circle 36.6 m in diameter, and the Breton examples of which Er Lannic (le Rouzic, 1930) is the best preserved. These sites have much in common with Cornish stone circles and must be considered related to them. But their associated artefacts indicate a date within the Early Bronze Age and this, as with the other continental stone circles, precludes them from being ancestral to those in Britain. It is necessary to look elsewhere for the origins of the latter.

3. RITUAL ENCLOSURES

As stone circles of the Late Neolithic period are entirely British monuments with only a few continental parallels it is probable that a source for them will also be British. As circular ritual enclosures are known in these islands from a very early time in the Neolithic the concept of erecting standing stones around a perimeter may have come from this tradition.

Our knowledge of the earliest peasant-farmers of Britain is slight. It is only lately that their immense long cairns have been considered centres for ritual rather than simple tombs for the burial of selected people. Their settlements and farmsteads are hardly known. Their religious beliefs are obscure. The sites may now be destroyed or overgrown or overlain by later constructions.

To seek a source for stone circles in these shadows is a quest undertaken by the optimistic or the desperate.

To the first agriculturalists of the British Isles, searching the strange, wild countryside for trees like the wych-elm that would indicate the presence of highly fertile soils, the need for propitiating the dangers of nature was great: lightning could start forest-fires; continual rain could make rivers impassable; diseases could kill families. The badger, the boar, the bear, the wolf, the snake, were the masters of the land; the deer could abandon its grazing-ground and leave starvation for its hunters; flint, so necessary for the tools of existence, could lie undetected beneath the chalk. The wheat had to ripen and be harvested, and a drought or heavy storm could destroy crops and then, more lingeringly, the people. To the newcomers with their primitive patch-farming there was no scientific safeguard or forewarning of disaster. Natural phenomena were part of man's experience and as unpredictable as man himself. Every bird, every tree, every thunderstorm had a life of its own and had to be communicated with personally, appeased and forestalled. 'Primitive man has only one mode of thought, one mode of expression, one part of speech—the personal.' It is within such a concept that the seeming irrationality of early religion has to be considered. Those ritual enclosures of the Early Neolithic that have been discovered contain evidence of superficially meaningless practices which may reveal the attempts of these people to obtain safety within their living and menacing world.

At one place, Goodland, Antrim, at the head of the cliffs above Murlough Bay, inside an oval ditched space, people had dug a score or more of pits over the years, pits holding nothing but earth, stones, charcoal, flints and pottery, 'the scraped up traces of abandoned settlements' (Case, 1969, 13). One pit with the Sandhills ware was dated to 2625 bc ±135 (UB-320E). Since many of the deposits were successive the 'shrine' must have been used over a long period, presumably for recurring ceremonies (Case, 1961, 203). Another ditched enclosure at Langford Lodge, forty miles south, had similar pits.

Such domestic deposits of earth and charcoal could have been obtained from former clearings where the freely growing weeds signified fertile ground. To use this powerful earth in rites of sympathetic magic would be understandable. To these practices was sometimes added the deposition of human bone, perhaps from another cult. Such open sites were occasionally superseded by stone-built tombs under which the original deposits were sealed. These burial-places acted as repositories for later material but also provided a formally enclosed area for the rituals, sometimes in circular forecourts. At Ballybriest, Tyrone, a court-cairn was built over a layer of dark earth with charcoal, broken pottery and cremated bone, the layer in its turn covering pits with earth, charcoal and broken sherds.

In other cases the 'shrine' was concealed beneath a huge cairn. At a site similar to Goodland, Knockiveagh, Down, a cairn had been built over a

8 mm thick layer of soil and charcoal with Lyles Hill pottery, broken stone axes and cremated bone. A date from this layer of 3070 bc ±170 (D-37) tentatively corrected to c. 3700 BC, shows how long a period one must consider when searching for the antecedents of megalithic ritual centres, the earliest of which may be unenclosed.

Crude pits filled with what might be offerings of domestic refuse are common at these sites. At others, particularly at some English Neolithic causewayed enclosures and later henges—huge earthwork rings used for 'tribal' meetings at particular times of the year—analogous pits holding settlement débris, charcoal and human bone were dug by these agriculturalists and then almost immediately refilled (I. F. Smith, 1971, 100). At South Cadbury hillfort, Somerset, the legendary hall of King Arthur, Neolithic pits held pottery, flint arrowheads, hazelnuts and a human lower jaw. One pit gave dates of 2510 bc ±120 (I-5970) and 2825 bc ±115 (I-5972). The pits had been refilled with clean red clay soon after being dug. The fifty-six Aubrey Holes of Stonehenge's first phase had been filled with chalk rubble and then reopened, only to be filled yet again with burnt soil and wood. One was dated to 1848 bc ±275 (C-602).

Many archaeologists have regarded these pits as indications of a cult of the underworld, being the means by which libations might be poured to the gods with other symbolic gifts. Such pits might be grotesquely proportioned. At Maumbury Rings henge, Dorset, the enormous bank ringed an area 36.6 m in diameter. At its inner edge were forty-four tapering pits up to 10.7 m in depth, containing antler picks, chalk phallic carvings and sherds of grooved ware, a form of Late Neolithic pottery often associated with henges in southern Britain. These pits, scores of cubic metres in capacity, had been filled in as quickly as the others. The history of Maumbury Rings demonstrates the changes to which prehistoric sites are prone for it was refashioned by the Romans into an amphitheatre. In the seventeenth-century Civil War the Parliamentarians used it as a defensive earthwork. And 'on the floor of the amphitheatre Mary Channing was executed by strangling and subsequently burnt, for poisoning her husband in the year 1706'.

The haphazard nature of pit-deposits in causewayed enclosures was replaced in the Late Neolithic by increasing formality. In henges like Maumbury and Stonehenge the pits were set just within the encircling bank, surrounding the open circular space that was used for the communal ceremonies. At most sites such pits were seldom dug more than once after which they were left undisturbed, and cannot have remained conspicuous unless the encroaching turf was regularly cut back. One wonders if they were marked to display their positions in succeeding years, perhaps by stakes or stones. If so, then their normal appearance would have been very like a timber or stone circle for which they might be the prototypes. Of late it has been suggested that such pits, so far from being allowed to revert to grassland, held posts that recorded precise astronomical alignments. Their main-

tenance would therefore be vital. Newham (1972, 18) makes a case for
regarding Stonehenge's Aubrey Holes in this way.

It may be remarked that the combination of pits and enclosures suggests
a dual purpose for the monuments, the ring being for meetings, the pits with
their domestic rubbish being relics of an ancient tradition of sympathetic
magic aimed at ensuring the continuing productivity of the land. In the same
millennium that such practices existed in Britain the builders of long tombs
were noting the movements of the sun and aligning the long axis of the
mound on it. Ultimately, elementary astronomical knowledge may have
been incorporated into the fertility ceremonies at the rings. Stonehenge I,
for example, and its counterparts may represent the fusion of three separate
elements: formalized meeting-place; fertility pits; and astronomical observation, all combining to form the complex ritual monuments of Late Neolithic
Britain.

Such monuments with their primary function of being foci for dispersed
groups that could meet, perhaps at Spring and Autumn, for trade and social
activities, were not mainly for any cult of the dead. There are other banked
and ditched circular enclosures of the period like those at Dorchester,
Oxfordshire (Atkinson, Piggott and Sandars, 1951), 13.7 m–24.4 m across,
with many human cremations in the central space and with peripheral pits.
Superficially they are similar to henges but they are really enclosed cremation
cemeteries related to later Bronze Age sites (J. N. G. Ritchie and MacLaren,
1972) and perhaps to those family cemeteries that occur beneath the covering
mounds of the mistitled 'single-grave' round barrows (Peterson, 1972). Each
of the Dorchester sites was possibly used by one family over a single
generation.

4. HENGES

Some of the earliest of the open stone circles may date from the last quarter of
the third millennium bc and may be found in Cumbria where they seem to
be the counterparts in stone of henges, the circular earthen enclosures with
bank and inner ditch of which Thornborough, Yorkshire, Maumbury Rings,
Dorset, and Avebury, Wiltshire, are examples. They were possibly meeting-
places to be attended at particular times of the year.

Just as in the early third millennium the Neolithic industrial manufacture
of stone axes shifted from Cornwall to north-western mountain sources
(Evens et al., 1962b; Evens, Smith and Wallis, 1972, 250) so at the same time
early henges were being built around the shores of the Irish Sea. In Wessex it
was only later that henges gradually superseded causewayed enclosures
which themselves, from dates obtained from Windmill Hill and Knap Hill,
Wiltshire, and Hambledon Hill, Dorset, seem to develop from about 2750 bc.
The succeeding southern English henges have been considered to be formalized
versions of these hilltop sites although the differences in situation and the
absence of henges from the causewayed enclosure areas of Sussex and
Middlesex complicate the possibility of a direct succession (D. R. Wilson,

1975). Instead, the Wessex henges with their grooved ware may ultimately have resulted from Irish influences, related to those earlier ritual enclosures, which in southern England replaced causewayed enclosures as the meeting-places for the scattered farming communities. Such an explanation would account for the proximity of Windmill Hill to the great circle-henge (a henge with a stone circle) of Avebury alongside the Ridgeway trade-route. The juxtaposition of other henges to causewayed enclosures (Ashbee, 1970, 104, 181) could have a similar explanation.

It is with causewayed enclosures that stone axes from north-west England are often associated. No fewer than thirty-one axes have been found in and near Windmill Hill (Stone and Wallis, 1951), including some from Cornwall, and others from the Group VI axe factory, Great Langdale, Westmorland; Group VII, Graig Llwyd, Caernarvon; Group VIII, Pembrokeshire; and Group IX, Tievebulliagh, north-east Ireland. Similar concentrations occur elsewhere: twenty-one near Avebury although only one came from the interior of that site; seven from the centre of Stonehenge; and thirteen in the Stourpaine region by Hambledon Hill. In Brittany, dolerite fragments from the factory at Sélèdin (Le Roux, 1971, 287) were abundant at the Camp-du-Lizo and, significantly, at the island of Er Lannic upon which stand two rare continental stone circles. Such clusters suggest that one of the functions of causewayed enclosures, henges and the great stone circles may have been axe-trading. Smith (1965, 19) observed: 'Such rallying-points play an essential role in the lives of some contemporary communities in a comparable stage of economic and technological development . . . Assembly of the scattered families . . . afford opportunities for the transaction of the necessary business of tribal life.' 'The most remarkable aspect of this phase is, however, the number and variety of stone implements then brought to the site. The Avebury district has been referred to as "the capital emporium of the whole axe-trade of the country". The real centre was Windmill Hill.'

Of the many stone axes found at Windmill Hill only 12 per cent each came from Cornish or Breton sources against at least 66 per cent from factories in North Wales and the Lake District, the sources that were being worked as the early henges were being built in their vicinity. An origin for henges in the north-west would account for the early dating c. 2650 bc of Llandegai I henge, Caernarvon. A Group VI polished axe in perfect condition had been deliberately buried beneath the bank. Llandegai lies in the first expanse of flat cultivable land on the coast eight miles west of the Graig Llwyd axe factory on Penmaenmawr, ideally situated for land or sea journeys. The idea that this henge might have been a place of pilgrimage for itinerant axe-traders (Houlder, 1968) or a seasonal gathering-place at which trading was one activity is attractive. What is improbable is that henges had only one purpose. Some vast enclosures like Durrington Walls, Wiltshire (Wainwright and Longworth, 1971), or Marden, Wiltshire (Wainwright, 1970a), may primarily have been secular centres, the foci of tribal areas. Trading, religious rites, tribal meetings and moots may all have been inextricably mixed at these monuments.

Henges may be found all over Britain (Burl, 1969). Yet only in the east did they proliferate. From Norfolk up to the Moray Firth they were built over a period of perhaps a thousand years. Along these coasts, as well as five or six indeterminate sites, there are at least thirty-two henges ranging from Arminghall, Norfolk, with a date for its internal timber structure of 2490 bc ± 150 (BM-129) to Cairnpapple, West Lothian, where the henge predates the overlying beaker cairn of the early second millennium bc, and up to Broomend of Crichie in Aberdeenshire, a probable two-phase monument whose urns and earlier beaker associations indicate a primary date as late as the seventeenth century bc.

It is pertinent to enquire why such a continuity is not apparent in the south-west or north-west in both of which areas the development of henges seems to have been stultified. An answer is that cognate sites do exist and with as long a history as the eastern henges but in the megalithic form of stone circles. In south-west England there are only three certain henges, all Class I (with only one entrance) and all near the coast south of the rock-strewn upland moors. One, Castlewitch, Cornwall, is within half a mile of Balston Down greenstone axe-factory. This and Castilly nearby, subsequently transmuted into a mediaeval *plen-an gwarry* for religious plays, are both small. The third, the Stripple Stones, on Bodmin Moor contains a stone circle. Yet in contrast to three henges, and even excluding Dartmoor with its insular sites, there are at least forty-three stone circles in the south-west peninsula, and it is clear that prehistoric people used the materials to hand for their building. On the high lands they built in the abundant stone.

Similarly in the north-west, although Llandegai I is early, there are few henges. Altogether in the Lake District only three are certainly known. These were built on low-lying land either in the Eden Valley or at the confluence of the rivers Eamont and Lowther near Penrith where Mayburgh, King Arthur's Round Table, and the uncertain site of the Little Round Table were to be found. The other great ritual monuments of the area are stone circles. There are at least fifty-six.

The explanation is plain. Even in regions outside the mountainous parts of the Lake District the digging of ditches and raising of banks could not have been easy, although the rock-cut ditches of Stenness and Brodgar must be borne in mind. The ditch at King Arthur's Round Table in soft river-silt with a low water-level provided only enough material for a 1.2 m high bank. At the Little Round Table the ditch was only 3.1 m wide and 1.2 m deep. And at Mayburgh no ditch at all was dug and the huge 6.4 m high bank was amassed from cobblestones. Purely in terms of mechanics it would have been more practicable to translate the earth bank of a henge into a 'wall' of stone. Differences in the difficulty of building a megalithic tomb instead of an earthen long barrow have been described (Atkinson, 1968, 91) and a similar problem might have existed in the context of henges and stone circles in the highlands. Several of the large stone circles are set within low earth banks, perhaps in recognition of a henge-ancestry, or perhaps evidence of multi-phase construction.

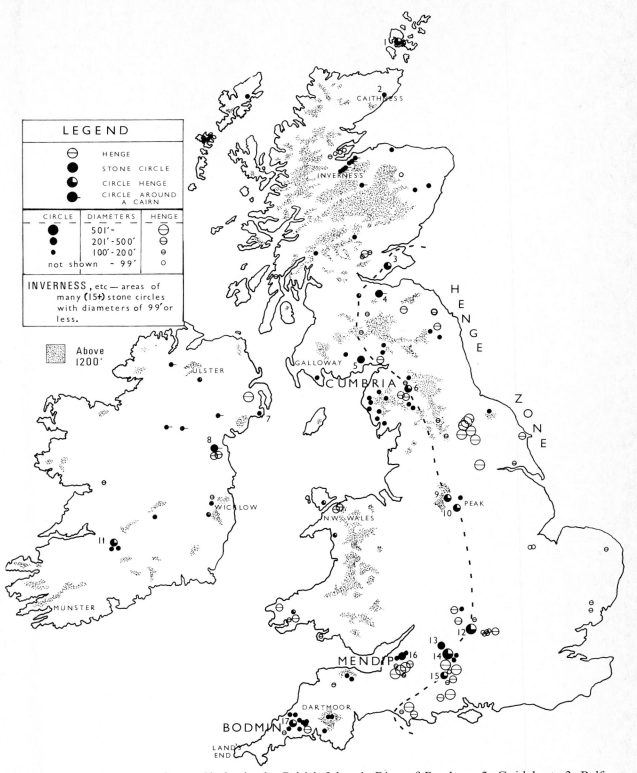

Fig. 2. Henges and Great Stone Circles in the British Isles. 1. Ring of Brodgar; 2. Guidebest; 3. Balfarg; 4. Cairnpapple; 5. Twelve Apostles; 6. Long Meg & Her Daughters; 7. Ballynoe; 8. New Grange; 9. Bull Ring; 10. Arbor Low; 11. Lios; 12. Devil's Quoits; 13. Winterbourne Bassett; 14. Avebury; 15. Stonehenge; 16. Stanton Drew; 17. Stripple Stones.

It is possible to draw a hypothetical line down the centre of the country (Fig. 2) from the Firth of Tay, through Penrith, the Peak District and Oxford to Dorset, which has all the old lowland zone to its east. Most of the large henges lie to its east, nearly all the stone circles to its west. Between the eastern and western areas may be interpolated a central zone about forty miles wide and along this 'spine' it is possible to see the gradual change from henge to stone circle as the geology alters from the soft chalks of the east amenable to the quarrying of ditches and the building of banks into the more intractable limestones and sandstones of the west where it would have been easier to transport and erect monoliths than to dig a ditch or even to scrape together material for a bank. The chambered tomb tradition, moreover, meant that generations of highland natives were more accustomed to manipulating large stones than grubbing up banks of soil.

Of the eighty-five henges now known forty-eight are over 61.0 m in diameter. Six of these large sites are either in northern Scotland or in Ireland. Of the others, thirteen lie to the east, nineteen in the central zone and ten in the west. With the exception of the Priddy henges all the western sites are close to the coast in areas of fertile land. Conversely of the large stone circles, excluding those of northern Scotland and Ireland because of their remoteness, only three are in the east, twenty-four in the centre and twenty-seven in the west.

There is a significant overlap in the central zone. Here there are eleven large henges and sixteen large stone circles. There are also eight circle-henges, sites that are a combination of henge and stone circle and which are to be found all along the central line from Balfarg, Fife, in the north, to Stonehenge in the south. They are restricted almost exclusively to this zone which, without distortion, could be extended northwards to include Broomend of Crichie, Aberdeenshire, and Stenness and Brodgar in the Orkneys. There is only one large circle-henge west of the line, the Stripple Stones on Bodmin just where south coast henges and moorland stone circles meet.

Although circles and henges do occupy generally separate areas these areas overlap and at the junction the types of construction are interchangeable. This is not to argue that in such sites the henge and the circle were erected simultaneously. At Avebury (I. F. Smith, 1965) they probably were. At Cairnpapple (Piggott, 1948) they possibly were not. At Stonehenge (Atkinson, 1960) they certainly were not. In many cases one imagines that the henge was the primary monument.

It is also noteworthy that the very largest of stone circles stand only just outside henge areas and never well away from them. The Twelve Apostles, Dumfries, 87.8×73.8 m in diameter, is seventeen miles west of Broadlee henge. Winterbourne Bassett, Wiltshire, 71.3 m was four miles north of Avebury. Stanton Drew, Somerset, 113.4 m is seven miles NNE. of the Priddy henges. Long Meg, Cumberland, 109.4×93.0 m across, is six miles north-east of the Penrith henges. Such associations give some indication of the densities of local population.

Pl. 3. *The Ring of Brodgar, Orkney Mainland.* The stones of the south-west arc inside the heather-covered ditch of this circle-henge with its large central space. The laminated middle Old Red Sandstone is easily split and has provided regularly-shaped flagstones like these two metre high pillars. The Loch of Harray in the background shows the nearness of the circle to water.

A third pointer to the henge-ancestry of some stone circles is that those areas in which there is a concentration of large stone circles invariably contain henges. In contrast, areas of many stone circles where there are no henges have only small circles that appear to be late: Caithness; Galloway; Wicklow; Dartmoor; Land's End: sites whose average diameter is closer to 15.0 m than 30.0 m. The association of large stone circles and henges and their overlap in the central zone points to a western transmutation into stone of an earlier tradition of circular earthworks.

Whether the large Cumbrian stone circles were built by newcomers to the district, henge-builders prospecting for stone outcrops, or adapted by axe-factory natives from foreign customs cannot yet be explained. Three C-14 dates averaging 2508 bc from the New Grange chambered tomb with its stone circle; a date of 2530 bc $\pm$ 145 (NPL-224) from Llandegai I henge; and two dates from a Group VI chipping-site near the Great Langdale factory of 2730 bc $\pm$ 135 (BM-231) and 2524 bc $\pm$ 52 (BM-676) show that stone sources in Cumbria were being exploited, and henges and stone-circles being built along the shores of the Irish Sea in the mid-third millennium bc. As the great Cumbrian stone circles are found along the stone-axe trade routes from the Lake District it is likely that these circles are local versions of henges and that they were connected with the distribution of stone axes.

5. TIMBER CIRCLES

It is possible that some of the British stone circles were copies of wooden originals. Since 1926 when Squadron-Leader Insall, on a flight from Nether-avon, Wiltshire, noticed the cropmarks of postholes at Woodhenge, aerial photography has revealed more remains of circular timber settings. Others have been discovered by excavation including that detected in 1850 at Beedon, Berkshire, when the Victorian diggers observed seven holes set in a circle beneath a round barrow. Many such settings of spaced timbers are known, both under mounds and freestanding.

(a) *Under barrows*

Timber circles beneath barrows are well known in Britain and abroad and have been described, *inter alia*, by Ashbee (1960) and Glasbergen (1954). In the Netherlands they were often concentric, sometimes within a surrounding ditch, and usually of the Bronze Age like the circle and avenue at the Noordse Veld, Drenthe, too late to be the forerunners of the British stone circles. There are also single circles associated with early beakers of the Late Neolithic, known in Britain also (Clarke, 1970, 76). The barrow at Radley, Berkshire, with its early (E) European beaker had a ring-ditch which could have been the foundation trench for a temporary palisade (ibid). Another, Amesbury G71, Earls Farm Down, Wiltshire, had three concentric stake-circles with a possible south-west entrance. Charcoal from the grave-pit gave a date of 2010 bc $\pm$ 110 (NPL-77) (Christie, 1967). At Brenig 41, in a Denbighshire valley, a concentric timber ring, perhaps wickerworked, replaced an earlier and freestanding stake circle built on ground that had been deturfed years beforehand. A pit inhumation was discovered at the centre of the concentric ring which eventually was covered by a turf mound (Waddell, 1974, 15).

Stone skeuomorphs of timber circles are found under some barrows. Circular stone settings under burial mounds are quite common on the North Yorkshire Moors where many cairns covered circles of boulders or slabs (Elgee, 1930, 102) like Obtrush Rook, Farndale, or the Old Wife's Howe with its Bronze Age urn. Food-vessels of the same period are occasionally associated with stone circles under round barrows. But although there may be a cousinly relationship these concealed circles are too late to be prototypes of the freestanding stone circles of western Britain.

(b) *Freestanding Timber Circles*

These are varied in plan and in function. Their architecture has been discussed by Musson (1971). Excavations inside the earthwork enclosures of Durrington Walls and Marden in Wiltshire, and Mount Pleasant, Dorset, uncovered circular settings of large postholes. The south setting at Durrington had six concentric rings with an outer diameter of 39.2 m; the northern in its second phase, a circle about 13.4 m across. At Marden there was a single ring, 10.5 m in size; and at Mount Pleasant five concentric rings with four cruciform corridors leading to the centre of the structure which was 38.1 m in diameter. This had some resemblance to the banked site of Woodhenge, Wiltshire, where there were six concentric ovals measuring 44.2 × 39.6 m.

C-14 determinations have been obtained from some and indicate their common chronological horizon. Durrington Walls South, phase 2, yielded three dates averaging 1950 bc; Durrington North, 1955 bc ± 110 (NPL-240); Mount Pleasant, three dates averaging 1995 bc; and Woodhenge, two dates from antler and bone in the henge ditch, averaging 1836 bc. All are Late Neolithic. And as all four were discovered inside earthwork rings with internal ditches, despite Durrington, Marden and Mount Pleasant being over 305 m in diameter whereas Woodhenge, adjacent to Durrington, is much smaller, it is feasible that these were secular roofed and walled buildings whose remains today present an attractive but misleading likeness to stone circles. They appear remarkably similar to the Irene Mound council-house of the Creek Indians, Georgia, that was used for meetings and ceremonies of a vivid character (Wainwright and Longworth, 1971, 232; Frazer, 1922, 484).

There are, however, other sites which seem most economically interpreted as freestanding settings of separated timber uprights, the wooden equivalents of stone circles. An 25.0 m circle of posts has been excavated at Caerloggas, Cornwall (H. Miles, 1972). Inside the double-ditched Class I henge at Arminghall, Norfolk (Clark, 1936) there was a horseshoe-shaped arrangement, 14.6 × 12.8 m open to the south-west, of eight holes up to 2.3 m deep, which had held huge oak posts averaging 84 cm in thickness. These posts were about 4.9 m apart. A C-14 assay from posthole 7 provided an early date of 2490 bc ± 150 (BM-129). There was no sign of a central posthole, and the thickness of the posts and the depth of the holes suggest an unroofed and open setting of tall timbers. At Bleasdale, Lancashire, (Varley, 1938) eleven oak posts had been erected in a ring 11.0 m across within a wooden palisade 45.7 m in diameter. At the centre of the circle was a grave containing two Pennine urns. One of the posts gave a date of 1810 bc ± 90 (NPL-69). The Sanctuary, Wiltshire (Cunnington, 1931) had a complex of concentric post-settings of different phases, the last including an outer ring 19.5 m wide. The site has been reconstructed as a series of huts (Piggott, 1940) but as, ultimately, the timberwork was replaced by a concentric stone circle 39.5 m in size, and connected to the circle-henge of Avebury by the long West Kennet avenue of standing stones, the Sanctuary may originally have been a freestanding circle of wooden uprights, particularly as some of the postholes were exceptionally deep for posts intended only as supports for a roof (Musson, 1971, 371). A burial with a B/W beaker (Fig. 10) by stone 12 may be crudely dated to a period within the seventeenth century bc.

Another site to have a comparable history of timber circle succeeded by a more permanent stone version is by Loch Tay, Perthshire at Croft Moraig (Piggott and Simpson, 1971). Like Arminghall the primary postholes were set out in a horseshoe open to the south-west. The fourteen posts were later replaced by an oval 7.6 × 6.1 m of standing stones, itself enclosed in a stone circle 12.2 m in diameter. At Stonehenge Atkinson (1960, 69) suggested that a wooden structure may have occupied the central space of phase I. If this were so then it could have been supplanted by the concentric bluestone circle of phase II, tentatively attributed to the makers of the decorated Early Bronze Age W/MR beakers (Clarke, 1970, 107) and dated by two C-14 determinations averaging 1670 bc.

The multi-phase monument at Lugg, Dublin (Kilbride-Jones, 1950) is interesting. On Saggart Hill, near slate outcrops suitable for building, excavators uncovered a 'sanctuary' site with about 160 postholes of varying size which may be the damaged remains of four concentric rings approximately 11.0 m in diameter, comparable to those at Durrington Walls and Marden. Two stone-slabbed 'hearths' with postholes at their corners and another without slabs were associated with this structure. Everything was overlain by a cairn of large, rough stones. Eight metres to the east was a habitation site with five huts, about three metres across, and with sherds of flat-rimmed ware, a form of pottery produced over a millennium from the Late Neolithic into the Later Bronze Age. Such a juxtaposition of ritual and settlement site is unusual.

It can be assumed that the two sites were contemporary for both were succeeded by a superimposed hengiform monument 49.4 m in diameter with an outer drystone wall, ditch, and inner earthen bank. At the centre of the enclosure was another drystone wall, ditch and inner mound 15.9 m across. There were three breaks in this inner wall at the north, north-east and south-east. That at the north-east had an avenue of posts leading towards the mound. Outside the wall were two pairs of massive postholes interpreted as the timber equivalents of trilithons, those constructions of two standing stones with lintel known at Stonehenge. Lugg, in its second phase, is clearly a ritual site with freestanding timber settings which may be related to better-known forms in stone.

In the present state of knowledge it cannot be claimed that the few known circular timber settings of this nature were the prototypes of stone circles. It is as possible that they were the equivalents in wood of the stone structures already existing in highland areas. It is noticeable that several were replaced by stone settings around the seventeenth century bc; Stonehenge II about 1670 bc; the Sanctuary with its B/W beaker, if this was a contemporary deposit; perhaps the stone circle at Croft Moraig whose presumptive graves were postulated to be of that period (Piggott and Simpson, 1971, 13); and the timber setting at Mount Pleasant which was replaced by a rectangular arrangement of stones, perhaps akin to the 'hearths' at Lugg, and dated to 1680 bc ±60 (BM-668). A similar rectangle has been found at Stenness, Orkney (J. N. G. Ritchie, 1973).

6. PASSAGE-GRAVES

The possibility of passage-graves being a source for the development of stone circles is interesting. These mounds with an orthostatic passage leading to a sepulchral chamber are widespread in the British Isles, especially in Ireland and Scotland. The Boyne cruciform-chambered tombs, of which New Grange, Meath, is the best-known, are concentrated in five great cemeteries (Boyne; Loughcrew; Carrowkeel; Carrowmore and Kilmonaster) across central Ireland. Some 200 sites are known, the earliest yet recognized being a small tomb near Knowth with a date of 2845 bc ±185 (UB-319). As well as the geometric art for which the Boyne and Loughcrew groups are famous, these tombs have large kerbstones. These contiguous kerbs, before the piling up of the cairn, must have made an impressive ring whose diameter was not always determined by the length of the passage. A cairn of 24.4 m radius, for example, would have sufficed to cover the passage and chamber at New Grange but, instead, the designers deliberately laid out a vast ring 82.3 m across (C. O'Kelly, 1971, 15), perhaps either to incorporate a second, smaller mound, or to make an enclosure large enough for all the participants before the completion of the cairn. At Knocklea, Dublin, a stone circle was actually concealed by the mound of the passage-grave. It may be that there were two stages in the building of such chambered tombs, the first dedicatory or propitiatory rites within a stone ring, followed by the completion of the tumulus.

Tombs were sometimes built over 'Goodland' sites which could also have provided an enclosure for the pre-tomb ceremonies. At Knockmany, Tyrone, there was burnt material and leaf-shaped flint arrowheads under the passage-grave; and at Baltinglass, Wicklow, with many quartz stones, the tomb stood on an area where fires had burned. There are too many instances in which religious monuments were built over earlier domestic sites for this to be fortuitous. It may be that previous land-use had left a convenient clearing in which the forest had not regenerated, or the land may have been considered 'sanctified' by people in antiquity, or, simply, that clearance had encouraged the growth of vegetation like mayweed that prehistoric man thought necessary for his rituals. But it is difficult to ascertain how long had elapsed before the second monument was built.

Sometimes the people of the open-ring traditions lived side by side with the Irish passage-grave builders but it seems that such co-existence was unusual. Sometimes circle and tomb could be adjacent as happened near Dowth, Meath, where a henge and the possible chambered tomb of Cloughlea were close together. Sometimes the passage-grave people adopted the idea of an enclosure to put round their tomb, a combination found at New Grange and in many of the Clava tombs of north-east Scotland. Oliver Davies (1938, 112), in discussing the affinities of Castledamph stone circle, remarked that some stone circles might have been put up by: '. . . descendants of the passage-grave folk, the circular peristaliths of whose cairns may have degenerated into free-standing circles . . . I have seen at Kilnavert a circular cairn with ditch and marked kerb close to a stone circle. Transitional forms may be discerned in this or another district outside the Six Counties of Northern Ireland.'

Nevertheless, stone circles are rare in areas of Irish passage-graves although chambered tombs with circles around them do occur in peripheral areas. Near the Boyne there is not only New Grange but the tombs of Killin Park, Louth; Killycluggin, Cavan; and Ballybrolly, Armagh, all inside freestanding circles. There are also many simple cairns within circles in this part of Ireland, including the destroyed Vicar's Cairn, Armagh, 40.2 m across, and with over fifty stones in the circle, one having concentric circles carved on it in passage-grave style. In 1797 the monument was almost complete but by 1868 the stone circle had been removed and today the cairn exists only in a mutilated form with some of its kerbstones in the adjacent field-bank.

But, in Ireland, it seems that the people of passage-grave customs and those of the open circles held inimical beliefs. They rarely mingled. The builders of the tombs seem motivated by a cult of the dead unrelated to the open rings which acted as foci for dispersed groups, and the dichotomy might have resulted from an hostility between one set of people and another that would explain the infrequent overlap of stone circle and passage-grave.

Quite often, in the boundary zones, a henge like Bryn Celli Ddu, Anglesey, or a stone circle like Callanish, was despoiled by the addition of a passage-grave. Often in the early second millennium cairns were put up inside an open ring, Dun Ruadh, Tyrone, or Cairnpapple, West Lothian, being good examples, as though a religion that demanded the presence of the dead was becoming widespread. Before 2000 bc in the Late Neolithic the two cults remained independent and it is only well into the second millennium that circle and burial were freely combined to create the composite Bronze Age cairn-circles and kerb-cairns of the western coasts of Britain.

7. CONCLUSIONS

It may be deduced that from the sources of early Neolithic ritual enclosures grew traditions of surrounding areas with circles of stone in highland regions, or posts or earth in the lowland zone. Such customs probably developed in the later centuries of the third millennium bc and it is easy to comprehend how standing stones would enhance some of the rather unimposing, weathered banks of henges. Whether the result was a single- or multi-phase monument can be decided only by excavation although, already, the Sanctuary, Croft

Moraig, and Stonehenge suggest that often stones were added to existing structures.

At the moment it is possible to indicate that the natural focus for the spreading traditions of ritual enclosures like Goodland, early henges like Llandegai, and the Boyne passage-graves, would be around the northern coasts of the Irish Sea and it is here that one may search for some of the earliest stone circles in the British Isles.

CHAPTER THREE

Stone Circles: Some Problems

*His Majestie commanded me to digg at the bottom of the stones . . . to try if I
could find any human bones, but I did not doe it.*

John Aubrey

The contrast between open stone circles which enclose areas free of mounds or
pits and those which have burials in them is fundamental to a study of circles
in the British Isles. The difference is not confined to the presence or absence
of deposited human remains but also involves the size of the circles, their
shapes, distribution, dating and the essential problem of their function, including the controversial question of astronomical use. Although these matters
are examined in the regional chapters where specific sites are discussed it is
necessary to establish the criteria upon which those chapters are written.

1. Open Circles

The majority of the largest open stone circles in the British Isles lie either along
the seaways of the western coast of England and Scotland or in north Wiltshire
by the Ridgeway and the Oxfordshire prehistoric track connecting the eastern
Cotswolds with Wessex (Fig. 3). Of the fourteen sites over 60.96 m in dia-
meter, five are close to the Atlantic coast: the Ring of Brodgar, Orkney;
Broubster, Caithness; the Twelve Apostles, Dumfriesshire; Long Meg and
Her Daughters, Cumberland; and Stanton Drew, Somerset; and to these it is
geographically legitimate to add the sea-sunken stone circles on the Île d'Er
Lannic in the Gulf of Morbihan and at Le Menec near Carnac, both in
Brittany.

Five other large circles were built near the Marlborough Downs, Wiltshire:
the three at Avebury; Winterbourne Bassett a few miles to the north; and the
Devil's Quoits circle-henge, Oxfordshire. Amongst the circles of Britain diameters exceeding 60.0 m are rare, less than 2 per cent of all sites, so that their
limited distribution either along the west coast or in north Wessex may be
significant. Only two possible sites occur outside these areas: Hethpool,
Northumberland, where eight tumbled stones form a rough horseshoe
61.0 × 42.7 m; and a ring in the Timoney Hills, Tipperary, where amongst
hundreds of fallen and displaced stones it is possible to discern sixteen stones
set in a circle 61.0 m across.

As well as their immense size the ten circles and Er Lannic have other

36

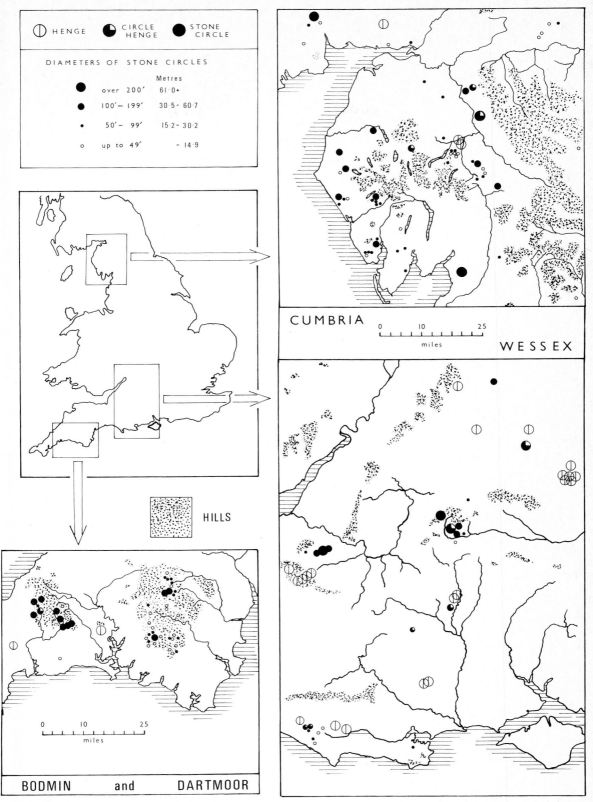

Fig. 3. Regions of Early Stone Circles.

features in common. They are almost all low-lying, in valleys or passes, in level situations, by stretches of water. The Ring of Brodgar stands on an isthmus between two lochs. The Twelve Apostles, like the Thornborough henges in Yorkshire, was erected between two rivers. Er Lannic must have been built close to a river-bank. The other circles are all within a few hundred yards of a river. This proximity to rivers and lakes is a characteristic they share with many henges (Atkinson, Piggott and Sandars, 1951, 84).

With the exception of the ruined circle at Broubster the stones are invariably tall, averaging 1.5 m or more in height. The shape of these huge megalithic rings is either that of a proper circle or of a circle with one flattened arc. Five sites are known to have conspicuous outlying stones. And half the circles contain evidence that their builders had some interest in establishing markers at one or more cardinal points, particularly east or west.

Several of these circles stand inside earth banks and are clearly related to henges. They also appear to represent the apogee of the 'open' or 'ceremonial' stone circle in the British Isles, surrounding no burial mound but simply enclosing an open space in which people could meet for social, economic and religious activities, the largest versions of the smaller and more numerous open circles of the western counties of England. These are most common in Cumbria and Cornwall but others exist in Wiltshire, Shropshire, Dorset, Wales and around the Wicklow Mountains, Ireland. The absence of dates makes it impossible to construct a reliable typology. It is a guess that the earliest may be the plain rings, about 30.5 m across, of many stones and with entrances where wider spaces were left in the circumference. Such 'entrance' circles are almost entirely limited to Cumberland.

Conversely, there are many local architectural variations in the British stone circles. Some in Inverness and Ireland surround chambered tombs. Others in Aberdeenshire and Cork have a recumbent stone, a block lying flat between two pillars. Parallel avenues of stones leading to circles are known in Westmorland and Wessex. Outlying stones are frequently associated with circles along the Atlantic coast. Lines of stones set along hill-ridges and running up to circles are common on Dartmoor. Embanked circles with stones set in a rubble bank are typical of the Peak District. The coasts on either side of the Irish Sea have several concentric stone circles, but great centre stones in circles have a distribution almost exclusive to south-west Scotland with some diminutive examples in south-west Ireland and Cornwall. It seems, therefore, that each locality developed its own form of megalithic ring, and attempts to establish taxonomic relationships may be misleading. There is, for example, no evidence that the builders of circles with small centre stones in Cork or in Cornwall were in any way associated with the makers of the more impressive centre-stone circles of Galloway. There could have been a movement of people from one area to another; or traders could have disseminated the idea; or the centre stones could be manifestations of the independent evolution of a similar concept. Without an accumulation of recurring data it is unsafe to

Pl. 4. *Castlerigg, Keswick, Cumberland*. The south-east arc of one of the finest stone circles in the British Isles. The tallest stone in the ring, a 2.25 metre high slate block is on the right, set radially to the circumference. The Derwent Fells are in the background.

assume that a single common architectural feature can be used as a cultural link between two distant areas.

There is, however, one quite clear division amongst the stone circles of the British Isles. The circles of north-west Britain, Ireland and Dartmoor normally contain burials however inconspicuous they may be. Those of western and southern England usually do not. Thus the term 'open' may rightly be used to distinguish these English circles. Those in England that do have burials are customarily smaller as can be seen from an analysis of circle diameters.

2. DIAMETERS AND 'BURIALS'

Abstracted from field-surveys, sometimes a hundred or more years old, Appendix 2A tabulates by country the recorded diameters of 657 stone circles in the British Isles of which 573 may be regarded as being reasonably reliable. Using the Imperial Foot of the original surveyors the diameters are presented in groups of 10 ft (3.048 m). It is impossible to be more precise as few surveyors had either the expertise or care of Thom (1967) and often they seem content to give the diameter to the nearest 10 ft (Fig. 4). This is manifested in Table 1 where diameters between 10 ft and 100 ft are dissected according to their terminal units: e.g. there are 51 rings between 10 ft and 100 ft ending in −2 ft, and 35 ending in −7 ft.

Diameters ending in	−1′	−2′	−3′	−4′	−5′	−6′	−7′	−8′	−9′	−0′
Total 573	26	51	34	41	86	40	35	33	34	193
%	4	9	6	7	15	7	6	6	6	34

Table 1. Diameters of Stone Circles in Imperial Feet

As it cannot be believed that prehistoric man measured in units of ten Imperial Feet with occasional 5 ft divisions it is evident that many modern surveyors have been content to approximate diameters to the nearest 10 ft, something noticed by Worth (1939, 326) in his study of the diameters of large circles on Dartmoor. Hence Appendix 2A uses this as the most refined grouping yet available for the majority of stone circles other than the 200 planned by Thom.

Before examining the diameters of 'burial' circles it must be stressed that 'burial' is used here as convenient shorthand for 'a deposit of human cremated bone' and does not imply that the relevant circle had a sepulchral function. It is also a truism that these burial-circles are those in which burials have been discovered. Probably some sites now recorded as open do, in fact, contain burials as yet unexcavated.

In England (Appendix 2B) 33 per cent of measured rings have burials; in Wales, 10 per cent; Ulster, 29 per cent; Eire, 20 per cent; and Scotland, 40 per cent. The similarity is illusory. Detailed examination of these burial circles shows diametral differences. Overall the average diameter of a stone circle in the British Isles is about 18.2 m; of a circle with a burial, 17.4 m; and of an open circle, 18.5 m. Yet whereas in Wales, Ulster, Eire and Scotland the average of the burial-circle is greater than that of the open circle the opposite is true in England where the burial average is only 14.5 m against the much larger 25.7 m for the open sites. This is because almost half the circles in Cornwall, Cumbria, Oxfordshire, Somerset and Wiltshire are over 31.0 m in diameter (48 per cent), yet of these thirty-one sites only one, Studfold in Cumberland, contains a burial. Whatever the purpose of the human

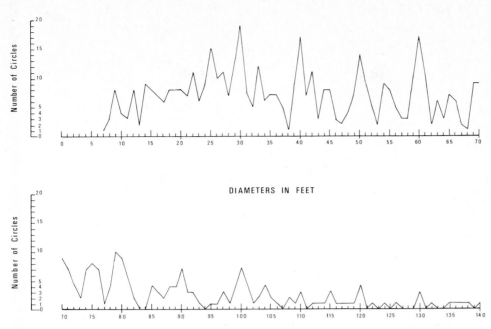

Fig. 4. The Diameters of Stone Circles. In Imperial Feet.

remains in the northern stone circles—whether dedicatory, propitiatory, sepulchral or sacrificial—it is clear that builders of the large English sites did not require such deposits.

3. SHAPES

Although it would be a misleading over-simplification to claim that the shapes of megalithic rings with burials differ from the open sites, it is true that the larger open rings tend to be circular whereas many of the Scottish and Irish rings having burials are oval. There is, however, an overlapping of shapes amongst all the smaller sites and it is very doubtful whether any valid geometrical distinction may be made between them.

Many earlier writers commented on the eccentric shapes of the so-called circles but it was Alexander Thom (1961a et seq.) who codified the majority of designs and proposed methods by which they might have been set out (Fig. 5). He suggested that among stone circles there are five main shapes: the circle, the flattened circle, the ellipse, the egg and the complex, based on the builders' utilization of geometrical designs. Although he did not include them there are also rectangles known as Four-Posters (Burl, 1971) derived from early second millennium bc Scottish circles with burials in them. They are approximately contemporary with ellipses. Their existence testifies to the variety of design employed by the builders of megalithic settings. Thom has put forward no order of development for the shapes but has theorized that the reason for abandoning the simple circle for more complicated designs

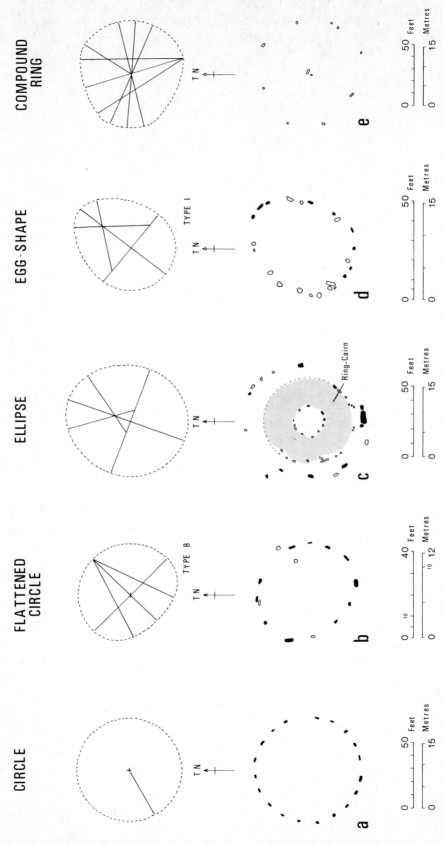

Fig. 5. Examples of the Shapes of Megalithic Rings. (a) Merry Maidens, Cornwall; (b) Barbrook I, Derbyshire; (c) Esslie the Greater, Kincardine; (d) Burgh Hill, Roxburgh; (e) Kerry Hill, Montgomery (Powys). (b)–(d), after Thom, 1967.

was the wish of the planners for circumferences that were multiples of the Megalithic Yard (M.Y.).

Cowan (1969) in conjecturing methods by which such designs might have been constructed concluded that the most probable order was: circle, flattened circle, ellipse, egg. It is possible to test this scheme by using artefactual evidence from the circles themselves. Such evidence includes C-14 dates and finds of pottery and datable implements.

Of the 900+ megalithic rings known in the British Isles the general proportions are 600 circles, 150 flattened circles, 100 ellipses and 50 eggs. Circles are the easiest to lay out, requiring only a central peg and a length of rope or thonging. It is not surprising that throughout the whole 'megalithic' period most rings were circular.

It is difficult, however, to provide a reason for flattened circles. (But see, Complex Sites, below). The flattened arc is unlikely to have been related to the straightened façade of a passage-grave for in stone rings there is no consistent orientation for the flat arc whereas tomb entrances were commonly in the eastern quadrant. Fleming (1972, 59) speculated that the designers of megalithic rings sometimes deliberately built non-circular enclosures so that two conditions, unavailable in a true circle, might be fulfilled: the audience could see all the rites; and the principals could occupy visually focal positions facing the spectators. The hypothesis is attractive. Yet, on the ground, the non-circular rings do not afford the requisite effects, particularly in the case of the flattened circles. So far from the straight arc 'providing a "back wall" which defines a linear area where the principals may perform' it is normally hardly noticeable, being marked neither by taller stones nor by stones set closely together. It is usually quite unobtrusive, apparent only in plan and with no dramatic focusing effect whatsoever. It does, however, stand on the lowest arc of the ring. It is true as Fleming says (1972, 60) that added definition may have been given by stretches of light hurdling but this is as unprovable as the derivation of monuments from unknown ancestral forms and can only remain a guess. If there was a functional reason for flattened rings it remains obscure.

The design of ellipses must have had a geometrical basis whether they are true ellipses, ovals or oblates but the methods of construction and the reasons for them remain in dispute (Thom, 1967; Cowan, 1969), and sceptics maintain that much of the 'proof' has no substantial foundation (Grossman, 1970). The majority of these sites are smaller than the earlier shapes.

For egg-shapes Thom suggests two designs. Although they appear to be contemporary with the oblates they are few in number and apparently unrelated to one another either spatially or culturally.

Despite Thom's contention that perhaps the ultimate development was that of the megalithic ring with several flattened sides it is possible they have another explanation. Nearly all of them have continuous boundaries either of earth banks like Avebury or contiguous stones like Delfour ring-cairn,

Pl. 5. *Avebury, Wiltshire*. The Sarsen slabs in the south-west arc of the outer circle just within the snow-covered ditch. Small concrete obelisks mark the positions of missing stones. The biggest stones, the huge blocks in the south circle, rise above the bank in the centre of the photograph.

Inverness. It is as likely that these are the result of haphazard construction as of nice mathematics.

The form is well exemplified by the flat cairn at Moel ty Uchaf, Merioneth (Thom, 1967, 84; Bowen and Gresham, 1967), in which the circle of touching kerbstones has three flattened arcs at north-west, north-east and south-east. Similarly Cairn 1, Chatton Sandyford, Northumberland (Jobey, 1968, 10) is flattened at south-east, south-west, WSW., north-west and north. Thom's explanation for Moel ty Uchaf is: 'They started with a circle 14 (megalithic) yards in diameter . . . They wanted to have a multiple of $2\frac{1}{2}$ yards in the perimeter (not 44 yards). So they proceeded to invent a method of drawing flattened portions on the ring which would reduce it to $42\frac{1}{2}$.' In contrast to this recondite activity there is an empirically persuasive argument to explain the construction of a kerb of contiguous stones. On the scribed circumference of the projected circle several stones could have been set diametrically opposite each other. The intervening spaces could then be filled in by separate work-gangs keeping as near the required curve as their judgements allowed. Deviations which might not be obvious in circles of spaced stones would be very apparent where there was a continuous line though, of course, only in plan and not to workers on the ground. (See The Lios, p. 228.)

This seems to be the explanation at Chatton Sandyford and it could also explain the irregularities in the shape of the ditch at Avebury. The excavator (I. F. Smith, 1965, 218) thought the work had been carried out by groups working in sections. This was likely at the adjacent causewayed enclosure of Windmill Hill (ibid, 7), and at the analogous site on Robin Hood's Ball, Wiltshire. Nicholas Thomas (1964) wrote, 'In plan this earthwork is very irregular and seems to have been designed in a series of straight sections.' So did the timber ring beneath barrow 41 in the Brenig valley, Denbighshire. 'This stake and wattle circle was somewhat irregular in plan, consisting really of a series of rather irregular rows of stakes, each row placed end to end to form a rough ring; it is possible that the structure was made in prefabricated sections.' (Waddell, 1974, 17.) It is arguable that Thom's complex sites reveal not intricate designs but only long-established practices for laying out earthwork ditches. It might also account for the flattened circles, thus leaving only two basic shapes, the early circle and the later ovoid.

4. DATING OF THE SHAPES

There are several methods by which a geometrical typology of megalithic rings might be composed. The first is architectural, postulating that the most imposing are amongst the earliest. The second relies on C-14 determinations. The third is based on artefacts found in the circles. Whereas the first has the disadvantage of being relative with no fixed chronological points the others come close to an absolute chronology. If all three reveal a similar pattern there is a likelihood that the geometrical model is valid.

(a) *Architecture*

Southern stone circles may have derived from henges which have average diameters well in excess of 31.0 m. Such an origin makes it likely that many of the primary circles would be of a comparable size and it is not entirely fanciful to consider that the larger stone rings, 31.0 m or more across, are amongst the earliest in the series. Of the ninety-one rings whose diameters exceed 31.0 m, sixty are sufficiently well preserved for their original shapes to be established. Of these thirty-five are circular and twelve are flattened but only ten are oval. There are three egg-shapes.

A further architectural criterion might be the size of the stones. Taking 1.0 m as an arbitrary height, amongst the forty-five great rings where the majority of the pillars are taller than that, there are twenty-eight circles and nine flattened circles with another six ovals and two eggs, a marked contrast with the seven circles, three flattened, four ovals and an egg-shape amongst the large rings with lower stones. True circles predominate in the impressive great megalithic rings.

In contrast, most ovals are less than 31.0 m along their greater axis (87.5

per cent). If there is any validity in the presumption that large diameters and an early date are correlated then the analysis tends to support the typology of: circle, flattened circle, oval, egg-shape. But it is only with caution that such an argument may be used. The imponderables of geology, size of population and type of ring militate against its uncritical acceptance.

(b) C-14 Determinations

At present the most precise archaeological dates come from radiocarbon determinations obtained from stratified material within the rings. Unfortunately, although what dates there are support the hypothetical typology there are too few for any conclusive scheme. The three earliest are those already cited for New Grange, the gigantic Irish passage-grave, and came from burnt material within the passage. Around this chambered tomb are the remains of a 103.6 m circle with stones up to 2.4 m high. As both cairn and stone circle share a common centre they are probably contemporary and the average C-14 date of 2508 bc may be extrapolated for the circle. At another circular site two assays of 2238 bc ± 70 (SRR-351) and 2356 bc ± 65 (SRR-350) came from the Standing Stones of Stenness, Orkney, a circle of twelve tall stones 31.1 m in diameter.

For Stonehenge II, the uncompleted 26.2 m concentric circular setting of bluestones up to 1.8 m high, there are two dates: 1720 bc ± 150 (BM-46) for the beginning of Phase III, and 1620 bc ± 110 (I-2384) for the abandonment of Phase II, averaging 1670 bc. A slightly later determination of 1500 bc ± 150 (BM-179) dates Barbrook II, Derbyshire, a flattened circle 13.4 m in diameter, of small stones within a low rubble bank. One might add Circle 278, Caernarvon, a 12.2×11.0 m ring-cairn with stones up to 1.4 m high lining a central space. This ring is flattened on the west. From it came two dates, 1520 bc ± 145 (NPL-11) and 1405 bc ± 155 (NPL-10), averaging 1462 bc. A late date of 1200 bc ± 150 (GaK-787) was obtained from a central cremation at Sandy Road, Scone, Perthshire, an oval 7.5×6.2 m of diminutive stones. Finally, an astronomical estimate of $c.1575$ bc (1800 BC) for midwinter sunset has been suggested for the great ellipse at Cultoon, Islay (MacKie, 1975, 6). Later phases at this site were dated to 765 bc ± 40 (SRR-500) and 278 bc ± 110 (SRR-499), providing a *terminus post quem* for this 41.0×33.5 m ring (ibid, 7).

The data show (Fig. 6) that C-14 dates do support the typology of circle, flattened circle, ovals, and also the supposition that large diameters and tall stones precede small sites of lower stones. But even including Circle 278 and Cultoon, a total of thirteen assays from seven sites is inadequate to construct a firm framework for the 900+ rings of the British Isles. Like the architectural considerations such agreement is helpful but not independently sufficient.

(c) *Artefacts*

It is the third method of dating that provides the most satisfactory data for establishing a probable sequence of geometrical shapes. Many megalithic rings, particularly in the north of Britain, contain cremated remains accompanied by artefacts. Some may be secondary additions to existing monuments but burials are so common, rising to over 44 per cent of sites in north-east Scotland (Burl, 1972, 33), that in most cases they were probably part of the primary ceremonies and so reliable for dating.

Pottery cannot provide the type of precise dating obtained from C-14 determinations. There is much uncertainty about the length of time a specific artefact was being produced and these periods vary in different parts of the country. Northern beakers in Scotland may have been produced during three centuries whereas their counterparts in Wessex began somewhat later and endured for barely a hundred years. It would be naïve, consequently, to say that Circle 4, Machrie Moor, Arran, should be dated about 1600 bc because it contained a Hiberno-Scottish food-vessel. What can be said is that, if the food-vessel was deposited in the central cist at the same time as the surrounding circle was erected, then it is likely that the circle was built at some period between about 1800 bc and 1400 bc when food-vessels flourished in Britain. For this reason, where an artefact has been discovered in a megalithic ring it has been placed at the middle of the span of production in Fig. 6 unless it is known to be earlier or later.

Some artefacts are not useful for such an analysis because they have too long a period of manufacture. Flat-rimmed ware is a good example. It may have been in use for the greater part of the second millennium bc. Such sherds found at Croft Moraig, Perthshire, or Loanhead of Daviot, Aberdeenshire, do not provide a helpful diagnostic of the age of the circle. Hence this ware is omitted from Fig. 6. Other material is of much greater value. Beakers have recently been studied by Clarke (1970), and Lanting and van der Waals (1972); collared urns by Longworth (1961); Irish Neolithic pottery by Case (1961); battle-axes by Roe (1966); Irish Bronze Age pottery by Harbison (1969) and Kavanagh (1973); Scottish urns by Morrison (1968); other Bronze Age material by Burgess (1969). It is upon these that the chronology is founded. Datable finds have been discovered at forty-nine sites, 29.5 per cent of the 166 megalithic rings whose shapes can accurately be established.

From Fig. 7 it seems that the circular rings are early and that ovals develop later with a general flourishing from about 1700 bc onwards—about 2100 BC in the calibrated bristlecone-pine chronology. It is also noticeable that the larger sites tend to be earlier, strengthening the hypothesis that imposing rings were amongst the first to be constructed. If the whole period from 2600 bc to 1100 bc is divided into three equal phases of 500 years then Phase A (2600–2100 bc) has only circles, mainly large, and flattened circles. Phase B (2100–1600 bc) still has a predominance of large circles with one large egg and a few small ovals. Phase C (1600–1100 bc) sees a sharp decrease in large circles but many more with small diameters, particularly ovals.

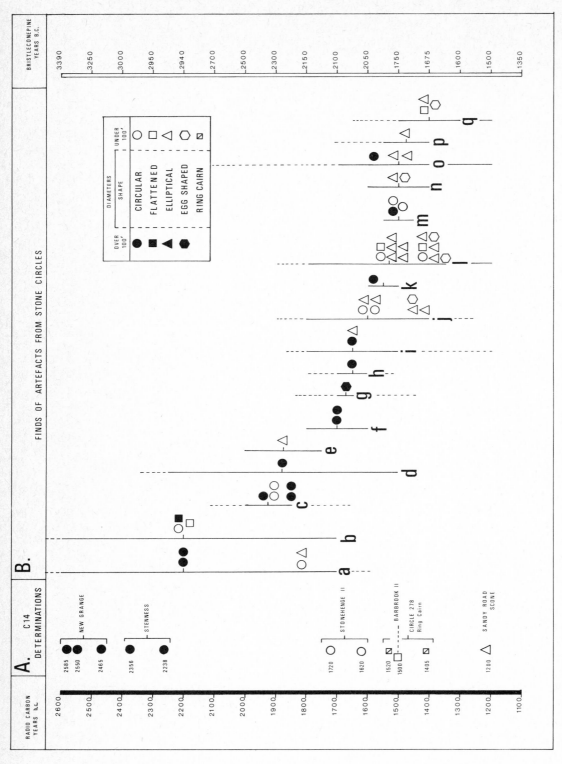

Fig. 6. A Possible Chronology for the Shapes of Megalithic Rings. Radio-carbon dates are shown on the left, a bristlecone-pine calibration on the right.

Types of artefact: (a) Western Neolithic pottery; (b) polished stone axes; (c) All-Over-Corded and European beakers; (d) Carrowkeel ware; (e) Rockbarton ware; (f) W/MR beakers; (g) N1/D beakers; (h) B/W beakers; (i) Knockadoon ware; (j) food-vessels; (k) S2/W beakers; (l) collared urns; (m) S3/W beakers; (n) faience beads; (o) incense and pygmy cups; (p) battle-axe, Group IV; (q) encrusted urns.

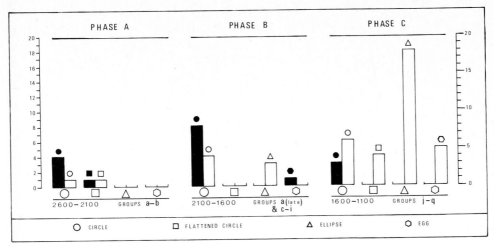

Fig. 7. Histogram of the Shapes and Phases of Megalithic Rings.

All the analyses appear to confirm that the most probable typology for geometrical shapes is circle and flattened circle followed by a later development of ovals. Yet there is still the possibility that each of the shapes reflects a different origin and that, rather than demonstrating an evolutionary typology, the analyses reveal only the individual time of emergence for each design, all being independent of the others. Such a possibility is diminished by the presence of the different shapes in monuments of the same type and locality.

This is most clearly seen in the Clava cairns, Inverness, where encircled passage-graves and penannular ring-cairns with surrounding stone circles intermingle in the same region. Thom in *Megalithic Sites in Britain* summarized his survey of these monuments (1967, Table 12.1, B6/1–B7/19), tabulating thirteen circles, three ovals, two flattened circles and one egg. The earliest of these sites (Henshall, 1972, 283) was probably built before all the shapes had evolved and it is possible that plans of the Clava cairns contain a full sequence of designs and are not just an accretion of shapes received from external sources.

As similar mixtures occur in the south of Britain on Bodmin Moor (Thom, 1967, 140, S1/1–S1/8); at Lands End (ibid, S1/10–S1/16); and on Dartmoor (ibid, S2/1–S2/8), one may conclude either that the layouts are accidental and not geometrical or that the megalithic rings did have intentional designs which were developed over the centuries and which it may be possible to disentangle. The archaeological picture is confused because it is not of a single evolution but of separate activities in different parts of Britain and it is also blurred by the near-absence of finds from southern England. Yet some conclusions can still be made.

Circles abound wherever there are megalithic rings. The largest appear to be among the earliest. Of the thirty-five known circles over 31.0 m 70 per cent do not contain burials and 65 per cent lie within the Atlantic province along the western coast from south-west Scotland to Cornwall, especially in the south-west peninsula. But with the exception of an overlap in Cornwall the flattened circles have a distribution distinct from circles. Only two, South Ythsie and Garrol Wood in north-east Scotland are not of the Irish Sea tradition or influenced by Wessex types of the same cultural pattern. There is a remarkable concentration around Cumbria. The larger rings are coastal whereas the smaller tend to be in the later, inland areas like the Peak District where the C-14 date of Barbrook II, 1500 bc ± 150 (BM-179) may be indicative of the later phases.

In contrast, only 15 per cent of ovals are in the Atlantic provinces. Nearly two-thirds are in north-east Scotland or in south-west Ireland. Over half contain burials. There are two important size-groups: a minor group of 25 per cent whose diameters average 21.9×20.7 m, and a major group of 58 per cent averaging 8.2×7.3 m. It is noticeable that the proportions are not grossly dissimilar. There is no discernible pattern to the distribution of the larger sites.

5. ASTRONOMY

Belief in the astronomical purpose of stone circles has been strong since the nineteenth century and perhaps received its most fervent advocacy in Lockyer's *Stonehenge and Other British Stone Monuments Astronomically Considered* (1906b). One of his tenets was that after a suitable site had been found the people erecting the circle would set out its major axis towards a place on the skyline where a celestial body—sun, moon or star—crossed the horizon on a particular day. Other writers gave similar credence to axial orientations: to alignments from circle-centres (Hyslop and Hyslop, 1912, 17–46); from one circle-stone to another (Somerville, 1923; Thom, 1965, 35; Hawkins, 1966a, 109); to outlying stones (Wilson and Garfitt, 1920); to mountain peaks and notches (A. L. Lewis, 1883; Thom, 1967 et seq.); and even to cairns, distant standing stones and chambered tombs whose contemporaneity with the circle had never been established.

It is only after the most rigorous analysis that such alignments should be accepted for, statistically, the odds are in favour of a good celestial sight-line occurring fortuitously in almost any circle. Examining a site like Grey Croft, Cumberland (Fletcher, 1957; Thom, 1967, L1/10), 27.1×24.4 m in diameter with twelve stones and an outlier, there appear to be so many possible lines and so many possible targets that to discover nothing would be improbable.

In a circle an alignment can theoretically be made between any two stones. In a twelve-stone site stone one can be aligned with each of the remaining eleven, and, excluding stone one, stone two with the other ten, and so down to stone eleven which, to avoid duplication, can only be aligned with stone twelve. There are sixty-six such lines and these must be multiplied by two because they can be used in reverse. A circle like Grey Croft offers 132 hypothetical sighting lines, one for every 2.7° of the horizon. Even axial alignments across this circle provide twelve lines. These have to be multiplied by three because one cannot be certain whether the alignment should be taken across their tops or from the left-hand side of the nearer stone to the right-hand of its opposite and the reverse. To these thirty-six alignments must be added another thirty-six: alignments can also be taken from the circle-centre to each side and top of the surrounding stones. Assuming that prehistoric man did build alignments into some of his megalithic settings there is no way at all by which a modern surveyor can be certain that he has detected that unique line from the remaining seventy-one in a circle like Grey Croft. He must take every one into account and it is obvious that there is a good chance of 'finding' at least one celestial line when there are observational lines for every 5° of the horizon. This is not considering the extra lines to the multitudinous notches and gaps in hills or their peaks or shoulders that are natural to the rugged horizons of most stone circles.

The hazards attendant on the detection of astronomical lines are shown in what initially seems to be a simple proposition, that a line might have been intended from the centre of a ring to a circle-stone. In an average 18.3 m circle with stones only 0.6 m wide if the observer chose a line from the centre to the left-hand side of a stone he would be in error by 4° had the prehistoric line been to the right-hand side. If projected to a skyline ten miles away this would represent a horizon difference of over two thirds of a mile. Or if one stood by mistake only 0.6 m away from the unmarked circle-centre, and most centres were unmarked, this could result in an horizon fix two-thirds of a mile from that intended by prehistoric man and if, as an example, this had been an orientation on the star Rigel (β Orionis) the error would have been in the order of 900 years for the time when the alignment was erected.

Potential celestial targets are numerous. The sun could be observed at its risings and settings at midsummer, midwinter and at the equinoxes. The moon could be descried at its azimuthal equivalents with the complication that there are lunar maxima and minima so that for the six solar positions there are, at the simplest, eight for the moon. Actually, allowing not only for the moon's maximum and minimum risings and settings at the solstices, but also for its oscillations (or perturbations) at its extrema, and the choice of its upper or lower limbs (but not its centre) for observations it provides no fewer than forty sightlines (Kendall, 1971, 311). For sun and moon there are forty-six possible alignments which have remained comparatively stationary since prehistoric times. Stars are different.

There are at least ten bright and easily observed stars of which nine might have been usefully observed at Grey Croft: Aldebaran; Rigel; Capella; Bellatrix; Antares; Altair; Procyon; Pollux and Spica. Over the nine centuries between 2500 and 1600 BC some of these altered their declinations considerably and moved a long way along the horizon. Rigel, for example, rose in 2500 BC at azimuth 132° in the latitude of Grey Croft, but by 1600 BC was rising at

124° a small shift of 8° when contrasted with the 18° of Capella (α Aurigae). The rising of a star has to be balanced by its setting so that Rigel over 900 years offered 8° × 2 of the horizon for possible sightlines.

Altogether, allowing for overlapping by two or more stars along the same part of the skyline, the nine stars cover 64° × 2 of the night-sky for the period concerned when most stone circles were probably built. To this 128° must be added the forty-six simple solar and lunar lines. These, even with allowance made for some coinciding with the stellar positions, add a further 8°. Thus of the 360° of the horizon no less than 136° might be utilized by someone searching for ancient alignments. For any single line the odds on having something to observe would be in the order of less than 3:1 against.

There are, however, not one but seventy-two lines at Grey Croft. The chances of finding one good alignment accurate to 1° is therefore 24:1 in favour of the surveyor. Even if the lines were reduced to an accuracy of 2 minutes, about the most refined focusing possible with the naked eye, the odds would still be about even. Because of this it behoves anyone examining circles to be absolutely certain that the orientations were intended by the builders through their erection of an otherwise meaningless outlier or row of stones. The existence of a convenient notch in the mountain range is inadequate. 'Whereas it is logical to suppose that a row of stones or a pair of archways were designed to point to some celestial object . . . it is unjustifiable at the present time to assume that natural objects were so used,' (Hawkins, 1966b, 6), and 'the problem is greatly alleviated by rejecting markers that are distinctly non-homogeneous, such as a burial tumulus viewed from a stone circle.' (ibid, 7.) This criterion needs strict application. There is little qualitative difference between hypothetical alignments using a mélange of stone circles, cairns, standing stones and hill-slopes, and the chimerical ley-lines of Watkins (1925) fabricated out of the innocent countryside from the imagined alignments of circles, mediaeval crosses, churches, hills, forests and green lanes. Even outliers can cause problems. At Grey Croft Thom has suggested that the outlying stone was nicely aligned on the setting of Deneb (1967, 105). This stone was buried about 1820 by James Fox, the tenant farmer, to save his plough and only replaced in 1949 by pupils of Pelham House School (Fletcher, 1957, 1). One cannot be certain of its original position.

The difficulties of archaeo-astronomy are considerable. This is not to claim that there is no evidence for astronomical awareness on the part of people in Neolithic and Bronze Age Britain, but only that precision is needed to establish former alignments intended for refined observation. Instances of more general orientations are plentiful. Many of the earliest monuments of Britain had plans in some way related to the movements of the sun. The majority of earthen long barrows had their burials at the higher end which was commonly towards the eastern quadrant of the horizon (Ashbee, 1970, 28–30). The same astronomical aspect is found in megalithic tombs whose entrances customarily were built between north-east and south-east. As it is in

Pl. 6. *The Merry Maidens, Cornwall*. From the NNW. A good example of the characteristic 'open' stone circle of western Britain. It was at this site that Lethbridge attempted an unorthodox method of dating.

this part of the horizon that the sun rises such alignments are unlikely to be coincidental. Certain groups of henges also have entrances which may be related to solar orientations. It is not improbable that some of the first stone circles, sites of ceremony and religion, continued the beliefs inferred from earlier monuments, and there is some evidence that in later, smaller sites, more elaborate observations were made. It must be added, however, that had prehistoric man's prime intention been to design an astronomical monument it is unlikely that he would have constructed a circle. A line of stones for an alignment or a horseshoe of pillars for calendrical computation would have been more appropriate. A circle is an enclosure, it would have been an effective fence either for containing or excluding something spiritual but it would not have been the most efficient of observatories. Whatever astronomical function it had was probably only a part of its overall purpose.

Penny and Wood (1973) provide a clear explanation of the ways in which astronomical phenomena occur and how they may be calculated.

This chapter has summarized some of the problems of distinguishing between types of circle, dating them and interpreting their function. Many of the differences were the results of local custom unrelated to national trends, developments by small bands of people largely unaffected by outside influences. Variations in architecture, in situation, in the depositing of cremated remains and of artefacts, all combine to fragment the study of stone circles into regional groups. It is these groups that form the background to the chapters that follow.

CHAPTER FOUR

The Stone Circles of Cumbria and their Function

The retriving of these forgotten Things from oblivion in some sort resembles the Art of a Conjurer.

John Aubrey

1. THE DISTRIBUTION OF OPEN CIRCLES IN BRITAIN

The majority of the large open stone circles are to be found all along the west coast of Britain, particularly in England in Cumbria and Cornwall. There are outlying examples on the east coast of Ireland. Intermingled with these are later and smaller circles, often containing burials and as they occupy the same general area some of the Cumbrian sites will be referred to in this chapter.

The coastal distribution of these large circles is better understood when it is realized that for prehistoric man travel by water was often easier than over-land. Seaways were preferable to the dense, trackless forests and widespread swamps of the countryside where even the higher routes along hill-ridges might be cut by lateral valleys and swirling rivers. Moreover, a boat was better than one's back for carrying heavy objects like stone axes, and it has been noticed that the distribution of axe-factory products was 'almost entirely riverine. It would seem that almost every river, tributary, coastal area and island was embraced in this ubiquitous trade' (Stone and Wallis, 1951, 118). And not only rivers. The seas along the western shores carried settlers and traders from Brittany to Ireland, from Galloway to the Orkneys, and the more treacherous tidal races and currents could be by-passed by short portages across isthmuses like that between Luce Bay and Loch Ryan or the Crinan peninsula (L. Scott, 1951). The building of small southern-derived megalithic tombs along these coasts and their later incorporation within eastern-inspired long mounds bear witness to the sea-crossings of these early people. The importance of Cumbria, containing the most mountainous region of England, the Lake District, is shown through its use by Neolithic groups passing through the Stainmore Gap in the Pennines on their way from Yorkshire to northern Ireland or to the north along the Tyne Gap towards south-west Scotland. What sort of boat was used is not known although it is clear that dug-out canoes were unsuitable, and experiments intimate that forms of timber-framed vessels as much as 8.0 m long and capable of carrying ten persons up to ninety miles a day may have been employed with their advantages of easy beaching and light construction.

Pl. 7. *Castlerigg, Cumberland.* The tall south stones are on the right, the low stones of the enigmatic rectangle are on the extreme left. In the centre of the picture is Threlkeld Knotts over which the equinoctial sun rises.

It was the combination of this maritime activity and the outgoing trade in stone axes that made the diffusion of stone circles along the western coasts of Britain almost inevitable. Once the first megalithic rings were erected, possibly in Cumbria itself, it was always probable that other areas would develop their own types of open circles, not as facsimiles but fundamentally of the same origin as those in north-west England. These Cumbrian circles are some of the most splendid in the British Isles. One of the finest at the Carles near Keswick, seen in the early morning with its tall entrance silhouetted against the mountains of Castlerigg and the distant Helvellyn, revives something of its ancient meaning. There is the meadow-wide space of Long Meg and Her Daughters; the close-set pillars of Swinside with its double portals; the tumbled Shap South, grotesquely close to the railway; Gunnerkeld, now best seen from the modern motorway; and the stones of Grey Croft, the Seascale nuclear power station to its north, the coast and the sea close on its west. Far to the south is the concentric circle of the Druids Temple, Birkrigg, also close to the sea, bracken encroaching on its outer stones, turf covering the burnt patches, the cremations, the pit where the little urn was placed. Such a variety makes this part of Britain a good starting-point for a study of stone circles. Useful general reviews of these circles may be found in Dymond (1881), Ferguson (1906), and R. G. Collingwood (1933).

Cumbria is a self-contained area bounded on the west by the Irish Sea, on the north by the Solway Firth, on the east by the Pennines, and on the south by Morecambe Bay. Yet on a clear day one can see from its highlands to Ireland and to south-west Scotland. Despite the central dome of mountains it was an attractive region to Neolithic man for the marine gravels along its coastlines offered well drained fertile areas, and it was along this littoral that some of the first people settled at sites like Ehenside Tarn, Seascale, and perhaps Skelmore Heads, Ulverston. Analysis of buried pollen grains has revealed a slight decline from the later fourth millennium bc in the number of elm trees, perhaps because of intensive grazing of farm-cattle, a decline that became marked from about 2500 bc onwards just at the time when the Lake District axe factories were being most actively worked. Such evidence from lowland sites 'suggests an initial settlement on the coasts by seaborne immigrants followed by a much more widespread but still not uniform settlement, resulting in larger clearances . . . [and it does] imply a wide-ranging nomadic economy, exploiting elms, and in places, oaks, over considerable distances.' (Pennington, 1970, 68.) Some clearance was affected by fire although this would be effective only amongst the higher-growing hazels and pines and not in the thick, damp oak forests of the valleys. It shows how even in these early times man was purposefully altering his environment.

Immigrants from Ireland or, indeed, travellers by sea would naturally be attracted by the coastal plain, later moving eastwards and inland along the limestone crescent of central Lakeland. People from the east would come first to the sandstones and rich soils of the north–south Eden Valley which soon became the main thoroughfare for traders and settlers in Cumbria, and it was along this valley that Bronze Age smiths and other people of the early centuries of the second millennium bc passed. Yet it was neither along the coast nor along the River Eden that the earliest stone circles seem to have been erected, but in and around the central dome, a mountainous district at first sight inimical to man but whose valley floors with their rich loams provided good though restricted grazing. The reason for the choice appears to be the connection with the stone-axe industry and with henges, a relationship that needs explanation.

2. THE DATING OF THE CUMBRIAN CIRCLES

Amongst the features of early henges (Burl, 1969) are circularity, a single entrance, portal stones, perhaps an outlying stone, and an open central area

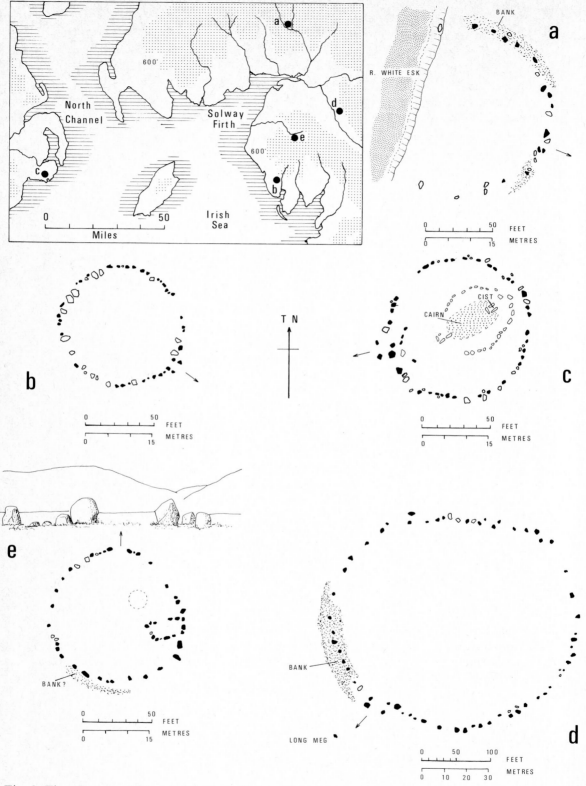

Fig. 8. Five 'Entrance' Circles. (a) Girdle Stanes, Dumfriess; (b) Swinside, Cumberland; (c) Ballynoe, Co. Down; (d) Long Meg & Her Daughters, Cumberland; (e) Carles, Castlerigg, Cumberland.

not more than about 61.0 m across. These traits occur in certain Cumbrian circles, and it is probable that they are related to henges and early in the development of stone circles. These megalithic rings are either circular or have one flattened arc; have entrances emphasized, as henges were, by the presence of either extra or very tall portal stones (Fig. 8); have outliers; have diameters well above average for stone circles, of 31.0 m or more; and are composed of many stones as though to create the effect of a continuous 'wall' of stone. Several circles like the Carles, Castlerigg, Keswick or Swinside or Long Meg or the Grey Yauds, all in Cumberland, have many of these characteristics and, tentatively, they may be assigned an early place amongst the stone circles built in north-west England. It may be noted that Ballynoe circle, Down, (Collins and Waterman, 1955) directly across the Irish Sea shares many of these features. Carrowkeel pottery of the Middle Neolithic period may have come from it.

It is possible to manufacture a diagnostic scheme in which such early traits are added in Column A, and presumably later features—small diameters, concentric circles and centre stones, ovoid shape and embanking—placed in Column B. The subtraction of the totals gives a crude but interesting indication of the chronological position of a circle (Table 2). Artefacts from the later circles are of the Early Bronze Age or after, suggesting that the principles behind the diagnosis were valid. The majority of burials occur in the later circles although this factor was not considered in the analysis. The earlier sites, broadly from the Carles to Broomrigg in the table, do not have Bronze Age material.

Because there have been so few good excavations the dating of stone circles in the British Isles is difficult. Of the thirty-three investigated since the introduction of radiocarbon determinations only six produced C-14 assays, one of which is improbably late. Cumbrian circles are no exceptions. Only four have been subjected to modern excavation: Lacra, 1947; Broomrigg, 1948–50; Grey Croft, 1949; and Gretigate, 1960. To these might be added Mosley Height, Lancashire, in 1950. As the C-14 method was not widely used until late in the 1950s there is no scientific 'date' for any of these sites.

In general it is the smaller, later Cumbrian circle with its cremation deposit that has provided artefacts. From Broomrigg C, a small 'circle' by a large megalithic ring, came a Pennine urn, indigenous to northern England, a plain pygmy cup and some jet disc beads. All these probably belong to the Early Bronze Age as does an unstratified V-perforated jet button. The 'circle' may originally have been a tumulus, presumably later than the great circle near which it lies (Hodgson, 1952).

From Lacra (Dixon and Fell, 1948) came a late collared urn. From the Druids Temple, Birkrigg (Gelderd, 1912; W. G. Atkinson, 1922) came an earlier urn, a sandstone disc or knife like others from Avebury, and Mosley Height, and a piece of raddle or red ochre possibly used for body decoration. A little circle at Moor Divock contained some indeterminate sherds and a

Site	(A) Early Traits								(B) Late Traits									GRAND TOTAL	Finds
	Diameter 27.0 m+	20+ Stones	Stones 1.0 m+ high	Entrance	Outlier	Circ./Flattened	Bank Around	+ TOTAL	Diameter 21.0 m−	10–15 Stones	Stones 1.0 m− high	Concentric	Centre Stone	Assoc. Circle	Oval	Embanked	− TOTAL		
PHASE 1																			
1. Carles, Keswick	1	1	1	1	1	F	1	7	x	x	x	x	x	x	x	x	0	+7	Stone Axe
2. Long Meg	1	1	1	1	1	F	1	7	x	x	x	x	x	x	x	x	0	+7	
3. Swinside	1	1	1	1	1	C	x	6	x	x	x	x	x	x	x	x	0	+6	
4. Grey Yauds	1	1	1	?	1	C	x	5½	x	x	x	x	x	x	x	x	0	+5½	
PHASE 2																			
1. Brats Hill	1	1	x	½	1	F	x	4½	x	x	x	x	x	x	x	x	0	+4½	Antlers
2. Elva Plain	1	1	x	x	1	C	x	4	x	x	x	x	x	x	x	x	0	+4	
3. Shap Centre	1	1	1	x	x	C	x	4	x	x	x	1	x	x	x	x	−1	+3	
4. Shap South	x	1	1	x	½	?	x	2½	x	x	x	x	x	x	?	x	−½	+2	
5. Grey Croft	x	x	1	x	1	F	x	3	x	1	x	x	x	x	x	x	−1	+2	Group VI Stone Axe
6. Gamelands	1	1	x	½	x	F	x	3½	x	x	1	x	x	x	x	1	−2	+1½	
7. Ash-house Wood	1	1	x	x	x	?	x	2½	x	x	1	x	x	x	?	x	−1½	+1	
8. Broomrigg A	1	x	x	x	½	?	x	2	x	x	1	x	x	x	?	x	−1½	+½	
PHASE 3																			
1. Studfold	1	1	x	x	x	x	x	2	x	x	1	x	x	x	0	x	−2	0	
2. Oddendale	x	1	x	x	x	C	x	2	x	x	1	1	x	x	x	x	−2	0	
3. Casterton	x	1	x	x	x	C	x	2	1	x	1	x	x	x	x	x	−2	0	?Beaker burial
4. Kirk, Kirkby Moor	x	½	x	x	½	C	x	2	x	x	1	x	x	x	x	1	−2	0	
5. Blakeley Raise	x	x	1	½	x	?	x	2	1	1	x	x	x	x	?	x	−2½	−½	
6. The Beacon	1	½	x	x	x	x	x	1½	x	x	1	x	x	x	x	1	−2	−½	
7. Shap North	x	1	x	x	x	x	x	1	1	x	1	x	x	x	x	x	−2	−1	
8. Lacra B	x	x	1	x	x	1	x	2	1	1	x	½	x	1	x	x	−3½	−1½	Flint flake
9. Kopstone	x	x	½	x	x	x	x	½	x	x	½	½	x	x	x	1	−2	−1½	
10. Birkrigg	x	1	x	x	x	x	x	½	x	x	1	1	x	x	0	x	−3	−2	Early Collared Urn
PHASE 4																			
1. White Moss NE.	x	x	x	x	x	C	x	1	1	1	1	x	x	1	x	x	−4	−3	
2. White Moss SW.	x	x	x	x	x	C	x	1	1	1	1	x	x	1	x	x	−4	−3	
3. Gretigate NW. (B)	x	x	x	x	x	x	x	0	x	1	x	x	x	1	0	x	−3	−3	
4. Gretigate NE. (C)	x	x	x	x	x	x	x	0	1	1	x	x	x	1	x	x	−3	−3	Haematite
5. Low Longrigg SW.	x	x	x	x	x	C	x	1	1	1	1	x	x	1	x	x	−4	−3	
6. Low Longrigg NE.	x	x	x	x	x	C	x	1	1	1	1	x	x	1	x	x	−4	−3	
7. Moor Divock 4	x	x	x	x	x	x	x	0	1	1	1	x	x	x	x	x	−3	−3	Food-Vessel
8. The Cockpit	x	x	x	x	x	x	x	0	x	x	1	1	x	x	0	1	−4	−4	
9. Lacra D	x	x	x	x	x	x	x	0	1	1	1	½	1	1	0	x	−6½	−6½	Late Collared Urn
10. Bleaberry Haws	x	x	x	x	x	x	x	0	1	1	1	x	x	x	0	1	−5	−5	Flints

Table 2. Analysis of Chronological Traits in the Cumbrian Stone Circles

food-vessel covered in herringbone decoration of the Yorkshire style. Flint flakes came from an encircled cairn at Gretigate and from Gamelands. All these artefacts probably belong to a period between about 1800 and 1400 bc. The only earlier implements are an unpolished stone axe and a stone 'club' (Williams, 1856a) which may have been one of the larger Cumbrian Neolithic axes (Fell, 1964b), both of which were unstratified at the Carles, Castlerigg circle at Keswick. A broken Group VI Stake Pass stone axe buried by stone 4 at the Grey Croft circle, Seascale, was presumably of the same Late Neolithic period. From Grey Croft, but in no discernible context, came a Bronze Age jet ring. Other than these there is no known datable material from the circles for which any chronology must be provisional.

3. SITUATION OF THE CUMBRIAN CIRCLES

Most of the open circles stand in situations easily approached by dispersed groups of people, unlike the later sites which occupy hillside positions either in the upper Eden valley or in south-west Cumbria. Some of the early circles are in natural passes like Grey Yauds, between steep fells a mile to its east and the wooded Eden valley two miles westwards and 500 ft lower. Others were close to rivers like Shap South (Kemp Howe), a few hundred yards east of the River Lowther. Some were in valley-bottoms: Gamelands stands at the foot of Knott Scar on the fertile moorlands around Orton and the River Lune.

This propensity for well-drained, easily accessible sites ultimately doomed some of these circles. Grey Yauds (Grey Horses) over 47.6 m across, was destroyed when the common was enclosed and today only the outlier survives. Kemp Howe, a 24.4 m circle, once had an avenue of stones leading southwards to it from a small barrow which was sketched as late as 1775. The circle was tumbled when the railway was laid. With the enclosure of the common in 1815 the avenue was ruined and only a few huge blocks like the Goggleby and Thunder Stones remain. The tumulus in Skellaw Field, 'The Hill of Skulls', was destroyed at the same time. In the *Gentleman's Magazine*, 1824, someone wrote, 'When the antiquary now views the remains of this remarkable monument he cannot but regret at what, perhaps, he may call the barbarous treatment it has met with.' Gamelands was no luckier. A ring 42.1 × 35.1 m in diameter of granitic glacial erratics, the whole interior was ploughed in 1862, some stones were buried, others blasted and destroyed.

The size and situation of these open circles support the belief that they were meant for use by quite large numbers of people. Quite different are the upland and remote positions of the later circles, many of which cluster together like tombs in a necropolis. On Askham Fell, 1050 ft O.D., on a wide and exposed plateau was the Moor Divock complex (Taylor, 1886) of small stone circles, avenues, ring-cairns and barrows. None of the five circles was more than 7.6 m across and at least one, excavated in 1866 by Canon Greenwell, contained a Yorkshire food-vessel. The whole megalithic group is strung out along a mile of moorland and is best explained as a familial cemetery used over several generations in the mid-second millennium with ritual and sepulchral monuments intermingled. Hut circles later found in the vicinity (Spence, 1934) may have been occupied by the builders.

Somewhat similar is the Lacra group of circles (Dixon and Fell, 1948), on a small plateau near a hilltop overlooking the Duddon Sands 450 ft below. The first circle was badly damaged but the second, 16.2 m in diameter, had a low central cairn covering a turf-stack over a fire-reddened patch by which were some fragments of cremated bone intermixed with birch and ash charcoal resting on the old land surface. The third circle also contained oak charcoal. The most complicated site was Circle D, 18.3 × 15.6 m, with a possible central stone, an avenue of stones extending WSW. with an opposing single stone row running ENE. from the circle. These settings, the conjectural central stone and traces of a concentric arrangement of stones on the south-east arc of the circle are reminiscent of the famous stone circle of Callanish, Lewis. By the north-west stone of Circle D was a broken and inverted over-hanging-rim urn (OHR) (Fig. 11) around which was oak and hazel charcoal and a hazelnut indicating that the urn had been placed in its shallow pit in the Autumn. Excavation of the fifth circle was unproductive but, like Moor Divock, the Lacra circles with their hints of seasonal ritual may be considered the products of a small local group although the sepulchral interpretation is more problematical. Cremated deposits in stone circles may well have been for supplicatory purposes.

A circle in which ritual and sepulchral functions may integrate is that at Oddendale, a concentric circle on the weatherblown top of Hardendale Fells, 1100 ft above sea level. The outer circle is 26.2 m across, of low stones and encircles a contiguous kerb, 7.0 m in diameter, which edged a mound over cremated bone and burnt material. A single stone stood midway between the circles almost exactly at the east.

The further south one goes in this region the more the stone-circle tradition overlaps with that of enclosed cremation cemeteries (Ritchie and MacLaren, 1972) and ring-cairns of the mid-second millennium, monuments in which several deposits of cremated bone were placed within a penannular bank. Such hengiform sites are common around the southern Pennines at sites like Banniside Moor, Lancashire (W. G. Collingwood, 1910), with its five pits and cremations and large stone at the south-west; or Blackheath, Yorkshire (Bu'lock, 1961), an earthen circular bank with several cremations in association with Pennine urns. At Mosley Height, Lancashire (Bennett, 1951), a circle of eighteen large boulders was irregularly spaced on a stony bank enclosing a paved space 12.8 m across beneath which were cremations, urns, grain rubbers and stone hammers of the Early Bronze Age, all in pits set haphazardly about a small central cist with the cremated remains of an adult female. Such a site, as its geographical position suggests, has demonstrable affinities both with enclosed cremation cemeteries and with stone circles.

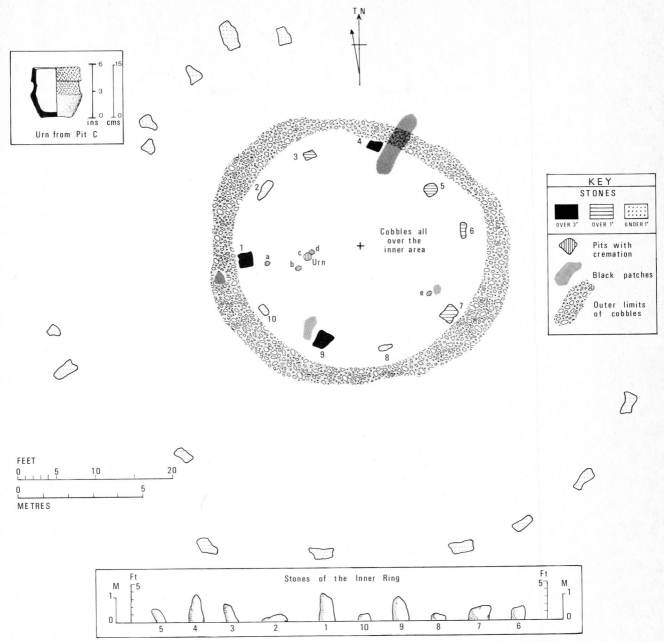

Fig. 9. The Druids Temple, Birkrigg Common, Lancashire-north-of-the-Sands (Cumbria).

So has Birkrigg Common, the 'Druid's Temple', in Lancashire-north-of-the-Sands (Fig. 9). This concentric stone circle, 25.9 m in diameter, superficially resembles the earlier circles but excavations in 1911 and 1921 revealed the whole area to be roughly paved like Mosley Height. And like that site it contained several cremations, one with an inverted OHR urn 15 cm high.

This digression indicates the variety of stone circle in any region of the British Isles, a diversity of function and cultural intermixing against which the analysis of the early open circles may be better judged, for it is from their own comparative uniformity and purpose as communal rallying-places that they can be isolated from other megalithic rings.

4. THE EARLY CIRCLES

The diameters of the earlier circles are smaller than the ancestral henges, averaging 36.6 m against about 73.0 m. This is because of the volume of henge banks and ditches. The central areas are little different in average size. A direct comparison between a henge and a stone circle of comparable diameters, King Arthur's Round Table henge at Penrith and Long Meg and Her Daughters circle six miles NNE., is instructive.

The 91.4 m henge has an earth bank about 10.4 m wide and some 1.2 m high. The material came from an inner ditch 9.8 m wide and 1.2 m deep. It can be calculated (R. J. C. Atkinson, 1961; J. M. Coles, 1973, 73) that it would have required about 55,000 man-hours to construct.

The 109.4×93.0 m circle contains some seventy stones of granite, ten tons in average weight. The remains of a wide bank runs around the stones. About sixty people would have been needed to drag each of the stones up the slope and haul it upright. If the time for locating a suitable stone, levering it onto the rollers or sled, lashing it securely, and dragging it as much as half a mile uphill to the site, digging the stonehole, erecting the stone and jamming it tightly with packing-stones, were to take only one ten-hour day—and some stones were much heavier, weighing as much as 28 tons—then the construction of the circle would have entailed $70 \times 60 \times 10$ working hours, 42,000 man-hours against the 55,000 for the henge. And to this has to be added the time taken to throw up the 3.6 m wide bank at Long Meg.

The equations are sufficiently similar to demonstrate that a stone circle demanded as much time to build as a henge of similar size and, indeed, may have demanded qualitatively more effort.

The circles in Cumberland are some of the largest in the British Isles and only to be approached as a group by the open circles of Cornwall. The features of the Cumberland circles are compatible with a henge ancestry. The sites are either circular or are flattened circles, probably early in the geometrical development of these megalithic sites. Some have earth banks. They also have entrances, a feature rarely found in any other cluster of circles. Yet their early construction remains inferential as no closed finds have come from them.

During successive periods in the Lake District incoming people occupied different areas. There were the Neolithic miners and traders of the stone axe factories within a time-span crudely expressed as 2500–1800 bc; users of beakers between about 2000 and 1400 bc; and food-vessel makers of the Early Bronze Age and the people with whom cinerary urns and bronze

Pl. 8. *King Arthur's Round Table, Westmorland.* From the south-west. The photograph of this double-entranced henge was taken in 1935 four years before Bersu's excavation and the site's subsequent destruction by road improvements. A cremation trench was discovered near the centre.

The central area is about fifty metres across, similar to the larger Cumbrian stone circles. It perhaps served the same function although here the bank is constructed of alluvial silt from the nearby River Lowther. The stone circle of Long Meg & Her Daughters is only six miles away.

implements can be associated, from about 1800–1300 bc. The great stone circles can persuasively be linked with the first of these and given a speculative origin towards the end of the third millennium bc.

Their distribution is significant. The probable high trackways used for transporting the stone axes from their mountain sources follow several routes defined by the presence of rough-outs (Plint, 1962; Manby, 1965). Several of the circles lie close to a track. Swinside is at the coastal end of the high route from the Great Langdale factories down the Duddon valley. Elva Plain is close to Derwentwater and the Bassenthwaite hills out towards the Cumbrian coast. The Carles is magnificently placed for travellers coming

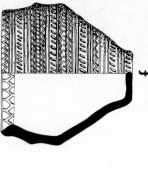

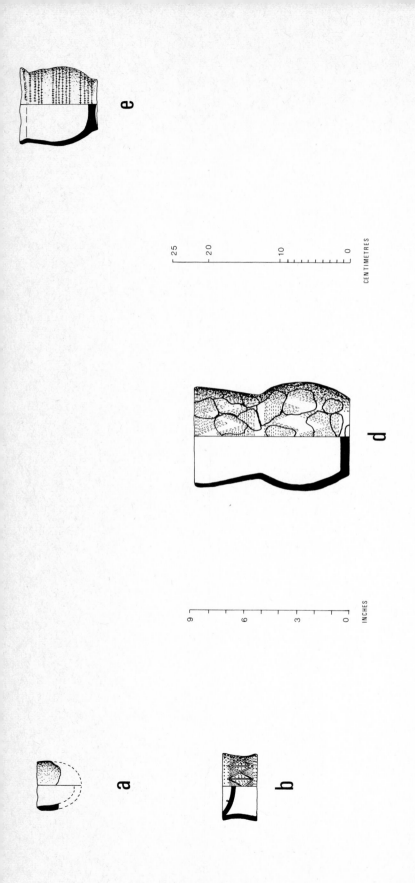

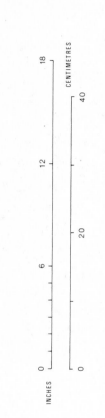

a

b

c

d

e

f

25
20
10
0

CENTIMETRES

9
6
3
0

INCHES

18
12
6
0

40
20
0

CENTIMETRES

INCHES

Fig. 10. Some Pottery from Stone Circles. I. (a) Neolithic cup, Lios, Co. Limerick; (b) vase-support, Er Lannic, Brittany; (c) grooved ware bowl, West Kennet Avenue, Avebury, Wiltshire; (d) S3/W beaker, Lios, Co. Limerick; (e) B/W beaker, The Sanctuary, Wiltshire; (f) food-vessel, Machrie Moor 4, Arran.

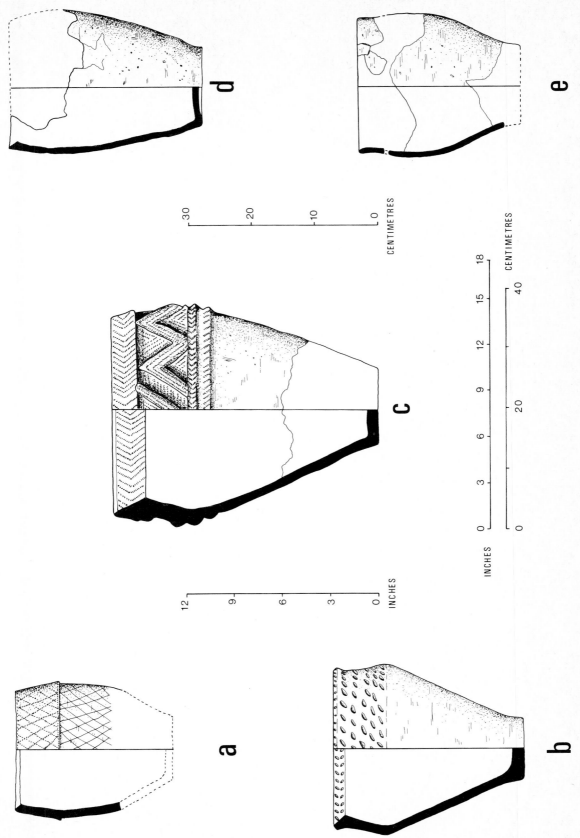

Fig. 11. Some Pottery from Stone Circles. II. (a) Collared urn, Lacra D, Cumberland; (b) enlarged food-vessel, Druids Circle, Caernarvon (Gwynedd); (c) encrusted urn, Sandy Road, Scone, Perthshire; (d) flat-rimmed urn, Glenballoch, Perthshire; (e) prehistoric (?) urn, Drombeg, Co. Cork.

northwards down Borrowdale either to go north-west along Derwentwater or to turn east towards the Penrith henges, themselves built at the focus of the mountain pass and river junction. Long Meg stands on the route towards the Tyne Gap and north-east England where so many Group VI Langdale axes have been discovered (Keen and Radley, 1971, 27). Grey Yauds, Brats Hill and the destroyed circle of Gretigate A may have been others of these early circles whose distribution is different from the other and later cultural groups such as the users of beakers (Fig. 10).

These fine funerary vessels were made by people intrusive to Britain in the early second millennium (Clarke, 1970). It has been concluded that there was probably no connection between the axe factories and users of this pottery (Fell, 1950; Clough, 1968). There are two main groups, an earlier of all-over-corded (AOC) pots (with rows of twisted cord or gut impressions over their whole body) around the south-west coast, probably not reaching Cumbria before the nineteenth century bc, and never penetrating the central massif. The other, more numerous group is entirely concentrated along the Eden valley and is composed of Northern beakers, particularly the late N/3 forms perhaps related to the westwards expansion, around the seventeenth century, of the rich N/2 Yorkshire beaker people. So far is it unlikely that these groups were connected with the axe factories that it has been suggested that their liking for shafted battle-axes actually led to the decline of the Lake District industry whose epidotized tuff was unsuited to perforation (Evens et al., 1962).

The native sepulchral food-vessels of the Early Bronze Age (Fig. 10), their enlarged versions, related encrusted urns, and some Irish bowls, are again concentrated in the Eden valley and its tributaries with a slight scattering along the west coast on the north and south of the Solway Firth (Fell, 1967). The main group appears to derive from Yorkshire, being characteristic of that style (Simpson, 1968), and their makers presumably entered Cumbria by either the Stainmore or Tyne Gaps. The other enlarged and encrusted food-vessels and Irish bowls are spread along the western littoral. In no case are they found in the mountain passes. Their distribution suggests a determination to avoid the highlands and to keep to the lower and more easily traversed valleys. Similarly, the contemporary collared urns in Cumbria have a clear-cut distribution along the south-west coast (Longworth, 1961, 301). Nor, except for a solitary bronze axe near Keswick, does any of the second millennium metalware lie within the mountains, and it must be concluded that, like their beaker and food-vessel counterparts, the people trading in this early metalwork preferred the more easily travelled routes. The elimination of these second millennium associations makes it necessary to turn to the Neolithic distributions if there are any discernible contexts into which the great circles can be placed. Here both stray finds and concentrations of stone axes at polishing sites provide a pattern that can be superimposed on the circles.

With the identification of the Lake District stone-axe factory sites (Bunch and Fell, 1949; Plint, 1962) it was possible to plot the probable mountain tracks along which the rough-outs were taken to their grinding and polishing sites where suitable sandstone was available. Several of these sites are close to the great circles: Portinscale to the Carles; Shap to the Westmorland circles; the grinding-floors at Clifton and at Belmont to the Penrith henges; and the Hunsonby rough-out group to Long Meg. Many axe flakes have been found on the gravel ridge at Seascale near Grey Croft. Kell Bank is in the same neighbourhood. The best-known site, Ehenside Tarn, was within three miles of a stone circle with ten large stones at Egremont, but this was removed in the nineteenth century and little is known of it. The stone circles can be linked to the mountain routes, and a circle sixteen miles across centred on Thirlmere will emphasize the Neolithic associations of this region. Inside are all the axe factories, three early circles with a fourth, Swinside, just outside, and the Penrith henges. In contrast, only two of the seventeen food-vessels, one of the seventeen beakers, and none of the eleven urns lie within this zone. The two food-vessels and the beaker are at its extreme edge (Fig. 12).

Although there are apparently no early stone circles along the west coast R. G. Collingwood (1933, 173), who noticed the correlation between axes and stone circles, thought that the coastal areas might have had timber and not megalithic structures. There has, in any case, been considerable destruction of stone circles along the coast in south-west Cumbria where a strip only a mile or so wide is available for agriculture. As well as the lost site of Egremont there were the three circles at Gretigate, dynamited and partly buried in the nineteenth century (Stout, 1961). Further south are the sites of three large circles: Annaside; Hall Foss; and the Kirkstones which existed in the eighteenth century but which since have almost entirely been demolished.

The distances separating the rings in the central region are approximately eight to ten miles. This is the distance from the factory sites to either the Carles or to Brats Hill; from the Carles to Elva Plain or to the vanished Motherby circle; and between Brats Hill and either Grey Croft or Swinside. Eight miles from Motherby are the Penrith henges, and roughly that distance separates them from Long Meg and from the Shap circles. Such comparatively regular spacing may indicate areas of settlement, the circles being the foci of 'tribal' territories. Extrapolating from hypotheses about the numbers of people involved in the ceremonies at a particular circle, varying from about 100 at Grey Croft up to 400–500 at Long Meg, and including the two Penrith henges, it might be guessed that some 2,000 people occupied the areas immediately around the Lake District mountains, living in the 200 square miles of cultivable land there. This would, at its most favourable, allow 64 acres (26 ha) per head of land to be cleared, planted and allowed to lie fallow, far more than was necessary for mere subsistence (Fleming, 1971, 10) so that 2,000 is not at all a high figure.

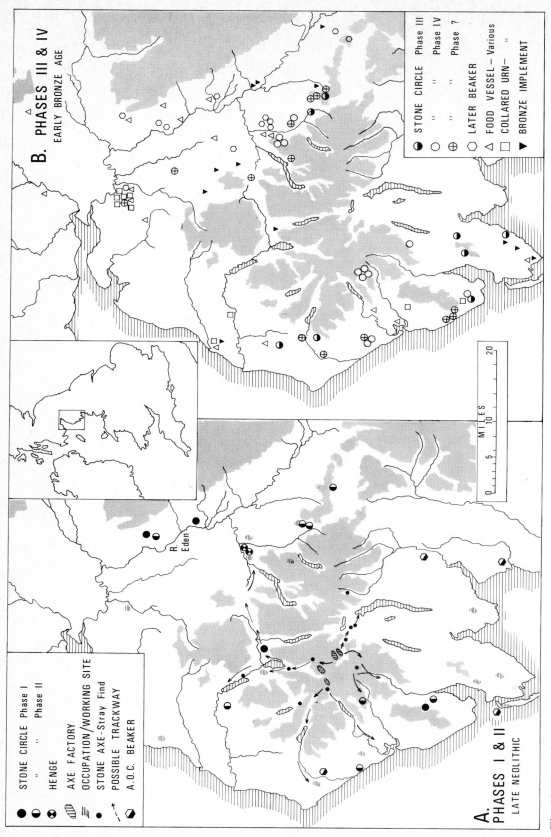

Fig. 12. The Distribution and Hypothetical Phases of Cumbrian Stone Circles.

5. CONSTRUCTION

Unsupported assertions that the great megalithic rings were seasonal rallying-points for dispersed farming groups are unsatisfactory. Nor does the essentially utilitarian nature of archaeological evidence, 'the discarded rubbish of antiquity', help very much. Tangential illumination of the purpose of these sites comes instead from the methods by which they were built and the numbers of people involved. It may be possible from this inferential data to reconstruct a dimmed image of these activities, a chiaroscuro of Late Neolithic society and its beliefs from a review of the stages by which a ring might have been constructed.

A convenient clearing was looked for, perhaps one already opened by earlier agriculture, large enough for the circle, flat like those at the Carles or Ash-house Wood, or on a slope as at Long Meg whose size may have precluded the choice of a more horizontal site. At Swinside, sometimes known as Sunken-kirk because the Devil is supposed to have caused the stones used in building a church by day to sink into the ground at night, the area may have been levelled, hinting that the effort was justified by the discovery of a spacious dry patch from which few heavy trees had to be removed. An important factor may have been the nearness of stones. Many circles are built of glacial boulders common locally.

Once the site had been found the circle would be scribed out from a central peg, its primary axis sometimes on an equinoctial alignment. In some cases the length of the radial rope may have been determined by multiples of the Megalithic Yard (M.Y.) of 0.829 m (Thom, 1955). Thom has claimed that measurements were made by standardized rods accurate to 0.03 in (Thom, 1967, 43), less than 1 mm or about the thickness of a wasp's leg. The unlikelihood of such a uniform length being used all over Britain in Neolithic times has caused many archaeologists, even the more numerate, to reject the hypothesis arbitrarily, the immutable accuracy of a rod susceptible neither to expansion nor distortion only fertilizing their scepticism. Even the Great Pyramid, always cited as a model of precision in antiquity, had an error of 0.05 per cent along its sides. And 4000 years after the first use of the M.Y., the mediaeval brass rod, now in Winchester Museum, manufactured by royal decree to fix the true length of the English yard, was in error by 0.04 in.

Yet several independent surveys have demonstrated that circle-diameters often conform to multiples of the M.Y. At New Grange the circle was calculated to be 103.6 m across (C. O'Kelly, 1971, 78), exactly 125 M.Y. like Brodgar and the inner rings at Avebury. At Aultan Broubster, Myatt (1973) found the diameter to be 78 M.Y. A field-analysis of thirteen megalithic rings on Dartmoor convinced the surveyors that 'the megalithic yard is a real and valid unit and that it was used to lay out the stone rings . . .' (Davidson and Seabrook, 1973, 31.) Replanning of Temple Wood, Argyll, of Torhousekie, Wigtown, and of the Bodmin rings by the writer and others has corroborated the extreme accuracy of Thom's original surveys.

Conversely, from a computerized analysis of stone circles in Cork and Kerry, Barber (1972, Section B, 63) concluded that for those rings 'there is no quantum, no megalithic yard'. 'However, the results from all three of the series of tests for a standard unit were such as to suggest that a common unit imprecisely defined was used. It is not possible, for the present, to prove this suggestion. However, it is probably fair to conclude, with respect to the standard unit of length employed in circle-building, that if it was used at all it was probably some rough measure like the human pace.' (ibid, 70.) And Kendall (1974), basing his work on Fourier analysis, thought that the Megalithic Fathom of 1.66 m might be valid for some of the Scottish sites but not at all certain for the English and Welsh rings. Freeman (1976), using different criteria, came to similar conclusions. As in both instances the examinations were thorough the national distribution of the Megalithic Yard must remain unproven. It is of interest to find that a unit of measurement, the Druid's Cubit of 20.8 in, had been proposed over two centuries before by Stukeley (1743, 11, 19, 31).

It is known that measuring-rods were used in prehistoric Europe. One, made of hazel, was found in the Danish Bronze Age tumulus of Borum Eshøj near Aarhus (Glob, 1974, 38; Klindt-Jensen, 1965, 65) alongside a central tree-trunk coffin. The rod measured 0.79 m and had three notches cut at 15 cm (6 in) intervals. It would be ironical if, after all, the linear measure used in stone circles was akin to the Imperial Foot. This is quite possible. The human foot was frequently taken as a unit of length, the English Rod being an aggregate of 16 men's feet, and although prehistoric Near Eastern civilizations employed longer units (the Egyptian Royal cubit of 524 mm; the Babylonian Kus of 531 mm), the simpler measure of a foot was preferred by many people nearer the British Isles, such as the Greeks whose 16 'fingers' equalled a foot of 12.17 in (309 mm) and the Romans with a foot of 11.66 in (296 mm). The Trelleborg Vikings of the late tenth century AD used a modification of this, 11.56 in (294 mm). The mediaeval French pied varied between a general 12.79 in (325 mm) and the Parisian 12.78 in. As 2/5 of the Megalithic Yard is 13.06 in (332 mm) which compares well with the 12.38 in of the Borum Eshøj rod when it too is subdivided, it is conceivable that it was variants and multiples of this foot measure that were known in prehistoric Britain.

As the Megalithic Yard remains uncorroborated nationally it becomes harder to accept Thom's statement that 'there must have been a headquarters from which standard rods were sent out' because 'if each small community had obtained the length by copying the rod of its neighbour to the south the accumulated error would have been much greater . . .' (1967, 43.) Ignoring the implication that all good things emanated from the south in prehistoric Britain another inference is that when a group wished to build a ring it either sent messengers to the national centre for a bundle of rods and a competent surveyor or that it waited for rod-carriers to visit the district which, in the remoter valleys of Caithness or Merioneth, might not have been for some centuries. Such a centre is unlikely. On the contrary, in each region of megalithic rings the standard lengths seem to differ slightly. As an example, amongst the recumbent stone circles of north-east Scotland the unit consistently falls short of 0.829 m. As this area also differs from others in its architecture it militates against the concept of one nationally accepted theocracy. So despite Thom's claim that the M.Y. was used throughout Britain and Brittany (Thom and Thom, 1973, 122), a surveying 'headquarters' is unlikely at Avebury (Baity, 1973, 396) or elsewhere, even in Ireland.

Irish influence was widespread during the later phases of the Neolithic and in the Bronze Age but metrological missions from there are improbable. Quite possibly 'Irish' customs were taken up by scattered, receptive groups and absorbed into their own socio-religious systems, an eclecticism paralleled by the mixing of architectural styles in megalithic tombs and by the miscellany of trade-goods found in some areas. It is true that Hiberno-Breton ritual practices may have had a common ancestry. It must be emphasized, however, that in both regions distinctive traits evolved—the art of the Boyne and Breton tombs, for example, is dissimilar—so that Thom's belief in a 'common culture' (Baity, 1973, 439) is mistaken. Geographically Ireland and Brittany are far apart. The Irish and Breton tombs have only a general resemblance to each other. Our ignorance of prehistoric languages, moreover, may obscure the linguistic difficulties experienced by early people in the communication of ideas.

The concept of a standardized length, however, could have been transmitted without being accompanied by artefacts or architecture or migrant settlers. Tests by the writer with students confirm that a pace or stride could have approximized to such a unit, varying from locality to locality. Ultimately the verification of the M.Y. must depend on statistical confirmation. Such acceptance is not affected by ultra-diffusionist claims that it was related to Mediterranean metric systems (Thom, 1967, 34; Baity, 1973, 395) and to the ancient Egyptian remen of 370 mm, one M.Y. equalling $\sqrt{5}$ remen (Ivimy, 1974, 132). The first pyramid, that of Zoser at Saqqara, was built about 2780 BC, 500 years after New Grange, and the builders of the early stone circles of the British Isles did not have olive-skinned Nilotic overseers when setting out those megalithic rings, whatever unit of measurement they used. Thom's work has gone a long way towards demonstrating that such units did exist. It is also becoming clear that contemporary prehistoric societies possessed an elementary numeracy enabling them to count the number of lengths when determining the radius of a ring. For these reasons, and for general interest, diameters in Megalithic Yards are quoted for many circles although the writer believes it improbable that such a length was unvaryingly adopted throughout the British Isles.

Hence in Cumbria one may imagine the meticulous designing of the ring, although, however nicely the site was marked out, the digging of holes and the heaving upright of vast stones would invariably cause some divergence from the plan. What can cogently be argued is that the size of the ring was determined by the size of the local population. The immense diameters of some henges and circles were far in excess of that needed by a few hierophants in ceremonies watched by uninitiated spectators who squatted on the distant banks or peered between the obstructive stones. Nor are the sites set in natural amphitheatres most convenient for such audiences, and it is improbable that a henge was a religious theatre-in-the-round with the audience seated on the banks, fidgeting uncomfortably on Mayburgh's cobbles or Thornborough's gypsum crystals. The enclosures are more convincingly explained as combinations of an outer setting demarcating the temenos, and a large, open interior for communal rites.

Several of the circles have a flattened arc. Such flattening is noticeable where the gradient alters, to the north-east at Long Meg, and where the ground falls away to the north-east at the Carles, to the SSE. at Swinside, and NNW. at Brats Hill. If such arcs are not accidental they may be the deliberate attempts to retain a level interior. Around the marked circumference shallow sockets were dug for the stones, not always equidistant from each other, and at some circles wider spaces or double settings of holes were left for entrances.

During this laying-out and clearing of scrub from the site other people would be dragging the stones to their positions, a task that would have been most simply achieved by putting them on sledges. These may have been pulled over wooden rollers using ropes of flax or nettle or bast (Atkinson, 1961; J. M. Coles, 1973, 82) but there is evidence that rollers are not very efficient on rough ground. Once at the site the undressed stones were levered and manhandled erect, small packing-stones being jammed around their bases.

Although population studies of prehistoric societies are based on little more than demographic guesswork, certain physical probabilities like the number of people needed to haul or raise a stone may change this into a near-respectable hypothesis. At the Carles the internal circumference is about 85 m. If one postulates, from ethnographic parallels, a ring of people dancing about one metre apart around a central group with the old, infirm and very young watching by the stones, then a total population of about 150 would be a median figure. At this circle the heaviest stone measures $2.3 \times 2.1 \times 1.2$ m (Woolacott, 1909), and weighs about 15 tons. An average stone weighs $2\frac{1}{2}$ tons. Most of these stones were local erratics but some had to be dragged up Chestnut Hill to the west, presumably by human beings because there is little evidence for heavy traction-animals in early prehistoric Britain (but see: Fowler and Evans, 1967, 294). Allowing six men per ton a heavy downhill stone might require 50–70 persons to move it. To raise the heaviest would demand as many for at an angle of 70° from the horizontal it would exert a pull of one-fifth its dead weight or 3 tons. Hauling at 100 lb (45 kg) per man with others desperately wedging timbers behind the stone to prevent its toppling backwards the smallest practicable construction team would have

Pl. 9. *Castlerigg, Cumberland*. From the north-west. Two massive stones four metres apart define the north entrance on the left. On the right are the slopes of Castlerigg.

been about 70 people. Even if this constituted every one of the able-bodied persons then at least as many again must be allowed for the infants, senile and unfit, a total population of 140, not dissimilar from the first speculative figure of 150. That for Swinside is much the same, for Long Meg about 250–400. Such numbers, based on mechanical demands, indicate only the minima involved, people who might have been professional work-gangs and not part of the population locally. Other data may reveal something of the activities within the circles.

If these circles were indeed for a concourse of people at special seasons the large rings might be expected to have conspicuous circumferential stones or outliers marking major solar positions, such orientations being not for esoteric calculations but more probably for seasonal observances, the summer and winter solstices or the vernal and autumnal equinoxes when the sun was midway between its extreme positions on the horizon. Autumnal gatherings are suspected from causewayed enclosures, the putative ancestors of henges, and the earliest stone circles may have had something of the same purpose, providing a place of meeting for scattered groups at special times of the year. What astronomical alignments they did contain would be calendrical. Thom (1967) lists several great open circles: the Rollright Stones; The Hurlers, Fernacre and Stannon, all in Cornwall, and Brats Hill, as large circles which are considered to have good solar alignments.

These lines might be fixed by outlying stones, entrances or especially tall circle-stones. Unindicated horizon points such as sides of mountains, hill-notches and peaks are not relevant as there is no extrinsic evidence that these natural phenomena were ever associated with the circle. If such celestial lines ever were incorporated into the Cumbrian circles they were upon the sun rather than the moon or stars. It is noticeable that in a study of fifteen sites (1967, 138, L1/1–L5/1) Thom proposed only five for astronomical use (ibid, 90) of which three were solar. The others are dubious. The re-erected outlier at Grey Croft and its doubtful orientation on Deneb has been mentioned earlier. At Brats Hill (Thom, 1967, L1/6, Circle E) only two of the nine lines submitted are Class A or 'to be accepted by any unbiased observer'. Both are to Arcturus (α Boötis). But as these are from the Circle E to two others, A and B, at Low Longrigg which cannot be seen from it their validity must also be in doubt, especially as the sightline beyond is completely obscured by the heavy mountainside of Whin Rigg. Nor, of course, would such alignments have been usable in the darkness. This leaves only the solar lines which may be basic to several circles.

Often in the large megalithic rings north, south, east and west are approximately marked by large stones. As such lines occur in many other open southern circles they are unlikely to be fortuitous (Thom, 1961a, 91; 1967, 95). At Long Meg two massive stones are at east and west; at Elva Plain where most are fallen the longest is at the west, the smallest at the east; at Swinside the tallest are at north and south; at Brats Hill at the south. These may be connected with elementary observations of important sun positions. There is direct evidence that sometimes north–south lines were related to solar positions. Of Wessex beaker burials Lanting and van der Waals (1972, 37) wrote, 'A N–S orientation must have been the rule in this area . . . Men were buried with their head toward the North, usually lying on their left side facing East . . . Women were usually buried with their head toward the South, lying on their right side, thus also facing East . . .' In Yorkshire an early north–south orientation was later replaced by the custom of aligning the bodies east–west, but with sex discrimination continued by placing men with their heads at the east, women's at the west (ibid, 40). It is remarkable how often these crude cardinal points occur. At the Spring and Autumn equinoxes the sun rises at the east and sets in the west, halfway between its summer and winter solstices, facts which when recognized would have been important to agriculturalists and stockbreeders urgently requiring the warmth of the year to return. A rudimentary equinoctial alignment would not have been hard to achieve once the sun's movements had been noted and its horizon or setting midpoint calculated. At the Spring or Autumn sunset two sticks could have been set in line with it about 15 m apart. This would provide an east–west axis. A cross-axial line would be only a little more difficult. Thonging stretched between the stakes could be folded in half to mark the midpoint. Longer thonging, its ends against the stakes, could have its midpoint marked by pulling it taut to make a temporary isosceles triangle. A rope laid from mid-point peg to midpoint peg would be at right-angles to the near-equinoctial line and would be roughly north–south. The more obvious occurrences of midsummer sunrise or midwinter sunset would need even less elaboration to fix. Or a north–south line could be obtained directly by similarly bisecting the angle between the rising and setting points of a star like Capella (α Aurigae) on a level horizon.

In the absence of explanatory evidence modern man is denied the likelihood of rediscovering the cosmology of prehistoric people. One may note that the Egyptians acknowledged the importance of a particular stellar group, the northern circumpolar stars, 'those that know no destruction', or 'those that know no weariness'. Such stars, that never disappeared below the horizon, were symbols of the dead who had triumphed over death and had passed into eternal life. To the Egyptians the north became a place of everlasting blessedness because there was no death there. Other prehistoric peoples, albeit with different interpretations, may also have looked on the north with awe and incorporated lines towards it in their megalithic monuments.

It has already been noted, however, how difficult it is to be certain that alignments discovered by modern surveyors were intended by the circle-builders. In the Cumbrian circles, outlying stones, often cited as being expressly for astronomical use, are common among the sites from Grey Yauds down to Cheetham Close, Lancashire, and of circles along the west coast of Britain. But of the seventy known outliers there are no constant orientations amongst the forty-two whose azimuths are properly recorded, and it is tenable that their function was sometimes directional for travellers to and from the site. Several of the Cumbrian sites have outliers, three at the south-west, one at the north-west. As these relate either to midwinter or midsummer sunset the circle-builders may have intended to record these events but if this is so the alignments are imprecise. At Long Meg the 3.7 m tall outlier stands in the right place, but only if seen from the middle of an irregular 109.4 × 93.0 m ring whose centre would have been difficult to determine. At the Carles and at Elva Plain both outliers stood several feet from the correct position for midwinter sunset. Like Grey Croft the outlier at the Carles had been buried, plough-scratches still being visible on it (Anderson, 1923), so that its present position must be suspect. At Brats Hill the very low outlier was erected fairly close to the line on the midsummer solstice. There is no outlier known at Swinside. Although it is credible that alignments were shown by these outliers they were rarely accurate.

All of them were placed where they would be useful as direction markers. Long Meg stands on a ridge above the valley. Elva Plain has steep slopes to north and south, and the outlier points south-west along the hogback that runs west towards the coast. The 0.9 m high outlier at the Carles leads to the gentlest slope downhill.

Entrances are even less satisfactory for astronomical purposes. That at Long Meg is at the same position as the outlier, at the south-west, and so possibly associated with the midwinter sunset, but at the Carles it is at the north and unconnected with the movement of any celestial body, although the Egyptian concept of an area of eternity has already been noted. At Swinside the entrance is at the south-east on an azimuth where the sun set a fortnight before the winter solstice. The radius of this circle is about 14.4 m and the entrance is 3.1 m wide affording an arc of vision 12° wide, quite unacceptable for any delicate alignment. The entrance at the Carles, however, leads to the eastern pass through the mountains along the River Greta. Long Meg has been discussed. At Swinside it leads down the gradual slope towards a stream and the sea. These gaps probably were simple entrances rather than astronomical windows. It has rarely been suggested that the gaps in henge-banks were anything but entrances. Similarly, there is not, at present, any evidence that the people who built stone circles intended more than a means of access to their monuments when they erected their portals. Where an avenue of stones is associated with a stone circle it almost invariably leads from a source of water, indicating the importance of water in the ceremonies that took place in the rings. The early Cumbrian portals may have had the same function, being at that point on the circumference where people approaching from the nearest stream or river would enter the circle: from the Greta north of the Carles; from the Eden south-west of Long Meg; and from the Black Beck south-east of Swinside.

6. FUNCTION

The most important question about stone circles, of course, is what they were used for, to discover what happened in them, and this can never be answered satisfactorily. Archaeological material provides only the feeblest of evidence upon which to base any speculation about the nature of pre-historic religion, a statement that remains true despite Fleming's comment (1973a, 177) that 'many prehistorians fall into the trap of saying "it is to do with ritual", therefore it must be connected with both unknowable and irrational ideas (in my own frame of reference), therefore I cannot hope to understand it.' This is not entirely correct. The rituals of prehistoric peoples may have been incomprehensible to us, or they might have been under-standable, but this is not the problem. The difficulty is to be certain that we can identify and define those beliefs from the fragments of tangible associations that remain. Speculation is easy; realization is almost impossible for an extinct society. Firth (1961, 229) has written of the elusive meanings of modern

Polynesian feasts, even when they have been explained; and Evans-Pritchard has remarked (1965, 112) 'that we have to account for religious facts in terms of the totality of the culture and society in which they are found . . . They must be seen as a relation of parts to one another within a coherent system, each part making sense only in relation to other institutional systems, as part of a wider set of relations.' And if this is despairingly true of extant primitive societies where customs may still be physically observed and participants spoken with, then how much harder it is to re-establish a pre-historic religion from which all the practices, taboos, social codes, ceremonies have gone, leaving only the fallen stones and broken artefacts. The archae-ologist must speculate to assess the size of a prehistoric population. He must be even more daring to propose a framework of kinship and tribal relation-ships because his models are usually founded on anthropologically dubious parallels. And to say anything detailed about religion within this vague society is almost wishful thinking. Yet archaeology is a tool of history and attempts at reconstruction should be made even if the theoretical structure has to be announced as jerry-built. Comfortingly, it is possible that some clues about early religion are available from study of later prehistoric groups whose ritual practices were historically recorded by classical authors like Caesar.

Centuries after the abandonment of stone circles the Celtic Druids of the Iron Age recorded the relationship between the sun's and moon's move-ments on the Coligny bronze calendar. This fractured first-century bc tablet carried a table of 62 lunar months possibly connected with the metonic cycle of 18.61 years. Of the same period the remarkable stone circle at Sarmizegetusa, Romania (Daicoviciu, 1960) is thought to be an architectural representation of the Dacian calendar of 360 days and a 12-month year. At Libeniče, Czechoslovakia (Piggott, 1968, 73, 224) the rectangular, ditched enclosure of the third century bc was oriented on the midwinter sunrise. At the south-east were pairs of posts, some perhaps carved in human form and adorned with bronze torcs. Pits, dug and redug over a long period, may have received libations of blood. An analogous rectangle at Aulnay-les-Planches, Marne, France, reached back to the eleventh century bc and a time when some stone circles were still in use. Both these Celtic enclosures are reminiscent of Neolithic cursuses in Britain, parallel banks of earth or chalk, just as the sixth-century bc Goloring circular bank and inner ditch near Coblenz is akin to a henge.

Such signs of cultural continuity are not an argument for inhabiting stone circles with Druids, but Caesar in Book VI, 2, of his *Gallic Wars* did write of the Druids as being British in origin, and their ancestry may have extended back well before Celtic times (Piggott, 1968, 235), stemming from a priest-hood much concerned with seasonal fertility ceremonies. Of late it has been suspected that many Iron Age hillforts were not for defence only but may have served as foci for tribal ceremonies just as the earlier causewayed enclosures and henges had done. The construction of forts like Maiden

Castle, Dorset, and the Trundle, Sussex, on the sites of causewayed enclosures might have arisen from the wish to perpetuate the traditional meeting-places of natives (Cunliffe, 1974, 248). Even a recently discovered causewayed enclosure at Briars Hill, Northampton, lies within a few hundred metres of Hunsbury hillfort. So far from breaking with the past there is much evidence of continuity of custom in the Celtic Iron Age (Chadwick, 1970, 164; Harding, 1974, 105). Ritual shafts, very like those of the Iron Age (Ross, 1968) but unequivocally dated to the Bronze Age, have been excavated at Wilsford, Wiltshire, and Swanwick, Hampshire, the latter with traces of dried flesh in it. It is permissible to suggest that the corpus of astronomical knowledge held by the Celts had, in part, a primitive origin in the practical observations hinted at in the architecture of the great open rings of Britain (MacKie, 1974, 188), just as Celtic festivals could have developed from earlier customs.[1] There is certainly a noticeable correlation between the postulated Iron Age provinces of the British Isles (Fig. 13) and architectural regions in stone circles which, presumably, reflect broad geographical territories as suggested by the chapters and sub-divisions in this book.

Early stone circles may contain within them simple orientations on the sun's or moon's major positions, or on stars, marking the time at which ceremonies of purification or propitiation were to be held. Such meetings for the appeasement of the elements survived in Europe even into mediaeval times and later, being held at special times of the year, usually Spring and Midsummer but, in north-west Europe, often at Samhuin or Halloween (31 October) and Beltane (1 May). In the hills around Callendar in central Scotland on the night before May Day, less than 200 years ago, people would cut a turf-circle on the hillside large enough to accommodate the participants. A bonfire was lit and an oatcake broken into pieces, one portion blackened with charcoal, and put in a bag. Blindfolded, each person took a piece, the black bit indicating who was to be the token sacrifice (Frazer, 1919, 150). Ceremonies of a similar nature also continued in Wales, north-east Scotland and Ireland down to the late eighteenth century AD. On other occasions, at Lent, villagers would leap through bonfires to help their crops ripen, blazing torches of straw would be carried into the fields, and straw effigies burnt as offerings (Frazer, 1922, 609). Such gatherings and seasonal activities are likely to have an antiquity that may reach back to the first farmers. 'In general, the evidence appears to indicate that astronomical lore, astra and deity symbolism, and seasonal rituals set by astra events and considered essential to successful agriculture and stockbreeding were part of the Neolithic mixed-farming tool kit', and 'the great emphasis on the summer solstice rituals in areas where the megalithic cultures were evident does imply a possible connection.' (Baity, 1973, 416.)

---

[1]This theme is discussed at much greater length by Hicks in his dissertation on the henges in Ireland (R. E. Hicks, 1975, 183).

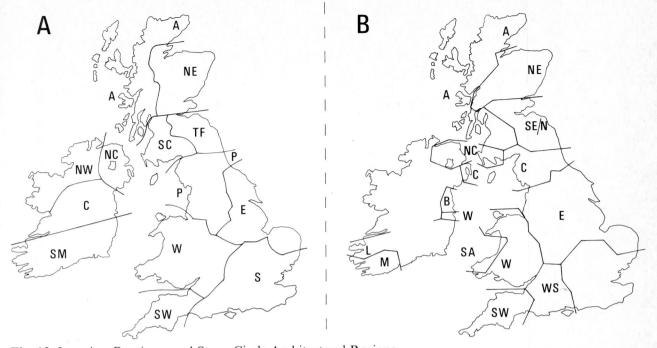

Fig. 13. Iron Age Provinces and Stone Circle Architectural Regions.
(A). Provinces of the British and Irish Pre-Roman Iron Age (after L. Alcock) in (ed. C. Thomas). *The Iron Age in the Irish Sea Province* (1972). A—Atlantic; C—Central; E—Eastern; NC—North Channel; NE—North-Eastern; NW—North-Western; P—Pennine; S—Southern; SC—Solway-Clyde; SM—Southern Mountain; SW—South-Western; W—Western.
(B). The Major Architectural Regions of Stone Circles. A—Atlantic (open rings); B—Boyne (passage-grave rings); C—Cumbria (entrance rings); E—Eastern (hengiform rings); L—Limerick (ditchless circle-henges); M—Munster (Cork-Kerry recumbent stone circles); NC—North Channel (many stones; centre stone rings); NE—North-East Scotland (Clava cairns; recumbent stone circles; Perthshire graded rings); SA—South Atlantic (ditchless, embanked rings); SE/N—South-East Scotland/Northern England (small ovals); SW—South-West Peninsula (paired and multiple rings); W—Western (mixed rings); WS—Wessex (avenues; circle-henges).

To the calendrical implications of the open circles can be added that many of them may have been associated with an axe-cult. Two stone axes were deliberately deposited at Llandegai henge, and one of bronze at Mount Pleasant, Dorset. Concentrations of stone axes have been noted around Avebury and the Ring of Brodgar, Orkney. Four Irish bronze axes were placed under a round barrow at Willerby Wold House, Yorkshire, in association with a burial with an AOC beaker. Such a cult was widespread in early prehistoric Europe. Maringer (1960, 169) cites several instances of the axe being associated with the sun in countries as far apart as Spain and Sweden. At Troldebjerg, Denmark, a hearth in a Middle Neolithic long house covered a pit with a complete pot and an axe with its cutting-edge upwards (Klindt-Jensen, 1957, 46). 'No doubt the ritual observed at Troldebjerg centred around the axe in association with the kindled fire. Both must have been symbols of the sky god who had sway over lightning and fire. It is the same god to which the peasant made offerings by placing them in the soil of his field, burying them in the earth, or hiding them under a stone.' (Maringer, 1960, 187.) Other deposits of axes were found in southern Sweden, in Denmark and in Brittany. Axes are common in Scandinavian rock-carvings. Double-axes of bronze like those from the Aegean, or copies in stone, widespread in Europe during the second millennium, may equally have been of cult significance (C. Hawkes, 1974, 211). It is extraordinary that even in the last century peasants in western Europe believed that stone axes found in their fields were thunderbolts and talismans. Several writers have expressed a belief in an axe-cult (Crawford, 1957, 76; Gelling and Davidson, 1969). Kühn (1966, 185) points out that even today an axe is considered a symbol of fertility in Germany. An axe which could be used to fell trees, to till fields and which struck sparks might be considered by Neolithic farmers to possess generative qualities and have a kinship with fire. A place where such axes were bartered would thus be not only a meeting-place and market but also a temple in which trade and ritual went hand in hand. The axe might become the symbol of the natural powers, particularly at a sun-important time of year. Such a cult was long-lasting for it endured well into Celtic times. Model axes were found at the ritual centre of Wood-eaton, Oxfordshire, built in the Romano-British period (Ross, 1967, 48).

An axe-cult gives extra significance to the famous carvings at Stonehenge III as well as the carvings at Drombeg recumbent stone circle, Ireland, and to the stone axes, engraved on the western stones at Er Lannic in line with the equinoctial sunset. It would explain the non-functional axes of chalk placed in Stonehenge and Woodhenge, Wiltshire, as it would the burial of beautiful jadeite axes at chambered tombs in Brittany like Mané er Hroek, and the manufacture of superb miniatures perforated perhaps for use as religious pendants. A beautiful specimen seems to have been laid by the Sweet wooden trackway, Somerset, around 3200 bc showing how far back into the Neolithic such a cult may extend (J. M. Coles, et al., 1974). The symmetrically patterned stone mace-heads of the Late Neolithic may also belong to this tradition, mounted on a shaft and borne by a priest or chieftain as a sign of his powers. Many of them are non-functional (Roe, 1968, 168) and may have been deliberately broken. Gimbutas (1953) shows the wide-spread cult-use of such objects.

The deposits of stone axes by many of the stones of the north circle at Er Lannic may reflect this belief. The site appeared to be an *atelier* for the manufacture of axes (le Rouzic, 1930), an observation in keeping with the hypothesis that circles and the axe trade were sometimes interconnected. The tallest stone at the south, and other cupmarked stones close to solar positions, show that Er Lannic may be a good example of the intermingling of ritual, social activity and trade in a stone circle. It can be added that a stone axe was discovered as a stray find in the interior of the Carles circle. More revealingly, a broken Group VI axe had been placed in a pit at the foot of the south stone in the Grey Croft stone circle.

Known as 'elf-shots' the prehistoric stone axe was placed in cattle troughs to protect the animals against ill-health even in the nineteenth century AD (Skeat, 1912, 65). It was used as a charm against the pangs of child-birth in Scotland. The connection with a sky-god is clear for in west England such axes were believed to be thunderbolts (J. Evans, 1872, 51) and, in an interesting association with fire, cottages in northern Ireland often had a stone axe placed in their rafters as protection against lightning. Showing how the early Christian church endeavoured to overcome native beliefs in paganism is the Anglo-Saxon incantation quoted by Skeat (1912, 67) whereby an invalid, having drunk a herbal mixture, had this chanted:

> This is thy remedy against the shot of the elves,
> This is thy remedy against the shot of the hag,
> I will help thee.
> [To the evil spirits.] Flee to the mountain-head.
> [To the patient.] Whole be thou. The Lord help thee.

The axe had become evil. The pagan goddess is evil. Yet how potent, even in the eighth century AD, the belief in them must have remained. But although a belief in a stone-circle axe-cult is justifiable, the same is not true of a religion that worshipped a mother-goddess, the 'hag' of the incantation.

In the past some archaeologists and art-historians have been led, because of the profusion of female figurines, engraved plaques and carved stones, to talk of a mother-goddess whose cult was widespread in Mediterranean countries and in western Europe. This female deity has been identified in regions as far apart as Anatolia and Ireland, often being represented not as a complete figure but symbolically through her eyes. 'It was a sometimes awe-inspiring face, dominated by excessively big eyes under arched brows . . .' (Cles-Reden, 1961, 58.) Hence the title of the 'Eye Goddess' (Crawford, 1957). Carved motifs, apparently of eyes, at New Grange caused Childe (1940, 67) to write of stones that 'disclose the chthonic deity to whose bosom the faithful dead returned'; and Robert Graves (1961, 102) in a collation of fancy speckled with fact envisaged New Grange as the home of Dagda who may 'be equated with Osiris, or Adonis, or Dionysus, who was born from a fir and mothered by the horned Moon-goddess Isis, or Io, or Hathur.'

Such analogies are exaggerated. What evidence there is for such a goddess seems limited to France (Fleming, 1969, 254) whereas in Ireland the megalithic carvings of the passage-graves are better placed in a religion that involved the sun. Careful analysis of Boyne art-motifs make the goddess-interpretation very unlikely (C. O'Kelly, 1973, 361) but the 'sun-dial' stone at Knowth, and the incidence of rays from the midwinter sunrise penetrating the chamber at New Grange (Patrick, 1974) show the tomb-builders to have beliefs involving, at the least, solar events. Elsewhere in Britain there are few signs of a female deity either in the form of figurines or of engravings on stone. Here again there is a division between Breton and Irish tombs. 'As the evidence stands, there are two great provinces of megalithic stone-cult art: Brittany and Ireland,

and although both share with the [Iberian] Peninsula a basic symbolism, both display such emphatic and large-scale divergent achievements that they cannot have relied solely on that one southern source.' (Powell, 1966, 114.) Stone circles are unlikely to have been temples of the mother-goddess. The activities within them were more probably directed towards fertility practices.

That these included dancing is an assumption that cannot be proved although such a communal activity is well recorded among primitive societies. Frazer (1922) gives many examples of ring-dancing around a Maypole in Europe at the leafing-time (ibid, 122); around bonfires at Lent (ibid, 610) when, in parts of Switzerland and elsewhere, burning wheels like sun-discs were rolled down hills and when witch-effigies were burnt on hilltops. In the Isle of Man a wren was killed at the Winter solstice and buried after which the people would dance in a ring to music (ibid, 537). Such circular group-dances were clearly customary at important divisions of the year.

Remembering the analogies made between the timber temple of the Creek Indians and that discovered at Durrington Walls, it is intriguing to find that many of the ceremonies of the Indians would have left the same sort of material evidence that occurs in the British circles. At the time of the first-fruits in July or August the whole Creek village would undergo a process of purification, followed by purging and a long fast (Frazer, 1922, 484). At sunset on the holy day all the people went indoors and a sacred fire was lit. During the festival that followed the warriors danced around the fire in its arbour of green wood. Men and women together finally formed three circles to dance again around the fire before bathing in running water to free themselves of their past sins. The Seminole Indians had rather similar rites. Much of these ceremonies would leave nothing behind, but, although no close parallel could be expected, there is evidence in some British circles of seasonal ceremonies, of bonfires, of rites at sunset, of associations with water. Like the Creeks, the builders of many circles were stone-using agriculturalists to whom the annual harvest was the great occasion of the year. Celebratory dancing would have been natural at such a festival.

In the same way the Iron Age Celts, some of whose customs must have descended from earlier societies (Piggott, 1965, 259; Chadwick, 1970, 32) also probably danced at their great festivals as some of their graceful bronze figurines show (Ross, 1972, 137). In the pre-literate Neolithic and Bronze Ages there is no direct record, even oral, of the activities inside the megalithic rings, but it is interesting to find a firm connection with dancing in the names of many stone circles. Both the Trippet Stones and the Merry Maidens, like several other Cornish circles, are reputedly young girls turned into stone for dancing on the Sabbath. A wedding party was similarly petrified at Stanton Drew, Somerset. Athgreany in Wicklow is supposedly a group of dancers and their piper who suffered for the same sacrilegious merry-making. The survival, from the most remote times, of other legends containing elements of truth (Thorpe, 1966, 18) suggests that folk-stories and names like these that tell of dancing in the rings may contain memories of ancient practices, a belief strengthened by the knowledge that dancing was part of the repertoire of prehistoric people in Britain. In the ditch around the sepulchral barrow at Winterbourne Whitchurch, Dorset, the ground had been worn smooth as though by dancers' feet (Grinsell, 1959, 157). At the barrow of Sutton 268, Glamorgan, dancers had repeatedly circled the primary burial before the covering mound was thrown over it (C. Fox, 1959, 98).

Pictorial evidence of early prehistoric dancing is absent from the non-representational megalithic art of the British Isles but is plentiful elsewhere from the Upper Palaeolithic onwards with the engraving of men dancing around two 'self-stranglers' at the cave of Monte Pellegrino, Sicily, and the nine skirted women dancing round a naked male in the Cogul rock-shelter in Catalonia. Bronze Age dancers occur in the rock-carvings at Val Camonica, Italy, in scenes of an agricultural world dominated by sun-signs (Kühn, 1966, 131). Formalized dancing plants are painted on the rock-face at the Cueva de los Letreros, Spain (ibid, 122). The well-known Scandinavian rock-carvings have many scenes of dancing, including some of men around a May-pole (ibid, 193). Even musical instruments have occasionally survived. Although it cannot be assumed that simple pipes like the swan's perforated leg-bone from a Bronze Age barrow at Wilsford G23, Wilts., were used to accompany a dance, or even the nine-piece pan-pipe from a shaman's grave of the eighth century bc at Przeczyce, Poland (Megaw, 1968, 340), there can be little doubt that the Neolithic pottery drums of northern Europe from the Trichterbecher cultures (ibid, 334) provided the rhythmic background for festival dancing such as is proposed here for the British stone circles.

None of this can be conclusive but the compiled evidence favours some form of dancing in the larger megalithic rings. Witchcraft at the Rollright Stones or at Soussons Common, Devon, where a hank of modern hair was found in the central cist (Worth, 1953, 191) may contribute something to the answer for, if Murray (1921) was correct, witchcraft was, in part, a post-Christian survival of pagan customs, 'the old pre-Christian religion of rural Europe which the new Asiatic religion of Christ had driven underground', although 'the fancies of the late Margaret Murray need not detain us. They were justly, if irritably, dismissed by a real scholar as "vapid balderdash"' (Trevor-Roper, 1969, 41). Yet mediaeval demonology did contain 'scattered fragments of paganism'. Dancing was common in witch-covens. 'The dances were the rapid, sexually exciting dances of the fertility cults. They were undoubtedly ancient and pre-Christian and were an integral part of the ritual. The most common were a round dance in which the performers faced outwards, or danced in pairs, back to back, in a ring, and a long processional in which all moved very fast . . .' (Hole, 1945, 31.) As it is very likely that the horned or antlered 'god' of the Bronze Age was ultimately transmuted into the Devil of the witches in Christian times his existence in such contexts is another indication that dancing was a part of Bronze Age religious practice. Evidence of the Christianization of pagan rituals may survive in the famous Horned Dance held at Abbots Bromley, Staffordshire, each year in early September, part of the annual Lammas Wake, itself possibly directly descended from the Celtic harvest festival of Lughnasa.

The very shape of the stone circles and their unlittered interiors accords with this interpretation of their use. Similar structures, whether made by the Indians of America, or in Gambia, or at Asota, India, were used for dancing, whatever the underlying reason for the ceremony and, as has been remarked by Piggott in his discussion on the use of the Sanctuary, Wiltshire (1940), a circle is an ideal shape for such communal participation.

Communal dancing would not exclude an axe-cult for this could have been an integral part of the ceremonies as some rock-carvings show. And simply because dancing is known in primitive societies this does not mean that a megalithic ring in which it took place could not have been elegantly designed.

Much of the opposition to the geometrical and astronomical hypotheses of Thom have been based on the unlikelihood of a Neolithic peasant society being capable of such erudition (Piggott, 1973, 324). Similar objections have been aimed against the later Druids as Pythagorean philosophers: 'We know that the Celts at this period, say 80 bc, were still practicing divination by human sacrifice and preserving the skulls of slain enemies by nailing them as trophies to the porches of their houses. Is it possible that they were at the same time living on the rarefied levels of Greek philosophy?' (Tierney, 1960, 223.) Correlation between miserable domestic, even savage ways of life and the possession of a high intellect is not impossible. Ross (1972, 161) has remarked:

As a people the Celts have always had a natural feeling for learning and intellectual exercise. It is an aspect of their temperament that has amazed and intrigued outsiders who have come into contact with them, and have found such a marked contrast between their frequently crude and often careless domestic arrangements and the refinement and elegance of their use of language and appreciation of linguistic subtlety.

In the same way the reeking midden around Skara Brae did not necessarily render its inhabitants incapable of abstract thought.

Yet before the student of the Late Neolithic sees it as a Euclidean Utopia he should recall the quite extensive evidence for fertility cults in British early prehistory whose practices would probably be obscene to modern thought, and try to reconcile these with Thom's astronomical magi. It is important to remember that many recorded Celtic customs like the horned god date back to at least the Bronze Age (Ross, 1967, 127ff; Swanton, 1974) when the stag, and perhaps the bull, were representative of the sun. The survival of horns and crotals from the Bronze Age votive hoard at Dowris, Ireland, suggests a bull-cult there in the later second millennium bc (J. M. Coles, 1971b).

It may be necessary, therefore, to visualize ceremonies of animal symbolism enacted in megalithic rings presumably by the same shamans or witch-doctors

—so much more evocative a word than 'priest'—who were also able to design complex geometrical plans for their enclosures. This is not impossible if the powers of the gods were considered such that it was essential to construct the nicest alignments to 'catch' these supernatural spirits before any social magic could be successful. But, fundamentally, if there is any validity in the triple assumption that Celtic beliefs were partly descended from earlier customs, that parallels may be made between other primitive people and British Bronze Age societies and that surviving artefacts are informative about Neolithic and Bronze Age customs, then the evidence is strong that religious rites in stone circles were very much concerned with fertility, their realization emanating from acts of sympathetic magic related to animals. The swan, for example, seems early to have been connected with solar cults. Equally, horned anthropomorphic deities are common, the antlered god in particular being suggestive of fertility (Ross, 1972, 213). An antler head-piece is known from the very early Mesolithic site of Star Carr, Yorkshire, with dates averaging 7572 bc. A chalk carving of a stag or elk was found in the Late Neolithic flint mine of Grimes Graves, Norfolk.

A stone circle, starkly simple on its hillside today, may be transformed into a prehistoric Mount Palomar without difficulty, but the wealth of Celtic animal mythology and the images on Scandinavian rock-carvings warn that it may be necessary to have the stones illuminated by night-fires and inhabited by antlered shamans holding axes on high, raising hands with outspread fingers, and performing acts of fertilization with domestic animals (Ross, 1972, 159) and with humans. 'The belief that it is possible to influence the fertility of the land and the abundance of crops by sexual intercourse on the part of human beings is too familiar to need elaboration.' (Gelling and Davidson, 1969, 68). 'In prehistoric times it would seem that the Sky father–Earth mother fertility ritual was enacted, doubtless by human instruments and agents of the respective god and goddess, to enhance the fecundity of the soil and the reproduction processes in nature generally.' (James, 1957, 224.) The shaman would 'become' the sun-god himself by imitative actions, practices more expected of bone-rattling witch-doctors than of Thom's grave and dispassionate astronomers. Body-painting may also have been practised as the lumps of ochre from Mosley Height, Skara Brae and other sites testify.

Much early religion was naturalistic, concerned with nature and its effects, sometimes requiring a shaman to intercede with nature on behalf of the community, less a witch-doctor than a medium who would dance himself into a drum-beaten ecstacy before passing into a trance.

A fire burns on the ground. Framed against the night by the red glow of the flickering flames, the shaman begins to move rhythmically, drumming, dancing, leaping and singing. The little bells on his robe tinkle, his iron ornaments clatter, and the Tungus sit there in the dim light, their attention riveted on his every move. The shaman's excitement communicates itself to the circle of spectators, and the larger the audience, the stronger the empathy between them and him. They all know each other, being inter-related and members of the same clan. Drawn together by the combination of night and firelight, they allow the monotonous rhythm of the drums to waft them irresistibly away from the everyday world. The excitement mounts, leaping like a spark from one man to the next, until all are near ecstacy and each is at once performer and spectator, doctor and patient, hammer and anvil. (Lissner, 1961, 274.)

Many of the Plains Indians of America had a form of Sun Dance—which had little to do with sun worship—which was prompted by the need for supernatural assistance. It involved slow, communal dancing in a circular enclosure around a 'killed' tree, the hardly moving 'dancers' going without food or water until they drifted into a trance. The Great Basin Indians, both men and women, also danced around a tree, singing songs about the animals they hunted. Even the post-Christian Indian Ghost Dance was a desperate attempt to invoke the old powers to bring back the buffalo and the Indians' dead tribesmen (La Farge, 1956).

The dancing is gone. But what does survive in Britain is evidence of fertility beliefs dating back to the Neolithic from flint mines, from causewayed enclosures and henges. Each of the mines, at Grimes Graves and at Black-patch, had a realistically carved chalk phallus (Piggott, 1954, 88). Also at Grimes Graves a crude statuette in chalk of a pregnant 'goddess' squatted on a niche in an area sterile of good flint. Other chalk phalli were discovered at Windmill Hill causewayed enclosure and, in bone, at the Trundle. Chalk figurines came from Windmill Hill and Maiden Castle, Dorset. A large chalk phallus was discovered at Maumbury Rings henge, Dorset, once more showing the association of fecundity and communal enclosure at this time. Of the same Late Neolithic period, from a repaired section of the Bell A timber trackway, Somerset, is the heterosexual ashwood figure with breasts and exaggerated penis, described discreetly as a god-dolly by the excavator (J. M. Coles, 1968). Another male figurine, but of pinewood, was unearthed at Dagenham, Essex, possibly of the Bronze Age, and with a hole for a detachable male organ very like other Late Bronze Age wooden figures with round shields from Roos Carr, Yorkshire. Four of these stand on a ship and may be compared with the Bronze Age rock-carvings from Ostfold and Bohuslän which have been tentatively linked with 'the hypothetical epiphany of the sun-god at a Spring festival' (Gelling and Davidson, 1969, 56).

Standing stones, especially those at the centre of a stone circle, have often been considered as representations of phalli for fertility ceremonies in which context the nineteenth century AD credence of Breton wives in the generative powers of the Carnac menhirs might be recalled. So might the small carving from the second millennium nuraghe culture of Sardinia which showed 'three naked women dancing a wild dance round a stone' (Cles-Reden, 1961, 133). Standing stones, occasionally associated with deposits of stone axes (Piggott, 1954, 166), exist in the forecourts of some chambered tombs, sometimes apparently chosen for their evocative shape, and such pillars and blocks have been interpreted as sexual symbols (Daniel, 1950, 120). If the centre stones of stone circles were indeed phallic representations then it becomes all the more likely that at such sites rituals of generation occurred, all traces of which have gone.

The paucity of finds from the circles means only that whatever the activities in the rings they did not demand permanent and tangible offerings being buried there. Astronomical observation would leave little except the stones themselves. But neither would the dancing of a community engaged in their imitative roles of god and animal and human. So far from astronomy and magic being mutually exclusive they were quite possibly complementary in many of the ceremonies that took place in the stone circles. It is unlikely, how- that these were occasions of pure science as has sometimes been claimed.

7. THE ANATOMY OF LONG MEG

At this point it will be advisable to summarize what has been claimed for the great open circles. This may be achieved appropriately by examining one of the largest though not earliest, Long Meg and Her Daughters (Fig. 8). The name comes from a legend that an indignant saint metamorphosed a local coven of witches into stones. Another more secular account claims that the smaller stones around Long Meg were her lovers. And yet another that if a piece were broken off Long Meg the stone would bleed. Attesting to the power of myth, the 'wondrous wizard', Michael Scott (c. 1175–1230) of Kelso, who practised astrology in Palermo, was somehow translated to seventeenth-century England where he is supposed not only to have 'cleft the Eildon Hills in twain' but also endowed Long Meg's stones with a magic power so that no one could count the stones twice alike. (The belief in uncountable stones was countrywide and is asserted for the Rollright Stones and as far away as the Countless Stones in Kent.)

Long Meg and Her Daughters is a huge site, 109.4 × 93.0 m, of massive stones set out in a flattened circle. It is on the edge of the wide sandstone terrace above the east bank of the Eden, six miles from the Penrith henges across the river, within three days' walk of the Langdale factory sites, and on the northern route to the Tyne Gap. The traces of earth bank around the stone circle attest to its affinities with henges. There is an entrance of double-stones at the south-west.

The heaviest stone, a huge block at the SSW., measures 3.4 × 2.1 × 1.5 m. It weighs about 28 tons and would have required at least 120 people to set it up. One may guess at a population of 250–400 to take part in the rites, perhaps held in the Spring or Autumn or at Midwinter. It is surely significant that two vast stones stand virtually due east and west in the equinoctial positions. They stand at opposite ends of Thom's primary diameter (1967, fig. 12.11) and it is tempting to believe that the circle was planned originally on this axis.

Pl. 10. *Long Meg & Her Daughters, Cumberland.* This view, from the north, of the western stones shows the considerable slope on which the ring was erected. The outlier, Long Meg, stands dark against the skyline, left-centre.

The standing stone in the foreground at the north corner weighs about four tons.

The circle is on a pronounced slope. At the highest point, 18 m beyond the entrance rises the thin, pointed column of the outlier, Long Meg herself, of red sandstone that may have had to be dragged uphill from the banks of the Eden one and a half miles west, a task made necessary by the absence of any pillarlike stone among the local granitic boulders. Long Meg is 3.7 m tall, 1.2 m higher than any other stone. The surfaces are smooth and tabular, and on the face nearest the circle are three markings (Fig. 14): a cup-and-ring with gutter; a spiral; and some incomplete concentric circles (Harvey, 1948). The signs are enigmatic and not necessarily contemporary with the erection of the stones, but there is increasing agreement that such markings are related to ideas of life and death through their frequent occurrence in tombs, on cist-slabs and in circles containing burials (Simpson and Thawley, 1972, 99; Burl, 1972, 37); and also that they are related to the sun because of the aligned stones on which they are sometimes carved (Morris, 1969, 51; Burl, 1974a, 65). 'As is normal in Scotland, most of the carvings are so sited

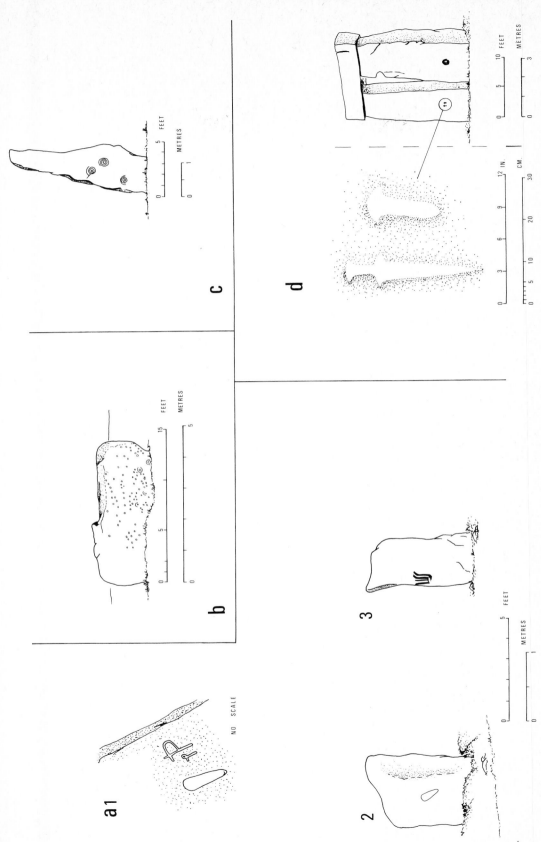

Fig. 14. Carvings on Some Stone Circles. (a) Er Lannic, Brittany: (1) Stone 2; (2) Stone 1; (3) Stone 3; (b) Rothiemay recumbent stone, Banffshire; (c) Long Meg outlier, Cumberland; (d) Stonehenge, Stone 53. (c) after Harvey, 1948.

as to be practically invisible in the midsummer noonday sun, but to show up very well indeed in a low midwinter sun.' (Morris, 1971, 54.) They affirm the rustic nature of the ceremonies in which the ebb of the seasons and the fertility of the ground may have been superstitiously associated with the need to placate or entice the sun in its journeyings. A connection between sun, death and fertility could be expected in the animistic world of these early farmers.

In 1586 William Camden reported that inside the ring were 'two heaps of stones, under which they say are dead bodies bury'd', but a footnote in the 1695 edition of the *Britannia* added that the heaps 'are no part of it; but have been gather'd off the plough'd lands adjoyning, and ... have been thrown up here in a waste corner of the field' (Camden, 1695, 831). Such cairns, which have long since vanished, cannot be assumed to have been prehistoric.

Long Meg's outlier stands at 223° 4′ from the hypothetical centre of the circle. This alignment is almost exactly that over which the midwinter sun would have set and this may account for the position of the outlier and its height for its tip would have had to rise clear of the skyline.

The stone also stands near the crest of the ridge beyond which the ground falls away steadily to the west, to the Eden and to the Lake District mountains. A traveller from that direction even a mile away can still see the top of Long Meg silhouetted against the sky when the other circle stones are concealed by the curve of the hill, and is led by the easiest path to the circle whose entrance of double stones is at the head of the slope. It is between these monumental portals that processions may have entered the circle, of people assembled from the many fells and valleys of the region, come to barter, to gossip and to celebrate, to exchange gifts, to reaffirm local custom and to supplicate that warmth, light and fertility might continue to attend their lives. Now only a few wandering visitors come here. They leave their cars in the shade of the trees along the lane, stroll around the stones, perhaps stand hopefully by Long Meg as Wordsworth once did in 1833:

> Speak Thou, whose massy strength and stature scorn
> The power of years—pre-eminent, and placed
> Apart, to overlook the circle vast—
> Speak, Giant-Mother!

But poet and visionary received no answer.

8. BURIAL AND CONTINUITY

A final question of these great Cumbrian circles is the presence of burials in some of them. Mention has been made of sites like Moor Divock, Lacra and Oddendale with their deposits of cremated bone. Hardly three and a half miles NNW. of the latter a cist was discovered at the centre of the concentric ovals of Gunnerkeld, a site, as Dymond (1878) remarked, very similar in appearance and position to Oddendale. Although such burials distinguish these megalithic rings from the larger and earlier circles it is to be wondered if this was not attributable to a change in custom rather than a difference in function.

The placing of a burial within a circular enclosure is known in other North Channel sites like the henges of the Giants Ring, Belfast; Longstone Rath, Kildare; and Ballymeanoch, Argyll. In the case of the latter the eccentrically placed ditched barrow and its two cists is such that it is likely to be a secondary mound made by beaker users some time in the mid-second millennium. The same intrusive element appears at Cairnpapple, West Lothian, and at Dun Ruadh, Tyrone, in both of which secondary tumuli were built in the interiors of older henges. In the same way, burial cists were added to Balbirnie stone circle, Fife (J. N. G. Ritchie, 1974b).

The first problem, then, is that of whether the interred cremations were contemporary with the construction of the circle. The second is the intention of the people who placed the bones there. Reference has already been made to mediaeval bonfires at seasonal festivals, pagan in ancestry, with their association between fire and the life-giving sun, and the fire-reddened patches in some circles like Lacra could be the relics of pyres the object of which may have been not only to consume the remains of the dead but also to invoke a sympathetic bond with the sun. It is an interpretation far removed from the funebrial explanations of earlier writers (J. Anderson, 1886) whereby stone circles of the Bronze Age were considered to be the sepulchres of noted chieftains, yet it would provide a continuum from the ceremonies of the earlier circles, ceremonies later enacted by smaller Bronze Age groups no longer journeying to distant centres but performing modified, analogous rites within their own local, less-imposing monuments.

In most of the open Cumbrian circles such a transition is not obvious although there is frequent evidence of cremation however slight. There may have been two cairns within Long Meg but in an area of almost 8,000 square metres they may not have been impressive. Within the Carles there may also have been cairns (B. Williams, 1856a). Otherwise the only trace of burial was at the west corner of the rectangular stone setting where a deep pit and charcoal was discovered (Dover, 1882). Fragments of charcoal and burnt bone were the only discoveries at Swinside. At Studfold, however, a megalithic ring more oval than the earlier examples, 35.1 × 28.4 m, had a low cairn centred 4.6 m from the focal point of the site (Mason and Valentine, 1925) which may be presumed to be secondary to the circle. No finds were recorded from the excavation.

More helpfully, at Brats Hill on Burn Moor five cairns occupy the interior of the circle and as there are four other circles nearby on this plateau it is worth considering whether this group is transitional between the early and the late circles (Fig. 15). Unlike many of the great circles Brats Hill is reached only after a hard walk up Gill Bank from the village of Boot in Eskdale, a

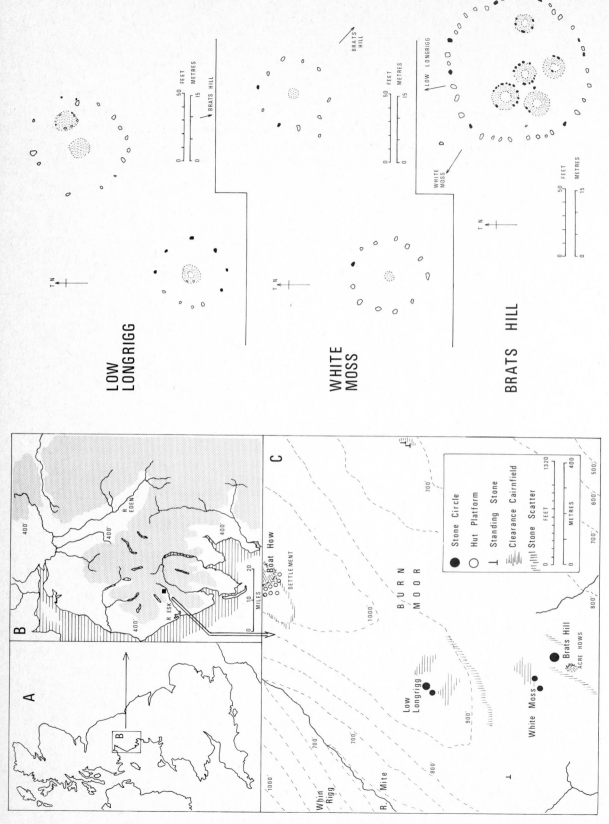

Fig. 15. The Complex of Stone Circles on Burn Moor, Eskdale, Cumberland (Cumbria).

three-quarter-mile climb along a footpath ascending a gradient of 1:5. The great circle stands to the west and just below Brats Hill knoll and measures 32.0×25.9 m, being flattened at the NNW, where the ground falls away. Of its forty-two stones most are now supine, the tallest 0.9 m high standing at the south. Ten metres to the north-west is an outlying stone barely 31 cm tall. It was suggested (Ferguson, 1906) that there was an entrance at the north-west but the gap is little wider than at any other part of the circumference.

The five internal cairns, 6.4–7.6 m in diameter, and now not more than 31 cm in height, were each once retained within kerbs of fourteen stones. When two cairns were opened in 1827 (B. Williams, 1856b) each had a central dome of five large stones covering human cremations, animal bones and antlers. What relationship these cairns had to the building of the circle is quite unknown but as a cluster it is likely they were built consecutively with the first being the mound just south of the circle centre. It is noticeable that the others crowd around it in such a way that almost the entire north-east sector of the circle is left open. Similar concentrations of cremation deposits in one half of a site have been noticed, *inter alia*, at the Old Parks barrow, Kirkoswald (Ferguson, 1895); at Cairnpapple henge (Piggott, 1948); and at two of the Dorchester henges (Atkinson, Piggott and Sandars, 1951, 58) where the burials also were thought to be successive. In the case of Brats Hill it is useless to speculate whether they represent succeeding generations or the deaths of important persons, singly or collectively, or even sporadic offerings in those seasons when the year had been bad. What can be inferred is that the concentration of cairns to the south-west was because the participants in the ceremonies wished to face in that direction.

About 130 m north-west of Brats Hill are two smaller stone circles arranged north-east–south-west on White Moss, the south-west site being 16.6 m in diameter of low stones of which the south one may be the tallest. At its centre are the remains of a cairn. Thirty metres north-east is the second, better-preserved circle, 15.9 m across, with the tallest stones up to 0.9 m high at the south-west. This also contains a low cairn. As well as a few scattered boulders to the south, many having been taken for the circles, there are also some unobtrusive cairns to the north. Hardly a quarter of a mile north on a hill 50 ft above White Moss is another pair of circles on Low Longrigg. The south-west site, from which White Moss and Brats Hill can be seen, is composed of a low stone circle 15.2 m across, with an internal cairn. Eighteen metres north-east is the second ring, all its stones prostrate, an ellipse 21.6×15.2 m in diameter, and with two cairns, one well defined. The dissimilarity in size of these circles, also on a north-east–south-west axis, suggests they also were built consecutively.

Surmises on the interconnections of such sites and Brats Hill or even between themselves is more a matter for the visionary than the archaeologist. If they are related at all and if they had corresponding functions, two inferences from ramshackle premises, the paired, smaller circles may be regarded as successors to Brats Hill. The warmer and drier weather of the Bronze Age together with an increase in population caused people to take up marginal land in many of the highlands of Britain (Simmons, 1969; Fleming, 1971a; S. P. Hicks, 1972) during the middle and later second millennium before a deteriorating climate and over-exploitation of the soil compelled its eventual abandonment. Signs of prehistoric settlement can be seen on moors whose present, thin acid soil offers no sustenance. From Burn Moor Tarn itself there are clear indications of a decrease in oak forest from about 1600 bc onwards and an expansion of grassland and the weeds that accompany it. The complete absence of cereal grains show this to result from pastoralists clearing grazing areas. But from about 1000 bc onwards worsening weather produced the beginnings of swampland conditions which would have forced settlers away from this upland (Pennington, 1970, 72–4). The smaller circles could be manifestations of men's attempts to extend their territory to land that even in their time provided little encouragement, and if they were indeed built consecutively this could testify to the gradual widening of forest clearance.

Intriguingly, if the star-lines of Thom were proved correct the chronological sequence of the stone circles on Burn Moor would be clear. There is a hypothetical alignment from Brats Hill to the north-east circle at Low Longrigg, directed towards Arcturus (α Boötis) in 1900 BC (c. 1575 bc) (Thom, 1967, 99). Another towards Low Longrigg south-west is for 1800 BC. A third from White Moss south-west to Brats Hill is orientated on Antares (α Scorpionis) in 1700 BC, and a fourth from Brats Hill to White Moss north-east might have been aligned on Pollux (β Geminorum) in 1600 BC (c. 1300 bc). Ignoring the remarkable century-spacing of these dates they correspond very closely to those obtained from independent pedological investigations already mentioned. Had the Brats Hill stone circle been built some 200 years before the earliest circle on Low Longrigg the span of occupation on Burn Moor could have been between about 1800 bc and 1000 bc, quite feasible archaeologically, and apparently confirmed by Thom's stellar lines. It must be added, however, that this may be misleading because of the deliberately restricted range of Thom's chronological limits.

Near both pairs of stone circles are small, low cairns. These cairnfields are comparatively recently recognized phenomena and their original status is debatable (A. Graham, 1957). Excavations have found few burials in these diminutive mounds, perhaps because of the acidity of the soil. If they are burial places this may imply that adjacent circles were not sepulchral despite their own cairns. Whereas similar cairnfields were associated with enclosed cremation cemeteries (ECCs) in south-west Scotland the excavators believed them to be the burial places of people who used the nearby ECC as a ritual centre (Scott-Elliot, 1967). But in Northumberland there were indications that comparable cairnfields might be the results of clearing stones from newly made fields (Jobey, 1968, 146). Other cairnfields have been recognized in Cumbria (Fell, 1964c). On the Yorkshire Moors they are often south-facing on dry ground and frequently associated with ring-cairns or stone circles under barrows (Fleming, 1971a), prompting the suggestion that the ring-cairns and circles were, at least in part, ritual centres, and that the cairnfields were piles of cleared stones that belonged to 'a late stage in the history of the moorland when the original forest soil had been truncated by erosion and surface stones were becoming a problem' (ibid, 22). An excavation by the writer in 1974 of a small cairn near Low Longrigg north-east confirmed its non-sepulchral nature. If broad chronological parallels may be made between Yorkshire and Cumbria then the small Burn Moor circles could belong to a period in the last centuries of the second millennium when people were making their final endeavours to obtain a living from the worsening moorland.

These unobtrusive stone circles have little resemblance to the great open stone circles of Lakeland and may be a millennium in time from them. Yet from the archaeological data one may deduce that their purpose was fundamentally little different. In other parts of the British Isles a similar continuity appears, though the architecture of the circles and the ceremonies within them are frequently unique to each region.

CHAPTER FIVE

Other Early Open Stone Circles

Now I come . . . to give a clear evidence these monuments were Pagan temples; which was not made-out before.

John Aubrey

1. INTRODUCTION

At one time it was thought that the makers of the fine beaker ware were the builders of stone circles. 'The probability is that they (the Beaker Folk) had some share in the inspiration of them all, and the raising of these temples throughout Britain is further proof of the widespread religious conformity that this people was able to impose.' (C. and J. Hawkes, 1943, 59.) Physically very different from the slighter, gracile Neolithic stock these powerfully built foreigners first came to the country at the beginning of the second millennium and settled around the meres and islets of eastern Britain before eventually moving inland up the rivers that offered them passage through the unknown forests. Over several centuries the intruders mingled increasingly with the natives, sometimes peacefully, sometimes as overlords, sometimes by conquest. Their efficient archery equipment, their copper and bronze knives which were the first metalware known in the British Isles, their custom of burying their dead singly, sometimes under round mounds, their elegant pottery, made these strangers awesome figures to the indigenous people.

Often skeletons of beaker-users together with their pots and the remains of a quiverful of flint-tipped arrows or a stone battle-axe are found at the foot of standing stones, occasionally in stone circles themselves. Sometimes, the second phase of Stonehenge being an example, they may have built a stone circle themselves. More commonly they used existing monuments for the deposition of their dead, perhaps because they considered such places to have acquired a sacred aura, though it must be added that the excavators of Gorsey Bigbury, Somerset, believed that beaker people had deliberately desecrated this henge before turning it into a squalid occupation site (S. J. Jones, 1938).

Apart from the absence of evidence within the circles the dates for the infiltration of these incomers across Britain militate against their having built the great circles. The districts containing several large open circles do not possess concentrations of early beaker material. In the Orkneys, in south-west Scotland, in Somerset, Devon or Cornwall, there are few early beaker remains, 70 per cent of the definable pottery in Somerset being of the seventeenth century or later, a time too late for the construction of the first stone circles in that county, particularly of the monumental Stanton Drew. In Cornwall there is a predominance of Bronze Age beaker material. On the other hand, the largest open stone circles of western Britain fit persuasively into Late Neolithic contexts and are very similar to those in Cumbria in their size, situation, architecture and in the forms of activity that took place within them. A cultural connection is likely.

Without invoking flotillas of missionaries disseminating the gospel of megalithic enclosures it is still possible to believe in the diffusion of native ideas along the western sea-lanes of Britain, and it is not strange that there is a resemblance between the circles of different areas. There are dissimilarities, more obvious in the smaller, later sites as local custom nurtured traits increasingly divergent from the earlier tradition. Several regions have two or three distinct types of megalithic ring within them that emphasize the polymorphic nature of society even in a small district. But as will be seen, whether in the Orkneys or at Land's End, the size of the circles, their shapes and their axial alignments indicate a common ancestry along the western seaboard. Examination of some of these large circles from north to south in the country demonstrates this.

2. ORKNEY MAINLAND

At one extreme of the Atlantic sea-route are the two most northerly circle-henges of the British Isles, the Standing Stones of Stenness and the Ring of Brodgar which is one of the biggest stone circles. They stand a mile apart at the ends of a narrow isthmus dividing the lochs of Stenness and Harray. Both sites are impressive, Brodgar having a 103.6 m circle inside a rock-cut ditch 142 m in diameter, and Stenness a 61 m bank around the remains of a 31.1 m circle. The diameter of Brodgar is almost exactly 125 Megalithic Yards, the same as the inner circles at Avebury (A. and A. S. Thom, 1973, 122) and at New Grange, Meath, the latter being dated to $c.$2500 bc. Brodgar is circular with an apparent north–south axis (ibid, 121). Similar meridional lines will be observed in other great circles. Particularly tall stones stand at west and south in Brodgar, perhaps as axial markers.

It is tempting to see this site and Stenness as meeting-places at the edges of separate social areas which the isthmus divided. The earlier suggestion that some chambered tombs and stone circles might be centres of complementary activities, the tomb being the repository for bones and other sepulchral material, the circle an area in which the community enacted its seasonal ceremonies—maybe even using some of the tomb-contents—is encouraged by the proximity to Stenness and Brodgar of huge passage-graves: the devastated Ring of Bookan on its ditched platform one mile north-west of Brodgar, and the magnificent Maes Howe, surely one of the most awe-inspiring monuments in Europe, also on a platform within an incomplete

Pl. 11. *The Standing Stones of Stenness, Orkney Mainland*. From the south showing three of the surviving pillars with the Loch of Harray behind them. A causeway at the NNW. provided the entrance to this circle-henge which originally had twelve stones. The thin, unshaped flagstones are about five metres high. About 1,300 tons of sandstone were quarried from the surrounding ditch.

rock-cut ditch, three-quarters of a mile east of Stenness. Whether there was any direct connection between tomb and circle is not certain but in both cases the paired sites are adjacent to the entry of the isthmus and a correlation is feasible. Comparable associations of tombs with henges have been noticed in Wessex at Mount Pleasant and Knowlton in Dorset and at Marden, Wiltshire, and it is arguable that such conjunctions might have been variants on the combination of burial and ritual site so common amongst the 'sepulchral' circles and henges of northern Britain.

The joining of henge and circle at both Stenness and Brodgar shows the affinities of these forms of enclosure. Both circles have stones of great size. Brodgar is in much better condition with many of its stones having been re-erected whereas Stenness has only four of its original twelve remaining (J. N. G. Ritchie, 1973). Which of the two is earlier is not yet known although the single NNW. entrance of Stenness, a Class I henge, may indicate its priority over the Ring of Brodgar, larger, farther to the north, a Class II site with opposed entrances at north-west and south-east. Within seven miles of Stenness are four chambered tombs other than Maes Howe, from Cuween to Wideford, of Neolithic origin, but there are only a few Bronze Age round cairns. Conversely, near Brodgar are only Bookan and the Stones of Via passage-grave and some twenty round cairns and a long mound in its immediate vicinity. The argument is treacherous but the differences in the type of neighbouring monument and their own architecture in these Orcadian circle-henges, as well as their positions, point to Stenness as the earlier. At the centre of this ring excavation has uncovered a small stone rectangle of supine slabs in which a post had stood. To the north-west were two stone holes and, beyond them, the ploughed-out remains of a little timber construction with a date of 1730 bc ±270 (SRR-592) (J. N. G. Ritchie, 1974a). Cremated bone was also found. The two stones had later been deliberately pulled from their sockets and the holes backfilled. Radiocarbon determinations of 2238 bc ±70 (SRR-351) from this area and of 2356 bc ±65 (SRR-350) from animal bone in the ditch suggest Stenness was constructed late in the third millennium bc in the Late Neolithic, a period in keeping with the belief that these great circles are early in the history of megalithic rings, well before the arrival of intrusive beaker-using people.

From a ditch terminal at Stenness came some sherds of grooved ware, Late Neolithic pottery also known in early Wessex henges and at Skara Brae only six miles north-west of Stenness. But at Brodgar the sole finds during the restoration of 1906 were a rough stone axe and a quartz hammerstone. To the suggestion that people using stone circles may have regarded the axe as a sun-symbol, a religious object to be used in their ceremonies, one may comment on 'the large number of broken axe-hammers found on Mainland in Orkney around the Stenness circles, suggesting that here too we may be concerned with a similar phenomenon of a Henge attracting the products of axe-factory sites' (Stone and Wallis, 1951, 135).

It has been claimed that the Ring of Brodgar was a complex lunar observatory (Thom and Thom, 1973), the situation being chosen because from it could be seen three natural foresights on different positions of the moon. There is indeed some evidence that megalithic lunar alignments preceded those upon the sun in parts of Britain, Stonehenge being a good example (Newham, 1972, 7). At Brodgar, many of the postulated orientations relate to the surrounding cairns and not to the megalithic ring itself and may be explained as an elaboration of an ancient ceremonial centre in the later second millennium. This could account for the hypothetical date, astronomically calculated, of 1560 BC (*c.* 1300 bc) (Thom and Thom, 1975, 113), some 1400 years after Stenness, extremely late for such a great circle-henge, especially with its concomitant axe-hammers which are unlikely to postdate the mid-second millennium bc (Roe, 1967, 69).

If Stenness and Brodgar stand at the edges of their territories then it is significant that each has an outlier between it and the isthmus, the Comet Stone on a low platform 137 m south-east of Brodgar, and the spectacular Watch Stone, 5.6 m high, to the north of Stenness at the narrowest part of the land. It may be that one function of such stones was to act as boundary-markers for land that had been settled. This might explain their frequent situation by steep slopes or at the head of river valleys by the edges of plateaux as in Cornwall.

3. THE TWELVE APOSTLES, DUMFRIES

Five hundred sea-miles south of the Orkney circles but within a few miles of the Solway Firth is the fifth largest stone circle in Britain, the Twelve Apostles just outside Dumfries, split by a hedge, spoiled in atmosphere by the road that edges the fields in which it stands. Typically it is low-lying between Cluden Water and the River Nith in the southern part of the valley, six square miles of flat, fertile ground with hills closing in the east and west, and in an excellent position to be the focus for a large and scattered community. This 87.8 × 73.8 m diameter flattened circle of eleven stones, the tallest at ENE. and WSW., should be regarded as a northern outlier of the Cumbrian group, only fifty miles by land along the shores of the Solway Firth from Long Meg. Like those circles a great number of stone axes, especially those of Group VI from the Lake District, have been found in its locality (J. Williams, 1970). A mile away by the Nith was another circle of nine large stones, 'unfortunately, and without the knowledge of the proprietor, Peter Johnston, Esq., of Carasalloch, they were broken up and applied to the purposes of building' (NSA Dumfries, 1845, 559).

The answer to why a circle of eleven stones should be called the Twelve Apostles may lie in a letter from H.M. Survey quoted in the Ordnance Memoirs of 1850. 'There should be only 11 stones. The drawn plan shows only this number; but there turns out to have been an accidental blue spot on this plan which has been reproduced by the zincography on the pub-

Pl. 12. *Stanton Drew, Somerset*. From the SSW. showing the ruined south-west circle isolated in the foreground. To the east of both the central and north-east rings are remains of stone avenues. The outlier, Hautville's Quoit, once stood near the farm buildings top-centre beyond the River Chew; and the Cove is just off left-centre of the photograph.

lished plans.' It is likely, however, that twelve was the original number.

It is striking to see the resemblance between this circle and Broadlee Class II henge seventeen miles to the east. Their diameters are very similar, Broadlee being 79.2 m across. The henge has entrances at north-west and south-east, the circle has a wide space, if not a formal entrance, also at the south-east. Both lie between rivers and are low-lying at the south of a river valley in level countryside. As Broadlee is only thirty miles north of Penrith it seems likely that both henge and stone circle had fundamentally the same purpose, the materials of their construction simply mirroring the local geology.

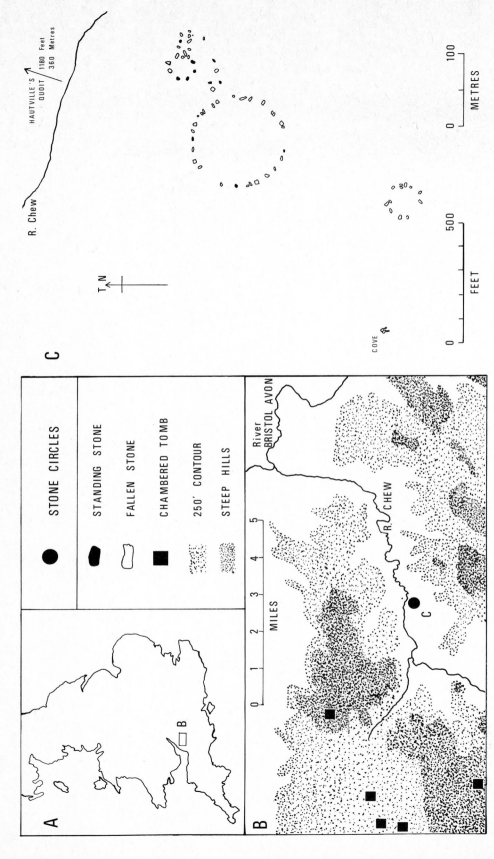

Fig. 16. Stanton Drew, Somerset (Avon).

4. STANTON DREW, SOMERSET

Further to the south, below Wales, by the side of the Bristol Channel is the second biggest stone circle in Britain after Avebury, Stanton Drew (the homestead by the stones), which as Stukeley remarked was 'vulgarly called the Weddings, and they say 'tis a company that assisted at a nuptial ceremony thus petrify'd.' (Fig. 16.) It consists of a complex of three circles, the central site being properly circular, 113.4 m across, and conforms to the pattern of the other great open sites in its low-lying position within what must have been the natural forest-zone. The complex is just over 90 m south of the River Chew in a valley, Broadfield Down rising steeply to the west, the Mendips to the south, slightly lower hills to the east. Predictably, it is in a pass which here connects the Yeo and the Bristol Avon valleys, the latter not only running down to the sea but also providing an easy route eastwards into the heartlands of prehistoric Wessex.

It is ironical that this great site, once so vital, now seems disappointingly unobtrusive, its very spaciousness reducing the impression it makes (Grinsell, 1956). The mighty and toppled stones seem almost without meaning, lying remote from each other in the quiet meadow on the low river-terrace. Once there were three circles on a bent north-east–south-west axis, a Cove to the west, and a pair of outliers to the north-east across the river. Of the circles, that at the centre is by far the largest, composed of massive unshaped blocks of local silicious breccia and a few oolitic limestones from a source three miles away in Dundry (Morgan, 1887; Kellaway, 1971, 34). From the circle a ruined avenue of eight stones goes east to the Chew. About 40 m to the north-east is a megalithic oval 32.3 × 29.9 m also with an avenue that appears to link with the former, and 137 m away across two fields is the third ring, another oval 43.1 × 39.8 m, its stones all tumbled, some almost completely grass-covered and lost.

241 m to the WSW. in the back garden of the whimsically named 'Druids Arms' public house are the remains of the Cove, three huge stones once set like the sides of an unroofed sentry-box facing south. The back stone has fallen outwards leaving the two others standing 2.1 m apart. Only three other Coves have been identified in the British Isles, all inside circle-henges, the robbed structure at Cairnpapple, facing east; the collapsed setting at Arbor Low, Derbyshire, facing SSW.; and the huge edifice at Avebury, facing north-east. There is a dubious example at Er Lannic, facing NNW. In their architecture they resemble the entrances and portal stones of mega-lithic tombs in whose forecourts the evidence of fires, pits and deposits composes a picture of ritual activity. If Coves were similarly used their presence in stone circles would once again link the circles with aspects of burial practice in Neolithic Britain. Because of the arrangement of its stones any rites occurring inside the Stanton Drew Cove would have been hidden from people in the great circle (Tratman, 1966; Fleming, 1972, 70), but the fact that it faces roughly south is interesting for, as will be seen, this orientation

was much favoured by builders of ritual sites in the south-west peninsula.

450 m NNE. on a higher ridge overlooking the circles lies Hautville's Quoit, perhaps once one of a pair of outlying stones but now a shattered stump by the hedge where it has been dragged from the field. Lockyer (1906b, 483) suggested that it was aligned on the star Arcturus (α Boötis) in 1620 BC (c. 1300 bc) but this seems exceptionally late.

As usual, the dating of this complex can only be inferential but its association with the river, its avenues, its size, its siting in a pass all suggest a function for large gatherings quite possibly within the Late Neolithic period, a view that is strengthened by the presence of early monuments in its locality. There are five Neolithic chambered tombs on the nearby western downs but only fourteen of the later Bronze Age round barrows whereas in the Mendips eight miles south there are at least 389 (Grinsell, 1971). Corcoran (1969, 27), remarking on the distribution of the chambered tombs on Broadfield Down, suggested that Neolithic people probably avoided the Mendips because of the higher rainfall there. 'During the Neolithic, at least, it would appear that there was insufficient pressure of population to induce settlement on less attractive soils', and Tratman (1967, 115) also has noted the absence of megalithic sites in the Mendips. The situation of Stanton Drew in a Neolithic area indicates that it too might be given a date nearer the beginning than the middle of the second millennium bc.

Remembering the south-facing Cove, it is of interest to find that of the nearby megalithic tombs the two transepted Cotswold-Severn sites, Felton Hill and the delightfully named Fairy's Toot at Nempnett Thrubwell were quite atypically orientated south–north. So is the strange, boat-shaped Soldier's Grave. The Waterstone portal dolmen has collapsed. Only the long mound at Red Hill is more traditionally aligned east–west.

The layout of Stanton Drew is intricate. A line drawn through the centres of the North-east and Centre circles extends directly to the Cove, and a line through the SSW. and Centre circles points to Hautville's Quoit. It is possible that the sites are successive with constructional alignments adapted to gradually changing beliefs. Some of the features at Stanton Drew are characteristic of circles in the south-west peninsula, and their implications will be discussed.

5. DARTMOOR

Although Stanton Drew is the last of the really large circles to be described in this chapter, there are so many other open circles in the south-west in the counties of Devon and Cornwall that some account of them must be given. It is not possible to examine them individually but their traits are such that a general analysis may provide intriguing glimpses of the concepts that contributed to their design. A summary of knowledge of these Dartmoor sites appears in Worth (1953), and Davidson and Seabrook (1973). The very absence of great circles implies not only a somewhat later period for the sites that do exist but also a smaller population to use them. On Dartmoor, a lozenge-shaped granitic mass extending over 160 square miles, there was a tendency to build circles for localized communities. The later Bronze Age sites customarily encircled a cairn with a cremation in a small cist. There are many diminutive cairn-circles (Lynch, 1972, 63) here in association with stone rows built in the middle and final centuries of the second millennium when there was considerable settlement on Dartmoor. Earlier there are the slightest signs of Mesolithic and Neolithic occupation around the very edges of what is now the moor but which, in 2000 bc, was very different with 'some growing bog on high ground . . . and . . . continuous forest which had only temporary clearances in it' (Simmons, 1969, 207).

In such an environment only a few large stone circles were built, the greatest being the south circle at the Grey Wethers, 33.2 m in diameter if one excludes the dubious Willing Walls Warren (Worth, 1942). Whereas these open circles were built around the perimeter of the present moorland, the smaller Bronze Age cairn-circles are usually to be found further into Dartmoor. Most of the larger circles are between 24.4 m and 30.5 m in diameter, occupying well-separated positions by rivers flowing to the south-east: Brisworthy on the south of the moor near the River Plym; Sherberton on the east close to the West Dart; and the others at the north-east around the headwaters of the Teign. There are no clues to their age. There are the remains of two chambered tombs, one the Spinsters Rock, Drewsteignton, by which there may once have been some cairn-circles and rows (Burnard, 1906, 348), and another ESE. of Chagford, but the dating of these is uncertain. Dartmoor seems to have been by-passed by the Cornish stone-axe trade, few implements being found east of the Tamar, very possibly because of the scarcity of settlers in the region, and it is reasonable to assume a rather late and indigenous development here, beginning in the drier north-east, the very area where the greatest concentration of open circles is to be seen.

Scorhill, a quarter of a mile from the North Teign, the two Buttern circles, Fernworthy, and the Grey Wethers are in this district. The last site is a pair of circles 6.1 m apart which, because of a nineteenth-century restoration, give a good impression of the original state of these monuments. Arranged almost exactly north-south, each over 32.0 m in diameter, they stand near the crest of a slope with Sittaford Tor to their west, its clitter of collapsed granite being the source of the circle stones. South of the crest the land falls to the deep valley of the East Dart a mile away, and the North Teign is only three-quarters of a mile north of the circles. This familiar situation for open circles suggests they were deliberately erected in a pass between the heads of the rivers.

'Wethers' is Old English for 'sheep' which the stones do resemble from a distance. It is said that for a joke a man called Debben actually sold them as a flock to a strange farmer in the Warren House Inn, saying the animals could plainly be seen grazing from Sittaford Tor (Crossing, 1965, 244). Other legends are less jocular.

Long ago faithless wives and fickle maidens were . . . compelled to expiate their misdeeds on the wilds of Dartmoor. Erring women had first to wash in Cranmere Pool then come back across the moor to Scorhill circle around which they had to run three times. Next they were driven down to the banks of the nearby Teign river where they were compelled to pass through the Tolmen—the holed stone in the river-bed. After this the unfortunate sinners toiled up the long weary way to the Grey Wethers circles. Here they fell on their knees and prayed for forgiveness. If their sins were too heinous for remission the huge stone fell slowly forward and crushed them. (St. Leger-Gordon, 1965, 59.)

One wonders if the Tolmen was not an aberrant version of the porthole entrances of earlier megalithic tombs (Clifford and Daniel, 1940) through which the bodies of the dead were transported, either inwards for interment or outwards as vital bones for forgotten ceremonies. The famous Cornish holed stone, the Men-an-Tol, was reputed to cure children passed through it of rickets. The nearby Tolvan stone had similar curative properties (Woolf, 1970, 25). If the association is correct the luckless Devon *immoraliae* were unwittingly perpetuating beliefs that had endured for 4000 years. In 1966 a ninety-year-old woman told a newspaper reporter how, as a crippled child, being passed through the hole in the Danish rag-tree at South Sjaelland had enabled her to walk for the first time in her life (Daniel, 1968). Other super-stitions asserted that at specific times of the year every stone in a circle would turn or shift, the Grey Wethers supposedly pivoting slowly on their bases at sunrise each day (St. Leger-Gordon, 1965, 75).

Such legends connecting circles with the sun may be of quite recent origin and reveal nothing of the sites' original function, although the presence of burnt material in some circles shows that fire played a part in the ceremonies. At Brisworthy there were fragments of charcoal. Ashes were found at the Grey Wethers. At Fernworthy, a mile north-east on another hill, the whole interior was strewn with charcoal (Burnard, 1906, 356). Unusually, the stones of this circle are graded in height with the tallest 1.2 m high wide block significantly at the south. A gradual increase in the heights of stones towards one arc of a megalithic ring, very different from the presence of one conspicuously taller stone, is not common amongst southern circles. Such a graduation can be seen at Gors Fawr circle, Pembrokeshire, where the largest stones are at SW.–WSW. The horseshoe of trilithons at Stonehenge III is graded towards the south-west. At the Nine Stones, Dorset, two enormous pillars flank a tiny stone at the exact north of a diminutive WNW-ESE. oval, and a similar com-bination of a north–south and north-east–south-west line occurs at the Druids Temple, Birkrigg Common, Lancashire, where the inner 8.4 m circle has its highest stone at the north and two tall stones flanking a smaller at the WSW. There is a little group of megalithic rings, including the oval Ninestone Rigg, Roxburgh, which have two noticeably bigger stones at the south-west of their circumferences but this is not true grading. The only general stone-circle culture to be consistently graded is the Clava group in Inverness, presumably related to the recumbent stone circles (RSCs) of north-east Scotland and of Cork and Kerry in south-west Ireland. Fernworthy's grading, therefore, is rather unusual. Its similarity to Gors Fawr may indicate communication between Dartmoor and south-west Wales, known perhaps in the Late Bronze Age (A. Fox, 1964, 102) but unclear for earlier periods.

At Fernworthy, several cairn-circles, some with low stone rows, existed around the circle, presumably erected when the ring had stood for some time. A spoiled double row approaches from the south leading to a cairn 9.1 m south of the circle. Another double row starts 90 m north, extending towards a round barrow. Altogether there were at least five cairn-circles nearby, the wrecked stones of one still being visible in the plantation to the east. One excavated in 1897 covered a rock-cut pit in which was a fine, long-necked s2/w beaker, pieces of a probable two-rivetted bronze dagger, a V-perforated lignite button and a flint knife, a collection of riches not unusual when members of the beaker group were buried by stone circles (Clarke, 1970, 224).

This nearness of beaker-burial and open circle demonstrates the fascination that megalithic rings had for these people, even at a time when forms of beaker had been made in Britain for at least 400 years. The Fernworthy beaker is unlikely to be earlier than $c.$ 1600 bc, whether placed in Clarke's framework or the Step 6 ($c.$ 1700–1550 bc) of Lanting and van der Waals (1972, 44), and provides a *terminus ante quem* for the great circle.

Although the Dartmoor open circles are not in themselves exceptional they do contain in their paired circles, their smaller territories, their crude north–south lines at the Grey Wethers and Fernworthy, some of the major traits of circles in the south-west. The charcoal in some circles may be the remnants of sweepings from bonfires or pyres outside the circle.

One unexpected fact is that, except for Brisworthy isolated in the south, these circles have approximately the same number of stones, between thirty and thirty-six, irrespective of the size of their circumferences. As similar phenomena, though with different numbers, occur in both the Bodmin and Lands End groups (Table 3) one may infer that the circle-builders not only wished to reproduce these numbers but also possessed, at the least, an elementary numeracy.

During the early centuries of the Bronze Age the landscape in occupied upland areas like Dartmoor was being changed from a patchwork of woodland clearings into wide deforested tracts on which more people were settling. Over 2000 hut-circles are known on Dartmoor. In general, the larger examples, dispersed amongst the stone-lined fields, are in the drier north-east, the smaller, frequently inside great cattle-pounds, in the south-west. Often ignoring the earlier megalithic monuments, the chambered tombs, the open circles, later people introduced other fashions in burial and in ritual. Bodies might be interred singly in large stone cists like Merrivale, broken in 1860 and a flint scraper found, and, better preserved, at Roundy Park near Postbridge, or they could be placed under impressive round cairns. All over

Dartmoor these Bronze Age tumuli survive, solitary in the contorted moorland, or in grouped cemeteries like Butterdon Hill, or set along a trackway at Hamel Down where one of the barrows contained the famous bronze dagger with a hilt studded with minute gold pins.

By the later second millennium (Fox and Britton, 1969, 226) the expansion of farming land and the influx of new people had created on Dartmoor the beginnings of a new culture blended from many sources, a vigorous and widespread society broadly related to other groups in the south-west peninsula. By the end of the Bronze Age deterioration of the soil and pasture forced the moorland people from their homes, but the five or six centuries before this had produced not only a pastoral population in the south-west of Dartmoor (Fleming and Collis, 1973, 16) but also a form of monument that cannot perfectly be matched elsewhere in the British Isles, the well-known stone rows, some of which have little cairn-circles at their higher ends.

Over sixty of these Dartmoor rows are recorded (Worth, 1953), as well as outlying examples like Wilmersham Common, Exmoor (Corney, 1967). Some are in good condition, most robbed of many of their stones for walls and roads, and now discernible amongst the hummocks of sour grass only by enthusiastic searchers, for these are not megalithic monuments and their knee-high, weathered stones have been half-engulfed by the rising peat. Nor is their architecture consistent. Some are single lines, as many are double, five are treble and, to compound confusion, some consist of single, double and treble rows intergrouped in a confused and damaged array whose components are difficult to separate.

Lengths vary. As well as Stall Moor whose two miles of stones are probably the conjunction of two individual lines that meet on the reedy, eroded river banks near Erme pound, the longest line is the single row on Butterdon Hill, 1914 m of stones that lead from a fallen menhir to a cairn-circle near the barrow-cemetery. The shortest complete setting is the 46.6 m double row at Cantrell. Perhaps twenty of the rows start at tall terminal stones. Certainly 80 per cent of them, and all of the single rows, are set along easy gradients and culminate in a small round cairn near the crest of the slope. As one walks along a ridge between the streams and sees the cairn at the end of the row, sometimes emphasized by stones increasing in height as they near the burial place, it is easy to imagine that these were processional ways affording a dignified approach to the sacred area. It might be speculated that the single rows were degenerate versions of the more monumental double and treble lines, but some of the tallest stones are in single rows like Staldon and Down Tor. And the double row at Sharpitor is only 15 cm wide, too narrow even for children.

They are not for astronomical observation. They are too low, too far-stretched across the waves of moorland, too sinuous for any sightings along them. Yet 76 per cent of them are very roughly laid out NNE/SSW, whatever the region of they moor they were built in, in complete contrast to stone cists on Dartmoor almost all of which were built north-west/south-east

(Worth, 1953, 178); Davidson and Seabrook, 1973, 31, 37).

The cairns they lead to are small, rarely more than 6.0 m in diameter, and presumably once covered a cremation in a cist or pit. Other than Fernworthy with its beaker, only Cholwichtown has been properly excavated and its 2.1 m wide, 46 cm deep pit contained only acid soil (Eogan, 1964). 81 per cent of the rows have cairns at their head but only half of these have stone rings of unimposing, low stones around them, although those at Down Tor or Ringmoor or the 16.6 m circle at Stall Moor stand impressively enough on their wild, empty hillsides. The last, sometimes known as the Dancers or, more hopefully, Kiss-in-the-Ring, has one stone 1.7 m high at the end of the row by the circle. It is visible from the tall Staldon row one and a quarter miles away across a valley; and from it Staldon can be seen distinctly on the skyline. These rings are not unlike their larger counterparts except for the cairn they enclose. Amongst their shapes are circles, ovals and eggs (Davidson and Seabrook 1973, 25).

The majority of the little cairns on Dartmoor, however, have neither ring nor even row attached to them and it is arguable that these peculiar cairn-circle-rows are the result of the mixing of traditions. As well as cairns unassociated with any other features there are, of course, circles without cairns, and cairn-circles without rows. There are even rows at Staldon and Black Tor and Merrivale and elsewhere without terminal cairn or circle and which may have served to demarcate territories or non-secular areas. The paired Merrivale double rows, for instance, now divided by a stream, have an open circle to one side and a group of hut-circles on the other. Their stones used to be known as the Plague Market for it was here, in 1665, that country-dwellers left provisions for the infected townsfolk of Tavistock.

The combining of burial place and stone circle was known in north-east Britain even in Late Neolithic times and became increasingly widespread in the south during the second millennium. As well as the banked Wessex barrows which may be cognate monuments, there is the lengthy Broad Down necropolis in Devon, not thirty miles from Dartmoor, where at least three of the large round barrows had stone circles around them (A. Fox, 1948). In other regions—Wales, Yorkshire, the Hebrides—people joined the barrow and the stone circle, perhaps because the Bronze Age cult of single cremation no longer permitted or required the removal of bones from a sepulchre, and it was no longer necessary to keep tomb and ritual circle apart.

This process is observable on Dartmoor where there are circles, cairns and cairn-circles. There are also the stone rows. The knowledge that some of these exist by themselves and that others are set askew to their circle-centre encourages the belief that some rows were later additions to circles even though most of the Dartmoor monuments were undoubtedly planned as units, the earlier perhaps being in the south-west. Although circle-rows exist in both south-west and north-east there are subtle differences. Of the twenty-two stone circles with rows, seventeen are in the south-west, about 9.8 m in diameter, and usually with a single long line of stones. In the north-east there are only five such circles, averaging 6.7 m, their rows always being double or treble. As there are many single rows in the south-west around the Plym, some of the oldest may be in this part of Dartmoor, the more elongated and elaborate versions being found in outlying areas where double and treble and grouped lines are more usual. Their origins remain in doubt.

Avenues of stakes associated with burial mounds, often with internal stake-circles, are known as far from Dartmoor as the Noordse Veld, Holland (Glasbergen, 1954); at Poole 37, Dorset (Grinsell, 1959); and Basingstoke, Hampshire (Robertson-Mackay, 1964, 7). These, however, are always double and not very like the Dartmoor types. Prototypes may be those timber avenues discovered with Neolithic barrows at Kilham, Yorkshire (Manby, 1971), and at Kemp Howe in the same county (Brewster, 1968, 13).

The fantastic megalithic lines at Carnac near the Gulf of Morbihan in Brittany are so much more monumental than the rows on Dartmoor that, although geographically and culturally there is no reason why there should not have been communication between the regions, a direct relationship appears unlikely. There are, however, simpler and shorter rows on the Crozon peninsula near Ushant to the west of Morbihan (Giot, 1960, 124); closer to Dartmoor, and some are set in rectangles perhaps akin to the ruined site at Mattocks Down, Exmoor (Grinsell, 1970, 45), thirty miles north of Dartmoor. These Crozon rows consist of three to seven lines, shorter than those at Carnac, and sometimes arranged in groups of three parallel rows like those at Raguénès, itself reminiscent of the rows at Corringdon Ball, Dartmoor, where there is a single line and two treble rows leading to a small cairn and another, larger cairn-circle. The Breton rows also lead to mounds or to semi-circular stone settings.

Like White Moss and Low Longrigg in Cumbria the Dartmoor stone rows belong to a period well into the second millennium when earlier traditions had become overlain with local variations in ceremonial. To visit the archi-tectural complexities of sites like Drizzlecombe (Worth, 1946, 292), deep in the moor near the head of the Plym, is to perceive something of the elaboration that had taken place in ritual for here, amongst the quiet tors, there are two large cairns, four smaller barrows, two of them in circles, three stone rows, four terminal pillars up to 4.3 m high, two pounds, five hut-circles and an isolated cist all combined in an interlocking series of alignments, symmetrical planning and unfinished projects that show how subsistence, burial and religion had become unified by these distant people of the Middle Bronze Age.

The little cairns inside their stone circles were the centres of ceremonies different from those in the open circles whose unencumbered interiors indicate communal participation impossible in the later sites. Yet, as the pollen analyses from Cholwichtown showed (Simmons, 1969), these circles and rows may have been built in areas cleared of trees at the very edges of cultivated

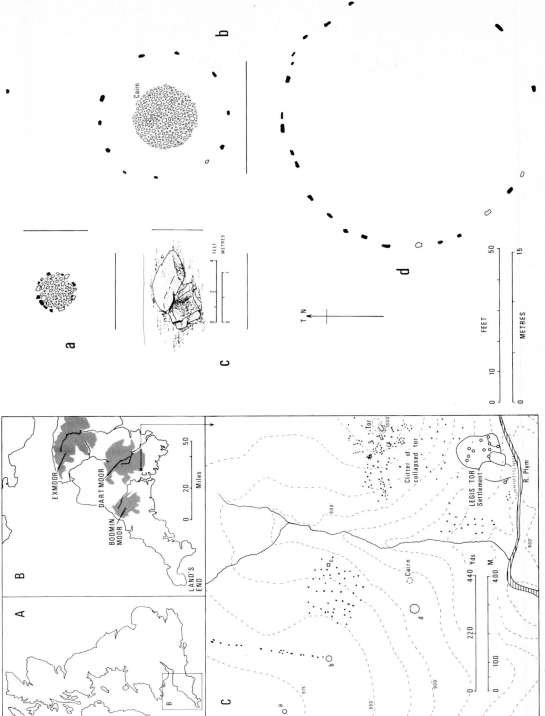

Fig. 17. Brisworthy and Its Environs, Dartmoor, Devon. (a) Ringmoor kerb-circle; (b) Ringmoor cairn-circle and stone row; (c) Ringmoor cist; (d) Brisworthy stone circle. (a), (b), (d) after Davidson & Seabrook, 1973; (c) after Worth, 1953.

land, cleared by familial groups whose need of good harvests and clement weather was as great as the people before them. The ceremonies may have changed but the intentions of the circle-builders may have been the same.

Something of the evolution in relationship between early circle, settlement, and later cairn-circle and row may be seen at Brisworthy, three miles ESE. of Yelverton, where all three monuments occur in the same district (Fig. 17). A 24.8 m open circle stands on an east-facing slope a quarter of a mile north of the River Plym. Its tallest stone, 1.4 m high, is at the north. Another, thinner, is at the WSW. This circle can be seen from Legis Tor pound-settlement, 550 m to the east, although it is not conspicuous against the hillside and probably was originally hidden by trees.

The settlement itself eventually covered 1.7 ha with drystone walls up to 2.4 m high to keep out wild animals and to prevent the livestock from straying. It lies at the foot of Legis Tor whose clitter of collapsed stones provided plentiful material for building. Of the four connected compounds the southern is the earliest, a mere 0.1 ha, a single hut being built into its wall. Altogether there are ten hut-circles, about 4.9 m across, with 1.2 m high stone walls that once supported a wigwam-like roof of branches and thatch or turves. The site is now a tumble of stones jumbled in wide confusion, but once cattle grazed by the river, children shouted in excitement in the trampled pound, smoke rose, people talked by their homes. Only the ruins, the broken pots, the tools they mislaid, remain as clues to their beliefs.

Several huts contained pottery of the early Trevisker style (ApSimon and Greenfield, 1972), characteristic of the south-west and of the second quarter of the second millennium. It has been suggested (Radford, 1952, 69) that some of the coarseware is related to similarly decorated pottery from the Late Neolithic settlement site in Brittany of Le Lizo, although some of the round-based vessels may be related to native types of Neolithic pottery (Piggott, 1954, 32).

Several hypotheses are tenable concerning the relationship between Legis Tor and the Brisworthy circle. They may never have been used by the same people. Or maybe the people of the earliest settlement built the circle. Although physically this would have been possible as the heaviest stone weighs only one and a half tons, the fact that there may have been only one hut for a family of about seven or eight people in the first pound makes it unlikely that the construction of such a large ring was achieved or even needed by them alone, and Brisworthy might be regarded as a focal site, one group of its dispersed community being these Legis Tor settlers of the Early Bronze Age. Intervening trees would not, in such a case, be a problem. The inter-visibility of monuments would have been irrelevant to people who were only part of a congregation, the majority of whom were too distant in the hills to have seen the circle.

A third possibility is that the later inhabitants of Legis Tor built the circle, not impossible if all ten huts were occupied simultaneously. Yet not only does a Middle Bronze Age date seem rather late but, more cogently, if the circle had been just for this settlement it would surely have been put up closer to the pounds where there was so much available stone.

Often these pounds have circle-rows near them and the two may be contemporary (Worth, 1947, 186). Legis Tor has such a cairn-circle and row at Ringmoor half a mile north-west. The single row, double in parts, is 530 m long and climbs easily to the NNE. towards a 12.5 m circle with its tallest stone at the south. The circle was reconstituted in 1909 when five extra stones were dragged off the moor to complete it. Inside is a 3.7 m cairn. The circle stands distinctly on the horizon of the hillside from Legis Tor. With the changing beliefs and contracting societies of the later second millennium the great circle at Brisworthy may have been abandoned by people who, by their own traditions, preferred the burial and the row in association with a stone circle that could be clearly seen across a countryside newly cleared of trees.

6. BODMIN MOOR

Less than twenty miles west of Dartmoor, but divided from it by the River Tamar and ten miles of prehistoric forest and swamp, is the granite moor of Bodmin, now largely cultivated but once a tree-covered upland out of which rose the northern crags of Rough Tor and Brown Willy. There is high rainfall here and exposure to the chilling Atlantic winds but today the purplish moor grassland makes for good walking and several of the Bodmin stone circles, still well preserved, merit inspection by anyone prepared to stroll a mile or so into the moor itself.

There are thirteen circles in this part of England, varying in size from Duloe in the south, 11.9×11.3 m in diameter, to the 46.0×43.3 m of Fernacre in the north. Except for Duloe, some small circles like Altarnun and the important site of the Hurlers, they tend to congregate around the north-west and, like the Dartmoor sites, they are close enough together to be local centres rather than foci for widely dispersed groups. Also like Dartmoor there appears to be some standardization in the number of their stones and it has been supposed that the two most northerly circles, Stannon and Fernacre, were earlier than the others because they had far more stones on their circumferences. This and their flattened arcs may be signs of an indirect connection with the early Cumbrian rings. There is no proof of date. What can be observed is that around Bodmin was a mixing of many traditions with two henges near the south coast, a circle-henge with a south-west entrance on the moor itself, and, in a ten-mile group of megalithic rings, a variety of shapes and architecture including six circles, two flattened circles, one egg-shaped ring, three circles with centre stones, three possible outliers, a circle around a barrow and a group of three associated circles. William Borlase in a letter of 1749 to Stukeley wrote: 'I found in a short time that though we had few remains about us of any striking beauty or magnificence, yet we

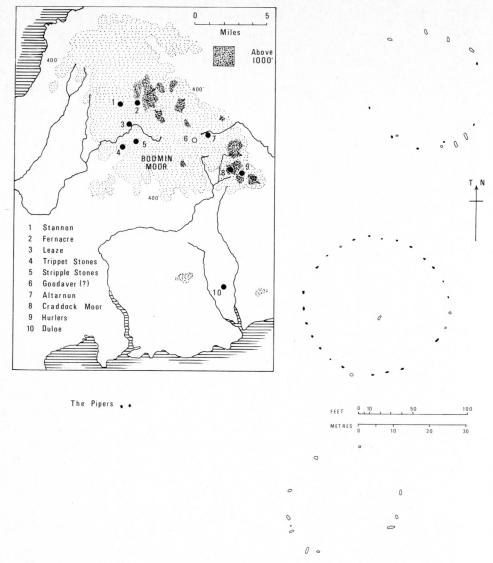

The Pipers

Fig. 18. The Hurlers, Bodmin Moor, Cornwall.

had a great variety of monuments here which were of the most remote antiquity.'

Of the circles to the east and south of Bodmin, sites like Smallacombe, so similar to many of the Dartmoor cairn-circles and likely to be of that tradition, and Altarnun and Goodaver need no description though Altarnun for its very remoteness is rewarding to see. Even the little circle of Duloe with its ribbon-handled urn of the mid-second millennium and its strewn charcoal can be overlooked, though its tall quartz stones make it a neat and attractive site to visit.

But the three circles four miles north of Liskeard need consideration (Fig. 18). 'The neighbouring Inhabitants terme them Hurlers, as being by devout and godly error perswaded that they had been men sometimes transformed into stones, for profaning the Lord's Day with hurling the ball,' wrote Camden. Few circles are so important. Few stand in such dispiriting surroundings in a mine-scarred landscape of derelict buildings and dreary industry. They lie, battered, one almost demolished, on a NNE.–SSW. line, their diameters being 34.7, 41.8 × 40.5 and 32.9 m respectively. The central, which may be egg-shaped with an east–west axis (Thom, 1966, 41) and its taller stones significantly to the south, has an off-centre stone. Uncommonly, its granite stones were smoothed by hammering, the crystals from the breakages being spread over the interior of the central circle. The stones themselves were placed in pits packed round with blocks to hold them secure, care being taken to ensure their tops were roughly level. During the 1936 excavations a pit with some crude paving was discovered on the south arc of the central circle between it and the wrecked southern site. No stone hole was noticed. The north circle was paved with granite. A stone pavement, 1.8 m wide, lay between it and the central ring. (Radford, 1938.)

120 m WSW. of the central site stand two stones, the Pipers, on an alignment pointing down a slope to the River Fowey two miles distant. Like so many other open circles the Hurlers were built in a pass, this time between the Fowey and the River Lynher, the steep sides of Stowe's Hill and Caradon rising to north and south. Not unexpectedly, there are no artefacts by which the circles can be dated. There are no hut-circles nearby. Trethevy Quoit, a fine portal dolmen, is two miles south. Although there are over twenty round burial mounds within a mile of the Hurlers, there are only two within half a mile, one being the famous Rillaton barrow whose unique, ribbed gold cup of the Early Bronze Age was discovered in 1818, misplaced for many years and later discovered in King George V's dressing-room (J. Hawkes, 1973, 172).

Multiple or associated circles are not unusual in the south-west where there are not only the Grey Wethers and the Hurlers but also the paired circles of Wendron, of Tregeseal, the four henges at Priddy in Somerset, and even Er Lannic in Brittany. There are the Knowlton henges in Dorset. Elsewhere in Britain there are the triple henges at Thornborough, Yorkshire North Riding, and the pair at Llandegai in North Wales. Only from these are there reliable dates. They show the henges to be successive, two C-14 dates from the Class I site averaging 2500 bc whereas the Class II was not built until 1790 bc ± 145 (NPL-222). It is not known why such multiple sites were constructed (Grimes, 1963, 106; Lynch, 1972, 66). One theory was that had the primary site been orientated on a star then the shift of that object over the centuries ultimately rendered the sightline obsolete. Men had to make a freshly aligned monument. But this would not be true of the Llandegai henges whose WSW. entrances were virtually on the same align-

Pl. 13. *Stannon, Bodmin Moor, Cornwall.* From the north-east showing the stones of the north-west arc. Although this open ring is over forty metres across very few stones exceed a metre in height.

ment, differing by less than 5° over the 1,250 years between 3400 to 2150 BC. There is no stellar declination to correspond with these dates.

At the Hurlers Thom (1966, 40; 1967, 100) noted the possibility not only of two solar but of three axial stellar lines from (a) South to North circle-centres towards Arcturus (α Boötis) at a declination of +41.5° in 1800 BC (1550 bc); and (b) from South to Centre circle-centres towards the same star, declination +41.9°, in 1860 BC (1575 bc). The chronological discrepancy is slight enough to be acceptable and could support the hypothesis that the North circle was built sixty years after the others simply because the star's rising position had shifted. But line (c) from Centre to North circle-centre with a declination of +40.7° was aligned not only on Arcturus (1660 BC) but also on Vega (α Lyrae) in 1650 BC (1350 bc). These dates correspond even more closely than (a) and (b), were surveyed as meticulously and carry the same statistical weight. The irreconcilable 200 year gap between 1860 and 1660 BC means that at least one pair, if not all, of the suspected alignments was never visualized by the circle-builders. This demonstrates the slipperiness of such back-datings even where modern observations have been most scrupulously recorded. Without independent data it is now impossible to decide not only which of the Hurlers' orientations are valid but even whether any of them were, and as both Arcturus and Vega were circumpolar in the latitude of Cornwall in the early second millennium it is feasible that neither of them has any astronomical relevance in these equinoctial circles.

It is necessary to recall that in the south-west peninsula these associated groups lie between rivers at suitable positions for converging people and traders. It is possible at the Hurlers as at Stanton Drew that the great central circle was the first monument and that the others were added at a later time perhaps to accommodate a greater population, or to allow for a more complicated ritual, or even to permit the beliefs of separate groups of people. Speculation at this stage is synonymous with fancy. Hints of ritual complexity come from the paved area between the circles, from the missing stone in the central circle as though more than one circle were to be used. Conjectures may miss answers. It should be remarked that at Stanton Drew the Cove stands to the WSW. So do the Pipers at the Hurlers. These WSW. lines will be found in other circles in the south-west, and seem to have been built into circles whose primary layout was on either an east–west or north–south axis.

Nine miles north-west of the Hurlers is a group of five megalithic rings in an area of four square miles below the heights of Hawks Tor and Brown Willy on Bodmin. There are hut-circles within half a mile of three of them but these are not necessarily contemporary structures. At the Stannon huts excavated recently (Mercer, 1970), two greenstone axes in strata earlier than the huts may be relics of forest clearance early in the second millennium. The huts and the field systems belonged to a later period somewhere between 1500 and 1200 bc. It is not possible at present to relate the building of Stannon or Fernacre stone circle to either of these periods.

The five rings are not on obvious trackways. All are of local granite, the largest, Fernacre and Stannon, having the smallest stones, and distinguished from the others by each having a flattened arc. Like Fernworthy in Devon, Stannon has its tallest stones at the south. The central site, Leaze, overlooking the River De Lank, is the smallest and is well preserved. Farther south is an almost perfect circle, 33.0 m in diameter, with stones well above average height for Cornwall. This circle, the Trippet or Dancing Stones, is one of many megalithic sites in Cornwall whose name stems from a puritan condemnation of sabbatical dances.

Leaze, the Trippet Stones and the circle-henge of the Stripple Stones to the east appear to have some standardization in the number of their stones. This tendency was noticed in Dartmoor and occurs again in the Land's End circles as Table 3 shows.

Area	Quantum of Stones	Site	Diameter in Metres	Approximate No. of Stones	Circumference of Circle in Metres	Spacing of Stones in Metres
DARTMOOR	30–36	Buttern East	24.5	30	77.0	2.6
		Fernworthy	18.3	30	57.5	1.9
		Grey Wethers N	32.0	29	100.5	3.5
		Grey Wethers S	33.2	33	104.3	3.2
		Scorhill	26.2	36	82.3	2.3
		Sherberton	30.0	36	94.3	2.6
BODMIN	26–28	Hurlers NE	34.7	28	109.0	3.9
		Hurlers Central	41.8 × 40.5	28	131.3	4.7
		Hurlers SW	32.9	26	103.4	4.0
		Leaze	25.0	28	78.5	2.8
		Stripple Stones	44.8	28	140.7	5.0
		Trippet Stones	33.0	26	103.7	4.0
LAND'S END	20–22	Boscawen-Un	25.3 × 22.3	20	77.1	3.9
		Boskednan	22.0	22	69.1	3.1
		Merry Maidens	23.8	20	74.8	3.7
		Tregeseal E	22.0 × 21.0	20	67.5	3.4

Table 3. Diameters and Numbers of Stones in Circles of the South-West Peninsula of Britain

The variation in the diameter suggests that neither this nor the radius was a vital measurement amongst the circle-builders of any particular locality, but the comparability in stone numbers is apparent even in these estimated figures. It was a common trait all over the British Isles. In Inverness and Aberdeenshire many of the circles have twelve stones. So do some of the circles in Cumberland. In Perthshire there are groups of six-stone and eight-stone circles as well as the tiny Four-Posters whose counterparts with a recumbent stone may be the five-stone circles of Cork. This conformity may have owed less to ritualism than to a conservative copying of older monuments, the perpetuation of a tradition whose numerical inception does not appear to be induced by metonic cycles or the prediction of eclipses. Such standardization does not exist in the early Cumbrian circles like Swinside, which possess many stones, but it seems to develop as the custom of stone circle building spread throughout Britain.

The question of diameters illustrates the difficulties involved in a research of stone circles. The Bodmin sites have been planned by at least six surveying teams. Their results are tabulated in Table 4 in Imperial Feet.

Except for Lukis and Borlase whose early measurements are incompatible with the others, there is no great discrepancy, less than 4 per cent even at Leaze. Yet this is important. Between the measurements of Gray and Thom, for example, there is hardly 0.2 per cent disagreement overall but this, minute as it is, would affect the credibility of the Megalithic Yard of 0.829 m. At the Trippet Stones Thom's diameter of 108.3 ft or 33 m is only 16 cm from an exact multiple of 40 M.Y. (108.8 ft or 33.16 m). But Gray's measurement of 107 ft or 32.6 m differs from this by 1 ft 9½ in or 55 cm, over ½ M.Y. reducing the diameter to 39 M.Y. +0.27 m. In practical terms Gray and Thom disagree by about half the thickness of any one of the unshaped rough stones some of which are either fallen or missing, yet it is upon such niceties of surveying that the precision of the Megalithic Yard is based. Lewis (1896, 9) believed the circles to have been measured in Egyptian cubits of 63.8 cm: 70 E.C. at Fernacre and the Stripple Stones; 66×60 at Stannon; 50 at the Trippet Stones; and 40 at Leaze (A. Lewis, 1896, 9). These lengths have the virtue of being multiples of ten as does the postulated distance between Fernacre and Stannon of 6275 ft or 3,000 cubits. One of the many objections to this theory is that the Egyptian Royal Cubit was not 63.8 cm but 52.4 cm (Ivimy, 1974, 132). It was the Hebraic or Sacred Cubit that measured 63.6 cm. It was codified too late for megaliths on Bodmin Moor.

This site at the south-east here, the Stripple Stones, is a circle-henge, the only one in the south-west peninsula. Two Class I henges are known near the south coast: the circular Castlewitch by the Group IV Balston Down greenstone-axe factory, with a south entrance; and the oval Castilly, eighteen miles west, with an entrance at the north. Neither is more than twelve miles from the Stripple Stones, suggesting that there might have been an expansion of henge-building from the south towards the rockstrewn moor.

The Stripple Stones lies sadly desolate below Hawk's Tor, its bank overgrown, its stones collapsed, a field-wall built contemptuously through it. Yet when it was excavated during a wet July fortnight in 1905 (St. G. Gray, 1908) it was possible to make a good plan. As usual, there was a wide ditch within the circular bank which was flattened at the north-east like the stone circles at Stannon and Fernacre. The single entrance was at the WSW. Almost uniquely, there were three apsidal alcoves set in the inner edge of the bank at the west, NNE. and east, the largest at the NNE. being about 11.28 m wide by 4.57 m

Site	Lukis & Borlase 1885	A. L. Lewis 1896	Tregelles 1906	Gray 1908	Hencken 1932	Thom 1967	Meg. Yds.
Fernacre	140′	147′ × 146′	146′	147′	150′	S1/7 (D) 150.7′	55
Leaze	–	83′ 6″	81′	84′	81′	S1/6 81.5′	30
Stannon	–	138′ × 125′ 6″	139′	140′	140′	S1/8 (S) 139.7′	51
Stripple Stones	145′	147′ × 146′	144′	148′	146′ 6″	S1/4 147′	54
Trippet Stones	104′ 7″	104′ 7″	108′	107′	108′	S1/5 108.3′	40

Table 4. Estimated Diameters of Bodmin Stone Circles in Imperial Feet

deep. Analogous recesses have been recorded at Durrington Walls earthwork enclosure, Wiltshire, and at a barrow near Amesbury (Wainwright and Longworth, 1971, 194).

Originally on the level interior was a 44.8 m stone circle of twenty-eight stones, its centre some 1.2 m north-east of the henge centre. The stones are rough granite from the nearby tor, up to 3.1 m high but frequently set barely 76 cm in the ground. Only four now stand. The fallen centre stone, once 4.0 m high, was set 4.3 m SSE. of the circle-centre. All that was found in the excavation were three flint flakes, burnt flints and some fragments of wood in the north section of the ditch.

If one stands in the east alcove and looks to a point midway between the western alcove and the entrance, one is facing directly westwards between two circle-stones. The north edge of the centre stone would have provided a convenient sighting-edge. Three empty holes near this stone may be the results of attempts to find the most effective position for it. Once the stone was set up it would have given a rough guide to the equinoxes. As Stukeley replied to Borlase in 1749: 'The Druids always celebrated their publick sacrifices exactly at the four great quarters of the year, the solstices and the equinoxes and that they might be right therein, they set up observatorys by great stones . . .'

The east–west and north–south alignments have been noticed in the great open circles from Long Meg to the Hurlers, and in the henge entrances in the south-west peninsula (Fig. 22), and seem to confirm an original interest of the builders in equinoctial positions that would indicate the onset of Autumn and Spring. The entrance of the Stripple Stones, however, is not at one of the cardinal points but at the WSW., an azimuth of about 252° from the henge centre. This has sometimes been explained as an alignment towards the Trippet Stones three-quarters of a mile to the WSW. If so, it is not a good line. And although one can see the Stripple Stones silhouetted on the hillside from the Trippet Stones, this circle cannot be seen from the circle-henge.

7. LAND'S END

The further to the south-west one travels the smaller the circles become. At Land's End, sixty square miles of low granitic hills and downs, the larger sites are only 18.3 m to 24.4 m in diameter. In some cases even smaller monuments, doubtful as true stone circles, are close to them. There appear to be four main areas of occupation, each with a large ring: the south-east with the Merry Maidens; central Penwith with Boscawen-Un; the north-west and the Tregeseal paired circles; and the North Downs where Boskednan was built. A long way to the east two further circles were erected on Wendron Down quite near the Camborne Group XVI greenstone-axe factory.

Tantalizing evidence has been uncovered recently of a former timber ritual circle at Caerloggas near St. Austell between Bodmin and Land's End (H. Miles, 1972). The site had three distinct phases. First there was a concentric circle, 25.0 m across, of posts within a bank, the south-west entrance being marked by larger posts. This circle was eventually replaced by a simple embanked timber circle, and this, in turn, was succeeded by a ring-cairn seemingly of the Early Bronze Age from the finds of a metal dagger and a piece of amber. Two round barrows lacking burials were in line to the south-east. The discovery of two pits, one with specks of burnt bone, and a spread of white pebbles and quartz by a central moorstone in the circle indicates the ritual nature of this long-lived and much adapted monument whose alterations warn that stone circles may not themselves be the simple structures they seem. One is also reminded that an ephemeral material like wood may have been as widely used as stone by people who never considered the imbalance this would cause on archaeological distribution maps.

Today the margin of cultivation in the Land's End peninsula is around the 400–450 ft contour, and it is interesting to observe how the stone circles, over 3700 years ago, were erected on the 350 ft contour or higher where, perhaps, the forests of the coastal plateau were becoming rather less dense. A facile typological sequence might impute a steady advance from the south coast to the higher land in the north: the Merry Maidens (Fig. 5), 320 ft O.D. is one mile from the sea; Boscawen-Un, 420 ft O.D., is three miles; Tregeseal, 540 ft O.D. and six miles; Boskednan, 730 ft O.D. and eight miles. But even if such a penetration occurred there is nothing to say how long it took or in what form. Circumspectly one may simply consider the four sites to be culturally related.

They have similar numbers of stones, twenty to twenty-two. There may be some rudimentary entrances in the form of wider gaps to the west at Boscawen-Un; and to the east at the Merry Maidens, a circle 23.8 m in diameter, sometimes known as the Dawn's Men, conspicuous in a wide field by the road. 320 m to the north-east is the first of two stones, the Pipers, 4.6 m and 4.0 m high, which were never visible from the circle even when an inconvenient stone wall was temporarily removed to facilitate an astronomical survey (Lockyer, 1906a). In contrast, the Goon Rith standing stone, 2.7 m high, can plainly be seen to the west. 'Dawn's Men' has nothing to do with sunrise. It is a corruption of Dans Maen or 'Stone Dance', a story of nineteen maidens dancing on a Sunday who were transformed into stones, the pipers that had played for them being petrified as they fled. The late Tom Lethbridge (Glyn Daniel described him as 'one of the last of that invaluable band of dilettante scholars and skilled devoted amateurs of whom we have had so many in Britain'), in what was even at his most enthusiastic an eccentric moment, attempted to date the Merry Maidens by holding a pendulum over one of the stones which soon 'felt as if it were rocking and almost dancing about. This was quite alarming . . .' (Lethbridge, 1973, 21.) By counting the inexplicable gyrations of the pendulum he arrived at a date of about 2540 BC (c. 2100 bc) for the construction of the circle, but there is not yet any independent verification of the results of this unorthodox experiment.

Pl. 14. *Boscawen-Un, Land's End, Cornwall.* An open ring like the others on this peninsula, Boscawen-Un, seen here from the south, has a 2.5 metre high quartz pillar near its centre, now leaning to the north-east. The position of the ring is low-lying and inconspicuous. A nineteenth-century trench across the central area produced no finds.

Further inland the 25.3 × 22.3 m flattened circle of Boscawen-Un, besieged by gorse, has been excellently restored. It has a tall central pillar as eccentrically placed as that at the Stripple Stones. Internal stones like these are unusual in the south-west although it is to be observed that they occur, as if by selection, only in the bigger sites like the Hurlers Centre, the Stripple Stones, and Boscawen-Un which is the largest of the Land's End group. It is around the coasts of the Irish North Sea that the most imposing centre stones can be seen in henges like Longstone Rath, or stone circles like Glenquickan in Kirkcudbright, and, when occurring in Cornwall, may be additions to circles just as the fallen Altar Stone was to Stonehenge or may even precede the rings. Their function is obscure. At Boscawen-Un the stone provides no astronomical orientation and no deposits were found near its base when the site was trenched in the mid-nineteenth century. Such single stones could have an ancestry deep in the Neolithic when foundation sacrifices may have been placed at the foot of standing posts which, whether carved or adorned with offerings, perhaps served as cult or phallic objects (Piggott, 1954, 49). Just as the wooden posts inside Goloring henge, Germany, or in stone circles like Ynys-Hir, Wales, could have been carved and painted, so offerings suspended from central stones, or colourful wickerwork effigies placed against them would have transformed these stones into obelisks as vivid as a totem pole and invested them with an attraction unapparent in the bare, weathered and slumping pillars of today. The custom of hanging pieces of cloth on posts survives even now. A tall tree with a hole through its middle is still super-stitiously festooned with modern rags in a forest in South Sjaelland, Denmark. And at Pitres, France, a prehistoric pillar in the churchyard of La Pierre de Saint Martin has had a Christian cross placed in front of it to support the rags and bits of cloth which people continue to bring to the pagan stone (Daniel, 1968). One of the things which condemned Joan of Arc of witchcraft was her habit as a girl in Domrémy of going in early Spring with other young people to a nearby tree by a fountain where they would dance and feast under the low branches which they had first hung with garlands. Of the astronomical circle at Sarmizegetusa, Romania, the excavators wrote: 'as for the two circles of posts inside the sanctuary, we believe the nails with big rings fixed into them were used to hang various decorations and votive offerings . . .' (Daicoviciu, 1960, 252). Centre stones in some British stone circles could have been adorned in the same way, as symbols of the god of its builders.

Of the remaining great Land's End circles, the pair at Tregeseal, the Dancing Stones, were set exactly east–west of each other; and Boskednan in the middle of North Down has a small cairn overlying it on the south-east. Near the remains of the cist were the fragments of an urn with small handles and twisted-cord decoration of the mid-second millennium. The circle should be earlier.

The large Land's End circles are spaced about two to three miles apart. The countryside within one and a half miles of each contains 73 per cent of the chambered tombs in west Cornwall, whether entrance passage-graves like Brane and Treen or portal dolmens capped with huge stones like Zennor or Lanyon Quoit, relatives of Trethevy Quoit which Norden in 1598 described as a 'little house raysed of mightie stones, standing on a little hill.' Artefactual evidence from these tombs is perplexing, being only miserable and possibly misleading scraps of Bronze Age material which could be the leftovers from centuries of prehistoric scavenging.

> The theory that the deposits in the chambers were cleared out at intervals has much to commend it . . . It follows that little or nothing belonging to the first burials may remain in the chamber, and indeed it is possible that the earliest burials were not accompanied by grave-goods . . . Another con-sequence is that most of the grave-goods . . . are likely to belong to the latest burials in the chambers . . . and may not be the slightest help in tracing the origins of the tomb-builders. (Henshall, 1972, 164–5.)

Bronze Age finds from portal dolmens like Sperris Quoit (Thomas and Wailes, 1967) or even early beakers from entrance-graves like Carrigalong in south-east Ireland (Powell, 1941) may therefore represent only the ultimate activities in a Neolithic tomb. This could be the case at Tregiffian, neighbour to the Merry Maidens, with its heavily cupmarked stone and another bearing a pair of 'eyebrow' motifs best known in the context of Irish Neolithic passage-graves (Piggott, 1954, 212). Excavation of this tomb produced only one sherd of Bronze Age pottery (Dudley, 1967). The contiguity of chambered tombs and stone circles in the Land's End peninsula carries no implication that the tomb-builders were connected with the circles but it may indicate the extent of land-usage in the Late Neolithic and Early Bronze Age of Cornwall. It is noteworthy that most of the smaller circles are more widely dispersed, and that of over 200 round barrows, the majority of which must be Bronze Age, only 45 per cent are within a one and a half mile radius of the large circles (A. C. Thomas, 1969, 11), suggesting a wider taking-up of land particularly along the St. Just littoral. That this is not true of all the Cornish monuments has been seen in the case of the chambered tombs. Neither is it true of the many standing stones or menhirs, 70 per cent of which stand within one mile of the circles. Particularly to the south it is noticeable how many of these stones stand at the head of little river valleys near the edge of the Downs very like boundary-markers.

One difficulty in the search for the chronology and function of these circles is to know which is, in fact, a circle. The Nine Maidens at Porthmeor, theoretically a megalithic ring of Flattened B design, was probably not a circle at all but a dilapidated walled hut-enclosure. And of Botallek in St. Just, Thom remarks (1967, 65–6), 'The layout of some of the multiple sites was apparently very complicated as is shown by Borlase's plan of the Botallek circles reproduced by Lockyer. One of the circles is evidently of the flattened type.' But the Botallek sites were almost certainly smallish hut-circles (Russell, 1959, 100) with no esoteric design—except by accident.

The Cornish stone circles appear related to the other great circles to the east and north. They are not essentially different. All the features of those open circles are to be found here. Visions of an invasion of circle-builders are needless for it is known that there was a sizeable Neolithic population here from the evidence of stone-axe sources at Mounts Bay (Group I), St. Ives (Group II) and Marazion (Group III) where outcrops of suitable stone were being exploited and axes exported as far as Wessex in the late third millennium. These products were not taken far overland (Cummins, 1974, 202). Like the fine Neolithic pottery of Cornish origin (Peacock, 1969) they by-passed east Cornwall where the stone axes from Balston Down were used, and were taken by sea to Wessex with its large prehistoric population. Here the traders competed with others from Cumbria, and it is easy to see this intermixing of distant peoples contributing to the spread of the idea of stone circles. Such conceptual models could even have derived directly from a knowledge of the gigantic circle-henge at Avebury in whose vicinity so many axes from Cumberland and Cornwall have been found.

From the disappointingly scanty evidence it appears that the rites in these

Cornish circles did not differ substantially from those in the even larger circles of the north. The very absence of finds shows that material gifts, unless of food and drink, were not part of the ceremonies. The presence of charcoal testifies to the lighting of fires outside the circles but the flames illuminate only the writhing shadows of the people; and the opaque light from the sunset or sunrise does no more than sharpen their distant silhouettes and touch the dark mound of the tomb, the rigid stones and the heavier blackness of the countryside and forest around them.

Some small clue to their beliefs comes with a study of the north–south and east–west lines noticed earlier in the Cumbrian circles and customary in the entrances of henges in the south-west (Burl, 1969, 9). These lines, which may be axial and used in the initial setting out of the circles, are also apparent in some of the larger circles of the south-west where the tallest stone was placed at the south in sites like the Hurlers and Fernworthy. It is possible that the east–west relationship of the Tregeseal circles was deliberate (Fig. 22).

But what is not instantly obvious is that many Cornish circles, whether in Bodmin or Land's End, have their tallest stone at the WSW., the heights being taken from Tregelles (1906). The difference in heights is not conspicuous but is consistent and would have been known to the builders. The azimuths of these taller stones vary between 236° and 254°. These non-equinoctial alignments, for the group is too clustered to be fortuitous, might be connected with the times of sunset in late Autumn and early Spring, periods inconsequential to agriculturalists concerned with sowing and reaping but times that:

> do deeply concern the European herdsman; for it is on the approach of Summer that he drives his cattle out into the open to crop the fresh grass, and it is on the approach of Winter that he heads them back to the safety and shelter of the stall. Accordingly, it seems not improbable that the Celtic bisection of the year into two halves at the beginning of May and the beginning of November dates from a time when the Celts were only a pastoral people. (Frazer, 1922, 633.)

Hence the celebration of Hallowe'en or the Eve of Samhuin on 31 October, the time of the kindling of fires, and when 'the souls of the departed were supposed to revisit their old homes' (ibid, 634). The Celts reckoned their periods of time by the number of nights, not days, day always following night, so that the setting of the sun was of more significance than its rising. Recent research on the henges of Ireland by Dr Ronald Hicks has shown that the entrances of these monuments, unlike most of those in Britain, were normally placed at the ENE. or WSW., like the tallest stones in Cornish circles, with

> distinct clusterings amongst the orientations (only two towards the solstices). The most popular was towards sunrise on May Eve, a line that if used in reverse would have fallen very near that required for Samhain sunset. An investigation of festival traditions produced the discovery that

the names of certain Celtic deities connected with the festivals are also connected with several of the henges. Some of the henges have related festival traditions as well (R. E. Hicks, personal communication).

Even to imply that Celtic festivals, historically recorded over a thousand years later than the time of stone circles, might have origins in Neolithic or Bronze Age beliefs is dangerous, particularly as even the Celtic rites are only imperfectly known. But certain elements are pre-Celtic (Ross, 1967, 145; 1972, 181), and even an austere recital of what is known of the pre-Christian festivals helps to repopulate the megalithic rings with people rather than with metempiric abstractions, and reminds the modern reader of the intimate interplay in early religion of the animal and supernatural worlds.

Of the four annual Celtic feasts: Imbolc, Beltane, Lughnasa and Samhuin, Beltane on 1 May was the celebration of the god Belenus, 'one of the more ancient and widespread Celtic gods associated with pastoralism' (Ross, 1967, 57), whose name supposedly means 'the shining one'. His is a solar cult that may reach back to the early farmers. At his festivals Druids drove cattle between two fires, perhaps as symbolic offerings to the sun. The other major pastoral celebration of the year held on the night before 1 November, Samhuin, was a time of malevolent spirits, often in the form of birds, when all the forces of the other world were loosened. Then countryside and human were threatened, the god mated with the raven-goddess, doom-ridden, and ceremonies and sacrifices had to be most solemnly performed to ward off the evils that came with the decline of the sun (Ross, 1972, 200; Powell, 1958, 116). A lesser-known pastoral festival, Imbolc or Oimelg, on 1 February, celebrated the coming into milk of ewes and the return of light.

For people earlier than the Celts, comparable though simpler, animistic beliefs may have caused the erection of stone circles. These open circles were planned, built and used by the peasant peoples of Britain in the later third and second millennia bc, people for most of the year cut off from others, their lives depending on their crops and cattle. They could ensure the continuation of their lives in part by their own muscular efforts. To these they added their own superstitious safeguards, a skull from a tomb, the building of a circle, the lighting of fires, watching the skies for signs that the sun would return, repeating regularly the ceremonies that had always been successful.

8. BRITTANY

The area around the Gulf of Morbihan, 250 miles south-east of Land's End, contains megalithic works that demanded the efforts of hundreds of people. Looking at the rows with their myriad stones, or the colossal standing stones, or Er Lannic's circles, one is aware of an obsessive fanaticism in the building of these monuments which are comparable in Europe only with the enormous sites around Avebury.

The prime function of the rows might have been ritualistic, providing an imposing approach to the elevated enclosure in which the ceremonies were to take place. The incorporation of a long barrow, or the juxtaposition of rows to chambered tombs like Kercado, which had a stone circle around it, by the Kermario alignments, or the enormous Tumulus St. Michel by the Lines of Menec, would be in keeping with the suspected association of ritual centre and burial place or ossuary in some of the open circles of Britain. The discovery of beautiful polished stone axes, some of them fashioned like their copper counterparts, in some of the large burial mounds like Mané er Hroek near the Locmariaquer necropolis or in the Tumulus St. Michel recall the hints of an axe-solar cult in the British circles, a connection supported by the restricted distribution of mounds with axe deposits and carvings in this Morbihan region (Lynch, 1967, 14). This makes all the more interesting the adjacency of the Er Lannic stone circles and the chambered tomb of Gavrinis. The stones of this passage-grave bear carvings both of spirals otherwise rare in Brittany but common in Irish tombs, and also of axes with splayed cutting-edges very like the real axes found in the large Carnac mounds mentioned above (Giot, 1960, 51). Tomb and circle were probably not contemporary. But the ceremonies in them may finally have intertwined. Brittany has been seen as a religious centre in which the cult of a mother-goddess and of the axe were juxtaposed, the solar alignments of the rows suggesting that pilgrims might have attended midsummer festivals at Menec or, in Spring and Autumn, at Kermario (James, 1957, 251). The combination of the rows with burial mounds also intimates practices connected with death.

Supposition that some of the single menhirs in the Carnac area may have been used as backsights for solar and lunar observations directed towards the Grand Menhir Brisé (A. and A. S. Thom, 1971–1972b) are mathematically credible, but archaeologically two problems need resolving. The former existence of mixed oak, hazel and birch forest is well attested (Giot, 1960, 18), its intensity encouraged by the heavy rainfall of the coastal lands. Even from the top of the raised mound of Le Moustoir it is to be wondered whether a clear view would have been available to the thin stone of the Grand Menhir six miles away unless a great amount of clearance had taken place. In 1970 AD it was still necessary to remark, 'today trees and huge banks of gorse and scrub make it impossible to see from any one of these stones to any one of the others' (A. and A. S. Thom, 1971, 148), and four millennia ago it was not likely to have been better, although land-clearance, sometimes by the use of fire, is known from that time onwards (Giot, 1971, 214; Atkinson, 1975, 44).

The other problem is that of Er Grah, the Grand Menhir Brisé itself, 20.6 m long, sometimes called the tallest standing stone in the world but actually four pieces of massive granite, prone and shattered, near the chambered tomb and the mound with stone row at Mané Lud on the Locmariaquer peninsula. The Grand Menhir, or Men er Hroeg, the Fairy Stone, is not only incredibly long, it also weighs an incredible 342 tons. Legends claim it was struck by lightning or was toppled by an earthquake but there is, in fact, no record of its ever having stood upright and it may have been broken in the process of erection. The raising of the Luxor obelisk in the Place de la Concorde, Paris, was considered an amazing feat of engineering in 1836 and that stone weighed only 220 tons. Comparisons are not inevitably odious and it is proper to recall the erection of another Egyptian obelisk, stolen by Caligula for his Circus in Rome. Centuries later in 1586 Pope Sixtus V ordered it to be put up in St. Peter's Square. The stone was 25.9 m long but weighed 20 tons less than the Grand Menhir. The task involved the lifting power of 850 men, 70 horses and 46 cranes. Even with this gigantic work-force the stone stopped rising as the straining ropes jammed in their blocks and it was only the celebrated shout of *Acqua alle funi* ('water on the ropes') by a watching sailor that averted the collapse and breaking of the stone. The tallest stone still standing in Brittany at Kerloas is over 11.6 m in height, a pygmy contrasted with the ambitious Men er Hroeg, and it is possible that the fragments of the Grand Menhir signify not an astronomical triumph but an engineering disaster.[1] Yet its very transportation from a suspected source on the Côte Sauvage nine miles to the SSW. was a tremendous accomplishment. An absolute minimum of a thousand people would have been needed. The discovery of several distant backsights (Thom and Thom, 1971) suggests that it was indeed intended for lunar observation by people quite capable of the mechanical engineering needed. It may also have been used as a landmark by seafarers, a true Colossus, guiding them to easy beaching on the sandy river banks near the Locmariaquer tombs, just as many of the Breton standing stones, especially those in pairs or threes, may have guided travellers along the forested valleys (Giot, 1960, 119).

Nearly four miles ESE. of the Grand Menhir, across the Gulf of Morbihan and beyond Île Longue, are the two stone rings of Er Lannic on an islet hardly 90 m across (Fig. 19). Gavrinis with its well-known chambered tomb is 550 m north. Other island-bound tombs in the Gulf: Île Longue, Ile aux Moines, Île d'Arz, Île du Tisserand, suggest that, before the region was inundated in post-Roman times, it had been a plain crossed by sluggish rivers, a fertile sandy district whose hills provided well-drained sites for occupation and for the burial places of Neolithic settlers. Since the rising of the sea, however, the area has become an archipelago of wooded islands hemmed at low tide by wide mudbanks and trapped by heavy currents when the sea is full. At high tide on Er Lannic all the south circle and a third of the north are submerged beneath tidal races that have not only forced the tall stones over but have shifted them from their proper positions so that it is now almost impossible to be certain of the original plan despite the re-erection of some stones after the excavations of 1923–6. In any case, what is probably the poorest plan of a megalithic ring ever published, almost indecipherable (le Rouzic, 1930, 4) makes the interpretation of the shape and size of this unique site exceptionally difficult.

[1]But see R. J. C. Atkinson, 1975, 43, for a contrary belief.

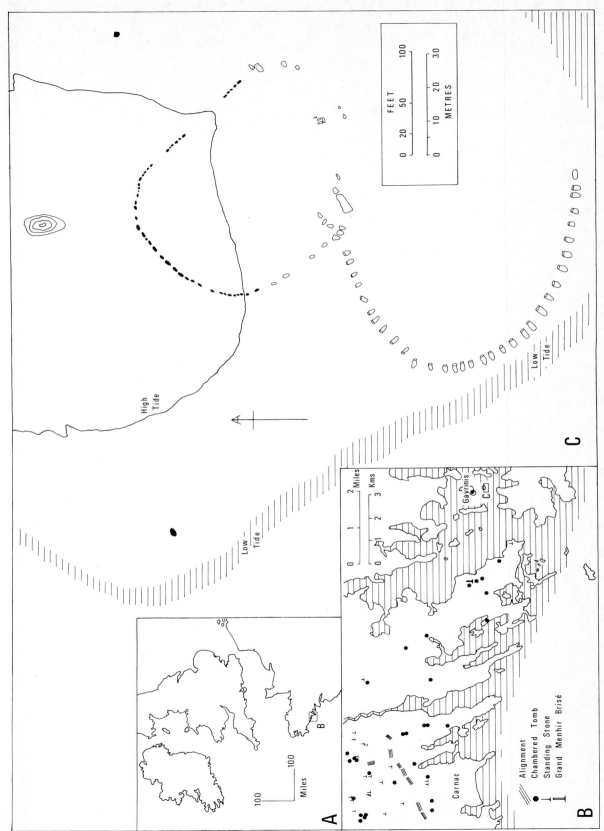

FEET

METRES

High
Tide

Low
Tide

Low
Tide

C

Gavrinis

C

Miles

Kms

Alignment
Chambered Tomb
Standing Stone
Grand Menhir Brisé

Carnac

B

A

B

100

100

Miles

Fig. 19. Er Lannic, Brittany. After le Rouzic, 1930.

The south ring may have been a 61 m semi-oval open to the east. The north ring was probably once a circle about 32.9 m (40 M.Y.?), in radius, sharply flattened at its north-east. The numerous stones average 2.3 m in height, are almost contiguous like some of the early Cumbrian rings, and are set in a low bank of earth and stones. One singularly high pillar, no. 14, stands at the north-west, 5.3 m tall, rising high above its neighbours. Another great stone stood where the rings touched at the south-west of the north circle.

On le Rouzic's plan there appears to be a NNW.-facing Cove just inside this circle at its south-east, but no details are given of this and the matter is unresolved although a Cove in the Morbihan with its profusion of megalithic tombs would not be surprising.

Outside the north circle are two outliers, one about 107 m WNW. of the circle-centre, the other 6.4 m high, 60 m from the centre on a line that precisely bisects the long, straight north-east chord of the ring. The stone weighs 21 tons. These outliers are almost due east–west of each other and form a tangent to the perimeter of the ring rather like the Station Stones at Stonehenge.

It is in the profusion of its finds that Er Lannic differs from the majority of the British stone circles (Fig. 20). Excavation revealed that beneath the encircling bank each pillar stood in a neat setting of packing-stones within which were scatters of bone, teeth of oxen, flint flakes, quartz implements, mauls, granite grinders and polishers, and masses of broken pottery. There were whole and broken stone axes.

Both inside and outside the bank were many rough cists or 'ritual hearths', the stones fire-reddened and holding charcoal and over three-quarters of a ton of pottery sherds as well as polished axes, polissoirs and querns, the relics of centuries of recurring ceremonies. Domestic debris, huts, traces of cultivated ground found to the north of the circle may belong to an earlier period, later people erecting the stone rings on land that had already been cleared, much as some chambered tombs in Ireland and Scotland were built on previously farmed land. Some of the stone of which the Er Lannic axes were made is dolerite whose axe-factory source has been identified at Sélèdin (le Roux, 1971) forty-eight miles north of Carnac near Corlay. First used *c*. 3000 bc, the site had a second industrial phase *c*. 2100 bc by people settling in its vicinity who used fire in the extraction of the stone. Three samples of this Group X stone have been found in southern England demonstrating the wide scope of the axe trade 4000 years ago. But many of the smaller fibrolite axes at Er Lannic came from a local outcrop at Port Navalo two miles south, and Er Lannic may once have been a working area where the roughed-out axes were polished before being bartered.

Of the sherds at Er Lannic a large proportion were from little vase-supports (Fig. 10) often decorated with pointillé triangles like the Aldbourne cups of Early Bronze Age Wessex. These ultimately derive from the early Neolithic

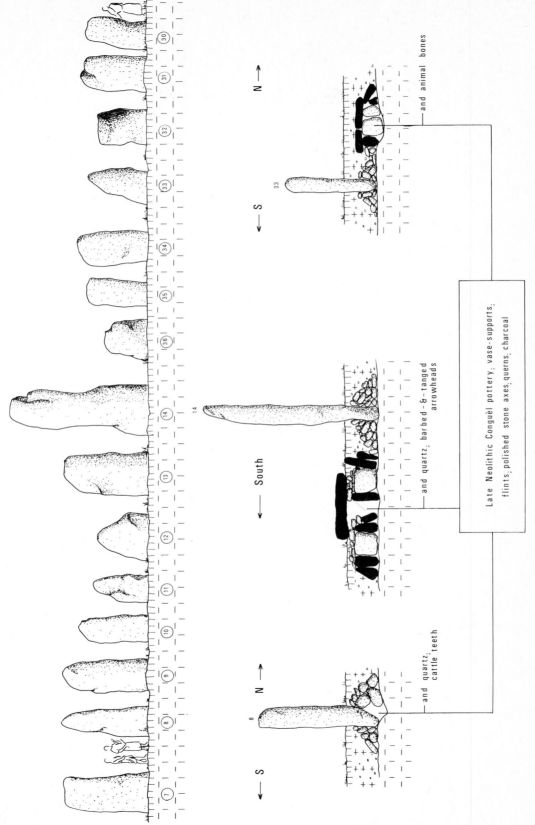

WEST

EAST

N

S

South

N

S

and quartz; cattle teeth

and quartz; barbed-&-tanged arrowheads

and animal bones

Late Neolithic Conguél pottery, vase-supports; flints; polished stone axes, querns, charcoal

Fig. 20. Er Lannic. Elevations of Stones on the North-West Arc, and Sections Through Some Cists.

Chassey cultures of south and east France, and may belong to a period before the mid-third millennium (Bailloud, 1974, 122). At Er Lannic, however, they were constantly associated with coarse, round-based Conguél ware very like the Irish Sandhills pottery (Case, 1963), produced from the Middle Neolithic to the Early Bronze Age between approximately 2500 to 1600 bc and which has been found at the Goodland ritual site and in some of the court-cairn ritual centres of north-east Ireland (Case, 1969, 16). Conguél pottery is probably Middle to Late Neolithic as its associations at the chambered tomb type-site and at the Camp du Lizo settlement only a few miles north-west of Er Lannic indicate (Giot, 1960, 71, 82; Case, 1969, 17). Vase-supports, moreover, are rare elsewhere in the Morbihan. At Er Lannic their juxtaposition with the other material, and the absence of stratified metalware, suggests a broad date around 2000 bc or earlier for the megalithic rings.

From the number and size of the stones and the area of the enclosure it is probable that a large population of several hundred people used Er Lannic for their midwinter ceremonies. If le Rouzic's plan can be trusted it seems that the north-east outlier was aligned on the maximum midwinter moonrise from the centre of the northern ring (Fig. 21). There is a wide gap between the stones at this point. To the north-west the tall Stone 14 may have marked the extreme midwinter moonset which, perhaps, was observed from the 'Cove' which apparently faced that direction. One of the packing-stones around Stone 14 had nine cupmarks on it, small artificial depressions common on circles in north-eastern Scotland but almost unknown in other megalithic rings. Le Rouzic (1930, 12) likened them to the pattern of the Great Bear in the constellation of Ursa Major, stars that shine near the North Pole and are circumpolar.

Despite the rich repertoire of representational engravings on Breton passage-graves—ellipses, half-circles, axes, bows, 'bucklers', 'yokes' or horns, and serpents—cupmarks are not common except around the Gulf of Morbihan (Péquart M. and St.-J., and le Rouzic, 1927, 74), confined significantly to tombs near Locmariaquer and the Grand Menhir Brisé: some cup-and-rings below ground-level at the Table des Marchands; a cupmark in the side-chamber of Les Pierres Plats at the sea's edge; inside Petit Mont whose architecture is unusually similar to some British passage-graves (Lynch, 1967, 15); at Kerpenhir; and cups all over the underside of the great capstone in the portal-dolmen of Kerveresse, all sites within four miles of Er Lannic and at the very south-east of the distribution of passage-graves in the Carnac region, reaffirming the local variations in ritual even within a rectangle only 15×8 miles in extent. The presence of cupmarks at Er Lannic emphasizes the individuality of these stone circles amongst the Breton megaliths.

What ceremonies were enacted in the rings cannot be told. There are many resemblances between Er Lannic and the rings of the south-west peninsula of Britain including the north–south and east–west orientations.

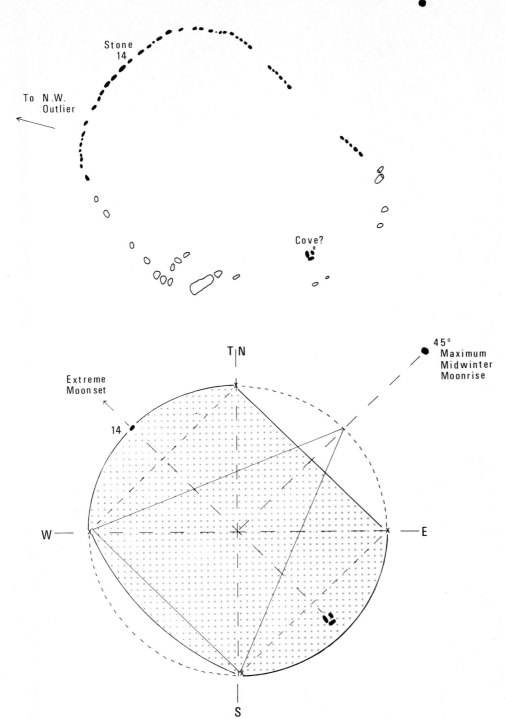

Fig. 21. A Possible Geometrical Basis for the Design of the North Ring at Er Lannic.

Le Rouzic pointed out that the huge, water-covered stone, Le Men er Gou, at the south of the semi-oval and the large pillar at the intersection of the rings lay on a north–south line and that the outliers were east–west of each other. It is also observable that the centre of the north circle is south of the north-west end of the ring's north-east chord and exactly west of its south-east corner. Er Lannic's flattened circle may be based on a rectangle whose cross-axial lines extend to Stone 14, the 'Cove', and the north-east outlier. The corners of this rectangle must be very close to the cardinal points.

Comparable meridional and equinoctial lines in the Morbihan are recorded from the megalithic rectangle at Crucuno (Thom *et al.*, 1973, 45) although this quadrilateral is suspected to be an eighteenth-century folly (see Glyn Daniel, *Antiquity* 49, 1975, 81).

The paired rings of Er Lannic are reminiscent of multiple sites like the Grey Wethers, the Hurlers, Stanton Drew where Er Lannic's 'Cove' has a positive counterpart. Some evidence for a solar axe-cult comes from the carvings of stone axes (Fig. 14) to be seen on stones 1 and 2 situated at the west of the northern ring (Péquart M. and St.-J., and le Rouzic Z., 1927, 42). Stone 3 carries an elaborate 'yoke' or horn motif (ibid, plate 9) akin to others at the passage-grave of Mané Lud where the stones also bear carvings of sun and axe. Such 'yokes' may have affinities with the 'sun-ploughs' of Scandinavian rock-art which represented 'presumably a ritual ploughing which formed part of a ceremony which took place when it was possible to work the land again in the Spring and which was designed to secure the success of the season's crops' (Gelling and Davidson, 1969, 79).

Whatever the validity of this interpretation, at Er Lannic the probable associations with water, the fierce fires, the outliers, the suggestion of an axe-cult, the north–south axial lines, all these serve to link these peculiar Breton rings with the great open circles of the British Isles, the broken pottery and remains of animal bones being analogous to the deposits discovered in the causewayed enclosures and later henges of Wessex. The exact nature of the rites at Er Lannic 5000 years ago as the moon rose in the midwinter night sky above the fire-sparkling river cannot be recaptured. But it is likely they were not dissimilar from those being performed in the other great stone rings of southern Britain.

9. CONCLUSIONS

Before leaving these open stone circles and turning to those of northern Britain with their central burials it will be appropriate to summarise what has been said here about these large megalithic rings.

They developed from the later third millennium onwards and were built and used by natives rather than by intrusive people. The paucity of artefacts makes such dating speculative but the C-14 dates from New Grange, the links with the stone-axe industry, the associative relationship of chambered tombs in the Orkneys, at Stanton Drew, Land's End, and with the mountainous Carnac tumuli like Mané Lud do point, however tenebrously, to a Late Neolithic horizon for many of these circles.

The larger sites are best interpreted as foci for dispersed and presumably small farming communities, not centres for adjacent settlements but for wider areas of the tree-covered countryside. The comparative nearness of some circles to passage-graves may indicate either that rites once entirely performed in and near a chambered tomb gradually became diverse enough to require two precincts, the older sepulchre and the new open circle, or that the two types of monument were built by different people of distinctly separate beliefs. During the second millennium with the increasing fragmentation of Bronze Age society into 'chieftain' groups, a social change perhaps connected with the intrusive beaker communities, smaller circles were built to serve the needs of their own locality. One regional distinction was the tendency towards standardization in the number of stones.

In the south-west peninsula associated circles are quite common amongst the larger sites from Stanton Drew southwards. These double or treble complexes, often near water and in passes, may be successive, manifestations of fresh cults being absorbed with older traditions or even the results of the growth of a more codified ritualism. The fact that these multiple sites are limited in number and usually near possible trackways suggests that they might be places where people of somewhat different beliefs could meet. That sites could be of several phases and stem from separate traditions is shown by the Stripple Stones circle-henge.

Of the beliefs and customs that impelled the building of these stone circles few tangible clues survive. One consistent element has been the recognition not only of east–west axial lines but also others to north and south (Fig. 22). Many circles are too badly damaged for any certainty of their original state but high stones stand at the south in the Hurlers Centre (Dymond, 1879), at the west at Stanton Drew (Dymond, 1877), and there are east–west lines at the Stripple Stones, Tregeseal and Er Lannic. Approximate north–south orientations are not only usual in the south-west peninsula amongst the henges like Priddy and Castilly but occur in some circles like the Grey Wethers and Er Lannic. In prehistoric and pre-compass times they were most likely obtained from baselines set out east–west at Autumn or Spring for there was no Pole Star (Polaris) to sight upon in that age though the stars Thuban (α Draconis) around 3000 BC (2400 bc) and Kochab (β Ursae Minoris) from 1500–300 BC (1250–300 bc) were flickering rather faintly in the northern sector of the sky. Thom has shown that the north and south stones at the Ring of Brodgar are each within a few inches of True North and South and although the ruinous state of this circle-henge precludes any certainty of its former condition, the tallest stones do seem to be west and south (Thom and Thom, 1973, 121).

Equinoctial alignments would be useful guides to the seasons for these peasant-farmers, and the setting out of a line at right-angles would have been simple. It is a practice known in other contexts. At the West Kennet long

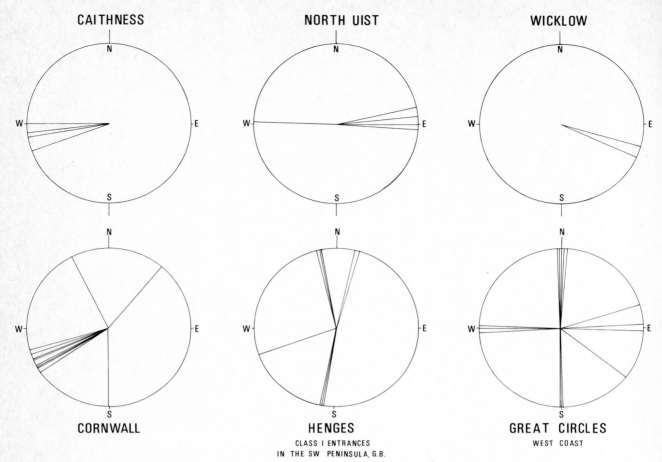

CAITHNESS   NORTH UIST   WICKLOW

CORNWALL

HENGES
CLASS I ENTRANCES
IN THE SW PENINSULA, G.B.

GREAT CIRCLES
WEST COAST

Fig. 22. Azimuthmal Positions of the Tallest Stones in Various Regions of the British Isles.

barrow near Avebury the passage was orientated east–west within an almost perfect isosceles triangle whose base was aligned north–south (Piggott, 1962b, 15). This may imply that north–south was only a secondary requirement to the prerequisite of an axis directed towards the vernal and autumnal equinoxes. Within this pattern of seasonal alignments upon the sun there is no incompatibility in the possibility of a change to a WSW. line in some Cornish stone circles, perhaps for herdsmen, though the data is slight.

In the design of all these megalithic sites, from Scotland down to Land's End, the circle and flattened ring are predominant and the oval virtually absent. The facts may be abstracted from Thom (1967, Table 12.1) for the three main areas of south-west Scotland, Cumbria and the south-west peninsula (Table 5).

As Thom has, in general, surveyed the bigger sites, those that are marked on the 1-in Ordnance Survey maps, this analysis supports the contention that the majority of larger rings are circular. A few have one flattened arc. The only possible ovals are the small Easthill site near Dumfries and the two outer

Area	Sites	All circles				All ovals		
		Circles	Flattened			Ovals		
			A	B	D	E	I	II
SW. Scotland	G4/3 – G8/2	7	3	2	0	?	0	0
Cumbria	L1/1 – L2/14	7	3	1	1	0	0	0
SW. England	S1/1 – S2/3 +S3/1	13	3	2	1	?2	0	1
	TOTALS	27	9	5	2	?3	0	1
GRAND TOTALS		43 Circles				4 Ovals		

Table 5. *Shapes of the Great Open Rings in Western Britain*

circles (later additions?) at Stanton Drew. There is an egg-shaped ring at the Hurlers. These represent fewer than 10 per cent of the sites.

The ceremonies within these equinoctial circles elude us. The evidence of fires at several circles like Brisworthy offers a frail connection with those later bonfires of fecundity in mediaeval Europe. The nocturnal leaping through the flames, the carrying of burning torches around the fields, the feasts and the token sacrifices may be as illusory as they are attractive. The absence both of human remains, except as secondary deposits, and of other material offerings leave only the tantalizing supposition that communication with nature in these circles was expected to be direct and had no need of buried gifts and, at the most, only the sweepings from a fire—a pyre?—were brought into the circle, perhaps accompanied by dances as evanescent as yesterday, with axes brandished ephemerally in the air, with thoughts that were never written down. The robed priest, masked witch-doctor, the shaman, the sacrifice, tethered beast, the whirling dancer, maenadic women, the imitative group-mimes . . . nothing remains for us to choose from.

Many of these circles must have stood in woodland clearings. Later, per-haps, they were built at the edges of cultivated land. Renfrew (1973a) has written of the Late Neolithic group-oriented chiefdoms that are revealed through community works like the henges, and of the individualizing chief-doms of the succeeding Bronze Age in which the architecture is less imposing and 'where the personal wealth of the chief and its prominent display assume as much importance to the community as did formerly the great tribal meet-ing-places'. If one adds to this the effect of an increase in population and the consequent disintegration of the large, loose-knit community into smaller and more self-contained chiefdoms, a hierarchical change perhaps initiated by the beaker-using people taking over whole territories and establishing minor kingships in place of the older egalitarian societies, then a social backcloth to the lesser, later and more numerous stone circles may be con-structed.

CHAPTER SIX

The Stone Circles of Northern and Western Scotland

How these curiosities would be quite forgott, did not such idle fellowes as I am putt them downe.

John Aubrey

1. THE WESTERN ISLES

Unlike the comparative uniformity of the southern ceremonial megalithic rings the stone circles of the western isles contain a diversity of architecture. In them may be found not only the familiar equinoctial lines but also several outliers and centre stones, a few concentric circles and at least one avenue. Integrated with these southern features is the northern custom of placing burials within the rings which themselves are rather smaller and frequently non-circular. The fact that the majority of the sites were erected close to the Atlantic explains this variety for it could be expected that their builders received ideas from the south and from Ireland via the trade in Tievebulliagh stone axes (P. R. Ritchie, 1968, 123), with some lesser influences from the east of Scotland.

No henges are known in these islands. Nor are there many large circles. There are either clusters of rings like the groups at Machrie Moor, Arran, and on Lewis, or individual circles on Coll and Tiree, Mull, central Argyll, Skye and North Uist, a pattern different from that of the south and suggesting smaller, more isolated settlements whose position was often determined by the demands of the sea route.

Just as the forests and swamps of the countryside hindered journeys so the seaways of the British Isles encouraged the careful traveller. Early prehistoric settlements in the north-west were frequently alongside coasts and estuaries or by navigable rivers. Trails were rare on land and not wide enough for pack animals. To travel, people used water, crossing land only to avoid dangerous tidal races and currents. It is possible to reconstruct a route from south-west Scotland up to the Orkneys (Scott, 1951, 22). The scatters of circles lie along-side it.

From the Solway Firth travellers crossed from Luce Bay in order to by-pass the perilous Mull of Galloway, and from there journeyed north to the Kintyre peninsula. No sensible seaman would have risked the Mull of Kintyre whose furious races inexorably destroyed any open boat in bad weather. So men moved up the protected eastern waters, passed by the west of Arran, and accepted the inconveniences of the short portage from Loch Fyne to Loch Crinan. It was at the north-east of this narrow, much-crossed neck of land that Neolithic people had settled in the fertile Kilmartin valley with its notable linear cemetery, henge, standing stones and the stone circle at Temple Wood, a compelling collection of monuments for the archaeologically minded visitor. Carvings of flat bronze axes and halberds, patterned cist-slabs and the discovery of later beakers and food-vessels show that the area was flourishing during the Early Bronze Age, and it may have acted as a convenient staging-post for trade-goods being taken northwards from southern Scotland and Ireland.

Once beyond Crinan a traveller found himself once more in Atlantic waters. Here the leather-sided and shallow-drafted vessels would be paddled between the islands and the mainland. Earlier tragedies warned seafarers to avoid the fatal Gulf of Corryvreckan between the islands of Jura and Scarba where the narrow channels create irresistible races. 'Any small craft . . . that is swept there by the flood (and there is no turning back) against the seas raised by a westerly gale, has little chance of survival in the terrific seas that break from the whirlpool for several miles to the west.' (Thom, 1971, 10.) So the boats kept near the coast, passed through the Sound of Mull up to the Ardnamurchan peninsula, crossing to the western coast of Skye to miss the tides running through the Sound of Sleat and the Kyle of Lochalsh.

Lonely circles like Loch Buie by a sheltered bay on Mull or Strontoiller by Loch Etive in Argyll demonstrate how distant the settlements may have been in this unfriendly region of rock and water. There are no more than three possible circles known on the 600 square miles of Skye, two of them by Loch Slapin, the first protected bay on the island from Ardnamurchan. Here voyagers may have waited for good weather before crossing the deep and storm-swept Minch that led them to the Outer Hebrides and ultimately to the Orkneys. And in this nerve-testing way the stone axes and the finer bronzes were carried sporadically from island to island, perhaps passed from settlement to settlement across waters normally only used by local fishermen but whose loneliness was sometimes touched by a few boats carrying people in their search for good land.

Such fragmented regions militated against any large-scale gatherings and the stone circles reflect this. They are mostly small, even on the well-populated islands of Arran and Lewis. Only on North Uist are there large ovals with longer diameters of over 36.6 m. The true circle becomes rare in these islands. On Arran there are more ovals and egg-shapes than proper circles. Such a consistent pattern is unlikely to be fortuitous. The possibility of men deliberately designing non-circular rings late in megalithic history is not unfeasible though it must be added that such designs are apparently not closely inter-related. Amongst the Loch Roag group on Lewis there is a 13.1×11.3 m circle with a flattened arc to the east; a 21.6×18.2 m oval with a long north–south axis; another, 12.9×9.2 m, with a north-west–south-east axis; and a

Pl. 15. *Loch Buie, Isle of Mull.* From the south-west showing the 2.7 metre high outlier, perhaps aligned on the midwinter sunset, and, just to its right, a second outlying stone to the south-east of the ring. This circle stands in a rare, cultivable patch of flat land on the mountainous southern coast of Mull.

17.4 × 14.1 m circle flattened at the north-east containing an inner north-west–south-east oval ring. Such a variety suggests independent planning.

So do the other architectural features, probably introduced from other areas along the Atlantic coasts. Outlying stones like those at Loch Buie may well be related to those in Cumbria. This well-preserved little circle has a low outlier at the south-east far too close for discriminating astronomical use, and a taller slab set edge-on 36.0 m to the south-west, well-placed both for observing the midwinter sunset and for directing people towards the sandy shores of Loch Buie half a mile away. Like the outlier at Long Meg it may have combined ceremonial and practical functions. 366 m NNW. another stone stands close to the entrance to the only good pass through the Torosay mountains and is most probably directional in character.

The avenues at Callanish, if they must be derived from another source, seem best paralleled by those around the Lake District at sites like Kemp Howe, Moor Divock, Broomrigg and Lacra. This geographical diversity of influences is extended by the discovery of a double-spiral carved on the north stone at Temple Wood, Argyll (Hadingham, 1974, 66). Apart from the significant position of the chosen stone it is notable that spirals are rarely found on stones in southern Scotland (Morris, 1967, 80; 1969, 41) but are common on the chambered tombs of eastern Ireland. It is interesting to learn that at the greatest accumulation of carvings on rocks in the British Isles, at Achnabreck, only five miles from Temple Wood, there were two standing stones exactly south of the site (Morris, 1971, 37).

The Temple Wood ring, almost perfectly circular and 13.2 m in diameter, close to 16 MY., stands at the west of the Kilmartin valley near Nether Largie South chambered tomb. To its east is the setting of standing stones thought by Thom (1971, 45) to form a lunar observatory, with the circle standing in line with a notch in the western mountains where the whole horizon looks as though it had been chewed by beavers. The circle was excavated by Craw (1930). The interior was covered with small boulders beneath which was a slightly off-centre cist aligned NNE.–SSW. like those on Machrie Moor, Arran, and of similar dimensions. The cist's capstone had been removed, but although nothing was found its affinities suggest an original food-vessel deposit of the earlier second millennium bc. Re-excavation by J. G. Scott revealed a small ring of stones around this cist like the central setting of a Clava ring-cairn. Another cist lay to the south-east. Traces of cremation were found in both cists (J. G. Scott, 1974). The approximate diameter for the inner ring of 3.5 m is within 18 cm of the 4 M.Y. calculated by Thom (1967, 36, A2/8).

Burial deposits are the most constant feature in northern stone circles, usually as cremations (Burl, 1972, 31) under central cairns in cists. That in some cases these were secondary additions may be inferred from the eccentric positions of the late beaker cairn at Ballymeanoch henge, Argyll (Craw, 1931), or the mound at Loch Roag, Lewis (J. Stuart, 1860), around which were pits paved with seashore pebbles. At the foot of some stones were other pits containing charcoal (Ellice, 1860, 202). But whereas there are good reasons for believing in such adaptations in some Hebridean circles this is less certain for the sites in Arran.

Near the west coast of this hilly island is a rare expanse of flat land crossed by the Machrie Water and joined by a mountain pass to east Arran. On this attractive patch of alluvium and sandstone are several chambered tombs of the later third millennium. These seem to have been built on hillsides by pastoralists indifferent to the fertile land below (Henshall, 1972, 25), although Renfrew has contended that the relative proximity of the majority to agricultural land is indicative of a crop-growing economy, each of the eighteen tombs being the focus of a separate 'territory' capable of supporting at the most a population of thirty-five to seventy people. Following his assumption that such upper figures are unrealistically high for early farming methods, a reduction by a factor of five produces a total of seven to fourteen people for each area, hardly more than a family group (Renfrew, 1973b, 134). In such terms a territory was little more than a croft, and one would think not of chieftains but of patriarchs ordering the affairs of their piece of land. The tombs were used into the early second millennium. A date of 2340 bc ± 110 (Q-676) was obtained from Monamore Clyde long cairn from material laid down just before the tomb was blocked, and some of the mounds, already old, may have had elaborate orthostatic façades and trapezoidal cairns added during the Late Neolithic period (Scott, 1969, 215).

There are indications that some territories coalesced during the Early Bronze Age. In several cases a single stone circle lies at the centre of two areas. But the concentration of circles on Machrie Moor (Fig. 23) may be evidence that the whole south-west littoral was combined into one great 'chiefdom' centred on a gigantic cairn at Blackwaterfoot. Like the Kilmartin valley, Machrie Moor became a cult centre raising once more the possibility that chambered tombs may have been ritual sites in Neolithic Britain. Two tombs, Tormore II and Moss Farm, stand on the moor itself in an area containing at least eight small stone circles. The main group is situated a mile inland on a slight east-facing slope. Their immediate territory lies within a hill-lined triangle of about three square miles (777 ha) which might have supported a prehistoric population of a hundred people. Allowing for under-exploitation this reduces to some twenty to fifty people for Machrie Moor in the earlier part of the second millennium, a number quite adequate to erect the circles yet not so large as to demand larger megalithic rings for their ceremonies.

From their artefacts the circles belong to the centuries around 1600 bc. Not three miles to the south-west by Drumadoon Bay there was once the Blackwaterfoot 'stupendous cairn' with several cists from one of which came a two-rivetted, lengthy bronze dagger with gold pommel like another of the Wessex culture (J. M. Coles, 1971a, 47), chronologically in keeping with the stone circle food-vessels, and a crescentic jet necklace from the Tormore cairn nearby. It is possible that here is yet another example of a chieftain society responding to the sea-trade in prestigious wares of the Bronze Age, the whole community welcoming their chief-priest's personal display of grandeur. It may have been such a person that was buried in the mountainous cairn.

Clarke (1970, 233) has suggested that such a phase marks a change from a beaker aristocracy to a society dominated by bronze-using chieftains.

No longer does local prestige safely emanate from the burnished beaker, the stone bracer, little bronze knives, jet buttons and belt-rings. In Wessex, and elsewhere, respect was now commanded by great bronze daggers with many rivets . . . The prestige of Wessex gear was as wide as the

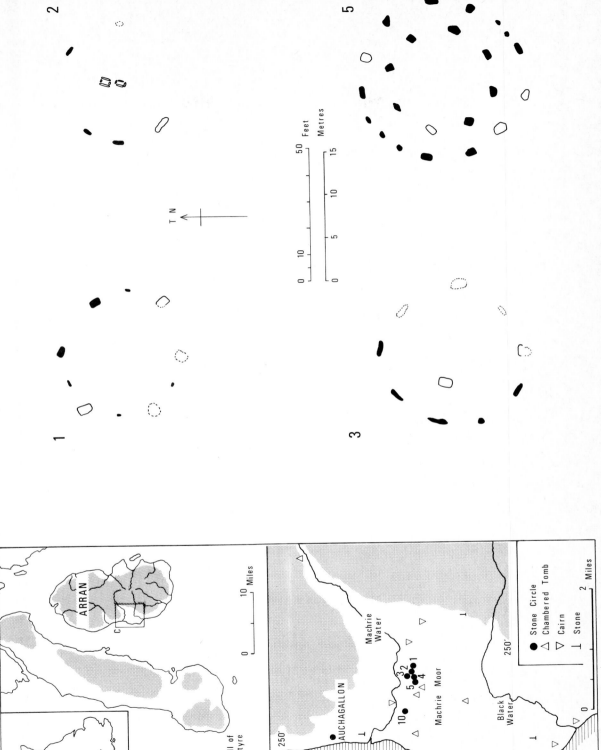

Fig. 23. The Complex of Stone Circles and Cairns at Machrie Moor, Arran. Plans after Roy, McGrail & Carmichael, 1963.

Pl. 16. *Machrie Moor 5, Arran.* From the west. A good example of a North Channel concentric circle whose origin may lie in the passage-grave tradition as the numerous low stones of the outer ring suggest. Excavated in 1861, the whole interior was found to be covered with small stones beneath which were two slabs like the sides of a cist. There were no finds.

The right-hand stone has a perforation where legend claims the giant Fingal leashed his dog, Bran, while he boiled a cauldron in the inner circle.

resources upon which it drew, from Brittany to Ireland, and from Northern Europe to Scotland.

He also suggested (ibid, 279) a deliberate alliance between the new chieftains and the native users of collared urns and food-vessels. This would fit well with the archaeological evidence from Arran.

Three of the Machrie Moor circles were dug into on a bright day in May, 1861 (J. Bryce, 1862, 506), and two, those with tall sandstone pillars, were each discovered to contain cists with food-vessels (Fig. 10), one cist having a skull of a twenty-two-year-old brachycephalic male, some long bones and a couple of flint arrowheads. In September Bryce returned on another lovely day and excelled himself by opening five more sites before nightfall. Only two cists were found, one food-vessel, some more arrowheads and a little bronze awl.

At least three of the circles are set in line like the Kilmartin cairns, pointing roughly to a conspicuous stone on a ridge a quarter of a mile west. This would direct a traveller towards the concealed Machrie Bay, but the line could never have been used astronomically because the horizon is obscured by Beinn an Tuirc mountain ten miles away on Kintyre and there is no hill-notch. The artefactual associations and the resemblance to a linear cemetery of round barrows are reminiscent of Wessex monuments and a simple interpretation of this complex would be that it was a series of successive Early Bronze Age sites, strongly influenced by southern customs, as was Kilmartin, in which burial by inhumation and cremation were intermingled.

The circles cannot represent territorial areas for there are five of them within 275 metres of each other. Their differing diameters from 6.4 m up to 18.1 m, their various shapes of oval and egg (Roy, McGrail and Carmichael, 1963), their structures including a concentric ring placed higher than the others, the distinct choices of either low granite blocks or thin, sandstone pillars, their six cists, all argue against a single, overall design. The intricacy of the shapes, even without the artefactual data, surely belongs to a time when the laying out of megalithic rings was well established.

The exactly central positions of the cists suggest they were contemporary with their circles but it must be said that two circles each had two cists; and whereas each cist was consistently aligned NNE.–SSW. the long axis of its megalithic ring never agreed with this but varied between north-west–south-east and north–south. It is possible that the circles were somewhat earlier than their food-vessel burials.

Emphasizing the mixture of influences to which Arran was open, hardly a mile to the north-west is another stone circle at Auchagallon with a recumbent kerbstone like others in north Argyll. Elsewhere on the island a circle at Lamlash and a Four-Poster at Aucheleffan, its superb view towards the sea-girt Ailsa Craig obscured by Forestry Commission conifers, have connections with north-east Scotland to be discussed later. Similar associations with distant areas occur in north Argyll where the circle of Strontoiller seems to be related to the Clava sites in Inverness-shire.

Space forbids more than a mention of the great megalithic ovals along the south coast of North Uist although the nearness of each to a chambered tomb is intriguing. Carinish, 41.5 × 39.0 m, is a quarter of a mile west of the Hebridean long cairn of the same name. Loch a Phobuill, 42.4 × 35.1 m, is close to Craonaval passage-grave with its tall peristaliths. And Pobull Fhinn, 37.8 × 28.0 m, by the lochside, is a quarter of a mile south-west of the fine Barpa Langass round tomb with its beaker sherds. Such associations are interesting on two counts. The first is the possible juxtaposition of tomb and circle noticed earlier. The second is that the circles by sea inlets are spaced about one and a half miles from each other and may have served areas about 320 acres (130 ha) in extent, areas that would have supported only a small agricultural population so that stock-breeding must also have been part of the economy of these people. Hints that this was so come from the bones of a calf, sheep or goat, and water fowl found at Rudh' an Dunain tomb, and the animal bones excavated at the Neolithic settlement at Northton on Harris. The large chambered tombs point to the needs of many people. In conclusion, all these circles and Cringraval, about 36.6 m across, stand on low plateaux and have their long axes approximately east–west with the tallest stone at the east (Fig. 22). Their unencumbered interiors, their size and positions present unequivocal parallels with the circles of southern Britain.

North of Uist is the island of Harris and Lewis known to have been settled since Neolithic times. Dates of 2461 bc ± 79 (BM-705) for birch forest clearance, and 1654 bc ± 70 (BM-706) for an oval beaker house have been recorded at Northton. (Simpson, 1973.) Outside contacts are confirmed by finds of other beakers in the Hebrides (Clarke, 1970, 578), by a bowl from the Uist habitation site of Eilean an Tighe exactly like others from the Orcadian tombs of Unstan and Mid Howe (Piggott, 1954, 230), and by the discovery of two Irish Group IX stone axes on Lewis (P. R. Ritchie, 1969, 124). Stone circles on Lewis cluster around the shores of Loch Roag, a rare and magnificent bay sheltered from Atlantic gales by the island of Great Bernera. Here the sandy beaches and dunes give way to the machair, level stretches of rich, calcareous soil, before reaching the rocks and mountains of the interior. Although today much of Lewis is covered by 1.5 m of peat caused by climatic deterioration, it cannot be doubted that the area around Loch Roag was very attractive to prehistoric man.

It is not surprising to find a group of circles here spread along two miles of the coast in the depths of the bay. None is more than half a mile from the sea and, like the Machrie Moor sites, all are different. Airidh nam Bidearan at the south-east may have been the largest but is now almost totally destroyed. Just to its north, Garynahine is an oval, 12.9×9.2 m, set north-west–south-east with a low central stone and cairn. Further north the largest surviving ring, Loch Roag, is close to the seashore. It is an oval about 21.6×18.2 m on a north–south axis and has an eccentrically placed cairn. Just inland from it Cnoc Fillibhir is a concentric ring, 17.4×14.1 m in diameter, its inmost tall stones arranged in a north-west–south-east oval. Half a mile, across a small bay, is one of the finest circles in Britain (Fig. 24).

The Standing Stones of Callanish form a small ring which with its thin pillars, chambered tomb, avenues and rows, has long excited the imagination since Martin Martin described it as 'ye Heathen temple' in 1695, wherein the Druid priest officiated by the imposing centre stone. Following the excavation by Matheson (Innes, 1860), it has been seen as a deliberately despoiled astronomical observatory (Somerville, 1913, 93); as a calendrical computer (Hawkins, 1966a, 186); as a fusion of burial and ceremonial

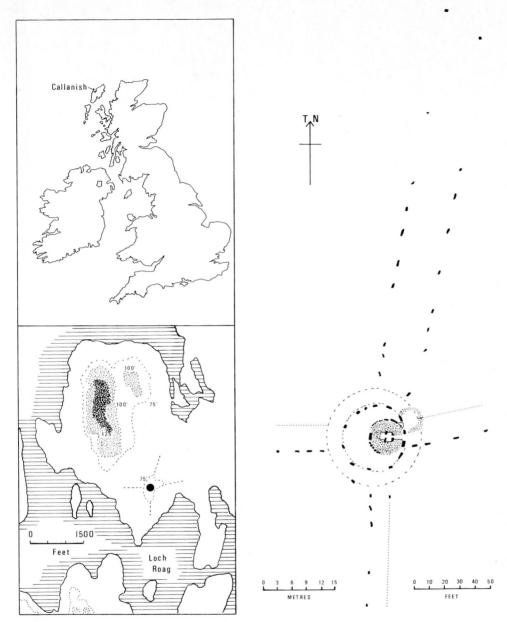

Fig. 24. Callanish, Lewis, Outer Hebrides.

architecture (Daniel, 1962, 72); and by Thom as a lunar and stellar site (1967, 122) susceptible of the most refined observations (1971, 68). It has been well described archaeologically by Henshall (1972, 138, 461).

The site is visible from a considerable distance for it stands on a promontory quite near the highest point where there is a rocky knoll. From the circle the waters of the surrounding lochs can be seen to east, west and north although the sea is almost totally hidden by higher land.

The stones of Lewissean gneiss came, if local legend can be trusted, from a stone-strewn ridge near Loch Baravat a mile north-east of Callanish. Even the largest, the central pillar 4.75 m high weighs no more than five tons and would have needed twenty people at the most to haul and erect it. The 13.1 × 11.3 m circle has thirteen stones, undressed and ungraded, and is noticeably flattened precisely towards the east. The tall stones are held upright in their holes by small packing-stones. The 'centre' stone is about 1.2 m north-west of the true centre and is at the back of a diminutive chambered tomb of Camster Orkney-Cromarty type (Piggott, 1954, 240) with a short passage and two little chambers divided by projecting slabs barely 0.9 m high. This was discovered deep beneath the peat in 1857 but only scraps of cremated human bone were unearthed from the chamber. It is accepted that this tomb is secondary much as some of the other Lewis cairns were added to circles, and just as the passage-grave at Bryn Celli Ddu, Anglesey, was built over a circle-henge (Lynch, 1970, 58), intimating that sometimes stone circles were deliberately altered or even destroyed by passage-grave builders. Pre-historic destruction of circles is not unknown. At Cultoon on Islay over 150 miles south of Callanish huge stones had been overthrown or dragged from their sockets before peat had begun to grow over the site during the second millennium (MacKie, 1975). Such demolition reveals antagonisms between prehistoric sects where irreconcilable beliefs demanded at least the adaptation if not destruction of the others' monuments. An embanked circle at Letterston in south-west Wales was concealed by a turf mound at a time when it was already old (Savory, 1964). Other circles had barrows or cairns placed over or overlapping their perimeters. At Callanish there seems to be the remains of a low cairn set against the ENE. stones. A single stone, 3 m to the south-west of the circle, may be part of an outer concentric ring.

Running NNE. from the circle is a damaged and slightly splayed avenue of high stones, 82.3 m long and terminating in two higher stones set at right-angles to the others like some of the Dartmoor 'blocking' stones at the end of the rows there. A single row of four stones leads exactly west for 12.2 m. Another, also of four stones, extends 15.2 m towards the ENE.; and what was probably intended as an avenue but is now a single stone and five stones in a 27.4 m line 3.7 m to its west leads southwards gently uphill towards the knoll of Cnoc An Tursa 91 m away.

Even on a drizzling day the stones straggle proudly along their ridge, stark against the western sky, and when the sun is shining the nearby houses hardly intrude upon the imagination which perceives how the setting of loch and hillside, sky and circle blend indivisibly together. Yet archaeologists have been taciturn about Callanish, seeing in it an enigma not easily solved by traditional methods.

In contrast, astronomers have welcomed the challenge, finding in each

Pl. 17. *Callanish, Lewis, Outer Hebrides*. From the north, showing the proximity of the ring and its rows to water.

stone row the possibility of a good celestial alignment. Toland had believed the two circles were intended for separate worship of the sun and the moon. Somerville (1913) thought the north avenue to be directed towards the rising of Capella (α Aurigae) between December and May in 1800 BC, the west row aligned on the equinoctial sunset, and the east on the Pleiades in 1750 BC. He also noted that two stones outside the circle at the north-east and south-west could have been directed towards the lunar maximum each nineteen years. Hawkins (1966a, 185) observed that the latitude of Callanish is close to that at which 'the moon at its extreme declination remains hidden just

below the southern horizon', and at Callanish the moon would appear just
to skim the horizon each eighteen to nineteen years if looked at along the
south row in 1500 BC. Thom (1966, 48; 1967, 122) commented on the re-
erection of some avenue stones and showed that the south row was set out
almost precisely towards the meridian, 180° 1′, that the east row could have
been orientated on the rising of Altair (α Aquilae) in 1760 BC, and the NNE.
avenue on Capella in 1790 BC, although such a star at its rising would be so
faint as to be almost unnoticeable (Hawkins, 1966a, 185). In a later work
Thom (1971, 68) added that an observer looking down the NNE. avenue
towards the SSW. would have seen the moon's maximum setting along the
slope of Mount Clisham 16 miles away on Harris. Chronologically one notes
that except for Hawkins' 1500 BC, the equivalent of a C-14 1250 bc, the other
proposed dates are close to 1800 BC (1550 bc) and therefore archaeologically
not improbable. It has to be realized, however, that Thom specifically limited
his entire archaeo-astronomical investigations in Britain to a period between
2000–1600 BC because 'it is generally agreed that the date of erection of
standing stones lies between 2100 and 1500 BC' (Thom, 1967, 101). These
archaeologically outmoded dates were, moreover, based on a radiocarbon
calendar and thus further distorted by the need for recalibration, making
2100–1500 BC the analogues of C-14 1675–1250 bc, and so part of only the
Early and Middle Bronze Age. Many of Thom's sites now need searching for
celestial alignments between 3250–1500 BC (Burl, 1973, 170), starting a
thousand years before the earliest of his hypothetical dates. It is only with
demonstrably Bronze Age sites that his astronomical chronology may be
applicable.

Legends about Callanish (Swire, 1966, 20) tell of a great priest-king, adorned
with mallard feathers, who came to Lewis with many ships and had the stones
erected by black slaves, many of whom died. Another folk-story is told of a
nineteenth-century antiquarian who as a boy visited the island and met an
old man in whose childhood people went to the stones secretly, especially at
Midsummer and on May Day. 'His parents had said that when they were
children people went openly to the circle but the Ministers had forbidden all
that—so now they went in secret for it would not do to neglect the stones . . .
And when the sun rose on Midsummer morning "Something" came to the
stones walking down the great avenue heralded by the cuckoo's call.'

> A voice so thrilling ne'er was heard,
> In spring-time from the Cuckoo-bird,
> Breaking the silence of the seas
> Among the farthest Hebrides.
>   Wordsworth, *The Solitary Reaper*

The cuckoo is the harbinger of Spring, and its call may have become associated
with the time of the Beltane May Festival.

The combination of ceremonial and astronomical practices at other sites has been suggested and it may be that such a fusion took place at Callanish. What is certain is that the construction, despite its complexity, contains only architectural traits well known elsewhere, its centre stone having a counterpart at Garynahine two miles away, its concentric circle matched by Cnoc Fillibhir nearby, both features of many other circles. Avenues are rarer in the north but occur in south Cumbria where parallel lines of stones connect the small rings at Moor Divock and where a splayed avenue ran uphill fron Shap South towards a tiny tumulus. A similar avenue may have existed at Broomrigg Plantation. The remains of a twisting avenue connect The Kirk, an enclosed cremation cemetery in Kirkby Moor, Lancashire, to a nearby cairn. A double row at Penhurrock once led towards a concentric circle; and at Lacra a 15.2 m wide avenue led 105 m to a stone circle which may have had a centre stone. This circle, like the concentric at Birkrigg Common, had a collared urn of the Early Bronze Age. In Scotland, the circle-henge at Broomend of Crichie, Aberdeenshire (J. Ritchie, 1920), once had a splayed avenue extending exactly northwards, first to the circle with its urn and Wessex stone battle-axe, and beyond to a concentric circle around a small cairn.

Callanish was probably never finished. Of the grandiose design involving a concentric circle with centre stone and four radiating avenues only the NNE. avenue was completed. It is significant that these stones are nicely aligned downhill towards Tob na Faodhail, the Bay of the Ford. Legends associating stone circles with water are common. The Oxfordshire Rollright Stones are said to go downhill to drink at a spring on New Year's Day (Manning, 1902, 293). On the same night in the Orkneys two great pillars near Stenness were believed 'to wrench themselves out of their places and roll down the slope to the sea. There having dipped themselves, they return and resume their accustomed position' (Gunn, 1915, 358). Isolated Breton standing stones are frequently to be found near wells, rivers, and brooks. Many henges as well as stone circles in Britain were built near water and this may not have been only for ease of transportation but also because water was intrinsic to the ceremonies. Cles-Reden (1961, 152) has pointed out the significance of water in the religious beliefs of people since Neolithic times from Mesopotamia to western Europe where the cult of sacred springs and offerings still persists in the throwing of coins into wishing-wells. Such prehistoric beliefs continued into the Iron Age. 'Springs, wells and rivers are of first and enduring importance as a focal point of Celtic cult practice' (Ross, 1967, 19), and are well attested by historical writers. Ross (ibid, 127) notes the association of Celtic horned fertility gods with water and adds (ibid, 218), 'the cult of wells and springs, and especially those at the source of some strong stream or river, cannot entirely be separated from the cult of river deities themselves . . .' Geoffrey of Monmouth relates a legend that the sick might be healed by taking water that had been poured over the stones of Stonehenge (Thorpe, 1966, 196).

Burgess (1974, 196) emphasizes the increase in water-orientated religious practices in the later Bronze Age, attributing this largely to a deterioration in the climate. There is no doubt, however, that water was essential in some Neolithic rituals. The stone axe was sometimes deposited in water, even the most perfect jadeite form (J. M. Coles *et al.*, 1974, 220). And whereas there is no obvious association with water in earlier Neolithic ritual monuments like the chambered and unchambered long mounds or causewayed enclosures, there is a marked change in the later henges in which 'many of the sites have been chosen for their proximity to streams' (Atkinson, Piggott and Sandars, 1951, 84). Such a transference from the former hilly locales to low-lying situations may have been occasioned by the increasing importance of water in the religious practices of Late Neolithic and Early Bronze Age people.

In the context of stone circles it is of interest to find that 'in the early Irish tradition, many of the goddesses are connected with rivers and springs . . . Perhaps the best-known example of this is the legend of Boand (She of the White Cows) who challenges the powers of a spring sacred to the king, Nechtan, and is destroyed by it. In its pursuit and destruction of the goddess it rises up to form the river Boyne.' There may be a whisper here of the mythology that once surrounded the great cemetery around New Grange (Chadwick, 1970, 173). Such legends, like those of birds and sacred animals, are the last and distorted words of an oral tradition that time has blown away, and knowledge of the past is all the weaker for its loss.

At Callanish the northern avenue may have linked the circle with a source of water for rites long since forgotten. Early Irish legends tell how the Samhuin feasts on 1 November were observed by lake shores and that it was at this time that water goddesses were metamorphosed into birds with chains of silver or gold. But the mental images of the people of Callanish are lost and one can only visualize, as on Dartmoor or at Stonehenge, a procession moving up the avenue from the bay towards the circle. Did its leader wear mallard-feathers? Modern folk-stories may, at best, be misleading if not entirely untrustworthy but the association of marsh-birds with religious activities was widespread in Britain in the Iron Age. 'The true significance of this cult of water-birds can only be imperfectly appreciated, but there is sufficient evidence to suggest that it was closely associated with solar deities in their role as gods of healing.' (Ross, 1967, 279.) How far back in time from the Iron Age such beliefs extend it is impossible to say but the proximity of many megalithic sites to water suggests that the builders of some circles may have held similar concepts.

Of the remaining structures at Callanish only one stone of the outer circle and one stone of the east side of the south avenue were put up. The south sides of the east and west avenues were completed, the other sides never started. That the project was abandoned and that these were not meant as single rows is indicated by the extra single stones; by the low causeway of cobbles leading from the circle towards the south avenue (Henshall, 1972,

462) rather like that at the Hurlers, Cornwall; and by the fact that the axial lines of the four intended avenues would have met at the circle-centre whereas the present single rows converge on a point well to its south.

Why the work was discontinued can only be speculated. Perhaps passage-grave builders deliberately desecrated the circle as others had done at Bryn Celli Ddu. The concentric circle of bluestones at Stonehenge II also was unfinished (Atkinson, 1960, 205), perhaps because of a change in the over-lordship of Wessex occasioned by the 'expulsion of late . . . beaker-users to regions outside Wessex' by chieftains using collared urns (Clarke, 1970, 224; Fleming, 1973b, 578). Or more prosaically people may have become dis-couraged by the work still to be done, or the death of a leader may have removed the driving-force for their labours.

The little circle and its centre stone provided a focus of attention upon one person rather than a place for communal activity, three avenues leading from lower ground where the sea-level was probably several feet lower in those days. 'On the shore of Bernera facing Callanish are two more standing stones looking as if they once marked a path across to the island where now is sea. It was probably dry land when the stones were put up for fresh-water Bronze Age peats can be seen round the shore today several feet below high tide mark.' (Lethbridge, 1973, 36.) The stone circle stands on its ridge just where the meeting gradients to NNE., east and west were easiest. Its southern row extended towards the meridian where the sun was at its highest and may have been meant to provide an approach to a culminating stage in the ceremonies like the analogous avenue at Broomend of Crichie. Although the stellar and lunar alignments may have been intended by the circle-builders the exactly east-facing flattened arc and flat face of the centre stone suggest the designers were primarily concerned with the sun's equinoctial rising.

Callanish today epitomizes most of the problems connected with stone circles. Its shape, its centre stone, its intrusive tomb, its astronomical lines merge into contradictions that may be modern over-complications. We should, perhaps, view the circle and its avenues as the result of solitude working upon the religious fervour of people whose lives were limited by their own island. As has been said of the Maltese temple-builders, 'this lonely people . . . in the midst of a boundless sea under a boundless sky in a world without beginning and without end, royally free and yet captives, may have concentrated increasingly on the mystic realms of the hereafter' (Cles-Reden, 1961, 74). Born of this seclusion came a monument whose architecture made it as insular as the elongated island tombs of the Orkneys, its seeds gathered from distant sources, its conception nurtured in the long, uninterrupted days on the sea-wrapped Hebrides.

2. NORTHERN SCOTLAND
Despite the large number of chambered tombs at the very north-east tip of

Scotland in Caithness there are few megalithic rings whether large or small. It does seem as though the builders of the Camster tombs of the Orkney-Cromarty group with their side-slabbed chambers would not erect circles even when their latest tombs were constructed in circle regions, unlike the Clava group in Inverness where circle and passage-grave combine to form unique monuments. In the Orkneys both Maes Howe cruciform-chamber tombs and Camster mounds co-exist, but the only circles are near Maes Howe on the mainland, never on the outlying islands like Rousay where Camster tombs predominate. On Lewis a Camster tomb was set inside Callanish; and in Caithness the circles and the tombs occupy complementary areas whereas there is a correlation between the distribution of the tombs and the several multiple settings of stone rows.

There are few large circles here but those that do exist are open rings, in passes and with large stones at the west (Fig. 22). They thus fall into the same category as the other ceremonial circles of the south and may owe their existence to their comparative nearness to the Atlantic route. The best known is Guidebest, so close to the Burn of Latheronwheel that the river has cut away the ground up to the circle itself. This ruined ring, surrounded by gorse bushes and in an inconspicuous hollow of pasture land, is 57.3 m in diameter, and has its tallest remaining stone, 1.5 m high, at the west on the very edge of the burn's high bank. A few stones of another large circle survive near Camster. Yet another has been found by Leslie Myatt (1973) at Aultan Broubster in the low land between Loch Calder and Forss Water to the west. It is 62.8 m across and, despite being badly damaged, appears to be flattened to the north-east. The tallest stone, 1.0 m in height, stands at the west. Small cairns have been built close to these circles. At Aultan Broubster there is even one near the centre but there is no reason to consider it any more than a later addition. Another circle, Achany, half-sunk in peat and about 26.8 m across, forty miles south-west of Guidebest near Lairg, has five boulders still in situ on the circumference of what seems to be an oval in a remote glen by the Gruidie Burn. In shape and situation it is quite different from the large Caithness circles.

Of the smaller sites little can be said. Lack of proper excavation leaves it uncertain whether some might not be the ruinous kerbs of erstwhile cairns. Several of them like Aberscross, The Mound, have cists or cairns inside them. This obscure 7.3 m circle has its most massive stone at the west and a tall, thin pillar opposite. Originally there were six stones. Now the natural platform on which it stands at the foot of Craigmore hill is half-covered in bracken and bushes, the hillside littered with boulders. Overhead, electricity cables stretch along the valley of the Fleet.

In May 1867, Lawson Tait cut an east–west trench across the site. At the exact centre there was a buried human cremation without pot or implement, the heads of a half-burnt humerus and radius showing it was an adult whose remains had been placed here on the covering slab of an oval stone cist aligned east–west. Despite evidence that this had never been disturbed it held only half an inch of rainwater on the rock bottom. Nor were there any deposits at the bases of two circle-stones. If anything else had been interred in the circle the acidic soil had destroyed it.

Three widely dispersed sites in Sutherland, Auchinduich, Cnoc an Liath-Bhaild and Dailharraild, possess the feature not recorded elsewhere, except at the strange site of Bowman Hillock near Huntly, Aberdeenshire, and Maughanclea, Cork, of having their stones set at right-angles to the circumference, surely another example of a local custom. These rings in their lonely river valleys are very small, not more than 9.1 m across, the first being a concentric. Cnoc an Liath-Bhaild, an ellipse 9.1 × 6.8 m, has a low cairn at its centre. A pronouncedly taller circle-stone stands at the west against a background of smoothed moorland hills. Note should also be made of the recent discovery of a 12.0 m circle with massive central boulder at Clachtoll by the coast in western Sutherland (Welsh, 1971).

Two badly damaged circles, one ring-marked, stood on the eastern slopes of Learable Hill, Sutherland, in Strath Ullie, one of the infrequent passes between the east and north coasts. The circles are not remarkable but one stands near to a complex of standing stones, cairns, parallel and splayed rows (RCAHM-S, 1911, nos. 374–381). Thom, who has posited that in 'megalithic' Britain people divided the year into sixteen months of twenty-two to twenty-four days (1967, 110), noted that two of the parallel rows were directed towards three of his sunrise declinations for 6 May, 30 August and the equinox (ibid, 158) although this entailed looking downhill, the reverse of what seems to be the case with rows elsewhere in Britain.

The stone rows of Caithness and Sutherland, which occupy roughly the same areas as the preceding Orkney-Cromarty tombs, particularly around Lybster on the coast, differ from those of Dartmoor in one respect. Whereas the latter are always parallel those in northern Scotland may be either parallel or splayed. Yet they have common traits with those in Devon. They are on hillsides, often connected to an unencircled cairn or cist, and are built of unobtrusive stones unlikely to have been chosen as sighting devices. The settings contain as many as twenty-three rows at Mid Clyth but these, like their southern counterparts, are composed of several groups. The orientations vary. With their short lengths, averaging about 36.6 m and their ankle-high stones they appear to be parochial variations as peculiar to the region as the megalithic horseshoe-shaped settings like Achavanich and Broubster, fifteen miles apart in central Caithness which, too, possess the local trait of having stones at right-angles to the perimeter. Another horseshoe setting, this time concentric, of hoary, moss-grown stones within two parallel rows, may have stood by the coast at Latheronwheel five miles south of Achavanich. They were shattered for dyke building a century ago (Gunn, 1915, 343). Horseshoe settings in stone, timber or earth with ends open approximately towards the south-west are known along the east coast of Britain (Burl, 1974a, 72) from Caithness down to Norfolk where Arminghall's post structure was dated to 2490 bc ± 150 (BM-129). The orientation is so different from that of the easterly facing chambered tombs that a distinct tradition may have existed that could explain the otherwise anomalous interest in the south-west of the ring-cairn builders of north-east Scotland.

Returning to the Caithness rows of tiny stones, these may be arrangements designed to lead the eye up the slope to a surmounting cairn just as the Dartmoor rows perhaps provided a line to walk along to the burial place. There are, however, more involved astronomical interpretations. At Mid Clyth, 'the hill of many stanes', the fanned rows have a central north–south axis. Thom (1967, 156) thought the rows might be aligned on the risings and settings of Capella (α Aurigae) between the years 1900 and 1760 BC. Certainly such observations, by bisecting the angle between them, could have established a north–south line much as the pyramid-builders of Egypt may have done (Edwards, 1947, 209), the more so as the need for a level horizon to ensure an accurate bisection is fulfilled at Mid Clyth. Little stones could then have been set in rows not for observation but to record the lines.

In a later study Thom (1971, 91) suggested a watcher looking south along the easternmost row would have seen the maximum winter moonrise and, north along the west row, the summer maximum moonrise. He interpreted the rows as extrapolating sectors enabling prehistoric man to compute almost undetectable perturbations in the moon's movements and so be able to predict eclipses (Thom, 1971, 83). Hutchinson (1972, 215) has analysed these findings succinctly and written, 'The presumption is that an attempt was being made to ascertain the limits of the effect of perturbation when the declination was otherwise varying very slowly. Moreover, it seems certain that a set of sightlines does imply particular interest in the absolute maximum declination (of the moon) . . . and also probably in the minimum.' He continued with the comment that the Caithness monuments 'certainly look like the ruins of mathematical instruments of some sort'. Heggie (1972, 46) in a detailed review of Thom's work in general agreed with this. There is no archaeological reason why this should not be so and one may conclude that prehistoric people whose megalithic monuments were analogous to others in the British Isles may have devised an intricate and esoteric use for them. If Thom's dates of c. 1650 BC are correct this could be equated with 1350 bc, well into the Middle Bronze Age at a time when even the latest beakers were becoming unfashionable.

None of this is incompatible with the belief that the rows were for socio-sepulchral customs. Yet they were not as finely laid out as has been claimed. Thom (1967, 156) wrote that he 'was immediately struck by the way in which each slab lies along the line in which it lies', but his own plan does not confirm this. The rows are only about 1.8 m wide so that a 60 cm misplacement of a stone would have been a great error, and a stone even by the edge of a row might be 30 cm from its theoretical position, a notable misalignment in stones only a few centimetres wide. At Mid Clyth the twenty-three rows can be split into three major groups and analysed:

			Percentages		
Group	No. of Rows	Surviving Stones	Exactly On line	Edge of Line	Up to 60 cm Off Line
East	?6	24	20	17	63
Centre	10	75	29	29	42
West	7	58	38	43	19
		+ 16 not planned			
TOTALS	23+	173	29%	30%	41%

Table 6. Positions of the Stones at Mid Clyth, Caithness (based on Thom, 1971, 92)

It is true that some of these stones may have been moved by solifluction but this would apply indiscriminately to correctly and incorrectly placed stones. That only 29 per cent of the stones are in their 'proper' places shows in practice how imprecise the construction of some of these monuments actually was.

Groups of stone rows, usually single and short but megalithic, are known in many other regions of the British Isles: Northumbria; Ulster; south-west Wales; Dartmoor; Cork and Kerry; as well as the awesome rows of Brittany, some of which are splayed. There are also isolated sites like the Old Castle Hill Stones on Moorsholm Moor, Yorkshire. Fan-shaped examples are uncommon outside northern Scotland but there are, of course, radiating avenues like that at Callanish and the four rows running to the Circles A and B at Beaghmore, Tyrone. One must conclude that each region developed local variants having only the most general resemblance to others.

The dating of the Caithness rows is unsure. Only at Garrywhin, seven miles SSW. of Wick, was there any artefactual evidence. Here seven or eight ruined rows lead uphill to a small cairn on a knoll. There is an obvious similarity between this site and those in Dartmoor. Although the rows are expectedly irregular like Mid Clyth and others at Dirlot, Yarrows and Camster (Thom, 1971, 92–100), here each stone had been fixed firmly between two smaller stones in a shallow pit making basal movement more difficult. Within the cairn, excavated in 1865, was a cist arranged east–west beneath a gigantic stone cover. In it were the remains of an inhumation and a cord-ornamented pot. If this were an All-Over-Corded beaker it could be dated as late as the early seventeenth century bc, but AOC beakers are rare in cists (Clarke, 1970, 62), and the east–west orientation is atypical for burials associated with them (ibid, 455). The pot may have been a food-vessel and of a somewhat later date. A time just in the latter half of the second millennium bc would be consonant with the horizons of stone rows elsewhere.

The scarcity of stone circles in northern Scotland may be an indication that the stone rows in some way fulfilled a comparable function. They could indeed have been used as celestial computers or for astronomical sightlines although the stones do seem low for this particular purpose and not helpfully aligned. Their very resemblance to the Dartmoor rows in their small stones, their associations with burials, their juxtaposition to cairns and standing stones is further augmented by the presence of a Dartmoor-style circular cattle-pound and hut-circles on the hillside at Cnoc na Moine near the Dounreay rows. But the cultural and chronological implications of this affinity, if it does in fact exist, have yet to be established.

3. MORAY FIRTH

Until now, whatever their architectural idiosyncracies, stone circles have seemed interrelated, open rings for ceremonies that involved the sun, the lighting of fires, the carrying of axes, with burials and fertility, held at special times of the year. Whether in Cornwall or in Caithness a fundamental commonalty appears, an underlying sameness about their use however much local variation might affect the designs. The sharpest difference arises from the recognition that the large, plain Late Neolithic rings probably encompassed rites by all the people, whereas from the beginning of the Bronze Age the smaller rings and their internal features imply a visual concentration upon one person, maybe a richly apparelled priest or headman. But with the circles of north-east Scotland there is a different tradition with different architecture, with a restricted distribution around the Grampians, a tradition in which the deposition of the dead was an essential component. The broad Inverness valley at the head of the Great Glen dividing Scotland from south-west to north-east is seminal to a study of these circles. Sheltered by mountains, its soil fertile, its rainfall low, it must have appeared to Neolithic arrivals ideal for settlement.

North-east Ireland had been entered during the mid-fourth millennium bc by stone-using farming communities whose economy depended on cattle-keeping, who began clearing the trees, and whose descendants ultimately built great tombs in which human bones were used for rituals. Their boats crossed and recrossed the waters of the Irish Sea, sometimes taking migrants to new parts, sometimes carrying prospectors searching for stone sources for their axes. At some time voyagers sailed up Loch Linnhe, an adventure in itself because of the Corran Narrows. Once beyond that, the pleasant

Pl. 18. *Balnuaran of Clava, Inverness.* The two large stones are part of the circle surrounding the north-east passage-grave. Right-centre is the low ring-cairn with its stone circle; and in the background is the cairn of the south-west passage-grave.

Lochy valley led north-east along the uninviting shores of Loch Ness into the wide, low-lying Inverness plain. Here on the sands and gravels of the gentle valley-sides some early farmers stayed by the River Nairn and twenty miles to the east in Strathspey.

Today one can see their ruined tombs, some of which must be composite monuments much as cathedrals are structures of successive styles. A magisterial synthesis of data on these and other Scottish chambered tombs is presented in Henshall (1963; 1972). In Inverness there are outliers of the Orkney-Cromarty group which possibly are the earlier; and the spectacular Clava cairns customarily built in low, inconspicuous positions. There are also infrequent long cairns, eastern in origin and probably late in the third millennium bc.

The Clava cairns are without doubt the best preserved and most rewarding to visit of these tombs. The necropolis at Balnuaran of Clava and Corrimony have been taken into State guardianship and may comfortably be inspected. Visually superb, despite recent excavations (Piggott, 1956) their dating, their origin and their function are in dispute. The group contains passage-graves and ring-cairns. The passage-graves have straight passages leading through a round cairn to a circular, exactly central chamber. The ring-cairns are uninterrupted, stony penannular banks with large kerbstones, enclosing an unroofed central space. Both types have graded kerbs highest around the SSW., and the majority of both have graded stone circles about 24.4 m in average diameter. There is no other collection of chambered tombs in the British Isles set inside circles, only atypical individual sites like New Grange in Ireland; nor, as has been discussed, is there any unrelated group with consistently graduated stones. Many of the Clava circles had twelve stones. Estimates are possible at sixteen sites and three seem to have been enclosed within eight stones; three may have had ten; and the remaining ten had twelve-stone circles although their circumferences varied from 72.3 m at Aviemore ring-cairn to 103.9 m at Balnuaran of Clava North-East. This is in keeping with the quanta recognized in some southern circles. As twelve-stone circles are also frequent amongst the recumbent stone circles (RSCs) of Aberdeenshire this is one indication of a relationship between the two areas.

Generally the passage-graves are smaller than the ring-cairns, and their chambers never exceed 4.9 m across whereas a ring-cairn's central space could be as wide as 10.7 m. Yet both share the unique traits of a SSW. orientation, cupmarking, stones graded in height, and have surrounding stone circles. The passage-graves have more compatible designs than the ring-cairns for, where the original plan may be inferred, the majority of their cairns and outer rings were circular. In contrast, there is a complete medley of designs amongst the 'circles' of ring-cairns from ovals to eggs (Thom, 1967, 137), and the cairns are often of a different shape again, including two, Bruaich and Cullearnie, that are simply irregular.

Whereas most Neolithic tombs had their entrances between north-east and south-east the passages and tallest stones in the Clava cairns were erected towards the south-west–south (Fig. 25), the ring-cairns especially clustering around the south-west. This may have been an as yet imperfectly perceived continuation of an older tradition. The passage-grave mounds were up to 3.1 m high, a height that would preclude sightings being taken across the circle. This is important, for claims have been made that the consistent south-west alignment of the Clava lines show their builders to be much concerned with the midwinter sunset, and, indeed, it is this Clava tradition in particular that offers the strongest support for the belief that astronomical orientations were essential parts of the religious ceremonies of some pre-historic people in the British Isles. Nevertheless, the Clava cairn lines are quite diffuse. Of the ten that can be established three are at the south-west, four at the SSW., and three at the south. The cairns do not reveal that precision claimed by devotees of prehistoric astronomy. Midwinter sunset can never have been at the south or even SSW. Even as far north as this latitude of 57° sunset can rarely have been more than 2° or 3° south of 223°, so that the builders of an average cairn 13.4 m in diameter, had they intended to sight their entrance on the midwinter sunset, would have made a vast error of at least 2.3 m if their tomb faced even SSW. If entrances were astronomically aligned it must have been towards a multiplicity of celestial targets.

Several cairns, like the Aberdeenshire RSCs, have cupmarks on some stones, basin-shaped depressions perhaps 75 mm across, made by grinding the surface with a small stone. Such markings afford another distinction between these sites and the undecorated southern circles. In the Clava passage-graves the cupmarks are mainly in the passage or chamber but in ring-cairns the predominantly southern distribution is evenly divided between kerbstones and circle-stones. The common association with burials and their presence on stones supposedly facing the sun suggests that cupmarks were sun-symbols of fertility.

The presence of cupmarks is one good diagnostic trait in establishing whether a stone circle is related to the Clava group. Very few circles in the British Isles are cupmarked, only just over 1 per cent for the 750+ circles outside north-east Scotland. But in that area there are forty-two cupmarked sites, 21 per cent of the regional total, a proportion increasing the nearer the circles are to Inverness. In Perthshire 13 per cent of circles are cupmarked, 19 per cent in Aberdeenshire, 43 per cent in Inverness. As these decorated north-east circles share other architectural traits it is likely that they are related.

Fig. 25. The Azimuths of Clava Cairns and Recumbent Stone Circles in North-East Scotland.

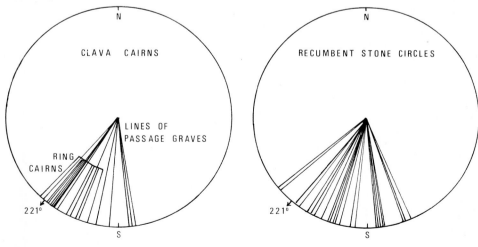

Within some Clava cairns there are other signs of ritual: scatters of quartz pebbles; cremated bone; a cist with a skull. But no dateable objects. Like cupmarking, the discovery of quartz pebbles is another probable indication that a circle belongs within the Clava tradition (Burl, 1972, 38). Excluding cairn-sites like Kintraw, Argyll, only fifteen circles in the British Isles have had quartz scatters recorded in them. Of these the Druids Circle and Circle 275 are in north Wales; and Clogherny Butterlope and Gortcorbies are in north-east Ireland. The remaining circles are related to Clava. In Inverness, Corrimony and Druidtemple had scatters of quartz; in Aberdeenshire, Castle Frazer contained quartz pebbles; so did Corrie Cairn and Culsh. Further south in Perthshire several sites like Croft Moraig and Monzie had quartz strewn round their stones. It is clear that this group is quite distinct from its neighbours in the practices of its builders.

Before looking into their purpose it is worth asking how many people were involved in the construction of the Clava cairns. At most cairns the stones are not heavy. The biggest kerb at Gask, the largest ring-cairn, weighs about half a ton. The west circle-stone at Balnuaran of Clava North-East, a sandstone block 3.4 m long, weighs seven tons and over level ground fifteen people could have moved it implying a minimum community of about thirty. One may guess at a total of fifty Clava cairns built over a period as long as a millennium. It is likely that the majority were put up in the later centuries as the population increased, and this might indicate that only two or three tombs belong to the early phases with a population of less than a hundred.

One of the most controversial problems of the Clava cairns is their origin because of the three distinct elements of chambered tomb, ring-cairn and stone circle. Ring-cairns are widespread in northern Britain (Henshall, 1972, 270; Kenworthy, 1972; Ritchie and MacLaren, 1972) but it is only within the Clava tradition that they occur in stone circles (Burl, 1972). Quite why passage-graves and ring-cairns so morphologically alike should merge in Inverness is not clear, but a plausible suggestion is that the ring-cairn builders were natives whose architectural practices were adopted by passage-grave incomers thus creating unique chambered tombs (Henshall, 1972, 276) whose central spaces were smaller than those in ring-cairns to permit corbelling of the chambers. Such a hypothesis explains the homogeneous orientation of the ring-cairns. A separate origin again for the stone circles, particularly if they were ungraded to begin with, would remove more of the problem, would account for the dissimilarity in cairn and ring shapes, and enable a Clava cairn to be regarded as the composite product of several traditions.

Two sites can easily be visited. Corrimony passage-grave in Glen Urqhart has a stone circle, 21.3 m in diameter, surrounding a 15.2 m cairn built on an artificial mound of small stones. Broken quartz had been strewn around the kerbstones during the cairn's construction. A gap in the stone circle at the ENE. revealed a cobbled area indicating that the space was intentional. The passage entrance is at the south-west and leads to a corbelled chamber, now roofless, 4.0 m across. On the floor was a slabbed area set on sand in which the excavators (Piggott, 1956) detected the stain of a crouched in-humation. A big slab on top of the cairn may have been the chamber's capstone and has many cupmarks.

The second site is the splendid Balnuaran of Clava cemetery near Culloden battlefield, Inverness (Fig. 26). Here there are two passage-graves and an intermediate ring-cairn on a bent north-east–south-west line about 122 m long. The south-west passage-grave has a graded stone circle in which there is no north-east stone, reminiscent of Corrimony's cobbled gap. Like that site the cairn is built on a mound. The entrance, between two large kerb-stones, is at the south-west. Cupmarks survive on a stone on the east side of the passage and on the first stone on the west in the chamber. In 1828 two probably flat-rimmed pots were discovered, one containing cremated bone.

The central site is a ring-cairn, its stones graded towards the south-west. Radiating out to three circle-stones are three enigmatic cobbled settings. There are cupmarks on two eastern kerbs. When excavated in 1953 the central area was found to be blackened by charcoal amongst which was a thin spread of cremated bone.

The north-east site is another passage-grave with a 16.5 m cairn also on a wide platform. Around this at ground level is a fine stone ring 31.6 × 29.7 m across. There is a notably cupmarked kerbstone at the NNW. In the passage, aligned south-west, is another cupmarked stone. A 'few bones' were found in the chamber about 1854.

Thom has suggested (1966, 18) that observers once squatted in the chambers of these cairns to observe the midwinter setting sun but comparable align-ments do not exist at most of the other Clava passage-graves (Fig. 25). One can only record at the Balnuaran complex evidence of the same rites seen elsewhere: cupmarked stones; cremations; stone circles enclosing areas for ritual, and assume that here also were sites magically used by early settlers for supernatural protection against the terrors and misfortunes of their lives. Nor at Balnuaran of Clava ring-cairn could the cupmarked kerbs have been seen from the central space because the cairn was at least 1.2 m high and the marked stones are lower. The marked kerb at Tordarroch faced inwards and could never have been viewed by the living. And the prolifically decorated capstone at Corrimony probably looked downwards into the blackness of the sepulchre.

This conflict between possible solar orientations and the impossibility of their ever having been used may be reconciled if they are considered to have been for the dead to whom the intervening cairn would literally have been immaterial. A 6.0 m thickness of cobbles, or the absence of a passage, or cupmarks invisible in the darkness, would be of no moment to the dead. Such a connection between death and the sun accords with the discovery that the roof-box over New Grange's entrance would have admitted sunlight to the

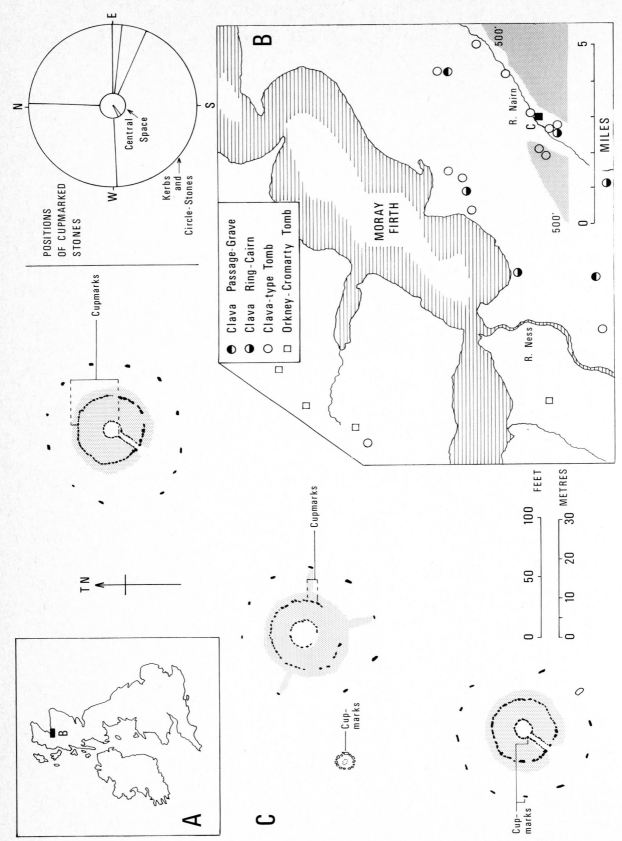

Fig. 26. The Complex of Two Passage-Graves and a Ring-Cairn at Balnuaran of Clava, Inverness (Highland). The small kerb-cairn is to the west of the ring-cairn.

central chamber at the winter solstice (Patrick, 1974) even when the tomb entrance was sealed.

In all these sites the stone circle seems no more than a barrier or demarcation of the temenos. No sightings could have been taken across it. Few stones are cupmarked. In Inverness it is the central burial mound that is impressive. But later, in two associated areas, specific elements of the architecture were emphasized. In Aberdeenshire the stone circle became dominant at the expense of the central cairn. And at the south-west of the Glen only the focal feature, the central space, of the Clava sites was retained.

Just west of the Balnuaran of Clava cairns is a small kerb-cairn (Ritchie and MacLaren, 1972, 8) architecturally related to them and with a close similarity to some sites in Argyll. At Clava the 3.7 m oval of fifteen close-set stones is flattened at the NNE. and the tallest stones are between south-east and south-west. There was a probable inhumation in a central pit where quartz pebbles had been scattered (Piggott, 1956, 192). The comparison between the diameters of such a kerb-cairn and others like Achacha and Strontoiller in Argyll or Monzie, Perthshire, which average about 4.5 m, and the central spaces of Clava passage-graves and ring-cairns averaging 4.0 m and 6.7 m respectively is apparent. The contiguity of the stones is like the Clava stone-lined interiors. It is not far-fetched to perceive that one development from Clava passage-graves was the construction of these small kerb-cairns based on the model of the central space, retaining not only its diameter but its graded heights of stones and astronomical alignments, diminutive and derivative cult sites of later Bronze Age families who had moved far from the homelands but who still preserved the essentials of the old religion.

Such cairns lie remotely to the south-west beyond Loch Ness. Around Inverness freestanding stone circles are few. There is one 5.2 m ring at Torbreck, and at Templestone in Moray there is a minute Four-Poster, besieged by over-reaching gorse bushes. At Innesmill in the same district there are remnants of a large circle in a field by the roadside, 33.5 m in diameter, the biggest stone at the south, perhaps all that survives of a recumbent stone circle. The ruins of a circle about 58 m across have been found at Edinkillie, Moray, quite close to a ford across the River Divie in a pass between the hills. Its recent discovery, like that of Aultan Broubster, Caithness, and of others in south-west Scotland, emphasizes how easily even great megalithic rings may be overlooked in unpopulated country.

4. ABERDEENSHIRE

Eighty miles east of the Clava cairns, clustered in the foothills of the Grampians along the coastal plain is a remarkable group of stone circles, the recumbent stone circles (RSCs) of north-east Scotland (Fig. 27). These circles have a ring of stones graded in height, the two tallest often in the south-west quadrant flanking a prostrate block. Inside the circle there may be a ring-cairn in whose central space human cremated bone was deposited. For centuries the unique recumbent stone has intrigued antiquarians.

> In the times of King Mainus . . . huge stones were erected in a ring and the biggest of them was stretched out on the south side to serve for an altar, whereon were burned the victims in sacrifice to the gods. In proof of the fact to this day there stand these mighty stones gathered together into circles— 'the old temples of the gods' they are called—and whoso sees them will assuredly marvel by what mechanical craft or by what bodily strength stones of such bulk have been collected to one spot. (Hector Boece, *History of Scotland*, 1527.)

The circles do indeed evoke our marvel even today when, 450 years after Boece, we can normally see only tatters of toppled stones testifying to nineteenth-century demolition. Midmar was 'christianized' by being enclosed in a churchyard where it stands today. Some stones from Culsalmond were similarly 'depaganized'. In 1860 there was a circle 24.4 m in diameter at Holywell, sometimes known as Sunkenkirk like Swinside in Cumbria. In the following year the tenant farmer hauled 500 cartloads of small boulders from its interior where two cists and an urn with cremated bone were dug out. The circle-stones were dragged off for barn foundations. One with at least thirty cupmarks was retrieved in 1879 and is now embedded in a stone wall at Tofthills farm. Nothing else survives.

Yet the group within a rectangle about 50 × 30 miles centred on Alford demands attention. They have been studied by F. R. Coles (1900–07), Keiller (1934), and Burl (1974a). The restricted enclave, the eccentric architecture, the consistent burials, the enigmatic relationship with the Cork-Kerry circles 500 miles away in south-west Ireland, provide the archaeologist and astronomer with substantial clues about their function and about the people who built them. Moreover, they and the related rings in central Scotland are the only group that quite regularly had artefacts placed in them that can be dated. Yet answers remain elusive. It is frequently a problem to establish the original structure. Some circles have been destroyed. Most, like Wantonwells or Kirkton of Bourtie, have been catastrophically damaged. Sometimes, as at Nether Corskie, only the two flanking pillars are left like a half-dismantled Hollywood set. Or just the recumbent and flankers at South Ley Lodge reminiscent of an elephantine head. Even where there are the stones of the outer circle at Rothiemay or Easter Aquorthies (Fig. 28) the smaller kerbs and stones of the cairn have gone. Even so, of seventy-four confirmed sites twelve still have unequivocal ring-cairns and it is manifest that these were never as conspicuous as those in Inverness. It is the stone circle that is dominant. But these RSCs share many traits in common with the Clava cairns: twelve-stone circles; comparable diameters; stone heights graded towards the SSW.; cup-

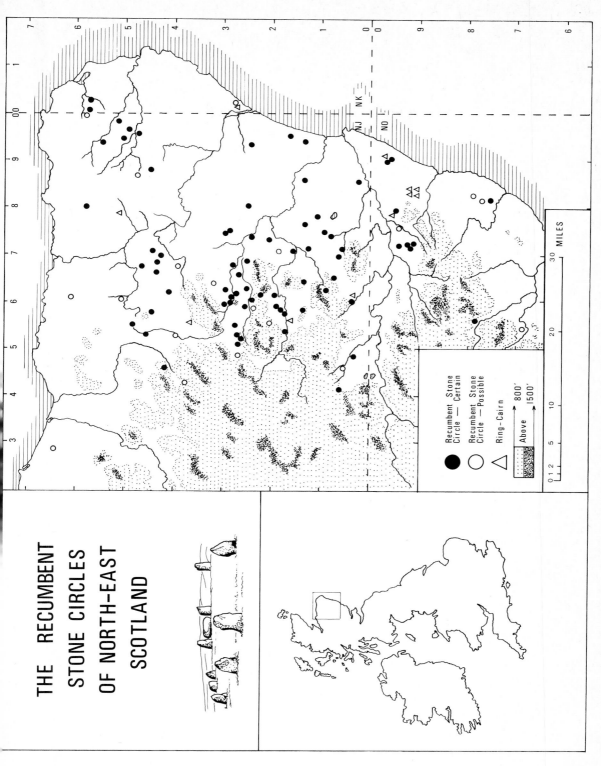

Fig. 27. The Distribution of Recumbent Stone Circles in North-East Scotland.

marks; quartz pebbles; ring-cairns; cremations; and pits with burnt material in the central space. Such connections are obvious. What is not so simple is to account for the dissimilarities.

Most Clava cairns are low-lying whereas RSCs normally stand on hillside terraces. Dyce looks across the valley of the Don. Tomnaverie, battered and wire fenced alongside a gorse-grown quarry, broods above the marshy, mossy land towards Loch Davan. These stepped positions, however, with their wide views are matched in some Clava cairns to the north-east of Inverness where one might expect sites intermediate between the 'classical' Clava forms and the RSCs. Easter Clune and Moyness are on slopes. So is Little Urchany, the only cupmarked Clava site outside the main group. Even farther east are Upper Lagmore on a sharp incline, and Marionburgh on a spur above the River Spey.

No Clava cairn, though, has a recumbent stone, and it is this that distinguishes the RSCs from their Inverness relatives. Search for the origin of these awesome and ponderous blocks has caused archaeologists to look to the lintel-stones over the passage entrance in Clava chambered tombs (Keiller, 1934); to the supine stones placed at the SSW. of the Sanctuary and Woodhenge circles in Wiltshire by makers of AOC beakers (Burl, 1974a, 58), another being suspected at Stonehenge (Atkinson, 1960, 33); and to the 'blind' entrances in the kerbs of cairns like Lyles Hill in north-east Ireland (Atkinson, 1962, 17). This last has no particular resemblance to the Aberdeen recumbents and is more akin to the 'false' entrances at cairns like Kintraw A, Argyll (Simpson, 1969), and stone circles like Temple Wood, Argyll (Craw, 1930). The two stones that protrude at right-angles from these sites are comparable with the blind entrances of some chambered tombs in England and Wales (Powell, 1969, 268), which are possibly skeuomorphs of timber mortuary platforms on which corpses were left exposed before interment (Atkinson, 1965, 130). Architecturally they are like the Coves known in some circles and henges, also with funereal associations.

If the origin of the recumbent does not lie with these an answer may stem from the highly decorated supine stones outside the entrances of at least two passage-graves in the Boyne valley of eastern Ireland. Outside New Grange (C. O'Kelly, 1971, 26) the Entrance Stone, 3.4 m long, was laid in front of the passage. It has five enormous spirals carved on it as well as arcs, lozenges and chevrons, and has a vertical channel pointing towards the tomb entrance. At Knowth, a mile to the north-west (Eogan, 1967, 302), a 3.1 m long stone decorated with concentric rectangles also had been laid outside the entrance. It too had a vertical line incised on it.

Contacts between north-east Ireland and north-east Scotland are well attested during the third and second millennium bc. Not only is Lyles Hill pottery to be found in Aberdeen cairns like East Finnercy in association with early beaker material (Atkinson, 1962, 17) but porcellanite axes from Tievebulliagh, Co. Antrim, are distributed along the south-east route through

Pl. 19. *Loanhead of Daviot, Aberdeenshire.* Taken from the south the photograph shows the recumbent stone, its flankers, the graded heights of the circle stones and the low, central ring-cairn.

Scotland via Loch Lomond and central Perthshire up into the Grampians (P. R. Ritchie, 1968, 124).

Although at the moment the parallels are tenuous, supine stones analogous to those in Ireland are also to be found outside the 'entrance' of some Scottish cairns on this south-east route. At Kintraw A, Argyll (Fig. 34), a 14.6 m cairn had been covered in brilliant white quartz crystals very much like New Grange. Set in its graded kerb was a blind south-west entrance of projecting stones. Two metres away was a 2.3 m long supine stone. At Culcharron, twenty miles north of Kintraw at the mouth of Loch Linnhe, a small cairn with graded kerbs had a blind entrance at the SSW., beyond which lay a cupmarked stone, 1.8 m long, parallel with the kerb. Quartz chippings had been strewn around the stones (Peltenburg, 1974). Such cairns appear to be related to the Clava group. Croft Moraig stone circle by Loch Tay on the direct route to Aberdeen has an outer bank at the SSW. of which lies a 2.1 m long cupmarked stone (Fig. 35). Many quartz pebbles were discovered in the circle. The Irish stone circle at Clogherny Butterlope, Tyrone, (Davies, 1939b) has a supine stone at the east. It is possible that once this stood erect but a significant number of white pebbles were found by it.

On the reasonable assumption that the 'supine stone' custom reached north-east Scotland, an RSC can be seen as a combination of two traditions which came together with the intermixing of settlers, traders and incomers in the first centuries of the second millennium. From Inverness, possibly by sea with a major entry along the River Don and its tributary the River Urie came builders of circles with stones graded towards the SSW. The fusion of this tradition with that of placing a prostrate stone at the entrance to a ritual monument could have been the origin of the characteristic RSC. If there were such a coalescence it is likely to have been in the low foothills around Alford. Here there seem to be the earliest RSCs (Fig. 28), the graded stones set around a perfect circle 18.2–24.4 m in diameter with tall flanking stones alongside a recumbent 4.0 m or more long and usually placed between south-west and south. Often there was an inner cairn. The later RSC-builders occupied peripheral areas to north, east and south down to the River Dee. These smaller rings, sometimes distorted, are composed of lower, ungraded stones and, peculiarly, the recumbent and its pillars were frequently placed not only well inside the circle and attached to the cairn but also set between south and SSE. Such sites as Garrol Wood or Auchquhorthies are very different from the 'classical' RSCs like Cothiemuir Wood or Castle Frazer on its long hillside.

Assumptions about the development of architectural forms are untrustworthy but the fact that the theoretically later RSCs do occupy outlying districts whereas the earlier are central offers some corroboration of this morphological framework. Artefacts provide firmer props. From early RSCs has come some early pottery. Loanhead of Daviot had Neolithic and AOC beaker sherds. Old Keig and Old Rayne also had fragments of beaker, the latter site containing a fine archer's wristguard of pale green polished stone, broken in half but still showing the three perforations for its wrist-binding. It was most probably associated with an N/MR beaker within Lanting and van der Waal's (1972) step 3 of c. 1900 bc or later. In contrast, the later RSCs have no early material, only pieces of coarse urn or perforated axe-hammers of the mid-second millennium.

Since Clarke's (1970) recent work on beaker pottery broad dates may be assigned to these pots although these must still be given with extreme reserve (Lanting and van der Waals, 1972, 44), particularly in north-east Scotland (ibid, 41). From early sherds it seems that RSCs were being built from about 1900 bc onwards. At Old Keig beaker sherds were found beneath the recumbent and with a pit cremation in the ring-cairn's central space. The greenstone wristguard came from Old Rayne's central pit. Even more beaker material came from Loanhead of Daviot, a finely preserved RSC now in State care, in the central space, under the cairn, near the recumbent and by some circle-stones (Kilbride-Jones, 1935).

Other, perhaps earlier, Neolithic round-based pottery including Irish-derived Lyles Hill ware was also found here, a combination that points to a construction date just after 2000 bc. Other, coarser bucket-shaped pots with flat rims were produced over as long as a thousand years so that discovery of these plain sherds is not chronologically helpful. Nor are the fragments of a 'clay urn with incised decoration' at the tiny quartz RSC of North Strone, or the urns of 'thick massive paste' at Castle Frazer except to suggest a crude terminal date in the mid-second millennium for the later circles. It must suffice,

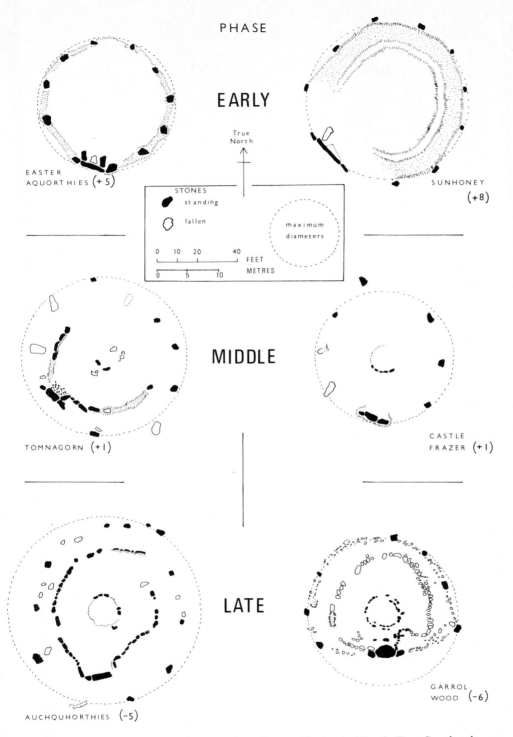

PHASE

EARLY

True
North

EASTER
AQUORTHIES (+5)

SUNHONEY
(+8)

STONES

● standing

◯ fallen

maximum
diameters

0 10 20   40
| | | | FEET
0   5   10   METRES

MIDDLE

TOMNAGORN (+1)

CASTLE
FRAZER (+1)

LATE

AUCHQUHORTHIES (−5)

GARROL
WOOD (−6)

Fig. 28. A Possible Typology of Recumbent Stone Circles in North-East Scotland.

with our present knowledge, to say that RSCs were being erected in north-Scotland between about 2000 and 1500 bc.

Some speculative comments may be made on the numbers of people involved in the use of RSCs. Many of the earliest circles in the heartlands around the Bennachie hills stand on the 350 ft contour on the protected southern slopes of soft hillsides. Although nearest-neighbour analysis shows an apparently random distribution each circle seems to have its own territory, several with long river frontages and with an overall area, including steep wooded hillsides, of about two square miles (518 ha). Within these are deep pockets of well-drained, fertile, sandy loam or till (Glentworth and Muir, 1963, 142), patches of 30–80 ha, an average 50 ha tract being capable of supporting about sixty people (Fleming, 1971, 10) if their economy were supplemented by hunting and stock-grazing in the woodlands and clearances. The RSCs are invariably close to but never on these rich soils.

Several considerations affected the choice of a site: the nearness of land suitable for growing crops; the availability of stone; and the need for a view to a far horizon. Many RSCs were built on hillsteps where the few trees that interrupted the horizon could easily be felled. Today a distant circle is often visible from lower ground but in antiquity forested valleys would probably have obscured a site whose present conspicuous position could be a phenomenon unconsidered by its builders.

Generally a secondary consideration was the availability of stone. At Dyce the stones came from a nearby quarry. At Hatton of Ardoyne there is an outcrop 45 m away. At Old Keig and Auchquhorthies the stones are presumed local. At Whitehill, however, the reddish porphyritic pillars were dragged from their hill-shoulder source to the spur on which they now stand and this task, involving much difficulty, shows that the position of the circle was of major importance.

So was the bulk of the recumbent. At many sites it is petrologically different from the other stones and had sometimes been brought from afar. It does not follow that this was for ritual reasons. Such a massive block might not be available locally. At Dyce, Loanend, Auchmachar, Easter Aquhorthies and several other RSCs the recumbent is 'foreign', the Old Keig stone coming from somewhere in the Don valley six miles away. This block of sillimanite gneiss is gigantic, $4.9 \times 2.1 \times 2.0$ m, and weighs about fifty-three tons. Though much of the journey from source to circle was over flattish ground the final haul had to be made uphill for nearly half a mile at a gradient of 1:14. This must have demanded the strength of well over a hundred people, an effort involving several communities for the occasion. At Balnacraig the recumbent weighs fifteen tons like those at Balquhain and Cothiemuir Wood. At Dyce and Kirkton of Bourtie they weigh twenty-four and thirty tons respectively. It is clear that the circle-builders were obsessed with the need for an impressive stone.

The smaller, local circle-stones caused little problem either in transportation or in erection. Once at the site some stones were 'dressed'. This is especially true of the flankers where it is easy to see how they were shaped to fit the configuration of the recumbent. The beautifully smoothed pillars at Cothiemuir Wood or at Midmar belie their Victorian description of 'rude stone monuments'. The bases of many stones were 'keeled' or stone-hammered into a rough beak to facilitate their tipping and erection (Kilbride-Jones, 1934).

It is known that at some circles—Castle Frazer, Druidsfield and Loanhead of Daviot—the site was levelled. Then the circle was laid out. As only very few sites were anything but circular (Thom, B1/1–B4/4) it may be presumed that the plan required nothing more than a central stake and a rope to inscribe a ring around it. A radius of 9.0–12.0 m would cause no appreciable eccentricity through the dragging of the radial rope over rough ground. There is, however, no indisputable proof of a measuring-rod being used. Multiples of the Megalithic Yard vary from fourteen at Ardlair (Thom, 1967, 37, B1/18) to thirty-four at Rothiemay (B4/4) with no significant peaking around any number. The unit, moreover, seems too long. At fifteen of the seventeen measured RSCs the circle-diameter falls short of its listed M.Y. multiple, the deviations ranging from −36 mm at Yonder Bognie (B1/23) to −39 cm at Easter Aquorthies (B1/6) with an average discrepancy of −18 cm or 1/5 M.Y.[1]

Having set out the circle the recumbent was levered into its hole on the chosen part of the circumference, and this statement carries with it a plague of controversy. So consistently is the recumbent stone in the south-west quadrant of the circle that its position must have been deliberately chosen, most probably decided by the astronomical superstitions of its labourers. RSCs have been studied for this possibility. After A. L. Lewis (1888, 52) and a speculative farrago, *On Some Antiquities in the Neighbourhood of Dunecht House, Aberdeenshire* (Cambridge, 1921), by Bishop Browne, Somerville (1923) discussed the possible calendrical function of the rings. Lockyer (1906b, 407f) predicated some alignments on either Capella (α Aurigae) or

[1] The relevant sites are B1/5; 1/6; 1/18; 1/23; 1/26; B2/1; 2/2; 2/3; 2/4; 2/6; 2/26; 2/17; 3/1; 3/7; 4/4. These all have a minus factor. Only B1/16 (+12 mm) and B2/5 (+24 mm) have diameters exceeding the proposed M.Y. length.

This is a very different statistical picture from that presented by the Clava cairns of Inverness. Here all five measured passage-graves have diameters exceeding their M.Y. length (B7/1a; 7/1b; 7/6; 7/18; 7/19) with an average discrepancy of +25 cm or $\frac{1}{3}$ M.Y. But the six allied ring-cairns have measurements as mixed as their designs. Three (B7/1c; 6/2; 7/15) have plus values, three (B7/2; 7/12; 7/16) have minus values, the final average for the six sites being −46 mm or 1/20 M.Y. Such variations between comparatively close areas seem to suggest the employment of different measures, or even paces, in each locality. In extension, had such divergent units existed then 0.820 m would fit better than 0.829 m for the RSCs; 0.838 m for the Clava passage-graves; and 0.826 m for the ring-cairns, the difference between the longest and shortest of these units being only 18 mm.

Arcturus (α Boötis). His dates for the latter star of 920 BC for Cothiemuir Wood, down to 250 BC for Braehead, a site at which only the recumbent stone survives, are far too late; and even those for Capella of 2000 BC at Braehead, down to 1300 BC at Cothiemuir Wood, are the chronological equivalents of c.1570–1000 bc, very late for monuments some of which contain early beaker pottery (Burl, 1974a, 73). More recently, Thom has found little of moment in the circles although the orientations he did note were either solar or lunar (Thom, 1967, 98, B1/18–B2/5).

It was once thought that all the recumbent stones were situated in relation to the midwinter sunset but this is not so. Of the seventy-four known RSCs thirty-five have determinable orientations, bearings being taken from Thom's accurate plans where possible. The azimuths through the recumbents lie between 230° and 156°. Alignments of Clava cairns are similar. Yet midwinter sunset here was about 223°, only varying where there was a high hill immediately south-west of the site. Over 75 per cent of the lines are farther to the south where the sun can never have set, and are not evenly spread but occur in little clusters as though directed towards several celestial targets.

No definitive statement can be made until not only the azimuth but also each monument's horizon altitude has been determined to establish a declination for it, but it seems significant that the azimuths towards the tallest stone in Clava ring-cairns, passage-graves and Aberdeen RSCs are all broadly towards the SSW., an horizon sector peculiar to these monuments. It is also noticeable that these three different types of monument progressively cover a wider arc, the approximate ranges being:

Clava ring-cairns	196°–224°	Arc = 28°
Clava passage-graves	171°–220°	Arc = 49°
Aberdeen RSCs	156°–230°	Arc = 74°

The most economical hypothesis would be that the earliest Clava cairns were aligned on obvious celestial targets, the settings of the sun and moon, and that over several centuries, as observational knowledge increased, later circle-builders sometimes preferred less apparent but more delicate alignments. Barber (1973) in an examination of thirty Cork-Kerry RSCs suggested not only that some of them had indeed been aligned on either midwinter sunset or midsummer sunset, but also that other circle-builders had 'orientated upon the maximum southern limit of the planet Venus' (ibid, 33), or were 'marking the southern limits of the zodiac', that area of the horizon in which no heavenly bodies rose or set.

This might explain the strangely wide scope of RSC orientations, the results of hundreds of years of nocturnal observations which inevitably culminated in a wide knowledge of the movements of many stars and planets. It may be added that such sky-watching was probably not at this time primarily intended to contribute to cosmological doctrines controlled by a 'druidical' hierarchy, but was simply empirical to establish marker-points on the horizon for the aboriginal ceremonies within the stone circles although ultimately the knowledge gained may have been seminal to the complex religions of the Celtic Iron Age. The objects sighted upon were probably chosen more for their symbolism, less because prehistoric man perceived a pragmatic relationship between those celestial bodies and terrestrial events. Although the connection between the warmth of summer and the northerly maxima of the sun was presumably apparent to him it is far less certain that 'at an early stage men living on the coasts of the Western Ocean must have noticed the connection between the tides and the Moon' (Thom, 1971, 11). This is to impose our own conditioned thinking upon the minds of an essentially alien culture. 'The truth is that magic is a symbolic activity, not a scientific one, and the elements used in it are selected because they are symbolically appropriate, not because they have been found by careful experiment to possess certain kinds of causal effectiveness.' (Beattie, 1966, 207.) There is considerable anthropological difference between the deduction that astronomical sightlines were built into some megalithic monuments and the guess that such lines were used specifically for the purpose of predicting eclipses, tides and for establishing a calendar.

Returning to the possible alignments in north-east Scotland, it is clear that in Clava ring-cairns only the simplest orientations are found, midwinter sunset at sites like Culdoich, Gask or Delfour (Thom, 1967, 98, B7/10), or maximum midsummer moonset at Culburnie or Tordarroch, although the remote Strathspey oval of Daviot may have been sighted on Venus.

It should be noted here that lunar lines are in one important respect very different from those for the sun. The solar solstice occurs annually, a repetition suggesting nothing more than yearly ceremonies at ring-cairns like Delfour. But the moon reaches its maximum only once each nineteen years in its metonic cycle. Nine or ten years later in the average ring-cairn stone circle of 27.7 m (Burl, 1972, 40) the moon would have been setting as much as 7.0 m to the west of the tallest stone and quite unrelated to it. It would seem, therefore, that although rites at these cairns may have been annual it is likely that special importance was given to the ceremonies each nineteen years when the moon reached its most southerly setting.

Most of the Clava passage-graves also were directed either to midwinter sunset as Thom noted for the Balnuaran of Clava tombs (1966, 18) or maximum moonset. Similar lines are found in the derivative kerb-cairns of Argyll and Perthshire (Fig. 34). But it is possible, as in Cork, that the people who built some outlying, perhaps later, cairns like Kinchyle of Dores, Croftcroy and Upper Lagmore, preferred newly realized alignments on the setting or rising of Venus, that shining planet whose most southerly maxima occurred approximately only each thirty years (Barber, 1973, 34). Venus can be as bright as −4.4 magnitude in those rare years when it is at perihelion near the end of December, twelve times as bright as the most brilliant star, Sirius (α Canis Majoris), although it is visible only briefly just before sunrise or just after sunset. Yet, to people accustomed to watching for the midwinter solstice and midsummer moonset, the brilliance of Venus in the night-sky can hardly have been unnoticed.[1] Venus may have seemed even more appropriate than the sun or moon for the ceremonies at the dead of the year. (It is a curious coincidence that I. Velikovsky in *Worlds in Collision* (London, 1950, 162) suggests that Venus was 'born' in the first half of the second millennium BC around 1500 bc, 'a stupendous prodigy in the sky' (ibid, 165) whose 'orbit crossed the orbit of the earth and endangered it every fifty years' (ibid, 195), and that the dramatic emergence of the planet caused consternation over all the world.)

Assuming that the builders of the earliest RSCs continued in the beliefs and practices of their Inverness forebears it is not surprising that the central Aberdeen sites have the same alignments as those of the Clava passage-graves (Burl, 1974a, 75). What different, novel orientations there were would be only in the later circles at the edges of RSC country and these do exist, including a whole group south of the Dee in Kincardine seemingly aligned on Venus rising. There are other alignments on the moon's minimum midsummer setting. One or two small circles like Ardlair or North Strone may have been directed towards the moon's maximum rising as though their builders were also incorporating new lines within the traditional framework. It is noticeable, however, that not one stellar line can be demonstrated in over eighty circles.

Such a hypothesis has the virtue of restricting the Clava-RSC orientations to the night-sky's three most brilliant bodies, the sun, moon and Venus, and the known azimuths of the monuments do appear to gather into clusters around the significant southerly settings and rising of these bodies. But it is one matter to analyse the lines, another to explain why they were chosen. There are implications of activities connected with nocturnal observation of events sometimes separated by a cycle of many years. It may be that these circles, like those of southern Britain, were intended for rites related to the passing of the year and with the cycle of life and death so well symbolized by the setting of the night's most splendid objects, or their emergence in midwinter darkness.

Such a belief is reinforced by inspection of the cupmarking in these rings. Whereas in Clava cairns cupmarks were carved almost indiscriminately, the fifteen decorated RSCs never have markings on their cairns but only on the recumbent or the circle-stones in its vicinity. Eight recumbent stones are cupmarked. So are six flankers and, in three cases, the stone by them. But

---

[1] The calculation of the declination and apparent brightness, which varies considerably, of this planet for any epoch in prehistory is exceptionally complex, and accurate computations would be needed before an alignment upon it for any site could be claimed with confidence.

not one cupmark occurs on any other stone or kerb. It is perhaps significant that the three most heavily marked stones, a westerly pillar at Balquhain and the recumbents at Sunhoney and Rothiemay, which has 119 cupmarks (Fig. 14), have azimuthal bearings of about 232°, 230°, and 226° respectively, very like the predominately south-west orientation of the Clava ring-cairns. The solar association of cupmarks have been affirmed by several investigators (Morris, 1969, 51; Gelling and Davidson, 1969, 103; Simpson and Thawley, 1972, 99), so that their appearance in sites whose builders were concerned with the movements of sun and moon need cause no surprise. From their positions on the stones it is likely that some at least were carved before the circle-stones were put up.

Once the recumbent had been manhandled into position the rest of the stones could quite easily be erected and packing-stones jammed around their bases, care being taken in the early sites to ensure the heights were graded down from the recumbent. The number of stones was often ten or eleven plus the recumbent itself. Only Candle Hill, Insch, has fewer than nine. Only North Strone has more than thirteen. This is compatible with the proposed Clava ancestry for those cairns also have a majority of twelve-stone circles.

Some of the central RSCs had a couple of stones projecting behind the recumbent, a feature sometimes known as a platform but which may be a representation of the passage in a chambered tomb. Still more have the remnants of a bank in which the circle-stones were set. Aikey Brae on a little hilltop, and Berrybrae in a laneside coppice, the stony bank half-stripped of turf by grazing cattle, are RSCs in the far north-east near Strichen which have well-preserved banks. Other banks up to 3 m wide and 1 m high have been recorded at Old Keig and Sunhoney, and ungraded embanked stone circles are known in Yorkshire, the Peak District and in Wales. Aikey Brae, with no trace of an inner cairn, was the only excavated RSC to have no deposit of cremated bone at its centre. Long before 1881, 'during a long summer day', labourers delved nearly 2.4 m into the centre of the circle but there was 'no trace of evidence that the soil had ever before been disturbed' (Stuart, 1856, xxii). Numerous small cairns around the RSC were also vainly demolished 'and the day closed without any trace of graves'. Charles Dalrymple who oversaw this operation plunged into the hearts of at least five other RSCs in the mid-Victorian decades.

When the embanked stones and the recumbent fenced off an open space, the builders performed the first rituals under the midwinter sky, setting up a large crib of wood either in or just outside the circle, a corpse being beneath it. And the pyre was lit. Fanned by the cold wind the fire flamed and flared until everything was transmuted into split and splintered bones, charcoal and ashes. The wide patches of burnt earth at Loanhead of Daviot, Old Keig and Hatton of Ardoyne with its reddened stones demonstrate the heat of the blaze. Carefully the bone-fragments were collected and, at Loanhead, one piece of bone, one broken sherd and one lump of charcoal were deposited in a small pit alongside the burnt-out pyre. Then, keeping the other human remains separate, the rest of the pyre and pottery, perhaps deliberately broken, was religiously buried by the circle-stones.

At this point the activities within the circle were very like those in some earlier passage-graves and in later enclosed cremation cemeteries or ECCS (Ritchie and MacLaren, 1972). At the Druid Stone, Ballintoy chambered tomb (Mogey, 1941), there was a burnt area containing pits, cremated bone and sherds of fine Neolithic shouldered bowls. (Other sites are mentioned in Chapter 2.) As with RSCS with their overlying cairns, a passage-grave was built on top of this. Perhaps a millennium later the custom emerged in north Britain of making a sub-circular bank within which ceremonies could be enacted. One such ECC, Weird Law, Peebles (RCAHM-S, 1967, 64), had a 2.4 m wide bank surrounding a pear-shaped stony mound. Beneath this was a burnt layer into which five pits had been dug. Four contained the cremated bones of what may have been a young mother and her child. The fifth held only earth and small stones, a practice recalling the 'libationary' pits of the Neolithic. Charcoal from Weird Law provided a date of 1490 ± 90 bc (NPL-57). From their affinities it is doubtful whether such unobtrusive Middle Bronze Age sites were *de facto* cemeteries. The analogous customs in RSCS suggest the cremations were dedicatory offerings rather than burials.

It is possible that a small rectangular timber structure at the centre of Loanhead of Daviot was the focus of the ceremonies during the early years of the stone circle and that the ring-cairn was a much later addition. 'There may be an indication of a "mortuary house" at Loanhead of Daviot where four shallow holes lie at the corners of a rectangle 4 ft × 2 ft [1.2 × 0.6 m] arranged NW–SE at the very middle of the central space. These holes were extremely shallow but this may be because the pit was subsequently cleaned out by the people who built a fire in the SE corner' (Burl, 1970, 163). In his excavation at Old Keig Childe noticed comparable fissures 'but considered they were natural as they were sealed beneath a clayey layer which held bones, sherds and a hearth much like Loanhead' (ibid, 164). Since then other enigmatic rectangles, sometimes of wood, sometimes of stone, have been noted at sites as far apart as Stenness, Orkney (J. N. G. Ritchie, 1974a); at the Sands of Forvie, Aberdeenshire (Kirk, 1953, 158); Mount Pleasant, Dorset (Wainwright, 1970c), and Balbirnie, Fife. In the excavation report of the latter, Ritchie (J.N.G., 1974b, 9) discussed the affinities of such structures.

Thus it may have been years after the pyre had been scraped up that the central ring-cairn was built within the stone circle at Loanhead of Daviot (Fig. 29). Such cairns, averaging 13.4 m across, with kerbstones graded towards the recumbent, were inconspicuous. Whitehill RSC had kerbstones 61 cm high but sometimes the 'cairn' consisted of little more than a floor of stones. At its centre there was a space, usually circular, about 4.9 m

Pl. 20. *The Standing Stones of Stenness. The Central Rectangle.* This strange feature is similar to another at Mount Pleasant, Dorset, and may be related to the small mortuary houses of Neolithic long mounds like Kilham, Yorkshire.

At Stenness a post had stood off-centre within the setting, and outside were the remains of a timber structure and pairs of standing stones. Imperfectly understood, this setting may demonstrate the continuity of tradition whereby ceremonies in stone circles derived from the funerary and fertility customs of the early Neolithic period.

Discovered during the Department of the Environment excavations, 1973–4.

across, and it was here that cremated bone was placed, often within a pit.

Such burials have been described in detail elsewhere (Burl, 1974a, 70) and a few examples much suffice here. Within the central space some pits were lined with stones. Others were simply cut into the soil. At Ardlair two flat stones were arranged 'like a roof' above a pit with a cremation. At Hatton of Ardoyne a large pit was paved with small boulders and held a cremation and a fire-reddened urn. Old Keig's pit, a rectangular trench that cut through a burnt area, was shallower. In it was dark earth, charcoal and cremated bone. There is record of a time before 1692 when they 'did see ashes of some burnt matter digged out of the bottom of a little circle . . . in the centre of one of those monuments . . . near the church of Keig' (Garden, 1766, 342).

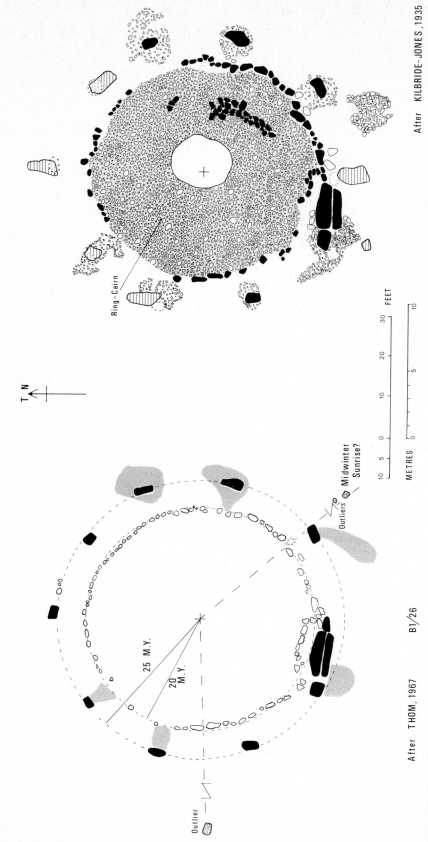

After KILBRIDE-JONES, 1935

Ring-Cairn

After THOM, 1967   B1/26

25 M.Y.

20 M.Y.

Outlier

Outliers

Midwinter
Sunrise?

N

METRES

FEET

Fig. 29. Two Plans of Loanhead of Daviot Recumbent Stone Circle, Aberdeenshire (Grampian).

No pits were discovered at Castle Frazer, Sunhoney or Auchquhorthies. The central space at the first had a paving of stones under which was black mould, charcoal and cremated bones. At Sunhoney eight deposits of burnt bone were found in the same area. Most of the stones surrounding the central space were fire-marked. The cairn was only 31 cm high. And in Auchquhorthies' centre was charcoal, half-burned ashes and urn fragments. Only very occasionally in RSCs were quartz pebbles strewn about. The heaping of soil in these centre spaces or in the pits, mixed with the charcoal and pottery, an apparently meaningless act, could have a symbolic essential, a form of sympathetic magic, to ensure the continuing fertility of the land. There was a tradition that 'pagan priests of old dwelt in that place' (Auchquhorthies) . . . and 'that the priests caused earth to be brought from adjacent places upon people's backs to Auchincorthie, for making the soil thereof deeper' (Garden, 1766, 340).

One strange feature of a few circles to the east of the Correen Hills near Alford is the reputed presence of a causeway leading to the site on the side opposite the recumbent. These RSCs within six miles of each other are on the extreme west of the enclave. At Crookmore, atypically in a hollow, the causeway led from the north-east. At Druidsfield nearby, a similar stretch was described as a long paved road of 'foreign stones' leading uphill from marshland at the NNE., ashes being scattered on it near the circle. The Clatt circles of Bankhead and Hillhead also had lengths of paving, the latter of stones 'so close that it was difficult to put in the pick'. At Nether Balfour, destroyed about 1847, there 'were remains of about 20 yards [18.3 m] of road paved with flat stones, evidently leading to the circle from the NE'. All these causeways were unarchaeologically stripped in the mid-nineteenth century so that the accounts are not reliable, but their consistent position around the north-east suggests a relationship with the north-east approaches at some of the Cork-Kerry RSCs of south-west Ireland where there had been constant trampling of the soil around the portalled entrances of recently excavated circles (Fahy, 1962, 67).

It is a long way in miles and in centuries from the fine RSCs of central Aberdeenshire via the putatively later, aberrant circles of Kincardine down to the possibly Middle Bronze Age RSCs of Cork and Kerry. To visit Loanhead of Daviot or Tomnagorn, emplanted with young conifers, or the walled-in Easter Aquorthies, is to see good 'blueprint' circles with large recumbents. Further south outlying sites like Garrol Wood (Fig. 28) in the dim green light of the trees, or Colmeallie, Angus, wrecked, neglected and littered with farm-rubbish, or Esslie the Greater (Fig. 5), is to see circles belonging to a time when the strength of the tradition was declining. Yet it is at Auchquhorthies in its wide field near the coast that perhaps the best-preserved ring-cairn and circle survives.

At circle after circle in these Scottish hills the tall stones have not been moved from where their prehistoric builders placed them over 4000 years ago, where the fires burned and where, in succeeding years, further human bones were put in the middle of the circle. There was no dancing here. There is no space within the stones and the platform would have been an obstruction. No priest predicted an eclipse. The recumbent is far too long to provide a finely aligned sighting-point. The orientations are calendrical to establish the time of year for the recurring ceremonies, times when fires were lit, perhaps more bodies incinerated. At Loanhead of Daviot 5 lbs (2.3 kg) of comminuted bone lay in the central space. They were not all adults. Over fifty fragments belong to the skulls of children between two and four years old. It is not possible to know whether these were victims of an epidemic, or a famine, or were sacrifices, although the indications of annual rites diminish beliefs in RSCs as family cemeteries. But the customs were local and persisted from the earliest centuries down to the end of the second millennium even during the moving and mixing of peoples. Such movements are detectable.

Within the rough rectangle of 140 square miles at the middle of the RSC lands there are at least twenty-eight RSCs. Most are early. If ten belong to the period of colonization the total population then might have been some 500–800 people, virtually a sub-tribe.

This demographic hypothesis can partly be tested by examining the RSCs around Old Deer near the River Ugie in Buchan, north-east Aberdeen, to see if the proposed populations are compatible with the numbers needed to build the rings. The seven sites lie in a triangle of seventeen square miles, the farthest only eight miles apart (Fig. 30) and are related by their characteristic stony banks which are possibly transitional between ring-cairns and the low banks of enclosed cremation cemeteries.

Loudon Wood, a circle 18.5 m across, and Strichen were possibly the primary rings in the area with a joint population of about 120 people at most. Loudon Wood's recumbent stone, $3.1 \times 1.2 \times 1.2$ m, weighed no more than twelve tons and could easily have been moved up its slight hillside by forty people.

Some of these Buchan rings seem late, Aikey Brae, on a hilltop, is an ellipse 16.6×12.8 m. Berrybrae, excavated by the writer in 1975 is another ellipse, 12.8×10.8 m, with its recumbent exactly on the short axis at 241° where, according to Lockyer (1906b, 481) it occupied a May Day solar alignment. (All the Buchan recumbents are unusually orientated: Aikey Brae, 184°; Loudon Wood, 191°; Netherton, 174°; and Strichen may have been mistakenly re-erected at the north because it had formerly stood at the south). Berrybrae was built on a level, artificial platform raised on a south-sloping hillside. Interestingly, its perimeter, using Thom's formula (1967, 31) is the product of $2 \times 2.8957 \times 6.42$ m $= 37.18$ m or almost exactly 18 Megalithic Rods of 2.07 m each. The error is only 0.13 m or 0.03 per cent. Flecks of charcoal, sherds of coarse pottery, quartz fragments and deposits of cremated bone suggest that the activities at Berrybrae were essentially no different from those in the earliest RSCs of previous centuries.

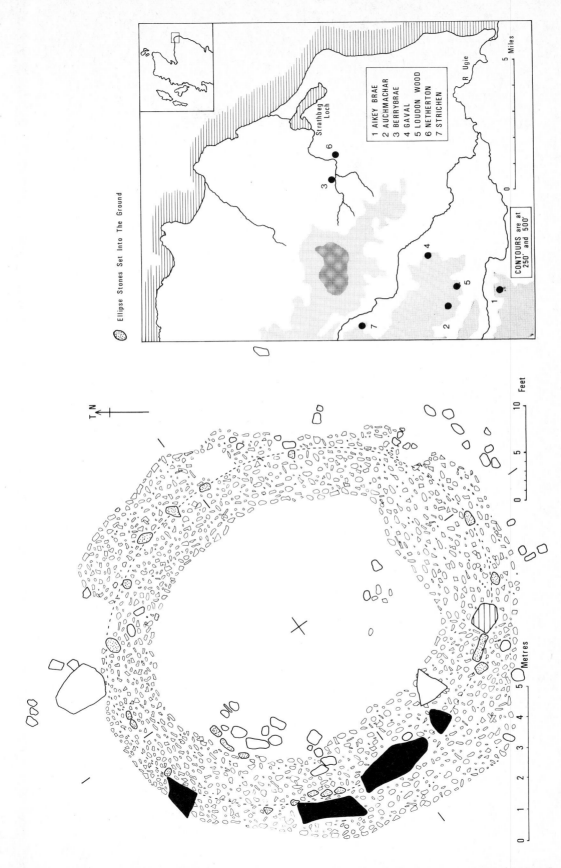

Ellipse Stones Set Into The Ground

CONTOURS are at 250' and 500'

1 AIKEY BRAE
2 AUCHMACHAR
3 BERRYBRAE
4 GAVAL
5 LOUDON WOOD
6 NETHERTON
7 STRICHEN

Strathbeg Loch

R Ugie

5 Miles

Fig. 30. The Ellipse of Berrybrae Recumbent Stone Circle, Aberdeenshire (Grampian).

Pl. 21. *Berrybrae, Aberdeenshire.* From the east. The excavation of this recumbent stone circle uncovered an elliptical bank of stones from which most of the standing stones had recently been removed. Such banks are a feature of the RSCs of the Buchan district and may mark a transition from ring-cairn to cremation cemetery type of enclosure.

Altogether in widely separated districts of north-east Scotland—Insch, Old Deer, Midmar and others—there may have been about fifteen RSCs initially. With developing land-clearance and productivity it is likely that the population gradually expanded and might have caused over any century a 50 per cent increase in the numbers of RSCs built by migrants whose original territories could not support the extra people. Such an increase, slow at first, would accelerate so that after 500 years there would have been well over a hundred circles (Fig. 31), of which seventy-four survive. Half of them would be of late, aberrant forms. It is instructive to find that a large proportion of late sites lies at the extremes of RSC country and to realise that even before outlying rings like Garrol Wood were being constructed some of the earliest RSCs could have been abandoned because of the deterioration of the soil

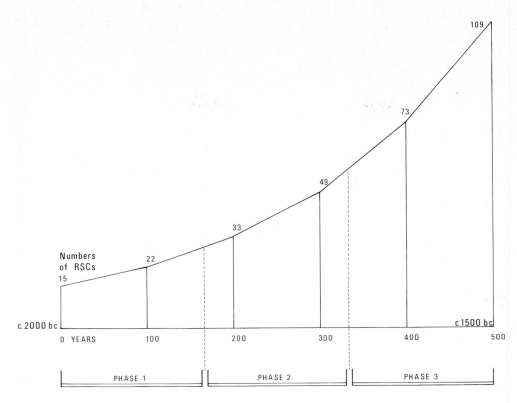

Numbers
of RSCs
15

22

33

49

73

109

c.2000 bc

c.1500 bc

0 YEARS   100   200   300   400   500

PHASE 1   PHASE 2   PHASE 3

Fig. 31. Hypothetical Curve of Increase in the
Number of Recumbent Stone Circles in North-East Scotland.

after several centuries of exploitation. But by the mid-second millennium in
Britain there can have been few vast areas left of unused, fertile, easily
worked soil. Once a whole district had been settled any large band of
migrants had only a few choices; forcibly to take over land already occupied;
to split into family groups that might search for unexploited glens and uplands; or to travel together to distant, hitherto unexplored parts, something
that might be forced on them by the hostility of other people reluctant to
allow strangers to settle on their borders. Trade and prospecting for stone and
metal ores had extended the knowledge of seaways to most parts of the British
Isles including the undeveloped countryside of south-west Ireland. Some
RSC groups may have journeyed here. Others drifted into southern Scotland
or northern England. Yet others mixed with neighbouring people of different
beliefs, and monuments lacking a recumbent stone but strongly influenced by
RSC customs were built.

   There are many other rings of stones in north-east Scotland, often small
ovals which from their graded stones appear related to the Clava tradition.
In general they stand at the edge of the RSC districts and, from such burial
finds as the decorated urn from Holywell, cordoned urn from Rappla Wood
or tripartite food-vessel from North Burreldales, seem late. They are very

varied. Sheldon near Inverurie may be a Clava-type circle without a recumbent stone. Rappla Wood's little circle stands on a stony platform. Farther south in Kincardine two of the four ring-cairns at Raedykes had stone circles around them. Noticeably, as in south-west England, there is often a standardized number of stones, six or eight being common, five or seven rare. Such circles are frequently graded on a south-west–north-east axis. Of the central sites Shethin, much ruined, was almost perfectly circular, about 5.2 m in diameter, with the tallest stone at the south-west. South Ythsie was a flattened circle, 8.5×7.9 m, with its largest stone at the south-west. Further south Image Wood was an oval six-stone site graded to the north-east; and Thorax, Banff, is 6.8×5.4 m of six stones which are not properly graded although the most massive block stands at the WSW. and has twenty-two cupmarks.

Cullerlie, proudly standing on the flat expanse of Leuchar Moss, not far south of the main RSC district, has eight boulders in a circle 10.1 m across, roughly graded to north-west–north (Fig. 48). At the centre was a small cairn with eleven kerbstones. The central, capstone-covered pit was 'much reddened, and there was charcoal at the bottom to a depth of 10 in (25 cm). Some of the charcoal was as large as a closed fist, and against it were fragments of calcined human bone. The pit had obviously contained a fire' (Kilbride-Jones, 1935, 219). Around this cairn were seven others, six with cremations. The ceremonies within this ring were like those of the earlier RSCs: the site had been levelled; the stones were erected, a fire of willow-branches lit within, ashes settling at the bases of the stones and around the uncovered kerbs; cremated bone was placed within these with oak-charcoal in five cairns and hazel in another showing they were probably not contemporary; then the cairns were built. From the excavation at Cullerlie and from inspection of the other small rings it seems the majority may be seen as later developments from the RSC tradition of central Aberdeenshire.

In the same way the occasional rectangles of four stones in north-east Scotland known as Four-Posters (Burl, 1971) appear to have the same ancestry. They also are graded towards the south-west or north-east. Most commonly found in Perthshire (Fig. 32) they have no good prototypes there whereas in Aberdeenshire the sites like Backhill of Drachlaw East, a six-stone circle, 8.5×7.4 m, graded to the south-west, has two small stones at its north and south, the removal of which would leave a good Four-Poster. Of six stones of South Ythsie two are noticeably shorter than the others. At Glassel, Kincardine, the oval 5.5×2.8 m has five stones, one to the south of the others which stand at the corners of a rectangle, the tallest at the south-west. Such circles are generally outside the central districts of RSCs and, from the urns at Newton of Montblairy, Broomend of Crichie and Tuack are of the Bronze Age. Diameters of the large Aberdeenshire Four-Posters, Howemill and the Hill of Bucharn, or Craighead, Kincardine, are much greater than those in Perth but are commensurate with those of nearby six- and eight-stone circles like Cullerlie. It is likely that Four-Posters have an Aberdeenshire ancestry.

These sites are not as far away from the RSCs as the very small ovals nor some of the multiple sites like Melgum at the extreme south-west, three large circles of tiny stones, or the three kerb-cairns at Logie Newton, mounds with massive kerbs, which have many blocks of white quartz amongst them. Standing high on Kirk Hill near Huntly, they have been called 'the most remarkable Druidical circle in the parish'. In appearance they are akin to the ring-cairn tradition.

It would seem that not only was north-east Scotland subject to influences from Inverness and from Ireland but also from the south-east whence the idea of some ring-cairns may have spread northwards. It is also probable that the tradition of building henges came from this direction for these earthwork enclosures are to be found all along the coast of east Britain with some very early sites like Arminghall, Norfolk, being known in the south as early as 2490 bc ±150 (BM-129). Several small hengiform rings are recorded in the north-east (Burl, 1969), some like the Muir of Ord on the Black Isle, Ross and Cromarty, and, as well as some isolated examples, another group around Inverurie at the confluence of the Don and Urie. Here there are three insignificant enclosures hardly 12.2 m in diameter at Tuack, Fullerton and Cairnhall, two with stone circles, and the more spectacular though wasted circle-henge of Broomend of Crichie, 35.5 m across, with north and south entrances through its outer bank. Inside are the remains of a six-stone circle which may have been added to the existing henge. There were cremated bones in pits or cists by each stone, some in cordoned urns of the sixteenth or fifteenth centuries bc. A sandstone battle-axe was found by a small circular cist in front of the north-west stone during the mid-nineteenth century excavation (Dalrymple, 1884), and this also has a mid-second millennium horizon (Roe, 1966, 241).

The encroaching town, a quarry, a housing estate, a juxtaposed main road, a railway and a factory chimney have not enhanced Broomend's setting yet it retains an almost unspoiled aura despite both this and the despoliation it has suffered whereby four of its stones have been taken and an interloper added, a Pictish symbol stone with well-preserved carvings of a questionable elephant, crescent and V-rods. This pillar came from a bank destroyed during the building of the railway. The avenue that led from a sandbank at the south very close to some cists with N2 beakers of the earlier second millennium has also been virtually demolished even though originally it was a 18.3 m wide double row running 412 m to the circle-henge and beyond to a larger circle at the north (Maitland, 1757, 154). The latter vanished during the construction of the Aberdeen turnpike road in the late eighteenth century.

The central burial at Broomend was unusual. At Fullerton nearby, five pits had been dug through a fire-marked patch and held a skull and inhumed and cremated bones. At Tuack, a mile away, four small pits with burnt bones had been set around a flat central stone. At Broomend, 46 cm down, was a layer of burnt material on top of a 4.6 m wide tapering pit filled with cobbles. Nearly 1.9 m down, the stones rested on three heavy slabs that made the top of a cist in which was a skull and leg bones as well as a deposit of cremated bone. It is rather like another pit at Old Parks Cairn, Kirkoswald, Cumbria (Ferguson, 1895), over two hundred miles away. Yet the builders of these earthen rings in north-east Scotland had clearly picked up the custom from the RSC users of placing death-offerings at the centres of their ritual sites. Despite the absence of pottery and artefacts from Broomend's medial pit, one is again reminded of the variety of burial traits amongst these Scottish stone circles.

5. CENTRAL SCOTLAND

Barely fifty miles from the aberrant Blue Cairn RSC near the River Dee is a cluster of small stone circles at the mouth of the Glenshee pass in Perthshire. From their grading towards the south-west, their cupmarks and their burials, they appear related to the Aberdeenshire RSCs. The scarcity of circles along Strathmore suggests that had there been any movement of people from the north-east it was not along the coastal strip but deep along the Dee to Glen Clunie near Braemar, then southwards on the long ascent between the mountains to the summit of the pass 2199 ft up, often snowbound in winter, then down the twisting glen to the hills around Blairgowrie. Today it is the highest main road in Britain. In the second millennium it was an important route from north-east Scotland.

The concentration of little circles near Glenshee shows this. There are at least six within four miles of each other, 800–900 ft up the western slopes of the Forest of Alyth, a cultural mixture of Four-Posters, six-stone circles and a larger ring of nine or ten stones at Broad Moss. In the same region are standing stones, hut-circles and enclosures, cairns on the steep, dividing hillsides, and here as on Dartmoor or in Caithness there arises the impression of families settling on tracts of unexploited land late in the second millennium bc.

The varied Glenshee group is a microcosm of Perthshire (Fig. 32) in which circles and ovals and rectangles intermix. Some stand in the desolate landscape north of the Tummel, or in the lowlands around Perth, or on the lovely hillsides overlooking Loch Tay, or still others suffer in inappropriately reconstituted surroundings: Ferntower on a golfcourse; Ardblair with a road running through it; Moncrieffe alongside an estate-drive; and Scone heatherset in the patio of Graystanes Close with modern houses and a suburban road around it.

Tigh-na-Ruaich in a cottage garden is one of a distinctive group of six-stone circles to be found almost exclusively in the west of Perthshire, although they have prototypes in Aberdeenshire. Despite their ruinous state they appear to be graded, Ardblair to the west, Wester Torrie and others to the SSW., Tigh-na-Ruaich to the north-east, and, supporting a belief in their north-eastern origin, the farther west they stand the smaller their diameter and the more

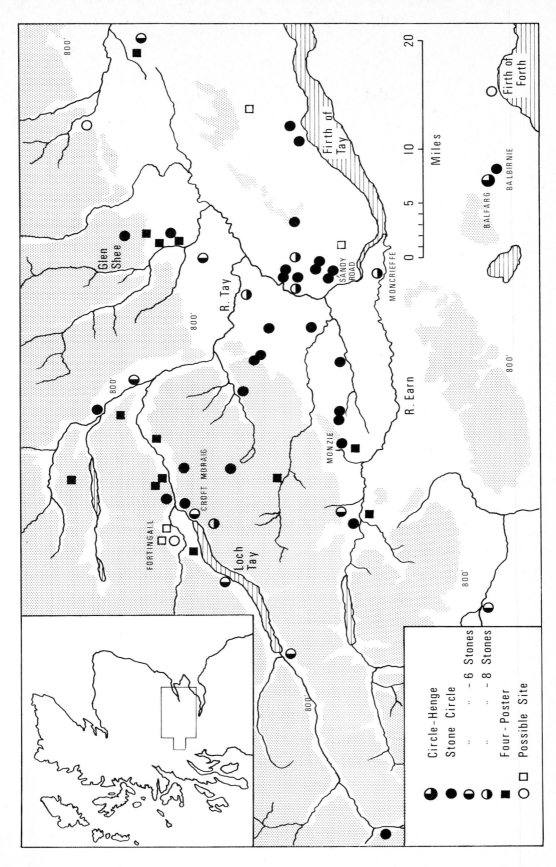

Fig. 32. The Distribution of Stone Circles in Perthshire (Tayside).

oval their shape. One of the best preserved is at Killin at the far south-west of Loch Tay, an oval, 10.0×8.4 m, with a massive stone at the SSW. Some like Machuinn, another graded oval by Loch Tay, and Pitscandlie stand on mounds, a feature that will be noticed amongst the Perthshire Four-Posters. Like so many of the rings dug into in the nineteenth century little is known of their contents. At Pitscandlie the mound was attacked and an 46 cm square of sandstone was found with two rough concentric circles scribed on it. An 'urn' was buried near one of the stones. At Tigh-na-Ruaich four huge urns filled with bone were discovered. One of the excavators in 1855 noted the soil within the ring was darker 'as if saturated with blood'. Rather more prosaically he probably saw the results of charcoal and burnt bone having been scattered in the central area. Remembering the Beltane bonfire ceremonies around Callendar in recent centuries so on 31 October, All Hallows Eve, the night of Samhuin, in many Perthshire villages the young people would make a large pile of ferns. Around it they placed a circle of stones, one for each family taking part. At sunset the fire was lit. Sometimes burning torches were carried into the fields (Frazer, 1919, 230). Near Callendar the ceremonies were similar but on the following morning the stones were inspected to see if any had been affected or moved for this would mean ill for its family. Such a combination of a festival when the sun was setting at the south-west, the charcoal of the fires, the ring of stones, the emphasis on the family, is very suggestive of a Bronze Age ancestry. This is more striking because on May 1 other villagers would cut not circular but square trenches and light a bonfire on the central rectangle (ibid. 152). Bronze Age rectangles, the Four-Posters, are common in Perthshire.

The Four-Posters of Perthshire and nearby counties (Fig. 33) are more centrally placed than the six-stone rings, although there is a far eastern example at Balkemback, Angus. They were built on hill-terraces like their ancestral RSCs and predictably were graded though sometimes the largest stone was at the north-east just as the Cork RSCs had their high portal stones opposite the recumbent rather than alongside it. The rectangles average only about 4.9×4.3 m, smaller than their Aberdeenshire counterparts, and were occasionally erected on an existing barrow at Lundin Farm, in a kerbed mound at Na Carraigean, or on an artificial platform at Dunmoid. Seven have been excavated and in five cremations were found. A sixth, Clach na Tiompan, seems late in the tradition. It is very small, its grading uncertain, and it lies in the remote reaches of Glen Almond far from any other Four-Poster. Yet even here there were quartz pebbles.

Burial relics varied elsewhere. At Glenballoch a cordoned urn filled with bone was 'protected by stones built round it in a beehive form'. At Dunmoid there was a stone cist containing a human thigh bone, at Carse Farm I a pit had been made by a stone, and at Lundin Farm a cremation pit was dug into a beaker barrow. Most of the pottery, the Dunmoid 'urn', a collared urn from Carse Farm, another from Lundin excavated in 1962 (Stewart,

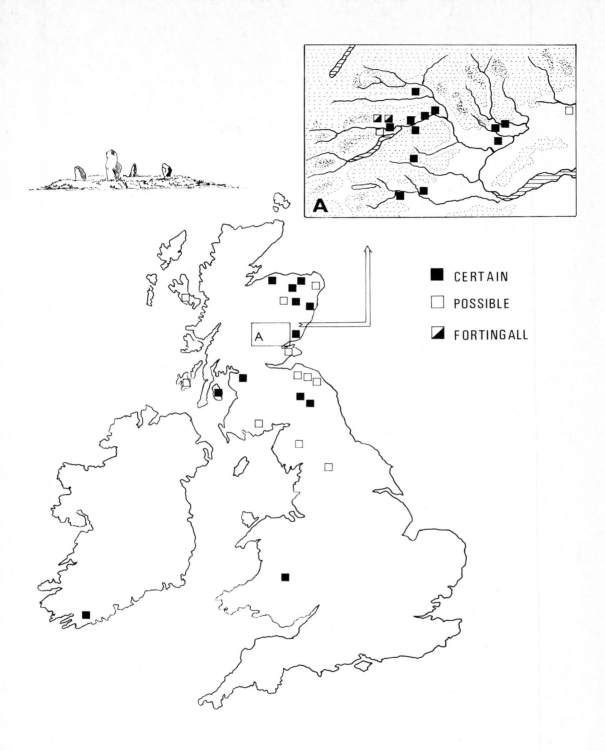

CERTAIN

POSSIBLE

FORTINGALL

Fig. 33. The Distribution of Four-Posters in the British Isles.

Pl. 22. *The Goatstones, Northumberland*. From the south-east. This Four-Poster may have a turf-covered ring-cairn inside it. The top of the east stone on the right (Plate 32) is cupmarked.
Although smaller in size this site is very like the Four-Posters of central and north-east Scotland.

1966b), and the cordoned urn from Glenballoch, are of the mid-second millennium. ApSimon (1969, 40) has pointed out the similarity of this cordoned urn to another from Lyles Hill, Antrim (E. Evans, 1953, 18, 48), also found protected by overlapping stones alongside the famous Neolithic cairn. Both urns have applied chevrons running round the neck below the rim, but the Glenballoch pot is a ceramic tragedy (Fig. 11). The ends of the zigzagging chevron do not join up but terminate assymetrically, a sad conclusion for a vessel that may offer evidence for the expansion of Scottish customs into Ireland during the second millennium (ApSimon, 1969, 54), an expansion revealed also by a concomitant spread of Four-Poster builders southwards.

A word should be added about Fortingall East and West, seven miles west of Aberfeldy. These are two of three megalithic sites close together on a terrace overlooking the River Lyon. Before excavation in 1970 they seemed to be Four-Posters from each of which one stone had been removed. Digging revealed that in reality they were sub-rectangular settings of eight stones with the largest stones at the corners. Flecks of charcoal and cremated bone were recovered. Both sites had had five stones deliberately overthrown and deeply buried presumably in the nineteenth century from the presence of a Victorian beer-bottle under one stone. Whether the smaller stones had been added to two juxtaposed Four-Posters is difficult to say but paired eight-stone circles are fairly common in central Scotland, and the Fortingall settings may be the results of a mixing of traditions. They stand by what may be a ruined and idiosyncratic RSC.

They could well be related to a larger, perhaps late, group of circles of which over half stand unusually on low land west of the Sidlaws. Some of these are eight-stone circles. The site at Murthly Hospital is 10.1 m in diameter, graded to the south-west, and contained a collared urn. The grading was retained here and this is also true of the oval Bandirran now in a wood, and the tiny, devastated Colen, with cupmarked south-west and SSW. stones, high on a hillstep above the Tay. Moncrieffe, thirteen miles south of Murthly, was also circular and graded. In it lay a profusely cupmarked stone which reputedly had once been in a central barrow with cremation. At this site meticulous excavations (Stewart, 1974) revealed the superficiality of judging stone circles only on their surface appearance, for Moncrieffe had undergone several alterations. The first monument here was a small, single-entrance henge with a timber setting rather like the first phase of Croft Moraig twenty-five miles to the north-west. Within the henge a later ring-cairn had been built surrounded by standing stones, a burial monument which in turn had been replaced by an even larger ring-cairn over which there was a heavy scatter of broken quartz. Around this cairn with its flat-rimmed ware was a circle of eight stones perfectly graded towards the south-west and between at least four of these the builders had placed recumbent stones. Whatever the relationships of this complex monument later people had not hesitated to despoil it for metallurgists cleared away part of the ring-cairn, smashed much of the pottery, and then used the space for bronze and iron working. The phase III ring has been re-erected nearer Moncrieffe House to permit the construction of a wider road but survives still as a vivid memorial to the confusion of purposes that prehistoric people put it to.

Elsewhere in east Perthshire there is even less uniformity. Only Faskally Cottages is graded. In other rings the SSW. orientation vanishes, there are many ovals and there are paired sites like the dishevelled kerb-cairns, 2 m apart, at Tullybeagles or the two at Shian Bank, both ovals, which had pillboxes built by them during the Second World War. Thom (1966, 15) believed alignments from centre to centre here were directed towards solar positions. What is likely in these individualistic rings with their haphazard number of ungraded stones, their dwarfed shapes, their unpredictable mixture of banks and outliers, their proliferation on low land, is that they are late, almost at the end of the megalithic tradition. This is supported by the paired Sandy Road, Scone, rings only one and a half miles WSW. of

Shian Bank, one of which now survives in a modern housing estate. Excavated in 1961 (Stewart, 1966a), the western oval had a central pit with a broken, nondescript, flat-rimmed urn (Fig. 11) half-filled with a token cremation and lumps of charcoal that gave a date of 1200 bc ± 150 (GaK-787). This low ring is many centuries from the monumental RSCs of Aberdeenshire. Paired and presumably late rings of easily handled boulders have been noticed elsewhere in Britain and will be observed in Ireland. It is not reasonable to suppose that there was a single, underlying cause for all such pairing. Some rings may have been successive because, for some reason, the first site was no longer adequate.

This may be the explanation for the two rings on the upland wastes at Fowlis Wester near Crieff (Fig. 34), which are almost certainly related to the Clava-derived kerb-cairns of Argyll. There is a very similar site at Monzie, three miles WSW. around Milquhanzie hill. This type of monument whether in Perthshire, Argyll or Inverness has contiguous kerbs graded to west-WSW., is small and often has cupmarkings, scatters of quartz pebbles and outlying stones standing in significant astronomical positions. There is customarily a central burial deposit, usually near an area of burning. At Fowlis Wester, on the highest point of the scruffy moorland ridge, the builders set up two stone rings. The eastern one enclosed just such a kerb-cairn. The west circle was begun by the people digging shallow pits into which they put white pebbles. The circle-stones were set in these inadequate holes and very soon tumbled or were toppled from them. The ceremonies in the ring were like those in north-east Scotland and included the lighting of fires, deposition of charcoal and of bone. The excavators' plan of the stone holes (Young, Lacaille and Zeuner, 1943, 177) show the ring to be circular, 7.3 m across, and Thom's supposition (1971, 54) that the site was an ellipse, 8.3 × 6.2 × 5.2 m, directed towards the midwinter maximum moonset is erroneously based on the present position of the fallen stones explaining why 'no foresight now appears on the horizon'. It once again reminds the archaeologist of the dangers inherent in accepting plans without excavation, particularly as there are circles like Hampton Down, Dorset (Wainwright, 1967), to which stones have actually been added since 1964.

Exactly east of the circle is the stone hole of a huge, prostrate outlier. Just beyond this is the eastern circle of low stones enclosing an oval setting of kerbstones which rest on quartz chippings amongst which are some implements perhaps from west Scotland. The SSW. kerb has three cupmarks hidden beneath the old ground surface. A small fire had burned on the laid clay floor and the expected lumps of charcoal and burnt bone were covered by some stone slabs which themselves were overlain with black earth and quartz capped with small stones. 9.5 m away at the NNE. a 1.8 m outlier stands edge-on to the site in line with its axis and the cupmarked kerbstone and pointing downhill to the distant River Almond.

The kerb-cairn at Monzie in a broad, flat field is similar. At its centre an

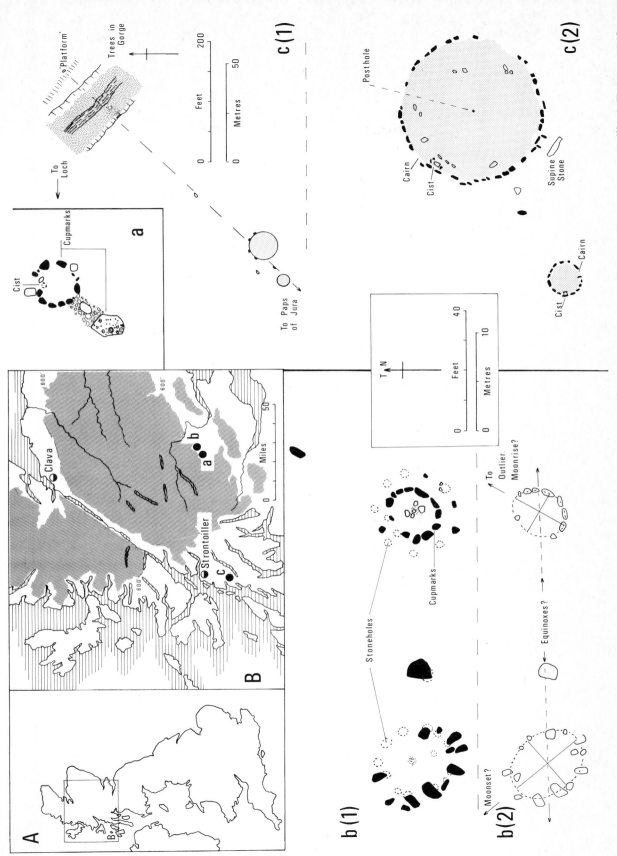

Fig. 34. Three Scottish Sites. (a) Monzie, Perthshire; (b) Fowlis Wester, Perthshire; (c) Kintraw, Argyll. (b1) after Young, Lacaille & Zeuner, 1943; (b2), after Thom, 1971; (c1), after Thom, 1971; (c2) after Simpson, 1969.

intense fire of hazelwood had reddened the earth and in a tiny cist at the north
the bones of an adult and a six-year-old child had been placed. Three metres
from the site at the south-west there is a remarkable outlier connected to the
kerb by a rough causeway (Mitchell and Young, 1939). This irregular 1.8 m
long boulder is decorated with forty-six cupmarks, cup-and-rings, grooves
and joined cups (Hadingham, 1974, 66). Such so-called 'Galician' art
(Simpson and Thawley, 1972, 86) is probably of great antiquity in Britain
and examples such as that at Monzie may have been taken and broken
from earlier monuments to incorporate the 'magic' into new settings. The
style is entirely different from the more geometrical motifs of the Irish
passage-graves (C. O'Kelly, 1973).

Kerb-cairns like Monzie in their architecture and rites are almost indistinguishable from others in Argyll and Inverness (J. N. G. Ritchie, 1971, 6),
being a development from the Clava cairns (Burl, 1972, 39). Previously it
has been noticed how the builders of those ring-cairns and chambered
tombs displayed a widening interest in the movements of sun, moon and
planet Venus so that it is not unexpected to find analogous observations in
these kerb-cairns, although here the alignments are revealed through the
positions of cupmarked stones and outliers. Table 7 summarizes this.
If the alignments are correct—and the bearings are taken from Thom where
possible—it shows that in many cases one end of a line was determined by
a cupmarked stone, the other by the outlier which was sometimes, as at

Table 7. An Analysis of some Scottish Kerb-Cairns

Site	County	Grid	Diameter (Metres)	No. of Stones	Quartz	Burnt Area	Inhumation or Cremation	Graded	Cupmarks	Axis	Outlier	Astronomical Line?
Clava	Inverness	NH 757444	3.7	15	/	x	In	SW.	ESE.	ESE.–WNW.	x	Equinoctial Sunset
Strontoiller B	Argyll	NM 907289	4.6 × 4.0	15	/	/	Cr	SSW.	x	NE.–SW.	NW. 11.6 m	Midsummer Sunset
Kintraw B	Argyll	NM 830030	3.4	14+	x	x	x	SW.?	x	SW.–NE.	ENE. 5.8 m	Midsummer Sunrise
Fowlis Wester W	Perth-shire	NN 923249	7.3	12?	/	/	Cr	WSW.?	x	WSW.–ENE.?	E. 5.5 m	Equinoctial Sunrise
Fowlis Wester E	Perth-shire	NN 923249	5.9	14?	/	/	Cr	SSW.	SSW.	SSW.–NNE.	NNE. 9.5 m	Midwinter Moonrise
Monzie	Perth-shire	NN 882243	4.9	10+	/	/	Cr	W.	E.	E.–W.	SW.? 3.1 m	Midwinter Sunset

Fowlis Wester, lined up like a playing-card with its thin edge towards the cairn to provide a sharp sighting-edge. This may have been true also at Monzie where the marked stone has probably fallen sideways. It may even have been dragged a little to the south. A cupmarked kerb and the tallest kerb stand opposed on an east–west axis and the tiny cist is due north. The outlier may have stood at the west, but the existence of an apparent causeway leading to its present position seems to contradict this and, for now, its calculated setting is taken from the published plans.

If the interpretation of these simple solar and lunar sightings is correct then two comments should be made. The invisible cupmarks at Fowlis Wester, like others in Clava cairns, imply that the alignment was fundamental to the construction but was unusable afterwards. The distances between kerb and outlier are, moreover, too short for unambiguous sightlines, never exceeding 11.6 m which permits overmuch lateral visual error. The kerb-cairns are unlikely to have been observatories in the sense that they were sites used for recurring observations. They were religious monuments incorporating astronomical alignments in their design. The other point is that despite this overall confirmation of Thom's astronomical analyses he may be wrong about Kintraw which he has claimed as one of the most important solstitial sites known to him (Thom, 1971, 36).

There are two cairns at Kintraw, kerb-cairn B, and A, the larger, to its north-east. These were excavated in 1959–60 (Simpson, 1969). Thom (1967, 155) suggested that from the hypothetically flat summit of the large cairn, looking across the top of a 4.0 m high leaning outlier, the midwinter sunset might have been seen behind the Paps of Jura twenty-seven miles away. He also postulated an artificial sighting-platform cut in a precipitous hillside to the north-east of the cairn but as this continues and widens for several hundred feet all around that side of the hill it is much more likely to be natural (but see MacKie, 1974, 181). In fact, as at Monzie and Fowlis Wester, the outlier probably belongs to the small kerb-cairn B, and provides a good alignment to the midsummer sunrise. Conversely, the large cairn has a blind entrance and a supine stone at the SSW. defining an orientation perhaps on the midsummer moon's maximum setting.

There may be here an explanation for the pair of monuments at Fowlis Wester. Both there and at Kintraw there seems to be a lunar and a solar site, and in both cases the solar alignment is obstructed: by the great cairn at Kintraw, by the eastern encircled cairn at Fowlis Wester. Was this deliberate? It may be more discreet to suppose that the sun-line was no longer important and, with indifference, the kerb-cairn builders set up their new monument alongside a site whose antiquity they respected but whose orientation was no longer of any interest. Nothing datable has come from any of these kerb-cairns, only two rim-sherds of flat-rimmed ware at Monzie. They are assumed to be late. They may reveal how an interest in astronomical observation deepened over the centuries of the second millennium from lines on the most simple solar movements to include, ultimately, lunar and even planetary orientations.

Presenting quite a different problem is the imposing stone circle of Croft Moraig, Perthshire, excavated in 1965 (Piggott and Simpson, 1971), at the north-east end of Loch Tay on the route between north-east and west Scotland (Fig. 35). Here the revealed sequence of phases emphasizes the naïveté of assuming that the visible features of any circle are contemporary. Initially fourteen posts were erected in a horseshoe setting 7.9 × 7.0 m open approximately to the south. Around it was a shallow ditch. It is not known whether this structure was roofed nor, of course, if the posts were painted or carved. It may be relevant to mention that not far away in Glen Lyon there still exists a stone-built shrine that was regularly unroofed and which may once have protected a wooden idol.

> The biennial thatching and unthatching of this shrine, . . . may find parallels in such early traditions as the ritual annual unroofing and re-roofing of a temple by the women of an island community near the mouth of the Loire. Here sacred rites were performed, no man was permitted to land on the island, and the woman who dropped her load in the roofing operations was torn to pieces by the other women and the remains carried round the temple in honour of the god. (Ross, 1967, 40.)

At Croft Moraig when the uprights weathered some were replaced more than once and it is tempting to visualize a freestanding timber setting with a central, flat boulder beside a hollow containing burnt bone. 1.5 m inside the 'entrance' and 3.4 m outside it were two posts aligned north–south. Outside the ditch and exactly east were two short rows of postholes. Such equinoctial and north–south alignments recall the layout of many southern stone circles. At this stage Croft Moraig resembled Bleasdale, Lancashire (Dawkins, 1900; Varley, 1938), where eleven posts enclosed a 11.0 m circle with a central pit containing urns, charcoal and burnt bone. A double row of posts at the ENE. marked the entrance. An assay from one of the posts gave a date of 1810 bc ±90 (NPL-69).

Croft Moraig was later translated into stone, the posts being replaced by eight stones, graded towards the SSW., arranged in a horseshoe 7.6 × 6.1 m, the NNE. stone being cupmarked. Some hollows in the interior and the ditch were stone-filled and had charcoal-laden earth and Neolithic sherds, fine ware and also flat-rimmed, that came possibly from the first phase whose position the stone-builders seem to have duplicated. Around the stones they threw up a stony bank. A long stretch of it has been robbed but at its SSW. is a 1.8 m long supine stone with over twenty cupmarks on its upper surface.

Finally a 12.2 m circle of large, ungraded stones was set up within the bank round the megalithic horseshoe. A pair of big outlying stones were put up at the ESE. like an entrance. In front of each was an empty hole which

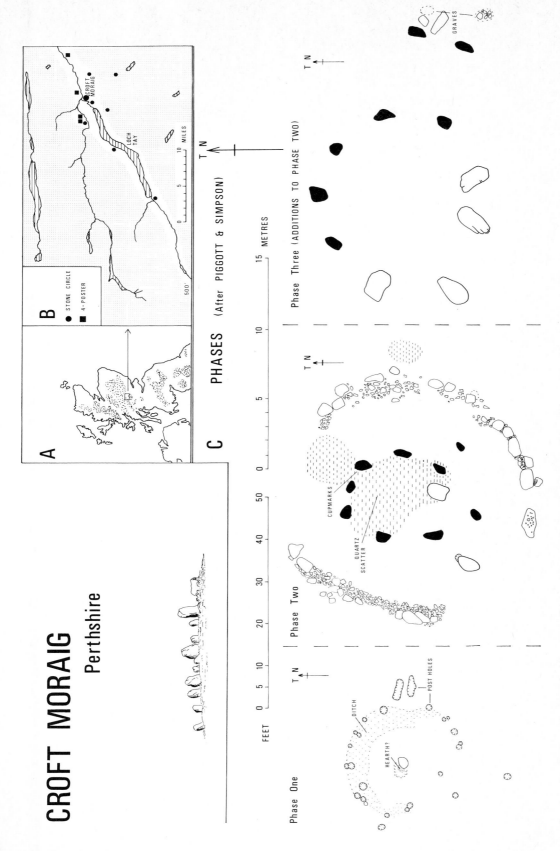

Fig. 35. Croft Moraig, Perthshire (Tayside). Phases of Development. After Piggott & Simpson, 1971.

may have held an inhumation long since destroyed by the acid soil. By the northern stone, and at the north-east of the outer circle, and within the horseshoe there were dense scatters of quartz fragments. Pairs of standing stones are common in Perthshire, twenty-six pairs being recorded from central Perthshire alone (Stewart, 1966b). In only three cases, Croft Moraig, Lundin Farm and Ferntower, are they associated with a stone circle. The fact that the two latter are Four-Posters is of interest because of their possible counterparts with pairs of stones amongst the five-stone circles of Cork.

Half-hidden by the hedgerow and by farm-buildings, diminished by tall trees, Croft Moraig is one of the most informative stone circles in the British Isles. Its Neolithic timber ring is one of the earliest known and may have affinities with the tradition that caused east–west lines to be incorporated into many early stone circles. But later the site was adapted by people following the Clava custom of grading stones, scattering quartz, cupmarking and aligning towards the SSW. The trait of placing a supine stone at this point may have derived from western Scotland rather than from Aberdeenshire, although the encircling banks are known there. There are certainly several 'Aberdeenshire' circles nearby. The etiolated remains of an RSC may survive at Fortingall South, three miles to the west, and at the 48.4 m Coilleachur on the slopes of Craig Formal to the east.

The variety of stone rings in Perthshire and the distribution of monuments along the hillsides down Loch Tay reveals something of the movement of people and of ideas passing along this prehistoric route that reached from Strath Tay through Glen Dochart and down to Loch Lomond and south-west Scotland (Scott, 1951, 35; Stewart, 1959). Croft Moraig reflects this in its several phases.

6. SOUTH-WEST SCOTLAND

At the mountainous head of Loch Lomond, twenty miles west of Kinnell in the Tay valley, is Inverarnon, a megalithic ring 31.1 m across which, like Coilleachur, may have RSC affinities. It stands on the route along which traders, prospectors and settlers may have passed. Yet for a hundred miles in the south there is hardly another circle.

Early prehistoric man appears to have by-passed the heavily forested lands of Ayrshire and the Clyde valley. Even the earliest of the chambered tombs, the late-fourth-millennium Bargrennan group with their small rectangular chambers and round cairns (Henshall, 1972, 277) were built to the south in western Galloway (Fig. 36). Other long-cairn builders who crossed the Pennines from eastern England settled in the eastern foothills between the rivers Liddel and Nith where sites like Lochhill (Masters, 1973) dated to 3120 bc ±105 (I-6409) testify to early occupation around Dumfries. Ultimately the two sepulchral traditions intermixed to produce some of the characteristic Clyde long chambered tombs whose elaborate concave façades,

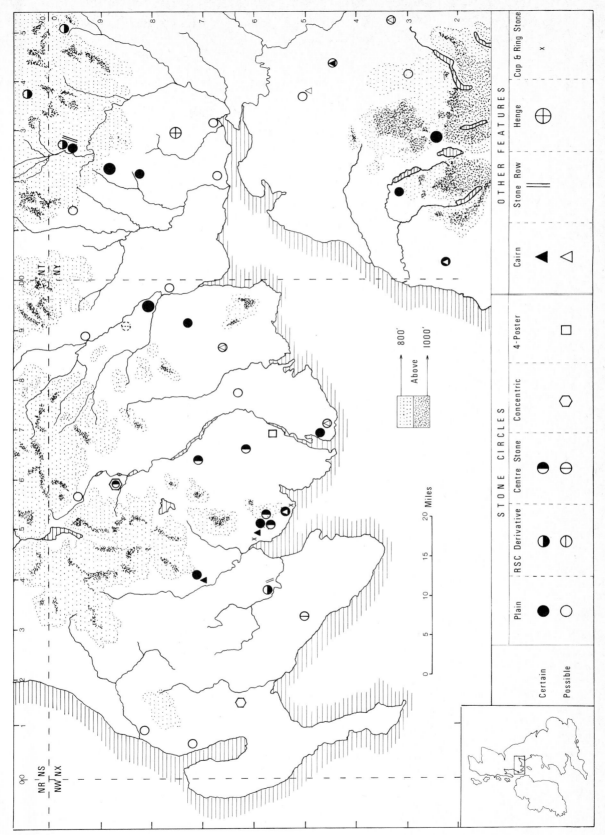

Fig. 36. The Distribution of Stone Circles Around the Solway Firth.

inspired by Irish prototypes, may not have been added before the late third millennium (J. Scott, 1969, 215).

Yet despite this Neolithic activity it was not until the Bronze Age that man affected the country around the Clyde estuary. Pollen analysis from Bloak Moss (Turner, 1965) shows only the slightest disturbance of the forest-cover during the third millennium whereas between 1800 and 1300 bc there were at least three phases of tree clearance, occasionally for cereal-growing, more frequently for the grazing of livestock (Turner, 1970, 100). Bloak Moss, just north-east of Kilwinning, is only a few miles from the possible enclosed cremation cemeteries of Gotter Burn, from Blackshaw Moor circle, and, most interestingly, not five miles from a damaged Four-Poster, the Four Stones, near Dunlop, from which cremated bones were dug around 1816 (Love, 1876, 291). This site, like the Four-Poster at Aucheleffan, Arran, and the graded six-stone ring with central cist at Lamlash on the same island, bears witness to the dissemination of ideas, if not of people, from the north-east and central Scotland during the mid-second millennium bc.

Nevertheless there are few identified circles along this inhospitable coast-line. The main concentration is in south-west Scotland between Luce Bay and Liddesdale (Fig. 36). There are three major divisions: an eastern group whose large open circles may be of Cumbrian origin; a west-central group; and an inland cluster of unusual sites that may in some way be related to RSCs. There is also the lonely, strange Torhousekie far to the west in Wigtown. Such a mixture reminds us of the mosaic of social beliefs that could exist even in a small area and of our present difficulty in separating them chronologically.

Unlike the ceramically rich RSCs of Aberdeenshire the Galloway circles have yielded almost nothing, pot, bronze, flint or burial. Conclusions about their dating, therefore, remain inferential.

At the north-east of the Solway Firth, besides some scattered inland out-lying examples, there are at least five large open rings which, from their low-lying positions in passes and by rivers, appear related to the Late Neolithic Cumbrian circles. The Twelve Apostles, the fifth largest ring in Britain, has already been described and it is sufficient here to remark on the number of Group VI Langdale stone axes that have been found in its vicinity (J. Williams, 1970, 114) re-affirming the possible religious as well as economic use of these implements.

Further north the River North Esk has cut away nearly a third of the 39.9 m circle-henge of the Girdle Stanes (Fig. 8) that stands, tree-ringed, in an inconspicuous hollow, its grassy outer bank showing clearly at the north. Several stones now lie in the river. Opposite there seems to be an eastern entrance of double portal stones. The diameter, the situation, bank and equinoctial entrance are characteristic of an open ring intended for the needs of dispersed groups. Not unexpectedly it contains no persuasive astronomical lines, for if it were built in the first centuries of the second millennium this would be early for subtle orientations. A survey made on Good Friday, 1911 (Hyslop and Hyslop, 1912, 30), claimed two solar lines towards natural features and two others on Capella for 1360 BC (c. 1100 bc) and 2150 BC (1775 bc) but these were not critically established, and the latter, which ironically is likely to be nearest the true construction date, was considered 'unacceptable' because it was aligned on one of two outliers 128 metres to the north-east on a rise, the other stone being low, this one almost buried so that it could not be properly used as a sighting device. A sinuous possible line of standing stones wanders from these outliers and around a knoll to the megalithic oval of the Loupin' Stanes nearly half a mile away.

Another huge ring, Whitcastles, 56.4 × 42.4 m, with its largest stones at north and south, is a collapsed ruin at the foot of Little Hartfell Hill. Thom (1967, 68) considered it a specialized form of his Type B flattened circle based on an approximate Pythagorean triangle whose height was half the circle-radius. As well as this and other open sites like Easthill there is also the pear-shaped block of the Lochmaben Stone on the shores of the Solway Firth looking across the estuary towards Cumbria. The name probably derives from *Locus Maponi*, and the site may have been used well into Iron Age and Roman times as a shrine of the hunter sun god whose Celtic name was Maponus (Ross, 1967, 458, 463), once more confirming the long use of some stone circles and the continuity of tradition whereby customs were perpetuated even by later incomers to the district. Once there was a 45.7 m megalithic oval here. Now all that remains is this enormous 2.4 m boulder and another making part of a stile nearby. In 1841 the Rev. James Roddick wrote: 'On the farm of Old Graitney . . . was seen not many years ago a number of white stones placed upright circling half an acre of ground in an oval form. One of them, the largest, is all that now remains, as some suppose, of a Druidical temple, the rest having been removed for the cultivation of the soil.' The stone on its terrace, conspicuous from Redkirk Point sea-lapped to the south-west, is the one survivor of a ring whose builders, perhaps, saw the axe traders coming from the Lake District mountains to the autumnal assemblies at territorial centres like Broadlee henge, the Twelve Apostles stone circle, and Whitcastles at a time when people still gathered to celebrate, trade, re-affirm laws and worship in such rings, whether at the southern Cheetham Close, Lancashire, with its outlying stone, or at the northern Girdle Stanes or even, just possibly, across to the unconvincing Holm of Daltallochan amongst the hills and drumlins of New Galloway.

Quite unlike these open sites is a lesser concentration of centre-stone circles halfway along the southern coast west of the Dee (Fig. 37). The architectural foible of erecting a stone within a circle seems directly related to the earlier Neolithic tradition of erecting posts or standing stones as cult monuments. Even in the Iron Age, temples often had a sacred tree as a focal point (Ross, 1967, 38). Circles with centre stones appear to be late and

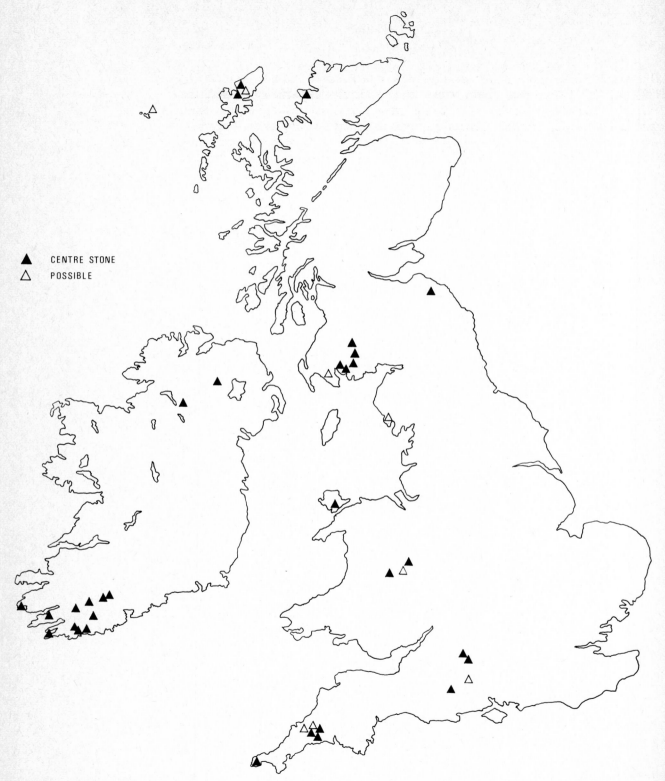

CENTRE STONE
POSSIBLE

Fig. 37. The Distribution of Stone Circles with Centre Stones.

frequently have a cremation deposit at the foot of the centre stone whether it is in a henge or a stone ring. Although little is known of the practice in stone circles, at Longstone Rath, Kildare (Macalister, Armstrong and Praeger, 1913), a 5.3 m granitic stone stood in a rock-cut basin at the centre of a henge with entrances to east and west. The central area had been flagged and this paving bore the detritus of numerous small fires. By the pillar a collapsed 2.4 m long cist, arranged north-east–south-west, held two well-cremated bodies which, from the signs of fire, had been burned *in situ* on a pyre of oak and hazel, and with them were fragments of coarse pottery and a type of bone wristguard sometimes associated with Northern beakers (Clarke, 1970, 261).

Similar deposits by centre stones occur in stone circles. At the circle-henge of Tisbury, Wiltshire, the central burial pit contained cremated bones and a pot now lost. At Callanish the chambered tomb had been squashed between the stone and the surrounding circle. At the neighbouring Garynahine the stone stood in a cairn. At Lacra D, Cumberland, there may have been a central stone by the late collared urn. Even at the great circle-henge of Avebury four ritual pits were discovered to the north of the Obelisk in the southern circle, and 'an urn full of bones was found towards the centre of the southern temple in 1880 . . . by Mr Pratt' (Smith, 1965, 200). Bryn Celli Ddu passage-grave, Anglesey, seems to have been built over a demolished circle-henge with central feature (Lynch, 1970, 58–60). Cremations, one of a young girl, had been buried at the foot of several stones and perhaps also in a central pit subsequently redug to receive a fire and the deposition of a burnt human ear-bone. Burial at the foot of a post or stone is known from the Neolithic period (Piggott, 1954, 49; J. N. G. Ritchie, 1974b, 8); standing stones are known in the forecourts of chambered tombs (Piggott and Powell, 1949, 131); central posts or stones are recorded in some chambers of megalithic tombs like Bryn Celli Ddu; Carrowkeel F, Sligo; Fourknocks, Meath (Hartnett, 1957), and others including at least twenty-two near Los Millares, Spain (G. and V. Leisner, 1943), where they may have been totemistic; and they continued to be set up well into the second millennium (Russell and Pool, 1964). The inclusion of such a feature in stone circles of the Bronze Age is not surprising.

Although centre stones are not found in the earliest areas for circles nor in north-east or central Scotland, it would be dangerous to assume they can be used to date a site for they are not necessarily contemporary with their surrounding bank or circle. At Stonehenge II, tentatively dated to around 1670 bc, the Altar Stone may originally have been set upright (Atkinson, 1960, 57) at a time different from the other bluestones, the majority of which came from another Pembrokeshire source on Carn Meini, Preseli (Kellaway, 1971, 33). That centre stones were sometimes added to circles is suggested by Thom's observations (1967, 62) that no stone stands at the exact centre of any site. It is possible sometimes that rings were built around an earlier standing stone. This happened at the Middle Bronze Age ring-cairn of Bedd Branwyn, Anglesey, centred on a great pillar, associated with beaker sherds, that became the focal point of the later ring-cairn (Lynch, 1970, 116, 123). Activities at these ritual centres sometimes continued well into the Christian period for it is written that St. Patrick angrily overthrew the Crom Cruiach, a centre stone richly adorned with gold and silver inside a twelve-stone circle (Ashbee, 1960, 182) in a district of Cavan that had long been a pagan cult centre (E. Evans, 1966, 67). Another large circle with centre stone at Boreray, St. Kilda, is supposed to have been destroyed by order of the mediaeval church. It has been suggested that such centre stones may have been decorated in some way or had effigies brought to them at special times of the year when they would become the focus of the ceremonies. The description of the lavish Crom Cruaich is explicable in such contexts. Burial offerings could be expected near such powerful stones.

There are several stone circles with rather unimposing centre stones in Cornwall and in Munster, that region of south-west Ireland where the Cork-Kerry RSCs are to be found. There are others in Wiltshire, Shropshire, Ulster and on Lewis. But the most concentrated group, now regrettably ruined, is in south-west Scotland. At these little rings in the hills around Cambret Moor and the Water of Ken the circles are composed of unobtrusive, rounded stones whereas the interior pillar is distinctly bigger. The best-preserved ring, Glenquickan near Creetown, has a stone 1.8 m high which stands in a cobble-strewn circle most of whose enclosing stones struggle for visibility in the thin, spiky grass. At Claughreid nearby, the 10.7 × 8.8 m oval also has low stones whereas the fallen stone at the centre is 1.65 m long. And at Lairdmannoch the circle itself at the south-east of a large cairn is virtually submerged in the lochside peat, and the 1.6 m centre stone lies half-covered beneath the creeping turf. The same may be said of two other centre-stone rings recently discovered to the north at Loch Roan and Stroangassel.

Such monuments can never have been conspicuous and were probably for local ceremonies. The circle-stones are demarcations. They are too close-set for dancing, their rings are too small to admit a big congregation and, like some of the other late megalithic rings, they are associated with cremation rites, the centre stone possibly providing a focus for the chief participant or perhaps itself embodying the religious symbolism required for the rituals.

The association of late megalithic ring and burial is further demonstrated by the adjacent cairn at Lairdmannoch, by the vestigial cairn suggested by Glenquickan's cobbles, and is valid for other small south-west Scottish sites without centre stones. The shattered monument of High Auchenlarie actually has the remnants of a platform-cairn inside it. Twenty-three metres to the south a cupmarked stone lies on a hillock against the background of the sea. The wretched slabs of Drannandow poke from the ground near

Drumfern cairn. Further inland still, just beyond a heather-grown swamp, the great cairn of Cauldside Burn, cist and all, overshadows a circle of thin slabs. One hundred and twenty metres north-north-east two stones, one fallen, lead to an overgrown ring-cairn, and, crossing the stream and continuing up the stone-walled hillside, one finds one of the most perfect decorated stones in Scotland, a 61 cm spiral carved on a heavy sub-rectangular block (Hadingham, 1974, 73).

If the central circles of the Galloway coast are indeed related to the passage-grave tradition, and they are unusually composed of many small stones like the other derivative rings in Ulster (p. 243), it is interesting to note that this is a rare area where passage-grave and 'Galician' rock-art overlap. Such intermingling is infrequent in cup-and-ring stone districts. In Munster only the isolated slab from Clear Island has passage-grave motifs. There are a few 'Boyne' stones in Wicklow. But Galloway possesses not only the densest group of cup-and-ring marked stones in the British Isles but at least six well-executed spirals suggesting direct coastal settlement from Ireland. This maritime contact is also recognized through the dissemination of cordoned urns (Morrison, 1968, 95), of food-vessels (Simpson, 1965, 37), and of mid-second millennium metalwork from Ireland (J. Coles, 1965, 88), a trade whose Hiberno-Scottish background may be highlighted by the observation that the concentration of decorated stones in Galloway, including spirals, are invariably within six miles of a copper-source (Morris, 1967, 86).

Increasingly during the second millennium in Wales, Cumbria, and Ireland (M. Davies, 1945) stone circles and cairns were combined to make composite monuments, and the centre-stone circles of Galloway appear to be one manifestation of this mingling of sepulchral and ceremonial practice along the coasts of the Irish Sea. That they are late sites emerges from their low perimeters, their diameters averaging only 13.4 m, their occasional ovals, factors they share with cognate monuments in this part of Scotland, the enclosed cremation cemeteries like the Whitestanes Muir group, Dumfriesshire (Scott-Elliot, 1967), where the sites were oval or egg-shaped, Site 1 with its eight cremations being dated to 1360 bc ±90 (GaK-461). Nith Lodge, Ayrshire, an embanked stone ring, 9.1 × 4.6 m, had three buried cremations associated with tiny pygmy cups and a collared urn and stone battle-axe both of which belong to the centuries around 1500 bc. Beoch, nearby, had nine large kerbstones around an egg-shaped enclosure with a late northern beaker. As elsewhere, the megalithic ring had been adapted to surround a series of cremation deposits at a time when the initially distinct architectural forms of henge, stone circle and kerbstone were being conflated in a bewilderment of regional types. Unlike the kerb-cairns and the Clava sites there are few signs of astronomical activity in the Galloway hillbound rings. It may be assumed that theirs was a socio-sepulchral function for kinship groups living by the rivers and lochs of southern Scotland.

Finally there are, in the extreme east of the region, three or four megalithic rings deep in the hills that climb above Eskdale and Liddesdale in the Cheviots, twenty miles from the sea, peculiar ovals of low stones with two startlingly tall pillars at their south-west, perhaps orientated towards midsummer minimum moonset. Whether this reveals a distant relationship with RSCs or with some earlier tradition is not clear. The builders, whatever their ancestry, probably approached from the valleys to the south-west rather than along the Tweed-Teviot rivers of south-east Scotland where there are no comparable sites in the 1000 square miles of occupied country.

The 7.0 m ring of Ninestone Rigg, Roxburgh, stands on a barren moorland hill, grassy tufts obscuring the ring except for the two tall south-west (232°) pillars with a half-hidden stone between them. It is like another oval—curiously, with the same name—the Nine Stones, Winterbourne Abbas, three hundred miles south in Dorset (Fig. 48), where two vast blocks 1.8 m and 2.1 m high flank a low stone at the north (Thom, 1955, fig. 3). This site has the expected north–south axis of southern circles, but it does resemble the Roxburgh ring in its architecture, shape and size. It is possibly coincidental that the Grey Mare and Her Colts, a long chambered tomb with concave façade like some Clyde long cairns of south-west Scotland, is only three miles to the SSW.

Ten miles from Ninestone Rigg across the high pass of Sandy Edge an egg-shaped ring of many stones was built alongside an outcrop almost at the brow of the steep Burgh Hill (Fig. 5). It has been ruined but alone among its little stones a 1.5 m pillar remains, fallen, at the south-west (238°) opposite a 1.1 m long, low, thin slab in appearance like a Cork recumbent stone. This 'recumbent' and the prostrate pillar are on the main axis of the site which was 'well explored but yielded nothing of a sepulchral nature'.

Across the bleak uplands to the west the Loupin' Stanes, Dumfriesshire, is another oval, this time of twelve stones set on an artificial platform rising to the south-west. Two enormous stones tower at the WSW. (246°). Just to the south-east may be the ruins of another ring. An erratic line of standing stones meanders southwards towards the Girdle Stanes circle-henge 550 metres down river, a line that may be the result of the linking of two stone circles of entirely different origins. Further south still near Langholm, the Seven Brethren, Whiteholm Rigg, also has its lowest stones at the north-east, but here, instead of two discrepantly high stones, there seems to be a normal grading in height towards the south-west in this flattened circle, 20.1 × 18.9 m, standing at the edge of a terrace overlooking the long, lovely valley of the Water of Milk. Such a ring may have RSC affinities but it is also probably related to the nearby open circles of Dumfries and Galloway, a supposition strengthened by the position of a pygmy outlier, prostrate at 358° 9′, indicating a north–south alignment (Thom, 1967, 95).

No astronomical lines have been detected at Ninestone Rigg, Burgh Hill or the Loupin' Stanes although their orientations seem appropriate either to late

Pl. 23. *Torhousekie, Wigtownshire*. From the north-east. The central setting and the graded heights of the stones towards the south-east are clearly shown. The numerous drumlins in the area provided easily-worked, rich agricultural soil for prehistoric settlers.

Autumn sunset or to the moon's minimum midwinter setting which, in these latitudes, would have been about 236° on a low horizon. The same may be true of the solitary Torhousekie, a superb ring far to the west by Wigtown Bay (Burl, 1974b). This circle, in State guardianship, was built on the Machars, an area of calcareous sandy soil and drumlins that would have provided excellent farming land.

Torhousekie is not only one of the best-preserved sites in Britain, it is also one of the most important being almost certainly a variant RSC whose location may indicate something of the spread of customs from north-east Scotland. On a manmade platform of earth and small stones nineteen local granitic boulders, graded towards the ESE., were set on the circumference of a flattened circle 21.4 × 20.0 m. The largest stone weighs about six tons and would not have required many people to move it. Within the circle, facing ESE. is a smallish central stone between two big boulders and that this setting is a variation of a recumbent stone and its flanking pillars is confirmed by the presence of a D-shaped ring-cairn attached behind it to the WNW. Torhouse-kie is unlike any other circle in south-west Scotland but has many resemblances to the later RSCs of Kincardine whose recumbents and pillars were placed at the SSE. and set well inside the stone circle. The position of the ring may be the result of a search for copper ores in the early centuries of the bronze industry. Standing on the Whithorn peninsula where there are many cup-and-ring marked stones convincingly associated with gold and copper deposits, Torhousekie itself is only four and a half miles from such a source at Kircowan.

The site can be seen as one facet of influences emanating from north-east Scotland, influences that included the making of pottery like the Glenballoch urn in Ireland, and that impelled the construction of Four-Posters in Northumberland, Arran and central Wales (Burl, 1971). And as the Cork-Kerry RSCs of south-west Ireland are also sometimes found near copper lodes (S. O'Nuallain, 1971, 27) it may be speculated that some prospectors, whose religious ceremonies were performed in circles with recumbent stones like those in north-east Scotland, ultimately reached the cupriferous regions of Munster and built their own forms of RSC. Torhousekie and the diffusion of Four-Posters shows something of the pattern of this movement (Fig. 33). As in south-west Ireland there are not only little RSCs but also five-stone circles like Four-Posters with recumbent stone attached, and at least one true Four-Poster at Lettergorman such an equation seems feasible. Torhousekie, therefore, provides some illumination on the extent of travel and communication in the early centuries of the Atlantic Bronze Age.

CHAPTER SEVEN

The Stone Circles of Ireland

The kingdom of Ireland he hath surveyed, and that with exactness . . . and those that he employed for the Geometricall part were ordinary fellowes . . . that circumnambulated with their box and needles, not knowing what they did.

John Aubrey

1. SOUTH-WEST IRELAND (MUNSTER)

The stone circles of Cork and Kerry, of which about eighty are known (Fig. 38), belong to the RSC tradition of north-east Scotland. There are studies by Condon (1916–18), Somerville (1930), O'Nuallain (1971), Burl (1970), and Barber (1972).[1] Nearly all the sites are very small. What is considered to be a large circle here is about 8.8 m in diameter. The larger sites tend to be placed along the coast in low-lying country with a concentration around Ross Carbery. In contrast, the smaller circles are generally inland near the Boggeragh hills.

Many of the bigger circles have a recumbent stone in their south-west quadrant, have tall portal stones, are graded, and contain occasional cup-marks or quartz pebbles. But their pillars are set opposite the recumbent, their grading is 'back to front', they lack an internal cairn, and consequently their direct connection with Scottish RSCs has been questioned, the doubts being strengthened by the 500 miles of land and sea between Aberdeenshire and Cork. Yet if the Irish sites have a separate ancestry it is unclear. The almost unique graded heights, the recumbent stone, cupmarks and quartz are persuasive links between Scotland and Ireland, particularly when the intermediate presence of Torhousekie and some four-Posters like the Four Stones, Walton in central Wales, is recalled.

The circles in which RSC elements are most obvious are those in coastal positions like the gorse-grown Bohonagh; or Drombeg overlooking a warped chessboard of fields; Dough and Brinny More. Their diameters range between 7.0 m and 10.5 m. The number of stones varies between eleven and seventeen. This is in contrast to the inland sites which frequently have only five stones and where diameters can be as little as 2.4 m.

The biggest coastal group is near Ross Carbery. Three sites, Templebryan, impressive in its tree-lined field, Drombeg and Bohonagh are very close to the

---

[1] I am very grateful to Mr John Barber who has generously allowed me to use the results of his extensive and detailed field-surveys in this region.

213

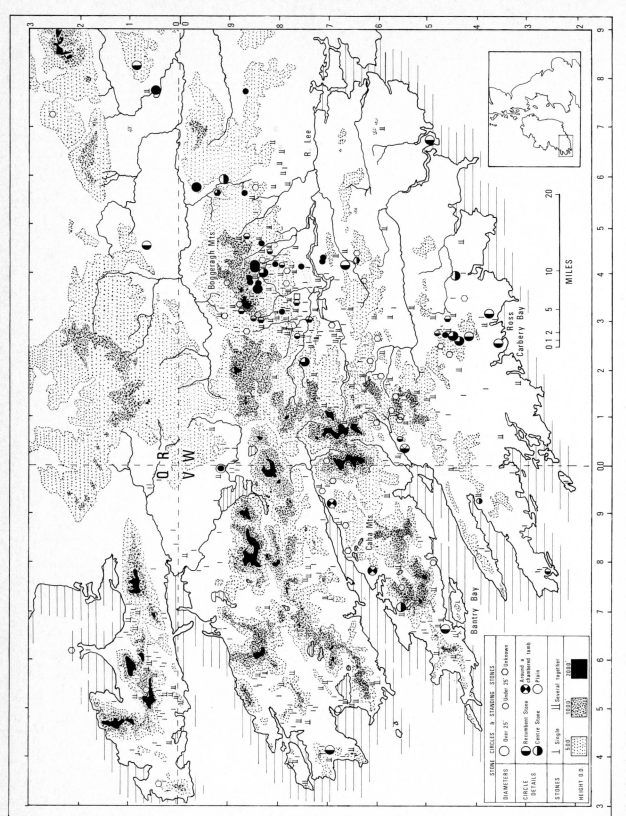

Fig. 38. The Distribution of Stone Circles in South-West Ireland.

Site	Miles from the Coast	Diameter (Metres)	Original Number of Stones	Type	Azimuth	Shape	Quartz	Centre stone	Central Burial	Portals Circum.	Portals Radial	External Stone	Hillside	Ditch	Graded Heights
Drombeg	1	9.1	17	RSC	225	Circ	x	?	1	1	x	x	1	x	1
Bohonagh	1½	9.1	13	RSC	268	Circ	x	x	1	x	1	x	1	x	1
Templebryan	1½	10.8	?13	RSC	199?	Circ	1	1	—	1	x	? Outlier to W	1	x	1
Reanascreena	3	9.1	13	RSC	258	Circ	?	x	1	1	x	x	1	1	1
Carrigagrenane	4	9.6	17?	RSC	205	Oval	x	1	?	x	1	x	x	x	1
Maulatanvalley	5	10.1	13?	RSC	258	Circ	1	1	?	x	1	x	1	x	1
Knocks A	5½	?	9–11	RSC	—	—	—	—	?	x	1	—	1	x	—
Knocks B	6	9.8 × 9.2	13?	RSC	264	Oval	x	x	—	x	1	x	x	x	1
Knockawadra	8	3.1	5	RSC	222	Circ	Outlier	x	?	1	x	Outlier to S	1	x	1
Lettergorman	8	5.4 × 2.3	4	4–P	245?	Rect	x	x	x	x	x	Outlier to W	x	x	1

Table 8. Architectural Traits in Stone Circles of the Ross Carberry Group, Cork.

coast suggesting early colonization here. Though they are mainly on low-lying land and inconspicuous, most, like Drombeg on a terrace overlooking the sea, are still placed on hill-slopes, often on spurs commanding wide views. Further inland other circles are near the gentle hills around Carrigfadda. The two smallest, Knockawadra and Lettergorman, significantly a Four-Poster, are in the extreme north. Table 8 shows how the circles vary, with the smallest farthest from the coast. Several RSCs have diameters of 9.1 m, very close to 11 M.Y.

Another group, with distinctive portal stones, is found on the north coast of the Caha peninsula, Ardgroom being only half a mile from the harbour on an open height 100 ft above the shore. The impression is of settlement by people approaching from the sea, perhaps after several seasons of cautious reconnaissance of the unknown wilderness. Some of these sites contain other features—central boulder-cists or stones, or an extra pair of stones outside the portals—which may be additions to the original RSCs, adaptations by people of differing beliefs.

Other groups occur near Bantry Bay. Such a distribution makes it probable that the primary colonization of Munster by RSC builders was along the south and south-west coasts by settlers searching for the light brown-earths that were easy to clear and farm.

The stone circles of inland regions are somewhat different. Though there are some large RSCs they often show considerable variation from the 'classic' form and their distribution is related to the River Lee and its tributaries, standing on easily worked soils above the valley-bottoms. The sites resemble those in Perthshire. This similarity is heightened by the presence of pairs of stones by some of the circles.

It is tempting to think of the few large inland RSCs as 'parent' sites from which the smaller circles may have developed. The position of Derreenataggart at the extreme south-west of the Kenmare peninsula; of Brinny More (Cappanaboul) at the head of Bantry Bay; of Gortanimill close to the Sullane along which settlers seem to have come; of Carrigagulla near to the Slaney, another settlement route; and of Shandagan only one and a half miles from the Lee, all these RSCs are situated where incomers might first have settled.

The larger sites are circular and have diameters much the same as some southern Scottish RSCs: Esslie the Greater, Kincardine, 25.0×23.2 m; and Binghill, 10.4 m, and Ardlair, 11.6 m, in Aberdeenshire. In Ireland the average diameter of seventeen large RSCs was about 9.0 m with the largest, Maughan-clea A in the hills by Bantry Bay, being just over 11.9 m across (Barber, 1972, 58). Many of the stones in these circles are 1.0 m high but inland sites like Carrigagrenane, well away from the coast, Gortanimill and Carrigagulla have no stone as high as this. An increase in the number of stones accompanied by a diminution in height is a general feature of later circles and, like their shapes, may be a factor in evaluating the relative chronology of megalithic rings. It may be significant, therefore, that the coastal rings tend to be circular whereas those inland are sometimes oval (Fig. 39).

The recumbent stone in the Munster sites remains in the south-west quadrant and is usually flat-topped. The longest is the 2.3 m stone at Derreenataggart looking between its portals to the hill-surrounded bay below. It is noticeable that Carrigagulla and Gortanimill have recumbents smaller than the average despite their being built in country where stone was more plentiful than by the coast.

Unlike the Aberdeenshire RSCs the recumbents have no flanking stones. They also are thin slabs rather than heavy blocks. There is nothing as impressive as the great squared stone at Cothiemuir Wood. Even Drombeg has a recumbent that, although 2.1 m long, is only 46 cm thick. This is the one Irish stone to be cupmarked, two carvings being placed on its upper surface.

It is the larger coastal circles that are most like the Scottish RSCs with their recumbent stones, grading and tall pillars but, unlike them, the pillars are erected opposite the recumbent, like entrances or portal stones. A similar arrangement may have existed at the strange oval at Burgh Hill, Roxburgh. Many of the Cork inland RSCs have these north-east portals set radially at right-angles to the circumference. Such pillars average only 1.4 m in height although those at Drombeg, Bohonagh and Derreenataggart, perhaps amongst the earliest, are over 2.4 m high. Not surprisingly, it is at Gortanimill

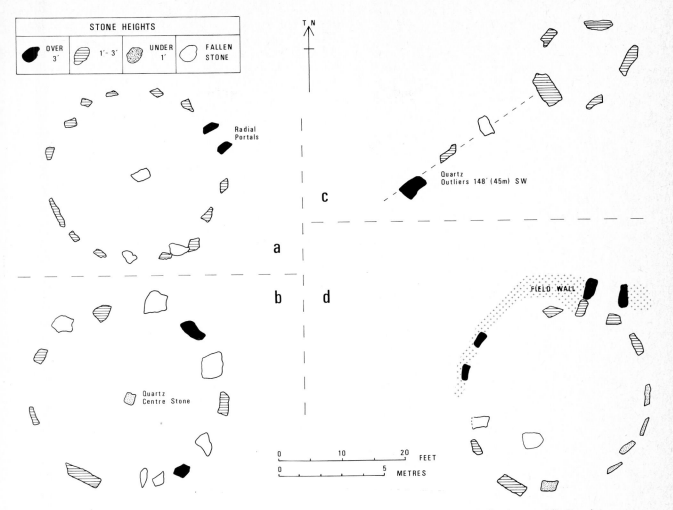

T N

Radial Portals

Quartz Outliers 148' (45m) S W

c

a

b   d

Quartz Centre Stone

FIELD WALL

| 0 | 10 | 20 | FEET |
| 0 | | 5 | METRES |

Fig. 39. Four Stone Circles in Cork. (a) Carrigagulla B; (b) Currebeha; (c) Knockraheen; (d) Carrigagrenane. After Barber, 1972.

and Carrigagulla that the lowest portals occur. From these stones the circles grade downwards towards the recumbent which, sometimes, is taller than its neighbouring stones. Yet stone 8 at Bohonagh seems to have had its top shaped so that it sloped upwards towards the adjacent recumbent. This was even more noticeable at Drombeg where stones 10, 11 and 12 had sockets whose depths had been graduated in order to give a sloping effect to the tops of the stones up towards the recumbent. It was at the same RSC that a huge lozenge-shaped stone at the NNE. had been dramatically placed alongside a very thin pillar like the 'male' and 'female' stones in the Kennet Avenue, Wiltshire, which could be forms of fertility symbolism (Smith, 1965, 197).

It can be seen that, albeit rearranged, nearly all the architectural traits of

Scottish RSCs exist in the Cork sites. Such variation could be expected if a long period had passed during the years of colonization before settlers had leisure once more to build their ritual monuments. Case (1970, 109) has argued that any cultural system transmitted from one area to another in this way will be an inexact copy and not identical with that of the homeland. This seems true in the case of the Cork-Kerry RSCs.

The one feature that completely distinguishes these circles from those in Scotland is the absence of any internal cairn although ring-cairns may exist alongside several circles (Barber, 1972, 65). At Drombeg, Fahy (1959) discovered that the site had been stripped, levelled and a gravel floor laid, 10 cm thick on the west. So intent were the builders on achieving a level surface that boulders had been removed and their pits filled with small stones. Beneath the gravel were burial pits. Drombeg is the only Irish RSC yet known with such a floor but at Bohonagh (Fahy, 1961) the site also was levelled with a step cut into the hillside like Druidsfield, Aberdeenshire. Around the portals and the recumbent were stony areas. Maulatanvalley may have been strewn with sandstone. Quartz pebbles had been spread around the portals of Mushera Beg (Gogan, 1931).

Only three of the large RSCs have been satisfactorily excavated. All contained central pits with cremated bone. At Bohonagh a low, central mound covered a shallow, carelessly dug pit holding soil, pebbles and fragments of bone. The embanked RSC at Reanascreena (Fahy, 1962) had an irregular central pit, filled with soil but no deposit. Instead, 3.1 m to the north was another small pit with a flat piece of shale over five or six pieces of burnt bone. The excavator speculated that the pyre had been to the east of the site as there was a heavy concentration of charcoal there. The very few bone-fragments under the shale suggest a token deposit similar to that in the primary pit at Loanhead of Daviot, Aberdeenshire.

At Drombeg there were two central pits. In the larger was bone and some flat-rimmed sherds (Fig. 11) like Lough Gur II (or Knockadoon) ware of the Early Bronze Age (Case, 1961, 198). The second pit had only a few charcoal flecks. It was possible to reconstruct the sequence of events. The pot had been broken before its deposition and perhaps wrapped in a cloth while hot burned bones were placed in it. Then it was put into the larger pit. Some sweepings from the pyre were added. The pot was pressed into place and a pinch of charcoal added before the pit was filled. Such rites are very like those known in Scottish RSCs.

What are not known in Aberdeenshire are centre stones whereas ten or more Munster circles have these, indicating the mélange of beliefs that resulted here during the second millennium bc. Most of these stones are lower than those of the circle and are quartz chosen perhaps because of their brilliance. At the hedge-bounded and thistlegrown Maulatanvalley, at Templebryan, Currebeha (Fig. 39), and Gortanimill observers have commented on the whiteness of the central stone. Even the ruined oval of Derrynafinchin in a remote valley

Pl. 24. *Drombeg, Cork*. From the north. The sea lies just beyond the hills. The tall stones on the left are the portals opposite the recumbent stone here partly obscured on the right by stones whose tops have been shaped to slope upwards to the recumbent itself. The flat stone in the ring marks the position of the central pit in which there was an urned cremation. The whole interior of the circle was covered with pebbles and gravel.

by Bantry Bay has a vivid quartz block by its central boulder-cist. Although the centre-stone circles of south-west Scotland should not be forgotten, Cornwall would seem the most probable source for the introduction of centre stones in south-west Ireland possibly by copper prospectors or traders. People knowing of Cornish circles like Boscawen-Un with its large quartz pillar, or the Hurlers Centre, or the Stripple Stone circle-henge, could well have added such a feature to the otherwise alien RSCs they encountered in Cork and Kerry.

Two sites, Reanascreena and Glentane East, are surrounded by banks and ditches. Other embanked stone circles can be found far to the north-west at the gigantic Lios henge and two others near Lough Gur, Limerick. Just to the south is Lissyviggeen, Kerry, a seven-stone circle 4.0 m across within an earth bank about 15 m from crest to crest. These sites, however, are low-lying whereas Reanascreena was built near the summit of a hill. In Kildare and Wicklow on the south-east coast of Ireland are several embanked circles on hilltops in situations reminiscent of many Irish passage-graves including some in Wicklow like Seefin and Baltinglass Hill. Stone circles such as the Piper's Stones, Kildare, or Castleruddery and Tournant, Wicklow, are on summits and are embanked. The former has many features in common with the Lios. At Reanascreena there may be a fusion of traits from chambered tombs, henges and RSCs.

The intermixing of features from Cornwall, Wicklow, Limerick and Scotland are explicable partly as a result of prospecting for copper in south-west Ireland in the mid-second millennium. 'The copper resources of the peninsulas and of Killarney were regarded as an attractive part of the potential of Kerry by prehistoric metalworkers . . .' (Herity, 1970.) Other incomers may have been seeking farming land.

As well as its stone circles Munster has many other prehistoric monuments, some of which belong to the same general period. There are settlement sites like Carrigillihy near Glandore where the remains of a small oval house contained artefacts of beaker affinities, and there were relics of huts near the RSCs of Bohonagh and Drombeg, although the latter, associated with a cooking-place, was dated to the fourth century AD. Yet a similar *fulacht fiadh* was excavated at Killeens thirty miles north-east and gave a date of 1556 bc ± 230 (C-877).

There are many wedge-shaped chambered tombs, questionably linked with the Breton *allées couvertes*, in the same region including that at Island, Cork, dated to 1160 bc ± 140 (D-49). Many of them have westerly orientations and grading, atypical of chambered tombs, but akin to RSCs. There is also the long wedge-cairn of Labbacallee where, in the gallery, there lay the headless skeleton of a woman, her skull being found with a male skeleton and a child in a super-imposed layer. Intriguingly, the modern name is a corruption of 'Leaba Caillighe', the 'Hag's Bed'.

All around the foothills are standing stones, often by the circles, some alone in settings of three to six pillars like the four arranged east–west at Eightercua near Waterville, Kerry, up to 3 m high and perhaps associated with a cairn. Such settings tend to stand at the edges of hills and may have marked tracks in and out of the area.

Industrial sites exist, in Kerry at Rose Island or Valentia, and in Cork at Derrycarhoon near Schull on the Mount Gabriel peninsula where six copper-mine shafts contained grooved egg-shaped mauls of gritstone up to 40 lbs (18 kg) in weight. On the same peninsula were 25 other mines with more grooved mauls (Jackson, 1968), one tip-heap providing a date of 1500 bc ± 120

(VRI-66). A similar axe-hammer was found in Moneen cairn where secondary cists held late Northern beaker sherds and food-vessels (M. O'Kelly, 1952). From another copper-mine at Ballyrisode came twelve polished stone axes, one of green chloritic grit.

Although none of these sites, domestic, ritual or industrial, can yet be directly connected with the stone circles their dating shows not only the wide extent of activity here during the second millennium but also the variety of custom, and this may explain some of the architectural idiosyncrasies of the circles.

The finds from the RSCs are limited to the broken pot from Drombeg, three small flints and four shale fragments from the same site, and a chisel-ended flint found outside Bohonagh's portals. There is also a perplexing C-14 assay from Drombeg's charcoal, of 13 bc $\pm$ 140 (TCD-38). This was later recalculated and is now cited as 600 AD $\pm$ 120 (D-62), improbably late for an RSC but in keeping with the neighbouring domestic site.

Turning from the large coastal RSCs to the smaller, inland sites, these still retain RSC traits even though only tenuously. The recumbent survives sometimes in a debased form hardly distinguishable from the other circle-stones. A lot of these circles have an outlier or a pair of stones by them either like a double entrance or at right-angles to the circle like a short row (Fig. 39) and are reminiscent of the Perthshire paired stones at the Four-Posters of Lundin Farm and Ferntower. Many of the sites, like Carrigaphooca, Macroom, are about 3.2 m across and of five stones including a westerly recumbent. 'To the east of the castle is a large stone placed upon a high rock, secured by wedges of other stones, and near it, the remains of a druid altar, encompassed with a circle of stones pitched endways.' The majority lie in the Boggeraghs where the Laney, Delehinagh and Dripsey flow into the Sullane. Each area has at least one large RSC but a riverine penetration from the east is probable rather than one overland from Ross Carbery, and the inland builders are likely to belong to a separate immigration.

Because of the retention of the recumbent stone in the five-stone sites, parallels may be made between them and Scottish Four-Posters, especially as in Perthshire the average diameter of eleven Four-Posters was 4.9 m, and in Cork twelve five-stone rings averaged 3.2 m. The suggestion that the five-stone circle is basically a Four-Poster with recumbent stone retained is supported by the presence of a genuine Four-Poster at Lettergorman with its tallest stone at the south-west.

Despite the wide distribution of the five-stone rings only two excavations are recorded. At Mushera Beg (Gogan, 1931) nothing was found in the hurried half-day of digging but a paved area was noticed around the outside of the stones and, like Corrimony and Castle Frazer in north-east Scotland, there was a concentration of quartz pebbles by the portal stones. At Kealkil (O'Riordain, 1939) no burial was found. Instead, at the centre of this site below a slope worn through with patches of naked rock were two shallow trenches crossing each other. 'They evidently served to contain two wooden beams which, we may suppose, served to support an upright post at the point where they crossed.' O'Riordain noted that the portals would have made a foresight through which the alignment past the central post and over the recumbent stone would be almost exactly north; and that a sighting along the edge of the recumbent to the side of a lately fallen member, once 5.3 m tall, of a pair of outlying stones, would have provided an easterly orientation. Kealkil is thus noteworthy as a site in which RSC architecture was combined with the pre-occupation of builders of open circles with north–south and equinoctial lines, another example of the mixing of influences here. Just to the ESE. of the ring was a cairn, 7.9 m in diameter, from which the only finds were three bits of scallop shell. This mound was interpreted as a ring-cairn like the circular remains at Maughanclea B, at Knocknakilla and Knockraheen. Without excavation these ruins cannot be resolved but it is interesting that they occur alongside diminutive five-stone rings (Barber, 1972, 65).

There have been claims that, like Kealkil, other Cork circles had an astronomical function. From an examination of five large RSCs Somerville (1930) suggested that Drombeg's recumbent would indicate the midwinter sunset, and Bohonagh's the equinoxes. He could find no good alignments at Reanascreena, Carrigagrenane or Maulatanvalley. Fahy, the excavator of Drombeg (1959) and Bohonagh (1961), agreed with these conclusions though he carefully noted that Drombeg's alignment did not pass through a distant hillgap but to one side of it. Reanascreena (Fahy, 1962) elicited only the comment that the recumbent may have marked a near-miss on the equinoxes—if an error of 12° may be considered 'near'. But the azimuth of 258° is akin to the WSW. lines noticed in many Cornish stone circles, and may be related to them as the presence of 'Cornish' centre stones in other Cork rings and Kealkil's north–south lines intimate.

The very lengths of the recumbents make it unlikely that the builders intended a precise sightline. At Bohonagh the stone is 1.8 m long. As the circle is only 9.1 m across there is a broad angle of vision over the diameter to the width of the recumbent of about 11°. As, in that latitude, the sun moves 3° along the horizon weekly, Bohonagh's recumbent could be used to determine a four-week equinoctial period in March and September but nothing more precise. This may have been the builders' wish but it is difficult to prove. At Drombeg the angle is about 14° because the stone is longer and the variation is for five weeks from mid-December to mid-January rather than precisely to the midwinter solstice.

Barber (1973) in a computerized analysis of thirty Irish RSCs found that seventeen contained orientations on the sun, moon and Venus which have subsequently been suspected in Scottish RSCs. Many of the large rings like Drombeg and Gortanimill had such lines. Of the exceptions ten had postulated stellar alignments. Three others were apparently related to no celestial event. From the example of Kealkil it is possible such deviations stem from two causes: one is the continuing expansion of lines already noted in north-east Scotland; the other is the integration of other astronomical traditions, especially those from the open circles of west Britain and the south-west peninsula.

Although the lack of artefactual evidence makes the dating of the Cork-Kerry rings almost a matter of guesswork yet if they did have an ancestry in the Scottish RSCs it is unlikely that the earliest of them was built much before 1600 bc. Support for this hypothesis may come from the proposed stellar dates ranging between about 1800–600 BC, the equivalents of *c.*1550–550 bc (Barber, 1973, 35), particularly as these include only one of the presumably early coastal rings, Derreenataggart. Hence it may be speculated that some time before the mid-second millennium bc people from outside the region arrived off the coasts of Munster, moving inland along the rivers, searching the wooded hillsides for easily worked soils. A distribution map shows

> that the bulk of the circles are sited on the now boggy lithosols of the highland areas of the south. These soils are the thin stony head or weathered fraction of the underlying sandstone. In the absence of the peat bogs they would have provided a thin light soil very well suited to peoples who did not have the heavy plough or the capacity to plough the heavier alluvial soils of the valley floors. This at once explains the distribution of the circles. The builders penetrated inland up the river valleys until they came to soils light enough to cultivate with the equipment they possessed, probably no more than the spade. Their upper limit would be set by the thin and infertile soils of the higher slopes. (Barber, 1972, 67.)

In this the rings resemble the Scottish RSCs also set on hillsides above the valleys. But everything seems half-size, their diameters, their 'territories'.

Around Ross Carbery the large coastal circles like Drombeg, Bohonagh and Templebryan are four to six miles from each other, close to convenient bays. A little farther inland six more rings, including Carrigagrenane, Reanascreena and Maulatanvally, crowd into a narrow strip of only four square miles. On the Beara peninsula large RSCs like Derreenataggart, Ardgroom, Shronebirrane, Drombohilly and Lohart stand some three miles apart. And in the foothills above Bantry Bay eight coastal rings were erected two to three miles from each other. Although it is not known whether all these neighbouring rings were contemporary it is not unreasonable to think of each having an approximate territory of one square mile (259 ha), of which perhaps (26 ha) was cultivable. This is about half the area for the Scottish RSCs. If the same demographic equation were applied to the Cork circles it would suggest that the Irish rings were used by groups of no more than about thirty people who understandably built rings about half the circumference of those in Aberdeenshire. That such a small number could have built a typical stone circle is not contradicted by the size of the heaviest recumbent, that at Derreenataggart, measuring $2.2 \times 1.5 \times 0.4$ m and weighing no more than 4 tons, easily moved by sixteen people even up a gentle slope. Drombeg's recumbent weighs even less, hardly 2 tons. Even the prostrate outlier at Kealkil which must have weighed about 4 tons was re-erected in the Spring of 1938 by only six labourers albeit 'with much difficulty' and with the aid of modern blocks and tackle.

The density of these Cork RSCs, like those in north-east Scotland and in Ulster, is very different from the uncrowded distribution of many circles in lowland Britain and implies different systems of land-owning, perhaps of independent families rather than fiefdoms or tribal areas communally worked.

These largely forgotten circles deep in the Boggeraghs or along the storm-drenched rocks of the western bays once were the most needed centres of people's lives, places that combined the mundane earth with the imagery of the night-sky, where a first burial sanctified the area, where people trod or danced around the portal stones as the layers of thick humus at Drombeg and Bohonagh testify, much as others may have done along the north-east causeways of some Scottish RSCs, looking towards the darkening, lowering horizon and the setting of the sun or moon. Now only the stones and the secrets survive.

2. WESTERN IRELAND

There are few stone circles along the western coasts of Ireland, well-scattered sites whose architecture is often a mixture of circle and burial structure. Around the Caha peninsula, Kerry, some RSCs like Dromroe or Gurteen have central boulder-cists, enormous slabs supported above ground by three or four low stones. It seems unlikely that they belong to the original circle because their heights customarily match that of the recumbent stone and would hinder astronomical observations. As they frequently occur without a circle along the coasts of Cork and Kerry (O'Nuallain, 1971, 25) their origins probably differ from those of the RSC-builders. No finds are recorded in Kerry but similar overground cists in Scotland at Moleigh, Argyll, or Collessie, Fife, held bronze daggers so that a second millennium date is probable.

A megalithic ring, Kenmare near Dromroe, surrounding a boulder-cist with a mighty seven-ton globular capstone, has no definite recumbent. The ring is of interest for, unlike any other in Munster, it is egg-shaped, measuring 17.4×15.8 m or about 21×19 M.Y. (Barber, 1972, 58). Such shapes are unusual. Thom (1967, 29, 68) lists only ten though subsequently others have been recognised on Arran, Dartmoor and elsewhere. The involved design is a late geometrical development and none of Thom's sites is likely to be earlier than the second millennium, including Woodhenge (ibid, 73), now with two C-14 assays averaging 1830 bc. Kenmare is unique in Kerry but does have some resemblance to another egg-shaped ring, Burgh Hill, Roxburgh (ibid, 70), previously noted for its affinities with the RSC tradition.

Further north is Lissyviggeen, already mentioned. Near Galway Bay is Masonbrook, 'The Seven Monuments', its stones set in a 21.3 m earth bank. Excavations in 1916 (Macalister, 1917) suggested that part at least of the central mound might be modern. In the county of Mayo what appears to be remnants of circles may actually be denuded passage-graves like those at Moytirra or Carrowreagh (Aldridge, 1970, 14) with a burial chamber at its centre. One or two genuine sites, Mullaghmore near a standing stone and three wedge-graves, or Rosdoagh (deValera, 1951, 80), or Summerhill House near Killala (N.M.I., No. 389) may be found here but this was never a rich area of stone circles perhaps because the passage-graves provided the necessary ceremonial sites. Even to the east in Tipperary circles are scarce. At Reardnogy More, a 4.5 m ring lay near the bottom of a hill on which was a four-stone alignment (Rynne, 1969). And in the Timoney Hills, spread across 100 acres (41 ha), over 200 stones lie in confusion after the depredations of road-makers. Sixteen may form the arc of a 61 m circle (N.M.I., No. 353).

Yet amongst this unpromising landscape there is the wealth of Lough Gur, twelve miles south-east of the Shannon estuary. Here where low-crowned limestone hills curve round the lough basin prehistoric people settled on the well-drained sheltered soils (S. P. O'Riordain, 1954). An early date of 2740 bc ± 40 (D-41) has come from one homestead. On the hillsides the black-budded ash and the hazel covered the slopes, overhanging the yellow celandine and the tall blue columbine. Red deer wandered in the trees alert for the wolf and the bear, for the barking of the hunters' dogs. At the forest edges, where the land had been cleared, whitebeam, hawthorn and cherry blossomed, white as quartz, in the Springtime. Overhead, reminding the villagers of the nearness of the Atlantic, they could see gulls and the soaring white-tailed eagle, flocks of cranes that flew slowly over the waters of the lough where mallards and little teals chuckled in the reeds.

For a thousand years or more timber houses, round and rectangular, and cairns, standing stones and wedge-graves were erected to the east of the mile-long lough, on Knockadoon peninsula, on the slopes of Knockfennel and Carrig Aille, and on Geroid Island where charcoal from one hearth was as late as 1730 bc ± 140 (D-34). While the men grazed their herds of oxen and a few pigs snuffled among the trees the women worked in the settlements. They made pots in the Early Neolithic style of north-east Ireland, fine round-based ware with decorated T-shaped rims for suspending the vessels by thonging, pots that gradually during the third millennium became simpler in shape and ornament until in the Bronze Age flat-bottomed coarseware became common. Such pots could have been used to store the grain from the terraced patches by some huts. Through the misting rains, the sunshine and the winds of centuries the slow life continued like a stone at the water's edge while the years drifted by. Contacts with the north-east were kept up, for traders, per-haps travelling overland and along the Shannon, brought axes of porcellanite from Tievebulliagh mountain in Antrim. And soon after 2000 bc the earliest British beaker-users came here (Clarke, 1970, 569, n. 28) at first maybe simply looking for farmland, but their descendants prospecting for the elusive copper sulphide ores that their smiths could transmute into the glowing daggers so favoured by their leaders. The wealthy aristocracy, with its ornate W/MR and N/MR beakers, established a community here, perhaps even a trading-post, whose occupants seem to have lived alongside the natives (Clarke, 1970, 94). Such contacts may have endured into the fifteenth century bc.

Except in the western lowlands there are burial sites and stone circles all around the lough and in the surrounding country. Four miles south-east is a large boulder-ring at Ballynamona, now cut by a farm lane. On the north shore of the lough itself by Knockfennel is an oval, 13.4 × 9.1 m, also of boulders. Just north-east of Lough Gur on Carrig Aille is a 55.5 m earth circle with a 4.3 m thick bank lined inside and out with tall stones. Half a mile south is a stupendous standing stone. Lewis (1909, 520) wrote how a local woman told him of a 'crock of gold under the stone which was guarded by a terrible ghost' that deterred nocturnal treasure-hunters. As the gold dematerialized during daylight hours the riches lay untouched.

On Knockadoon, as well as the huts, there is an enclosed sepulchral site, 31 m in diameter, again with a double kerb filled with rubble, with a small stone ring containing a cist with two skeletons, one a child. Such rings are not formally concentric stone circles inasmuch as they are freestanding but are double walls to support a bank. In this they differ from rings like Machrie Moor 5, Arran, or Winterbourne Bassett, Wiltshire, in which each ring is independent of the other.

Half a mile across the water from Knockadoon in Grange townland is a complex of monuments that, although only two of them are true stone circles, deserves description. At the north-east is an oval, 22.9 × 16.2 m, of fifteen stones within a slight earth bank. There is a wide gap, apparently an entrance, on the south-west axis. Immediately by it there used to be a great open circle about 52 m across. In 1826 it was a ring of seventy-two stones. Cottages stood in it. Now only nine close-set pillars remain on its south-west arc, all low and maybe not in their correct positions. Alongside are traces of a chambered tomb.

Hardly 30 metres south is the Lios henge (Fig. 40), a massive bank of gravelly clay, 9 m wide, 1.2 m high, and 64 m in diameter, lined inside with stones that stand shoulder to shoulder around the wide interior. There is no ditch. Today trees grow on the Lios and a field-wall brushes it. It was excavated in 1939 (S. P. O'Riordain, 1951).

In layout these three Grange rings have some likeness to other triple settings like Balnuaran of Clava, Inverness, whose central ring-cairn has been broadly compared with the Lios (Henshall, 1972, 275); like the Hurlers, Cornwall; and even more like Stanton Drew, Somerset, where, as at Grange, the alignment is not straight and where the north-east ring is the smallest. As there are constructional parallels between some Lough Gur monuments and the Priddy henges, Somerset (Tratman, 1967, 111), only seven miles south-west of Stanton Drew, such comparisons may contribute to an understanding of the somewhat puzzling associations of finds from the Lios

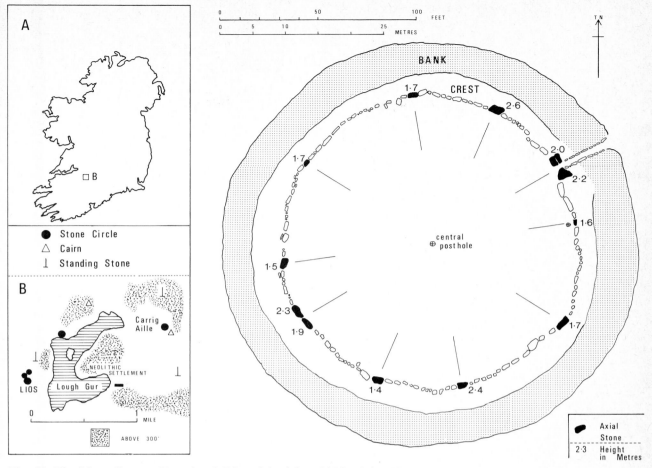

Fig. 40. The Lios, Grange Townland, Limerick. After O'Riordain, 1951.

with others around the Bristol Channel in south-west Wales and Wessex. The ring is more than architecturally wondrous. If it can ever be interpreted it may one day reveal how much the large British open rings, stone or earth, are compositions of commerce and ceremony in which native and foreigner freely commingled.

The Lios is not a stone circle. The stones that fringe its bank are contiguous, mostly local limestone but some of volcanic breccia from Grange Hill a mile away. Hiding their lumpy packing-stones is a thick layer of gravelly clay, now heavy with grass, over the 47.6 m wide interior. At the ENE. (78°) is a thin, stone-lined passage, gravel-floored, that terminates in two gigantic inner portal stones. The site may stand on previously farmed land. What looks like the remnants of a field-wall pass under it (O'Riordain, 1951, 44).[1]

[1] I am informed by Mr John Barber that the Lios has probably been added to in modern times, but the alterations do not affect the most important aspects of the architecture.

Pl. 25 *The Lios, Limerick*. From the SSW. showing the great ring and the small stone circle to its north. A large circle once stood between the small site and the trees to its left.

The entrance to the Lios has a leafless tree by it. Just to the left is the largest stone in the ring, of volcanic breccia. It is four metres tall and weighs over sixty tons. It was probably brought from Grange Hill a mile to the north.

The Lios is instructive about prehistoric working methods. At the exact centre on the old land surface beneath the clay the excavators found a posthole 13 cm across, too slight for a totem pole but adequate for a focal post from which the 23.8 m radius of the inner bank could be marked out. This was done not by scribing an entire circle in the turf but by extending the rope to five roughly equidistant places on the eastern circumference and then to five others opposite. The ten spots were marked with poles. One socket survived by stone 17. In this way five diameters were fixed, the most important being that from the entrance to its opposing pair of stones for this was the major axis. If Somerville's calculations were correct (Windle, 1912, 287) it was aligned to 258° on the moon's minimum midsummer setting about 2500 BC (c. 2000 bc). There is a crude east–west axis between stone 17, with its posthole, and 74, and, at right-angles, a meridional line between stones 41 and 106. The design looked like one of Thom's compound rings (1967, 84) but more haphazardly achieved. The distances between the posts varied: 9.5 m, 17.1 m, 18.6 m, 14.0 m and 15.2 m, measuring clockwise from the entrance.

Meanwhile twelve heavy stones were being dragged to the site. Holes were dug for them by each post, two at the entrance, two opposite where touching stones were set up, their tops making a V-notch ideal for sightings. The other eight stones replaced the circumferential posts and at this stage the Lios looked like any large stone circle. But then, using the stones as end-markers, the first straightish section of the bank was piled up over the edges of the filled stone holes, 1.2 m high and flat-topped but with a vertical inner face that was supported by propping extra stones against it, their bases resting on the ground and held secure by heaped up cobbles. There was a squalid camp for the hundred or more workers on the west where fires burned and where refuse and filth gathered, occasionally strewn over with earth as the months of labour continued. People carried baskets of clay from the shores of the lough. Others dragged stones whose weight tore and gouged the interior of the circle. Yet more manhandled the packing-stones to the pillars that were being pulled upright by gangs hauling heel-deep on the bank's top. And so, stretch by stretch, the Lios was completed. Finally the level clay floor was laid.

Such a reconstruction is not fanciful. The average marking stone is 1.9 m high and stands in a prepared hole whereas the intermediate stones, 1.0 m tall, stand on the surface and can only have been erected by leaning them against the bank which, itself, is irregular with kinks where section joined section. Hearths, pottery, and layers of turf were uncovered in its western sector. The heaviest stone, at the north-east, weighs over 60 tons and 120 persons or more would have had to heave it over a mile from its hillside. The clay for the bank and floor came from a drift deposit to the south-east by the lough. With an average basketload of 30 lbs (13.6 kg) (Coles, 1973, 73) some 300,000 loads would have been needed, taking a hundred workers sixty to seventy workdays from midsummer well into the Autumn.

The uneven heights of the lining stones makes it unlikely that the bank was intended as a viewing-platform for the uninitiated. The Lios is more like a temenos in which many might participate. Its inner space, with a circumference of 149.5 m, could accommodate a hundred or more dancers so that a population figure of 200–300 is feasible. This would be sufficient to move the stones but is too many for the adjacent Lough Gur occupation sites even if the nine or ten known houses were contemporary and had as many as eight people each. Nor would local people have required a camp. But within twelve miles are many other prehistoric sites: huts; ring-barrows

at Ballingoola, Cahercorney, Lissard and Rathjordan with its early beakers;
and the most south-westerly of all Irish passage-graves at Duntryleague; so
that, as with the open stone circles of west Britain, the Lios could well have
been a meeting-place for scattered groups.

The forgotten ceremonies included the deliberate breaking of pots. This
practice was widespread. It has been seen at the RSCs of Loanhead of Daviot,
Aberdeenshire, and Drombeg, Cork. It occurred in chambered tombs like
Audleystown, Down; in the stone circles of the Sanctuary, Wiltshire and
Carneddau Hengwm, Merioneth; and in earthwork enclosures like Durrington Walls, Wiltshire. (Wainwright and Longworth, 1971, 217.) At the
Lios many sherds were found under the bank and by the western stones
near the lunar notch, and from these fragments a date for the monument
can be estimated.

There is a dichotomy. Whereas in the camp beneath the bank there was
only native pottery (Fig. 10), simple fineware and the later coarse bucket-
shapes, such pottery was accompanied, in the interior, by a few sherds of
Ebbsfleet, beaker and grooved ware. This may mean that the ring is a native
work that preceded the arrival of newcomers. The 'European' beaker and
English Ebbsfleet fragments are probably no later than 1800 bc. This agrees
quite well with the grooved ware and its characteristic accompaniment of
lopsided arrowheads and end-scrapers which formed a large proportion of
the flints near the stones. Such ware is of special relevance because it has
been found not only in Wessex henges like Stonehenge I, Maumbury Rings,
Woodhenge, and the great enclosures of Durrington Walls, Marden and
Mount Pleasant, but also in the circle-henge of Stenness in Orkney. If a date
were hazarded for the Lios within a century of 1900 bc this would accord
with the evidence of the Irish pottery. Any later material, including food-
vessels and a bronze awl, may be accounted for as a sign of the monument's
continuing use well into the second millennium when a late, long-necked
s3/w beaker was broken by the entrance (Fig. 10). It would also agree with
Somerville's hypothetical lunar date of 2500 BC (c. 2000 bc).

What impulses caused the building of the Lios cannot yet be explained
for it is not known which of the three Grange rings is the earliest or if they
were used simultaneously. What may be inferred is that it stemmed from the
henge and circle tradition around the Irish Sea. In a time when prospectors
from Wessex were reaching out to south-west Wales and to Wicklow it
may have been they who described the ceremonial rings they themselves
had first seen in Ireland. Or the axe traders, for stone axes were discovered
beneath the clay floor (S. P. O'Riordain, 1951, 50), could have been responsible. What part makers of grooved ware, perhaps related to the Boyne
passage-grave culture, played in the custom of henge building is uncertain.
It may be noted that, like the Lios, Stonehenge I, with such pottery, also
seems to have been a lunar site (Newham, 1972), its date of 2180 bc ± 105
(I-2328) making it a possible contemporary of the Lough Gur ring.

'The precise relationship of Irish passage-graves, Maes Howe-type tombs, Skara Brae, Rinyo, and the Grooved Ware cultures in general, may be obscure at present, but it would be hard to deny that it exists.' (Henshall, 1972, 286.) In the flux of the early second millennium when new routes were being opened, many novel ideas tangled across the seaways, carried by trader, prospector, settler, by beaker, grooved-ware and native potter. The Lios belongs to the tradition of open circles, not to the Clava-RSC culture of north-east Scotland. Its affinities lie to the east, in the Wicklows, in south-west Wales, in Wessex whence its newcomers travelled. It is more probable that they followed Irish rivers inland than that they sailed round the tempestuous peninsulas of Kerry. From Milford Haven across St. George's Channel is only eighty miles of sea before the shelter of Waterford. From there they could follow the River Suir towards the landmark of Galtymore mountain then paddle westwards along the tree-darkened Aberlow between the towering Galtees and Slievenamuck and into the forested Golden Vale of Tipperary. A short portage would reach the headwaters of the Maigue flowing northwards past Ballynamona only a few miles from Lough Gur. Once explored, this Welsh-Irish route would soon become established.

Certainly the s3/w beaker at the Lios is like another from the trading-post of Merthyr Mawr Warren on the south Welsh coast and virtually identical with a pot from the Wick barrow, Somerset (Savory, 1965, 78), made within 150 years after 1700 bc according to Lanting and van der Waals' (1972) provisional chronology. The earlier combination of AOC, E and W/MR beakers at the Lios is only matched in Ireland or Wales at New Grange and this demonstrates the attraction Lough Gur had for these immigrants.

The site most closely resembling it is Castleruddery (Fig. 41) in the western Wicklows near Baltinglass. This little-known ring near the Slaney (Leask, 1945) also has a stone-lined bank, an easterly entrance, huge portal stones, here of quartz, and an open space about 29 m across. Like the Lios it has no ditch and its earth bank must have been scraped up. Situated as it is in an area of gold-bearing gravels, of passage-graves, and of open stone circles, its likeness to the Lios is intriguing, especially as the Slaney flows southwards into Wexford harbour close to Waterford and the rivers that led to Lough Gur.

Along the shores of the Irish Sea cognate, possibly related enclosures, unditched and low-lying, were built: large henges near the Boyne valley like Monknewton, Micknanstown, and several sites near New Grange (Burl, 1969, 25), or further north at the Giant's Ring, Belfast. And across the sea is Meini-Gwyr embanked circle with its stone-built entrance; Ysbyty Cynfyn, Cardigan, now in a churchyard; and perhaps the enormous circle-henge at Mayburgh near Penrith, Cumberland, also ditchless, its huge cobbled bank having a megalithic entrance at the ENE. Such rings may be one facet of the social disturbances of the Late Neolithic and Early Bronze Age in the British Isles when the products of mining and manufacture in Ireland were traded in Scotland, Wales and England, bringing with the prosaic axes and daggers new ideas and rites. The Lios may be one of these enclosures, constructed by natives in their own building style but belonging fundamentally to the traditions of the open henges and stone circles of western Britain.

3. EASTERN IRELAND

These traditions can be seen even more clearly in the open rings dispersed along the coast of the Irish Sea from the Wicklows up to the fine stone circle of Ballynoe beyond the mountains of Mourne. Large open circles are rare anywhere in Ireland even along the east coast where influences from Scotland, Wales and England were strongest and where the majority of henges and open rings are to be found. The indigenous passage-grave custom of combining tomb and temple in one monument was not easily reconciled with the concept of the simple, open ceremonial circle, so that where such intrusive monuments were built near passage-grave domains tombs were quite often added to them, sometimes many years later. Such seems to have happened at the henge with passage-grave at Bryn Celli Ddu, Anglesey; at the unditched Giant's Ring henge near Belfast with its off-centre portal dolmen; at Dun Ruadh, Tyrone, where cists and cairn were added to an oval circle-henge; and, possibly, even at New Grange itself. There is, therefore, a scarcity of open rings in Ireland.

The thickest cluster with henges and circles interspersed developed below the steeper north-west slopes of the granitic Wicklows. The well-known copper lodes lie many miles to the south-east in the drab wastes around Arklow. And the fabled Wicklow gold, of which a 22 oz (0.62 kg) nugget was discovered in 1795, is likely to have been washed down by east-flowing streams although its source is still untraced. The circle-builders, apparently, were more attracted to the fertile soils of the Curragh than to the presence of mineral deposits.

Within fifteen miles of Naas on this plain are hengiform monuments; several stone circles; passage-graves, perched like Seefin on hill summits; portal dolmens, simple megalithic tombs with tall entrance stones and a massive capstone; and at least three of the tallest standing stones in the British Isles.

Remembering the mooted relationship of Castleruddery, just to the south of the Naas concentration, with the Lios it is relevant to mention its nearness to two portal dolmens, one at Haroldstown, Carlow, the other at Browne's Hill with its incredible capstone weighing about 100 tons. Across the sea, Dyffryn Ardudwy is one of several cognate portal dolmens in north Wales. It contained, probably as secondary material, pottery closely related to that at Lough Gur (Lynch, 1969, 169; Powell, 1973, 46). However this is interpreted, and there is still dispute about the general date of portal dolmens, it does confirm the trans-marine connections between British and Irish people who 'may prove by virtue of their land and sea routes, and their stone

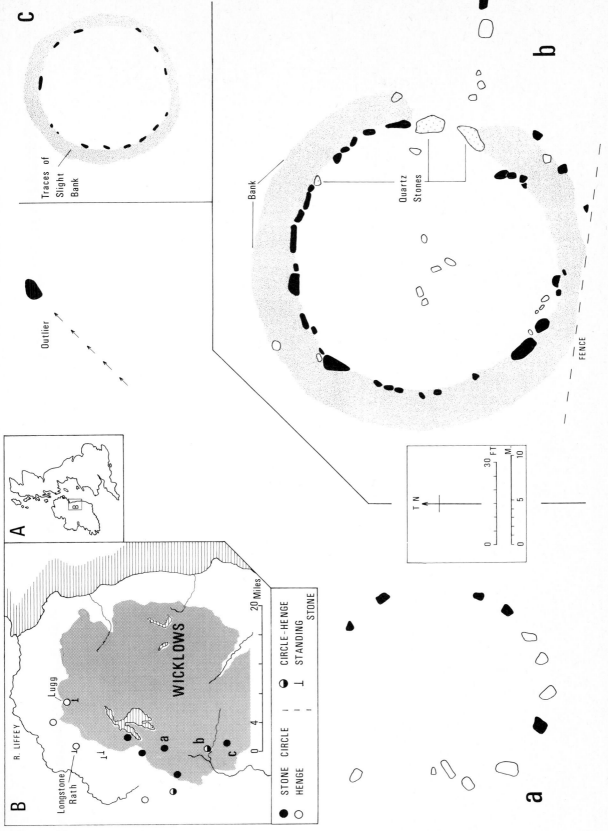

Fig. 41. Three Stone Circles in Wicklow. (a) Athgreany; (b) Castleruddery; (c) Boleycarrigeen. (a) and (c) after plans by J. Patrick.

industries, to have been more potent in the dissemination of ideas . . . than the material evidence from excavations can at present substantiate' (Powell, 1973, 38).

The Curragh seems to have been as much a cult centre in prehistoric times as the more famous Tara in Meath or Killycluggin, Cavan. Its great stones like Craddockstown, 4.4 m in height, or that at Longstone Rath with its cist and beaker bracer, or the monster at Punchestown, 7 m high with an empty cist at its foot, the second tallest standing stone in the British Isles after Rudston in Yorkshire, are matched in Carlow to the south by the pillars at Mullaghmast, Aghade or Ardristan, all with artificial grooves like others in Brittany. Their distribution along the Slaney from Wexford may indicate the approach taken by their builders.

There is an obvious distinction between earth and rock in the Wicklow plain. On the rich soils near the Bog of Allan there are henges with wide banks and deep ditches at Longstone Rath; at Lugg near Dublin with its rings; at Carbury where the sites seem late and atypical; and at the Curragh itself, now a racecourse, where there are at least two henges. Sites 4 (S. P. O'Riordain, 1950, 254), 33.5 m across with entrances at east and west, had a central oval pit in which it seemed a young woman had voluntarily been buried alive.

In contrast, the few stone circles are in the western foothills. Boleycarrigeen, the Griddle Stones, 14.0 m in diameter, near Baltinglass, stands in a north–south pass between the mountains, its twelve ragged slabs inside a low bank and seemingly graded, the tallest, 1.8 m high, to the east where a gap may indicate a rudimentary entrance. Further north is the shattered Tournant on its platform; the Piper's Stones in Kildare, ruined and overgrown with pines; Broadleas with its contiguous, low boulders; and the splendidly preserved Athgreany near Hollywood (Fig. 41), perfectly circular, 23.0 m in diameter—a length not related to the M.Y.—and perhaps originally of twenty-four ungraded stones placed on a hill-terrace. Like Boleycarrigeen the taller stones are on either side of an eastern gap making it likely that this was intended as an entrance. Two gnarled trees interrupt its circumference. To the north-east a lower outlier could point the expectant eye to a nearby hillside in which there is no notch, but more convincingly leads down to the river and the broad pass climbing to the Wicklow Gap and the long, narrow Glendalough, beautiful with its lakes, rocks and woods, that reaches the River Avonmore and the coast at Arklow.

Neither Boleycarrigeen's bank nor Athgreany's outlier are easily paralleled in this part of Ireland, and although lack of excavation, even of meticulous fieldwork, makes assumptions about these rings hazardous it is probable that they resulted from contacts with north-west Britain where, in Cumbria, stone circles with banks, outliers and entrances are also known.

One must travel almost a hundred miles north through passage-grave country before coming to Strangford Lough, Down, and the next open circles.

Pl. 26. *Athgreany (The Piper's Stones)*, *Wicklow*. From the south. The stones are of unshaped granite. The outlier is on the right of the middle ground. It is now fallen but even when erect was no more than 1.5 metres high, far too low for astronomical use, particularly against the mass of Slievecorragh Hill, 1379 ft (420 m) in height.

Here, by a good crossing of the Laggan, is a henge, the Giant's Ring (Collins, 1957), egg-shaped, its gravel bank revetted with boulders like the Lios, similarly unditched, and very like Mayburgh 120 miles to the east across the Irish Sea. Some miles south-east of the Giant's Ring is Castle Mahon stone circle, attractively placed on a mountainside near the coast with magnificent views down to the lough. It was excavated in 1953 (Collins, 1956).

It is an oval, 21.3 × 19.8 m, of lowish stones (Fig. 48), the broken stump at the WNW. having a pit by it with some slabs of shale, oak charcoal and nine indeterminate sherds of Western Neolithic pottery. Just touching the ring's centre a large, steep-sided pit had been reddened by a fierce fire of ashwood which had been extinguished by laying clean clay over it. People had then manoeuvred a large block, now prostrate, into the pit, resting it on four thin shale slabs before filling the pit with a mixture of loam and oak charcoal. Nearby, charcoal had been strewn thickly on the ground. The only bone in the ring was found in a neat cist just north of the fire-pit. Hazel charcoal lay around the intensely burned bones of a child. By it was a well-made flint plano-convex knife, also fire-burned.

To seek parallels for Castle Mahon in other stone circles one might look all over Britain. Cullerlie, Aberdeenshire, had a central fire-pit. Monzie, Perthshire, had a strong fire and tiny cist with an adult and a child. Reanascreena, the embanked RSC in Cork, had a central pit with a shale slab over a cremation, and this may reveal a little of the practices at Castle Mahon because it seems as though a central stone had been removed from the Cork pit. Several Cork RSCs have low centre stones, 76 cm high at Templebryan, 51 cm at Maulatanvalley. The pit at Reanascreena could have contained a similar one resting on the shale slab before being taken away and the cavity filled with earth and charcoal as the excavated section shows (Fahy, 1962, 61). At the centre of Croft Moraig, Perthshire, was 'a flat natural boulder, embedded in the old surface, and near it a shallow hollow . . . with a sparse scatter of comminuted charcoal in the filling, suggestive of a hearth' (Piggott and Simpson, 1971, 5). Over the much crossed Irish Sea, referred to by Mackinder as the British Mediterranean (Bowen, 1970, 20), the henge at Bryn Celli Ddu, Anglesey, also had a central pit whose filling had been 'put in around a central feature such as a stone or wooden post which was later withdrawn or which decayed' (C. O'Kelly, 1969, 27).

At Castle Mahon the large stone would have stood about 30 cm high originally and apparently aligned north–south. It was not removed but was pushed over by the people who had built the circle and lit the fire, and not long after these activities for there were no signs of silting around it. Then the pit was filled with charcoal from a different fire, perhaps at a different time of the year. Imagination allows a picture of fires in May when the ash trees came into leaf, the setting up of the stone, and then, months later, the burning of oak with its winter acorns, the toppling of the stone and the filling of the pit with scraped up earth and charcoal. Trees like the oak, the ash and hazel were venerated by the Celts many centuries later. The Atlantic distribution of centre stones has already been referred to as a practice that may reach back to early Neolithic times. At Castle Mahon the circle is almost certainly later but the Western Neolithic sherds by stone 5 may indicate a date no later than the early second millennium at a time when north and south-west Ireland were connected by the trade in copper ores.

The little cist at Castle Mahon may be an addition to the circle by food-vessel users. Such funerary vessels, which seem to combine characteristics from late beaker and indigenous late Neolithic pottery in England, were prolific in Yorkshire where a mixing of native and Dutch incomers might be expected. Users of this Early Bronze Age ware gradually opened up routes to the west through the Peak District and across the Pennines to the western coast down rivers like the Aire, Ribble, Mersey, Weaver and Conway. Increasingly they mixed with other groups: users of Irish bowls with their multiple-cist burials on hilltops; users of collared urns penetrating northwards along the Welsh coastlands. Food-vessel people put no rich repertoire of material possessions with their burials, though the plano-convex flint knife found at Castle Mahon was popular with them. So was cremation and cist burial in their later phases (Simpson, 1968, 202), often as an addition to a circle. Secondary food-vessel cremations have been discovered, *inter alia*, at Balbirnie, Fife (J. N. G. Ritchie, 1974b); at Dun Ruadh, Tyrone (Davies, 1936); at Gortcorbies ring, Londonderry (May, 1947); and at Mosley Height, Lancashire (Bennett, 1951), where the 12.8 circle near a prehistoric trackway had a primary cist burial with an early collared urn and then several later food-vessel cremations. By analogy the little cist with its burned hazelwood at Castle Mahon may not be part of the first planning of the stone ring.

The Irish Sea in the Neolithic and early second millennium was not a barrier but a trackway across which people travelled freely. Customs intertwined. Then, later, perhaps as the 'chiefdom' societies settled down in their small territories, the flux subsided.

It is true that in the Copper Age and Early Bronze Age *c.* 1900–1500 bc, the spread of specialized groups of 'beaker' ware and even, to some extent, of certain types of food-vessel, encourages us to believe in limited folk-movements, in either direction, across the Irish Channel. But increasingly we become aware of a process of regional consolidation which gives to the works of man which have survived an 'Irish' or a 'British' look, in other words, of cultural provinces which only marginally overlap with each other or with continental groups. By the end of the Early Bronze Age, Wales as a whole is part of a southern British province in which the 'collared' or 'overhanging-rim' cinerary urn predominates in complete contrast to Ireland, where nearly all the cinerary urns follow the 'food-vessel' or 'cordoned urn' traditions. The western sea-board of Britain now seems to become a frontier area, locally affected by maritime contracts, but not apparently crossed, from east or west, by major movements of population. (Savory, 1970, 38.)

Castle Mahon belongs to the earlier period and may be one of the last of the open rings that were built on the coasts around Cumbria from the third into the early second millennium bc.

The outer stone circle here, Ballynoe (Fig. 8), ten miles to the south-west, on the pleasant Lecale peninsula by Dumdrum Bay with its Neolithic remains, is probably much earlier for it is reminiscent of the very large stone rings of Cumbria, the meeting-places for dispersed groups of people. Ballynoe's low-lying position by a river is in agreement with this, as is its architecture. It is a rewarding site to visit in its sloping field with the dramatic peaks of the Mourne mountains to the south-west.

Pl. 27. *Ballynoe, Down*. From the east. This ring with its close-set stones of irregular height is very like some of those in Cumberland. Just discernible on the right is the entrance of double stones on the far side of the circle. Two outliers can be seen in the middle ground, right of centre.

It is a circle, perhaps slightly flattened at the north-west, with a diameter of some 33.5 m. Originally there may have been up to seventy stones in the ring, close-set and up to 1.8 m high, of glacial erratics which litter the slopes here. The tallest stones are at north and south with four more forming a double entrance at the WSW. (250°). There are two pairs of outliers angled from the circle at NNE. and SSW., the nearer of which in both cases is exactly ten M.Y. from the circumference. All these features: the large diameter, many stones, the north–south line, the entrance, the outliers, are 'Cumbrian' in style, very like Swinside 100 miles ESE. (28.7 m across, of close-set stones, tallest at north and south, and, at the SSE., double-portals which, like Ballynoe's, lead downhill). It is likely, therefore, that Ballynoe is one of the earlier circles. The discovery of a sherd of Carrowkeel Late Neolithic pottery (Case, 1961, 225) of passage-grave affinities from a cremation pocket inside the ring (Evans, 1966, 94) supports this for the pottery may postdate the construction of the circle. The ring was excavated in 1937-8. Unfortunately the work was never adequately published, nor will it ever be now, and it was left to Collins

Pl. 28. *Millin Bay*, *Down*. From the north showing the 'pulpit' in the forefront, open to the north and facing southwards into the D-shaped cairn with its long cist. Many of the stones here were decorated with cupmarks, pecked grooves and lines. A Neolithic field-wall runs along the axis of this strange monument.

and Waterman (1955) to accumulate what information they could about this important and complex site.

Eccentrically placed to the east inside the ring is a kerbed mound covering a cairn with cists at its east and, possibly, at its west. Outside the cairn but under the mound were several stone balls or betyls. The mound in many ways is like another at Millin Bay seventeen miles to the north-east by the sea (Collins and Waterman, 1955) in which a cairn-covered long cist was surrounded by an irregular oval bank lined with contiguous stones, some of which were decorated with motifs like those in the Loughcrew passage-grave cemetery. The whole monument had been built over a field-wall, possibly Neolithic, like another group of stone circles at Beaghmore, Tyrone (May, 1953). The construction of Millin Bay, if not its shape, and its underlying wall recall the Lios. It has connections with the ring-cairns of north Britain.

In the long cist there were the disarticulated bones of about sixteen individuals of whom up to twelve were children. Care had been taken to stack skulls and long bones neatly, even to the extent of replacing teeth in their sockets—sometimes wrongly. Millin Bay is a good example of a monument in which the connection between death and ritualism in the prehistoric mind is manifest. Although it contained nothing—except some unstratified Carrowkeel ware—that could accurately be dated it has affinities with the cairn at Old Parks, Kirkoswald, Cumberland (Ferguson, 1895), and, more vaguely, with Balnabraid cairn, Argyll (J. N. G. Ritchie, 1967), both with material of the mid-second millennium. If Millin Bay is of the same chronological horizon it might once again emphasize the variety of contact around the Irish Sea at this time.

It cannot be absolutely certain at Ballynoe that the mound-kerb was contemporary with the mound itself. It may be earlier. It is now horseshoe-shaped and open to the WSW. Outside it near the entrance is an opposing arc of six stones. There is a similar construction at Millin Bay which incorporates a pulpit-like structure facing south (Collins and Waterman, 1955, 18), and there is at least one other stone ring in which an arc had no connecting cairn. At Croft Moraig, Perthshire, (Piggott and Simpson, 1971, 7), an arc of three stones may have stood to the south-west of the stone horseshoe. Although the purpose of such settings is unknown there may be a connection between them and the discontinuous façade outside the northern timber ring at the south-west at Durrington Walls, Wilts. (Wainwright and Longworth, 1971, 43) and which is linked to an avenue of posts in the same relationship as Ballynoe's entrance is to its arc. Hypothetically the arc and the stone horseshoe could be early features to which the cairn and mound were added later, perhaps by people of passage-grave origins.

4. NEW GRANGE
Looking southwards from Down the stone circle around New Grange, Meath, may provide clues to the nature of the small circles in Ulster to be

described next. Circles of standing stones around chambered tombs are rare in the British Isles except for the Clava cairns of Inverness. In Ireland there is another small and scattered group within the area of passage-graves. The best-known site is New Grange, the magnificent chambered tomb in the prehistoric necropolis on the bend of the River Boyne. Good descriptions appear in Daniel and O'Riordain (1964), and C. O'Kelly (1971).

This tomb with its finely decorated kerbstones and passage originally stood inside a circle of about thirty-five stones though now only twelve survive. The circle itself, slightly flattened at the south-east, was about 103.6 m in diameter (125 M.Y.). The shape of the mound inside is still uncertain but it is deeply flattened at the south-east where the entrance is aligned exactly on the midwinter sunrise (Patrick, 1974). Hicks (R.E., 1975, 195) has speculated that the etymology of New Grange is *An Uamh Greine*, the 'Cave of the Sun', from *grian*, 'the sun', and remarks that Grange Townland in Limerick, in which the Lios stands may have a similar origin, and that 'a line from the Grange circle to the peak of the hill identified . . . as Cnoc Greine yields a sunrise alignment at or very near Beltaine' (ibid, 196). It is relevant, therefore, that the four small satellite passage-graves around New Grange also face towards the south-east, the ruined chamber of one containing a stone basin with a rayed circle chiselled on it like a sun-pattern facing down the passage towards the midwinter sunrise, further evidence of the association of the sun and death in the mind of prehistoric man.

At New Grange neither the sides nor the bases of the circle-stones were 'dressed'. They are massive, rough blocks, mainly of local stone. Four remain outside the entrance, the tallest about 2.4 m high. Virtually all the stone for New Grange could have been collected within ten miles but some of the circle-stones were syenite, the nearest source of which is close to Pomeroy sixty miles north. If they were dragged from there, rather than moved glacially, the efforts of these early wheat-growing peasants must be ranked with the later chieftains of Stonehenge whose sarsens, though larger, were much closer.

Although excavations have taken place by some of the circle-stones (O'Riordain and O'hEochaidhe, 1956) there were no datable finds. Within the tomb, however, burnt material provided three C-14 determinations of 2585 bc $\pm$ 105 (UB-361); 2475 bc $\pm$ 45 (GrN-5462); and 2465 bc $\pm$ 40 (GrN-5463), approximately equivalent to 3300 BC. Though it is difficult to prove that the stone circle is contemporary with the passage-grave yet supporting the belief that it is not later than the mound, O'Riordain's excavations revealed that although cairn material had soon slipped down the monument's sides and had reached the north-east stone none of the slip was found beneath the stone or in its socket. Equally, it appears that both mound and circle share a common centre. Conversely, it has been argued that circle and tomb are of different periods because of the lack of Boyne art on the circle-stones, although the north-east stone did have a line of cupmarks along its base. But such passage-grave art rarely exists in any circle in the British Isles, and at New

Grange it may be assumed that the ornamented kerbs had a function different from those of the outer circle which fenced them off from the world outside. A stone circle is supposed to have existed around the 'temple' at Stanydale, Shetland (Calder, 1950, 198), again probably as a demarcation. It seems likely that New Grange's outer circle is no later than the passage-grave and therefore the earliest stone ring yet recognised.

If it is indeed very early it is strange that similar sites in Ireland are uncommon. One possibility is that the passage-grave was deliberately built inside a stone ring which already stood by the Boyne alongside this first stretch of non-tidal water. There are also nine or ten henges here which could be analogous rings and evidence of pre-tomb settlement but these have yet to be dated. The antipathy of passage-grave builders to open rings could have inhibited the building of further circles. There does seem to be a distribution inland to the north and west of encircled burials, a distribution that follows the lowland routes towards Loughcrew, Carrowkeel and Carrowmore passage-grave cemeteries. Stone circles surround the chambered tombs of Killin, Louth, and Ballybrolly, Armagh, and the possible passage-grave of Killycluggin, Cavan. They surround the Vicar's Cairn, Armagh, and Druid's Temple cairn, Fermanagh. Just as the average diameters of passage-graves diminished from east to west in Ireland (Piggott, 1954, 194) so the diameter of the encircled mounds decreases the further inland they are found, making it probable that the circles do not precede the cairns. None of the rings seems to be early and New Grange remains unique, isolated from the remainder of the stone circles of the British Isles, one of the finest chambered tombs in western Europe. It is in total contrast to the little, ditched and embanked cairns around Kilnavert, Cavan (Paterson, Gaffikin and Davies, 1938, 149), some standing against small stone rings (Davies, 1938, 112).

5. NORTHERN IRELAND

Over 110 stone circles of the Bronze Age are known on northern Ireland, mainly in Ulster. Unlike the distribution of the earlier Mesolithic and Neolithic occupation sites and tombs there, they were built not in the northeastern counties like Antrim but around the central Sperrin mountains, on the hillsides some 500 ft or more above sea-level. If their construction is to be attributed to incomers then these probably approached from the north from Lough Foyle and through the Butterlope Glen into the rising, rounded countryside, much of it now peat-covered, of Tyrone and Londonderry, an infiltration by people seeking land in this largely undeveloped part of Ireland. It was not until the Late Neolithic that there was much settlement here (Case, 1969, 18), but during the first half of the second millennium many different groups arrived, early and late beaker-users from south-west Scotland (Clarke, 1970, 75, 182); from North Wales (ibid, 228); makers of northern English food-vessels (ApSimon, 1969, 38); of native Irish bowls (ibid, 36); and even some collared-urn people from the east and south whose custom of urned cremations seems to have been adopted by the food-vessel group. 'Short sea crossings made Ulster . . . the region where intrusive elements were strongest and the region where fusion with native elements produced distinctly insular cultures'. (ibid. 57.) The presence of the indigenous Neolithic court-cairns in Tyrone, like Legland or Clady Halliday with its Sandhills pottery, to the south of the circle areas shows how such blending of native and intrusive beliefs might have occurred.

This is clearly true of the stone circles whose architecture displays a mixture of sources. Often they were built on protected southern slopes, on a small plateau or terrace. They tend to be grouped about five miles apart in little territories above the dense forests of the lowland plain. Useful studies of them appear in O. Davies (1939a) and Chart (1940). In general, these rings of low stones are small, averaging only 10.7 m across, some so little that a healthy sheep could leap them. Over half are in pairs or in clusters of three or four particularly in Tyrone where nineteen such groups occur. In this they are similar to the later Cumbrian sites of White Moss or Moor Divock; to Drizzlecombe and others on Dartmoor; to the Arran complex on Machrie Moor; and to Welsh pairs like Nant Tarw, small in size and presumably of the later second millennium. But unlike any other region of the British Isles many of these Ulster sites were composed of many stones, 41 per cent of the inland rings having forty-five or more close-set stones whereas in other areas of stone circles it is quite unusual to find a ring with more than twenty stones. Such a dissimilarity suggests a possible development from the low and numerous contiguous kerbstones of passage-graves and cairns. The resultant rings are irregular and unmegalithic. Many remain unknown under the creeping peat and it is likely that a complete map of their distribution would explain much about land-use and territorial patterns in the mid and late Bronze Age in northern Ireland.

As could be expected, many are associated with cairns or cists. Twenty or more are very close to megalithic tombs or round mounds, and sixteen rings are known to have burials in them. Showing the diversity of influence in the Sperrins, in the north, there are at least eight concentric rings like Owenreagh or Ballyholly. Yet others, like Aghalane, have centre stones. Two in Tyrone have pronounced entrances. Such a variety of architecture emphasizes the mixed traditions here. It is the stone row, however, that distinguishes these Irish sites. A number, especially in the eastern Sperrins, have single lines of stones that join the ring tangentially. Others like Knockna-horna have truncated avenues, tangential at Davagh Lower, splayed at Beaghmore, leading to cairns like those in Dartmoor and Caithness.

A few rows joined to circles consist of three tall stones. These are rare in the western Sperrins, more common in the central regions where one of the three circles at Tremoge has three enormous slabs lying by it, and another nearby has three small stones in a line 7.6 m away (Chart, 1940, 238). Towards the east coast such three-stone settings stand as isolated monuments with

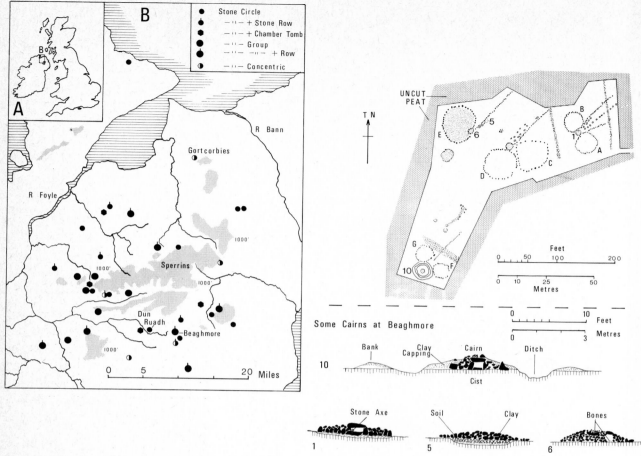

Fig. 42. The Complex of Stone Circles at Beaghmore, Tyrone.

no circle at all, a fact that implies an independent origin for these lines. Three, Tomagrough, Kilgreel and West Division, are within a few miles of Belfast Lough and less than eighty miles along the North Channel from Ballachroy, Argyll. This three-stone row has been interpreted as a solar observatory (Thom, 1967, 151; 1971, 36), although MacKie (1974, 177), whilst agreeing with the major alignments here, has pointed out the hazards of uncritical acceptance of other 'sightlines' that a cairn, now vanished, would have blocked. Quite possibly the Irish triple stones are culturally related to Ballachroy and it would be illuminating to make astronomical analyses of them. Thom's date of c.1800 BC (c.1575 bc) for the Scottish stones fits quite well with the postulated second millennium dates for the Belfast rows. The little rings, farther inland, seem to be of that period.

Amongst the Sperrins, part heather, part grass, sombre expanses of boggy upland thick with peat, one comes almost by accident on the circles, un-obtrusive even when they stand by roadsides like the diminutive rings at

Pl. 29. *Beaghmore, Tyrone.* From the east. The depth and extent of the peat-cover is apparent in this aerial photograph. Two Neolithic field-walls are just detectable running north-south below the near and middle pairs of rings.

Aughlish in Londonderry, one a concentric with tall stones at north and south, others with tangential alignments; or Corick, ten miles south-east near a ford where five more circles, a huge centre stone, alignments and a ruined chambered tomb huddle by the river bank; or Cavancarragh in Fermanagh where peat-cutting has exposed a 6.1 m ring and a tangential double row, very like some in Dartmoor, that passes by the circle and by two wrecked round cairns from which food-vessels and cremations were extracted in the nineteenth century.

Probably the best known of these complexes is Beaghmore, Tyrone (Fig. 42). It is also one of the most enigmatic, its interrelated circles, cairns and rows having no obvious pattern. Once buried beneath peat, the site was half uncovered in 1945-9 (May, 1953) and 1269 stones revealed. Further work was undertaken in 1965 (Pilcher, 1969). It is now known that the monuments were built on a terrace of light, sandy soil that overlooked a wide, tree-topped valley to the north-west whose river ultimately flowed into the Foyle and the sea thirty miles to the north. It is a region of circles. Nearby are the rings of Davagh, the Evishbracks and, just to the west, the multi-phase ring-cairn of Dun Ruadh.

Some of the stone rows at Beaghmore pass over straight stretches of stony rubble that could be the collapsed walls of Neolithic fields. That agriculture took place here was shown by pollen analysis (Pilcher, 1969, 89). Around 3250 bc clearances for cereal cultivation were made in the heavy forest of pine, oak, birch and hazel by people using carinated Neolithic pottery, some of which had been brushed smooth inside, maybe with rush leaves. These farmers apparently performed their ceremonies in a type of Goodland site, burying pottery and charcoal in shallow pits in the clearing they had made. Gradually agriculture gave way to pastoralism. Early in the third millennium the people went away and the land reverted to forest. Over the centuries the climate became drier and by 2000 bc heaths had replaced much of the wood-land although, already, peat was forming on the ill-drained uplands whose impoverished soils supported only bog-mosses like the yellow sphagnum, cotton-sedge and slender shoots of heather. By 800 bc peat was everywhere, glistening with pools left by the grey rains, its dying vegetation piling up against the stones of rows and circles built on the preceding Bronze Age heathlands.

At Beaghmore, the moor of birches, there are isolated cairns, three pairs of circles associated with cairns and rows; and a single circle, also with cairn and row. May's plan (1953) has the rare archaeological virtue of showing True North and it is noticeable that four of the long rows extend towards the cairns at 223° (declinations −25.0° to −25.9°), astronomically un-related to sun, moon, Venus or even megalithic calendar. The rows, 19.5 m to 25.6 m long, are of little stones but have much shorter rows of tall stones beside them. Whereas the rows lead directly to the cairns the circles are tangential to their ends and it is very possible that the rings were built alongside earlier cairn-rows.

At the east of the site four splayed rows reach up the slope to a cairn whose cist contained a Group IX porcellanite axe. Rings A and B, 11.9 × 9.6 m and 10.0 × 9.8 m, flank the cairn. Thirty-seven metres west are the two biggest rings, C and D, with formal diameters of 16.0 m but both irregular. Ring D touches a cisted cairn with two rows of stones. Ring C looks as though it had been erected during a dark midwinter night it is so buckled at north-east and south-west. It is 17.1 × 15.9 m in diameter and its eccentricities are deliberate. At the north-east its stones curve out to encompass a flat natural stone. At the south-west it has a convex alcove of three circle-stones set on a bank of small pebbles. Below the circle floor here were pits with hearths, charcoal, flint and broken pottery, the remains of a Goodland site part of which was incorporated in the later ring.

To the north-west, 23 metres away, is another little cairn, only 3.1 m across, with the usual long and short rows. In it was a miniature corbelled cist with a cremation. On top of this were the remains of vegetation gathered from the nearby peat bog: fungus, moss and some birch twigs. A flagstone had been placed on this, and on the stone were the cremated fragments of a skull. Such a separation of skull from body was noticed in an urned cremation in a round barrow at Winterbourne Steepleton 4A, Dorset (Grinsell, 1959, 155), and at Sutton 268, Glamorgan (C. Fox, 1959, 100), also of the Middle Bronze Age.

Circle E at Beaghmore absorbs this cairn like an amoeba ingesting. Unlike the other rings it is megalithic for some of its stones are chest-high. The interior of the ring is embedded like a fakir's bed of nails with 884 upright sharpish stones. Nearby is a cairn 2.4 m across in which an oak stem has been deposited in a pit, a practice very much akin to the branches sometimes found in Celtic ritual shafts, strengthening the supposition that the Celts 'were carrying on and elaborating a tradition which had its roots in Bronze Age Britain and, perhaps, in the entire early Indo-European world' (Ross, 1968, 279).

Eighty metres to the SSW. is the last excavated pair of rings although others probably remain peat-hidden on either side of the country road. Here the cairn has a bank and inner ditch. Soil under the cairn yielded a C-14 determination of 1535 bc ± 55 (UB-11). Peat that filled the ditch provided an assay of 775 bc ± 55 (UB-163). The cairn's construction should lie between the two dates, perhaps closer to the former. This is indirectly confirmed by the discovery of a deposit of patinated flints 1.2 m from the end of the cairn's single row (Pilcher, 1969, 80). These had been stuck upright in the soil beneath the peat, the soil being dated to 1605 bc ± 45 (UB-23). If they were contemporary with the row and the row with the cairn then the latter might have been built around 1575 bc.

Both the north-west and south-east rings here, F and G, respect the cairn's ditch. Circle G has an apparent entrance of tall stones at its south-east, but these may be the adapted remains of the customary short row of tall stones otherwise absent here.

The Beaghmore complex has been described in some detail because it demonstrates the intricacies of these later sites. It seems unlikely that the cairns, rows and circles were a unitary design, and several stages of construction can be visualized culminating in the erection of the rings. Similar multiphase monuments have been postulated for Dartmoor where the circles belong to the same general period in the later second millennium, and where the practices also not only reached back to the Neolithic but foreshadowed others of the Iron Age.

Mysteries exist at Beaghmore. The rings, at first inspection merely irregular and quite unimpressive, possess alcoves or recesses like those at the Stripple Stones, Cornwall. That in circle C has been mentioned. It does not fit the geometry of egg-shapes (Thom, 1967, 29). There is a distinct alcove 2.1 m deep at the south-west. There are others at all the rings except E. They may have been recesses for the officiating 'priest' or shaman, but overall they do not appear to contain astronomical alignments, nor are the ring-diameters related to the Megalithic Yard (Table 9). If they were not for some scientific purpose such as astronomical observations then the alcoves may never be satisfactorily explained. As well as the Stripple Stones, others are known at the earthwork of Durrington Walls, spacious and irregular, and at the Amesbury barrow, Wiltshire. A cairn by Drumskinny circle, Fermanagh, thirty miles west of Beaghmore also has an apse.

Excavated in 1962 (Waterman, 1964) this circle of rough stones, 14.0 × 13.0 m, is in a fenced corral through which hens scuttle, some of its stones deep in the reed grass of the scrubby field (Fig. 48). It could not be dated. One small sherd of Western Neolithic ware lay near the east stone. Otherwise, only crudely made flints were found. Even the cairn at the WNW. had no deposits, nor did the row of low stones that led to the cairn from the SSE. But the cairn did have a diminutive oval setting of upright stones at its centre and a pronounced alcove by its WNW. kerbstones at an azimuth of 290°. Like those at Beaghmore this has no obvious purpose. It does, however, provide an oblique method of dating Drumskinny. A very similar cairn was excavated at Wind Hill, Lancashire (Tyson, 1972), across the Irish Sea, 10.4 m in diameter, with an alcove at its east and an oval stone setting at its centre. Two cremations were found, and a flint scraper and knife, a pebble hammer, and a V-perforated lignite button, a typical beaker collection around 1600 bc. In the same way the complicated platform-cairn, Brenig 51, Merioneth, had a semi-circular cairn which held a collared urn added at its north-east (Lynch and Allen, 1975, 8). A C-14 assay of 1470 ± 70 bc (H-802) is not far in time from Wind Hill, and if Drumskinny is of the same period it has a similar chronological horizon to Beaghmore.

Table 9. *Diameters and Azimuths at Beaghmore, Tyrone*

Site	Diam.	M.Y. ?	Error in M.Y. (Metres)	Azimuth (Alcove)	Declinations		Astronomical Alignment ?
					0° Alt.	1° Alt.	
A	11.9 × 9.6	14 × 12	+0.35 × −0.42	243°	−15°12′	−14°21′	—
B	10.0 × 9.8	12 × 12	+0·06 × −0.18	206°	−31°17′	−30°20′	31°6′ = Venus, midsummer set
C	17.1 × 15.9	21 × 19	−0.37 × +0.18	227°	−23°13′	−22°19′	−23°9′ = midwinter sunset
D	16.8 × 16.2	20 × 20	+0.27 × −0.46	244°	−14°40′	−13°50′	—
E	19.5 × 16.8	24 × 20	−0.48 × +0.27	—	—	—	—
F	8.5	10	+0.25	293°	+13°03′	+13°53′	—
G	9.8	12	−0.18	227°	−23°13′	−22°19′	−23°9′ = midwinter sunset

Such alcoves are unlikely to be the results of careless building for they are quite regular. They remain as difficult to explain as the problem of the contemporaneity of circles and cairns in Ulster. At Gortcorbies, Londonderry, close to the mouth of the Bann, a concentric circle, 13.4 m across with its tallest stone at the E, had a central cist with hazel, willow and oak charcoal in it that had been set in a heavily burned layer within the inner ring (May, 1947). A cairn, with a food-vessel and a N/NR beaker, and quartz pebbles overlay the circle at the east and was clearly secondary to it. A time around 1700 bc would not be inappropriate. But the relationship of the circle to a large cairn 27 m south-west is uncertain.

A similar conflation of different monuments may be seen at Clogherny Meenerrigal, Tyrone (O. Davies, 1939b, 36). Here seventeen tallish stones set in rough paving had been arranged in a 18.3 m circle around a wedge-grave in a round cairn. A quarter of a mile to the east on a mountain shelf above Butterlope Glen is another circle, 12.2 m across, of well-spaced up-rights. This had a nearly central posthole (ibid, 40). Other pits were empty but hazel charcoal seemed to have been scattered about the interior. At the ENE. was a fallen outlier with white pebbles lying by it.

Although there is a common pattern of cremation, of charcoal and of burnt areas in these circles it would be rash to claim any close cultural links between them. The underlying similarity is very much modified by local practices. This applies also to the further question of paired sites. At least ten associated circles are recorded in Tyrone, always with a related cairn. In this they differ from the Perthshire eight-stone pairs. The Ulster rings have many more stones and average 11.6 m across against the Scottish 7.3 m. What 'burials' the Perthshire rings have are in pits rather than under mounds. But the paired circles at White Moss and at Low Longrigg, Cumberland, have cairns albeit these are inside the rings rather than alongside it. Thom has suggested that a pair of circles might provide a sightline from centre to centre towards some celestial event and he lists several monuments where such a possibility exists (Thom, 1967, 97ff): (Table 10). It is surprising how many of these have solar alignments but it must be remembered that there are many other paired sites, not included in this list, where there is no orientation on the sun. The non-solar exception in Table 10, Glenquicken, may be irrelevant because the second circle has long since been destroyed (RCAHM-S, 1914, No. 292) so that Thom's line from it is figurative.

Despite Table 10 the centroid lines at Beaghmore are not astronomically persuasive. Only from rings F–G is there a major solar orientation. Regrettably there has been little investigation of the centres of these rings so that it is not known whether there were posts or other sighting-devices there, but in Circle C it seems there were not (May, 1953, 196), a fact that diminishes any astronomical possibility. Certainly the axial lines differ from pair to pair. At present it is arguable that two rings were needed for complementary activities, hinted at in the paving beneath the north and middle circles at the

Thom's Number	Site	County	Azimuth	Alignment
B3/3	Raedykes	Kincardine	314°	Sun
G4/12	Glenquickan	Kirkcud--bright	116° 7′	Antares, 1860 BC. But second circle gone.
G7/4	Loupin¹ Stanes	Dumfries	306°	Sun
L1/6 D–C	White Moss	Cumberland	243°	Sun
L1/6 C–D	White Moss	Cumberland	63° 6′	Moon
P1/14	Tullybeagles	Perthshire	264°	Sun
P2/8	Shian Bank	Perthshire	317°	Sun
W11/4	Nant Tarw	Brecknocks.	295°	Sun
W11/2	Trecastle Mt	Brecknocks.	53°	Sun

Table 10. Azimuths of Paired Stone Circles, Centre to Centre

Hurlers in Cornwall. The Beaghmore complex remains an enigma. Yet its date is quite well established, and its paired circles, their concomitant cairns, the avenues, the 'entrance' of ring G, these are all features to be found among the later circles of Cumbria, and it may be in that region that the ceremonies enacted in these Ulster rings first evolved. If such a continuity did exist it could explain the discovery of stone axes at several sites, a hammerstone at Gortcorbies, at Wind Hill, the Tievebulliagh axe from the cairn at Beaghmore. Five others, four of them Group IX, came from the neighbourhood of the circles. It is possible that these artefacts reveal an enduring axe-cult whose origins were discussed earlier.

In parallel, the unusual ring at Kiltierney, Fermanagh, not far from Lough Erne, could be related to the Scottish RSC tradition (Chart, 1940, 146; Burl, 1974b, 31). The association is not at all certain but this 11.1 × 10.2 m oval stands on a raised platform, has a cupmarked pillar at its ESE., and a re-cumbent-looking stone flanked by taller pillars at its WNW. Kiltierney, standing close to a crowd of little cairns and a larger banked barrow with megalithic art indicates some of the intermixing of traditions in northern Ireland during the early second millennium. But it is at Dun Ruadh, Tyrone, not four miles west of Beaghmore, beneath the stone-scattered Crockneill Hill near the Owenkillew that these incoming beliefs were unequivocally conflated, custom following custom at the same site, the last builders totally altering the previous structure (O. Davies, 1936).

As at Beaghmore it seems that there was a Neolithic Goodland 'sanctuary' here. The excavators found many stone-filled pits with charcoal, flints and Neolithic sherds, some in the Ballymarlagh style of north-east Ireland. Upon this simple site a henge was built in the centuries close to 2000 bc, its inner ditch providing the yellow clay for an oval bank 53.0 × 46.3 m, whose outer edge was vertically revetted with stakes. There was an entrance at the SSW., a rather unusual bearing for henges most of which favour NNW. and SSE. if double-entrances, north-west, north-east or south-east if Class I (Atkinson, Piggott and Sandars, 1951, 86), but there are exceptions. As well as two of the Priddy rings with timber-revetted walls (Tratman, 1967, 104) there are several smaller henges around the Irish Sea coasts that do have entrances in their south-west quadrants (Burl, 1969, 9). Most of these are in Wales or Cornwall. Another, Ballymeanoch, Kilmartin, is in the same Argyll valley as Temple Wood circle which has some resemblance to Gortcorbies, twenty-five miles north of Dun Ruadh. Interconnections between Scotland and Ireland in the earlier second millennium provide the cultural background to some of the northern Irish rings, and the henge at Dun Ruadh may be of the same general period as Ballymeanoch which must predate its secondary N3 beaker burial of the seventeenth century bc. And recent work has revealed that many Irish henges, of a later period than most of those in Britain, are orientated ENE.– WSW (Hicks, R. E., 1975, 98).

It was food-vessel people who caused the final changes at Dun Ruadh. Either with the wish to destroy the open central space or because they wished to use this 'sanctified' area for quite different purposes they erected an off-centre 10.4 × 9.1 m ring of thin, irregular stones connected by drystone walling. Two other stones formed an approach at the SSW. aligned on the henge entrance. Rectangular cists were placed seemingly at random around these stones, some with cremations, some with native bowl food-vessels, one with a Hiberno-Scottish food-vessel common on both sides of the North Channel (ApSimon, 1969, 40). All this was eventually covered with a 2.1 m high ring-cairn with a paved passage and cobbled centre. Bronze Age cemetery mounds of various kinds are well known in Ireland (Waddell, 1970, 101) and seem to have the same underlying sepulchral function as the flat multiple cemeteries of the Middle Bronze Age in Britain, although the ceremonies that preceded the raising of the cairn and which continued in its central space were perhaps connected to those of the simpler stone circles of Northern Ireland. The increasing regionalization of society at this time makes it easier to acknowledge local idiosyncrasies than to perceive any cohesive national religious belief.

Even in one group there is evidence of several opposing traditions. At Castledamph overlooking the low Glenelly valley in Tyrone there are two contiguous circles whose stones are especially tall where the circles touch, a feature duplicated only at Er Lannic in Brittany. A hundred metres south-east is a ruined concentric circle of which there are examples in south-west Scotland, in the Hebrides and in Cumbria, but which were also common in Wessex. Just to the west is a 23 m long line of big stones like a Dartmoor row. Like them it marches uphill to a cairn. The line is almost exactly north–

south and has a subsidiary parallel row of lower stones. This may have re-placed an earlier timber row, for excavation revealed three deep pits very like postholes alongside it (O. Davies, 1938). The north end of the stone row touched the circumference of a 19.8 m concentric circle around the cairn. The 4.6 m space between the rings of low stones was set with cobbles as though for participants to move or dance around the central space with its 3.7 m ditched cairn whose cist held the cremated bones of an eighteen-year old youth. A cupmarked stone nearby may have been the cist cover.

Such 'paving' or 'floor' has been claimed in several Lancastrian and south Cumbrian rings like Bleaberry Haws, only 5.2 × 4.0 m, which was dug into in the absence of the excavator (Cowper, 1893, 419). The interior was covered with cobbles. A cairn stood nearby. At Mosley Height (Bennett, 1951) there was rough paving over pits and cists with cremations and Bronze Age Pennine urns. A little circle at the centre held the primary burial of a young woman. A more positive concentric circle, the Druids Circle, Birkrigg Common (W. G. Atkinson, 1922) had similar cobbling. Cremations, one with an early urn, were found in the inner ring. By them were some lumps of red ochre perhaps used for body-painting.

It is remarkable how many concentric circles have such a layer of stones. The 'Stonehenge layer' of bluestone and other chippings may be an analogous 'floor' though this is disputable (R. J. C. Atkinson, 1960, 64). From south-west Scotland, another region that affected northern Ireland, at the con-centric circle on Machrie Moor, Arran, 'under the thin sward we found a complete floor of stones, of various sizes, mostly small, but placed without any such arrangement as would be found in a pavement . . .' (J. Bryce, 1862, 509). At Temple Wood, Argyll, the surface of the circle was covered with a layer of boulders 15–23 cm in thickness. Thus whereas at Castledamph the penannular cobbling might have been for ceremonial movements it seems generally that these layers were no more suitable for such an activity than the spiky setting inside Beaghmore E and might be better interpreted as coverings for the sealed, burned layers and multiple pits, cists and cremations so wide-spread in Middle Bronze Age Britain.

Far to the west from Castledamph, miles from any other circle, is Beltany Tops, Donegal, as idiosyncratic a ring as any in the north. In the flat land south of Raphoe is an isolated hill. Its summit has been flattened to make a wide boulder-littered platform edged with a ring of contiguous stones that hardly project above the platform. One 2.7 m tall pillar at the WSW. by an alcove faces a triangular stone at the ENE. whose inner surface is covered with cup-marks. It has been thought that these stones define an orientation on sunrise in early May, the time of Beltane, and that there is another alignment, this time on midwinter sunrise, between a tall circle-stone at the north-west and an outlier 20.4 m away from the ring at the south-east (Somerville, 1923, 212). Quite what Beltany is is unclear. Unscientific digging has left it in appalling confusion. It has been thought to be a despoiled cairn (E. Evans, 1966, 85).

Two stone axes, one from Tievebulliagh, have been found near it but no finds have come from its mutilated interior except a Celtic stone head (Ross, 1967, 115). The recital of such a combination of stone ring and cairn, of astronomy, of Neolithic and Iron Age artefacts (or ritual objects) creates a fittingly inconclusive epilogue to the description of the stone circles of northern Ireland.

CHAPTER EIGHT

The Stone Circles of Wales

Mr. Camden much studied the Welch language, and kept a Welch servant to improve him in the language, for the better understanding of our Antiquities.

John Aubrey

1. INTRODUCTION

Whereas Ireland contains over a quarter of the megalithic rings and Scotland has almost half, Wales has only about 5 per cent of the circles of the British Isles, not fifty rings, few of which are to be compared with the great circles of Cumberland or Ireland. Nor do they show innovations but, in general, derive their features from outside sources. The ridges of mountains, the swift rivers, the steep, dead-ended valleys imposed here on prehistoric man a pattern of dispersed, semi-isolated occupation where conservatism was normal. Some megalithic rings like Banc Du in Radnor, (Powys[1]) perhaps the highest stone circle of the British Isles, lie desolate under moorland winds far from pass or major river in parts where few strangers ever came. Others like Pennybridge or Penbedw Park or Pen y Wern stood alongside trackways and their architecture mirrors the fashion of the countries from which people travelled: outlying stones common in the circles of western Britain; avenues, perhaps from Wessex sources; centre stones; and circles built inside the unditched banks of the west coast. Good studies of these Welsh megalithic rings appear in Allcroft (1927, I, 233–44) and Grimes (1963).

Most of them were small. The largest at Ffridd Newydd, Merioneth (Gwynedd), is only 50.6 m in diameter. The average is just over 18.6 m, rings of low stones set up in non-circular designs of ovals or eggs that concentrate in five main areas: Pembrokeshire (south-west Dyfed); Merioneth (Gwynedd) on the west coast; the mountains of Mynydd Eppynt in central Wales; the Shropshire border on the east; and the north coast of Caernarvon (Gwynedd) where several Bronze Age rings were built near the Neolithic axe factory at Penmaenmawr and the Llandegai henges.

In four of these areas the circle-builders were occupying regions settled in the Neolithic, for megalithic tombs existed here whether long mounds like Pipton in the Mynydd Eppynt, the elaborated Dyffryn Ardudwy in Merioneth (Gwynedd) or Capel Garmon in the north, or portal dolmens in south-west

---

[1]Because of the rapid adoption of the new County names in Wales these have been added in parentheses wherever an old County is mentioned in this chapter.

Wales. It is only in Shropshire that such tombs are not to be found and even here there was Neolithic settlement on the Breiddyn Hill.

2. SOUTH-WEST WALES

The open oak forests of the south Welsh coast had attracted crop-growers and pastoralists early in the third millennium (Webley, 1969) as chambered tombs like Tinkinswood near Cardiff or the Nevern group of portal dolmens like Pentre Ifan near Cardigan show. Beneath an Iron Age hillfort at Coygan Camp, Carmarthen Bay, lay remains of a settlement dated to 3050 bc ±95 (NPL-132); and timber houses of the Neolithic period at Mount Pleasant, Glamorgan, or Clegyr Boia, Pembroke (Dyfed), or a stopover trading-post on the sand-dunes at Merthyr Mawr Warren near Porthcawl with broken polished axes from at least four axe factories tell the same story of Neolithic land-use and sea-trade along this quiet and lovely coastline. An axe-flake of rhyolitic tuff from the factory at Ramsey Island, Pembroke (Dyfed) (Group VIII) at the extreme south-west tip of Wales, discovered at Coygan, suggests an early date for the exploitation of this source. Another more famous site of a later period is Carn Meini (Group XIII) in the Preseli mountains with its spotted dolerite used not only for the axes and axe-hammers that were for a short while bartered in south-west Wales and Wessex but also for the celebrated bluestones of Stonehenge's second phase. From the calm of Milford Haven, described by Nelson as the best natural harbour in the world after Ceylon's Trincomalee, the stones could have been safely shipped along the coast through the erratic tidal waters off Barry and then inland along the Bristol Avon.

Yet despite this millennium of activity there are few circles or henges here, one little group near the Preselis, and perhaps four other sites recorded along the 100 miles of coast. In the far west was Pennybridge, destroyed in 1918, alongside a Pembrokeshire (Dyfed) trackway near the great barrow-cemetery of Dry Burrows. In south-east Wales is Grey Hill in Monmouth (Gwent), a dubious small ring on a bracken-covered moorland with a tall outlier to its north-west. Between, there is only Mynydd y Gelli on a hill-shoulder with what may be a disturbed cist; and the 18.3 Y Naw Carreg, demolished in the First World War. Legend claimed that these stones could not be counted, a belief known from other megalithic rings like the Rollright Stones in Oxford-shire. It is notable that young people would gather to count the stones 'on a Sunday about Midsummer' (Grimes, 1963, 141).

The one concentration of sites, whether stone circle or henge, is to be found at the south-west foot of the Preselis just where travellers between Ireland and England might cross the peninsula to avoid the currents and wild seas around St. David's Head where strong westerly winds drive waves into numberless rocky coves and the spray bursts and spreads against the cliffs. A safer passage could be made between Fishguard and Carmarthen Bays, passing by the brooding Preselis, and it is here that rings like Meini-Gwyr stand.

Inconspicuous in an untidy field this 18.3 m ring once had about seventeen tall stones of which two remain set in a low, stone-lined clay bank, 36.6 m across, with a narrow entrance, also stone-lined, at the west. There is no ditch. In front of the entrance was a pit holding only grey clay and much fine charcoal, but food-vessel people had later lit a fire on top of the disused bank (Grimes, 1938) and thus provided evidence that Meini-Gwyr had probably been built during the earlier part of the second millennium. Sites most resembling it are in Ireland, Castleruddery in the Wicklows, and the Lios near Lough Gur, and this may provide a clue to the builders.

At Lough Gur the fragments of a N/MR beaker, like others along the shores of the Severn Basin and the British Channel (Clarke, 1970, 112), could have been left by copper prospectors in the early second millennium moving westwards along the Thames north of Wessex, into South Wales and ultimately to Ireland. There the prospect of the stone-lined earthworks may have moved them to emulation in their own settlements. In south-west Wales there are hengiform sites like Dan Y Coed, Ffynnon Brodyr and Castle Bucket, all unditched and with westerly entrances. As the beaker people may have maintained their German homeland tradition of enclosing burials in timber circles it is neither surprising to find a similar barrow in Pembrokeshire (Dyfed) at South Hill, Talbenny, nor difficult to believe that they might have adopted stone circle building in Britain for their own beliefs.

Twelve miles west of Meini-Gwyr was Letterston (Savory, 1964), another embanked circle of twenty stones, 12.2 m in diameter. 12.2 m beyond its east entrance of big radial stones was a ritual pit filled with oak and ash charcoal, comparable to the pit at Meini-Gwyr. Quartz had been spread over the interior of the ring. Some of Letterston's features are akin to those in the Cork RSCs and may be related to them. Here, as at Meini-Gwyr, the influences seem to come eastwards from Ireland rather than from Wessex, though not necessarily all transmitted by the makers of beaker pottery. Letterston may also have belonged to the earlier second millennium for, eventually, when it was becoming a ruin and its stones were leaning or had even fallen people heaped a huge turf mound over it, possibly after an urned cremation had been placed between its neglected portal stones.

How closely the beaker groups in south Wales were associated with the later trade in stone axes from Preseli is uncertain although several funnel-necked s2/w vessels with bar chevron decoration have been found in this region and at Stonehenge, a type of pot that may not have been manufactured much before the seventeenth century bc (Lanting and van der Waals, 1972, 43). As Clarke has written, these people show 'a distinct interest in the henge and stone circle monuments, especially those with free-standing uprights' (1970, 224), and he has hypothesized that it was they who introduced circle-building into central and south Wessex as copies of forms that they had seen in the west. If true then it may have been they, or the earlier W/MR people, who used the megalithic ring at Gors Fawr less than two miles from Carn Meini.

Here on a peat-drenched and drab low-lying common is a fine 22.3 m open circle of stones graded towards the SSW., a custom that seems to have become popular in the mid-second millennium in southern Britain if the similar grading at Fernworthy, Devon or Stonehenge III can be used as a chronological guide. Two tall stones, 13.7 m apart on a WSW.–ENE. axis, stand 134 m to the NNE. of Gors Fawr. Bushell (1911), who did a lot of fieldwork in the Preseli region in the early twentieth century, thought the circle to be like a gigantic sun dial with the stones set at 24° intervals for calendrical purposes (ibid, 319)—an observation which is inaccurate—and perceived among the scatter of natural boulders a chimerical avenue directed towards the outliers and an orientation on the rising of Arcturus in 1420 BC (c. 1125 bc). Thom considered the outliers to contain their own axial alignment on midsummer sunrise over the nearby Foel-drych hilltop. Yet it was Bushell who likened the Preseli region to a prehistoric Westminister which, in the sense of a cult-centre, it may have been.

Hardly five miles to the west of Gors Fawr is the damaged Dyffryn Syfynwy ring on an ENE. slope overlooking a deep valley. The tall, jagged stones, many fallen long ago, stood in an 22.0 × 18.9 m oval around a 0.9 m high cairn of small boulders. This once impressive ring is now ruinously confused, stones lying on the cairn which itself has been despoiled and much disturbed centrally and at the west. Its association with an internal cairn may demonstrate the variety of adaptation to which such monuments are susceptible.

3. WEST COAST

Far north of the Preselis is the second region of Welsh megalithic rings, the coast around Tremadoc and Barmouth bays to the east of the Lleyn peninsula, another major area of Neolithic settlement. Pollen analysis has shown a portal dolmen at Dyffryn Ardudwy near the coast to have been built in a clearing amidst thick hazel woods that had already been disturbed by earlier farmers. Less than two miles to the east on what is now bleak upland peat two embanked stone circles were erected in a stretch of wet alder woodland first attacked by man in the Neolithic but more widely cleared for agriculture in the second millennium before, slowly, the wood, mutilated by the clearance and then by the local grazing of cattle, degenerated in open bogland that persists to the present (Moore, 1973).

Many axes and flakes from the Graig Lwyd axe factory (Group VII) near Penmaenmawr have been found in the vicinity of these Ffridd Newydd circles on the Hengwm moorland whose surrounding mountains offered the prospector copper, lead and gold. Major trackways defined by standing stones guided traders across the uplands from west to east, from Ireland through the mountains to the south-flowing rivers that would lead to Wessex. One such track starting at Llanbedr just south of Harlech has a 3.4 m monolith on the flat land at the tidal limit of the Afon Artro, marking a safe landing-place, and from here the track climbs north-east into the high, empty wastes, tall stones fixing its route past Bala lake and ultimately to the River Severn (Bowen and Gresham, 1967, 57). Another, lesser track may have reached south-east from Llanbedr past the Hengwm circles to Cerrig Arthur, another embanked ring, and on to a prehistoric way from Barmouth Bay.

On the moorland to the north-east of the Carneddau Hengwm portal dolmens the two Ffridd Newydd rings were built within 27.4 m of each other. Hardly noticeable now, both were embanked stone circles, the northern 32.9 m in diameter with a 1.5 m wide ditch outside the rubble bank. No holes were dug for its large stones which have now all gone. To the south was an even larger ring, 50.6 m across, its low stones strangely set in the outer edge of the bank. Both rings were partly excavated in the autumn of 1919 (Crawford, 1920). The south ring yielded nothing but small sherds of what seem to be late beaker ware from a south-east stone hole but the north circle had a fire-pit near its centre filled with red ash heaped on a flat stone and covered by another. Nearby were eighteen rusticated beaker sherds similar to those from the adjoining ring.

These paired circles are less than half a mile from Llecheiddior, an egg-shaped ring, 19.8 × 15.2 m, of short stones also supported in a stony bank. Not far to the south of Ffridd Newydd is another embanked oval, Cerrig

Fig. 43. Two Welsh Stone Circles. (a) Cerrig Arthur, Merioneth (Gynedd); (b) Ynys-Hir, Brecknockshire (Powys). (a) after Bowen & Gresham, 1967; (b) after Dunning, 1943.

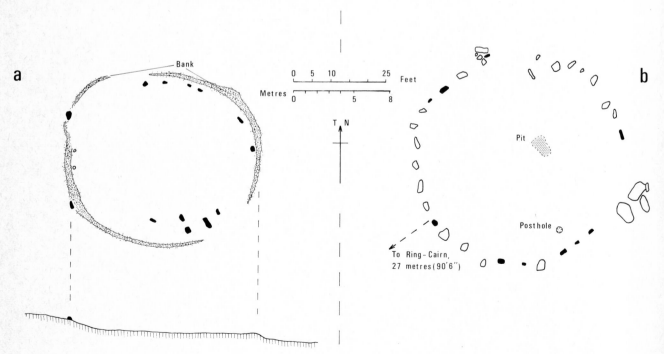

Arthur (Fig. 43), on a site cut into the hillside. Such monuments shade imperceptibly into complex ring-cairns (Lynch, 1972, 63) whose stones are not as pillarlike as those in embanked stone rings but which nevertheless are set in banks and which, in turn, are sometimes indistinguishable from stone-lined ring-cairns like Banniside, Lancashire, or Froggatt Edge, Derbyshire, which has six low stones at the inner edge of a rubble bank with entrances at north and south.

True embanked stone circles are not common in the British Isles, perhaps thirty being known, Pobull Fhinn and Loch a Phobuill on North Uist being the largest. Five sites in Ireland, including the Lios and Castleruddery, average 24.7 m across their banks whereas the six Welsh rings are much smaller, averaging only 14.9 m. What concentrations of such monuments as can be established are in central and northern England where embanked stone circles, complex and simple ring-cairns intermix on the moors of the Peak District and Yorkshire. One large ring is known at Gamelands near the Lake District, a site having some affinities with the Druids Circle, Caernarvon (Gwynedd), but much more characteristic are little rings like the 10.1 m Nine Ladies on Stanton Moor, Derbyshire, enclosed in an ugly modern wall, or the 15.9 m Twelve Apostles, high on Ilkley Moor in Yorkshire.

In them there is repeated evidence of Bronze Age burial, perhaps for ritual reasons. Although quite early beaker material came from the Lios elsewhere the finds are of the mid-second millennium: food-vessels from Cunninghar, Clackmannan, and the Druids Circle; late beakers from Ffridd Newydd; collared urns from Danby Rigg, Yorkshire, and Nith Lodge, Ayrshire; Pennine urns from Mosley Height, Lancashire, and Todmorden, Yorkshire; and pygmy cups from Nith Lodge, Mosley Height and Todmorden, associated with faience beads at the last two sites. It seems unlikely that such cognate Bronze Age artefacts should consistently be added to these widely dispersed sites, so that it seems safe to regard the majority as late in the history of stone circles, particularly as at the complex ring-cairn of Barbrook II, Derbyshire, two Pennine urns were found with charcoal dated to 1500 bc ± 150 (BM-179).

Whether such rings originate from sites like the Lios is unclear though the stone-built entrances at Meini-Gwyr, at Letterston, and at the Druids Circle, may have been constructed in imitation of earlier orthostatic passages. But the impact of henge-building must have been strong in eastern districts of Britain and may account for some of the eccentricities of embanked rings in the Peak District and in Yorkshire, just as Fullerton in Aberdeenshire may have had its stones set in a bank to resemble the circle-henge of Broomend of Crichie a mile away.

Nearly thirty miles south of the Ffridd Newydd rings is a ravaged circle-henge, typically without a ditch like several other henges along these western coasts, at Ysbyty Cynfyn, Cardigan (Dyfed), one stone still standing in its bank which now surrounds a church. Such Christianization of a pagan monument, noticed before, is paralleled in the same county by the discovery of a megalithic stone supporting the pulpit in Llandysiliogogo church (Bowen, 1971).

Elsewhere in this region there is the oval Cefn Coch on a ridge near Tremadoc Bay within a mile of the doomed Cwm Mawr ring 'blown up in recent times'. There are occasional well-scattered diminutive rings like Pen y Stryd. And far inland along the Dovey valley, fifteen miles from any other circle are the associated rings of Cerrig Gaerau and Lled-Croen-yr-Ych on a broad flat saddle in the mountains of Montgomery (Powys). The large stones of the former, a 21.0 m ring, are fallen but some of the lesser pillars of Lled-Croen still stand in an oval 24.7 × 22.9 m. A low outlier stands edge on to the ring 31.7 m to the south-east. Such paired sites have been interpreted elsewhere in Britain as successive, as their different shapes and sizes suggests, and the presence of what must have appeared an unusual megalithic circle at Cerrig Gaerau so far into the centre of Wales points to the mixture of influences here.

4. Mynydd Eppynt

In the worn, smoothed hills of the Mynydd Eppynt in south central Wales are some similarly paired sites whose major trait is the presence of associated alignments (Fig. 44). At Nant Tarw on an extensive flat terrace overlooking former marshland two unobtrusive rings are within 90 m of each other. The one at the WNW. is an oval 20.7 × 19.0 m, its biggest pillar 0.9 m high at the south-east end of the major axis but inexplicably 91 cm inside the theoretical perimeter (Thom, 1967, 82). 107 m to the WNW. is a large fallen monolith with two much smaller stones just beyond it, perhaps a separate monument but more probably related to the ring even if put up at a different time. A line from the ring's centre through the stone to the skyline beyond produces a declination of 10° 1′ and a fair line on Spica (α Virginis) setting in 1900 BC (c.1575 bc) (Thom, 1967, 101).

The ESE. ring is an ellipse, 20.7 × 17.8 m. There is a similar prostrate outlier with a small stone 85.3 m to the WNW. of this ring as there was at the other, but this fallen stone is now within 3.1 m of the WNW. oval, an uneasy proximity which suggests that the circle and its outlier may have preceded the oval. It is noticeable that this second outlier would have stood against the skyline of the gentle hillock on which the WNW. ring was placed. The azimuth of this stone from the centre of the ESE. circle gives a declination of about −16° 46′ which has no astronomical significance.

Across the Usk valley three and a half miles NNE. of the Nant Tarw pair and near a Roman road and temporary camps are two other rings on Trecastle Mountain, again quite dissimilar from each other. The ENE. circle is 23.2 m across of inconspicuous stones with an eccentric mound in its interior. Close by is the second ring, only 7.3 m across, ruined and incomplete. To its WSW.

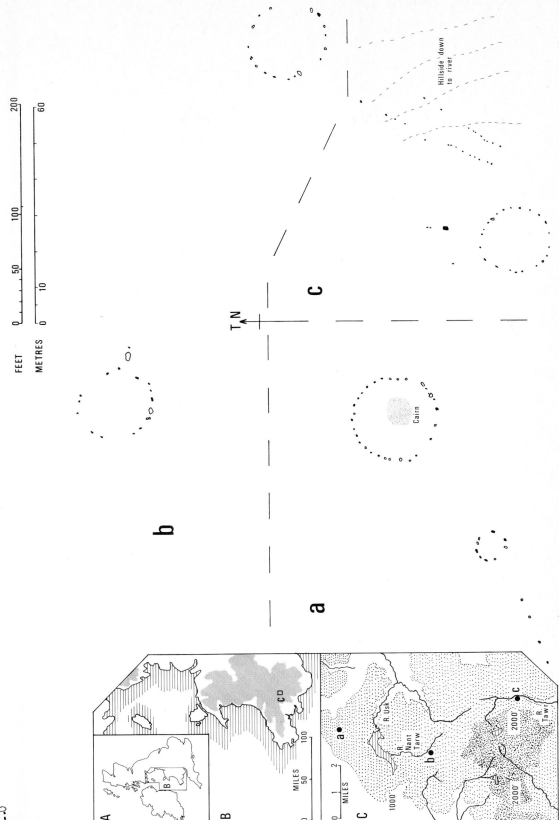

Fig. 44. Three Stone Circle Sites in Brecknockshire (Powys). (a) Trecastle Mountain; (b) Nant Tarw; (c) Cerrig Duon. After Grimes, 1963.

is a miserable alignment crawling towards the circle, its stones now just perceptible in the wet ground. Even allowing for a rise in the ground level it is unlikely that such a setting could have been made for astronomical observation, and it is significant that though proposing three possible solar lines in these rings Thom overlooked this row altogether (1967, 101, W11/2).

It is with the third site, Cerrig Duon, four miles SSE. of Nant Tarw in the narrow, dark Tawe valley that one purpose of such idiosyncratic rows is shown. This egg-shaped ring stands on a platform above the little river to its east. Although its stones are low there is a massive rectangular block of sandstone, 1.8 m high and measuring 1.5 × 0.9 m along its sides, only 9.1 m NNE. of the ring and quite dominating the scene. Just like the outliers at Nant Tarw this stone, Maen Mawr, has two little stones in line with its axis behind it (Grimes, 1963, 138; Thom, 1966, 46). It may mark the rising of Arcturus in 1950 BC (Thom, 1967, 101), but it is more probably directional. It can be seen from a great distance to the south and also to the east across the river even when the ring is hidden. From the north it stands out solidly on the near horizon against the far-off hills. About half a mile northwards on the eastern valleyside is another standing stone set like a playing-card, its long axis pointing directly towards Maen Mawr. Less than 185 m beyond this stone and past the shoulder of the hill Maen Mawr can be seen on its low spur and its usefulness as a guidestone is literally apparent.

No finds are recorded from these lonely Welsh rings, and at first they seem quite unaffected by any outside influence. That this is not so is shown by the avenue at Cerrig Duon, 45.7 m long, narrowing to about 4.9 m across as it nears the ring. Today it is only just noticeable even in the short grass but, like the avenue at Callanish, it follows the easiest line of approach up the hillside from the river 70 ft below.

Just as there are single lines of stones in Wales without circles like that at Parc y Meirw, Pembrokeshire (Dyfed), so there are unassociated avenues like Hwlfa'r Ceirw, Caernarvon (Gwynedd), a double row of small stones leading from the foot of a scarp to the edge of the sea-cliff. In this it is like the double Yelland row, Devon, 34.4 m long, in the Taw estuary and often submerged by the incoming tide (Grinsell, 1970, 43). Such settings, therefore, may be of a tradition separate from that of the circles to which they are sometimes attached. The avenue at Cerrig Duon, for example, does not lead to the ring but, if extended, would pass over 6 m away from the eastern-most stone.

The only other avenue connected with a stone circle in Wales is at Rhos y Beddau, a 12.8 m circle of little stones on a hillside in Montgomery (Powys). An avenue overgrown with heather and bracken creeps up the hill from the river. Like Cerrig Duon and Callanish it narrows as it approaches the ring, in this case leading towards the southern arc but stopping some 7.6 m short of the circumference. Cerrig Duon also stopped short, an additional reason for believing that ring and avenue were the work of different people.

Cognate settings of standing stones connected to stone circles are a feature of several north Wessex rings where they may have developed from the short stone settings at the entrances of some henges like Stonehenge I. Balfarg, Fife, had a similar approach. Timber double rows which may be analogous are recorded from Neolithic burial sites like Kemp Howe and Kilham in Yorkshire as well as at henges such as Lugg, Dublin, and Durrington Walls, Wiltshire, in whose excavation-report their affinities are discussed (Wainwright and Longworth, 1971, 228). Thus, avenues may have had a considerable history before the development of stone circles. Earth versions exist at Stonehenge II, at Arbor Low, Derbyshire, and perhaps at the Bull Ring in the same county.

Other circles with avenues may be found rarely in Scotland: Broomend of Crichie, and Callanish; and more commonly in Westmorland and the eastern marches of Wales, a distribution along the Severn valley suggesting some relationship with those in Wessex. As many of these avenues lead up the easiest slope from a river their deliberate association with water, noted at Callanish, is re-affirmed, the two avenues to the River Chew at Stanton Drew in Somerset becoming all the more significant in this context, although the mile and three-quarters separating Stonehenge from the Christchurch Avon suggests that at that site at least the avenue was for a directional purpose.

Even more remote than Cerrig Duon or Trecastle is Ynys-Hir (Fig. 43) on a bleak ridge deep in the mountains at a height of 1300 ft. Here the stones stand in an almost perfect circle 18.0 m in diameter. They were set shallowly with only a few packing-stones so that by the time the site was excavated in 1940 (Dunning, 1943) they were nearly all fallen. Wider gaps at east and west may have marked entrances but however the site was used it seems not to have had a long life. There were no datable finds. One stone-lined posthole was discovered 1.5 m inside the circle near to the south-east stone. Just to the south-west of the ring was a ring-cairn which had been converted into a barrow by people who placed Bronze Age pottery, including a small, coarse pygmy cup, in it. At the centre was a pit with a token cremation and charcoal beneath a flat stone like the deposit at Ffridd Newydd. Ring-cairns alongside stone circles have been noticed elsewhere in Wales (Lynch, 1972, 64), but their distribution is by no means identical, overlapping only in the north and south-west of the country. Their juxtaposition at Ynys-Hir may be attributed to the use of the same territory at different times by people who seemingly respected an older monument. There is just such a pairing at Cheetham Close, Lancashire, where a 15.5 m ring and a 22.0 m ring-cairn were built alongside each other. Other pairs occur on Extwhistle Moor, Lancashire. And on Danby Rigg, Yorkshire, the moor has a stone circle on the northern spur near a multitude of little clearance cairns; and a large ring-cairn in a contiguous uncleared area, bordered to north and south by deep defensive ditches (Elgee, 1930, 134). Half a mile separates circle from ring-cairn. We have as yet no knowledge of whether they were contemporary, built by the same people, had the same purpose or were for complementary practices.

A similar but closer association occurs thirteen miles WNW. at Cefn Gwernffrwd deep in the Cambrian mountains where a 24.0 m circle of shattered stones stands within 60 m of a rather larger ring-cairn whose builders, like so many others, showed an interest in the south-west quadrant (Henshall, 1972, 272), this time by placing a huge stone there. Tangential to the east of the ring-cairn is a short three-stone row akin to those at Cerrig Duon and Trecastle Mountain fifteen miles SSE.

Twenty miles north-east of Ynys-Hir is another group of rings around the heights of Radnor Forest: Rhos Maen; the oval of Gelli Hill, 21.3 × 19.5 m, with an outlier on the western skyline; and the heatherthick Six Stones; and, lower down the Lugg valley, the Four Stones near Walton, reported by Camden to be a circle ruined in the reign of King John. It is, in reality, a small Four-Poster, a surprising 300 miles south of Perthshire and part of a thinning southward distribution of these monuments established by sites like Aucheleffan on Arran; the Goatstones and the Three Kings in Northumberland; Grassington in Yorkshire; and Lettergorman, Cork (Burl, 1974b, 31). The Four Stones, Walton, rounded, lichen-marked boulders possibly dragged from the volcanic Stanner Rocks two miles to the south, is an isolated site, remote from any other circle, in a hill-flanked basin, and its presence in an area of Neolithic occupation is puzzling. Yet it carries hints of a Scottish association in its cupmarked south-west stone and perhaps also in the uncommon occurrence of standing stones in its neighbourhood. To the west at Llanerch Farm is one of the few cupmarked stones in Wales.

5. SHROPSHIRE–MONTGOMERY (POWYS)

It will be clear what a variety of form exists among these Welsh rings to which the term 'megalithic' seldom applies. Although the number of stones may be as many as forty-five at Ffridd Newydd South, or as few as eight at Pen y Stryd, Merioneth (Gwynedd), it is uncommon for them to be large. Sixty per cent of the Welsh sites have no stone as tall as 0.9 m. Of the others, four stones at Trecastle Mountain that still stand average only 89 cm, and twelve at Nant Tarw West, 41 cm. Yet in the vicinity of most of these low rings are big stones so that it may be assumed that often the number of people was inadequate to move them and that the sites were used by only a few participants. Although dating is difficult there is nothing to suggest that any of these rings precedes the second millennium. Probably many of them were built in the Bronze Age by which time the construction of non-circular enclosures was well established. Where the design can be determined nearly two-thirds of the Welsh rings are ovals. Their architecture also reflects a choice of features: some are embanked, others have outliers or avenues. And to this mélange may be added those with centre stones.

On the eastern border of Wales in a region which includes the important

Clun-Clee trackway and the Hyssington axe factory the rings at Kerry Hill, Montgomery (Powys) and at the Hoarstones, Shropshire, both have pillars inside them. Immediately to the north of Corndon hill towering 1000 ft above the valley of the W. Onny were five megalithic rings in an area of four square miles in the north–south pass between Stapeley and Stiperstone hills. Three of them have been destroyed. Traces of Shelve may survive to the north of the church but Druid Castle and the Whetstones have gone, the last blown up in the 1860s when the land was enclosed. 'Under the Whetstones when they were dug up was found a mass of black . . . human bones.' As usual, there is little guide to the date of these sites. Under one stone at Druid Castle, moved about 1884 during the extension of farm-buildings, was a broken three-handled pot which was later lost. A bronze dagger was found near the Whetstones, a bronze palstave close to Druid Castle, and a looped palstave and a sand-stone axe-hammer have been discovered near other circles here, a collection which may point to the use of the rings in the centuries of the mid-second millennium. Within a mile of Corndon was the Cwm-Mawr axe factory by Hyssington (Group XII) from which picrite axe-hammers and battle-axes were distributed locally and along the Severn from the nineteenth century bc on-wards, some being known in South Devon and even as far as Land's End. These heavy perforated implements were used from late beaker times, some-times for metalworking. Deposits of copper also occur in the neighbourhood of Corndon (N. Thomas, 1972) where the frequent round barrows and cairns also compose a picture of settlement during the Bronze Age.

The two circles which survive here are both large flattened rings (Fig. 45). Mitchell's Fold, 28.4 × 25.9 m in diameter, to the north-west of a cairn with a standing stone, is attractively placed on a high, dry heathland in a clearing

Fig. 45. Two Shropshire (Salop) Stone Circles. (a) Hoarstones; (b) Mitchell's Fold.

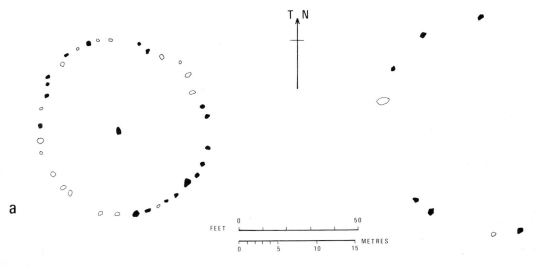

a

b

T N

0   50
FEET

0   5   10   15
METRES

in the bracken, its sixteen dolerite stones coming from Stapeley Hill on whose lower slopes it was built. Several of the pillars are tall, and are impressive against their background of whale-backed hills and wide valleys. There is a doubtful tradition that once the ring with its north-east flattened arc had a central stone and the Ordnance Survey, Southampton, has a record that this was located in 1955, fallen and turf-covered inside the ring.

Sometimes called Black Marsh or Hemford, the Hoarstones, one and a half miles north-east of Mitchell's Fold, has an indisputable centre stone. This 23.2 × 19.8 m ring, the most northerly of the Corndon group, also is flattened, this time towards the WSW., but unlike Mitchell's Fold the circle has a low-lying situation in a muddy field overgrown with gorse and tufts of marsh-grass. Several of its stones are now overlain with peat and even the tallest at the south-east rises only 76 cm above the ground. Nearly at the true centre is an unshaped boulder, 97 cm high. Most of the stones are set closely together but there are larger gaps at north, east and south-west, and which, if original, may have been intentionally aligned on the peaks of the great hills of Broom-low Callow, 1247 ft, Stiperstones, 1647 ft and Corndon, 1684 ft respectively (Chitty, 1926, 251), and it has been speculated that these hills could have been, to the prehistoric mind, places of magical import within whose ambience a stone circle would become the more powerful.

Other comments have been made about this ring's design. 'It is interesting to see that in the Type A circle at Black Marsh one end of the axis of symmetry is marked by a stone with a hole cut in it, and one end of the cross-axis by a stone with two cut holes. In neither case do the holes go right through.' (Thom, 1967, 68.) The implication that the marks were the work of the pre-historic circle-designers is mistaken.

It may perhaps be thought slightly suggestive of a tradition of public ceremonies having been performed at this place that, when a wedding occurs in the neighbourhood, the miners repair to these stones, and, having drilled a hole or holes, load them with powder, and fire them instead of cannons. Accidents frequently happen on these occasions, but it is satis-factory to know that the miners suffer from them more than the stones do; the latter are, however, full of the holes made in this manner, which must not be mistaken for ancient markings or wedge holes. (Lewis, 1882, 3.)

Previously it has been noticed that legends have associated circles with dancing or with weddings like the petrified guests at Stanton Drew. At the Hoarstones there may have endured fading murmurs of fertility ceremonies and, obliquely, rites to do with fire. If these rings were once places where such activities occurred it is less surprising that at most circles no memory of them has persisted than to find occasionally, after 3000 years or more, that there are rings to which folk-memory still attaches whispers of their ancient use.

Eleven miles south-west of Corndon the ring of Kerry Hill (Fig. 5) lay near the Clun-Clee trackway, an important prehistoric route between the Irish

Sea and the Severn Basin from Early Bronze Age times, used by axe-hammer
traders and bronzesmiths until 'with the onset of wetter conditions its use
declined: from the Late Bronze Age the district was either deserted, or isolated,
the older levels being sealed in parts by the growth of hill-peat' (Chitty,
1963, 191). Pen-y-Wern may have been a circle on this trackway. Kerry Hill is
farther to the west on a southern hillslope. Like Mitchell's Fold it is a large
site, 26.5 m in maximum diameter, of only nine stones, some thin slabs,
some great boulders but none more than 53 cm high, with a 1.2 m long stone
lying near the centre. This, the centre stone at the Hoarstones, and perhaps
at Mitchell's Fold, may be related to others with centre stones in Wessex.
Influence, through trade, certainly extended northwards along the Severn
valley from Wessex and the avenues at Cerrig Duon and Rhos y Beddau, and
the Shropshire-Montgomery centre stones could derive from examples of such
architecture seen on the rich plains to the south.

Other clusters of centre-stone circles exist, of course, in south-west Scotland
and in the Cork-Kerry area, but it is extremely unlikely that there was direct
contact between places so distant from a remote ring like Kerry Hill, whereas the Clun-Clee trackway on which it stood extended eastwards to the fringe
of the Birmingham plateau and thence southwards into Wessex (Seaby, 1949)
where megalithic rings like Avebury and Winterbourne Bassett with their
great centre stones must have been well known. Such contacts between Wessex
and east Wales along the edges of the Severn valley do much to explain architectural features like centre stones and avenues in both areas.

Three large flattened rings in one district also indicates a probable relationship between them though the arc in each case is differently placed. Thom
diagnosed Kerry Hill as a compound ring with flattening to north-west and
south-west and remarked, 'that while the axis is not east and west the line
KT is very nearly due north' (1967, 88), a persistent trait in the open rings of
western Britain.

6. NORTH WALES

On Cefn Coch, the red ridge that stands above the great stone headland of
Penmaenmawr where the Graig Lwyd axe factory (Group VII) was located,
is a shattered line of cairn-cemeteries, mounds, ring-cairns and stone circles
across the junction of three moorland tracks which themselves are defined in
places by standing stones. Just north of Graig Lwyd at least twelve monuments
crowd along half a mile of the track. The chief of them is the famous Druids
Circle.

Two miles away the well-preserved ring of Cerrig Pryfaid stands on a more
southerly route, a 91 cm high outlier marking the way north-west past cairns
towards the tall stones at Bwlch y Ddenfaen and westwards to the coast.
With the exception of this ring and those by Penmaenmawr the only other
megalithic rings in north Wales may have been on Anglesey (Ynys Mon)
where the two Bryngwyn Stones are reputedly the largest standing stones in

Wales. The taller is a thin 4.0 m pillar, 91 cm above its companion to the east. It has been claimed that only these survive of a 12.2 m circle once surrounded by a ditch and outer bank, a form of circle-henge. 'Farther westward . . . there are stones pitch'd on end, about twelve in number, whereof three are very considerable, the largest of them being twelve foot high . . .' (Edward Lhwyd in Camden, 1695, 676.) 275 m away is Castell Bryn-Gwyn, a henge that was used well into the Bronze Age. As Bryn Celli Ddu, the passage-grave built over a ravaged circle-henge, is only three miles to the north-east this low-lying south-east coast of Anglesey may have been settled quite early by circle and henge builders. Eight and a half miles to the east across the Menai Straits, Llandegai I henge has been dated from cremation pits outside its single entrance to 2530 bc $\pm$ 145 (NPL-224) and 2470 bc $\pm$ 140 (NPL-221), a time when the exploitation of the Neolithic axe sources on Penmaenmawr had already begun.

The circles above Graig Lwyd, however, are later than this. Dates from them show they were built in the Bronze Age when trade between Ireland and north-east England was strong. Thirty miles to the east five big stones remain of a 35.4 m circle on a valleyside at Penbedw Park, Flintshire (Clywd), on the same route from Yorkshire, past the Clywdian and Halkyn hills to Penmaenmawr. Trees have been planted in the ring where stones once stood. There is an outlier to the west towards the first mountains, the forested valley of the Clywd and then the sharp hillsides of the Cambrian highlands.

Here, 1300 ft above the sea, is the Cefn Coch group. A mile to the east the 12.2 m ring of Hafoty lies half-collapsed on the flank of a ridge in mountain pasture. The trackway passes through this circle, by a cemetery of small cairns and on to the knee-high stones that are all that is left of a ring, maybe once 30.1 m across, near the ruined cairn at Red Farm. The trackway continues climbing slowly westwards over half a mile of rock and grass to Circle 275, five rounded slabs on the circumference of a circle 3.1 m across, a site to which many visitors give no glance in their hurry to reach the Druids Circle. Yet when it was excavated during a cold, wet May in 1958 (Griffiths, 1960, 317) it produced tantalizing evidence. Between the east and south boulders were crude spreads of stones like a bank. The interior of the circle was covered with quartz fragments and near the centre was a shallow pit densely packed with quartz. The diameter, the number of stones and the quartz all recall the diminutive five-stone circles of Cork in south-west Ireland like Faranfada, Belmont A and B, and Cousane, none more than 4.0 m across, erected on the high slopes of the Boggeragh mountains. Like Circle 275, excavations at Kealkil and Mushera Beg uncovered no burials but, like the Welsh ring, much quartz was found at the latter. The known trading contacts between Munster and north Wales during the Bronze Age may have caused a little Irish ring to have been put up in these Welsh moors on the major trading route between Ireland and eastern England.

Farther west, almost hidden in a dip 145 m beyond the Druids Circle is

Circle 278, an irregular ring-cairn about 15.9 m in diameter, its central space walled with flat-topped stones but, even though enclosing a space some 12.2 m across, completely empty of finds, except hard by the stones themselves, once more reminding us that these monuments are unlikely to have been essentially sepulchral. By the south-east stone a fire had burned and a female cremation had been placed in the wall. Exactly opposite was another area of burning and a slab-covered pit with a small collared urn but no burial. The tallest stone of the ring-cairn had once stood at the SSW. Opposite this on the NNE. quadrant was 'an elaborate setting of stones that looked rather like a small armchair' but only 30 cm wide, which the excavator thought 'might have been intended to support the base of a wooden image or totem' (Griffiths, 1960, 321), and perhaps for the same purpose as the 'pulpit' at Millin Bay, Down, a hundred miles to the north-west on the opposite coastline of the Irish Sea. From wood beneath the bank two C-14 assays of 1520 bc ±145 (NPL-11) and 1405 bc ±155 (NPL-10) were obtained. Such dates, of course, relate only to the erection of the ring-cairn and not necessarily to the subsequent activities in it. Another ring-cairn, Brenig 44, twenty miles to the south-east in the Glyndwr mountains and which may have been surrounded by a timber circle, had been used over several centuries for fire ceremonies that involved the laying down of charcoal in the ring, activities dated as early as 1680 bc ±100 (H-501) and as late as 1280 bc ±70 (H-503), 400 years of rites that had little to do with burial (Lynch, Waddell, Allen and Grealey, 1974, 30). The Cefn Coch ring-cairn may likewise have been employed for a long period after its construction in the fifteenth century. Indirect confirmation is given by wood from a fire-pit in a cairn alongside it which was dated to 1130 bc ±145 (NPL-12).

More stone circles, tumbled and almost unrecognisable, may have stood to the west of Circle 278 but it is the famous Druids Circle to its east that compels attention (Fig. 46). Whereas the ring-cairn is virtually concealed in a hollow the embanked stone circle stands conspicuously in a shallow saddle right against the trackway, its stones, still upright and bleak against the sky-line. Some of these granitic monoliths are nearly 1.8 m high and despite the despoliation of treasure-seekers and the blasting operations of nineteenth-century wall-builders the ring retains a wild dignity.

Having first erected the thirty pillars the Bronze Age workers piled up a boulder bank 46 cm high and up to 1.7 m wide all around the ring except at the south-west where a 2.4 m gap with two great portals at each terminal made a prominent entrance. Once birches had grown in the locality of the site. Even at the time the circle was built a few trees probably stood near the trackway that today can still be seen as a hollow trail that goes directly past the ring before dropping down to a stream on the west. The Druids Circle seems to have been put up at the juncture of several such tracks, a fact that points to its status as a meeting-place.

In plan Thom (1967, 77) has defined it as an oval 25.7 × 24.5 m (31 × 29½ M.Y.) on a major WNW.–ESE. axis but Griffiths (1960, 307) considered it to

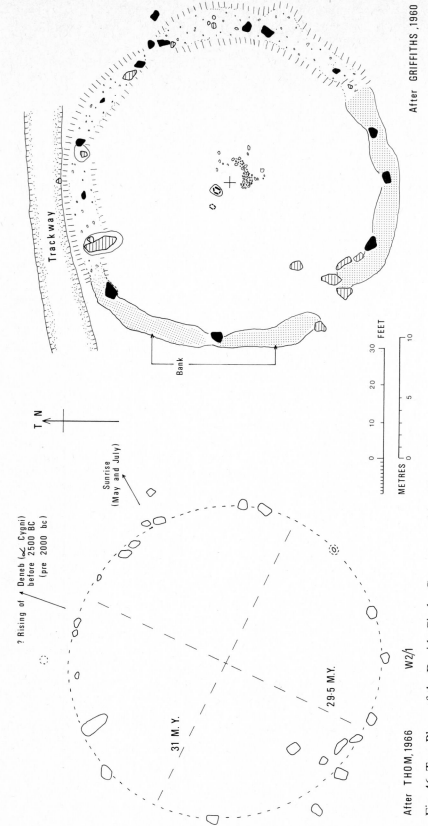

After GRIFFITHS, 1960

Trackway

Bank

T N

? Rising of Deneb (α Cygni)
before 2500 BC
(pre 2000 bc)

Sunrise
(May and July)

31 M.Y.

29.5 M.Y.

After THOM, 1966   W2/1

FEET
30   20   10   0
METRES
0   5   10

Fig. 46. Two Plans of the Druids Circle, Caernarvonshire (Gwynedd).

be flattened at the north where its circumference was contiguous with the track. Certainly the small standing stone, No. 7, exactly at the north, is on a flattened arc 91 cm within Thom's hypothetical perimeter which takes no cognizance of the concentric bank which also is flattened here. Had the builders wished to place their monument as close to the track as they could, then stone 7's position becomes explicable as a reluctance on their part to erect it on the worn track itself. The flattening results from this and not from the desire to create a perimeter that was a full multiple of the Megalithic Yard—95 M.Y. in the case of the Druids Circle though here Thom's plan shows the ellipse passing through the centres of some stones, the outsides of others and along the inner edge of No. 25 at the south, a difference of at least 0.61 m which could alter the length of the circumference by about 4 M.Y. It must also be remarked that the excavator considered the most significant arcs to be not at WNW. and ESE., Thom's major axis, but quite differently at the WSW. entrance and at the ENE. where stone 16, tall and perhaps the only artificially shaped monolith, and a strange outlying stone stand. The outer face of stone 16 has a little shoulder which 'local tradition, ever ready to take full advantage of the opportunities offered by the circle, states . . . was the "altar" on which the slain bodies of infants were placed during sacrificial ceremonies' (Griffiths, 1960, 310). Such folk-stories add as much to the confusion as to the fascination that the stone circles create in the modern mind.

As with other open rings of the coasts of western Britain no structure occupied the great central space of the Druids Circle, but at ground level very close to the middle the excavators found the capstone of a finely made cist around which stones, including some quartz, had been unevenly scattered. Inverted in the cist was an enlarged food-vessel (Fig. 11) holding the cremated bones of a ten- to twelve-year old child. To the WNW. was a pit with a plain enlarged food-vessel containing a second child cremation, this time with a small bronze knife. Another pot stood in a third pit from which a slight trench led south-west to a hollow lined with overlapping hones of sandstone on which lay a poorly preserved cremation deposit. Such whetstones, like axes, may on occasion have been worn as amulets or talismen. One tiny perforated example was found with a cremation at Ffridd y Garreg Wen, Flints. (Clywd).

Other enlarged food-vessels are known in Yorkshire, in Cornwall and in south-west Scotland but there is something of a concentration in Wessex suggesting that their makers had contacts with that region. Yet the situation of the Druids Circle on its vital east–west trackway and its enclosing bank are suggestive of eastern influences where embanked stone rings are more common. In Wessex, except far south in Dorset, they are unknown. The sites most resembling the Druids Circle are to the north and to the east. At Carperby near Aysgarth in west Yorkshire there are the remains of an embanked oval 28.0 × 23.8 m, its fallen pillars of local gritstone up to 1.2 m long, lying on an overgrown stony bank. There is one slight, disturbed mound, 30 cm high, at the centre. At Gamelands in Westmorland the flattened ring, about 42 m along its maximum diameter, has a low bank on which at one time forty stones stood, broken only at the south-east where there was an entrance. Ploughing, around 1862, dragged up what may have been the stones of a central cist.

The Druids Circle, so picturesquely placed, may be regarded as a monument in which at least two traditions combined, just as the dramatic cairn-circles at Bryn Cader Faner with its outward-tilted stones, or Carn Caca, are combinations of stone circle and burial mound. This is a phenomenon often observed in the later rings of Wales. But the significance of the child burials is obscure. Elsewhere, at Pond Cairn, Glamorgan, and at the ring-cairn, Aber Cwmddyr, Cardigan (Dyfed), there are child burials, the latter site having 'within the central area the unburnt body of a headless child' (Lynch, 1972, 72). At Bedd Branwyn cairn, Anglesey, only thirty-one miles west of the Druids Circle, amongst other burials there were three separate deposits of infants' ear-bones. Within the barrow at Treiorwerth nearby there were the ear-bones of a six-year-old. 'It is suggestive of some unpleasant ritual, probably sacrifice, accompanying the funerals of certain special individuals . . .' (Lynch, 1970, 129.) It will be remembered that directly across the Irish Sea, the central cist at Castle Mahon stone circle, Down, contained a child's cremation. Other sacrifices are suspected from Bronze Age cist-burials in Ireland (Waddell, 1970, 98).

It may be wondered whether the cremations at the Druids Circle are similarly the evidence of sacrifice as the slain child at Woodhenge, relics of a darkening past that the visitor to a stone circle must remember, telling him he may be standing not in a scientific observatory but in a place where people, fearful in a precarious world, offered fire and death in return for protection.

CHAPTER NINE

Late Stone Circles of Eastern and Southern Britain

Though this be writt, as I rode, a gallop; yet the novelty of it, and the faithfulness of the delivery, may make some amends for the uncorrectness of the Stile.

John Aubrey

1. INTRODUCTION

This region is a paradox. Covering nearly half of the 121,000 square miles of the British Isles, much of it low-lying, fertile, patterned with slow, wide rivers, some of its territories were the most heavily populated in the country. Yet only 12 per cent of stone circles are located here. Whether as tiny as Mayshiel, East Lothian, in a rubble ring only 2.7 m across, high on a Lammermuir hillside, or as vast as Avebury, so enormous that a longbow arrow could not be fired from one side to the other, these rings are few, just over a hundred being known from Fife down to Dorset.

This is partly because much of this prehistoric landscape was avoided by man.

> Southern Britain presented an illimitable forest of 'damp oakwood', ash and thorn and bramble, largely untrodden. This forest was in a sense unbroken, for without emerging from its canopy a squirrel could traverse the country from end to end; but in another sense it was limited, for the downs and heaths which here and there touched the sea or navigable rivers . . . were the terminals of far-reaching stretches of open and semi-open country, grassland and parkland . . . This open country was some-times at valley level but more often consisted of low hills, plateaux, or ridges of moderate elevation but dominant; so that Man moved on his vocations above the environing forest, and his eye ranged over wide spaces. (C. Fox, 1933, 82.)

And although this panorama of a widely hostile land is being modified by discoveries of henge and settlement on the heavy clays of the midlands it remains largely true.

But the major reason for the scarcity of stone circles in eastern and southern Britain was the presence locally of alternative forms of building material. Here there was timber in plenty and it is significant that, difficult though it is to rediscover such an ephemeral monument as a circle of posts, long rotted and overgrown, the majority of those known are in this area: Moncrieffe and Croft Moraig in Scotland; Arminghall in East Anglia; Mount Pleasant, the Sanctuary and Woodhenge in southern England. It is noteworthy that in at least four of these rings the posts were replaced by standing stones, a reminder of the complexity of such multi-phase sites.

The monuments men built were fashioned by custom and by the easiest material nearby. Stone is scarce in the earths and chalks of the east and south. Timber is plentiful. So is easily dug land. Hence the same area that contains only 12 per cent of the stone circles has well over 50 per cent of the henges, including most of the great enclosures whether the Thornborough earthworks on the north, 244 m from outer ditch to outer ditch, or the stupendous Avebury, or the southern henge at Knowlton in Dorset, 213 m from crest to crest of its bank, weathered and farmed away, the eye misled by the hedges, road, fields and farm that mar its interior.

These henges distort the picture of stone circles, being so much bigger that the megalithic rings are diminished by comparison with them, and it seems apparent that especially on the eastern side of the region people preferred to have ritual centres inside a ring of posts, almost undiscoverable today, or within earthen banks like the little-known henges of Coupland in Northumbria, Little Bromley, Essex, or Eggardon in Dorset. Stone circles are rare here. It is only where rock appears, the millstone grit and limestone of the Pennines, sandstone sarsen of the Marlborough Downs, that megalithic rings were erected along this hard north–south spine, and here some of the most impressive were built inside encircling banks: circle-henges like Balfarg, Arbor Low, Avebury and Stonehenge, the most spectacular prehistoric monuments in the British Isles.

2. THE CIRCLE-HENGES

Of these uncommon sites (Fig. 2) some like Brodgar and Stenness in the Orkneys are far away from other areas but, down the centre of Britain, along the 350 miles which separate Fife from Wiltshire are seven circle-henges—eight if Long Meg is included—which share the characteristics of having large open rings within smallish henges, of being near trackways, in areas of Neolithic occupation, their builders displaying the same interest in north–south lines as those of western Britain. Most of the henges are Class II. It is only those at the extremes, Balfarg at the north, Stonehenge at the south, that have single entrances.

Strangely, in every case the megalithic ring is wrecked. At Avebury, the Devil's Quoits, at Balfarg, even the Stripple Stones in Cornwall, many of the stones have been smashed and removed, often by pious mediaeval Christians; and, worse, at Stonehenge both bluestone concentric rings were dismantled. Nor is there any stone now at the Bull Ring or Cairnpapple. Only at Arbor Low do the stones remain, all collapsed, slumping on the turf like cards blown over by a north wind. From the size of the henges it seems they served large populations for the open interior is never less than

46 m across with no burial mound to reduce its spaciousness, room enough for a hundred people or more, although Cairnpapple, Arbor Low and Avebury did have Coves near their centres, a type of structure otherwise known only at Stanton Drew and, just possibly, at Er Lannic.

One of the major problems of these circle-henges is to decide whether henge and stone circle are contemporary. At Stonehenge the bluestones are believed to have been added as much as 800 years after the construction of the earthwork. At Avebury the bank and the stones are considered coeval. But at Arbor Low and Cairnpapple, despite the exact reconstruction of their plans it is not possible to say more than that the shape of the stone ring and of its enclosing henge differ, as do their centres, making it feasible that these are earthworks to which the stone setting was secondary. Against this, there is such a similarity between them that they are almost duplicates in reverse, making it unlikely that the builders of one were unacquainted with the other or that the megalithic rings were put up by a separate group. Their shapes intimate that they belong after the early phases of stone-ring building and they may well be unitary designs of the early second millennium when henge and stone circle could be merged to embrace the beliefs of people from east and west.

There is no close likeness between the others. Little is known of the low-lying Balfarg (Atkinson, 1952, 58). Discovered by aerial photograph its bank is so ploughed that it is a mere 15–20 cm high, and its ditch could be detected only by probing. Yet it surrounds a circular area 57.9 m across which once had a proud ring of stones. Today only two are left, one 2.0 m tall at the north-west entrance, the survivor, like Stonehenge's Slaughter Stone, of a pair of portal stones that were customary in early henges (Burl, 1969, 6; Catherall, 1972, 153).

The Devil's Quoits, Oxfordshire, had similar portals at its east and west entrances to an oval enclosure 165 × 146 m with over twenty-four big stones set in an ellipse 85.3 × 76.2 m in diameter. The site was partly excavated when it was being levelled for a wartime aerodrome (Grimes, 1944), and, because of an encroaching quarry, was further investigated when a slight central structure of timber was discovered (M. Gray, 1973; 1975). Typically it stood by an important trackway from the midlands which avoided the forested clays near Wantage, passed the henge of Deadman's Burial, and stretched down to Uffington and the route into Wessex (Case et al., 1965). Most probably it was a trail used both by highland stone-axe merchants bringing their wares to Wessex and by north Wessex flint-traders travelling northwards from the Avebury district past the henges, the Rollright Stones circle, the cursuses in the Vale of Evesham, across Charnwood Forest and up into the Peak District where they would have come to the Derbyshire circle-henges of Arbor Low and the Bull Ring.

This quarried site behind the mining village of Doveholes stands at a height of 1100 ft on the limestone plateau above the wooded valley of the

Dove, ten miles NNW. of Arbor Low on the same trackway that leads down to Whaley Bridge and the Mersey flowing out to the Irish Sea. Not one stone is left of the circle but the 76.2 m bank is upstanding and the ditch, from which some possible Neolithic coarseware came (Alcock, 1950), can still be clearly seen with its north and south entrances even though hacked and scarred by miners. This henge and its southern counterpart, Arbor Low, occupy that limestone area of the Peak District chosen by the builders of Neolithic chambered tombs like Green Low, Liffs Low and Five Wells, quite distinct from the millstone grit moors east of the Derwent where the majority of Bronze Age sites were built (S. E. Hicks, 1972, 1) and where many of the food-vessels and most of the collared urns have been discovered. The fact that two neatly cisted food-vessels were in a barrow built onto Arbor Low's bank equally suggests an early second millennium date for the henge, for similar satellite Late Neolithic and Early Bronze Age barrows have been noted elsewhere in Derbyshire (Radley, 1966b).

The highly situated site of Arbor Low (O. E. eorðburh-hlaw, 'the earth-work mound') is evocative to visit, walking up the slope from the farm towards the green bank, the stones hidden, the mound of Gib Hill barrow, broken-topped from its many excavations, rising to view on the right. The excavation of Arbor Low was part of a wider scheme. In 1899 'the British Association set up a committee to enquire into the "Age of Stone Circles", a project that I began with the digging of the Stripple Stones, Cornwall' (St. G. Gray, 1908), and concluded with an investigation of Avebury, Wiltshire, between 1908 and 1922 (St. G. Gray, 1935). Funds were never plentiful: 'The two grants made by the British Association for the work at Arbor Low amounted to £50' (ibid, 105).

Arbor Low's oval bank, 82.9 × 75.0 m across its crests, in places 2.1 m high, undulating, footworn, has entrances at NNW. and SSE. (Fig. 47). They are not in line with the henge centre but are 5.5 m to its west. The food-vessel barrow, its top hollowed like a dented table tennis ball, is outside a terminal of the southern entrance, a long earthen row starting at the other terminal and curving south and west for a great distance towards Gib Hill, with a heavy cist perched near its summit, and to the remains of what may have been an earlier henge ultimately replaced by Arbor Low (Radley, 1969a).

Inside Arbor Low's bank is the ditch, now smoothed with turf but from which 50,000 cu ft (1475 m³) of solid limestone was gouged and manhandled up crude ramps and rock steps onto the bank where boulders weighing up to a ton testify to the labour of the henge-builders. The ditch encloses an irregular 48.8 m area on which forty-two limestone pillars lie white and car-buncled by millennia of weathering. It was not from the fresh ditch but from an exposed outcrop that the stones were obtained so that 'their pot-holes and crevices were worn away by Nature ages before the day on which they were set up'.

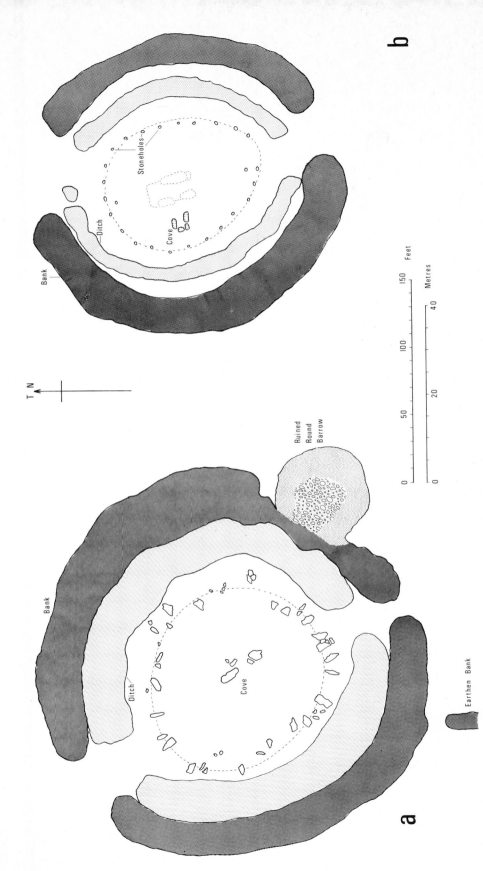

Fig. 47. Two Similar Circle-Henges: (a) Arbor Low, Derbyshire, and (b) Cairnpapple, West Lothian. After St. G. H. Gray, 1903; and S. Piggott, 1948.

Pl. 30. *Arbor Low, Derbyshire*. From the west. The only stone of this circle-henge that is not prostrate leans over in the middle of the nearer arc. The collapsed Cove is in the centre of the ring.

Top right is the round barrow added to the bank during the Early Bronze Age. Between 1761 and 1845 there were five attempts to discover a burial in it, Bateman finally locating a cist with a cremation and two food-vessels. Almost a century earlier Rooke had unearthed the antler picks used by the builders of the mound.

The circle-stones are not from the ditch's bedrock and may have been brought from a distance to add to an existing henge.

Whether the stones ever did stand has been questioned despite the unreliable eighteenth-century testimony of William Normanshaw that he had seen some erect as late as the 1740s. Certainly during his two excavations St. G. Gray (1903) found no stoneholes. Fortunately one large stone at the WSW. is not totally prostrate and it can be assumed that inadequate sockets in the hard bedrock left the stones, many 3.0 m to 3.7 m long, precariously and briefly balanced around an egg-shaped ring measuring approximately 37.2 × 41.5 m (45 × 50 M.Y.) on a major ESE.–WNW. axis. A wider gap at the north-west near the henge's northerly causeway may be an 'entrance'.

At the centre of the site are the remnants of a Cove that once faced SSW. towards the heaviest stone, a 3.7 m long eight-ton block now almost overhanging the lip of the ditch. An extended male burial surrounded by stones was discovered just to the east of the Cove. An area up to 4.9 m east of the Cove had been dug out, in one place to a depth of 2.4 m and refilled with earth. Fragments of a human ulna were found in the infill (St. G. Gray, 1903, 480) but the excavation-report does not give further details of what seems to be a rock-cut pit very like another at Cairnpapple near the Cove there. A pit dug 1.5 m into the bedrock was excavated under the multiple-burial cairn at Harland Edge eight and a half miles east of Arbor Low. In its filling was cremated bone and charcoal which provided a date of 1750 bc ±150 (BM-210). Eight other rock-cut inhumation pits in Derbyshire, that at Shuttlestone being 2.4 m deep, are cited in the excavation-report (Riley, 1966, 43), four with bronze daggers, another at Smerrill Moor with a s2/w beaker so that an Early Bronze Age horizon for them is probable. If the cavity at Arbor Low is analogous and the result of secondary activity along-side the focal Cove, then the first phase of this circle-henge would appear to be in the early centuries of the second millennium.

The dating of Arbor Low presents the same problem as in other sites though the food-vessel burial does provide a *terminus ante quem* for the bank.

In his excavations Gray made few finds. At the extreme terminal of the henge's SSE. entrance there was an antler pick and thirteen ox-teeth on the ditch floor. The NNW. entrance was more productive. Six large flint flakes and scrapers had been deliberately set on a ledge low on the ditch wall 'perhaps purposely concealed; they could not have come by accident into the position in which they were found' (St. G. Gray, 470). That they were a votive offering is indicated by their mint condition like the axes from other henges. As well as flint implements in the opposite terminal there was a barbed and tanged arrowhead on the ditch bottom near a blackened hearth. It is reported that a magnificent flint knife, 15 cm long, was found in the nineteenth century at Arbor Low (J. Evans, 1872, 314). If this could be associated with the arrow-head and the other flints it would form a typical early southern beaker as-semblage (Clarke, 1970, 203) very similar to that from the Green Low round barrow on the limestone of Alsop Moor five miles south of Arbor Low where a rock-cut pit held an inhumation with flints and an s1 beaker. Such southern beakers flourished in the eighteenth century bc, and it is possible that Arbor Low's Class II henge was built around that time, well after the primary phase of western stone circles as its egg-shape suggests, perhaps superseding the smaller henge to its south-west.

Except that it is a little larger, Arbor Low closely resembles Cairnpapple, West Lothian, 200 miles to the north, a circle henge that was excavated over two seasons in 1947 and 1948 (Piggott, 1948). Both sites are oval Class II henges with rock-cut ditches, stone rings, Coves and entrances. There are more subtle similarities.

		Henge					Stone Ring				
	O.D. Height (feet)	Entrances	Henge shape	Diameters (Metres)	Axis of Entrances	Distance of Axis from True Centre	Diameters (Metres)	Shape	Major Axis	Entrance	Direction of Cove
Arbor Low	1230′	2	Oval	83 × 75	327° × 147°	5.5 m to W.	41.5 × 37.2	Egg	294° × 114°	5.8 m wide at NW.	SW.
Cairnpapple	1000′	2	Oval	65 × 57	356° × 176°	5.5 m to E.	35.1 × 28.0	Egg	335° × 115°	7.6 m wide at SSE.	E

Table 11. Comparisons between Arbor Low and Cairnpapple

A grave dug in the rock at Cairnpapple is like that at Arbor Low and at Green Low nearby and 'is precisely the manner of digging Early Bronze Age graves in the chalk country of the south of England . . . The technique may constitute another link with the south' (Piggott, 1948, 115).

Cairnpapple (Fig. 47) stands on a basalt hill west of Edinburgh, and on a clear day one can see the Bass Rock to the east and the Arran mountains to the west, from coast to coast across southern Scotland. On such a propitious site a ritual centre was established in the Late Neolithic when seven pits, which may originally have held stones, were dug on three sides of a trapezium open to the WSW. Like the Aubrey Holes at Stonehenge these pits were infilled and then redug to receive token cremations, one with a broken bone pin like those in four or five of the Aubrey Holes. On the old land surface were fragments of two stone axes, one from Great Langdale (Group VI), the other from Graig Lwyd (Group VII), tools that may have been broken during the clearance of the site in the late third millennium.

Years later people from the south built the henge here above the oak and hazel woodlands, gangs digging rough sections of ditch into the basalt and heaping up superimposed layers of clay, turves, stones, earth and boulders to make the oval bank that was set back from the ditch like the bermed henges of southern and eastern England. Wide entrances were left at north and south but, as at Arbor Low, on a line well away from the axis of the henge. The Northumbrian henge of Coupland fifty miles east of Cairnpapple is asymmetrical in the same way (Atkinson, 1952, 64). On Cairnpapple's central area an egg-shaped ring, 35.1 × 28.0 m, of twenty-four large stones, 1.2–1.5 m high, was erected, its apex at the SSW. opposite from that at Arbor Low. Its perimeter measured $122\frac{1}{2}$ M.Y. (Thom, 1967, 68). A 7.6 m gap here seems to be an entrance not quite in line with the henge causeway, again like Arbor Low in reverse and, rather unusually, despite analogous pillars at rings like Pobull Fhinn, North Uist, two single stones stood just inside the perimeter at north and south, making angled portals for henge and stone ring. It is either to this period or, less probably, to the first that a Cove of three huge stones belonged, a construction well off-centre facing almost directly east. Near the Cove and also near the circumference of the stone ring were five burnt areas, one by a ditch terminal like the hearth at Arbor Low. In front of the Cove were some mysterious rectangular pits, in places dug 0.8 m into the bedrock and which resemble quarry-pits. These might be the remains of a rectangular structure akin to those at Loanhead of Daviot RSC (J. N. G. Ritchie, 1974b, 10). Yet at Cairnpapple 'scattered scraps of cremated bone' in the infill of these trenches may correspond in some way with the isolated ulna at Arbor Low. Two sherds of un-decorated beaker in the north-west trench suggest these might be rock-cut graves like those noted in Derbyshire, the proportions being not dissimilar, disturbed at the time the Cove was destroyed by a second group of beaker people intent on constructing a new burial place. How long this circle-henge was used before this destructive interference is hard to estimate. The burial by an eastern stone of a child with an N/NR beaker probably in the nineteenth century bc might be no more than a repetition of the well-known liking of beaker users for placing burials by megalithic pillars. The ring could be much earlier.

Quite different is the pit-burial by the Cove whose stones must have been removed by that time because one of them seems to have been used as a marker or headstone for an oval setting of contiguous stones within which was an extended inhumation reminiscent of that by Arbor Low's Cove. The body may have had a wooden mask placed over its face (Piggott, 1948, 115). Such burials with large standing stones have affinities with the Clava kerb-cairns and the associated sites like Monzie in Perthshire (Ritchie and Mac-Laren, 1972, 10), a tradition that is known to be related to stone rings in Inverness but never with Coves, and which may have caused its adherents to respect the ring at Cairnpapple but to adapt the Cove for their own needs. With the body were two N2/L beakers of the eighteenth and seventeenth centuries bc, one with a base impressed with the bracken on which it stood before firing.

In turn the little cairn over this burial could not have had a long life. Food-vessel users with no need for megalithic rings came to the site, ripped up the standing stones for use as kerbs for a new cairn, 15 m across, that overlay the former Cove, beaker cairn and western stoneholes. There was a further enlargement effected by taking boulders from the henge bank to extend the food-vessel cairn to a diameter of 30 m, overlapping the silted ditch. Burials in inverted collared urns were placed in the extension. It is probable that Cairnpapple was used for yet more burials in the Iron Age when four long graves were dug at the east, destroying one of the old stone-holes. Centuries later the Ravenna Geographer referred to a place, *Medio Nemeton*, somewhere near the Roman Antonine Wall from Forth to Clyde where Britain was at her narrowest. 'Nemeton . . . had the significance of an open sanctuary in the Celtic religious tradition' (Piggott, 1948, 118), and it is tempting to see in Cairnpapple direct evidence of that continuity of custom that is only hinted at elsewhere, the Middle Sanctuary on a hill in lowland Scotland where one could see from coast to coast, and where people had come to supplicate, to bury and to pray for over two thousand years.[1] Cairnpapple is worth visiting. The first food-vessel cairn has been reconstructed and can be penetrated down an iron ladder to see a cist and the beaker grave. Outside, the cairn-enlargement has been reduced to a cobbled plateau pitted with the stoneholes of the henge like grey Gruyère. The custodian's hut has an explanatory model of the site, almost unique in the British Isles at the present.

The accumulated evidence from these circle-henges along the routes connecting northern and southern Britain is that of monumental sites being built in the early centuries of the second millennium for purposes of communal gatherings, for trade and religion in the same manner as the great open circles of the west but much more susceptible to interference and destruction by makers of the native food-vessels.

3. THE SMALLER RINGS OF THE NORTH-EAST AND MIDLANDS

Equally, the ring at Balbirnie, Fife, close to Balfarg, was subjected to food-vessel interference. When the site, first dug into in 1883, was re-excavated in 1970 and 1971 because of the widening of the Perth road (J. N. G. Ritchie, 1974b) a central rectangular setting of slabs was discovered within this 15×14 m ellipse whose ten stones were graded to the south. Sherds of grooved ware were found by Stone 10 in the north-east arc and suggest a date in the second quarter of the second millennium for the ring, a supposition supported by its elliptical shape and by a C-14 assay of 1330 ±90 bc (Ga-K-3425) for later activity here. The open rectangle was very like those at Stenness, Orkney, and at the earthwork enclosure of Mount Pleasant, Dorset, the latter aligned north–south with outlying stones at west, north and east (Wainwright, 1970c, 323), and dated to 1680 ±60 bc (BM-668), having replaced a Wood-henge-type building whose ditch contained grooved ware and which yielded three dates averaging 2000 bc. Such rectangular settings might be related to the 'hearth' at Lugg henge, Dublin, and to the timber mortuary houses known under some Neolithic long graves and beaker burials.

At Balbirnie patches of cremated bone lay underneath some circle-stones. Whatever the ceremonies here they were interrupted when cists associated with a late beaker and a jet button were constructed within the ring. The date of c.1330 bc came from wood alongside the beaker. It may have been in this phase that stretches of low walling were put up between the stones

[1]But see R. W. Feachem, 'Medionemeton on the Limes of Antoninus Pius, Scotland' in *Collection Latomus* 103, 1969, 210–16.

Pl. 31. *Balbirnie, Fife.* A general view from the NNE. of the 1970–1 excavations, Department of the Environment. Surrounding the central rectangular setting are three cists. No. 3 on the right had a cupmarked stone and a food-vessel; no. 2 in the foreground had a bone bead; and behind it, no. 1 had a sidestone with cupmarks and cup-and-ring marks. Both nos 1 and 2 had cremations of a woman and child.

The site is only 300 metres east of Balfarg circle-henge.

forming a continuous barrier in much the same way as the prostrate connecting stones at Moncrieffe thirteen miles north-west, and analogous to the embanked stone circles elsewhere in Britain that seem generally to belong to a period in the mid-second millennium. The artefacts at Balbirnie agree with such an horizon.

But the first cists did not long remain undisturbed and were seemingly rifled when later cists were built (J. N. G. Ritchie, 1974b, 13) that contained the cremations of women and children like the pits of Weird Law enclosed cremation cemetery forty-five miles to the south. One of these later cists held a food-vessel and a flint knife.

Like Cairnpapple, the stone circle was further abused. A low cairn was piled over all the cists. Sherds of deliberately-broken urns, one with barley impressions (Jessen and Helbaek, 1944, 20) were scattered amongst the boulders, intermingled with small coagulations of burnt human bone. It would seem that this last phase at Balbirnie occurred rather late in the second millennium, for a C-14 determination of 890 ±80 bc (Ga-K-3426) came from the land surface that had built up within the ring during the centuries while the stone circle remained open to the weather.

Although it must not be overstated it seems that the makers of food-vessels in particular regarded megalithic rings as little more than desirable locations for their cists, a duality in the people's attitudes permitting a recognition of the monument's sacred character whilst allowing them to transform its essential openness into a cairn-filled ring. Such cairns whether at Balbirnie and Cairnpapple or even at Dun Ruadh or Gortcorbies in Ireland tell the same story of the integration of an ancient sanctuary into a later sepulchre. It follows that food-vessel cists at other rings like Machrie Moor, Arran, Cunninghar, Clackmannan, or the 12.2 m oval of Marchwell, Midlothian, do not provide conclusive proof for the dating of these sites. In the same way the large barrow at Newbridge outside Edinburgh with its fine rivetted bronze dagger may not be of the same date as its three surrounding stones. These could be all that is left of a circle, 54.9 m across, but they may equally simply be single monoliths.

The three, thin writhing pillars at Lundin Links, Fife, are just as questionable. Ringed in battered iron railings on a golf-course, they huddle like captured triffids, more reminiscent of standing stones than of a ravaged circle. An obsequious eighteenth-century factor described them: 'some of them over 20 ft in height, beneath which my ingenious and honoured patron, Baron Clark, having employed men to dig, several coffins were found, containing bones of men . . .' Thom (1971, 56) deduced from their impressive heights that the stones were intended for observations on the minimum moonrise and moonset. Whether they were ever part of a circle remains debatable.

Indeed, whether in south-east Scotland or north-east England stone circles are uncommon, and great megalithic rings hardly exist. There are henges here: Coupland; Overhowden; Weston; Normangill and Rachan Slack as well as Balfarg and Cairnpapple, but only two large stone rings. Both these are egg-shaped, and on either side of the Merse-Teviot valley along which a traveller could cross the Cheviots, past Burgh Hill oval and down Liddesdale to the Solway Firth. Both sites are close to a henge. Borrowston Rigg, north of the Teviot, 41.5×36.6 m on a WNW.–ESE. axis, lies overgrown on a moorland. Of its low stones none more than 60 cm high, one lies exactly at the north 3.1 m inside the circumference like an inlier at Cairnpapple. Thirty-seven metres north-west two stones may mark an alignment on Capella in 1930 BC (Thom, 1967, 98). Five miles WSW. across the Leader Water is Overhowden henge, a large oval with a north-west entrance.

Thirty miles south-east of Borrowston Rigg is the other, more impressive ring of Threestoneburn, Ilderton, standing on a pronounced slope like Overhowden henge near which excavations unearthed many flints and a stone macehead (Atkinson, 1952). Overlooking the spacious valley to its ESE., Threestoneburn, 36.0×29.3 m, stands on a north-west–south-east axis with its biggest surviving stones up to 1.7 m high in its northern arc. Inside this open ring Victorian investigators uncovered spreads of charcoal like those in the southern rings of Fernworthy on Dartmoor, the traces of fire-rituals perhaps connected with seasonal sun festivals. Eight miles north of Threestoneburn is Coupland henge in the Till valley, similar in size to Overhowden but with NNW. and SSE. entrances. In the same neighbourhood are the Standing Stones of Hethpool on a level knoll between a steep-sided burn and a hillside, all the stones toppled, which may have formed a vast horseshoe or an oval of unshaped stones on a north-east–south-west axis.

Elsewhere there are no great circles. This was not a region of much Neolithic activity. Chambered tombs and long mounds are few. It is only around 2000 bc that settlement of land around the Forth estuary became wide-spread. 'The apparent sparseness of neolithic occupation in south-east Scotland may be contrasted with the increase in activity in the area in the 2nd and 1st millennia.' (J. N. G. and A. Ritchie, 1972, 19.) In England, burial cairns like the round Copt Hill, Durham, or the long Bellshiel Law, Northumberland, are singular Neolithic sites amongst the numerous Bronze Age monuments of this part of Britain: round barrows like Kirkhaugh with an AOC beaker and a gold ear-ring (Tait, 1965, 16); standing stones like the 3.7 m high cupmarked pillar at Swinburn Castle; stone rows like the Five Kings with two stones at right-angles to the alignment; and the hundreds of cup-and-ring marked rocks in Northumberland (Beckensall, 1974) at one of which, Fowberry Moor, 'the remains of a round burial mound include stones carved with the same symbols as those on the natural rock underneath' (ibid, 9). Even the large henges with their two entrances and oval shapes are more probably of the early second than of the third millennium.

Thus in the eastern Lammermuirs there are no large open rings, only little ring-cairns high in the hills, embanked ovals like Mayshiel or Spartleton Edge, 12.8 m across, with seven stones just showing above the peat and heather. This is the very fringe of stone-circle country. Forty miles south-west is the Burgh Hill group with their tall south-west stones. Thirty miles west is the once isolated six-stone ring of the Harestones, now hedged round in a cottage garden, intermediate between the small ovals of Perthshire and those of the Cheviots where Duddo Four Stones, the destroyed Fairnington, the Five Stanes and others hint at wide cultural connections between the lands to north and south of the Forth estuary. Embanked rings like Yadlee, only 8.2 m across, or Nether Dod, 12.2 m in diameter with a south-west entrance, are as much ring-cairns as stone circles. Kingside Hill on an open moorside 1000 ft up, its thirty stones enclosing an 11.6 × 10.7 m space with a south-west entrance is very like the enclosed cremation cemetery of Weird Law forty miles west. Both sites had central mounds. Charcoal from a cremation at Weird Law was dated to 1490 bc ± 90 (NPL-57). Such a period or even later is likely for many of these monuments with their mixture of stone circle and earthwork.

The Perthshire affinities are accentuated by the Four-Posters in Northumberland: the Goatstones with a cupmarked south-east stone, and the

Pl. 32. *The Goatstones, Northumberland.* The thirteen cupmarks on the east stone, seen from the north. The top of the stone slopes towards the south-west.

Three Kings in Redesdale which was shown to have a pillaged ring-cairn inside it when it was excavated in 1971 (Burl and Jones, 1972). Neither site is likely to be earlier than the mid-second millennium and may be 'family' monuments built by small groups that had wandered southwards in search of good land.

Farther south in Yorkshire the pattern is the same. There are great henges like the double-ditched trio at Thornborough, built on the gravel between the rivers Swale and Ure, their north-west–south-east entrances aligned through the sites. Other henges: Cana; Nunwick; Hutton Moor crowd into the same few square miles between the rivers. There are standing stones such as the Devil's Arrows, Boroughbridge, monsters of millstone grit dragged five miles to a spot leading down to the best fording of the Ure. There is the tallest standing stone in the British Isles at Rudston, in the churchyard, a monolithic gritstone, its tip broken but still standing 7.9 m above the ground. This twenty-six-ton giant was hauled from Cayton Bay ten miles away. Significantly it rises at the eastern end of a chalk ridge near Bridlington where many stone axes have been found. The ridge begins at Rudston with its cursuses, its henge and long barrows, and bends down to Newbald by the

Humber where there is another henge. At Rudston early beaker sherds came from one of several cursuses converging on the ridge (D. P. Dymond, 1966, 92). The tall pillar, which stood in a rectangular ditched enclosure, once had a smaller stone to its east much like Maen Mawr in Wales and seems to have served the same directional purpose as a towering landmark on the trackway that led through one of the most densely populated areas of Neolithic Britain. Just as a pillar at St. Asaph's church, Bernera in the Hebrides is supposedly 'part of a small stone circle in which the Druids stood to observe the ravens and from their doings to draw auguries' (Swire, 1966, 205), so the monolith at Rudston has been 'christianized' by enclosing it in the churchyard, another example of the persistence of paganism into mediaeval times.

But stone circles are rare. This is henge country and the very existence of the monstrous stones at Rudston and Boroughbridge is a contradiction as though to emphasize the scarcity of stone. Rings that have been called stone circles turn out not to be so. One in the east on the North Yorkshire Moors at Danby Rigg was actually a complex ring-cairn, its rubble bank worn down, one of its four tall stones remaining. Excavators found two late collared urns at its centre, upside down and holding cremated bone and charcoal.

Another so-called pair of circles at the High Bridestones is better interpreted as the wreckage of stone rows across 137 m of heather-thick moor. Only Commondale on a gentle slope may be a genuine oval, 31.7 m across, the tallest of its stones a mere 61 cm high at the ESE. and set radially like its neighbours. Digging here has resulted only in the discovery of a few, ill-recorded flint flakes (Pearson, 1970, 240). Another misnamed stone circle at Kirkmoor Beck Farm with ten stones just protruding through the turf around a 4.6 m space covered a few urn sherds, a flint and scraps of cremated bone (Radley, 1969b). Such a site has more in common with ring-cairns than with the splendid open megalithic rings of western Britain.

If the North Yorkshire Moors are not fruitful territory for the seeker of stone circles the hills of western Yorkshire are only slightly more productive. The rings show the same mixture of stone circle and ring-cairn, two being adjacent at Dumpit Hill on Mossy Moor Ridge near Hebden, small and ravaged for wall-building. The Twelve Apostles on Ilkley Moor near the crest of a ridge is perhaps the best preserved of several such embanked rings in an area better known for its cup-and-ring-marked rocks. A slight earth bank surrounds a true circle, 15.9 m across, many of the stones fallen or missing. Of those still standing one over 1.2 m high leans at the north-east, its moorland setting contrasting against the cultivated hillsides of Wharfedale in the distance. To find truly megalithic circles it is necessary to go deeper into the Pennines where 1225 ft up in the hills on a characteristic terrace is the Druids Altar, Grassington, three standing stones remaining of a 'Scottish' Four-Poster, built like other Perthshire examples on a cairn, here badly disturbed at its south. The site has been misinterpreted as a ruined embanked circle (Allcroft, 1927, 225), its name coming from a large, flat stone within, but this seems to be the broken south-west pillar whose stump still survives at the corner of a 4 × 3.5 m rectangle set almost north–south. Being seventy miles south of the nearest Four-Poster at the Goatstones, Northumberland, the Druids Altar is as isolated from its fellows as the Four Stones, Walton. Such is the ruinous state of this monument that it has also been visualized as the remains of a small chambered tomb with a crescentic façade (Feather and Manby, 1970, 397). The embanked oval of Carperby, immediately below the towering Ivy Scar, with its likeness to the Welsh Druids Circle, is fifteen miles to the north.

Of twenty or more rings in Yorkshire only three or four have stones more than 0.9 m high. Most stand in low, overgrown banks about 11 m across and enclose areas of multiple burials like the enclosed cremation cemeteries to which they are related. Four urns and a pygmy cup came from the 7.6 m Harden Moor. And to the south, despite the proud claim that no county has more stone circles than Derbyshire where at least twenty can be visited (Andrews, 1907), the same criticism can be made, that most of them are simple or complex ring-cairns. Even though the county can boast more general studies of its 'stone circles' than any other—Lewis, 1903; J. Ward, 1905; Andrews, 1907; Radley, 1966a—there seem never to have been more than five or six megalithic rings in the Peak District.

This lovely and spectacular region rises at the south end of the Pennine Chain, divided by the Derwent, rich in forested valleys pushing between the moors and worn hills from Dovedale to High Peak and beyond. The stone rings demonstrate clearly the development and change that occurred in these monuments during the second millennium, starting as wide circles of heavy stones and concluding as tiny earthen enclosures with slab-revetted interiors.

Early settlement in the Peak concentrated on the rich soils of the western limestone where Neolithic people built chambered tombs like Five Wells, its circular cairn overlying two earlier passage-graves (Corcoran, 1969, 90), and where many stone axes from the Lake District, from north Wales and from Charnwood Forest (Group XX) just below Derbyshire, indicate the distant contacts of this district in the third millennium (Moore & Cummins, 1974, 74). After 2000 bc people for a while occupied the same areas west of the Derwent with increasing numbers of beaker burials often as contracted inhumations in deep, rock-cut pits. At least thirty of their round cairns are known and 'there can be little doubt that the new importance and prosperity of the Peak area depended on its strategic central position, linking the new North Welsh and North Irish expansion, with Yorkshire to the north and the Fen Margin to the south. This network would seem the most likely for the growing trade in Irish gold and bronze equipment' (Clarke, 1970, 216). Makers of food-vessels, their burials in ground-level cists twice as numerous as the beaker barrows, came in from Yorkshire and also from the west, but now, from about 1700 bc onwards, there was the first exploitation of the poorer millstone grit country east of the river, a colonization increased by the settlement of other groups using collared urns for their cremated burials. These were the people mainly responsible for the widespread clearance of the mixed oak forest on the eastern uplands between 1500 and 1000 bc (S. P. Hicks, 1972, 17), and this was the time of the cremation cemeteries whose antecedents may be to the north-west of the Peak where the multiple cremations in the stone-lined enclosures of Todmorden and Mosley Height were accompanied by Pennine urns, pygmy cups, faience beads and fragments of bronze ware of what Bu'lock has called his late Peak II/III horizon from the mid-second millennium onwards (Bu'lock, 1961, 3; Varley, 1964, 53; Burgess, 1974, 189).

In the Peak District the sequence of stone circles mirrors these chronological, environmental and cultural changes both from the limestone to the millstone grit, and from open megalithic rings to minute ring-banks around burial pits. The farther to the east one travels the smaller the height of the stones until at the edge of districts like Big Moor the rings consist of low rubble banks with no standing stone anywhere in them. The only great Peak stone circles are on the limestone itself at the circle-henges of Arbor Low and the Bull Ring, attributable at the latest to a time of quite early beakers. The few other stone rings without banks, albeit much smaller, are very close to the limestone edge at the sites of Doll Tor and Ninestone Close where four enormous blocks, the largest stones in Derbyshire, remain of a 13.1 m ring at the side of a little terrace. It was dug into by Bateman in March, 1847, when he found some badly fired sherds and a worked flint. The site is over-risen by the eroded crag of Hart Hill to the south-west.

Less than a mile to the east across a valley is the lonely plateau of Stanton Moor like a lost world, its top covered with a prehistoric necropolis of cairns, ring-cairns, standing stones and stone circles. Doll Tor at its west was another rare unbanked ring, 6.1 m in diameter of six fair-sized stones. At some time the intervals between the stones were joined by drystone walling, and several urned cremations with pygmy cups were buried in the interior. Later the east stone was encapsulated in a ring-cairn like Gortcorbies, Londonderry. Under a flat slab at the centre a female cremation lay in a pit with a segmented faience bead. Other cremations, three with collared urns, one with a star-shaped faience bead, had been placed around the inner edge of the stone bank which eventually was filled in to make a flat-topped platform cairn (Heathcote, 1939). The faience beads broadly indicate the date of Doll Tor's ring-cairn. Whether they were exotic imports from the eastern Mediterranean or whether they were of native manufacture, (Newton and Renfrew, 1970, 203) which thermal neutron activation analysis of their tin content and of others from the continent strongly suggests, their associations in Britain point to a date around the fifteenth century (McKerrell, 1972, 299). This is in a late relationship with other finds—at least twenty-five collared urns, seventeen early in the tradition (Longworth, 1961, 298, 305), a food-vessel, four incense cups,

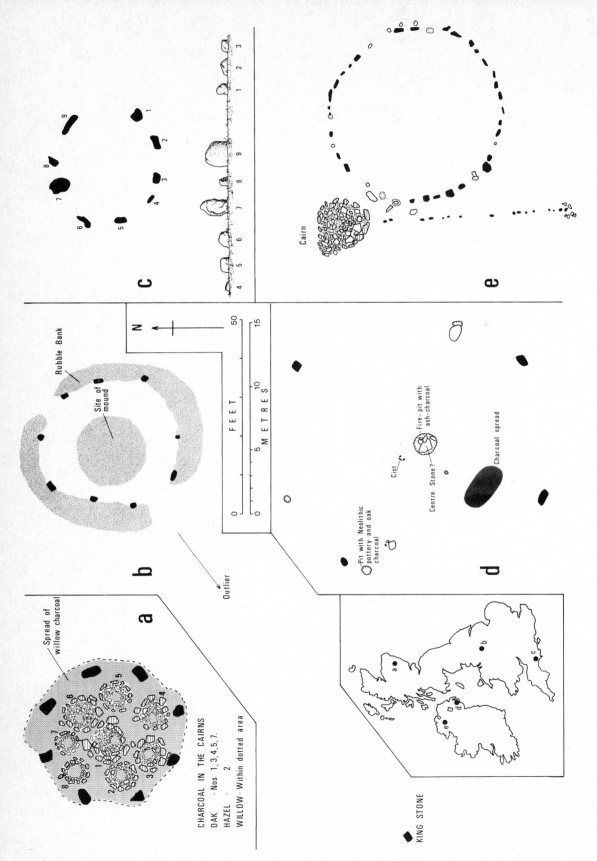

Fig. 48. Five Small Stone Circles in the British Isles. (a) Cullerlie, Aberdeenshire; (b) Nine Ladies, Derbyshire; (c) Nine Stones, Winterbourne Abbas, Dorset; (d) Castle Mahon, Down; (e) Drumskinny, Fermanagh. The variety of architecture and ritual in the British stone circles is shown in these plans. (a) after Kilbride-Jones, 1935; (c) after Collins, 1956; (d) after Waterman, 1964.

fragments of bronze, a jet ring and late battle-axes (Roe, 1966, 226), all of the Bronze Age—on Stanton Moor where 'on a rocky and uncultivated waste, about two miles in length and one-and-a-half in breadth, are numerous remains of antiquity, as rocking-stones, barrows, circles of erect stones etc., of undoubted British origin' (Bateman, 1848, 116).

At the north is the embanked stone circle of the Nine Ladies, small, its unremarkable stones, like so many of the later rings in Derbyshire, set in a low rubble bank that is difficult to appreciate, like its entrances at north-west and south-east, because of an ugly stone wall that has been built around it (Fig. 48). To the south-west is an outlier, the slablike King Stone, 58 cm of millstone grit, scratched with graffiti, trapped meaninglessly inside another wall. Perhaps even later than the Nine Ladies is the line of three ring-cairns close by, from 12.2 m to 24.4 m in diameter, with north and south gaps in their banks, two with large tumbled stones along their inner edges. From the most northerly, half-hidden by trees, came four Pennine urns (Radley, 1966a).

The juxtaposition of stone rings, complex ring-cairns and earth circles occur elsewhere. The flattened stone circle of the Seven Stones in Hordron, its stones entirely lost in towering summer bracken, is close to Moscar Moor ring-cairn which in turn is not far from the 30.5 m enclosed cremation cemetery of Bamford Moor whose bank is little more than 15 cm high. This is like another ECC at Wet Withens on Eyam Moor, 29.9 m across, enigmatically described by Thom as a Circle+ (1967, 137, D1/2). A few stones lie on its thick and heathery bank. In the wide interior once supposedly supporting a nearly central stone, Bateman dug up a cist with an urn. The cairn of Round Hillock to the NNE. was robbed in 1759 by road-builders who found a large urn, amber beads and a perforated jet pendant of the mid-second millennium. In an interesting note on the method of making astronomical records Wilson and Garfitt (1920) suggested there might be alignments towards hilltops and the midsummer and equinoctial sunrise.

On Big Moor the typological sequence of Derbyshire rings is explicit. At the west a complex ring-cairn, Stoke Flat, stands by the steep Froggatt Edge. A conspicuously taller stone, 1.1 m high, marks a south-west entrance through the bracken-grown bank. Two miles to the east across the moor Barbrook I, an embanked stone circle (Fig. 5), is a flattened ring 14.6 × 12.5 m across its bank with a taller stone at the south-west where the ground starts to fall from the vast, flat grassland. No finds are recorded from the two robbing-trenches dug by the Duke of Rutland's gamekeeper before 1939. A low, gnarled outlier pokes from the spiky grass and heather to the WSW. Thom (1967, 98) noted a good orientation to an even lower outlier on the setting of Spica (α Virginis) in 2000 BC, somewhere between 1550 and 1500 bc which correlates markedly with the C-14 assay obtained independently from Barbrook II, a complex ring-cairn to the north. This was the period of the major clearance by pastoralists of the oak and alder forests on this upland. It should be remarked however, that any remaining tree-cover might have negated such a low-set sight-line.

The bank at Barbrook II of small stones was retained by kerbs and, internally, by a drystone wall against which nine or ten stones stood. In the western half of the ring was a cairn over a pit in which there was a collared urn, two flint scrapers, a flint knife and a cremation from whose charcoal a date of 1500 bc ± 150 (BM-179) was obtained. There was evidence that a ritual fire had been lit after the cremation had been buried. To its east was a disturbed cist, its cover cupmarked (G. Lewis, 1966). On the same moor, two miles NNE. of Barbrook II, another ring-cairn at Brown Edge, Totley Moor, had no standing stones but within its stony bank was a foot-high cairn, cremations in pits with Pennine urns, and pygmy cups, the site yielding a series of dates from 1530 bc ± 150 (BM-212), 1250 bc ± 150 (BM-211) down to as late as 1050 bc ± 150 (BM-177) for the cremated burial of a youth with a Pennine urn (Radley, 1966a), a time when already the moorland was being abandoned. This 12.2 m, grass-high ring with its multiple burials is a long way in time from the awesome circle-henges of the limestone plateau.

4. THE ROLLRIGHT STONES

South of Derbyshire there are no big groups of stone circles, only clusters in Dorset, Exmoor and north Wessex (Fig. 1). There is also the oddly remote Rollright Stones (Fig. 49) in Oxfordshire, one of the most famous circles in the British Isles, 'a great monument of Antiquity, a number of vastly great stones placed in a circular figure, which the country-people call Rolle-rich stones, and have a tradition that they were once men thus turn'd into stones' (Camden, 1695, 254). The name has nothing to do with any supernatural rotation of the stones but may derive from *Hrolla-landriht* as early spellings like Rollindricht and Rollendri intimate, 'the land belonging to Hrolla'.

This circle was placed at the narrowing edge of a limestone plateau with an outlier, the King Stone, at the top of the steep slope to the north-east, and, 357 m ESE., the ruins of a portal dolmen called the Whispering Knights. These leaning pillars have been considered a Cove like that at Stanton Drew (Grinsell, 1956, 2) but eighteenth-century descriptions of an erstwhile round mound and the arrangement of the five stones make the interpretation of a despoiled tomb more likely.

The Rollright Stones seem innumerable, seventy-seven stones, stumps and lumps of leprous limestone, some nearly lost in the short turf, others 2.1 m high, in a perfect circle, 31.6 m or 38 M.Y. in diameter, with a possible entrance at the north. Although local legends claim that the stones cannot be counted the circle may originally have had no more than about twenty-two tall monoliths. Centuries of weathering have eroded them into fragments that lie by or behind their rotting bases. Many of these manageable pieces were removed for building but, before 1886, some were replaced in convenient gaps around the circumference (Ravenhill, 1932, 14), creating the neat confusion of today's monument, described marvellously by Stukeley as 'the greatest Antiquity we have yet seen . . . corroded like wormeaten wood by the harsh Jaws of Time'.

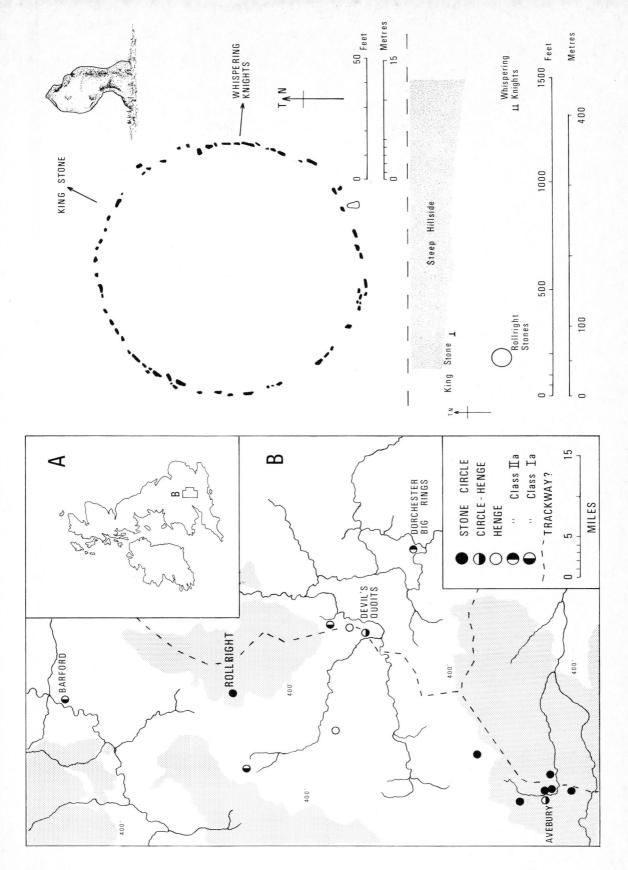

Fig. 49. The Rollright Stones, Oxfordshire.

There is no other stone ring near the Rollright Stones. It stands on a track-way leading south from the midlands past Hunsbury and Tadmarton with their later hillforts and onwards either to the western Cotswolds or to the basin of the Upper Thames. Like some of the stone rings of north-east Britain the circle is in an area of henges. The possible site of Hampton Lucy is sixteen miles NNW. by the Avon (Webster and Hobley, 1965, 18), and beyond there is the hengiform Barford with a date of 2416 bc ± 64 (Birm-7). The double-entranced Westwell is thirteen miles SSW. of the Rollright Stones; the ovals of the Deadman's Burial near a beaker cemetery, and the Devil's Quoits, both about sixteen miles SSE. on the Oxfordshire trackway; and Condicote, double-ditched and with a south entrance, eight miles WSW. at the start of the Cots-wolds. The Rollright Stones are at the extreme north-east corner of stone-building country, here in company with such chambered tombs as the Hoar-stones or Adlestrop Hill at the outer limits of the crowd of Neolithic megalithic barrows in the north Cotswolds (Corcoran, 1969, 36). Builders of stone rarely settled farther east. Only at the Devil's Quoits is there a stone setting inside the henge, and there the stones were almost fanatically quarried from intractable gravel conglomerate.

The well-drained gravels of the Upper Thames seem to have supported a large and prosperous population in the Late Neolithic and Early Bronze Age along the land and river routes to Wessex and East Anglia but the Rollright Stones were built on a high ridge above the forests, on an area of shallow, clay loams always susceptible to summer drought and more suited to pastoralists than crop-growers, people unlikely to be numerous. If each of the henges and the stone circle were at the edges of their 'territories' where the land merges into the fringe of forests, as seems to be the case with the Middle and Late Neolithic causewayed enclosures of Wessex (Renfrew, 1937b, 229) and the RSCs of north-east Scotland, then each might be the focus of some twenty square miles of inhabited land, separated from each other, and quite sufficient to support several hundred people in the richer, low-lying soils of the henges, perhaps between 100 and 200 on the limestone upland.

The Rollright Stones are at the narrowest south-west point here. East is the undulating landscape of Great Rollright, westwards the downcurving hillsides to the Evenlode plain where, eight miles south the chambered long barrow of Ascott under Wychwood was erected in a cleared stretch of open woodland on which people had farmed as much as two centuries before. The barrow was put up around 2785 bc ± 70 (BM-492). Neolithic axes from Enstone and Witney also show the presence of Neolithic people in Oxfordshire. The associa-tion of an outlying portal dolmen and the occupation of the high country suggests that the Rollright Stones were put up in the early second millennium when the midlands route was being increasingly used.

Seventy-three metres north-east of the perimeter, across the hedged country lane, is the King Stone, a 2.4 m high outlier, twisted and bent like a hunched hag. This has been thought to be a stone from a chambered

Pl. 33. *The Rollright Stones, Oxfordshire*. From the north. The outlying King Stone is just off the photograph where a path on the extreme left leads to it.

tomb but despite Stukeley calling a long mound near it the 'Archdruid's Barrow' the rise is natural (Ravenhill, 1932, 17) and the King Stone may be taken as one more example of the outlying stones well known among the great open rings of western Britain. An alignment on the rising of Capella in 1790 BC (*c.* 1550 bc) is feasible (Thom, 1967, 100) but seems late for such a site, particularly when an alternative purpose can readily be tested. Go down the sloping field to the north a few hundred yards where the hill's curvature hides the circle even if the modern hedge were removed. The King Stone is clear against the skyline. Go to the King Stone and the circle is visible. An outlier is not needed elsewhere here for the ground is quite level and the Rollright Stones may be seen from a long way away. It is another instance, like Long Meg, the Heel Stone and Maen Mawr, of a sensible reason for these outlying stones.

Local stories say the outlier is a king turned to stone, as were his men, by a witch who owned the land over which the ambitious conqueror marched. 'Go forward,' she cackled,

> 'Seven long strides shalt thou take.
> If Long Compton thou canst see
> King of England thou shalt be.'

And the king shouted,

> 'Stick, stock, stone,
> As King of England I shall be known.'

But the unsuspected mound, Stukeley's 'long barrow', humped on the downslope between his view and Long Compton and, malevolently triumphant, the witch cried,

> 'As Long Compton thou canst not see,
> King of England thou shalt not be,
> Rise up stick, and stand still, stone,
> For King of England thou shalt be none;
> Thou and thy men hoar stones shall be
> And I myself an eldern tree.'

The king became the King Stone, his warriors the circle, and some far-off muttering traitors the Whispering Knights.

One wonders what time-thin truths survive. 'The past has left marks deep in the human mind as real as the tangible marks which we search out among our fields and hills.' (J. Hawkes, 1973, 186.) At other stone circles, a hundred or more miles distant, there are legends to do with water, white blossoms, of midsummer, of sun, of fertility practices, all of which combine in the stories of the Rollright Stones to create a tantalus of shadows. It may be coincidental that the witch changed herself into an elder tree with its June clusters of creamy-white flowers, but notice that 'on Midsummer Eve when the eldern tree was in blossom, it was the custom for people to come up to the King Stone and stand in a circle. Then the eldern was cut, and as it bled the king moved his head' (A. J. Evans, 1895). In other accounts the stones of the circle moved downhill during the night to drink at a spring, especially at midnight on New Year's Day (Manning, 1902), the time of the winter gatherings suspected elsewhere. If a young Oxfordshire wife were infertile she would visit the circle at midnight and press the tips of her breasts against the stones just as women did at Carnac 300 miles away across the English Channel. Stukeley wrote that the young people would meet at the Rollright Stones 'at a special time and make merry with cakes and ale'. The seasonal gatherings on winter nights and summer days, the processions from a source of water, the belief in the fecund power of the stones, the celebrations and merrymaking of young men and women, these are flashes of an ancient world glimpsed now through the frosted glass of time.

Expectedly in a ring where the activities were vital but left so little of substance behind excavations have not been helpful. 'Besides, that curious Antiquary Ralph Sheldon Esq., making a diligent search in the middle, after anything that might lead us to the first design of it, and particularly bones, found himself disappointed.' (Camden, 1695, 268.) No bones. No burials. On the prehistoric track the open circle of the Rollright Stones with its north entrance, its outlier, its mouldering stones, lingered in use for two thousand years, the earliest ceremonies never entirely forgotten even when they had declined into the mummeries of witchcraft. In Tudor times there were reports of sabbaths being held there and rumours were muttered that Warwickshire witches went naked to the stones for their rites. As late as 12 May, 1949, the night of a full moon nearest Walpurgis night, the night of Beltane, two observers saw dark figures moving around the King Stone, dancing, perhaps half a dozen bodies, couples back to back.

> There was more a mumbling than any talking or singing . . . When they were still the leader appeared to make signs and gestures as he stood by the King Stone. He had some kind of disguise. I could have sworn it was a goat's face mask . . . but I did not mention this before as I thought someone would think I was suffering from some kind of madness, or hallucinations. (McCormick, 1968, 110.)

There is, however, no reputable evidence that other stone circles were used for witchcraft practices in mediaeval, Tudor or Stuart times, and modern suggestions that they were meeting-places for the covens are probably witchful thinking.

The Rollright Stones are now supposedly free from such visitations. Some say that the ritual murder of a hedgecutter at Lower Quinton made the nearby sanctuary of the Rollright Stones too obvious and the covens moved elsewhere (*Daily Mirror*, 13 February, 1954). Others said that the nocturnal practitioners within the stones were discouraged by cheerful calls from passing motorists of, 'Lovely night for the witches, then!' (Daniel, 1966).

5. THE SMALL RINGS OF SOUTHERN AND WESTERN ENGLAND

There are not many stone circles south of the Rollright Stones. In the Cotswolds where so many megalithic tombs were constructed there is none unless the doubtful Bathampton is accepted (Tratman, 1958, 110), although folklore does claim that until the early nineteenth century a stone circle stood at the Devil's Churchyard near Cherington, Gloucestershire, a ghostly site where headless horsemen and black dogs still appeared to night travellers (Partridge, 1912).

Skirting north Wessex with its important group of circles there is only a thin scatter of rings along the Dorset coast, some strange circles in south Devon, three on Exmoor, and the isolated circles in south Wiltshire of Tisbury and Stonehenge.

The Dorset rings are strung along the coast from Rempstone to Little Cheney, a distribution about thirty miles long with a mere nine sites in it, most at the west end, and all within five miles of the sea. Their comparatively small diameters are in noticeable contrast to the size of the huge earthworks of Mount Pleasant, Maumbury, Knowlton and Eggardon in this region. In passing it may be asked whether the enormous enclosure of Mount Pleasant, Dorchester, with two dates of 1784 bc ± 41 (BM-645) and 1778 bc ± 59 (BM-646), might not have been a settlement of people using the much smaller henge of Maumbury Rings a mile to the west for their religious ceremonies, a site that had replaced the causewayed enclosure of Maiden Castle just to the south-west. Grooved ware has come from all three sites as it has from Durrington Walls and Stonehenge where a similar relationship of settlement and 'temple' may have obtained. Knowlton South and Centre in Dorset could be associated in the same way.

Whatever the truth the Dorset henges are on average four times the diameter of the megalithic rings. Characteristically these are oval, rather small, and lie at the edge of hillsides near but not in the cemeteries of round barrows along the Dorset Ridgeway for which this part of the country is famous. A majority of the rings are near Little Bredy where, at the foot of Crow Hill, is the Valley of Stones, a convenient source of sarsen and conglomerate slabs for the megalithic tombs and stone circles in the neighbourhood. Two-thirds of the tombs and of the rings lie within four miles of this valley although the total distribution extends up to sixteen miles away, clear indication that geological expediency underlay prehistoric man's choice of materials. It is probable therefore that timber rings await discovery farther east along the south Dorset Downs.

The most easterly of the rings, at Rempstone, now lies wrecked at the margin of a wood amongst the bracken, quite close to the fine linear cemetery of the Nine Barrows. Typically, Rempstone is oval, 24.4×20.7 m. 'In August, 1957, the remains of a stone avenue were revealed by deep ploughing about half a mile west of this circle and aligned on it.' (Grinsell, 1958, 77.) The existence of such a feature, linked with the ring or not, is of interest in Dorset because at the long-smashed ring of Little Mayne. Roger Gale in 1728 wrote that there were 'two avenues of pitcht stones leading up to it, one from the South, the other from the East'. Piggott who made notes on many of these Dorset rings (S. and C. M. Piggott, 1939) commented that Gale was a reliable fieldworker who had already seen Avebury and the fragmented avenue there. Quite possibly in this part of Dorset there were megalithic features in common with north Wiltshire.

Farther west near the Valley of Stones, Kingston Russell, a flattened circle about 27.7×20.6 m (Thom, 1955, 281), the longest stones at the north, is entirely fallen. So is the much smaller oval of Hampton Down to the east by the rim of Portesham Hill overlooking the coast 700 ft below. Its history illuminates the perils of superficial fieldwork. In 1939 there were sixteen stones in a ring about 10.7 m across. Thom (1967, 40) found it difficult to establish an accurate diameter, which is not surprising for when Wainwright examined it in 1964 there were twenty-eight stones. Even more disturbing than this evidence of modern interference was the discovery during excavation that not only was the number of stones wrong but the site also. The true prehistoric ring had stood to the west where there was now a hedge, and had consisted of an oval, about 7.6 × 6.1 m, of eight or nine stones. A track led to its north-east entrance marked by stakes and two sections of ditch (Wainwright, 1967). No finds came from this excavation. Like many other southern rings burials were not customary here.

In much better condition is the atypical Nine Stones, Winterbourne Abbas (Fig. 48), shaded by trees alongside a road, enclosed in iron railings. Unusually it is in a valley. Thom (1955, 281) described it as a flattened circle of precisely the same proportions as Kingston Russell two and a half miles south-west, so identical that he was able to superimpose their plans (ibid, Fig. 3) although the Nine Stones was much smaller with axes of 9.1 × 7.6 m. Later he re-interpreted the ring as an ellipse 9.1 × 7.9 m or 11 × 9½ M.Y. (Thom, 1967, 72). There is, in fact, a resemblance to Kingston Russell for both sites were once graded to the north, the Nine Stones having two conspicuously taller stones, 1.2 m and 2.1 m high, on either side of a low block at the True North. In many ways the Nine Stones is like the group of rings in south-west Scotland of which the flattened Loupin' Stanes (Thom, 1967, 137) is a good example, but whereas those sites have their tallest stones at the south-west the builders of the Nine Stones in southern England adopted the accepted north–south lines of that region.

These scattered Dorset ovals are probably of the Bronze Age. Although they cannot be directly associated with the barrow cemeteries neither can they be related to any distribution of Neolithic sites (Grinsell, 1959, Map 1). At the Nine Stones the biggest of the stones, eight tons in weight, needed many people to move and erect it but the ring itself could accommodate only a few. This is even more true of the diminutive Hampton Down. Both these rings might more suitably be seen as focal points for one or two participants, the remainder of the small community outside watching ceremonies that here, unlike the north of Britain, required no cremation deposits.

Miles to the west in southern Devon an old map of 1789 referred to a stone circle near Sidmouth near the significantly named Seven Stones Lane. Nothing remains although many flint implements have been ploughed up in the vicinity of this reputed site (E. E. Smith, 1947). Five miles north-east in a linear cemetery of round barrows extending over three miles from Gittesham Hill to Broad Down three barrows had stone circles around them (A. Fox, 1948), each well away from the mound and its ditch. At their centres were small cairns with rough cists containing cremations, a bronze dagger, a shale cup and an imitation segmented faience bead, an assemblage of the later Early Bronze Age at a time when in the west of the country burial mounds and stone rings were both being conjoined in the cairn-circle-rows of Dartmoor with their cist burials, at Carn Caca in Wales, even as far north as Penrith where 'almost opposite to Mayborough (henge) on the Cumberland side of the Eimot is a vast cairn or tumulus, composed of round stones, and surrounded with large grit stones . . . which altogether form a circle 60 ft in diameter' (Pennant, 1774).

But showing no internal mounds or cists are the three rings on Exmoor, a boss of slates, shales, grits and sandstones, in north Somerset, little used during the Neolithic but with increasing occupation in the later second millennium (Grinsell, 1970, 30). None of these rings can be directly dated. They are all ruined and the stones generally are tiny, those at Almsworthy being noticed for the first time during peat-burning in 1931. All have been described by St. G. Gray: Withypool (1907); Almsworthy (1931); and Porlock (1929; 1950). The most southerly, Withypool, is a circle 36.4 m (?44 M.Y.) across, a diameter that diminishes what stature its little heatherset stones have. Beyond Greenlands Hill four and a half miles north is Almsworthy, its stones just as lost in the blowing bracken and grass. It allegedly consists of three concentric ovals, the outer measuring 34.1 × 28.7 m, but of the sixteen or more stones of this theoretical ring only six exist, only three of the central, and four of the inner circle, a total of thirteen stones with one other 4.9 m ESE. of the setting. If the site is truly a triple concentric then it is unique amongst the freestanding stone rings of the British Isles. In 1939 Way re-assessed it as perhaps a number of parallel stone rows (Grinsell, 1970, 41), a type of monument known elsewhere in Exmoor and very common fifty miles south on Dartmoor. It certainly has a likeness to some like those on Corringdon Ball and Yar Tor. And the last of the Exmoor sites, Porlock, two miles from the coast and the same distance north of Almsworthy, stood near the edge of the moor on a gentle slope, many of its stones fallen around a 24.4 m circle, one about 1.9 m at the SSE. The circle was greatly disturbed during the 1939–45 war.

One remarkable 'feature' of these Exmoor sites is that they lie almost north–south on a straight line six and a half miles long, even though they are not intervisible. Such a phenomenon would be welcome to believers in ley-lines, those supra-natural alignments mystically perceived by Mr Alfred Watkins of Hereford who

> saw through the surface of the landscape to a layer deposited in some remote prehistoric age. The barrier of time melted and, spread across the country, he saw a web of lines linking the holy places and sites of antiquity. Mounds, old stones, crosses and old crossroads, churches placed on pre-Christian sites, legendary trees, moats and holy wells stood in exact alignments that ran over beacon hills to cairns and mountain peaks. In one moment of transcendant perception Watkins entered the magic world of prehistoric Britain, a world whose very existence had been forgotten. (Michell, 1973, 9.)

Plotted on maps these aggregations of summits, circles, spires and cross-roads, leaping for miles from crag and cromlech to castles and crosses, some-times, inevitably, passed by places with certain names: 'Red, White and

Black are common: so are Cold or Cole, Dod, Merry and Ley. This last gave Watkins the name of the lines which he called leys,' (ibid). This latter polyglottal prefix derives variously from: Norman, La Haye; Old Norse, hly—a shelter; and Old English, lād—a stream; leāc—leek; læge—fallow; leg—fire; and a batch of personal names like Leik, Lēofstan, Lylla and Lulla, so that 'ley' has no single significance whatsoever.

As it happens, between Withypool and Almsworthy a farm called Ley stands 91 m east of the line just west of Exford. But against the assumption that this proves the existence of a Watkins ancient trackway—and one of the most precipitous as it splashes across three river valleys—ley-liners must reconcile this one building against the widespread presence from half to three miles to east or west of the line of: White Cross, White Post and the Whit Stones, Red Stone Hill, Red Deer Farm, Black Hill, Black Barrow, Blackland and Black Ball, which in concert create a track more compatible with the rolling English drunkard than with ley-tracks or 'streams of the sacred current . . . for the spiritual irrigation of the countryside' (ibid, 199).

From Porlock let the reader meander, unstraightly, along the Quantock and Polden hills, over unlaid paths to north Wessex.

CHAPTER TEN

The Stone Circles of Wessex

In September following I survey'd that old Monument of Aubury with a plaine table and afterwards took a Review of Stonehenge.
It is very strange that so eminent an Antiquitie [as Avebury] *should lye so long unregarded by our Chorographers.*

John Aubrey

1. INTRODUCTION

It is ironical that the two most famous stone circles of the British Isles, Stonehenge and Avebury, (Fig. 50) are not at the centre of a megalithic region but at its edges. Wessex is interesting architecturally. In it there are all sorts of building materials: chalk at Maumbury Rings; timber rings at the early Sanctuary and Mount Pleasant; stone circles at Winterbourne Bassett; even an intermixing of all three at Woodhenge with its chalk banks, timber ovals and recumbent south-west sarsen.

As befits an area visited by people from all parts of Britain, bringing stone axes from Cornwall, Wales, Cumbria; copper and gold from Ireland; jet from Yorkshire, the stone rings have many different features: outliers; centre stones; concentric circles; avenues, sometimes blending together in unique forms of monument. The two greatest stand at the meeting points of natural routeways, the rivers, overland ridges that converge on Avebury, the central position of Stonehenge between the south coast and the Bristol Channel to the west, the Thames flowing eastwards towards the North Sea and the continent. But Avebury and Stonehenge differ in almost every respect.

2. STONEHENGE

At some time around 2700 BC on a slope of the chalk downs one and a half miles west of the Christchurch Avon people began building what was to become the most famous of Britain's prehistoric monuments, described in the twelfth century by Henry of Huntingdon as one of the four wonders of the island, *Stanenges*, the place of the stone gallows or hanging-stones, so-called because the inner trilithons resembled mediaeval gibbets. Starting, like others put up by makers of grooved ware, as an ordinary henge Stonehenge had a concentric stone circle added to it during the time beaker people were in Wessex, a feature which in turn was superseded in the late third millennium by a sarsen peristyle around a horseshoe of five trilithons, the Giants Ring, dragged sarsen by sarsen twenty back-breaking miles from the Marlborough

302

Downs by a multitude of labourers a thousand years or more after the first digging of the ditch.

Wrecked in antiquity, chipped for mementoes in the eighteenth and nineteenth centuries, threatened with demolition in the 1914–18 war, sold at auction in 1915 for £6,600, the annual scene of mock-Druid midsummer masquerades, excavated by Cunnington in 1801, by Gowland in 1901, Hawley, 1919–26, and, selectively, by Atkinson, Piggott and Stone since 1950, this ravaged colossus rests like a cage of sand-scoured ribs on the shores of eternity, its flesh forever lost. Stonehenge grudges its secrets. Each one explained—the date, the source of the stones, the builders—leads to greater amazements, a spiralling complexity that even now eludes our understanding so that our studies remain two-dimensional and incomplete.

There is not space to describe Stonehenge in detail. The admirable book by R. J. C. Atkinson (1960) should be read for this. But some of the aspects are so relevant to this examination of the stone circles of the British Isles, especially the question of astronomical usage, that they demand notice. For from its beginning the monument had such definite sightlines built into it that its designers obviously considered them essential to their ceremonies.

At first impression what is known of the henge is not remarkable. People, perhaps those who lived in round timber huts in the vast Durrington Walls earthwork two miles east by the Avon, heaped up its circular bank, 97.5 m across. Both Stonehenge and Durrington contained grooved ware. Their dates (1848 bc ± 275 (C-602) and 2180 bc ± 105 (I-2328) from Stonehenge; 2050 bc ± 90 (BM-400), 2015 bc ± 90 (BM-399) and 2000 bc ± 90 (BM-396) et al. from Durrington) centre around 2000 bc (c. 2700–2500 BC) and establish a cultural and chronological connection between these neighbouring monuments, one the settlement, the other the 'temple' for the people's yearly ceremonies. Already the population must have been great. Durrington took well over 900,000 man-hours to construct (Wainwright and Longworth, 1971, 197), the work of years even for several hundred people. The 6.1 m wide, 1.8 m high bank at Stonehenge, its outer ditch segmented like the earlier causewayed enclosures, must have needed at least 30,000 hours of labour. For as many as 500 people, many unable to dig, drag or carry, this represented weeks of effort. The only pottery known from this phase, five sherds of grooved ware, were discovered deep in the ditch. Not a mile away many similar sherds lay in a pit with two chalk plaques (Vatcher, 1969) whose incised patterns were akin to others at Skara Brae where pottery with Boyne motifs (Piggott, 1954, 329) re-inforces the belief that the grooved-ware potters had connections, however tenuous, with Ireland. At Stonehenge, moreover, geometrical carvings in the Boyne style were noticed low down on a sarsen stone of the last phase (Atkinson, 1960, 209).

In the henge an entrance flanked by two portal stones, one the fallen Slaughter Stone, was left at the north-east with an outlier, the 4.9 m high pustular Heel Stone beyond, sometimes mispelled as the Hele Stone by

Pl. 34. *Stonehenge, Wiltshire*. From the north-east showing the Heel Stone, the ditch and bank of the early henge, the central sarsen ring and the white marks of the Aubrey Holes first noticed as 'cavities' by John Aubrey in 1666. The entrance to the henge is just to the right of the fallen Slaughter Stone.

believers in its solar use, but actually wrongly identified as a stone hurled by the Devil at a friar whose heel left an imprint on the pillar. The real stone of this legend lies at the SSW. of the outer sarsen ring.

Just inside the circumference of the bank fifty-six pits were dug, refilled and dug again, many to receive human cremations accompanied by long bone pins and flints. Although the circumference of their circle is 271.6 m or 131 Megalithic Rods of 2.07 m (6.8 ft) (Thom. Thom and Thom, 1974, 83) its radius of 43.2 m can only crudely be equated with 52 M.Y. or 43.1 m, some of the holes deviating a lot from the perimeter. Yet each of the cardinal points and the four intermediate points such as north-east 'lie midway between holes' (ibid). These Aubrey Holes, named after John Aubrey who first noticed them, may be the results of several centuries of activity and not necessarily part of a single phase. Their contents of artefacts, human remains, earth and charred wood, even a 'ritual' axe of chalk, are very like those at Cairnpapple and at Cadbury Castle, Somerset, where pit P154 had Neolithic sherds, flint arrowheads, a human jawbone and an antler which was dated to 2510 bc ± 120 (I-5970). Other pits simply held red clay (Alcock, 1972, 109), very much like the symbolic soil deposits suspected in allied fertility ceremonies of the Neolithic.

At the centre of this first phase of Stonehenge may have been a timber building like that at Woodhenge or Mount Pleasant, but this area has been so badly dug in the past that only a few postholes have been noted of this hypothetical structure (Atkinson, 1960, 61).

Hawkins made a significant step forward in a paper in *Nature*, 1963, subsequently reprinted in *Stonehenge Decoded* (Hawkins 1966a) with his discovery of the alignments of post holes, stones and archways at Stonehenge to the extreme risings and settings of the sun and moon. It is difficult to doubt that Stonehenge was an observatory at this time in which extreme risings of the moon and sun were recorded for calendrical purposes. The midsummer sunrise alignment from the henge centre to the Heel Stone has been known since the eighteenth century even if it is not precise (Newham, 1972, 5), this stone, moreover, acting equally well as a directional marker from the long downwards slope to the NNE. where the low bank would have been out of sight, and the stone may have served a dual purpose as guidestone and sun-marker. Less equivocal are the otherwise inexplicable fifty-three stakeholes (Fig. 50) across the entrance in eleven incomplete rows, six deep (Hawley, 1925, 22), convincingly orientated on the shifting extreme midwinter risings of the moon from its maximum to its intersection with midsummer sunrise nine years later (Newham, 1966; 1972, 15). It would seem that such observations were taken for well over a century (6 lines × 18.61 years of the metonic cycle), but once recorded fixed the times of the midsummer daylight celebrations and the midwinter nocturnal ceremonies. If this interpretation is correct then the henge must have been planned after these sightings were completed for the stakehole vectors fill the causeway between the ditch terminals and must have been removed before the bank was finished, being replaced by a single line of heavier posts to the north-east alongside the Heel Stone where the entrance would not be obstructed (Atkinson, 1960, 66). As an antler in the ditch was dated to about 2180 bc (2900–2600 BC) this suggests that such observations had been a part of Neolithic religious practices for many centuries, as the sunrise phenomenon at New Grange (*c.* 3300 BC) confirms, and that midsummer and midwinter gatherings had a long history amongst the prehistoric inhabitants of the British Isles.

Three great postholes to the north-west outside the henge (L. and F. Vatcher, 1975) each about 76 cm across, may have served as 9.14 m high alignments on midsummer sunset and midwinter moonset (Newham, 1972, 24), or to support a platform level with the horizon for signalling the time of moonset (Thom, Thom and Thom, 1974, 89). These postholes, now marked in concrete, yielded mesolithic C-14 dates, but seem astronomically significant. Interestingly, the distance from the centre of Stonehenge to the centre post is very close to $17\frac{1}{2}$ of Newham's 'Lunar Measures' of 14.5 m, each of which is exactly $17\frac{1}{2}$ M.Y.

One more astronomical facet of Stonehenge I emerges from its location. Underwood (1969, 13) seeking to prove that the henge was specifically situated at the confluence of several subterranean streams, wrote, 'no conclusive explanation has ever been given for the site of Stonehenge'. This is not true. It was Newham (*Yorkshire Post*, 16 March 1963) who pointed out that the latitude here is virtually unique in that the extreme northern and southern risings and settings of sun and moon are at right-angles to one another whereas, a few miles north or south, such cross-alignments would lie along the sides of a skewed parallelogram. Thus the Four Stations, stones set just within the bank at the corners of a rectangle 79.3 × 33.5 m, provide orientations both on the sun and the moon for their maximum midsummer and midwinter positions. 'It would appear that the site chosen satisfied the necessarily stringent foresight conditions except that the horizon for the line needed for the Moon setting . . . seems nearer than the ideal. However, any attempt to raise the site by more than a few feet would have brought up distant hills or ridges too far away for use; the midsummer sun, for example, would have then risen on a horizon so far away that a very large artificial foresight would have been needed.' (Thom, Thom and Thom, 1974, 89.)

Over a century ago Duke noticed how the heights of particular stones were related to the slope on which Stonehenge stood. From the henge centre the top of the 4.9 m high Heel Stone coincided with the distant skyline. But because it was farther uphill the south-east Station Stone (no. 91), 2.7 m long, if erect and observed from the mound of the SSE. Station (92) would also have been level with the horizon. Observations to the south-west had to be made from a downhill marker-stone. Hence the Station Stone at the west (93) is only 1.2 m tall but still just touches to the horizon when seen from the worn-down NNW. Station (94). 'This plainly tells the fact that these differing heights of the . . . gnomons is for the purpose of accommodating the eye of the astronomic observer to the horizon over its apex.' (Duke, 1846, 145.)

For centuries before the erection of the bluestone circle the midsummer and midwinter ceremonies were performed in the henge, the chalk fillings of the Aubrey Holes showing whitely around the central space. Perhaps on special occasions the rituals were accompanied by the placing of a human cremation in a re-opened hole or elsewhere (Atkinson, 1960, 28). If of the sixty or so probable deposits one had been made each time the moon reached its maximum midwinter rising and midswing, twice in 18.61 years, such a practice might have continued over some five centuries, approximately the period between the estimated construction of the henge and the beginning of the bluestone circle (2700–2150 BC).

Such speculation is unverifiable. More certain is that in the early eighteenth century bc (*c.*2150 BC) the interior of Stonehenge was transformed. People

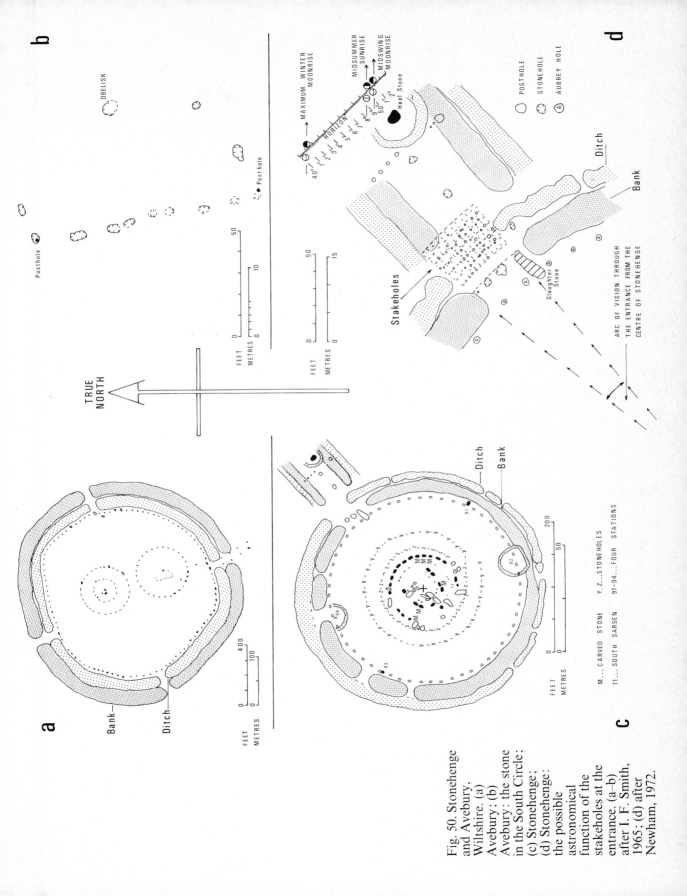

b

OBELISK

Posthole

Posthole

TRUE NORTH

FEET
METRES

FEET
METRES

MAXIMUM WINTER MOONRISE

MIDSUMMER SUNRISE

MIDSWING MOONRISE

HORIZON

Heel Stone

POSTHOLE

STONEHOLE

(A) AUBREY HOLE

Stakeholes

Ditch

Bank

ARC OF VISION THROUGH
THE ENTRANCE FROM THE
CENTRE OF STONEHENGE

Slaughter Stone

d

a

Bank

Ditch

FEET
METRES

c

Ditch

Bank

FEET
METRES

M...CARVED STONE   Y, Z...STONEHOLES

11...SOUTH SARSEN   91-94...FOUR STATIONS

Fig. 50. Stonehenge and Avebury, Wiltshire. (a) Avebury; (b) Avebury: the stone in the South Circle; (c) Stonehenge; (d) Stonehenge: the possible astronomical function of the stakeholes at the entrance. (a–b) after I. F. Smith, 1965; (d) after Newham, 1972.

began to build a concentric circle there of 26.2 and 22.6 m diameters; they made a 12.2 m wide earth avenue one and three-quarter miles long from the Avon to the henge where they filled in part of the ditch to widen the entrance; they dug a ditch around the Heel Stone but, showing how little beliefs had changed, immediately refilled it with packed chalk. And along the avenue they dragged the stones, 4-ton blocks, mostly of dolerite but with some softer volcanic and calcareous ash, rhyolite and sandstone, eighty-two stones from the Preseli mountains of south-west Wales.

Whether these stones were transported by men along the 200 miles of water and land between Carn Meini and Salisbury Plain or whether they were moved at least part of the way by glaciation (Kellaway, 1971) is undecided, although analysis of river-gravels near Stonehenge shows no relevant glacial material (Green 1973). As far as present knowledge can tell no other circle in the British Isles contains stones that were brought more than a few miles at the most. Against this, so few bluestones have been discovered elsewhere on Salisbury Plain that acceptance of the glaciation theory for Stonehenge implies that the second-millennium builders scavenged the whole area for these stones, some of which are very different in appearance from the majority of the dolerites and which, perplexingly, were not hard-wearing. Conversely— and legends are no longer dismissed as entire fiction—Geoffrey of Monmouth states categorically that the stones came from Ireland, a meaningless assertion if the stones had been discovered as erratics in Wiltshire or even in Somerset, but explicable if folk-stories sustained the memory of their transportation from a situation on the Wessex–Irish trade-route. Carn Meini has been described as a sacred mountain, a landmark between Ireland and Wales that seafaring copper prospectors might have regarded with superstition and thanksgiving, a reverence impelling them to remove stones from the mountain-top to build a holy circle in their homeland.

> To the traveller humping his pack along the ridgeways of south Pembrokeshire on the last stages of the land-route to the West, its cloud-wrapped summit must have seemed no less the home of gods than did Mount Ida to a voyager in the Cretan plain; and to the trader returning home across the sea from Ireland, shielding his eyes from the spray as he peered across the bows of his laden boat, the same summit would be the first welcome sign of land ahead. I believe, therefore, that the awe-inspiring character of Prescelly Mountain is alone sufficient to account for the special significance of the rocks which crop out along its crest. (Atkinson, 1960, 176.)

It is strange that Geoffrey of Monmouth should be so specific about the source of stones, having Merlin say, 'Send for the Giant's Ring which is on Mount Killaurus in Ireland' (Thorpe, 1966, 196). The Irish development of copper-working may be associated with the intrusion of w/MR beaker people there (Clarke, 1970, 91; Case, 1967, 168). Sherds of their pottery have been found at New Grange, at the Lios circle by Lough Gur and in an undatable context at Stonehenge where there were also pieces of Niedermendig lava brought from their German homeland. Alternatively it may have been the makers of the rather later s2/w beakers that inspired the building of the bluestone circle. Clarke (1970, 216) has noted 'the territorial link between Wessex and South Wales in this phase, as well as the simple axe-hammers of Prescelly stone with strong Southern beaker affinities'. A revised chronology would place these pots between 1800 and 1550 bc (Lanting and van der Waals, 1972, 36). Such sherds were found by Hawley in the ditch-filling, presumably contemporary with the widening of the entrance.

An s2/w beaker was discovered by the Lios entrance. A mile to the north near Carrig Aille hill (Fig. 40) is a large concentric circle, 55.5 m across, the outer ring inside a great bank, the inner ring consisting of thirty-three nearly contiguous stones none more than 1.2 m high (Windle, 1912, 302). It is possible, therefore, that the concept of Stonehenge's concentric bluestone circle had an Irish origin as Geoffrey of Monmouth tells, beaker metal-traders voyaging homewards from Lough Gur towards the cloud-misted Carn Meini, eager to enhance a native chalk sanctuary in Wessex with a spectacular ring of magical stones.

There are at least two objections to this somewhat romantic picture. The first is that it is probable that some at least of the bluestones were in Wessex long before the building of the concentric circle at Stonehenge. The second is that the distribution of concentric circles does not support the Irish theory. Such rings were never common, only about thirty being known from Cnoc Fillibhir on Lewis, down to Stonehenge, what concentrations there are being around the coasts of the North Channel and in Wiltshire in areas where centre-stone circles also exist although the latter reach further into the south-west peninsula. Half of the concentrics cluster in the North Channel region, and many are unimpressively small in diameter and stone-heights, little ovals like Coolnasillagh, Londonderry, or the 19.8 m Castledamph, Tyrone, with its small central cairn, a sepulchral feature which may reveal the origin of this group of concentrics whose inner stone settings are basically surrounds for burials. This is as true of the big Druids Temple, Birkrigg, with five cremations and a primary urn within the central setting, or Gunnerkeld, Shap, where the middle ring encloses a low mound with a cist, as it is for the many lesser ovals. A concentric ring is very like the chamber and kerbstones of a passage-grave before it was hidden under its cairn or barrow, an appearance which could account for the frequent scatters of stones or cobbles or 'paving' in the inner ring as figurative representations of the cairn. As these North Channel concentrics are most common at the fringes of passage-grave areas their derivation may be sought in the chambered tomb tradition.

It is unlikely that the Wiltshire concentrics have the same origin. Here an explanation of the rings as megalithic skeuomorphs of timber settings is more probable whether the wooden prototypes were roofed like Woodhenge or freestanding like Arminghall, Norfolk, or Caerloggas, Cornwall. Translations of timber into stone rings are known as far away as Croft Moraig and Moncrieffe in Perthshire. Significantly, one of the Wiltshire concentrics, the Sanctuary near Avebury, 39.5 m and 19.7 m, is known to have replaced such a multiple timber ring, and there is indirect evidence of woodworking techniques at Stonehenge in the delicately fashioned sarsens with their joints and rebates.

From this simple explanation for concentric rings it is understandable that there are several on the Wiltshire chalklands whereas in regions of stone there are few: none in Cornwall, one in the Lake District. 'On the Moor Green farm are 30 stones, called Kirkstones, forming part of two circles, similar in position to those at Stonehenge.' The site has been destroyed. In Devon and Cornwall there are one or two multiple rings of very low stones such as Yellowmead or Shovel Down which may once have lain beneath cairns.

It would be unreasonable to expect concentric rings so widely dispersed in Britain to be close in date. Many, especially in the north, are oval or even egg-shaped like Machrie Moor 5, Arran, and if the chronological scheme proposed in Chapter 3 is reliable, may be of the seventeenth century or later. In Wiltshire a b/w beaker by a stonehole at the Sanctuary could be as early as 1800 bc. Two C-14 determinations of 1720 bc and 1620 bc at Stonehenge suggest the bluestone circle was abandoned early in the seventeenth century bc. In the woodland regions of Wessex the development of stone rings may have been retarded by the continuing use of concentric settings of timber whose great posts might have resisted rot for up to two centuries (Wainwright and Longworth, 1971, 225), semi-permanent structures that could easily have been maintained for 500–600 years with only occasional renovation, thus explaining the rather belated prevalence of concentric stone rings there: Winterbourne Bassett; the Sanctuary; the North Circle, Avebury, and may be additional reason for believing that a post-ring existed within Stonehenge I, ultimately replaced by the bluestone concentric, its quintuple portals at the north-east, the tall Altar Stone on the opposite perimeter (Atkinson, 1960, 206) with a Cornish Group I greenstone axe in its stonehole.

The change from open henge to circle-henge may have been accompanied by a fundamental change in the ceremonies. It is possible, as Newham suggests (1972, 7), that the earliest alignments in Stonehenge were lunar. Gimbutas has described how, in the beginnings of agriculture, the moon was regarded as a 'Goddess . . . encompassing the archetypal unity and multiplicity of feminine nature. She was giver of life and all that promotes fertility, and at the same time she was the wilder of the destructive powers of nature. The feminine nature, like the moon, is light as well as dark' (Gimbutas, 1974, 152). It is this association with darkness and regeneration that may be the reason that the first moon-lines were for midwinter occasions (Newham, 1972, 21), and may also account for the frequent relationship between the circular sanctuaries and water, the interrelation of water and life being deep-rooted in prehistoric beliefs (Gimbutas, 1974, 95). Such Neolithic concepts were in contrast to the later Indo-European belief in earth and sky gods whereby the moon diminished in importance. 'As a supreme Creator who creates from her substance she is the primary goddess of the Old European pantheon. In this she contrasts with the Indo-European Earth-Mother, who is the impalpable sacred earth-spirit and is not in herself a creative principle; only through the interaction of the male sky-god does she become pregnant.' (ibid, 196.) Yet underlying both theosophies is the idea of renewal enacted in the festivals of winter and spring. 'Since many elements of the year-god's festivals are represented in the sculptural art of Old Europe, it seems not unreasonable to assume that festivals took place in Neolithic and Chalcolithic Europe. Possibly the central idea of ritual drama, the "Sacred Marriage", the ritual coition of the male god and a female goddess, is reflected in the little sculpture from Cascioarele.' (ibid, 228.)

> The task of sustaining life was the dominating motif in the mythical imagery of Old Europe, hence regeneration was one of the foremost manifestations. Naturally, the goddess who was responsible for the transformation from death to life became the central figure in the pantheon of gods. She, the Great Goddess, is associated with moon crescents, quadripartite designs and bull's horns, symbols of continuous creation and change . . . The ubiquity of phallic symbols connotes the glorification of the spontaneous life powers. Phallicism certainly had no obscene allusion; in the context of religious ritual it was a form of catharsis, not of symbolic procreation.' (ibid, 236.)

From Neolithic Britain there are only a few examples of mobiliary art: chalk phalli, a goddess from Grimes' Graves, a 'god-dolly' from a Somerset trackway. Art in the Irish passage-graves is not representational. There is nothing comparable with the profusion of figurines in Eastern Europe during the Neolithic. But from the fragments of prehistory there comes an impression of an archetypal presence created from the need to sustain life, a presence not always revealed through carved or clay-moulded images, sometimes elusively held in the mind only, whether such belief was in moon-goddess or sun-father. And the two could be made one. What may have happened with the arrival of beaker incomers is not the destruction but the lessening and integration of Neolithic beliefs into the Indo-European concepts, the moon-lines being subordinated to the new emphasis on the sun. At Stonehenge the ancient lunar alignments were not destroyed, but the major axis of the monument towards the Heel Stone was accentuated by the concentric circle with its entrance heavily lined with five pillars along each side (Atkinson, 1960, 205) down which the midsummer rising of the sun would shine across the ring to the conspicuous Altar Stone.

This bluestone circle was never finished. An antler dated to 1620 bc ± 110

(I-2384) has come from one of its half-dug stoneholes. Another antler, 1720 bc ± 150 (BM-46), from the ramp of the Great Trilithon shows that the well-known sarsen circle had been commenced about the same time and it is reasonable to assume that the beginning of one caused the abandonment of the other. Why there was a change is unknown. For centuries, while Stonehenge had remained a provincial henge to which, finally, a minor stone circle was being added, only eighteen miles to the north the great circle-henge of Avebury at the conjunction of several trackways had all this time been a brilliant and stupendous monument amid such wonders as the West Kennet long barrow, the Sanctuary, the manmade mountain of Silbury Hill, itself a contemporary of Stonehenge I, a complex of enormous megalithic works that could well have been the wonder and envy of the inhabitants of Salisbury Plain. The incredible sarsens of Stonehenge III may have been a response to this. They are the products of people accustomed to working in wood but also people who had resources of manpower and food-supply and organization and who were determined that their new monument should outdo Avebury as a megalithic circle yet be modern enough to act as a centre-piece for a few participants only.

It has been proposed that coupled with the expansion of the trade in copper, bronze and gold there arose in the Early Bronze Age a splendid Wessex culture represented by foreign chieftains whose rich dagger-burials adorn the bell-barrow cemeteries like Normanton, Lake and Wilsford around Stonehenge, powerful merchant-princes who broke the beaker overlordship in Wessex. Work on the bluestones ceased. 'By the ensuing Late and Final beaker phases there seems to have been competition for territory between the new full Bronze Age Wessex culture and the retreating beaker groups.' (Clarke, 1970, 224.) Whatever the truth about the length and nature of this aristocratic society whose 'opulent single-grave' burials are neither particularly wealthy (Coles and Taylor, 1971, 12; Burgess, 1974, 189) nor necessarily single (Peterson, 1972, 40), it may not have been these people who inaugurated the final and most glorious phase of Stonehenge but earlier groups such as the s2/w beaker users already mentioned or the makers of grooved ware who, in consort with beaker people, built a gigantic earthwork at Mount Pleasant, Dorset, not fifty miles from Stonehenge, as late as c. 1780 bc (Burleigh, Longworth and Wainwright, 1972, 402).

Whoever they were, whoever the genius who planned it, Stonehenge was a marvel of design and administration that demanded the labours of hundreds, perhaps thousands, over many years. From the Marlborough Downs seventy-seven sarsens were achingly hauled, each an average of twenty-six dragging tons, over grass, stream, downslope, long pulls around the Pewsey marshes, up the inch-inch-inch backstraining steepness of Redhorn Hill, and more miles across the West Down, ropes greasy-black with sweat, day by day, to the last exhausted exultant sight of the Heel Stone, two months of strain for a thousand or more people, fed by others, the settlements for miles empty

Pl. 35. *Stonehenge, Wiltshire*. From the east. Just beyond the ditch in the foreground. is the fallen Station Stone 91, once about 2.5 metres tall.

The truncated south sarsen, no. 11, leans outwards on the left of the ring.

The fourth, fifth and sixth sarsens from the right have carvings on their faces.

of all but the old. One stone a year may have been all. The stones were dressed, pounded with mauls, sides ground into shallow flutings, rubbed smooth, more months of work, heaved erect into their holes, stones forty tons or more, first the uprights of the trilithons, their lintel-pegs bashed from the rock, then their lintels levered plank by plank upwards on heavy hardwood cribs, then the outer circle of uprights, the inner and outer faces contained within perfect circles with perimeters of 45 and 48 Megalithic Rods (Thom, Thom and Thom, 1974, 79), and finally, their lintels placed on top, tongued and grooved, mortised and tenoned, rebated, curved to the line of the circle. Somewhere lay the discarded bluestones, rejected.

The modern technological age reveres Stonehenge for the engineering of its stones, just as, at Knossos in Crete, the cunning parabolas of the drains from the Queen's lavatory, distract attention from the vitality of the frescoes. Yet the people who struggled to shape, to create the sarsens were primarily building a monument for their lives. Statistically, it was a 29.6 m circle of thirty stones, 4.1 m high, surmounted by thirty lintels. Inside was a horseshoe of five trilithons open to the north-east. Such trilithons are unique amongst the British stone circles and would seem to be stone replicas of wooden frames, maybe like those assumed at Lugg henge, Dublin (Kilbride-Jones, 1950). But Stonehenge was not merely for technocratic admiration, it was for use by the people who built it.

At some time the bluestones were replaced. New stoneholes were dug around the lintel-circle in apparent concentric rings but actually in a spiral (Sale, 1965), entered at the SSE., circling the sarsens and curving into them almost exactly at the south where sarsen no. 11 is much shorter and thinner (Atkinson, 1960, 38), and supports no lintel though there is a peg for one on the adjoining sarsen, perhaps having been intentionally removed in this phase to establish an entrance near the Great Trilithon itself. Such spirals are common in rock-art and have been suspected in the ground plan of Bryn Celli Ddu passage-grave, Anglesey, and at the Druids Circle, Penmaenmawr. But at Stonehenge the scheme was never completed. An antler found in one of the unused Y and Z holes was dated to 1240 bc $\pm$ 105 (I-2445), a date in keeping with others from dagger-graves of the later Wessex culture (Burgess, 1974, 228). It was then that the bluestones were placed where many of them stand now, about sixty in an irregular circle around the trilithons, nineteen others, tooled and shaped, in a horseshoe setting within them, the Altar Stone alone and erect near the centre of the completed monument.

There was nothing like it. It was a truly megalithic temple, its lintelled stones of incomparable size in Britain, an undertaking that had involved a great part of the population of Wessex for many seasons. Renfrew (1973c, 554) has suggested that such a commitment is an indication that by this time Wessex had possibly become a single, unified chiefdom with a large population, specialist craftsmen, a priesthood, and with 'frequent ceremonies and rituals serving wide social purposes' (ibid, 543).

In the magnitude of its labour force Stonehenge was similar to the communal works of the Late Neolithic, the henges, great circles, the earthwork enclosures that had demanded the efforts of hundreds. Yet it was different. Whereas the great open rings had space enough for all their builders Stonehenge had room for only a few within the sarsens, no more than twenty or thirty at most in the confines of the bluestone horseshoe and Altar Stone surrounded by the enclosing trilithons at the heart of the monument.

There is something else. The axis had changed slightly, the sarsen centre being about 30 cm to the left of that for the Aubrey Hole circle, perhaps because the midsummer rising of the sun had changed a little over the centuries. More important, as in some other later stone circles there seems to be greater interest in the midwinter sunset. Now the pillars of the bluestone horseshoe were graded in height towards the south-west. So were the sarsen trilithons, rising to the 7.3 m height of the Great Trilithon between whose pillars the midwinter sunset would have been framed. On some of the sarsens are carvings of Irish bronze axes (Fig. 14). Such carvings show not only the continuation of the solar axe-cult into the Bronze Age but also carry on the tradition of north–south and east–west lines in the great stone circles. Four carvings are on the south trilithon; three other groups cluster together on the east stones of the sarsen circle (Atkinson, 1960, 43; 208). As if to emphasize the point, two carvings in the Breton style of shield-escutcheons, also sun-symbols, have been noticed on a trilithon and a lintel at the west (ibid, 44, 209), just as carvings of stone axes were noticed on the western stones of Er Lannic, Brittany. The persistence of custom is clearly shown in these positions as it may be in the truncated sarsen at the exact south. It is also quite possible that, at some time during this third phase, distant positions, sometimes as much as nine miles away, had posts or platforms erected at the exact points on the horizon where the moon rose or set in each of its eight extremes, dramatically grazing the edges of hills, the site at Hanging Langford camp, for example, SU 401135, marking the minimum midsummer moonset around 2000 BC (Thom, Thom and Thom, 1975, 23), the equivalent of c. 1570 bc, at a time when the great sarsen circle and trilithons had been built. Other positions at Gibbet Knoll, Figsbury Rings and Chain Hill, all of the same period (ibid, 20, 25, 26) around 1600 bc, seem so precisely established that the likelihood of coincidence must be small.

Stonehenge was a native monument. There is no need to seek Mycenaean architects for its design, and the possible carving of a dagger from Mycenae on one of its stones is no more relevant to its origins than the scratched signature of Charles Dickens on a windowpane of Shakespeare's birthplace. However modified they were the customs at Stonehenge were the elemental ones of supplication for the continuance of life. At first in the midwinter darkness of a tree-scattered landscape, paths marked by animal tracks, nights disturbed by the baying of wolves, everyone performed the rituals in an open enclosure. In later centuries perhaps only a few priests enacted more formalized rites within a monument planned mathematically in accordance with their more arcane cosmogony. But still the sun and moon were paramount and the symbolism of fire and axe and water survived, the stones acquiring by association properties not only of averting ill but, more positively, of possessing curative powers. Geoffrey of Monmouth wrote that people would pour water over the stones to cure the sick. 'There is not a single stone among them which hasn't some medicinal virtue.' (Thorpe, 1966, 196.)

As late as the fourth century bc Hecateus of Abdera was reported by Diodorus Siculus as having written: 'Opposite to the land of the Celts [Gaul?] there exists in the ocean an island no smaller than Sicily . . . the inhabitants honour Apollo more than any other. A sacred enclosure is dedicated to him in the island, as well as a magnificent circular [astronomical?] temple adorned with many rich offerings.' There has been much speculation about this passage but the island could be Britain, the enclosure Stonehenge's bank, the temple the sarsen circle in which Apollo, the sun, was worshipped even into the Iron Age. Centuries later in the Auvergne at the time of Beltane bonfires were lit around which the villagers would dance and sing, burning torches of straw which they called 'granno-mio'. 'Granno . . . may be no other than the ancient Celtic god, Grannus, whom the Romans identified with Apollo,' (Frazer, 1922, 611) here clearly associated with the primitive fire-festivals, probably connected in some way with the *Grianainech*, 'Sun-countenance', of Irish mythology (Ross, 1967, 477), and referred to as *Apollini Granno* on an inscribed Roman slab from Scotland 'indicating some confusion with Belinus. Granno seems to derive from the Celtic *grian*, sun' (R. E. Hicks, 1975, 189).

It may have been the continuing use of Stonehenge by Celtic priests of the Iron Age, the Druids, with their opposition to foreign authority that caused the Romans to wreck the monument. Although they normally endeavoured to incorporate native cults within their own pliant pantheon the Romans did not tolerate subversion of their rule, and destroyed places they suspected of being centres of hostility. For this reason they decapitated the pillars of the astronomical circle at Sarmizegetusa, Romania (Daicoviciu, 1960, 235). When the Druids incited a rebellion on their sacred island of Anglesey the Britons were slaughtered 'and the groves sacred to their savage rites were cut down'. The same may have happened at Stonehenge. Tacitus does not tell us. Toppled, robbed, chipped, fallen stones worn by two thousand years of visitors' feet, alongside a major road, approached along an umbilical tunnel, Stonehenge retains something of its solemnity even in the nonsense of neo-Druidical visitations which on occasion have evoked unpleasantness. 'The fall of one of the Stonehenge uprights in 1900 caused the owner, Sir Edward Antrobus, to fence the monument and to charge entry, and a contretemps then ensued at the next Solstice ceremony, when the chief Druid was ejected by the police, and publicly and ritually cursed Sir Edward.' (Piggott, 1968, 180.) Sir Edward survived. Stonehenge remains an awesome member of the stone and timber circles of the British Isles.

3. THE LESSER STONE RINGS

Other than Stonehenge and Avebury there are not many stone circles in Wiltshire. Every one is ruined, in some cases not one stone remaining of what was an impressive site. The centre stone at Tisbury, the outlier at Winterbourne Bassett, the 'several great stones' at Clatford, these are all gone as is Falkner's Circle and the Sanctuary near Avebury, leaving only frustrating descriptions and vague positions behind. Yet they make a background for the two great rings, and their architecture reveals the influences to which stone-circle builders in Wessex were susceptible.

Most of the rings were low-lying. Tisbury, just north of the River Nadder twelves miles WSW. of Stonehenge, appears to have been a circle-henge, 'a circular work with a vallum set round with stones, and a large stone set erect in the centre. On removing the stone (which was 12 ft high and 4 ft wide) by Lord Arundel's order, to the old castle at Wardour, a skeleton was found at the depth of 18 in under the surface, deposited close to the centre stone' (Hoare, 1812, 251). Such inhumations have been noticed by other centre stones like that at Longstone Rath henge, Kildare.

Nothing is left of Tisbury. Nor is the small concentration of rings in Wiltshire, the group around Avebury, any more impressive. This district, at the meeting-point of the Kennet river and the Ridgeway, hard by the Marlborough Downs on which abundant sarsen stones lay, had long been an area of Neolithic occupation as the earthen long barrows and chambered tombs attest. Round barrows, mostly of the second millennium, line the Ridgeway itself, many of them heavy with trees planted by Gothick romanticists 200 years ago. But the stone rings have suffered.

Four miles east by the Kennet, probably in Broadstone West Meadows, eight huge stones stood in a wrecked circle of which Stukeley wrote, 'over against Clatford at a flexure in the river, we met with several great stones'. These had gone by 1890, including four that may have formed a short avenue down to the river. Another avenue and little ring might have existed at Langdean Bottom three miles south of Avebury. Only a few indeterminate stones exist today. Below the slope of the Ridgeway and very close to Avebury was Falkner's Circle, twelve stones set in a 36.6 m ring. One stone has survived the intensive farming of the nineteenth and twentieth centuries. Nine miles north-east of Avebury by a little stream is the wreckage of Coate circle, first noticed by Richard Jefferies, its stones now fallen and almost overgrown.

Even the largest of them at Winterbourne Bassett has gone. In the early eighteenth century a large concentric stone circle stood here, 71.3 m in diameter. The stones were quite small but at the centre was a higher pillar and to the west was 'a single broad flat and high stone standing by itself'. There is little left today, just a jumble of stones at the middle of the broad plateau between the eastern downs and the lower land to the west.

The mixture of outliers, centre stones and avenues recalls the architecture of other regions, especially those where great open rings were erected in passes and valleys as meeting-places for scattered farming groups. Whether any of these Wiltshire rings had this purpose is difficult to answer for they are ruined and unexcavated. But quite different is the Sanctuary on Overton Hill at the point where the Ridgeway begins to drop from the Marlborough Downs to a ford across the Kennet before climbing Furze Hill past East Kennet long barrow and Langdean Bottom on its way to central Wiltshire and Stonehenge. The Sanctuary does not excite the casual visitor. The A4 roars past its iron railings, a lorry-loaded transport café faces it, and the greying concrete blocks and cylinders marking the positions of the former posts and stones do little for the uninstructed imagination.

Yet this site is almost a chronicle of the history of stone rings in Wiltshire, their origin, their modifications, their destruction, their quiet mysteries.

From a small roofed hut it was successively changed into a timber and then a stone concentric ring linked to Avebury by a serpentine avenue of stones. When John Aubrey saw it about 1670 it still survived, its stones 1.2–1.5 m high, respected and visited by local people. Within fifty years it was gone. Stukeley went to it in 1724 before a farmer, Griffin, smashed it up, 'the person that gain'd a little dirty profit'. 'This Overton Hill, from time immemorial, the country-people have a high notion of. It was (alas! it was!) a very few years ago crown'd with a most beautiful temple of the Druids. They still call it the sanctuary.' (Stukeley, 1743, Preface.) It was excavated in 1930 (Cunnington, 1931).

To claim to have disentangled a definitive sequence for its phases of eleven rings, some overlapping, some of wood, some stone, would only be presumptuous. Studies by Piggott (1940) and Musson (1971) have already provided varying possibilities based on detailed examinations of the excavation-report. It is reasonable to suppose that in such a prolific area of stone, timber was used for the first building because it was to be roofed, a conjecture improved by the discovery of mollusca (*Lymnaea peregra* and *Planorbis leucostoma* among others) in some postholes, water-loving fauna which may have been carried to the site on reeds and rushes intended for thatching. Many of these samples came from Circle G, a 4.1 m ring of six heavy posts which could be the remains of a cramped round hut built high on the hillside by Neolithic people part of whose rituals included the deposition of broken pottery by the posts. So few antlers and animal bones have been found here that it must be assumed that from the beginning the Sanctuary was a place of ritual and not a domestic dwelling.

Table 12. The Sanctuary, Wiltshire. Suggested Diameters in Imperial Feet

Ring	Cunnington 1931		Musson 1971, 368	Smith 1965, 244	Thom 1967, 38. (S5/2).		
	M	ft	ft	ft	ft	M.Y.	Error
A	40.2	131 ft 4 in	129 ft	132 ft	129.7	48	−0.86 ft
B	20.1	65 ft 8 in	64 ft 6 in	66 ft	64.8	24	−0.48 ft
C	13.7	44 ft 9 in	46 ft 6 in	—	46.8	17	+0.56 ft
D	11.5	37 ft 9 in	32 ft	38 ft	34.3 30.9	13 11	−1.06 ft +0.98 ft
E	6.4	21 ft	19 ft 10 in	—	19.3	7	+0.26 ft
F	4.5	14 ft 9 in	14 ft 2 in	14 ft	13.6	5	0.00 ft
G	3.9	12 ft 9 in	13 ft 6 in	—	12.0	4	+1.12 ft

In its second phase this simple building was replaced by a larger with a roof supported on concentric rings of big posts, E and D, respectively 6.0 m and 9.8 m across, a construction that was rebuilt at least once (Musson, 1971, 368). It should be added that because different surveyors have measured either to the inside, centre or outside of posts, have used the original excavation plan or plotted the concrete stumps on the site itself, even the diameters of the Sanctuary are not certain as Table 12 demonstrates.

The earliest pottery suggests that the first activities at the Sanctuary were conducted by people contemporary, perhaps identical with those using the causewayed enclosure at Windmill Hill three miles north-west and the gigantic chambered tomb of West Kennet three-quarters of a mile west across the Kennet, places where human bones were vital to the rituals (I. F. Smith, 1971, 100) and where similar mixtures of Windmill Hill and Ebbsfleet pottery occur, Windmill Hill causewayed enclosure having a C-14 assay of 2580 bc ± 150 (BM-74). For centuries people went seasonally to such centres but, early in the second millennium, perhaps stimulated by the arrival of other groups, new monuments took the place of the causewayed enclosures, henges were built in the river valleys and consistently in them— at Stonehenge; at Avebury; at the enclosures of Marden; Durrington Walls; Mount Pleasant; at Waulud's Bank, Bedfordshire, where the henge was four miles from a causewayed enclosure at Maiden Bower (Selkirk, 1972, 173)—grooved ware has been found. This pottery, made by people whose antecedents are still very little understood, has also been discovered in timber structures of the period: the north and south rings at Durrington Walls and at Mount Pleasant, sometimes with a very few early beaker sherds, C-14 determinations indicating dates very early in the second millennium. During the excavation of 1930 such sherds, as well as Late Neolithic Mortlake ware and AOC beaker fragments, were discovered in several postholes at the Sanctuary.

Change from causewayed enclosure to henge, from Windmill Hill to Avebury, may also have meant a change in the practices at the Sanctuary as the pottery may imply, the thatched building being succeeded by freestanding timber rings at some time just after 2000 bc. Though respecting the ancient Ridgeway site people now put up an unroofed concentric post-circle, F and B, 4.3 m and 19.7 m, both with postholes so deep as to suggest they were for very tall and non-structural posts. Four postholes of the same size flanked a recumbent stone at the SSW. just inside the inner ring. Two much heavier posts at the north-west marked an entrance seemingly aligned on the settings of midsummer sun and midwinter moon. A deep-set central post could also belong to this phase.

Such slender posts probably did not survive long. They were replaced first by an even larger concentric circle of heavier timbers, C and A, 14.2 m and 39.3 m across, on the same axis as before; and then by megalithic rings of the same diameters but with the axis 10° or so to the west where three stone pillars, set radially on the outer circumference, joined a splayed avenue of stones that led downhill towards Avebury. These were the circles that John Aubrey saw nearly 4000 years later. A burial with a B/W beaker by an east stone (Fig. 10) shows this last phase to have been completed by 1700 bc at the latest. Another stone hole contained over twenty bits of Niedermendig lava often found with sherds of E/ and W/MR beakers of the eighteenth century bc or earlier (Clarke, 1970, 100).

Whatever the ceremonies at the Sanctuary it is of interest to find a mathematical relationship between each of the postulated phases whereby either the number of posts or the diameter is approximately double that of its predecessor: Phase I = six posts, 4.1 m across; II = 12 posts, 9.8 m; III = 34 posts, 19.7 m; IV = 42 posts, 39.3 m. Were other interpretations to be preferred there would still be 'a tendency towards recognisable patterns in the number of postholes' (Musson, 1971, 375). As there is no structural necessity for such numerical elegance it is likely that the mathematical models were employed in much the same way as the standardized number of stones in some Cornish groups of stone rings for ritualistic reasons. Close to the Sanctuary, the massive stone chambers at West Kennet, which were unlikely to have been built later than about 2500 bc, were laid out in an almost perfect isosceles triangle whose base was exactly half its height (Piggott, 1962b, 15). A comparable geometrical design has been proposed for Parc le Breos Cwm, Gwent (R. J. C. Atkinson, 1961, 296). And Ashbee (1966, 36) was at pains to point out the mathematical properties of the Fussell's Lodge long barrow where the proportions of the trapezoidal mound were $1:2:3\frac{1}{2}$.

At West Kennet, finely reconstructed after the excavations of 1955 and 1956 (Piggott, 1962b), it was evident that prehistoric people had taken away selected human skulls and long bones from the tomb, and 'it is possible . . . to compose the ghoulish picture of a visitor to the barrow picking up a partly decomposed arm, detaching the humerus, and flinging the other bones into a dark corner' (ibid, 81). What was done with the chosen bones is unknown although finds of human bones, some already old and dry before being broken, in the ditches of Windmill Hill suggest that they too had been taken from an ossuary for use as fetishes or mementoes (I. F. Smith, 1965, 137). There are records of skeletal robbery at other megalithic tombs (Gresham, 1972). Knowledge of this custom, as well as the recognition of a geometrical design at West Kennet, is relevant because similar practices have been detected at the circle-henge of Avebury one and a quarter miles north of the chambered long mound.

4. Avebury

It is fitting that a book about the stone circles of the British Isles should conclude with Avebury for it is the mightiest in size and grandeur of all of them. John Aubrey, who came upon it by accident while fox-hunting, wrote that Avebury 'does as much exceed in greatness the so renowned Stoneheng

Pl. 36. *Avebury, Wiltshire*. From the NNW. Camden mentioned the earthwork in 1610 but it was John Aubrey who first recorded the megaliths on January 7, 1648/9 when he 'was wonderfully surprized at the sight of those vast stones' [and] 'some segments of rude circles'.

Silbury Hill is on the right with the tree-lined Winterbourne stream meandering by it, roughly paralleled by the waverings of the West Kennet Avenue on the other side of Waden Hill.

as a Cathedral doeth a parish Church'. The comment is perceptive for whereas the early Stonehenge had a parochial plainness Avebury was a national monument whose magnificent complexity is now obscured by its size and the village, trees and roads inside it (Fig. 50).

Itemized it sounds ordinary. It consisted of: two avenues of standing stones leading to: a chalk bank broken by four entrances whose causeways across the ditch provided access to a central plateau where: the largest stone circle in the British Isles surrounded: two smaller circles which contained: a Cove and a central stone. But even the most Gothick of poetry could not evoke the impact that this colossus has upon any mind sensitive to the lingerings of prehistory. It is so vast that half a village sprawls within its boundaries, cottages and fields, a main road buckling through its anatomy. There is little peace here. Perhaps there never was. As long ago as 1289 the earthwork was called Waledich (O. E. weala-dic, the dyke of the Britons), from the time of the Saxon penetration of Wessex when such enclosures were helpful defences for either Briton or invader. It is not coincidence that the herepath, the Saxon army-road, marches over the downs straight through Avebury and westwards towards the Bristol Channel.

Yet the site was little damaged until the fourteenth century AD when many stones of this pagan place were meticulously buried by Christians, one a barber-surgeon who was crushed beneath a giant pillar at the south. Some of the stones have been re-erected this century. But, mainly in the eighteenth century, the economics of destruction smashed more stones for walls and roads and houses. Stukeley saw it.

> The barbarous massacre of a stone here with leavers and hammers, sledges and fire, is as terrible a sight as a Spanish Atto de fe. The vast cave they dig around it, the hollow under the stone like a glass-house furnace or a baker's oven, the huge chasms made through the body of the stone, the straw, the faggots, the smoak, the prongs, and the squallor of the fellows looks like a knot of devills grilling the soul of a sinner.

Part of the bank was levelled by the local squire. The SSE. entrance was widened to allow stage-coaches to pass. Trees grew thickly on the bank.

Since 1865 there have been intermittent excavations, the major investigations being by St. G. Gray (1935) between 1908 and 1922, and by Keiller and Piggott, 1934–5 and 1939 (I. F. Smith, 1965), the former doing so much to restore Avebury and its Kennet avenue to something of their first splendour, his Hispano-Suiza roaring down the quiet lanes of the 1930s awakening the consciences of the archaeologically unaware.

Today Avebury is tidier, cleaner. With resolution one may sidestep the cars and dodge through the swing-gate to walk along the ditch where the bank engulfs the sky like a swelling wave. One may see stones as big as house-walls, stare between cottages across the henge to the farther bank a quarter of a mile of grass and stone away. Avebury is not easy to comprehend. 'For a village of the same name being built within the circumference of it and (by the by) out of it's stones too, what by gardens, orchards, inclosures, and such like, the prospect is so interrupted, that it is very hard to discover the form of it.' (Camden, 1695, 111.) Simple statistics, however, tell its magnitude. The henge was built below Windmill Hill in a level area, once thickly wooded but for some centuries largely cleared of trees for grazing and agriculture (J. G. Evans, 1971, 268). Avebury is situated centrally on a low, natural dome from which it slopes down in all directions. Its flat-bottomed ditch, hacked from the chalk, measures 347.5 m, nearly a quarter of a mile, across its inner diameter and encloses $28\frac{1}{2}$ acres (11.5 ha). The ditch varies between 7.0 m and 10.1 m in depth and is 21.3 m wide at the

top. There is an irregular berm, a narrow flat space, between the edge of
the ditch and the outer bank which has a median circumference of 1353 m.
At its base it is 22.9 to 30.5 m broad and was once about 6.7 m high. Four
entrances, each 15.2 m wide, stand at NNW., ENE., SSE. and WSW. Here
the bank was higher and wider, its terminals revetted with timbers. In such
dimensions Avebury is like some other Wessex enclosures:

Table 13. Wessex Earthwork Enclosures

Site	Approx. Shape	Diameter/s (Metres)	Acres Enclosed	Main Pottery	Average C-14
Marden	Oval	527 × 357	35 (14.2 ha)	Grooved	1988 bc (2400 BC)
Durrington Walls	Oval	490 × 472	30+ (12.1+ ha)	Grooved	2014 bc (2500 BC)
Avebury	Circular	421	28½ (11.5 ha)	Mortlake	—
Waulud's Bank	Circular?	310	18 (7.3 ha)	Grooved	—
Mount Pleasant	Oval	290 × 260	13.8 (5.6 ha)	Grooved	1772 bc (2150 BC)
Knowlton South	Circular	229	9.8 (4.0 ha)	?	—

   Knowlton has not been formally excavated but the other five sites have
yielded grooved ware. A hypothetical date for the construction of Avebury's
bank and ditch, around 2000 bc, suggested by the C-14 assays from Durrington
and Marden nearby, is supported by the presence of much native Mortlake
pottery beneath the bank and on the ditch-bottom, in both instances accompanied by a few sherds of Windmill Hill, Ebbsfleet and grooved ware, a
ceramic mixture which together with typical Late Neolithic flintwork points
to a time of building near 2000 bc before users of beakers came to the site,
for their pottery is found only in later levels at Avebury.
   It is possible that Avebury had a function comparable with the other
enclosures, places where large numbers of people might gather either for
occupation, unlikely at Avebury because of the absence of domestic rubbish,
or for ceremonial purposes as its stone rings suggest. A big population cannot
be doubted. It has been estimated that Durrington Walls took some 900,000
man-hours to build. The causewayed enclosure at Windmill Hill near
Avebury enclosed 21 acres (8.5 ha) and must have required at least 120,000
man-hours of labour to dig its uneven and segmented triple ditches yet, if
the date of 2580 bc ± 150 (BM-74) can be relied on (c. 3400 BC), it was constructed in the Neolithic nearly 1000 years before Avebury when, presumably,
there were far fewer people (R. J. C. Atkinson, 1968, 87).

From Avebury's ditch was prised an almost unbelievable 3,950,000 cu ft of chalk, about 200,000 tons to be broken, lifted and carried to the bank. Thom's analysis of the geometry of the henge postulated an intricate design based on a right-angled triangle with sides of 75, 100 and 125 M.Y. (Thom, 1967, 89). The great megalithic ring had a main radius of 200 M.Y. (165.8 m). According to Thom (1971, 101) the scheme was so involved that of necessity it took years of setting out and correction, two of its radii each being an astonishing 750 M.Y. in length (622 m). 'The elasticity of a rope of this length would alone have prohibited its use (ibid) and measuring rods had to be used.' As this meant laying down and picking up a 2.07 m long rod or rods, end to end, 300 times 'with an accuracy approaching 1 in a 1000' (Thom, 1967, 1), an error of no more than 2 mm each time the rod was placed on uneven ground and springing grass—and one wonders how this 622 m of separate rods was kept so absolutely, so undeviatingly straight— it is more discriminating to seek another explanation for Avebury's irregular shape.

The site lies a quarter of a mile east of the Winterbourne stream. It may be assumed that at the crest of the dome a line from a focal peg was used to scratch a wavering circle, 173.7 m in radius, for the inner edge of the ditch, a NNW.–SSE. axis being set exactly at right-angles to another lying WSW.– ENE. to establish the positions of the four causeways. A massive post-socket in the SSE. entrance may be all that remains of one of the markers (I. F. Smith, 1965, 204). Then with antler-picks, ox shoulder-blades, baskets, ropes of leather or animal hide or even grass, the ditches were quarried, quadrant by quadrant, in sections, gangs of workers driving the antler tines into fissures, levering, pushing, until the chalk broke, was shoved aside, dragged into a basket, hefted up ladders and chalk-cut terraces, hauled and dumped onto the bank where turf, cut from the virgin ground, formed a core for the rising layers of rubble, rock and soil. The more the work pro-gressed the harder it became as the ditches delved into solid chalk, and the ragged white bank rose higher, until, when a ditch-section was finished, the jagged balk between it and its neighbour was hacked down and the antler picks flung away.

It is possible to calculate how long this took, using Atkinson's (1961) formula of: $\text{Man-Hours} = \dfrac{\text{Volume } (120 + 8L + 2F)}{1000}$, where L=the mean vertical distance for material to be carried, and F=the mean horizontal distance. At Avebury this amounted to 1,560,000 man-hours of effort for the ditch and bank alone. On the much less certain hypothesis that 750 people laboured there, ten hours a day, for two months each year after the harvest was in, the enclosure would have taken about four years to complete.

With a total population of 1500 in this region, an average $2\frac{1}{2}$ acres (1 ha) of land per head under cultivation, as much lying fallow, and perhaps seven times this area unexploited because of rock, marsh, hillside, river and forest,

valley between Waden Hill and the Ridgeway, the stones increasing in height where the line kinked sharply at Avebury's SSE. entrance to make a direct and dignified approach across the causeway. Both the avenues are connected with water, the Beckhampton stones crossing a stream, the other coming within 91.4 m of the Kennet although there is no proof that it ever went down to the riverside. Each pair of stones in this Kennet avenue has a thin pillar opposite a squatter lozenge, and pillar and lozenge alternate along each of the two rows (Keiller and Piggott, 1936, 420). So regular and noticeable is this that the phenomenon must have been deliberate, perhaps as male and female symbols to express the fertility beliefs with which the stone circles of the British Isles are so intimately associated, all the more appropriate if related to the life-giving water nearby.

Despite being of stone instead of earth the Kennet avenue has a similarity to the avenue at Stonehenge and it may be wondered if, like that, it was not a later addition to its circle-henge. Both lines have an end near the major river of their region, both are associated with beaker pottery, and both led to a concentric circle, the Sanctuary and the Stonehenge bluestones. By coincidence, their lengths are comparable, one and a half and one and three-quarter miles respectively.

The contemporaneity of the earth avenue with Stonehenge II was proved by excavation and it can be dated to c.1750–1700 bc before the concentric's abandonment, a period in tune with the w/MR and s2/w beakers there. Only indirect dating is available for the Kennet avenue but a B/w beaker at the Sanctuary shows the stone circle to be probably earlier than 1700 bc. Two other beakers buried by stones in the Kennet avenue, an N2 in a grave dug after the erection of stone 25b, an E beaker alongside a flexed skeleton, as well as a carinated grooved-ware bowl in another grave, make a date much later than 1750 bc hard to accept. That communal work continued for years around Avebury is proved by Silbury Hill a mile to the south, the primary mound of this 39.6 m high artificial mound having a date of 2145 bc ±95 (I-4136). As Silbury Hill took about 18,000,000 man-hours to complete it can be reckoned that even with 500 labourers working through each autumn the project would have endured for well over fifty years, probably longer. Even with a year-long labour-force the earthwork would have taken fifteen years to build (Atkinson, 1974, 128). There is no reason why the Kennet avenue should not have been another undertaking, a double row of stones passing by the tree-darkened ground to the east, perhaps first intended as an approach from the Kennet, awkwardly linked to the short setting of portal stones at Avebury—outside which there may have been a great post or stone or cremation cemetery to be avoided—but later adapted to link two precincts, the circle-henge and the long-known Sanctuary now newly translated into stone.

Inside Avebury's great stone ring stands a pair of smaller rings on the same NNW.–SSE. alignment but, like Cairnpapple and Arbor Low, away from the axis through the entrances. They are small only by contrast. Both are among the biggest of stone rings. Both are circular, 103.6 m in diameter or 125 M.Y. (Thom, 1967, 90). It may be that, whereas even for 1500 people an enclosure of 28½ acres (11.5 ha), 366 m across, would have reduced everything to a distant insignificance, a lesser ring 103.6 m across would have been ideal for the ritual dancing of several hundred participants, the remainder of the vast enclosure being used for the accustomed activities of the earlier causewayed enclosures, the gathering of dispersed groups, trade, systems of gift and exchange from remote areas (I. F. Smith, 1971, 103).

The NNW. circle inside Avebury was a concentric with twenty-nine to thirty stones, 3.4–4.0 m high, on its outer circumference, the inner ring 42.7 m across having twelve equally tall stones (I. F. Smith, 1965, 223). At its centre was a north-east-facing Cove two of whose tremendous stones still stand.

Sixty feet SSE. of the perimeter of the first ring was a similar circle probably of thirty high, broad sarsens in whose stoneholes were some weathered Late Neolithic sherds showing that this ring was quite likely to be contemporary with the ditch and bank. This was not a concentric. Instead, just off-centre, it had a thick, 5.5 m high pillar, the Obelisk, which, perhaps fortuitously, was precisely north of one causeway and east of another. Four pits to its north contained no chalk but were filled with dark brown earth, a practice reminiscent of other Neolithic soil-deposits. An urn full of bones was found near the Obelisk in 1880 when a flagstaff was being put up but the 'fragments were carried off by the children' and nothing more is known of this burial. Just inside the circle at the SSW. was another stone but this, like the Obelisk 44.2 m away and like three-quarters of the stones of this circle, has been removed with only a marker now to show where it stood.

Perhaps the most enigmatic of all Avebury's architectural features was a setting of twelve low stones 15 m west of the Obelisk (Fig. 50). Nine of them, six surviving 0.9–1.5 m tall, stood in a straightish line 31.2 m long, 342°–162°, each of whose ends was marked by a stout post. Other stones stood to the east at right-angles to the terminals. Smith speculated that the setting might represent the peristalithic forecourt of a symbolic long barrow, the rest not constructed, the Obelisk occupying 'the place of the burials in an actual tomb' (ibid, 250). Fleming (1972, 70) felt this degraded the planners to the role of 'half-witted copiers' instead of showing them as the ingenious and visionary people that, in actuality, they were. Both writers could be correct. Many acts of symbolism were probably performed inside megalithic rings including mimes of customs long-known from earlier burial and fertility practices so that a model of an orthostatic forecourt would be quite appropriate. Conversely, into such a traditional structure might be incorporated novel astronomical lines. Or the setting might be analogous to the unexplained rectangle inside the Carles at Keswick; or the megalithic rectangles of Brittany and King Arthur's Hall on Bodmin; or the sarsen rectangles at Mount Pleasant and Stenness. Without complete excavation of the disturbed centre of the SSE. circle only guesses may be made of its purpose.

17.7 m to the SSE. of the ring was another pillar, the Ring Stone, described by Stukeley as 'an odd stone standing, not of great bulk. It has a hole wrought in it . . .'. From the size of its pit it appears to have been substituted for a former and larger outlier, possibly being preferred because of its natural perforation. Only the stump of the Ring Stone was left by its eighteenth-century breakers.

Nearly 200,000 tons of chalk was quarried to make Avebury's bank. Over 190 stones, weighing up to 47 tons, awkward 4.9 m wide 0.9 m thick slabs were tugged crawlingly from Avebury Down, some 4000 tons or more of rough sarsens, more again for the avenues during the gold and crimson of Autumn after Autumn, ropes rain-wettened, shoulders aching with the levering of the stones. To ask the reason for this voluntary hardship is to examine again the strange society of Late Neolithic Britain, a society of prehistoric farmers capable of arithmetical calculations, stone-workers who made a sun-symbol of the axe, an egalitarian people who banded together for years of labour while their great circles were being built, peasant families who cleared the forests and tilled the soil, grazed their cattle, but who looked to the sky for their calendar and back into ancestral times for the protection and assurance their lives needed. That they used some unit of measurement for their circles and ovals seems indisputable, and that the inner circles at Avebury have similar diameters need cause no surprise considering the example of the mathematics and geometry involved in the design of West Kennet chambered tomb eight or more centuries before by the forefathers of the Avebury builders. The elegance of an arithmetical model would surely have conferred an extra gloss to the plan of this vast circle-henge.

Whether Avebury had an astronomical function is not clear. So many stones have gone that alignments could have been destroyed. Thom (1967, 105) detected a possible line through the circle-centres towards the mid-winter setting of the bright star Deneb (α Cygni) but, as well as the absence of any adequate foresight, Deneb had the necessary declination of 36° 5′ around 2000 BC (c. 1575 bc), far too late to be compatible with the Neolithic pottery in the stoneholes of the SSE. circle, especially as early beaker sherds were stratified above them (I. F. Smith, 1965, 227), and the proposed align-ment must be considered doubtful. In general, the hypotheses for stellar orientations in stone rings rely on such fragile evidence and offer such nebulously optimistic reasons for their existence that they are far less satis-factory than the strongly based arguments in favour of alignments on the sun, moon or even the brilliant planet, Venus.

Possibly the Cove in the NNW. circle was open to the midsummer sunrise. (It would be very interesting to learn in which direction the Beckhampton Cove, if it were such, faced.) It is also possible that seen from the central Obelisk in the southern circle, the terminals of the stone-setting defined the position of the midwinter minimum moonset to the north-west and the maximum midsummer moonset to the south-west, but this must remain speculative until the horizon altitudes can be determined. It would hardly be more than wishful thinking to attribute a solar, midsummer function to one circle, a lunar, midwinter use to the other as Toland did for Callanish 250 years ago. Olson (Baity, 1973, 445) has claimed the multiple rings at Stanton Drew marked seasonal risings of the sun and moon and that circle-builders in Britain had a preference for specific numbers of stones in their rings: twenty-nine and thirty; twelve and thirteen; eighteen and nineteen; numbers which, in that order, were related to the days in a month; lunar months in a year; and years in a metonic cycle. More comprehensive studies do not verify this thesis for the British stone circles (Appendix 3). Quanta have indeed been noticed in some regional groups (Cornwall; Inverness; Aberdeenshire; Cork *inter alia*) but these stem more from a predisposition towards mathematical gracefulness than from an intention to establish any form of megalithic calendar. The fact that the inner circles at Avebury had twenty-nine to thirty stones each does not signify any wish to record days in a month— which in prehistoric Britain would have been the synodic or lunar month of twenty-eight days[1] and not the Julian or Gregorian months of modern times— but is more probably connected with stone numbers in other regions like Bodmin and Dartmoor (Table 3).

As in other rings, whether the great circles of western Britain or the graded recumbents with their cremations in north-east Scotland, seasonal gatherings must be suspected at Avebury as the evidence of hazelnut shells at Windmill Hill or in the ritual pits of the Kennet avenue imply, Autumn perhaps being the most convenient time for a concourse when the harvest was in, the beasts stalled, when the axe-traders might arrive with the stone tools that could be axe, hoe, plough-share or religious token. There are no axe-carvings at Avebury, or any other carvings on the stones, but scores of stone axes have been found in the district, axes from all parts of Britain: Cornwall; Cumberland; north and south Wales; Shropshire; and it is 'tempting to associate the trade in some measure with the magico-religious ceremonial connected with the great Avebury complex itself and with the well-known axe-cults of Neolithic and Early Bronze Age Europe' (Stone and Wallis, 1951, 134).

People met at Avebury in part to order their lives, to make social agreements, partly simply for the pleasure of meeting again, partly to trade, partly to express ritually what their lives needed, creating no dichotomy between the natural and supernatural worlds although the latter had to be expressed symbolically through rites that embodied beliefs providing 'explanations for events which otherwise would be inexplicable' (Beattie, 1966, 206). This was their method of coping with what might ordinarily be disasters against which they had no power. In such terms the 'male' and 'female' stones of the Kennet avenue become symbols of fecundity, an integral element of the beliefs and ceremonies within Avebury, for here was the essence of their dread, that life might cease or be threatened so fearsomely that only by

[1]But see Thom, 1967, 107, for 'months' of twenty-two to twenty-four days each in megalithic Britain.

invoking every possible force, totally and repeatedly, only then could they balance their precarious world, coming together at the time of warmth and light, of cold and darkness, making caricatures and carvings of sun and moon, lighting fires, offering good soil, calling upon their ancestors for protection, making sacrifices. Like Wagnerian music the primitive themes blend in a richness more emotional than scientific, all the more evocative and compelling to the group-mind.

Outside Avebury there are the paired stones, pillar and lozenge, and on the Kennet avenue there are pits and holes in an 'occupation' area that from its 600 weathered sherds of Mortlake, Ebbsfleet and grooved ware, should be of the same period as the circle-henge. The two pits held dark soil 'more or less heavily charged with charcoal', and of the ten smaller holes which also were soil-filled, five were clay-lined like postholes but contained twigs of hazel, blackthorn and hawthorn. Such low and spreading trees, growing at the edges of woodland, bear Spring blossom, and in Autumn produce the edible nuts, sloes and red berries which may have been offered, soil-sprinkled, in these little holes less than half a mile from Avebury's southern entrance.

The interior of Avebury itself was deliberately kept clean. A few pottery sherds in the ditch-bottom, some antler picks, are almost all the artefacts discovered during Gray's limited excavations. Like so many other southern British stone circles the activities did not include the deposition of oblations within the enclosure. There were, however, fourteen separate finds of human bones in the ditches (St. G. Gray, 1935, 148), detached long bones: femurs; humeri; fibulae; radii; and mandibles; fragments of skulls; all reminiscent of the skeletal remains in the ditches of Windmill Hill where long bones also predominated (I. F. Smith, 1965, 136; 1971, 100).

Avebury epitomizes the open megalithic rings of southern Britain. Every architectural trait of those circles has been integrated into Avebury, and when the axe-traders came, or people from distant parts, they would recognize here, raised in mighty stones, likenesses of their own stone circles. If the composition of Avebury is dissected it is revealed as an aggregation of features from its own native Wessex and Somerset, from Cornwall and the south-west peninsula; and, more tenuously, from the farther Shropshire, Cumbria and the coasts of the Irish Sea, all areas from which stone axes were brought, sometimes directly, sometimes passing from group to group over a hundred miles or more.

Avebury was a long time building. Many of its features must have been added to accommodate the differing beliefs of people foreign to Wessex, absorbed into the architecture over some centuries. From Wessex itself came the concept of the huge circle-henge with its open arena, its size determined by the number of people nearby, its design a mixture of lowland henge and western stone circle. Also from Wessex came the concentric stones of the NNW. circle derived from timber prototypes which may have existed at Avebury itself. The Cove also could be Wessex in inspiration, embodying in its open stones the forecourt and tomb ceremonies of the megalithic barrows and cairns of the Cotswold-Severn group.

But the other features in Avebury: the paired circles; the centre stone; the outlier; the avenues; the holed stone; these are not native to Wessex but are better known in the south-west peninsula and must be regarded as cultural importations. Paired rings are characteristic of the south-west peninsula where there are multiple circles like the Grey Wethers, the Wendron circles, the Hurlers, Er Lannic in Brittany, even Stanton Drew and the Priddy henges. It is hardly coincidence that the number of stones in the Avebury rings is so like those of the Bodmin and Dartmoor sites. Centre stones, too, are found in the south-west where Boscawen-Un and the Stripple Stones are typical. Other centre stones, shrunken and unemphatic, are known in Shropshire where Black Marsh stands on the ancient Clun-Clee trackway. The Kennet and Beckhampton avenues at Avebury may have counterparts in the short stretches nearby at Clatford and Langdean or, farther afield, in the idiosyncratic rows of Dartmoor, but are more similar to sites in Westmorland, Shap, Moor Divock and Broomrigg. Also in the Lake District the outlying stones of the Carles and Long Meg, like the King Stone outside the Rollright Stones, may be equated with the Ring Stone at Avebury though the substitution of this perforated stone may point to a stronger Cornish influence, for outliers are also known in Cornwall. So are holed stones, the famous Men-an-Tol and the Tolvan Stone with a reputation for having curative properties as did the speckled Tobernaveen holed stone of Sligo where 'children suffering from infant maladies were formerly passed through the aperture for a cure' (E. E. Evans, 1966, 192). Similarly, if 'children are passed through a hole in the Long Stone, near Minchinhampton, Gloucestershire, they are cured of, or prevented from getting, measles, whooping cough and other infantile diseases' (Grinsell, 1936, 54). The therapeutic reputation derives, surely, from the porthole entrances of Neolithic chambered tombs like Avening and Rodmarton, and is another reminder of the intricate association between death, burial and the life-giving ceremonies in the megalithic rings. One may imagine at Avebury witch-doctors brandishing human bones, people dancing within the stones, the old and the very young seated, swaying, hands and drums beaten rhythmically, flaming effigies carried around the stalk-cut fields of Autumn, fires reddening the midwinter night, an image reflecting the other great rings of the British Isles, for the ceremonies here seem fundamentally those of the other open circles. Avebury is a pantheon. It is a compilation of regional customs, a cult-centre where hundreds of people combined to deflect danger and engender safety. Stukeley was not in error when he marvelled at 'those remarkable circles of stones which we find all over the kingdom' and exaggerated only a little when with the visionary's eye he called Avebury 'the most august work at this day upon the globe of the earth'.

It lingered in use like many of the stone circles into the first millennium bc when with new customs and sometimes new people coming into the country such rings were less favoured. But still folk came to them. Even into Christian times some of the old practices endured and a fourteenth-century barber-surgeon died while despoiling this pagan place. Where once all the people had danced, celebrated, burned winter fires, watched the sun rising on the midsummer hills, now only young persons came, and sometimes, more furtively, wives remembering half-giggled, half-serious gossip that the grey, fallen stones had powers to make life if one dared still to go to them. Youths and maidens took cakes and ale to the rings not knowing that food and drink had been buried there 4000 years or more ago. With the irony of the old gods, at Avebury where the Obelisk had stood, maypoles were put up each year even into the nineteenth century and Victorian children innocently danced and wreathed their ribands where millennia before other people had danced, as innocently but more serious in their rising, driving ecstacies. Even in the 1500s Stubbs could write of the maypole, 'And then fall they to daunce about it, like as the heathen people did at the dedication of the Idols . . . I have heard it credibly reported . . . that of fortie, threescore, or a hundred maidens going to the wood overnight, there have scaresly the third part returned home again undefiled.'

Whether what Stubbs would have condemned as orgiastic depravity followed upon the ceremonies at Avebury and the other great circles can never be known. What remains for the archaeologist are the tangible relics, the twigs of the first-fruits, the charcoal in the open rings, the human bones, 'the accumulation of factual detail' that so far from distracting attention from any vision of the past serves to give this vision shape and substance even though it is realized that the matter which most concerns us, the mind of man, is the least likely of all the mysteries of stone circles to be revealed. Where the stone came from, how the pillars were erected, and when, these problems may be answered by scientific deduction. Geometrical designs can be examined. Burials and offerings, carvings, may with difficulty and diffidence be interpreted. Future work may be concerned with accurate planning, and with geographical analysis of territorial patterns, the relationship of stone circles to other monuments in their locality. But the sounds and the colours are gone forever.

Now only the stones remain, bleak, leaning against the winds that blow across their silence. The fires are out. The midsummer sun has for years risen above empty, fallen rings. The people and their fears are gone. There are only the stones and they have no message for the visitor, misquoting Swinburne:

> The fields fall southward, abrupt and broken,
> To the last low edge of the long lone land.
> If a step should sound or a word be spoken
> Would a ghost not rise at the strange guest's hand?
> So long have the grey bare stones lain guestless,
> Through branches and briars if a man make way
> He shall find no life but the sea-wind, restless
> Night and day.

County Concordance

For those not familiar with the new (1974) counties the following, alphabetical list gives the equivalents of the unrevised names used in this book.

New Name (also cited in the Gazetteer)   *Former Name (used in the text)*

Annandale and Eskdale, Dumfries and Galloway	Dumfriesshire, Scotland
Avon	Somerset, England
Clwyd	Flintshire, Wales
Cumbria	Cumberland; Westmorland, England
Cumnock and Doon Valley, Strathclyde	Ayrshire, Scotland
Cunninghame, Central	Clackmannan, Scotland
Dyfed	Pembrokeshire; Carmarthenshire, Wales
Grampian	Aberdeenshire, Scotland
Greater Manchester	Lancashire, England
Gwent	Monmouthshire, Wales
Gwynedd	Caernarvonshire; Merioneth, Wales
Highland Kyle and Carrick, Strathclyde	Caithness; Sutherland; Inverness, Scotland
	Ayrshire, Scotland
Merrick, Dumfries and Galloway	Wigtownshire, Scotland
Powys	Radnor; Brecknockshire; Montgomery, Wales
Salop	Shropshire, England
Strathclyde	Argyllshire, Scotland
Tayside	Perthshire, Scotland
Tweeddale, Borders	Roxburgh; Peeblesshire, Scotland

334

APPENDIX ONE

A County Gazetteer of the Stone Circles in the British Isles

Sites are arranged alphabetically under old county names for: Eire; England; Scotland; Ulster; and Wales. The most important details are given for each site in the following order.

1 The customary name for the ring.

2 The condition of the site:
    (1) Good. Worth visiting
    (2) Restored
    (3) Ruined but recognisable
    (4) Destroyed or unrecognisable
    (5) Uncertain status, including misidentified sites and hybrid rings such as complex ring-cairns (Lynch, 1972)
    (6) Possibly a fake

3 Grid reference.

4 Diameter (where known) in metres. Two diameters are given if the ring is non-circular. Where available Thom's (1967) classification is given:

CA; CB; CD = Flattened circles   CE = Ellipses
CI; CII = Egg-shaped rings   Complex Sites

5 Architectural details, using these abbreviations:

A	Avenue	P2 etc.	Adjacent sites
B	External bank	Pf	Platform
BD	Internal boulder-dolmen	PG	Internal passage-grave
C	Concentric ring	Pl	A plain ring
CH	Circle-henge	Pt	Portals or entrance
Cm	Cupmarkings	Q	Quartz
CN	Internal cairn or barrow	R	A single row of stones
Cr	Cup-and-ring markings	2R	Two separate rows
Crem	Cremations	RC	Internal ring-cairn
CT	Internal cist	RPt	Radial portal stones
Em	Embanked circle	RSC	Recumbent stone circle
Exc	Excavated	S	Centre stone
Gr	Stones graded in height	V	Cove
O	Outlying stone/s	WG	Internal wedge-grave
4P	Four-Poster	6	6-stone ring
5	5-stone RSC	8	8-stone ring

6 Other details:

    i. Where applicable, date of excavation; finds; and C-14 determinations with laboratory numbers.

    ii. References. These are given by author's name if the work is cited in the Bibliography, adding a date only if the author appears more than once; or by volume, number, date and page. All Thom's (1967) catalogue numbers are given followed by his name for the ring if this differs from the customary one.

    iii. Astronomical details are abstracted from Thom's 'A' lines (1967, 97ff) and, selectively, from other sources. The following abbreviations are employed:

MR	Moonrise	SR	Sunrise
MS	Moonset	SS	Sunset

Stars are given by name.

EIRE

CAVAN

1 Crom Cruaich / (4) / H 21.12.? / ? / S / *PRIA* 36 (1921–4) 23; Evans E. (1966) 67; Ashbee (1960) 182; Ross (1972) 194

2 Killycluggin a / (3) / H 239160 / 30.5? / O? / Davies (1939a) 13; Paterson *et al.*, 148; *JRSAI* 52 (1922) 113

3 Killycluggin b / (4) / H 238160? / 18.3 × 12.2 / ? / *JRSAI* 52 (1922) 113

4a Kilnavert A / (3) / H 22.15. / 12.5 / P2 / Davies (1939a) 13

4b Kilnavert B / (3) / H 22.15. / 12.5 / P2 / ibid

5 Lissanover / (3) / H 22.15. / ? / ? / Evans (1966) 67

CLARE

1 Ballyalla Lake / (5) / R 34.81. / ? / ? / *JRSAI* 46 (1916) 99

CORK

1 Adrigole / (5) / V 81.48. / ? / ? / Private information

2a Annagannihy A / (5) / W 385851 / 7.5 × 5.5 / O, P2 / Condon (1916) 161; Barber (1972), 50 (C 49)

2b Annagannihy B / (5) / W 386852 / ? / P2 / Barber (1972), 50 (C 48)

3 Ardgroom / (2) / V 701552 / 7.6 × 7.2 / RSC, Pt, Gr / *JRSAI* 35 (1905) 171; Barber (1972), 24 (C 2). Ast: MS (Barber, 1973)

4 Ballvackey / (3) / W 34.42. / ? / ? / Inf. E. M. Fahy

5 Baurgaum / (3) / W 15.47. / ? / RSC / O'Nuallain, 24

6 Bellmount Lower / (3) / W 427643 / 4.0 / RSC, Pt, Gr / Barber (1972), 41 (C 26). Ast: Venus set (Barber, 1973).

7 Bellmount Upper / (4) / W 43.64. / 4.0 / RSC, 5, Pt / Barber (1972), 42 (C 27); Borlase W. C., I, 35. Ast: SS (Barber, 1973)

8 Bohonagh / (1) / W 308368 / 9.1 / RSC, RPt. / Exc. 1959, crem. Fahy, 1961; Somerville, 1930

9 Brinny More / (3) / W 035533 / 10.5 × 9.6 / RSC, BD, B / Barber (1972) 28 (C 4) *NMI* no. 450; Borlase W. C., I, 43

10 BROOK PARK E. / (1) / W 325876 / ? / O / Killanin & Duignan, 373

11 CAPPABOY BEG / (3) / W 09.60. / ? / O / Barber (1972) 32 (C 12)

12 CARRIGAGRENANE / (3) / W 253431 / 9.6 / RSC, RPt, S? / Barber (1972) 38 (C 23) Somerville (1930) 81. Ast: Venus set (Barber, 1973)

13 CARRIGAGRENANE A / (4) / W 258438 / ? / ? / Barber (1972) 39 (C 25)

14 CARRIGAGULLA A / (1) / W 373837 / 3.0 / RSC, 5, Pt / Barber (1972) 46 (C 36) Condon, 1917, 157.

15 CARRIGAGULLA B / (3) / W 389822 / 8.2 / RSC, S, RPt / Barber (1972) 46 (C 37) Condon, 1917, 156

16 CARRIGAPHOOCA / (4) / W 294735 / ? / RSC, 5 / Barber (1972) 47 (C 39)

17 CLOGHBOLLA / (3) / W 274872 / 3.1 / RSC, 5, O / ibid 48 (C 41)

18 CLOGHBOOLA BEG / (4) / W 28.88 / ? / ? / ibid 51 (C 50)

19 CLONLEIGH / (5) / W 67.49. / ? / RSC? / Inf. C. McCarthy

20 COOLCLEVANE / (1) / W 287639 / 8.7×7.7 / RSC, RPt / Barber (1972) 30 (C 11)

21 COOLMOUNTAIN / (3) / W 19.60. / ? / ? / ibid 32 (C 10)

22 COUSANE / (1) / W 113566 / 3.6 / RSC, 5, Pt / ibid 29 (C 8)

23 CUPPOGE / (1) / R 77.04. / c.21.3 / Pl? / JRSAI 62 (1932) 115

24 CURRAGHROE / (3) / W 77.86. / 4.6 / Pl / ibid 116

25 CURREBEHA / (3) / W 407640 / 9.1 / RSC, Pt, S / Barber (1972) 41 (C 28); Borlase W. C., II, 505. Ast: Venus set (Barber, 1973)

26 DERREENATAGGART / (1) / V 665465 / 8.4 / RSC, Pt, S? / Barber (1972) 23 (C 1); JRSAI 50 (1920) 158; Borlase W. C., II, 504

27 DERRYNAFINCHIN / (3) / W 048623 / 9.5 / RSC?, BD, S / Barber (1972) 30 (C 13)

28 DOONEENS / (5) / W 383814 / 2.8 / RC?, R / ibid 43 (C 41)

29 DOUGH / (3) / V 784256 / 7.0 / RSC, 5 / Inf. C. McCarthy

30 DROMBEG / (1) / W 247352 / 9.1 / RSC, Pt, Cm / Exc. 1957–8, urn. C-14: 13bc $\pm$ 140 (TCD-38), recalculated as: AD 600 $\pm$ 120 (D-62). Fahy (1959); (1960); Somerville (1923) 211; (1930) 72. Ast: SS (Somerville, 1923, 211, Barber, 1973)

31 DUNBEACON / (3) / V 928409 / 8.5 / RSC, S / Barber (1972) 31 (C 14)

32 DURRAGHALICKY / (4) / W 223453 / ? / ? / Inf. E. M. Fahy

33 FARANFADA / (3) / V 65.54. / ? / RSC?, BD? / Barber (1972) 24 (C 3)

34 GERTROE / (3) / V 92.81. / ? / Pl / O'Nuallain (1971) 23

35 GLANCARNEY / (4) / W 14.56. / ? / RSC?, 5? / Barber (1972) 32, (C 9)

36 GLENLEIGH / (3) / W 316901 / 3.6 / RSC, R / ibid 44 (C 33). Ast: Venus set (Barber, 1973).

37 GLENTANE E. / (3) / W 292828 / ? / B, O / Killanin & Duignan 373

38 GORTANIMILL / (3) / W 208738 / 7.6 / RSC, Pt, S / Barber (1972) 45 (C 34); Condon (1917) 125

39 GOWLANE N. / (3) / W 47.86. / 9.5 / RSC, RPt $\times 2$ / Barber (1972) 49 (C 47); JCHAS 15 (1909) 59

40 GRENAGH S. / (3) / W 58.84. / ? / ? / Killanin & Duignan 166; Borlase W. C. I, 35

41 KEALKIL / (1) / W 054556 / 3.1 / RSC, 5, O / Exc. 1938, no finds. O'Riordain (1939); Borlase W. C. II, 419; Barber (1972) 28 (C 5). Ast: Equinoxes (O'Riordain, 1939)

42 KEEL CROSS / (3) / W 413799 / 2.7 / RSC, Gr / Barber (1972) 47 (C 47); Condon (1916) 152. Ast: MS (Barber, 1973)

43 KILBOULTRAGH / (5) / W 33.76. / ? / RSC? / Inf. C. McCarthy
44 KIPPAGH / (5) / W 24.47. / ? / ? / Inf. E. M. Fahy
45 KNOCKANE / (5) / R 513048 / 12.2? / RSC? / Inf. C. McCarthy
46 KNOCKANEIRK A / (3) / W 374625 / 10.4 / RSC, Pt, Gr / Barber (1972)
40 (C 29). Ast: MS (Barber, 1973)
47 KNOCKANEIRK B / (1) / W 368632 / 4.0 / RSC, 5, Pt / Barber (1972) 40
(C 30). Ast: Venus set (Barber, 1973)
48 KNOCKAVULLIG E / (3) / W 430701 / 2.3 / RSC, 5 / Barber (1972) 48
(C 43); Condon (1916) 161
49 KNOCKAVULLIG W / (3) / W 430701 / 3.0 / RSC, 5 / ibid 48 (C 44)
50 KNOCKAWADRA / (3) / W 263457 / 3.1 / RSC, 5, Pt / Barber (1972) 37
(C 17)
51 KNOCKEENADARA / (5) / R 816087 / 9.1 / RSC?, / RPt? / *JCHAS* 34
(1929) 43
52 KNOCKS A / (3) / W 300445 / ? / RSC, RPt, S / Barber (1972) 38 (C 16)
Ast: MS (Barber, 1973
53 KNOCKS B / (3) / W 300456 / 9.8 × 9.2 / RSC, RPt. / Barber (1972) 36
(C 21)
54 LACKADUV / (1) / W 303800 / 4.3 × 3.4 / RSC, 5, R / Barber (1972) 49
(C 45)
55 LAHARANKEEL / (3) / W 393772 / ? / RSC, 5, Pt / ibid 47 (C 40). Ast: MS
(Barber, 1973)
56 LETTERGORMAN / (3) / W 263455 / 5.4 × 2.3 / 4P?, O / Barber (1972) 39
(C 24)
57 LISSARD / (4) / W 57.900 / *c*.8.2 / Pl? / Condon (1916) 69
58 LOUGHATOOMA N / (4) / W 401838 / 8.5 × 5.8 / Pl / ibid 156
59 MAUGHANCLEA A / (3) / W 107564 / 11.9 / RSC, BD? / Barber (1972) 29
(C 6). Ast: MS (Barber, 1973)
60 MAUGHANCLEA B / (?) / W 10.56. / 6.7? / Em? / Barber (1972) 31 (C 7)
61 MAULATANVALLY / (3) / W 263443 / 10.1 / RSC, RPt, S / ibid 36 (C 15);
Somerville (1930) 79, 96; Borlase W. C., II, 420
62 MAULMORE / (5) / W 3..8.. / 2.7 / RSC, 5 / Inf: C. McCarthy
63 MUSHERA BEG / (1) / W 294842 / 3.5 / RSC, 5, Em? / Exc. 1930, quartz.
Gogan (1931); *JRSAI* 45 (1915) 316; *NMI* no. 420.
64 OUGHTIHERY B / (4) / W 41.79. / 2.6 / RSC, 5 / Barber (1972) 49 (C 46)
65 REANASCREENA / (2) / W 265410 / 9.1 / RSC, Pt, B / Exc. 1960, crem.
Fahy (1962); Somerville (1930) 77
66 REIM NA GAOITHE / (3) / W 56.92. / ? / RSC, S / Killanin & Duignan 367
67 ROSNASCALP / (3) / W 41.75. / 2.7 / Pl? / Condon (1917) 157
68 RYLANE / (1) / W 438816 / 3.5 / RSC, 5, Pt / Barber (1972) 48 (C 42);
Condon (1916) 152. Ast: MS (Barber, 1973)
69 SCRONGARE / (3) / W 269754 / 2.4 / RSC, 5 / Inf. C. McCarthy
70 SHANDAGAN / (3) / W 41.66. / 7.6 / RSC / Inf. E. M. Fahy
71 TEERGAY / (5) / W 4..7.. / 8.3 / Pl? / Barber (1972) 45 (C 35)
72 TEMPLEBRYAN / (3) / W 386438 / 10.8 / RSC, Pt, S / ibid 37 (C 19);
JRSAI 36 (1906) 262

DONEGAL

1 Beltany / (5) / C 254003 / 44.8 / CN, O / Somerville (1923) 212; *UJA* 2 (1939) 293; Ross (1967) 115. Ast: SR (Somerville, 1923, 213)
2 Culdaff / (3) / C 54.47. / *c*.21.3 / C?, O? / *JRSAI* 59 (1929) 152. Ast: SS (*JRSAI* 59 (1929) 153)

DUBLIN

1 Knockanvinidee / (5) / O 06.23. / 9.8 × 9.1 / C, P2? / *JRSAI* 55 (1925) 126
2 Piperstown K / (5) / O 11.23. / 4.3 × 3.4 / CN / Exc. 1962, crem. Rynne & O'hEailidhe

GALWAY

1 Masonbrook / (2) / M 658147 / 21.3 / Em, CN? / Exc. 1916, no finds. Macalister (1917)

KERRY

1 Doughill / (5) / V 962696 / ? / ? / O.S. Sheet 184
2 Dromatouk / (5) / V 947709 / ? / ? / ibid
3 Drombohilly / (1) / V 790607 / 9.0 / RSC, RPt / Barber (1972) 20 (K 1). Ast: MS (Barber, 1973)
4 Dromod / (3) / V 545694 / 4.0 / RSC, 5 / O'Nuallain 21
5 Dromroe / (1) / V 875650 / 10.5 / RSC, BD / ibid 18; Barber (1972) 21 (K 3). Ast: SS (Barber, 1973, 32)
6 Drumminboy / (?) / V 754555 / 7.5 / RSC, Gr / O'Nuallain 20; Barber (1972) 22 (K 4)
7 Gurteen / (1) / W 006698 / 10.5 / RSC, BD? / O'Nuallain 16; Barber (1972) 22 (K 5). Ast: MS (Barber, 1973)
8 Illaunimnal / (5) / Q 60.21. / ? / ? / Killanin & Duignan 142
9 Kenmare / (1) / V 907707 / 17.4 × 15.8 CE / BD, Cm / O'Nuallain 13; Borlase W. C. I, 6; Barber (1972) 23, B58 (K 6)
10 Killowen / (4) / V 924716 / ? / RSC?, BD? / O'Nuallain 16; Barber (1972) 25 (C 56)
11 Leabaleaha / (5) / V 41.69. / 11.0 / S / *JRSAI* 32 (1902) 338
12 Lissyviggeen / (1) / V 997906 / 4.0 / B, O / *JRSAI* 16 (1883) 306; O'Nuallain 21
13 Spunkane / (5) / V 49.67. / ? / ? / Killanin & Duignan 457
14 Teeravane / (?) / Q 340037 / ? / RSC?, S? / Inf. M. Sibley
15 Tinnies Upper / (5) / V 38.77. / ? / ? / Killanin & Duignan 450
16 Tuosist / (2) / V 824663 / 10.8 / BD? / O'Nuallain 19; Barber (1972) 21 (K 2)

KILDARE

1 Broadleas / (3) / N 96.11. / 31.5 × 30.0 / Pl / Walshe 130
2 Piper's Stones / (4) / N 83.01. / ? / B / Walshe 126
3 Whiteleas / (4) / N 92.08. / 23.8 / Pl? / ibid 127

KILKENNY

1 BRANDON HILL / (?) / S 69.40. / ? / CN? / Killanin & Duignan 300

LAOISE

1 DRUIDS ALTAR / (4) / S 60.91. / ? / ? / Borlase W. C. II, 374

LIMERICK

1 BALLYNAMONA / (3) / R 696384 / ? / Pl / Evans E. (1966) 143
2 LIOS / (2) / R 640410 / 47.6 / Em, Pt / Exc. 1939, Knockadoon I and II
ware (Case (1961) 224, 227, 228); E and s3/w beakers (Clarke (1970) 1901F, 1903F),
bronze. O'Riordain (1951); Savory (1964). Ast: SS (Somerville, in: Windle, 1912,
287); Capella, 1950 BC (Lewis A. L., 1909)
3 LOUGH GUR C / (3) / R 641411 / 22.9 × 16.2 / B / Windle (1912) 292
4 LOUGH GUR D / (3) / R 640411 / c.51.8 / Pl, A? / ibid 293
5 LOUGH GUR O / (3) / R 661419 / 55.5 / C, B / ibid 302
6 LOUGH GUR T / (3) / R 646417 / 13.4 × 9.1 / Pl / ibid 304
7 SLIEVEREAGH / (5) / R 73.25. / ? / ? / Priv. inf.

LOUTH

1 KILLIN / (3) / J 01.10. / ? / ? / Davies (1939a) 12
2 RAVENSDALE PARK / (6) / O 05.98. / ? / C? / ibid 13; Borlase W. C. II, 421

MAYO

1 CARROWREAGH / (3) / ? / ? / BD? / *TGHAS* 31 (1964–5) 14
2 MULLAGHMORE / (3) / G 17.32. / ? / ? / *JRSAI* 81 (1951) 180
3 ROSSPORT / (3) / F 82.39. / c.16.5 / C / *NMI* no. 386
4 SUMMERHILL HOUSE / (3) / G 19.34. / ? / ? / *JRSAI* 81 (1951) 180

MEATH

1 DONAGHMORE / (4) / N 86.68. / ? / ? / *JRSAI* 22 (1892–3) 126
2 GREENANSTOWN / (4) / O 110637 / ? / ? / *PRIA* 58 (1957) 264
3 NEW GRANGE / (3) / O 007727 / 103.6 / PG / Exc. 1954, no finds. C-14:
2585bc ± 105 (UB-361), 2475bc ± 45 (GrN-5462), 2465bc ± 40 (GrN-5463).
O'Riordain & O'Eochaide; O'Kelly C. (1971): Daniel & O'Riordain. Ast: SR
(Patrick, 1974).

TIPPERARY

1 BALLYANNY / (3) / R 83.85. / ? / C / O'Riordain (1964) 90
2 FIRBREAGA / (3) / R 83.68. / ?/ /? / Killanin & Duignan 386
3 REARDNOGY MORE / (3) / R 84.59. / 4.5 / O, R / Rynne
4 TIMONEY / (3) / S 193838 / c.61.0 / Pl? / *NMI* no. 353; Evans E. (1966) 196

WEXFORD

1 CARRICKBYRNE / (5) / S 82.24. / 6.1 × 4.9 / 8 / *JRSAI* 16 (1883–4) 41

2 WHITECHURCH / (4) / S 71.19. / ? / ? / Killanin & Duignan 123

WICKLOW

1 ATHGREANY / (1) / N 930032 / 23.0 / O, Cm? / *JRSAI* 61 (1931) 128
2 BOLEYCARRIGEEN / (3) / S 94.90. / *c*.14.0 / B? / *PRIA* 42 (1934) 39
3 CASTLERUDDERY / (3) / S 92.94. / 29.3 / B, A, Pt / *JRSAI* 75 (1945) 266
4 RATHGALL / (5) / S 90.73. / ? / ? / *PRIA* 42 (1934) 40
5 TOURNANT / (5) / N 87.00. / 13.4+ / O, S? / ibid 38

ENGLAND

CORNWALL

1 ALTARNUN / (1) / SX 236781 / 15.2 / S, R / Tregelles 396; Thom (1967)
S1/2 (Nine Stones); Ast: MS (1967, 100)
2 BOSCAWEN-UN / (2) / SW 412274 / 25.3 × 22.3 CB / S, O / Exc. pre-1879,
no finds. Tregelles 379; Thom (1961a) 86, S1/13
3 BOSILIACK / (4) / SW 44.32. / ? / ? / *CA* 3 (1964) 91
4 BOSKEDNAN / (3) / SW 434353 / 22.0 / Pl / Tregelles 386; Lewis A. L.
(1905) 433; Thom (1967) S1/11 (Nine Maidens)
5 CRADDOCK MOOR / (3) / SX 248718 / 38.0 / Pl / *JRIC* 25 (1938) 61
6 DULOE / (1) / SX 235583 / 11.9 × 11.3 CA / Pl / Exc. *c*.1863, urn. *JBAA* 38
(1882) 149; Thom (1967) S1/3 (Duloo)
7 FERNACRE / (1) / SX 144800 / 46.0 × 43.4 CD / O? / Tregelles 394; Thom
(1967) 57, S1/7 (Rough Tor)
8 GOODAVER / (5) / SX 208751 / 31.7 / Pl / *JRIC* 25 (1938) 61
9 HR CARWYNNEN / (5) / SW 652372 / 16.8 / Pl / *CA* 9 (1970) 137
   THE HURLERS
10a NE. / (3) / SX 258714 / 34.7 / P3 / Dymond (1879)
10b SW. / (3) / SX 258714 / 32.9 / P3 / Dymond (1879)
10c CENTRE / (2) / SX 258714 / 41.8 × 40.5 CII / P3, S, O / Exc. 1936, flints.
Radford (1938); Dymond (1879); Thom (1966) 40, S1/1
11 LEAZE / (1) / SX 137773 / 25.0 / Pl / Tregelles 392; Thom (1967) S1/6;
Ast: SR (1967, 100)
12 MERRY MAIDENS / (1) / SW 432245 / 23.8 / O / Tregelles 382; Thom
(1967) / S1/14. Ast: Lockyer, 1906a
13 NEW DOWNS / (5) / SW 701507 / ? / ? / *CA* 1 (1962) 114
14 PORTHMEOR / (5) / SW 444366 / ?34.0 × ? CB / S? / *CA* 6 (1967 86; Lukis
& Borlase 28; Thom (1967) S1/12
15 ROSEMERGY / (4) / SW 417363? / ? / ? / *CA* 5 (1966) 64
16 STANNON / (1) / SX 126800 / 42.7 × 40.5 CA / O? / Tregelles 395; Thom
(1967) 58, S1/8 (Dinnever Hill)
17 STRIPPLE STONES / (3) / SX 144752 / 44.8 / CH, S / Exc. 1905, flints. Gray
H. St. G (1908); Thom (1967) S1/4
18 TREDINNICK / (5) / SW 442349 / *c*.9.1 / P2? / *CA* 4 (1965) 71
19 TREEN / (4) / SW 397222 / ? / ? / *PWCFC* 2, 183

TREGESEAL

20a EAST / (3) / SW 387324 / 22.0 × 21.0 CA / P2 / Tregelles 385; Thom (1967) S1/16 (Botallack)

20b WEST / (4) / SW 386323 / ? / P2 / Tregelles 385

21 TREGESEAL C. / (4) / SW 385323 / ? / ? / *PWCFC* 2, 99

22 TREVELLO / (5) / SW 449263 / ? / ? / *CA* 2 (1963) 65

23 TRIPPET STONES / (1) / SX 131750 / 33.0 / Pl / Tregelles 389; Thom (1967) S1/5 (Treswigger)

WENDRON

24a NORTH / (3) / SW 683365 / *c.*18.3 / P2 / Tregelles 388

24b SOUTH / (4) / SW 683365 / 16.5 / P2 / Tregelles 388; Thom (1967) S1/10 (Nine Maidens)

25 WHITESAND BAY / (5) / SW 35.26.? / ? / ? / *PWCFC* 2 186

CUMBERLAND (Cumbria)

1 ANNASIDE / (4) / SD 098853 / *c.*18.3 / ? / Parker & Collingwood 18

2 ASH-HOUSE WOOD / (4) / SD 192873 / 30.5 / Pl / *TCWAAS* 29 (1929) 257

3 BLAKELEY RAISE / (6) / NY 060140 / 16.6 / Pl / *O.S. Southampton* NY 01 SE 1; Thom (1971) L1/16 (Blakeley Moss). Ast: MS

4 BRATS HILL / (1) / NY 173023 / 32.0 × 25.9 CA / O?, CN / Exc. 1827, antlers. Williams B. (1856b); Dymond (1881); Thom (1967) 60, L1/6 (Burnmoor E). Ast: Arcturus setting

5 BROAD FLAT / (5) / NY 425445 / *c.*19.2 / ?Pl, ?CN / Collingwood W. (1923) 23

6 BROOMRIGG A / (3) / NY 548466 / 50.9 × 50.0 CE / O or A; CH? / Exc. 1934, 1950, no finds. *TCWAAS* 35 (1935) 77; *TCWAAS* 53 (1953) 5

7 BROUGHAM HALL / (5) / NY 52.28. / 18.3? / CN? / Pennant (1774)

8 CASTLERIGG / (1) / NY 292236 / 32.9 × 29.9 CA / CH?, O, Pt / Exc. 1882, no finds. *TCWAAS* (O.S.) VI (1883) 505; Dymond (1881); Thom (1966) fig. 39; (1967) 145, L1/1. Ast: SS, SR, MR (1967, 99)

9 CHAPEL FLAT / (4) / NY 37.50. / 24.4? / ? / Ferguson (1906) 248

10 DACRE PARISH / (4) / NY 493277 / ? / ? / *TCWAAS* (O.S.) VI (1883) 113

11 EGREMONT / (4) / NX 995107 / ? / ? / Parker & Collingwood 8

12 ELVA PLAIN / (3) / NY 176317 / 34.4? / O / *TCWAAS* 63 (1963) 301; Thom (1967) L1/2

GRETIGATE

13a A / (4) / NY 057036 / 31.7 / P3 / Stout (1961)

13b B / (4) / NY 057036 / 22.0 × 18.9 CE / P3, CN / Exc. 1960 Stout (1961)

13c C / (4) / NY 057036 / 7.3 / P3 / Exc. 1960, flints. Stout (1961)

14 GREY CROFT / (2) / NY 034024 / 27.1 × 24.4 CD / O, CN / Exc. 1949, stone axe (Gp. VI), jet ring. Fletcher (1957); Thom (1967) L1/10 (Seascale). Ast: Deneb setting (1967, 99)

15 GREY YAUDS / (4) / NY 544486 / 47.6? / O / *TCWAAS* 35 (1935) 171

16 HALL FOSS / (4) / SD 112857 / 22.9? / ? / *TCWAAS* (O.S.) I (1874) 278

17 KIRKSTONES / (4) / SD 106843 / ? / ? / *TCWAAS* (O.S.) I (1874) 278

18 LACRA A / (4) / SD 150814 / 15.2 / Pl / Dixon & Fell

19 LACRA B / (3) / SD 149809 / 16.2? / CN, S? / Exc. 1947, crem. Dixon & Fell; Thom (1967) L1/13

20 LACRA C / (3) / SD 150810 / 21.3? / Pl / Dixon & Fell

21 LACRA D / (3) / SD 151812 / 18.3 × 15.6 CE / A or R, S? / Exc. 1947, urn (Longworth (1961) no 341); Dixon & Fell

22 LE WHELES / (5) / NX 989180 / ? / ? / *TCWAAS, SW Regional Group Report* (1958) 4

23 LONG MEG AND HER DAUGHTERS / (1) / NY 571373 / 109.4 × 93.0 CB / CH, O, Pt, Cr, S / Dymond (1881) 39; Harvey (1948); Thom (1967) 151, L1/7. Ast: SS (1967, 99)

LOW LONGRIGG

24a NE. / (3) / NY 172028 / 21.6 × 15.2 CE / P2, CN / Dymond (1881) 55; Thom (1966) 37, L1/6 (Burnmoor A)

24b SW. / (3) / NY 172027 / 15.2 / P2, CN / Dymond (1881) 55; Thom (1966) 37, L1/6 (Burnmoor B)

25 LAMPLUGH / (4) / NY 065177 / 30.5? / Pl? / Ferguson (1906) 248

26 MOTHERBY / (4) / NY 419282 / 15.2? / Pl? / Ferguson (1906) 248

27 STUDFOLD / (3) / NY 040224 / 35.1 × 28.4 CE / Pl? / Exc. pre-1924, no finds. *TCWAAS* 23 (1923) 34; Thom (1967) L1/14 (Dean Moor)

28 SWINSIDE / (1) / SD 172883 / 28.7 / Pt / Exc. 1901, no finds. Dymond (1902); Dymond (1881) 47; Thom (1967) L1/3 (Sunkenkirk)

WHITE MOSS

29a NE. / (3) / NY 172024 / 15.9 / P2, CN / Dymond (1881); Thom (1967) L1/6 (Burnmoor D)

29b SW. / (3) / NY 172023 / 16.6 / P2, CN / Dymond (1881); Thom (1967) L1/6 (Burnmoor C)

DERBYSHIRE

ABNEY MOOR

1a I / (5) / SK 18.79. / 14.6 / P2, Em / Radley (1966a) 18

1b II / (5) / SK 18.79. / 15.3 / P2, Em / Radley (1966a) 18

2 ARBOR LOW / (3) / SK 160636 / 41.5 × 37.2 CII? / CH, R, V / Exc. 1901–2, flints. Gray St. G. (1903); Radley (1969a); Thompson (1963)

3 BARBROOK I / (1) / SK 278755 / 14.6 × 12.5 CB / Em, O, Cm? / Ward (1905) 183; Thom (1967) 66, D1/7. Ast: Spica setting (1967, 98)

4 BARBROOK II / (3) / SK 277758 / 13.4 / Em, CN / Exc. 1966, urn, flints. C-14: 1500 ± 150 (BM-179) Lewis G. (1966); Sheffield Museum display

5 BARBROOK III / (5) / SK 283772 / 26.5 × 24.0 CB / Em / Radley (1966a); Thom (1967) D1/8 (Owler Bar)

BRASSINGTON MOOR

6a A / (4) / SK 23.54. / 11.9 / P2? / Ward (1905) 183

6b B / (4) / SK 23.54. / 6.7 / P2? / Ward (1905) 183

7 BROOMHEAD I / (3) / SK 238966 / 18.8 / Em / Radley (1966a) 19

8 BULL RING / (3) / SK 078783 / 46.0? / CH, R? / Exc. 1949, Neo sherds? Alcock (1950)

9 DOLL TOR / (3) / SK 238628 / 6.1 / Pl + CN / Exc. 1852, 1931, Pennine urns. Bateman (1861) 84; Heathcote (1939); Bu'lock 25

10 FORD / (5) / SK 06.54. / ? / C / Andrew 74, 80

11 FROGGATT EDGE / (5) / SK 249768 / 11.0 / Em or RC? / Exc. pre-1939, urn, crem. Radley (1966a) 17; Ward (1905) 183

12 LAWRENCE FIELD / (5) / SK 252797 / ? / ? / *THAS* 4 (1930–7) 263

13 MOSCAR MOOR / (5) / SK 221845 / 11.0 / Em / Radley (1966a) 18
14 NINE LADIES / (1) / SK 247634 / 10.1 / Em, O, CN / *Arch* VI (1782) 112;
Bateman (1848) 112; Andrew 82; Thom (1967) D1/3
15 NINESTONE CLOSE / (3) / SK 225625 / 13.1 / Pl? / Exc. 1847, sherds,
flints. Bateman (1848) 102, 111; Ward (1905) 183; Thom (1967) D1/4
16 OFFERTON MOOR / (5) / SK 212806 / 29.3 × 24.4 / Em, C? / Ward (1905)
183
17 PARK GATE / (5) / SK 281685 / 13.7 / Em, C? / Radley (1966a) 16
18 SEVEN STONES IN HORDRON / (3) / SK 215868 / 16.5 / Pl / Ward (1905)
183; Thom (1967) D1/9 (Moscar Moor)
19 SMELTING HILL / (5) / SK 202803 / 10.1 / Em / Ward (1905) 394
20 TOP OF RILEY / (4) / SK 226768 / ? / Em / Radley (1966a) 18
21 TUNSTEAD / (4) / SK 026792 / 10.1 = 9.1 / Em, O? / Exc. *c.*1905, no finds.
Andrew 82–4; Allcroft 228
22 WET WITHENS / (5) / SK 225790 / 29.9 / Em, CT, S? / Exc. 1840?, no
finds. Bateman (1848) 113; Lewis A. L. (1903) 135; Thom (1967) D1/2 (Wet
Withers)

DEVON

1 BRISWORTHY / (2) / SX 565655 / 24.8 / Pl / Exc. 1909, charcoal. *TDA* 48
(1916) 99; Thom (1967) S2/3
2 BROAD DOWN D / (3) / SY 172933 / ? / CN / Exc. 1868, crem. *TDA* 4
(1870); Fox A. (1948)
3 BROAD DOWN 45 / (3) / SY 172933 / ? / CN / Fox A. (1948)
4 BROCKHILL FORD / (5) / SX678656 / 8.7 × 7.1 CE / CN / Worth (1953
190; Davidson & Seabrook 28
5 BROWN HEATH / (5) / SX 649653 / 10.1 × 9.2 CA / CN, CT, 2R / Davidson
& Seabrook 26; Worth (1953) 206
6 BUCKLAND FORD / (5) / SX 657660 / 9.6 × 8.2 CII / CN / Worth (1953) 458;
Davidson & Seabrook 26
7 BURFORD DOWN / (5) / SX 637601 / 5.3 / CT / Davidson & Seabrook 25
8 BURFORD ROW / (5) / SX 637601 / 9.9 × 8.6 CB / CN, R / Davidson &
Seabrook 28, 35. Ast: MR
9 BUTTERDON / (5) / SX 656588 / 11.1 / CN, R / Worth (1953) 205; Davidson
& Seabrook 25
10 BUTTERN EAST / (4) / SX 649885 / 24.5 / Pl / *TDA* 26 (1894) 303
11 BUTTERN WEST / (3) / SX 643886 / 28.5 / ?S / *TDA* 26 (1894) 303
12 CHOLWICHTOWN / (4) / SX 584622 / 5.8 × 4.8 CE / R / Exc. 1961, no
finds. Eogan (1964); Simmons (1969) 217; Thom (1967) 72, S2/7 (Lee Moor)
13 COLLARD TOR / (5) / SX 558620 / 8.1 / CN, R / Worth (1953) 208
14 CORRINGDON BALL / (4) / SX 666612 / 11.1 / 2 × 3R / Worth (1953) 231;
Davidson & Seabrook 25
15 COSDON BEACON / (5) / SX 643916 / 7.9 / CN, CT, 3R / Worth (1953) 218
16 DOWN RIDGE / (5) / SX 655721 / 24.7 / ? / Worth (1939) 322
17 DOWN TOR / (1) / SX 587694 / 11.0 / CN, R / Worth (1953) 212
18 DRIZZLECOMBE C / (5) / SX 592671 / 10.4 / CN, R / Worth (1953) 182
19 FERNWORTHY / (1) / SX 655841 / 18.3 / Gr, R + 2R / Exc. 1897, charcoal.
TDA 30 (1898) 107; Burnard (356)

GREY WETHERS

20a NORTH / (2) / SX 638832 / 32.0 / P2 / Worth (1939) 326; Thom (1966) 43, S2/1

20b SOUTH / (2) / SX 638832 / 33.2 / P2 / ibid

21 HARTER NORTH / (5) / SX 577717 / 8.8 / CN, 2R / Worth (1953) 213

22 LAKEHEAD / (2) / SX 647774 / 7.6 / CT, R / Worth (1953) 229

23 LAKEHEAD NEWTAKE / (5) / SX 644778 / 5.8 / Pl / Worth (1953) 182

24 LANGSTONE MOOR / (4) / SX 557782 / 20.4 / C, R? / Brailsford 448; Worth (1953) 217; Crossing 151

25 LOWER PILES / (5) / SX 645602 / 4.2 × 3.8 CII / CT, O? / Davidson & Seabrook 28

26 MERRIVALE / (1) / SX 555744 / 19.8 × 17.8 CB / O / *JBAA* (1860; Crossing 94; Thom (1955); (1967) 95, S2/2

27 RINGMOOR / (2) / SX 563658 / 12.5 / CN, R / Worth (1953) 209; Thom (1967) S2/4

28 SCORHILL / (1) / SX 655874 / 26.2 / R / Worth (1953) 249

29 SEVEN STONES / (4) / SY 109878 / ? / ? / Smith E. E.

30 SHARPITOR / (5) / SX 558707 / 3.5 / CN, 2R / Worth (1953) 213

31 SHAUGH MOOR / (5) / SX 554635 / 15.2 / CN, R / Worth (1953) 208

32 SHELL TOP / (5) / SX 598638 / ? / ? / *CBA Arch. Rev. Gps* XII & XIII (1972) 18

33 SHERBERTON / (3) / SX 639732 / 30.0 / Pl / Worth (1939) 321

34 SHOVEL DOWN / (5) / SX 660860 / 8.4 / CN, 2R / Worth (1953) 188, 220

35 SPURRELL'S CROSS / (5) / SX 656594 / 15.2 / CN, 2R / Worth (1953) 205

36 STALL MOOR / (3) / SX 635644 / 16.6 / CN, R / Worth (1953) 182, 204; Crossing 403; *TDA* 93 (1961) 65; Davidson & Seabrook 25 (Erme Row)

37 STALL MOOR SOUTH / (5) / SX 632632 / 6.5 × 5.6 CI / CT / Davidson & Seabrook 28, 33. Ast: SR 1800 BC

TROWLESWORTHY WARREN

38a EAST / (5) / SX 577640 / 6.7 / CN, 2R / Worth (1953) 209

38b WEST / (5) / SX 577640 / 6.1 / CN, R / Worth (1953) 209

39 WHITE MOOR DOWN / (2) / SX 634896 / 20.0 / Pl / Worth (1953) 248

40 WILLING WALLS WARREN / (4) / SX 587652 / 41.9 / Pl / Worth (1953) 261

41 YAR TOR / (5) / SX 682738 / 11.0 / CN, 3R / Worth (1953) 188

DORSET

1 HAMPTON DOWN / (3) / SY 596865 / 7.6 × 6.1 / A? / Exc. 1965, no finds. Wainwright (1967); Piggott S. & C. M. 152; Thom (1967), S4/3

2 KINGSTON RUSSELL / (3) / SY 577878 / 27.7 × 20.6 CB / Pl / Piggott S. & C. M. 142; Thom (1955) S4/2

3 LITTLE MAYNE / (4) / SY 72.87. / ? / 2A? / Piggott S. & C. M. 149

4 LULWORTH / (4) / SY 87.81.? / ? / Pl? / ibid 150

5 NINE STONES / (1) / SY 611904 / 9.1 × 7.9 CE / Pt / ibid 146; Thom (1955) S4/1 (Winterbourne Abbas); (1967) 72

6 REMPSTONE / (4) / SY 994821 / 24.4 × 20.7 / A? / Piggott S. & C. M. 146; Grinsell (1958) 77

7 WINTERBOURNE ABBAS / (4) / SY 6..9.. / ? / ? / Piggott S. & C. M. 150

Co. DURHAM

1 EGGLESTON / (4) / NY 982252 / ? / Em?, CN? / Hutchinson *Hist. of Co. Durham* III (1794), 277

LANCASHIRE (Cumbria)

1 THE BEACON / (5) / SD 280842 / 29.9 × 27.4 / Em / *Arch* 53 (1889) 418
2 BLEABERRY HAWS / (5) / SD 264946 / 5.2 × 4.0 / CN? / Exc. 1886, flints. *TCWAAS* (O.S.) IX (1888) 499; *Arch* 53 (1893) 419
3 CHEETHAM CLOSE / (3) / SD 716158 / 15.5 / O / *TLCAS* 12 (1894) 42
4 DELF HILL / (5) / SD 914331 / 4.6? / Em? / Exc. 1842, urns, crems. *Gents Mag.* (1842) 413
5 DRUIDS TEMPLE / (1) / SD 292739 / 25.9 / C, Gr? / Exc. 1911. 1921, Pennine urn (*TCWAAS* 70, 1970, 2). Gelderd; Atkinson W. G.; Thom (1967) L5/1 (Birkrigg Common)
6 EXTWISTLE MOOR / (5) / SD 900337 / ? / ? / Exc. 1887?, urn, flint battle-axe. *TLCAS* 11 (1893) 158
7 HELLCLOUGH / (5) / SD 914333 / ? / ? / Exc. 1886, urn. *TLCAS* 5 (1886) 272
8 THE KIRK / (5) / SD 251827 / 22.9 / Em, A? / *Arch* 53 (1893) 417
9 MOSLEY HEIGHT / (3) / SD 881302 / 12.8 / Em, Pt? / Exc. 1950, Pennine urns, pygmy cups, faience, bronze, crems. Bennett; Bu'lock 15; Radley (1966a) 20ff
10 RING STONES HILL / (4) / SD 892367 / ? / ? / *TLCAS* 9 (1856) 33
SUMMERHOUSE HILL / (–) / SD 501744 / Not a circle. Tor debris mistaken for a ruin. *North & Spence.*
11 WORSTHORNE / (4) / SD 885329 / ? / ? / Exc. 1887, crem. *TLCAS* 11, 1893, 158
12 WORSTHORNE MOOR / (4) / SD 884327 / ? / ? / Bu'lock 39

NORTHUMBERLAND

1 BIDDLESTONE / (3) / NT 954074 / ? / ? / O.S. Southampton, NT 90 NE
2 CARTINGTON / (3) / NU 056046 / 4.4 / Pl / Greenwell W. *British Barrows* (1877) 429, no. CCVII
3 DODDINGTON MOOR / (3) / NU 012317 / 12.2 / Pl / *NCH* XIV 21
4 DUDDO FOUR STONES / (3) / NT 931437 / 9.8 / Pl, Cm? / Exc. *c.*1890, crem. *TBFC* 28 (1932) 84; Thom (1967) L3/1
5 DUNMORE HILL / (5) / NT 98.18. / ? / O? / *NCH* XIV 21
6 ELSDON / (3) / NT 70.06.? / ? / ? / *NCH* XV 60
7 GOATSTONES / (1) / NY 829748 / 4.9 / 4P, Cm, CN? / Burl (1971)
8 HETHPOOL / (5) / NT 892278 / 61.0 × 42.7 / O?, Cr / *PSAN* 6 (1935) 116
9 ILDERTON / (3) / NT 971205 / 36.0 × 29.3 CB / Pl / Exc. pre-1862, charcoal. *TBCF* 4 (1856–62) 450; *NCH* XIV 21; Thom (1967) L3/4 (Lilburn)
10 NUNWICK PARK / (4) / NY 885741 / 8.7? / Pl? / *NCH* XV 60
11 RIDLEY COMMON / (3) / NY 778698 / ? / Pl? / O.S. Southampton, NY 76 NE 44
12 SIMONBURN / (5) / NY 802712 / 9.0 / Gr?, CN? / O.S. Southampton, NY 87 SW 18
13 THREE KINGS / (1) / NT 774009 / 4.3 / 4P, RC / Exc. 1971, flint, crem?

Burl & Jones; *PSAN* 5 (1911–12) 234; Burl (1971)
14 YEAVERING BELL / (5) / NT 918270 / 12.2? / Pl? / *NCH* XIV 21

OXFORDSHIRE

1 DEVIL'S QUOITS / (4) / SP 411048 / 85.3 × 76.2 / CH / Exc. 1940, 1973, animal bone. Grimes (1944); Gray M. (1973); (1975)
2 ROLLRIGHT STONES / (1) / SP 296308 / 31.6 / O / Exc. pre-1610, no finds. Ravenhill; Allcroft; Camden (1695) 268; Thom (1967) 63, S6/1 Ast: SR, Capella rise (1967, 100)

SHROPSHIRE (Salop)

1 HOARSTONES / (3) / SO 324999 / 23.2 × 19.8 CA / S / Chitty (1926); Lewis A. L. (1882); Grimes (1963) 127; Thom (1967) 65, D2/2 (Black Marsh)
2 MITCHELL'S FOLD / (3) / SO 304983 / 28.4 × 25.9 CA / O, S? / Grimes (1963) 125; Thom (1967) D2/1
3 DRUID CASTLE / (4) / SO 305981 / ? / ? / *TSNHAS* 16 (1931–2) 203
4 PEN-Y-WERN HILL / (5) / SO 313788 / 27.4 / O / Chitty (1963) 178
5 SHELVE / (4) / SO 335992 / ? / ? / O.S. Southampton, SO 39 NW 13

SOMERSET (incl. Avon)

1 ALMSWORTHY / (3) / SS 844417 / 34.1 × 28.7 / C?, O? / Gray St. G. (1931); Grinsell (1970) 41
  BATHAMPTON
2a A / (4) / ST 772652 / ? / P2?, A? / Tratman (1958) 110
2b B / (4) / ST 772652 / ? / P2?, A? / Tratman (1958) 110
3 CHEW STOKE / (4) / ST 560616 / ? / ? / ibid 112
4 LEIGH DOWN / (4) / ST 542639 / 18.3? / ? / ibid 112
5 MATTOCKS DOWN / (4) / SS 602439 / ? / ? / Grinsell (1970) 41
6 PORLOCK / (4) / SS 844447 / 24.4 / O? / Gray St. G. (1929); (1950)
  STANTON DREW
7a NE. / (3) / ST 603630 / 32.3 × 29.9 CE / P3, A / Thom (1966) 43, S3/1
7b CENTRE / (3) / ST 603630 / 113.4 / P3, V, A, O / Thom (1966) 43, S3/1
7c SW. / (4) / ST 603630 / 43.1 × 39.8 CE / P3 / Grinsell (1956); Dymond (1877); Tratman (1966); *PSANHS* 33 (1887) 37; Thom (1966) 43, S3/1; (1967) 72. Ast: Arcturus 1690 BC (Lockyer, 1906b, 174)
8 TWINHOE / (5) / ST 73.59. / ? / ? / *Bath & Cambourn Arch Soc.* (1966) 7–12
9 WITHYPOOL HILL / (3) / SS 836343 / 36.4 / Pl / Gray St. G. (1907)

WESTMORLAND (Cumbria)

1 CASTERTON / (5) / SD 640799 / 18.0 / Em? / *RCAHM-E* (1936) 66
2 CASTLEHOWE SCAR / (3) / NY 587155 / 6.4? / Pl / *RCAHM-E* (1936) 90; Thom (1967) L2/11
3 GAMELANDS / (3) / NY 640082 / 42.1 × 35.1 CA / Em, CT? / Ploughed *c.*1862, flints. Fell (1964a); Thom (1967) L2/14 (Orton)
4 GUNNERKELD / (3) / NY 568178 / 32.0 × 29.0 / C, CT / *TCWAAS* (O.S.) IV (1878–9) 537; Thom (1967) L2/10

5 HERD WOOD / (5) / NY 41.06. / 19.8? / ? / *TCWAAS* 34 (1934) 92

6 IRON HILL / (5) / NY 596147 / 7.1 × 6.2 CE? / CN / Exc. pre-1861, antler, animal bone. *Arch J* 18 (1861) 36; *RCAHM-E* (1936) 90; Thom (1967) 72, L2/12 (Harberwain)

7 KEMP HOWE / (3) / NY 567133 / *c*.24.4 / Pl, A / *RCAHM-E* (1936) 206

8 KOPSTONE / (5) / NY 496216 / 23.2 / Em, C? / Taylor 326

9 MAYBURGH / (4) / NY 519234 / ? / CH?, Pt / Clark (1936) 43

10 MOOR DIVOCK 3 / (3) / NY 497217 / 3.4+ / CN / Taylor 327

11 MOOR DIVOCK 4 / (3) / NY 494219 / 5.8 / CN / Exc. 1866, food-vessel. Greenwell W. *British Barrows* (1877) 400; Taylor 328

12 MOOR DIVOCK 6 / (3) / NY 491227 / 7.6 / A / Taylor 333

13 MOOR DIVOCK 7 / (3) / NY 490226 / 4.3 / C / Taylor 333

14 MOOR DIVOCK 8 / (3) / NY 490227 / 2.7 / A? / Taylor 334

15 ODDENDALE / (3) / NY 593129 / 26.2 / C, CN / Exc. pre-1879, crem. *JBAA* 35 (1879) 369; *TCWAAS* (O.S.) VI (1883) 178; Thom (1967 L2/13)

16 RAWTHEY BRIDGE / (5) / SD 71.97.? / ? / ? / *TCWAAS* 26 (1926) 5

17 SWARTH FELL / (4) / NY 457192 / 17.4 / Pl / *RCAHM-E* (1936) 40

18 WHITE HAG / (3) / NY 607115 / ? / Pl? / *RCAHM-E* (1936) 89

19 WILSON SCAR / (4) / NY 549182 / 18.3 / Pl? / Exc. *c*.1943, local grammar school. Inhum. *TCWAAS* 35 (1935) 69

WILTSHIRE

AVEBURY

1a NORTH / (4) / SU 103700 / 103.6 / C, V, P2 / Smith I. F. (1965) 201

1b SOUTH / (3) / SU 103700 / 103.6 / S, O, P2 / Smith I. F. (1965) 198

1c OUTER / (3) / SU 103700 / 331.6 Complex / CH, 2A / Exc. 1833, 1865, 1894, 1908, 1934 et seq. Ebbfleet, grooved ware, beakers, E?, FN, N/MR (Clarke, 1970, nos. 1049F–1054F). Smith I. F. (1965); Gray St. G. (1935); Thom (1967) 89, S5/3. Ast: Deneb set (1967, 100)

2 BROADSTONES / (4) / SU 161685? / ? / ? / *WAM* 56 (1955) 192; *VCH Wilts I* 96

3 COATE / (4) / SU 181824 / 68.6 / Pl / *VCH Wilts I* 56 112; Grinsell (1958) 58; Thom (1967) S5/6 (Day House Lane) Passmore (1894)

4 FALKNER'S CIRCLE / (4) / SU 109693 / 36.6 / Pl? / *WAM* 19 (1881) 55

5 LANGDEAN BOTTOM / (4) / SU 118657 / 10.1 / A? / *VCH Wilts I* 67

6 SANCTUARY / (4) / SU 118679 / 39.5 / C, A, O / Exc. 1930, Ebbsfleet, beakers, AOC, BW (Clarke, 1970, nos 1063, 1064F). Cunnington (1931); Musson (1971) 368; Thom (1967) S5/2. Ast: MS (1967, 100)

7 STONEHENGE / (3) / SU 123422 / 29.6 / CH, A, O / Exc. 1901, 1919, 1950 et seq. Grooved ware, beakers, W/MR, S2/W (Clarke, 1970, nos. 1047F, 1048F). C-14: phase I, 2180bc ± 105 (I-2328), 1848bc ± 275 (C-602); phase II, 1620bc ± 110 (I-2384); phase IIIa, 1720bc ± 150 (BM-46); phase IIIb/c, 1240bc ± 105 (I-2445). Atkinson R. J. C. (1960); *WAM* 32 (1902) 1ff; *Ant J* 4 (1924)–8 (1928); Hawkins (1966a); Thom A., A.S. & A.S. (1974); (1975); Newham (1972) Ast: Hawkins, (1966a); Thom *et al.* (1975); Newham (1972)

8 TISBURY / (4) / ST 951299 / ? / CH?, S / *VCH Wilts I* 114

9 WINTERBOURNE BASSETT / (4) / SU 094755 / 71.3? / CH?, O, S / *VCH Wilts I* 125; Thom (1967) S5/5

YORKSHIRE

1 APPLETREEWICK / (3) / SE 065632 / 9.1 / P2?+C / *YAJ* 41 (1963–6) 317

2 BLAKEY TOPPING / (5) / SE 873934 / 16.5? / Pl? / Elgee 105

3 BRACKENHALL GREEN / (5) / SE 13.39. / 'Large' / ? / *Bradford Ant*, 7 (O.S.) (1902) 117; Raistrick 358

4 BRADUP / (3) / SE 089439 / 9.2 / Em / Raistrick 356

5 BRANSDALE MOOR / (5) / SE 604998 / ? / ? / Wilson *Yorkshire Moors & Dales* (1912) 17

6 CARPERBY / (3) / SD 990904 / 28.0×23.8 / Em, CN / Raistrick 354

7 COMMONDALE / (3) / NZ 637108 / *c*.31.7 / C?, O? / Exc. *c*.1968, flints. *YAJ* 42 (1969) 240; Elgee 104

8 DANBY RIGG N. / (4) / NZ 708065 / 12.8 / Em / Exc. pre-1860, 2 collared urns. *Gent's Mag* 14 (1863) 440; Elgee 104

9 DRUID'S ALTAR / (3) / SD 949652 / 4.0×3.5 / 4P / Raistrick 356; Allcroft 225

10 DUMPIT HILL / (3) / SE 029639 / 9.8 / Em / *YAJ* 41 (1963–6) 325

11 GRASSINGTON A / (5) / SE 025666 / 9.1×7.6 / Em / *YAJ* 41 (1963–6) 324

12 GRASSINGTON B / (5) / SE 025667 / 8.5 / Em / ibid

13 HARDEN MOOR / (5) / SE 073388 / 7.6 / Em / Exc. (date?), 4 urns, pygmy cup. Radley (1966a) 19, 23, 26

14 HOUSE CRAG / (5) / SE 816981 / 29.6 / ? / O.S. Southampton, SE 89 NW 36.

15 KILNSEY / (3) / SD 951680 / 5.5 / Em / *YAJ* 41 (1963–6) 326

16 KIRKMOOR BECK FARM / (5) / NZ 924030 / 4.6 / CN / Exc. 1968, urn, crem. Radley (1969b)

17 MUKER / (5) / SD 911973 / 22.9 / Em? / O.S. Southampton, SD 99 NW 1

18 NAB RIDGE / (5) / SE 575979 / 9.8×8.5 / CN / ibid SE 59 NE 8

19 NETTLEHOLE RIDGE / (3) / SD 979563 / 25.0 / Em, CN / *YAJ* 41 (1963–6) 322

20 TODMORDEN / (3) / SD 943253 / 27.4 / Em / Exc. 1898, Pennine urns, pygmy cup, faience etc. Roth *Yorkshire Coiners . . .* (1906) 307; Bu'lock 41

21 TWELVE APOSTLES / (3) / SE 126451 / 15.9 / Em / Raistrick 357

22 WALSHAW DEAN RESERVOIR / (4) / SD 967342 / 11.0 / Pl / Roth *Yorkshire Coiners . . .* (1906) 304

23 WEECHER RESERVOIR / (4) / SE 11.42. / 24.7 / ? / Raistrick 358

24 YOCKENTHWAITE / (5) / SD 899794 / 7.6 / Pl / Raistrick 355

SCOTLAND

ABERDEEN (Grampian)

1 AIKEY BRAE / (3) / NJ 959471 / 16.6×12.8 / RSC, Em, Gr / Exc. pre-1881, no finds. *Great North of Scotland Railway Guide* (1881) 105; Coles F. (1904) no. 13

2 ARDLAIR / (3) / NJ 552279 / 11.6 / RSC, Pf, RC / Exc. *c*.1821. 1857, crem. Stuart (1856) xxii; Coles F. (1902) no. 53; Thom (1967) 144, B1/18

3 ARNHILL / (4) / NJ 531456 / *c*.18.3 / RSC, Pf, Cm / Coles F. (1902) no. 64

4 AUCHMACHAR / (4) / NJ 948503 / *c*.15.2 / RSC, Em / Coles F. (1904) no. 15

5 AUCHMALIDDIE / (4) / NJ 881448 / ? / RSC / Coles F. (1904) no. 9

6 AULD KIRK O'TOUGH / (3) / NJ 625092 / 31.3 / RSC, Cm, Cr / Coles F. (1900) no. 14; Ritchie J. (1918) 90

7 BACKHILL OF DRACHLAW EAST / (1) / NJ 672463 / 8.5 × 7.4 CR / 6 / Coles F (1903) no. 29; Thom (1967) B1/24 (Blackhill)

8 BACKHILL OF DRACHLAW WEST / (4) / NJ 672463 / ? / 6? / Coles F. (1903) no. 30

9 BALNACRAIG / (4) / NJ 603035 / 13.7 / RSC, Cm / Coles F. (1900) no. 13; Ritchie J. (1918) 87; *PSAS* 53 (1918–19) 68

10 BALQUHAIN / (3) / NJ 735241 / *c*.20.4 / RSC, Cm, O / Exc. 1900, no finds. Coles F. (1901) no. 17; Ritchie J. (1918) 91; Thom (1967) B1/11

11 BERRYBRAE / (3) / NK 028572 / 12.8 × 10.8 / RSC, Em / Exc. 1975, crem. D & E (1975); Coles F. (1904) no. 19

12 BINGHILL / (4) / NJ 855023 / 10.4 / RSC / Coles F. (1900) no. 21

13 BLUE CAIRN / (3) / NJ 411063 / 23.2 / RSC, CN / Exc. 1875, urn, animal bones. Ogston *Prehistoric Antiquities of the Howe of Cromar* (1931) 108; *Aberdeen Univ. Rev.* 33 (1950) 428

14 BOWMAN HILLOCK / (4) / NJ 480398 / 20.4? / Pl / D & E (1973) 60

15 BRAEHEAD / (4) / NJ 592255 / ? / RSC, Pf, Cm / Coles F. (1902) no. 46; Ritchie J. (1918) 99

16 BRANDSBUTT / (4) / NJ 760223 / 27.4? / Pl? / Coles F. (1901) No. 16

17 BROOMEND / (4) / NJ 63.25. / ? / RSC? / Keiller (1934) 20

18 BROOMEND OF CRICHIE / (3) / NJ 779196 / *c*.13.7 / CH, 6?, A / Exc. 1855, urns, axe-hammer (Roe, 1966, no. 350, IV EN). *PSAS* 18 (1883–4) 319; 54 (1919–20) 154

19 BURRELDALES / (5) / NJ 739396 / ? / ? / Coles F. (1903) no. 16

20 CAIRNHALL / (4) / NJ 785175 / ? / Em / Coles F. (1901) no. 12

21 CAIRN RIV / (4) / NJ 674466 / *c*.29.0 / RSC, CN? / Exc. (no date), axe-hammer, bronze. Coles F. (1903) no. 32

22 CAIRNTON / (4) / NJ 58.44. / ? / RSC / Coles F. (1903) no. 36

23 CANDLE HILL / (3) / NJ 599299 / 13.1 / RSC, CN / Coles F. (1902) no. 41

24 CANDY / (4) / NJ 533303 / ? / Pl? / Coles F. (1902) no. 60

25 CASTLE FRAZER / (3) / NJ 715125 / 20.4 / RSC, Pf, RC, Gr / Exc. pre-1855, urns. Coles F. (1904) 299; (1901) no. 4; Thom (1967) B2/3

26 CHAPEL O'SINK / (4) / NJ 706189 / 14.9 / RSC?, RC? / *PSAS* 51 (1916–17) 40; Thom (1967) B1/16 (Westerton)

27 CLATT, BANKHEAD / (4) / NJ 529270 / ? / RSC, A? / Coles F. (1902) no. 51; Keiller (1934) 18; *NSA Aberdeen* 12, 851

28 CLATT, HILLHEAD / (4) / NJ 528265 / 22.9? / RSC, A? / Coles F. (1902) no. 50; *NSA Aberdeen* 12, 851

29 CLOCHFORBIE / (4) / NJ 80.58. / ? / RSC / Coles F. (1904) no. 25

30 COLPY / (4) / NJ 63.32. / ? / P2? / Exc. pre-1843, urns? *NSA Aberdeen* 12, 732; Coles F. (1902) no. 67

31 CORRIE CAIRN / (5) / NJ 552205 / 18.9? / RSC?, Q / Exc. pre-1868, urn, food-vessel?, beaker?, *PSAS* 7 (1866–8) 24–5; Stuart (1867) lix

32 CORRSTONE WOOD / (4) / NJ 510271 / ? / RSC / Coles F. (1902) no. 54; Thom (1967) B1/21, (Mains of Druminnor)

33 CORRYDOWN / (3) / NJ 707445 / *c*.22.9 / RSC, CN? / Coles F. (1903) no. 25

34 CORTES / (5) / NJ 99.58. / ? / RSC? / *NSA Aberdeen* 12, 293

35 COTHIEMUIR WOOD / (3) / NJ 617198 / 21.3 × 18.9 ? / RSC, Cm, CN ? / Coles F. (1901) no. 10; Keiller (1934) 8, 11, 13; *NSA Aberdeen* 12, 946

36 CROOKMORE / (4) / NJ 588184? / ? / RSC, A ? / Keiller (1934) 18, 19

37 CULLERLIE / (2) / NJ 785043 / 10.1 / 8, RC, Gr / Exc. 1934, 1 sherd, flints. Killbride-Jones (1935); Thom (1967) B2/7

38 CULSALMOND / (4) / NJ 64.32. / ? / RSC? / Coles F. (1902) no. 68

39 CULSH / (4) / NJ 87.48. / 9.1? / RSC?, Q / Exc. 1913, flints, stone axe. *PSAS* 48 (1913–14) 191; Coles F. (1904) no. 10

40 DEER PARK / (3) / NJ 684156 / ? / Pl? / Keiller (1934) 3, 5

41 DOUNE HILL / (4) / NJ 48.06. / ? (Pl? / *PSAS* I (1851–4) 260

42 DRUIDSFIELD / (4) / NJ 578177 / 15.2 / RSC, A? / *NSA Aberdeen* 12, 449; Wilson (1863) 159

43 DRUIDSTONE / (3) / NJ 616222 / 16.8? / RSC, O? / Coles F. (1901) no. 18

44 DRUMFOURS / (4) / NJ 561110 / ? / Cm?, O? / Coles F. (1902) no. 1; Keiller (1934) 6, 20; Ritchie J. (1918) 191

45 DUNNIDEER / (4) / NJ 608284 / ? / RSC / Coles F. (1902) no. 39

46 DYCE / (1) / NJ 860133 / 18.0 / RSC, RC, Gr / Coles F. (1900) no. 22; Keiller (1934) 9, 13, 15; Thom (1967) B2/1 (Tyrebagger)

47 EASTER AQUORTHIES / NJ 732208 / 19.5 / RSC, Pf, CT, Gr / Coles F. (1901) no. 15; Keiller (1934) 8, 9, 12, 16, 17; Thom (1967) 143, B1/6

48 ELLON / (4) / NJ 954302 / 6.1 / Pl / *PSAS* 51 (1916–17) 34; Godsman *History of the Burgh & Parish of Ellon* (1958) 23

49 FORVIE / (5) / NK 101260 / 19.9 / RSC? / *Aberdeen Univ. Review* 35 (1953) 150; Thom (1967) 72, 79, B1/27

50 FRENDRAUGHT / (4) / NJ 62.41. / 25.9? / RSC / *PSAS* 51 (1916–17) 30

51 FULLERTON / (3) / NJ 62.41. / 25.9? / B, 6? / Exc. 1850?, flat-rimmed ware, inhum. Kilbride-Jones (1935) 445; Coles F. (1901) no. 13

52 GASK / (4) / NJ 802064 / ? / Cm, Cr? / *PSAS* 53 (1918–19) 65

53 GAVAL / (4) / NJ 981515 / ? / RSC, Em? / Coles F. (1904) no. 19

54 GINGOMYRES / (4) / NJ 46.42. / c.18.3 / RSC / Exc. pre-1853, charcoal, animal bones. *PSAS* 1 (1851–4) 141; Coles F. (1906) no. 12

55 GREENHILL / (5) / NK 097401 / ? / ? / Coles F. (1904) no. 2

56 GREY MUIR CAIRN / (5) / NJ 675452 / c.16.8 / Pl? / Coles F. (1903) no. 33

57 HATTON / (4) / NK 050364 / ? / RSC? / Destr. 1831, 2 urns, flints, bracer. Coles F. (1904) no. 1

58 HATTON OF ARDOYNE / (1) / NJ 659268 / 24.4 / RSC, Pf, RC / Exc. pre-1856, urn beaker, crem. Stuart (1856) xxii; Coles F. (1901) no. 21

59 HILL OF BUCHARN / (4) / NJ 518360 / 7.9 / 4P / Exc. c.1810, bones. O.S. Edinburgh, NJ 53 NW 13; Burl (1971) 42

60 HILL OF FIDDES / (4) / NJ 934243 / 14.0? / RSC, Pf, Em / *Arch* 5 (1777) 246; Fergusson (1872) 264; Coles F. (1902) no. 23

61 HOLYWELL / (4) / NJ 549270 / c.24.4 / Cm, CT / Destr. c.1861, urn. Coles F. (1902) no. 52; Ritchie J. (1918) 99

62 HOWEMILL / (3) / NJ 580107 / 9.1 × 7.0 / 4P? / Coles F. (1902) no. 2; Burl (1971) 42

63 HUNTLY / (4) / NJ 529399 / c.13.7 / RSC? / Coles F. (1902) no. 63a

64 IMAGE WOOD / (3) / NO 52.99. / 4.0 × 3.1 / 6 / Exc. pre-1904, no finds. Coles F. (1905b) no. 1

65 INCHBAIRE / (4) / NO 61.96. / ? / ? / *PSAS* 53 (1918–19) 69

66 INSCHFIELD / (4) / NJ 624294 / 27.4 / RSC / Coles F. (1902) no. 45; Thom (1967) B1/14

67 KIRKTON OF BOURTIE / (4) / NJ 801250 / 21.6? / RSC / Coles F. (1902) no. 25; Thom (1967) B1/7

68 LESLIE / (4) / NJ 59.24. / ? / ? / *NSA Aberdeen* 12, 1022

69 LOANEND / (4) / NJ 604242 / ? / RSC, Cm / Coles F. (1901) no. 19; Ritchie J. (1918) 98; Keiller (1934) 12, 13, 19

70 LOANHEAD OF DAVIOT / (1) / NJ 747288 / 20.5 / RSC, RC, Gr / Exc. 1932, Neo pottery, AOC beaker, etc. (Clarke, 1970, 1467F–1469F), pygmy cup. Kilbride-Jones (1935); *PSAS* 70 (1935–6) 279; Coles F. (1902) no. 29; Burl (1974a) 71, 72; Thom (1967) 61, B1/26

71 LOGIE COLDSTONE / (4) / NJ 459055 / ? / 4P? / O.S. Edinburgh, NJ 40 NE 4

72a LOGIE NEWTON WEST / (3) / NJ 657392 / 6.4 / P3 / Coles F. (1903) no. 13

72b LOGIE NEWTON CENTRE / (3) / NJ 657392 / 7.0 / P3 / ibid

72c LOGIE NEWTON EAST / (3) / NJ 657392 / 6.4 / P3 / ibid

73 LOUDON WOOD / (3) / NJ 962497 / 18.5 / RSC, Em / Coles F. (1904) no. 26; Keiller (1934) 10, 13, 14

74 MAINS OF HATTON / (3) / NJ 699425 / 20.4 / RSC / Coles F. (1903) / no. 26; Thom (1967) B1/25 / (Charlesfield)

75a MELGUM A / (5) / NJ 472052 / 28.0 / P3 / *PSAS* 61 (1926) 265

75b MELGUM B / (5) / NJ 472052 / 22.6 / P3 / ibid; Thom (1967) B2/8 (Tarland)

75c MELGUM C / (5) / NJ 472052 / 29.0 / P3 / *PSAS* 61 (1926) 265

76 MIDMAR KIRK / (1) / NJ 699064 / 17.4 / RSC, Gr / Coles F. (1900) no. 16; *PSAS* 53 (1918–19) 64; Keiller (1934) 13; Thom (1967) 146, B2/17

77 MILL OF CARDEN / (4) / NJ 69.25. / ? / RSC? / Coles F. (1902) no. 34

78 MUNDURNO / (4) / NJ 940131 / ? / RSC? / Keiller (1934) 20

79 NETHER BALFOUR / (4) / NJ 539172 / ? / RSC, A? / Destr. *c*.1847, stone cup? *ONB* 88 (1867) 107; *PSAS* 10 (1872–4) 196

80 NETHER CORSKIE / (4) / NJ 749096 / ? / RSC, Cm / Coles F. (1903) no. 1; Ritchie J. (1918) 87

81 NETHER COULLIE / (4) / NJ 709156 / ? / RSC / Coles F. (1901) no. 5a

82 NETHER DUMEATH / (4) / NJ 425378 / *c*.12.2 / RSC? / Coles F. (1906) no. 11

83 NETHERTON / (3) / NK 043573 / 17.4 / RSC, RC / Coles F. (1904) no. 22

84 NEW CRAIG / (4) / NJ 745296 / ? / RSC, Pf, Cm / Coles F. (1902) no. 30; Ritchie J. (1918) 94

85 NORTH STRONE / (4) / NJ 584138 / 20.4 × 18.9? / RSC, Em? / Exc. pre-1902, urn. *Scottish Notes & Queries* (May 1897) 178; Coles F. (1902) no. 3

86 OLD KEIG / (3) / NJ 593195 / 25.6? / RSC, Em / Exc. pre-1692, 1931, flat-rimmed ware, beaker (Clarke, 1970, 1479F). Garden (1766); Childe (1934); *PSAS* 47 (1932-3) 37

87 OLD RAYNE (3) / NJ 679280 / 26.2? / RSC / Exc. pre-1856, 'reddish urn', bracer (B3). Clarke (1970) 570; Stuart (1856) xxi; Coles F. (1902) no. 33; Thom (1967) B1/13

88 PITGLASSIE (3) / NJ 686434 / 18.3 / RSC, Cm / Coles F. (1903) no. 24; Keiller (1934) 12; Ritchie J. (1918) 99

89 POTTERTON / (4) / NJ 952163 / ? / RSC, Cm, Pf? / *PSAS* 51 (1916–17); Ritchie J. (1918) 91

90 RAICH / (3) / NJ 618436 / 4.3 × 3.7 / CN / Coles F. (1903) no. 34

91 RAPPLABUM / (4) / NJ 726405 / ? / RSC? / O.S. Edinburgh, NJ 74 SW 7

92 RAPPLA WOOD / (3) / NJ 736402 / 15.2? / RSC?, CN / Exc. (no date), urn, bronze. Coles F. (1903) no. 17; *PSAS* 4 (1860–2) 429

93 SCHIVAS / (4) / NJ 902352 / 27.4 / ? / Coles F. (1903) no. 10

94 SHELDON / (3) / NJ 823249 / 32.9 / RSC?, O / Coles F. (1902) no. 24; Thom (1966) 28, B1/8

95 SHETHIN / (3) / NJ 882328 / 5.2 / 4P? / Coles F. (1902) no. 32; Thom (1967) B1/10 (Fountain Hill)

96 SHIELBURN / (4) / NJ 675463 / ? / ? / Coles F. (1903) no. 28

97 SOUTH FORNET / (3) / NJ 782109 / 26.8 / RSC / Coles F. (1902) no. 4

98 SOUTH LEY LODGE / (4) / NJ 767132 / 29.6? / RSC / Coles F. (1902) no. 11; Thom (1967) B2/14 (Leylodge)

99 SOUTH YTHSIE / (3) / NJ 885304 / 8.5 × 7.9 CB / 6, O? / Coles F. (1902) no. 31; Thom (1967) B1/9. Ast. SR (1967, 98)

100 STONEHEAD / (3) / NJ 601287 / ? / RSC / Coles F. (1902) no. 40

101 STONYFIELD / (3) / NJ 589376 / 13.7 / ? / Coles F. (1902) no. 66

102 STRICHEN HOUSE / (4) / NJ 937545 / 13.4 / RSC / Coles F. (1904) no. 18; *PSAS* 19 (1883–4) 372; Browne *Antiquities in the neighbourhood of Dunecht House* (1921) pl. xxxi; Keiller (1934) 15; Thom (1967) 142, B1/1

103 SUNHONEY / (1) / NJ 716058 / 25.3 / RSC, RC, Cm / Exc. 1855, urn. Stuart (1856) xxi; *Arch* 22 (1829) 198; Coles F. (1900) no. 18; Ritchie J. (1918) 88; Thom (1967) 145, B2/2

104 TOMNAGORN / (3) / NJ 651077 / 22.3 / RSC, RC, Pf / Coles F. (1900) no. 15; Thom (1967) B2/16 (Tannagorn)

105 TOMNAVERIE / (3) / NJ 486034 / 17.1 / RSC, RC, Pf? / Coles F. (1905) no. 2; Thom (1967) B2/9

106 TUACK / (4) / NJ 795154 / 7.3 / B, 6 / Exc. pre-1855?, cordoned urn, bronze. Coles F. (1901) no. 1; Stuart (1856) xxii; *PSAS* 54 (1919–20) 154

107 UPPER AUCHNAGORTH / (3) / NJ 839563 / 13.7 / Pl? / Coles F. (1904) no. 21; Keiller (1934) 6; Thom (1967) B1/5

108 UPPER ORD / (4) / NJ 484269? / 22.6? / RSC?, O? / Coles F. (1902) no. 56f

109 UPPER THIRD / (4) / NJ 677394 / ? / RSC? / Coles F. (1903) no. 14

110 WANTONWELLS / (4) / NJ 619273 / ? / RSC, Pf / Coles F. (1902) no. 37; Thom (1967) B1/12

111 WAULKMILL / (4) / NJ 473052 / ? / ? / Coles F. (1905) no. 3

112 WESTER ECHT / (3) / NJ 739084 / 29.3? / RSC / *Arch Scot* 2 (1822) 324; *PSAS* 53 (1918–19) 64

113 WEST HAUGHS / (4) / NJ 68.38. / 23.2? / 6? / Coles F. (1903) no. 15

114 WHEEDLEMONT / (4) / NJ 482262 / 26.5+ / ? / Coles F. (1902) no. 55

115 WHITEHILL / (3) / NJ 643135 / 22.0? / RSC, RC / *NSA Aberdeen* 12, 613; *PSAS* 1 (1851–4) 141; Coles F. (1901) no. 6; Keiller (1934) 8, 16, 17, 19; Thom (1967) 136, B2/18 (Tillyfourie Hill)

116 WHITEHILL WOOD A / NJ 678505 / 8.2 / 6? / Coles F. (1903) no. 39; Thom (1967) 40, B4/1 (Carnoussie House)

117 WHITEHILL WOOD B / (3) / NJ 678505 / 25.6 / ? / Thom (1967) / 137, 40 B4/1 / (Carnoussie House)

118 YONDER BOGNIE / (3) / NJ 601458 / 24.4 / RSC, RC? / Coles F. (1903) no. 35; Thom (1967) B1/23

ANGUS (Tayside)

1 BALGARTHNO / (3) / NO 353316 / 6.1 / Pl / Exc. *c*.1850, jet ring, flint. Stuart (1856); Warden (1884) IV, 177

2 BALKEMBACK / (3) / NO 382384 / 8.5 / 4P?, Cm, Cr / Coutts, 18

3 CARSE GRAY / (3) / NO 462538 / 3.7 / 4P? / O.S. Edinburgh, NO 45 SE 1

4 COLMEALLIE / (3) / NO 565781 / 15.2 / RSC, RC / Keiller (1934) 1; *NSA Angus* 623; Warden (1884) III, 226

5 COROGLE BURN / (5) / NO 348601 / ? / R? / Coutts, 19; Thom (1967) P3/1 (Glen Prosen)

6 DALBOG / (4) / NO 587719 / ? / CT / Jervise *The Land of the Lindsays*, I (1853) li

7 EASTER PITFORTHIE / (4) / NO 619614 / ? / ? / O.S. Edinburgh, NO 66 SW 9.

8 MYLNEFIELD / (?) / NO 334301 / ? CE / 6? / Elliot *Lochee, As It Was and Is* (1911) 203–4

9 NEWBIGGING / (4) / NO 541693 / *c*.16.8 / RSC?, CN? / *ONB Angus* 61

10 PITSCANDLIE / (3) / NO 484528 / 15.2 / CN, Cr / Exc. ?, pre-1850, urn, incised sandstone. Warden (1884) V, 98; *PSAS* 2 (1854–7) 190; Coutts, 18; Thom (1967) P3/2 (Blackgate)

ARGYLL (Strathclyde)

1 STRONTOILLER / (1) / NM 906292 / 19.8 / O / *PSAS* 9 (1870–2) 104; Thom (1967) A1/2 (Loch Nell)

2 TEMPLE WOOD / (1) / NR 826979 / 13.4 / CT / Exc. 1928, 1974, crem. Craw (1930); Scott J. (1974); Thom (1966) 21, A2/8; (1971) 45. Ast: MS (Thom, 1971, 45)

ARRAN (Strathclyde)

1 AUCHAGALLON / (1) / NR 893346 / 14.9 / CT? / Exc. pre-1910, no finds? Bryce T. H. (1910) 119; Thom (1967) 72 (Auchengallon)

2 AUCHELEFFAN / (1) / NR 978251 / 4.9 / 4P / Exc. 1902, no finds. *PSAS* 37 (1902–3) 66

3 DRUMIDOON / (5) / NR 886292 / ? / ? / *PSAS* 36 (1901–2) 128

4 GLEN SHIRAG / (4) / NS 00.37. / ? / ? / Bryce J. (1862) 505

5 KILDONAN / (5) / NS 031208 / ? / ? / Bryce T. H. 125

6 LAMLASH / (1) / NS 018336 / 6.4 / 6, O / Exc. *c*.1861, flint. Bryce J. 505; Bryce T. H. 121; *PSAS* 40 (1905–6) 296

7 MACHRIE MOOR I / (3) / NR 912324 / 14.6 × 12.7 CE / Pl / Exc. 1861, no finds. Bryce J. 502; Bryce T. H. 117; Roy *et al*. 64; Thom (1967) 72 (Tormore)

8 MACHRIE MOOR 2 (3) / NR 911324 / 13.7 / 2CT / Exc. 1861, food-vessel, flint arrowheads. Bryce J. 502

9 MACHRIE MOOR 3 / (3) / NR 910325 / 15.2 CI / 2CT / Exc. 1861, food-vessel. Bryce J.; Roy *et al*. 62

10 MACHRIE MOOR 4 / (3) / NR 910324 / 6.4 × 5.5? / Pl? / Exc. 1861, food-vessel. Bryce J. 503

11 MACHRIE MOOR 5 / (1) / NR 909324 / 18.1 CI / C / Exc. 1861, no finds. Bryce J. 504; Roy *et al*. 60

12 MACHRIE MOOR 10 / (3) / NR 900327 / 19.2 / Pl / Exc. pre-1861?, no finds? Bryce J. 505; Bryce T. H. 151

13 SOUTH SANNOX / (4) / NS 01.45. / ? / C / Exc. 1909, no finds. Bryce J. 505; Bryce T. H. 117

AYRSHIRE (Strathclyde)

1 BEOCH / (3) / NS 53.09. / 11.3 / Em, CN, Cr / Exc. 1937, 3 urns (Morrison, no. 48), beaker (Clarke, 1970, no. 1557F) *PSAS* 72 (1937–8) 235
2 BLACKSHAW MOOR / (5) / NS 25.47. / ? / C?, Cr? / Smith J. (1895) 12
3 FOUR STONES / (4) / NS 379550 / 4.9 / 4P / Exc. *c.*1816, crem. *PSAS* 11 (1874–6) 291
4 GRAY STANES / (5) / NX 09.82? / ? / ? / Smith J. (1895) 222
5 HAGGSTONE MOOR / (5) / NX 06.72.? / 13.4? / ? / ibid 223
6 NITH LODGE / (3) / NS 54.10. / 9.1 × 4.6 / Em / Exc. 1937, urn (Morrison, no. 45), pygmy cups (Morrison, nos. 46, 47), battle-axe (Roe, 1966, no. 371, IV D N). *PSAS* 72 (1937–8) 241
7 MOLMONT / (4) / NS 514371 / 18.3 / Pl? / Smith J. (1895) 101

BANFF (Grampian)

1 BELLMAN'S WOOD / (4) / NJ 605505 / ? / ? / Coles F. (1906) no. 9
2 DOUNE OF DALMORE / (3) / NJ 185308 / 15.9 / RC / Coles F. (1907) no. 6
3a GAUL CROSS N. / (5) / NJ 535639 / ? / P2, 6? / Coles F. (1906) no. 15
3b GAUL CROSS S. / (5) / NJ 535639 / ? / P2, 6? / ibid
4 HARESTANE / (4) / NJ 664438 / 18.3 / RSC?, Cm / Coles F. (1903) no. 27; Ritchie J. (1918) 108
5 HATTON / (4) / NJ 270418 / 11.00 / Pl? / Coles F. (1906) no. 21
6 LOWER LAGMORE / (3) / NJ 180359 / 19.8 / PG?, Cm / Henshall (1963) 390
7 MARIONBURGH / (3) / NJ 183364 / 22.6 / RC? / Henshall (1963) 391
8 NEWTON OF MONTBLAIRY / (4) / NJ 68.55. / ? / ? / Exc. pre-1886, food-vessel? Anderson (1886) fig. 128
9 NORTH BURRELDALES / (3) / NJ 676549 / 6.4 / 4P? / Coles F. (1906) no. 1; Thom (1967) B4/2
10 ROTHIEMAY / (3) / NJ 550487 / 28.0 / RSC, Cm / Coles F. (1903) no. 38; Ritchie J. (1918) 104; Thom (1967) B4/4 (Millton)
11 ST. BRANDAN'S STANES / (4) / NJ 608611 / ? / RSC?, Cm / Coles F. (1906) no. 4; Ritchie J. (1918) 104
12a SANDEND BAY A / (5) / NJ 560658 / 18.3? / P2? / Coles F. (1906) no. 3
12b SANDEND BAY B / (5) / NJ 560658 / ? / P2? / ibid
13 THORAX / (3) / NJ 582549 / 6.8 × 5.4 CE / 6, Cm / Coles F. (1906) no. 6; Ritchie J. (1918) 102
14 UPPER LAGMORE / (3) / NJ 176358 / 16.5 / PG / Coles F. (1907) no. 8; Henshall (1963) 389

BERWICK (Borders)

1 BORROWSTON RIGG / (3) / NT 560521 / 41.5 × 36.6 CII / Pl / *RCAHM-S*, (1915) no. 226; Thom (1967) 69, G9/10. Ast: Capella set (1967, 98)
2 KIRKTONHILL / (4) / NT 47.54. / ? / ? / O.S. Edinburgh, NT 45 SE 21

BUTE (Strathclyde)

1 ETTRICK BAY / (3) / NS 03.66. / 14.9 × 11.1 CE / O? / Hewison *Bute in the Olden Times, I* (1893) 81; Thom (1967) 72, A9/2
2 KINGARTH / (3) / NS 092554 / 26.2 / Q / Exc. ? date, flint scraper? Hewison *Bute in the Olden Times* (1893) 78
3 ST. COLMAC'S / (?) / NS 04.66. / ? / ? / D. Marshall *A History of Bute (Museum Guide)* (no date) 15

CAITHNESS (Highland)

1 ACHANARRAS HILL / (3) / ND 145552 / 18.3 / Pl? / *RCAHM-S* (1911a) no. 141
2 ACHEROLE / (4) / ND 22.51. / ? / ? / *RCAHM-S* (1911a) no. 484
3 AULTAN BROUBSTER / (3) / ND 045599 / 62.8 / Pl / Myatt (1973)
4 BACKLASS / (3) / ND 079423 / 6.7 / Pl? / *RCAHM-S* (1911a) no. 142
5 GUIDEBEST / (3) / ND 181351 / 57.3 / Pl / *RCAHM-S* (1911a) no. 279; Thom (1967) N1/13 (Latheron Wheel). Ast: MS (1967, 100)
6 OLD HALL OF DUNN / (4) / ND 204564 / ? / ? / *RCAHM-S* (1911a) no. 483
7 SHURRERY / (5) / ND 04.57. / ? / ? / *RCAHM-S* (1911a) no. 381
8 WARTH HILL / (5) / ND 371698 / 15.9? / C?, / CN / *RCAHM-S* (1911a) no. 41

CLACKMANNAN (Central)

1 CUNNINGHAR / (4) / NS 92.97. / 32.3 × 29.3? / CT, Cr / Exc. 1894, urns. *PSAS* 29 (1894–5) 190; *PSAS* 33 (1898–9) 361
2 HAWK HILL / (4) / NS 92.92. / ? / ? / *RCAHM-S* (1933) no. 601

COLONSAY

1 SCALASAIG / (3) / NR 388943 / ? / ? / *D & E* (1970) 5
2 SCALASAIG S. / (4) / NR 386937 / ? / O? / ibid

DUMFRIES (Dumfries & Galloway)

1 GIRDLE STANES / (3) / NY 254961 / 39.9? / CH, Pt, R? / Hyslop & Hyslop 17; *RCAHM-S* (1920) no. 198; *PSAS* 31 (1896–7), 281; Thom (1967) G7/5
2 GREYSTONE PARK / (4) / NX 98.76. / ? / ? / Exc. pre-1886, pygmy cup (Morrison, no. 94); *TDGNHAS* 5 (1886) 38
3 KIRKBOG / (4) / NX 877939 / ? / ? / *RCAHM-S* (1920) no. 81
4 KIRKHILL / (3) / NY 140960 / 11.6? / Pl / *RCAHM-S* (1920) no. 625; Thom (1967) G7/3 (Wamphray)
5 KIRKSLIGHT RIG / (3) / NY 223885 / 16.0 / 2CT? / *D & E* (1973) 23
6 LOCHMABEN STONE / (4) / NY 311660 / 45.7? / Pl / *Old Statistical Account, Dumfriess* (1841) 266; Ross (1967) 458
7 LOUPIN' STANES E. / (2) / NY 257966 / 13.4 × 10.9 CA / R? / *RCAHM-S* (1920) no. 199; Hyslop & Hyslop; *PSAS* 31, (1896–7), 283; Thom (1967) G7/4. Ast: SS (1967, 98)
8 LOUPIN' STANES SE. / (4) / NY 258965 / ? / ? / Hyslop & Hyslop; Thom (1967) 137. G7/4

9 TWELVE APOSTLES / (3) / NX 947794 / 87.8 × 73.8 CB / Pl / *RCAHM-S* (1920) no. 284; *PSAS* 28 (1893–4) 84; Thom (1967) G6/1

10 WHITCASTLES / (3) / NY 224881 / 56.4 × 42.4 CB / Pl / *RCAHM-S* (1920) no. 307; Thom (1967) 68, G7/6

11 WHITEHOLM RIGG / (3) / NY 217827 / 20.1 × 18.9? CA / O? / *RCAHM-S* (1920) no. 603; Thom (1967) G7/2 (Seven Brethen)

12 WOODHEAD / (5) / NY 21.66. / ? / ? / *RCAHM-S* (1920) no. 5

EAST LOTHIAN (Lothian)

1 KINGSIDE HILL / (5) / NT 627650 / 11.6 × 10.7 / CN, S? / *RCAHM-S* (1924) no. 240

2 MAYSHIEL / (3) / NT 617646 / 2.7 / Em / ibid no. 238

3 NINE STONES / (3) / NT 626650 / 6.4 / Pl? / ibid no. 239; Thom (1967) G8/2

4 PENSHIEL / (5) / NT 641631 / ? / ? / *RCAHM-S* (1924) no. 243

5 PENSHIEL GRANGE / (5) / NT 641632 / 8.2 × 4.6 / 4P? / ibid no. 242

6 PENSHIEL HILL / (3) / NT 632642 / ? / S? / ibid no. 241

7 SPARTLETON EDGE / (3) / NT 64.67. / 12.8 / Em?, S? / ibid no. 185

8 YADLEE / (3) / NT 654673 / 8.2 / Pl / ibid no 172; Feachem 76

FIFE

1 BALBIRNIE / (2) / NO 285030 / 15.0 × 14.0 CE / CN, CT, Cm / Exc. 1883; 1970–1, grooved ware, S4 beaker, food vessel, urns, jet button. C-14: 1330 ± 90 bc (Ga-K-3425); 890 ± 80 bc (Ga-K-3426). Ritchie J. N. G., 1974b; *RCAHM-S*, 1933, no. 418. Ast: SR?

2 BALFARG / (3) / NO 281032 / 36.6 / CH, Pt / *RCAHM-S* (1933) no. 420; Atkinson R. J. C. (1952) 58

3 DUNINO / (4) / NO 53.11. / ? / ? / *RCAHM-S* (1933) no. 221

4 LUNDIN LINKS / (3) / NO 404026 / 16.5? / Pl? / Exc. pre-1790, stone button? *PSAS* 37 (1902–3) 212; *RCAHM-S* (1933) no. 379; Thom (1971) P4/1. Ast: MS (1971, 56)

HEBRIDES (Western Isles)

Benbecula

1 GRAMISDALE / (4) / NF 824552 / 26.5 / Pl? / *RCAHM-S* (1928) no. 353; Thom (1967) H4/1

2 SUIDHEACHADH SEALG / (3) / NF 825552 / 26.8 / Pl? / *RCAHM-S* (1928) no. 352; Thom (1967) H4/2 (Gramisdale S)

Berneray

1 BHRUIST / (3) / NF 92.82. / ? / ? / *RCAHM-S* (1928) no. 132

Harris

1 BORVEMORE / (3) / NG 020939 / ? / Pl / Exc. 1864, inhum? *RCAHM-S* (1928) no. 136

Lewis

1 AIRD SLEITENISH / (3) / NB 031198 / 6.6 / C?, CN? / *D & E* (1973) 48

2 AIRIDH NAM BIDEARAN / (3) / NB 234299 / ? / Pl / *RCAHM-S* (1928) no. 94; *PSAS* 38 (1903–4) 193; Thom (1967) 128, H1/5 (Callanish V). Ast: MR (1971, 68)

3 CALLANISH / (2) / NB 213330 / 13.1 × 11.3 CA / PG, S, A, R / Exc. 1857, crem. *PSAS* 3 (1857–60) 110; Somerville (1923); *RCAHM-S* (1928) no. 89; Henshall (1972) 461; Thom (1967) 96, 123, H1/1. Ast: Capella 1800 BC, Pleiades 1750BC (Somerville, 1913); SR, SS, MR, MS 1500 BC (Hawkins, 1966a, 185); Altair 1800 BC, Capella 1790 BC (Thom, 1967, 124); MS, MR (Thom, 1971, 68)

4 CNOC FILLIBHIR / (3) / NB 225325 / 17.4 × 14.1 CE / C / *RCAHM-S* (1928) no. 91; *PSAS* 38 (1903–4) 189; Thom (1967) 126, H1/3 (Callanish III)

5 CUL A CHLEIT / (5) / NB 247303 / ? / Pl / *RCAHM-S* (1928) no. 95

6 DRUIM NAM EUM / (3) / NB 22.33. / ? / C? / ibid no. 92

7 GARYNAHINE / (3) / NB 230303 / 12.9 × 9.2 CE / S / ibid no. 93; *PSAS* 38 (1903–4) 189; Thom (1967) 126, H1/4 (Callanish IV)

8 LOCH ROAG / (3) / NB 222325 / 21.6 × 18.2 CE / CN / Exc. 1858, postholes? *RCAHM-S* (1928) no. 90; *PSAS* 3 (1857–60) 127, 212; Thom (1967) 126, H1/2 (Callanish II)

9 LOCH SEAFORTH / (5) / NB 26.170 / 16.5 / Pl / *PSAS* 70 (1935–6) 122

10 PRIESTS GLEN / (5) / NB 40.35. / 45.7? / ? / *RCAHM-S* (1928) no. 56

North Uist

1 BEINN A CHAOLAIS / (5) / NF 90.77 / 18.3 / ? / *RCAHM-S* (1928) no. 241

2 CARINISH / (3) / NF 832603 / 41.5 × 39.0 / Pl / ibid no. 248; Beveridge (1911) 260

3 CRINGRAVAL / (3) / NF 808643 / 36.6 / Pl / *RCAHM-S* (1928) no. 251

4 LOCH A PHOBUILL / (3) / NF 829630 / 42.4 × 35.1 / Em / ibid no. 249; Beveridge (1911) 260; Thom (1966) 29; (1967) 131, H3/18 (Sornach Coir Fhinn)

5 POBULL FHINN / (3) / NF 844650 / 37.8 × 28.0 / Em?, O? / *RCAHM-S* (1928) no. 250; Beveridge (1911) 259; Thom (1967) H3/17. Ast: SS (1967, 99)

St. Kilda

1 BORERAY / (4) / NA 150049 / ? / S / Macaulay *History of St. Kildas* (1764) 53

Skye

1 CLACHAN ERISCO / (5) / NG 451480 / ? / ? / *RCAHM-S* (1928) no. 636

2 KILBRIDE / (4) / NG 58.20. / ? / ? / ibid no. 676

3 NA CLACHAN BHREIGE / (3) / NG 543176 / 6.6 / 4P? / ibid no. 667; Thom, (1967) 4, 43, H7/9 (Strathaird)

INVERNESS (Highland)

1 AVIEMORE / (3) / NH 896134 / 23.2 / RC, Gr / Henshall (1963) 360; Thom (1967) 81, B7/12

2a BALNUARAN OF CLAVA SW. / (2) / NH 756443 / 31.8 / PG, Gr, Cm / Exc. *c.*1828, flat-rimmed ware. Henshall (1963) 364; Thom (1966) 18, B7/1 (2). Ast: SS (1967, 98)

2b BALNUARAN OF CLAVA CENTRE / (2) / NH 757444 / 31.6 / RC, Cm? / Exc. 1953, flints. Piggott (1956) 188; Henshall (1963) 361; Thom (1966) 18, B7/1 (1)

2c BALNUARAN OF CLAVA NE. / (2) / NH 757444 / 31.6 × 29.7 CI / PG, Gr, Cm / Exc. *c.*1854, bones. *PSAS* 18 (1883–4) 345; Henshall (1963) 362; Thom (1966) 18, B7/1 (3). Ast: SS (1967, 98)

3 BOBLAINY / (4) / NH 493396 / 13.7 / PG or RC? / Henshall (1963) 366

4 BRUAICH / (1) / NH 499414 / 22.3 / RC, Cm / Henshall (1963) 366

5 CARN DALEY / (3) / NH 494314 / 18.3? / PG / Henshall (1963) 367

6 CLAVA / (5) / NH 757444 / 3.7 / Q, Cm / Exc. 1953, crem. Piggott (1956) 192

7 CORRIMONY / (2) / NH 383303 / 21.3 / PG, Q, Cm / Exc. 1952, bone pin. Piggott (1956) 174; Henshall (1963) 368

8 CROFTCROY / (4) / NH 682332 / 9.8+ / PG / Henshall (1963) 370; Thom (1967) B7/17 (Farr P. O.)

9 CULBURNIE / (1) / NH 491418 / c.21.3 / RC, Cm? / Henshall (1963) 370

10 CULCHUNAIG / (4) / NH 742442 / ? / PG or RC? / ibid 371

11 CULDOICH / (3) / NH 751437 / 30.5? / RC, Cm / Exc. 1953, crem. Piggott (1956) 190; Henshall (1963) 371; Thom (1967) B7/2 (Miltown of Clava)

12 CULLEARNIE / (3) / NH 725476 / ? / PG or RC? / Henshall (1963) 372

13 DALCROSS MAINS / (3) / NH 779484 / c.21.3 / PG / ibid 374; Piggott (1956) 194; Thom (1967) B7/6

14 DAVIOT / (3) / NH 727411 / c.27.4 / RC, CT / Exc. 1820?, skull. Henshall (1963) 374; *PSAS* 16 (1881–2) 293; Thom (1967) 76, B7/5.

15 DELFOUR / (3) / NH 844085 / 34.1? / RC / Henshall (1963) 375; Thom (1967) 87, B7/10. Ast: SS (1967, 98)

16 DRUIDTEMPLE / (3) / NH 685420 / 22.6×? CI / PG, CT, Q / Exc. c.1882, 1952, crem. Piggott (1956) 185; Henshall (1963) 375; Thom (1967) 69, B7/18

17 GASK / (3) / NH 679358 / 36.6 / RC, Cm / Henshall (1963) 378; (1972) 558; Thom (1967) 148, B7/15 (Mains of Gask)

18 GRENISH / (4) / NH 907154 / 31.4? / RC / Henshall (1963) 378; Thom (1967) B7/13 (Loch na Carraigean)

19 KINCHYLE OF DORES / (3) / NH 621388 / 21.0 / PG / Exc. 1952, crem. Piggott (1956) 185; Henshall (1963) 381; Thom (1967) B7/19 (River Ness)

20 LEANACH / (4) / NH 743444 / 29.3 / PG or RC? / Henshall (1963) 382

21 MAINS OF CLAVA SW. / (4) / NH 759446 / ? / PG or RC? / Henshall (1963) 382; Thom (1967) B7/11

22 MIDLAIRGS / (4) / NH 714368 / c.15.2 / PG or RC? / Henshall (1963) 382

23 MILLTOWN OF CLAVA / (4) / NH 752439 / ? / PG or RC? / Henshall (1963) 383

24 NEWTON OF PETTY / (3) / NH 734485 / 24.4 / PG or RC? / ibid 383

25 TORBRECK / (1) / NH 644404 / 5.2 / Gr / *PSAS* 18 (1883–4) 355; Henshall (1963) 385

26 TORDARROCH / (3) / NH 679334 / 34.4×? CA / RC, Cm / Henshall (1963) 385; *PSAS* 18 (1883–4) 331; Thom (1967) B7/16 (Farr, West)

27 TULLOCHGORM / (4) / NH 965214 / 23.9 CE? / RC, Cm / Henshall (1963) 386; Thom (1967) 78, B7/4 (Boat of Garten)

ISLAY

1 ARDILISTRY / (3) / NR 442493 / ? / ? / Priv. inf.

2 CULTOON / (3) / NR 196570 / 41.0×33.5 CE / Pl / Exc. 1974, 1975, flints. C-14, pre-765bc±40 (SRR-500). MacKie, 1975. Ast: SS c.1800 BC (MacKie, 1975, 6)

3 LOSSIT BURN / (5) / NR 202560 / 12.8 / Em? / *D & E* (1961) 19

KINCARDINE (Grampian)

1 AUCHQUHORTHIES / (1) / NO 901963 / 22.9 / RSC, RC / Exc. 1858?, urn? Stuart (1856) xix; Coles F. (1900) 145; Keiller (1934) 3, 8ff; Thom (1967) 147, B3/1 (Aquorthies, N.)

2 CAIRNFAULD / (3) / NO 754941 / 22.9 / RSC?, Gr / Exc. pre-1900, bones. Coles F. (1900) Thom (1967) 40, B2/11

3 CAIRNWELL / (3) / NO 907974 / 9.1 / RC / Exc. 1858, urns. *PSAS* 5 (1862–4) 131; Henshall (1963) 400; *JRAI* 17 (1888) 47

4 THE CAMP / (4) / NO 816772 / 24.4 / RSC?, RC? / Coles F. (1903) 193

5 COTBANK OF BARRAS / (4) / NO 827791 / 18.3 / RSC? / ibid 198

6 CRAIGHEAD / (2) / NO 912977 / 8.5 × 7.3 / 4P / Exc. 1858, bones. *PSAS* 5 (1862–4) 130; Coles F. (1900) 152

7 DUNNOTAR / (4) / NO 836833 / ? / ? / *ONB Kincardine* 6 (1865) 71

8 ESSLIE THE GREATER / (3) / NO 717916 / 25.0 × 23.3 CE / RSC, RC / Exc. 1873, bone. *PSAS* 14 (1879–80) 301; Thom (1961b) 300, B2/4 (Esslie South) Ast: SR, MS (1967, 98)

9 ESSLIE THE LESSER / (3) / NO 722921 / 13.4 / RSC?, RC? / Exc. *c*.1873, no finds? *PSAS* 14 (1879–80) 303; Thom (1967) B2/5 (Esslie N.) Ast: SS (1967, 98)

10 GARROL WOOD / (3) / NO 725912 / 18.0 × 14.6 CB / RSC, RC, Pf / Exc. 1904, urn. Coles F. (1905a); (1900) no. 7; Thom (1967) B2/6

11 GLASSEL / (1) / NO 64.99. / 5.5 × 2.8 Oval / O? / Exc. 1904, flint. Coles F. (1905a); (1900) no. 11; Thom (1967) B3/6

12 MILLPLOUGH / (4) / NO 819754 / ? / RSC? / Coles F. (1903) 196

13 OLD BOURTREEBUSH / (4) / NO 902964 / 30.5 × 22.6? / RSC / Exc. 1863, no finds. Coles F. (1900) no. 1; Thom (1967) B3/2

14a RAEDYKES SE. / (3) / NO 832905 / 14.3 / RC, P4 / Exc. 1965, no finds. *D & E* (1965) 24; *PSAS* 57 (1922–3) 20; Henshall (1963) 401; Thom (1967) B3/3

14b RAEDYKES NW. / (3) / NO 832906 / 14.3 / RC, P4 / *PSAS* 57 (1922–3) 20; Henshall (1963) 401; Thom (1967) B3/4

15 RAES OF CLUNE / (3) / NO 833905 / 17.1 / RSC / Henshall (1963) 39, 400; *PSAS* 53 (1918–19) 71; Thom (1967) B3/7 (Clune Wood)

16 TILQUHILLIE / (4) / NO 72.940 / ? / RSC, O? / *PSAS* 53 (1918–19) 71

KIRKCUDBRIGHT (Dumfries & Galloway)

1 CAULDSIDE BURN / (3) / NX 529571 / 25.0 / Pl / *RCAHM-S* (1914) no. 16; Thom (1966) 25, G4/14; (1967) 59. Ast: SR (1967, 98)

2 CLAUGHREID / (3) / NX 517560 / 10.7 × 8.8 CE / S / *RCAHM-S* (1914) no. 293; Thom (1967) 72

3 DRANNANDOW / (3) / NX 401711 / 27.1 / Pl / *RCAHM-S* (1914) no. 366; Thom (1967) G4/3

4 DRUMMORE / (3) / NX 688459 / *c*.25.9? / ? / *RCAHM-S* / (1914) no. 237

5 EASTHILL / (3) / NX 919739 / 21.3 × 18.3? CE / Cm? / *RCAHM-S* (1914) no. 332; *PSAS* 29 (1894–5) 309; Thom (1967) G5/9 (Maxwellton)

6 ERNESPIE / (4) / NX 774632 / ? / ? / *RCAHM-S* (1914) no. 202.

7 GLENQUICKAN N. / (1) / NX 509582 / 16.8 × 14.6 CA / S / *RCAHM-S* (1914) no. 292; *PSAS* 29 (1894–5) 307; Thom (1967) 64, G4/12 (Cambret). Ast: Antares 1860 BC (1967, 98)

8 GLENQUICKAN S. / (4) / NX 508583 / ? / ? / Thom (1967) 64, G4/12

9 HIGH AUCHENLARIE / (3) / NX 539534 / 13.7? / CN / *RCAHM-S* (1914) no. 18

10 HOLM OF DALTALLOCHAN / (5) / NX 554942 / 24.9 × 18.5 CE / ? / *RCAHM-S* (1914) 97; *PSAS* 29 (1894–5) 310; Thom (1967) G4/1 (Carsphairn)

11 KIRKGUNZEON / (4) / NX 865666 / 9.1 / ? / O.S. Edinburgh, NX 86 NE 7

12 LAIRDMANNOCH / (3) / NX 662614 / 6.4 / S / *RCAHM-S* (1914) no. 446; Thom (1967) G4/9 (Loch Mannoch)

13 LITTLE BALMAE / (5) / NX 68.44. / 27.4? / ? / *PSAS* 29 (1894–5) 304

14 LOCH ROAN / (3) / NX 640709 / 21.0 × 18.0 CE? / S / *TDGNHAS* 22 (1938–40) 164

15 PARK OF TONGLAND / (2) / NX 699560 / 4.9 / 4P? / *RCAHM-S* (1914) no. 445, 164; *PSAS* 29 (1894–5) 305

16 STROANGASSEL / (3) / NX 589869 / 22.1 / S, C? / Priv. inf.

N.B. (Omitted. Not circles: Knockshinnie, NX 681450, *PSAS* 29 (1894–5) 304; Lochrinnie, NX 721869, ibid 312.)

MIDLOTHIAN (Lothian)

1 MARCHWELL / (5) / NT 22.61. / 12.2? / CN? / Exc. (no date), food-vessel. *RCAHM-S* (1929) no. 105; *PSAS* 75 (1940–1) 220

2 NEWBRIDGE / (5) / NT 123726 / 54.9? / CN / Exc. 1830, bronze dagger (Coles J., 1969, 90). *PSAS* 12 (1876–8) 449; *RCAHM-S* (1929) no. 131

MORAY (Grampian)

1 ALVES / (3) / NJ 162628 / 6.7 × ? CE / 6, Gr? / *D & E* (1970) 33

2 BOGTON MILL / (3) / NJ 274608 / 15.2 / ? / Coles F. (1906) no. 23

3 CHAPEL HILL / (5) / NJ 03.46. / 10.7 / ? / Coles F. (1907) no. 20

4 DRUM DIVAN / (4) / NJ 192431 / ? / ? / Coles F. (1907) no. 12

5 EDINKILLIE / (3) / NJ 048414 / *c*.58.0 / Pl / *D & E* (1972) 30

6 INNESMILL / (3) / NJ 289641 / 33.5 / RSC?, Cm / Coles F. (1906) no. 22; Thom (1967) B5/1 (Urquhart)

7 TEMPLESTONE / (3) / NJ 068568 / 3.4 × 2.7 / 4P, RC? / Coles F. (1907) no. 19

MULL

1 BALLISCATE / (5) / NM 499541 / ? / ? / Thom (1967) M1/8; O.S. Edinburgh, NM 45 SE 1

2 DERVAIG / (3) / NM 439520 / 6.1 × 3.7 / 4P? / O.S. Edinburgh, NM 45 SW 4; Thom (1967) M1/6

3 LOCH BUIE / (3) / NM 618251 / 13.4 / O / *Arch J* 5 (1848) 217; Thom (1967) M2/14. Ast: Arcturus 1740 BC, 1980 BC; Antares 1850 BC (1967, 100)

4 MAOL MOR / (5) / NM 435531 / ? / ? / O.S. Edinburgh, NM 45 SW 5; Thom (1966) M1/4

5 TENGA / (3) / NM 502462 / ? / ? / Priv. inf.

NAIRN (Highland)

1 AULDEARN / (3) / NH 924553 / 16.8 / PG or RC? / Henshall (1963) 387

2 LITTLE URCHANY / (3) / NH 866485 / 20.7? / PG OR RC? / Henshall (1963) 388; Thom (1967) B6/1

3 LITTLE URCHANY E. / (4) / NH 866485 / ? / PG OR RC? / *PSAS* 16 (1881–2) 328

4 MOYNESS / (4) / NH 952536 / 30.2? / RC / Exc. 1856, 'clay urn'. Henshall (1963) 388; Stuart (1867) xxii; Thom (1967) B6/2

ORKNEYS

1 RING OF BRODGAR / (2) / HY 294132 / 103.6 / CH, O / *RCAHM-S* (1946) II, no. 875; Thom A. & A. S. (1973). Ast: MR, MS *c*.1560 BC. (Thom A. & A. S., 1973, 120)

2 STENNESS / (3) / HY 306125 / 31.1 / CH, O / Exc. 1973, 1974, grooved ware. C-14: 2356bc ± 65 (SRR-350), 2238bc ± 70 (SRR-351), 1730bc ± 270 (SRR-592). *D & E* (1973) 68; (1974) 79; *RCAHM-S* (1946) II, no. 876

PEEBLES-SHIRE (Borders)

1 HARESTANES / (3) / NT 124443 / 4.6 / Pl / *RCAHM-S* (1967) no. 107
2 NETHER DOD / (3) / NT 080228 / 12.2 / Em / ibid no. 108

PERTHSHIRE (Tayside)

1 AIRLICH / (3) / NN 959386 / 7.9 × 6.7 CE / Em, C / Coles F. (1910) no. 20; Thom (1967) P1/16 (Meikle Findowie)

2 ARDBLAIR / (2) / NO 160439 / 14.9 / 6 / Stewart (1966a) 20; Coles F. (1909) no. 19; Thom (1967) P2/1 (Leys of Marlee)

3 BACHILTON / (4) / NO 005241 / ? / ? / Coles F. (1911) no. 37

4 BALMUICK / (3) / NN 785247 / 4.0 / 4P? / ibid no. 5

5 BANDIRRAN / (3) / NO 207310 / 8.5 × 7.6 / Pl? / Stewart (1966a) 20

6a BLACKFAULDS A / (3) / NO 145317 / 10.0 × 7.0 / P2, Cm? / *PSAS* 24 (1890–1) 223; Stewart (1966a) 20; Thom (1967) P2/9 (Guildtown)

6b BLACKFAULDS B / (3) / NO 145317 / ? / P2 / *PSAS* 24 (1890–1) 223

7 BROAD MOSS / (3) / NO 197487 / 6.7 / ? / Coles F. (1909) no. 12

8 CARSE FARM I / (3) / NN 802488 / 4.7 / 4P, Cm / Exc. 1964, urn. *D & E* (1964) 39; Coles F. (1908) no. 18; Thom (1967) 40, P1/4 (Weem)

9 CARSE FARM II / (4) / NN 797484 / 23.2? / Cm / Exc. 1964, crem. *D & E* (1964) 40; Coles F. (1911) 386; Thom (1967) P1/5 (Weem)

10 CLACH NA TIOMPAN / (3) / NN 831329 / 4.3 / 4P, Q / Exc. 1954, no finds. Henshall & Stewart 122; Coles F. (1911) no. 35; Thom (1967) P1/9 (Clach na Tromp-pan)

11 COILLEACHUR / (3) / NN 845466 / *c*.48.8 / RSC?, Cr? / Coles F. (1910) no. 14

12 COLEN / (4) / NO 110311 / 6.4 / 8, Cm / *PSAS* 26 (1891–2) 222; Thom (1967) P2/6

13 COMMONBANK / (5) / NO 177247 / ? / Cm / *D & E* (1973) 44

14 COMRIE BRIDGE / (4) / NN 787468 / 7.9 / Pl / Coles F. (1910) no. 11

15 CRAMRAR / (3) / NN 725455 / 7.6? / 4P?, Cm / Burl (1971) 50, no. 17

16 CROFT MORAIG / (3) / NN 797472 / 12.2 / Em, Cm, Gr / Exc. 1965, Neo sherds, flat-rimmed ware. Piggott & Simpson; Coles F. (1910) no. 13; Thom (1967) P1/19

17 DRUIDS SEAT / (3) / NO 125313 / 8.5 / Pl / *PSAS* 26 (1891–2) 223; Thom (1967) P2/3 (Blindwells)

18 DUNMOID / (2) / NN 780212 / 4.6 / 4P, CT / Exc. *c*.1840, 'urn'. Coles F. (1911) no. 9

19 FASKALLY COTTAGES / (3) / NN 930589 / *c*.6.4 / Pl / Coles F. (1908) no. 14; Dixon *Pitlochry Past & Present* (1925) 62

20 FERNTOWER / (1) / NN 874226 / 5.5 / 4P / Coles F. (1911) no. 24

21 FONAB MOOR / (3) / NN 925553 / 3.7 / 4P / Coles F. (1908) no. 12

22 FORTINGALL E. / (3) / NN 747470 / c.5.2 / 4P / Exc. 1970, crem? Burl (1974b) 30; Thom (1967) P1/6

23 FORTINGALL W. / (3) / NN 746470 / 7.0 × 5.5 / 4P / Exc. 1970, no finds. Burl (1974b) 30; Coles F. (1908) no. 17; Thom (1967) P1/6

24 FORTINGALL S. / (4) / NN 746469 / 22.9? / RSC? / Burl (1974b) 30; Thom (1967) P1/6

25a FOWLIS WESTER W. / (3) / NN 923249 / 7.3 / P2, Q, O / Exc. 1939, crem. Young et al.; Coles F. (1911) no. 33; Thom (1967) P1/10; Ast: MS (1971, 53)

25b FOWLIS WESTER W. / (3) / NN 923249 / 5.9 / RC, P2, Cm / Exc. 1939, quartz. Young et al.; Coles F. (1911) no. 33; Thom (1967) P1/10. Ast: MR (1971, 53)

26 GLENBALLOCH / (1) / NO 185481 / 4.9 / 4P / Exc. c.1870, urn (ApSimon, 1969, 40). PSAS 15 (1880–1) 89; Coles F. (1909) no. 10; Thom (1967) P2/4 (Courthill)

27 GREENLAND / (3) / NN 767427 / 8.3 / ? / Coles F. (1910) no. 10; PSAS 43 (1908–9) 271

28 INVERARNON / (3) / NN 316185 / c.31.1 / C, O / PSAS 63 (1928–9) 339

29 KILLIN / (3) / NN 576327 / 10.0 × 8.4 CE / 6 / Coles F. (1910) no. 9; Thom (1967) P1/3

30 LUNDIN FARM / (1) / NN 882505 / 4.0 × 3.4 / 4P, CN / Exc. 1962, AOC beaker (Clarke, 1970, no. 1737.1), urn. Stewart (1966b)

31 MACHUINN / (3) / NN 682401 / 6.7 × 5.8 / 6 / Coles F. (1910) no. 8

32 MONCRIEFFE / (2) / NO 133193 (9.1 / RC, Q, Cm / Exc. c.1830, 1974 beaker, flat-rimmed ware. D & E (1974) 86; PSAS 16 (1881–2) 92

33 MONEYDIE / (4) / NO 059288 / c.27.4 / ? / Coles F. (1911) no. 38

34 MONZIE / (5) / NN 882243 / 4.9 / O, CT, Cm, Q / Exc. 1938, flat-rimmed ware. Mitchell & Young; Coles F. (1911) no. 29; Thom (1967) P1/13

35 MURTHLY / (2?) / NO 103386 / 10.1 / Em, 6? / PSAS 9 (1870–2) 268; Coles F. (1908) no. 38; Stewart (1966a) 20

36 NA CARRAIGEAN EDINTIAN / (1) / NN 839620 / 4.9 / 4P / Coles F. (1908) no. 10; Dixon Pitlochry Past & Present (1925) 57

37 PARKNEUK / (3) / NO 195515 / 4.3 × 3.1 / 4P / Coles F. (1909) no. 3

38 PITSUNDRY / (3) / NO 056345 / c.12.2 / S / Coles F. (1908) no. 36

39 ST. MARTINS / (3) / NO 160312 / 7.5 / 4P? / Stewart (1966a) 21

40a SANDY ROAD W. / (2) / NO 132265 / 7.5 × 6.2 CE / P2, Gr / Exc. 1961, flat-rimmed ware. C-14: 1200bc ± 150 (GaK-787). Stewart (1966a); Thom (1967) P2/11 (Scone)

40b SANDY ROAD E. / (4) / NO 132265 / ? / P2 / Stewart (1966a) 11

41 SHIAN / (5) / NN 844408 / c.20.7 / ? / PSAS 45 (1910–11) 395

42a SHIAN BANK NW. / (3) / NO 156273 / 8.4 / P2 / Stewart (1966a) 21; Thom (1966) 39, P2/8. Ast: SR (1967, 100)

42b SHIAN BANK SE. / (3) / NO 156273 / 8.4 / P2 / Stewart (1966a) 21; Thom (1966) 39, P2/8. Ast: SS (1967, 100)

43 TEGARMUCHD / (3) / NN 803486 / ? / 4P?, CT? / Coles F. (1910) no. 15

44 TIGH NA RUAICH / (3) / NN 976534 / 7.9 × 6.4 CE / 6 / Exc. 1855, 4 urns. J Kilkenny Arch Soc (1854–5); Coles F. (1908) no. 15; Thom (1967) P2/2 (Ballin-luig)

45 Tom na Chessaig / (5) / NN 770220 / ? / ? / Coles F. (1911) no. 7
46a Tullybeagles E. / (3) / NO 013362 / 7.0? / P2 / Coles F. (1911) no. 36a; Thom (1967) P1/14
46b Tullybeagles W. / (3) / NO 013362 / 9.5 / P2 / Coles F. (1911) no. 36a; Thom (1967) P1/14
47 Tullymurdoch / (3) / NO 194514 / 13.7 / ? / Coles F. (1909) no. 4
48 Wester Torrie / (3) / NN 646045 / 6.7 × 5.5? / 6? / *PSAS* 36 (1901–2) 618
49 Woodside / (3) / NO 185501 / 4.9 / 4P? / Coles F. (1909) no. 6; Thom (1967) P2/5 (Hill of Drimmie)

RENFREWSHIRE (Strathclyde)

1 Covenanter's Stone / (5) / NS 477532 / 7.6 / Pl / *D & E* (1963) 45

ROSS (Highland)

1 Carn Urnan / (3) / NH 566523 / 22.3 / PG / Henshall (1963) 343
2 Lochalsh / (4) / NG 831274 / ? / ? / O.S. Edinburgh, NG 82 NW 5

ROXBURGH (Borders)

1 Burgh Hill / (3) / NT 470062 / 16.1 × 13.3 CI / Pl / Exc. pre-1873, no finds. *TBFC* 7 (1873) 78; *RCAHM-S* (1956) II, no. 1011; Thom (1967) 70, G9/15 (Allan Water)
2 Fairnington / (4) / NT 667285 / ? / ? / *RCAHM-S* (1956) II, no. 911
3 Five Stanes / (3) / NT 752168 / c.5.8 / Pl? / ibid I, no. 349; Thom (1967) G8/7 (Dere Street III)
4 Frogden / (4) / NT 774292? / ? / ? / *RCAHM-S* (1956) I, no. 549
5 Harestanes / (4) / NT 64.24. / ? / ? / ibid no. 22
6 Ninestone Rigg / (1) / NY 518973 / 7.0 / Pl / ibid no. 113; Thom (1967) G8/2

SHETLAND

1 Doom Rings / (?) / HU 166596 / ? / ? / O.S. Edinburgh, HU 15 NE 18
2 Stanydale / (5) / HU 285503 / 73.2? / ? / *PSAS* 84 (1949–50) 198

SUTHERLAND (Highland)

1 Aberscross / (3) / NH 771990 / 7.3 / CT / Exc. 1867, crem. *PSAS* 7 1866–8) 473; *RCAHM-S* (1911b) no. 291; Thom (1967) N2/2 (The Mound)
2 Achany / (3) / NC 560029 / 26.8 / Pl / *RCAHM-S* (1911b) no. 461
3 Auchinduich / (3) / NC 584002 / 8.5 / C? / *RCAHM-S* (1911b) no. 91
4 Clachtoll / (3) / NC 037278 / c.12.0 / S / *D & E* (1971) 45
5 Cnoc an Liath-Bhaid / (3) / NC 728102 / 9.1 × 6.8 CE / C, CN? / Exc., finds? *RCAHM-S* (1911b) no 518
6 Dailharraild / (3) / NC 678390 / 6.7 / CN / *RCAHM-S* (1911b) no. 247
7 Learable Hill N. / (3) / NC 895241 / 17.1 / Cm, Cr? / ibid no. 375
8 Learable Hill S. / (3) / NC 893235 / 19.8 × ? CE / CN? / ibid no. 374; Thom (1967) 72
9 Linsidemore / (3) / NH 545992? / 16.8? / C? / *RCAHM-S* (1911b) no. 92

10a RIVER SHIN A / (3) / NC 582049 / 4.3 / P2 / ibid no. 462; Thom (1967) N2/3

10b RIVER SHIN B / (3) / NC 582049 / 6.3 / P2 / Thom (1967) 36, 139, N2/3

TIREE

1 LOCH A'BHLEOGHAN / (5) / NM 03.45. / 23.8 / CN / Beveridge *Coll & Tiree* (1903) 130

2 LOCH A CHAPUIL / (5) / NM 02.45. / 23.8? / CN, CT? / ibid 130

3a MOSS A / (5) / NL 95.45. / 23.8+ / P2 / ibid 130

3b MOSS B / (5) / NL 95.45. / 23.8+ / P2 / ibid 130

WEST LOTHIAN (Lothian)

1 CAIRNPAPPLE / (4) / NS 987717 / 35.1 × 28.0 CI / CH, Pt / Exc. 1947–8, Neo. pottery, bone pins, stone axes (Groups VI, VII), N/NR, 2 N2/L beakers (Clarke, 1970, nos. 1790–1793F). Piggott (1948); Ross (1967) 63; Thom (1967) P7/1

WIGTOWNSHIRE (Dumfries & Galloway)

1 ELDRIG LOCH / (4) / NX 324498 / ? / S? / *RCAHM-S* (1912) no. 230

2 GLENTIRROW / (3) / NX 145625 / ? / C / ibid no. 48

3 LAGGANGARN / (4) / NX 22.71. / 12.8 × 10.1? / Cm? / *PSAS* 10 (1872–4) 56; (1898–9) 170

4 STEEPS PARK / (4) / NX 245527 / ? / ? / *PSAS* 33 (1898–9) 170

5 TORHOUSEKIE / (1) / NX 383565 / 21.4 × 20.0 CA / RSC, RC / Burl (1974b); *RCAHM-S* (1912) no. 531; *PSAS* 31, (1896–7), 90; Thom (1967) G3/7

6 TORHOUSEKIE N. / (5) / NX 382566 / ? / ? / *RCAHM-S* (1912) no. 532

N.B. (Omitted: Wren's Egg, NX 362415. *RCAHM-S* (1912) no. 12; Thom (1967) G3/13. A glacial erratic.)

ULSTER

ANTRIM

1 LISNAMANNY / (5) / D 13.15. / ? / ? / *UJA* 8 (1945) 102, no. 45

2 MOYADAM / (4) / J 23.87. / ? / ? / *UJA* 9 (1946) 79

3 SLIEVENAGH / (3) / C 99.02. / ? / ? / *UJA* 8 (1945) 103, no. 56

4 TUREAGH / (?) / J 35.96. / ? / PG? / ibid 103, no. 66

ARMAGH

1 BALLYBROLLY / (3) / H 84.46. / 21.3 / PG / *NMI* II (1963) 46

2 VICAR'S CAIRN / (4) / H 91.39. / 40.2 / CN / Exc. 1795, 1815, finds? Borlase W. C. I, 297; Chart 70

DOWN

1 BALLYNOE / (1) / J 481404 / 33.5 / Pt, O, CN / Exc. 1937–8, Carrowkeel ware (Case, 1961, 225). Collins & Waterman 46

2 CASTLE MAHON / (3) / J 552470 / 21.3 × 19.8 / 6, CT / Exc. 1953, Neolithic sherds (Case, 1961, 224), flint knife. Collins (1956)

3 MILLIN BAY / (3) / J 628495 / 22.9 × 15.2 / CN, CT, Cr / Exc. 1953, food-vessels. Collins & Waterman

4 NEWCASTLE / (6?) / J 37.31. / 45.1 × 42.7 / Pl / Davies (1939a) 11; Chart 135; Evans E. & O'Nuaillain S *Archaeological Survey of Co. Down* (H.M.S.O., 1966) No. 4

FERMANAGH

1 AGHASTIROUKE / (5) / H 16.31. / ? / ? / Chart 177

2 BROUGHER / (3) / H 356529 / 11.3 × 8.5 / O, R / Chart 156

3 CAVANCARRAGH / (4) / H 305435 / 6.1 / R / *JRSAI* 4 (1876–8) 499; Evans E. (1966) 114; Davies (1939a) 12

4 CLOGHASTUCKANE / (3) / H 059416 / 3.8 / O / Chart 169

5 CLOGHBRACK / (3) / H 08.40. / ? / ? / Chart 169

6 CORRADERRYBROCK / (3) / H 03.42. / ? / S / Chart 158

7 DRUID'S TEMPLE / (4) / H 43.19. / 38.4 / CN, CT / Destr. 1712, burials. *JRSAI* 5 (1881) 538; Chart 184

8 DRUMSKINNY / (2) / H 201707 / 14.0 × 13.0 / R / Exc. 1962, no finds. Waterman

9 ESHBRALLEY / (4) / H 41.35. / ? / ? / Chart 181

10 FORMIL / (3) / H 16.68. / ? / R / Davies (1939a) 11

11 GREENAN / (5) / H 19.35. / ? / ? / Chart 182

12 KILCOO / (3) / G 97.47. / ? / ? / ibid 157

13 KILLEE A / (5) / H 31.46. / 24.4 / O / ibid 167

14 KILLEE B / (3) / H 31.46.? / ? / ? / Davies (1939a) 12

15 KILTIERNEY / (3) / H 216625 / 11.1 × 10.2 / RSC?, Cm / *JRSAI* 13 (1874–5) 467; Borlase W. C. I, 219; Chart 146

16 KILTOBER / (3) / H 43.20. / ? / O? / Davies (1939a) 14

17 MONTIAGHROE A / (3) / H 193693 / 15.2 / R / Chart 144

18 MONTIAGHROE B / (3) / H 193693? / 13.1 × 11.6 / R / Waterman 23

19 MONTIAGHROE C / (3) / H 193693? / ? / ? / Davies (1939a) 10

20 RATORAN / (5) / H 33.46. / ? / ? / Chart 166

21 SHEEMULDOON / (3) / H 25.62. / ? / ? / ibid 147

22 TROMOGAGH / (3) / H 11.34. / 18.3 / S / ibid 177

LONDONDERRY

1 ALTAGHONEY / (3) / C 515013 / 12.2 / R / Davies (1939a) 11

2a AUGHLISH A / (3) / C 64.04. / 7.0 / Pl, P5 / ibid 10; Chart 204

2b AUGHLISH B / (3) / C 64.04. / 15.2 / C, P5 / Chart 204

2c AUGHLISH C / (3) / C 64.04. / 5.5 / R, P5 / ibid

2d AUGHLÏSH D / (3) / C 64.04. / ? / ?, P5 / ibid

2e AUGHLISH E / (3) / C 64.04. / ? / R, P5 / ibid

3 BALLYBRIEST / (3) / H 760880 / 5.8 / ? / Evans E. (1966) 149

4a BALLYGROLL WSW. / (3) / C 533146 / 10.7 / C, Pt, P2 / Chart 198

4b BALLYGROLL ENE. / (3) / C 533146 / 9.1 / PG?, P2 / ibid; Davies (1939a) 14

5 BALLYHOLLY NE. / (3) / C 577118 / 6.1 / R / Chart 199
6a BALLYHOLLY A / (3) / C 57.11. / ? / ?, P3 / ibid
6b BALLYHOLLY B / (3) / C 57.11. / 13.7 / C, R, P3 / Davies (1939a) 9
6c BALLYHOLLY C / (3) / C 57.11. / ? / ?, P3 / ibid
7 CARBALINTOBER / (4) / C 83.11. / ? / ? / Davies (1939a) 14
8 COOLNASILLAGH / (3) / C 785003 / 18.3 × 13.7 / C, R / ibid; Chart 208
9a CORICK A / (3) / H 778897 / ? / R, P5 / Chart 211
9b CORICK B / (3) / H 778897 / ? / R, P5 / ibid; Davies (1939a) 10
9c CORICK C / (3) / H 778897 / ? / R, P5 / ibid
9d CORICK D / (3) / H 778897 / ? / S, P5 / ibid
9e CORICK E / (3) / H 778897 / ? / P5 / ibid
10 CUILBANE / (3) / C 82.13. / 12.8 / PG? / Chart 201
11 ERVEY / (5) / C 52.12. / ? / Pl / Davies (1939a) 14
12 GORTCORBIES / (3) / C 741259 / 13.4 / C, CT / Exc. 1945, flints. May
(1947); *JRSAI* 99 (1969) 63
13 LACKAGH / (3) / C 47.08. / 11.4 / Pl / Davies (1939a) 12
14 LETTERAN / (3) / H 81.86. / ? / ? / ibid 10
15 MAGHERAMORE / (3) / C 69.04. / ? / ? / ibid 14
16 OWENREAGH / (3) / H 741903 / 8.2 / C, O / ibid 11; Chart 210

TYRONE

1a AGHALANE A / (3) / H 48.94. / ? / CT, P3 / Chart 218
1b AGHALANE B / (3) / H 48.84. / ? / S, P3 / ibid
1c AGHALANE C / (3) / H 48.84 / ? / Pl, P3 / ibid
2 AGHASCREBAGH / (3) / H 61.84. / 7.6 / C / Davies (1939a) 7
3a BEAGHMORE A / (2) / H 685842 / 11.9 × 9.6 / R, A, P2 / Exc. 1945–9. May
(1953)
3b BEAGHMORE B / (2) / H 685842 / 10.0 × 9.8 / R, A, P2 / ibid
4a BEAGHMORE C / (2) / H 685842 / 17.1 × 15.9 / A, P2 / ibid
4b BEAGHMORE D / (2) / H 685842 / 16.8 × 16.2 / A, CN, P2 / ibid
5 BEAGHMORE E / (2) / H 685842 / 19.5 × 16.8 CB? / R, CT / Exc. 1945–9,
crem. May (1953)
6a BEAGHMORE F / (2) / H 685842 / 8.5 / R, P2. / Exc. 1945–9, no finds.
C-14 from assoc. cairn: 1535bc ± 55 (UB-11); pre-circle: 775bc ± 55 (UB-163);
post-circle: 1605bc ± 45 (UB-23), flint hoard. Pilcher (1969); May (1953)
6b BEAGHMORE G / (2) / H 685842 / 9.8 / Pt, A / ibid
7 BELEEVNABEG / (3) / H 693827 / ? / Pl / Davies (1939a) 7
8 BELEEVNA EVISHBRACK / H 695828 / ? / C, R / ibid 7
9a BUTTERLOPE A / (3) / H 49.94. / 5.8 / P4 / Chart 217
9b BUTTERLOPE B / (3) / H 49.94. / 7.6 / P4 / ibid
9c BUTTERLOPE C / (3) / H 49.94 / 7.6 / P4 / ibid
9d BUTTERLOPE D / (3) / H 49.94 / 15.6 / P4 / ibid
10 CASTLEDAMPH S. / (3) / H 522925 / 19.8 / CN, CT, R, C / Exc. 1937,
crem. Davies (1938); Evans E. (1966) 199
11 CASTLEDAMPH SE. / (3) / H 522925? / 5.5+ / C / Davies (1938) 106
12a CASTLEDAMPH N. / (3) / H 522925? / 12.2 / P2 / ibid 106

12b CASTLEDAMPH SW. / (3) / H 522925? / 12.2 / P2 / ibid

13 CASTLEMERVYN / (3) / H 336573 / 12.2 / S / Davies (1939a) 9

14 CLOGHERNY BUTTERLOPE / (3) / H 493947 / 12.2 / O / Exc. 1937, no finds. Davies (1939b) 40; Chart 217

15 CLOGHERNY MEENERRIGAL / (3) / H 488945 / 18.3 / WG / Exc. 1937, charcoal. Davies (1939b) 36

16a CORNAMADDY A / (3) / H 685698 / 9.1 / R, P2 / Davies (1939a) 10

16b CORNAMADDY B / (3) / H 685698 / 9.1 / R, P2 / ibid

17 CREGGANCONROE / (5) / H 662758 / 12.2? / R? / ibid 7; Chart 237

18 CREGGANDEVESKY / (3) / H 63.73. / 10.7 / O / Chart 238

19 CULVACULLION N / (3) / H 505888 / 9.8 / O / Davies (1939a) 6

20a CULVACULLION A / (3) / H 505888 / 9.5 / P2 / Chart 224

20b CULVACULLION B / (3) / H 505888 / 10.4 / P2 / ibid

21 CULVACULLION S / (3) / H 505888 / 18.3 / CN? / ibid

22 DAVAGH LOWER A / (3) / H 70.87. / 16.2 / C, A / ibid 226

23 DAVAGH LOWER B / (3) / H 70.87. / 13.1×11.3 / R / ibid

24 DOOISH / (3) / H 31.69. / 4.6 / R / ibid 243; Davies (1939a) 9

25a DOORAT W. / (3) / H 50.97 / 12.2 / CN / Davies (1939a) 11

25b DOORAT E. / (3) / H 50.97. / 12.8 / CN / ibid; Chart 216

26a DUNBUNRAWER A / (3) / H 48.84. / ? / R, P3 / Davies (1939a) 7

26b DUNBUNRAWER B / (3) / H 48.84. / ? / Pl, P3 / ibid

26c DUNBUNRAWER C / (3) / H 48.84. / ? / Pl, P3 / ibid

27 DUN RUADH / (3) / H 624845 / 10.4×9.1 / CH, CT, RC / Exc. 1909, 1934, food-vessels (ApSimon, 1969, 35, 37, 43). Davies (1936); Evans E. (1966) 201; Waddell (1970) 131

28a GLASMULLAGH A / (3) / H 387805 / 7.6 / R, P4 / Davies (1939a) 10

28b GLASMULLAGH B / (3) / H 387805 / 7.6 / R, P4 / ibid

28c GLASMULLAGH C / (3) / H 387805 / 7.6 / Pl, P4 / ibid

28d GLASMULLAGH D / (3) / H 387805 / 7.6 / Pl, P4 / ibid

29 GLASMULLAGH E / (3) / H 387805? / 7.9 / R / ibid

30 GLENGEEN / (3) / H 37.56. / 12.5 / R / Chart 250

31a GOLAN A / (4) / H 44.81. / ? / P2 / ibid 231

31b GOLAN B / (3) / H 44.81. / 8.8 / P2 / ibid

32 KNOCKNAHORNA / (3) / H 410989 / 15.2 / Pt or A?, CN? / Davies (1939a) 7; Chart 215

33 LOUGHMACRORY / (3) / H 58.77. / 12.2 / C? / Chart 232

34a MEENDAMPH A / (3) / H 46.97. / 17.1 / P2, CN / Davies (1939a) / 11

34b MEENDAMPH B / (4) / H 46.97. / ? / CN, P2 / ibid

35a MOYMORE A / (3) / H 712745 / ? / R, P7 / Davies (1939a) 7

35b MOYMORE B / (3) / H 712745 / ? / R, P7 / ibid

35c MOYMORE C / (3) / H 712745 / ? / R, P7 / ibid

35d MOYMORE D / (3) / H 712745 / ? / R, P7 / ibid

35e MOYMORE E / (3) / H 712745 / ? / R, P7 / ibid

35f MOYMORE F / (3) / H 712745 / ? / R, P7 / ibid

35g MOYMORE G / (3) / H 712745 / ? / PL, P7 / ibid

36 MULLANMORE / (3) / H 59.75. / 15.2 / Pl / Chart 236

37a OUGHTBOY A / (3) / H 59.93. / 4.9 / P2 / ibid 218
37b OUGHTBOY B / (3) / H 59.93. / 4.9 / P2 / ibid
38a SCRAGHY A / (3) / H 22.73. / 18.3 / Pl, P2 / Davies (1939a) 7
38b SCRAGHY B / (3) / H 22.73. / ? / C, P2 / ibid
39a TREMOGE A / (3) / H 655735 / 9.1 / R, P2 / Davies (1939a) 8; Chart 238
39b TREMOGE B / (3) / H 655735 / 9.1 / P2 / Chart 239
40 TREMOGE S / (3) / H 655733 / 12.2 / R / Davies (1939a) 8
41 TURNABARSON / (3) / H 68.69. / ? / R / ibid 11

WALES

ANGLESEY (Ynys Mon)

1 BRYN CELLI DDU / (4) / SH 508702 / 17.7? / CH? / Exc. 1927–8, crems.
Arch 80 (1930) 179; O'Kelly C. (1969) 29; Lynch (1970) 58
2 BRYNGWN STONES / (4) / SH 462669 / 12.2? / CH? / *RCAHM-W* (1937)
103; Grimes (1963) 112; Lynch (1970) 115
3 TRE'R DRYW BACH / (5) / SH 468673 / ? / ? / Lynch (1970) 115

BRECKNOCKSHIRE (Powys)

1 CERRIG DUON / (1) / SN 852206 / 18.3 × 16.8 CI / O, A / Grimes (1963)
138; Thom (1966) 46, W11/3 (Maen Mawr). Ast: SS (1967, 101)
2a NANT TARW E. / (3) / SN 819258 / 20.7 × 17.8 CE / O, P2 / Grimes (1963)
136; Thom (1967) 82, W11/4 (Usk River). Ast: SS (1967, 101)
2b NANT TARW W. / (3) / SN 819258 / 20.7 × 19.00 / O?, P2 / Grimes (1963)
136; Thom (1967) 82, W11/4 (Usk River). Ast: SR (1967, 101)
3 PEN Y BEACON / (4) / SO 239373 / 29.5 / Pl / *Archaeology in Wales* 13
(1973) 62
4a TRECASTLE MOUNTAIN E. / (3) / SN 833311 / 23.2 / P2 / Grimes (1963)
135; Thom (1967) W11/2 (Y Pigwn)
4b TRECASTLE MOUNTAIN W. / (3) / SN 833311 / 7.3 / R, P2 / Grimes (1963)
135; Thom (1967) W11/2 (Y Pigwn)
5 YNYS-HIR / (3) / SN 921383 / 18.0 / Pl / Exc. 1940, no finds. Dunning
(1943) 169; Grimes (1963) 134; Thom (1967) W11/5

CAERNARVONSHIRE (Gwynedd)

1 CEFN COCH / (3) / SH 548427 / 20.1 × 16.5 / O? / Grimes (1963) 113
2 CERRIG PRYFAID / (1) / SH 724713 / 21.3 × 19.8 / O / Grimes (1963) 115;
RCAHM-W (1956) no. 177
3 CIRCLE 275 / (3) / SH 725747 / 3.1 / Em?, Q / Griffiths 305
4 CORS Y CARNEDDAU / (3) / SH 718746 / 16.5 / Pl? / Grimes (1963) 118
5 CWM MAWR / (4) / SH 553414 / 20.1 × 16.5? / ? / Grimes (1963) 113
6 DRUIDS CIRCLE / (3) / SH 722746 / 25.7 × 24.5 CE / Em, Pt / Exc. 1958,
enlarged food-vessel, food-vessel, bronze knife, 3 whetstones. Griffiths (1960);
Grimes (1963) 116; Thom (1967) 77, W2/1 (Penmaenmawr) Ast: SR (1967, 100)
7 HAFOTY / (3) / SH 747752 / *c*.12.2 / Pl, O? / Grimes (1963) 118
8 RED FARM / (3) / SH 732750 / 30.5? / ? / ibid 117

CARDIGANSHIRE (Dyfed)

1 HIRNANT / (5) / SN 753839 / 5.9 / CN? / Priv. inf.
2 YSBYTY CYNFYN / (4) / SN 752791 / ? / CH? / Grimes (1963) 127

CARMARTHENSHIRE (Dyfed)

1 CEFN GWERNFFRWD / (3) / SN 737493 / 24.0 / R? / Inf. S. Briggs
2 MEINI-GWYR / (3) / SN 142267 / 18.3+ / Em, Pt / Exc. 1938, no finds.
PPS 4 (1938) 324; Grimes (1963) 141
3 Y NAW CARREG / (4) / SN 561099 / 18.3? / Pl? / Grimes (1963) 139

DENBIGHSHIRE (Clwyd)

1 CAPEL HIRAETHOG III / (5) / SJ 032545 / *c*.18.3 / CN / Priv. inf.

FLINTSHIRE (Clwyd)

1 PENBEDW PARK / (6?) / SJ 171679 / 35.4? / O / Grimes (1963) 118; Thom
(1967) W4/1

GLAMORGAN

1 MYNYDD Y GELLI / (1) / SS 975942 / 9.1 / CT / *Archaeology in Wales* 6
(1966) 30

MERIONETH (Gwynedd)

1 CERRIG ARTHUR / (3) / SH 631188 / 15.9 × 12.8 / B? / Bowen & Gresham 38
2a FFRIDD NEWYDD N. / (3) / SH 616213 / 32.9 / B, P2 / Exc. 1919, FP beaker
(Clarke, 1970, no. 1871F). Crawford (1920); Grimes (1963) 119
2b FFRIDD NEWYDD S. / (4) / SH 616213 / 50.6 / Em, P2 / Exc. 1919, FP
beaker (Clarke, 1970, no. 1872F). Crawford (1920); Grimes (1963) 119
3 LLECHEIDDIOR / (4) / SH 611217 / 19.8 × 15.2 / Em? / Bowen & Gresham 37
4 LLYN EIDDEW BACH III / (3) / SH 642346 / *c*.12.8 / Pl / Priv. inf.
5 MOEL GOEDOG W. / (5) / SH 610324 / 7.6 / Pl / Bowen & Gresham 88
6 PABELL LLYWARCH HEN / (4) / SH 940366 / ? / Pl / ibid 283
7 PEN-Y-STRYD / (3) / SH 725312 / 17.1 / Pl / ibid / 39

MONMOUTH (Gwent)

1 GREY HILL / (3) / ST 438935 / 9.8 / CT?, O / Daniel (1950) 212

MONTGOMERYSHIRE (Powys)

1a CERRIG GAERAU / (3) / SH 904005 / 21.0 / P2 / Grimes (1963) 122
1b LLED-CROEN-YR-YCH / (3) / SH 903005 / 24.7 × 22.9 / P2, O / ibid 122
2 KERRY HILL / (1) / SO 158860 / 26.5 (Compound) / S / ibid 123; Thom,
(1967) W6/1 (Kerry Pole)
3 RHOS-Y-BEDDAU / (3) / SJ 058303 / 12.8 / A / Grimes (1963) 120; Thom
(1967) 149, W6/2. Ast: Spica 2000 BC (1967, 100)

4 WHETSTONES / (4) / SO 305976 / 29.6 × ? / ? / Destr. *c*.1860, 'ashes and bones'. Grimes (1963) 124; *TSANHS* 10 (1926) xxix

PEMBROKESHIRE (Dyfed)

1 DYFFRYN / (3) / SN 059284 / 22.0 × 18.9 / CN / *RCAHM-W* (1925)
2 GORS FAWR / (1) / SN 134294 / 22.3 / Gr, O / Grimes (1963) 145; / Bushell (1911) 318; *RCAHM-W* (1925) no. 731; Thom (1967) W9/2
3 LETTERSTON III / (4) / SM 937294 / *c*.12.2 / Em, Pt / Exc. 1961, urn. Savory (1964); Lynch (1972) 75
4 PENNYBRIDGE / (4) / SM 953001 / *c*.9.1 / ? / Grimes (1963) 146
5 WAUN MAWN / (4) / SN 084341 / 45.7? / Pl? / ibid 149; *RCAHM-W* (1925) no. 768

RADNORSHIRE (Powys)

1 BANC DU / (5) / SO 042792 / 12.8? / ? / Grimes (1963) 128
2 FOUR STONES / (1) / SO 245607 / 5.2 / 4P, Cm / *Arch Camb* 6 (1911) 103; *RCAHM-W* (1913) no. 615b; Thom (1967) W8/3
3 GELLI HILL / (3) / SO 095583 / 21.3 × 19.5 / O? / Grimes (1963) 130
4 RHOS-MAEN / (4) / SO 143579 / 24.1 / ? / ibid 131; Thom, (1967) W8/2
5 SIX STONES / (3) / SO 163516 / *c*.24.1 / Pl / Grimes (1963) 133

The Diameters of Stone Circles

Table 14. The Diameter of Stone Circles in the British Isles

Country	Number of Circles	Diameters Known	Not	Diameters in Feet																	Known Burials	%
				−9	10+	20+	30+	40+	50+	60+	70+	80+	90+	100	110	120	130	140	150+	200+		
England	243	180	63	1	10	20	21	14	18	16	14	18	5	13	8	2	4	3	5	8	59	33
Wales	49	41	8	0	2	3	3	5	4	10	8	3	2	0	0	0	0	0	1	0	4	10
Brittany	3	3	0	0	0	0	0	0	0	0	0	0	0	0	0	0	0	0	1	2	0	0
Ulster	128	76	52	0	7	13	18	16	8	7	3	1	0	0	1	1	1	0	0	0	22	30
Eire	133	74	59	9	14	13	14	4	4	1	4	0	2	3	0	0	0	0	4	2	15	20
Scotland	407	286	121	1	30	46	22	31	31	33	29	17	14	12	4	4	3	0	5	4	115	40
TOTALS	963	660	303	11	63	95	78	70	65	67	58	39	23	28	13	7	8	3	16	16	215	33

Table 15. Burials in Stone Circles whose Diameters are Known

Country	Number			−9	10+	20+	30+	40+	50+	60+	70+	80+	90+	100	110	120	130	140	150+	200+	Known Burials	%
England	59			0	7	11	11	6	8	5	2	4	2	2	1	0	0	0	0	0	59	33
Wales	4			0	0	0	0	0	0	1	2	1	0	0	0	0	0	0	0	0	4	10
Brittany	0			0	0	0	0	0	0	0	0	0	0	0	0	0	0	0	0	0	0	0
Ulster	22			0	0	1	4	3	4	4	3	0	0	0	1	1	1	0	0	0	22	30
Eire	15			1	1	0	6	0	3	0	1	0	0	1	0	0	0	0	1	1	15	20
Scotland	115			0	12	9	8	12	15	19	19	6	5	8	1	0	0	0	0	1	115	40
TOTALS	215			1	20	21	29	21	30	29	27	11	7	11	3	1	1	0	1	2	215	33

Country	Median $\frac{1}{2}(n+1)$	Average of All			Average of Burial Circles			Average of Open Circles		
		No.	Total	Average Diameter	No.	Total	Average Diameter	No.	Total	Average Diameter
Eire	9.8	74	1027	13.9	15	285	19.0	59	742	12.6
England	19.8	180	3959	22.0	59	855	14.5	121	3140	25.7
Scotland	16.8	286	5150	18.0	115	2089	18.2	171	3060	17.9
Ulster	11.9	76	1024	13.5	22	421	19.1	54	604	11.2
Wales	19.8	41	764	18.6	4	91	22.9	37	672	18.2
TOTALS		657	11924	18.2	215	3741	17.4	442	8182	18.5

Table 16. *Stone Circles. Known Diameters for Countries in the British Isles.*
(Metres.)

APPENDIX THREE

The Significance of the Number of Stones in the Stone Circles of the British Isles

Because of collapse and destruction it is uncertain how many stones there were in most megalithic rings. Nevertheless, reasonable estimates can be made for over a third of the sites and these are given below in Table 17.

There are some clear preferences. Peaks around 4, 6, 12, 16, 20 and 30 suggest that there was a liking for a simple arithmetical elegance as the successive rings at the Sanctuary in Wiltshire indicate. Ten per cent of all the circles are of twelve stones, but while this number accounts for 11 per cent of the English rings, over 19 per cent of the sites in that country had over thirty-six stones. In Scotland there are many Four-Posters, six-stone and eight-stone circles. In Eire, particularly in Cork and Kerry, there are several five-stone and seven-stone smaller rings. Such preferences, as has been noticed, are even more apparent when applied to specific regions like Cornwall or Inverness.

But there is little support for Olson's thesis (Baity, 1973, 445) that there was a predilection towards twenty-nine and thirty; twelve and thirteen; eighteen and nineteen, because these numbers would be useful calendrically in determining: days in a month; months in a year; or years in the moon's great cycle. Even lumping together as one group all the rings with more than thirty-six stones there are thirty-four numbers listed in Table 17. Olson's six figures, if they represent more than a random choice, should be significantly more than $\frac{6}{34}$ or 17 per cent of the total but, in fact, they are $\frac{63}{316}$ or 20 per cent, only slightly above a straightforward arithmetical average and markedly less than the proportion of 4-, 5-, 6-, 7-, 8- and 9-stone rings (42 per cent), numbers which possess no apparent astronomical potential.

From Table 17 it can be seen that while a claim could be made that some circles had stone numbers related to calendrical months, only three sites had stones connected with the much more obvious number of twenty-eight nights in a lunar month. Nor were circle-builders very interested in recording the eighteen/nineteen year metonic cycle or the other theoretical megalithic calendar of sixteen months of twenty-two to four days each (Thom, 1967, 109). Moreover, of the putative 'months in a year' circles, there are far fewer of the necessary thirteen-stone rings which would accurately account for the thirteen annual lunar months of four weeks each, than of twelve-stone circles in which annual computations would be in error after the first forty-eight weeks. All in all, the quanta are more feasibly related to local custom than to astronomical calculation. It is observable that there was some preference for an even number of stones. There are half as many again (170) of these as there are of odd numbers (112), perhaps because symmetry was easily achieved by pairing stones opposite each other on the circumference of a ring. This tendency is even more pronounced when it is realized that many of the five-stone, eleven- and thirteen-stone circles are actually four-, ten- and twelve-stone rings with an extra recumbent stone. Thus, from this preliminary study it may be stated that the rings contain evidence of elementary numeracy with a partiality for mathematical elegance but show little sign of having been numerically designed as any form of astronomical computer or record.

Table 17. Estimates of the Numbers of Stones in the Stone Circles of the British Isles

	Numbers of Stones																																		Totals
	4	5	6	7	8	9	10	11	12	13	14	15	16	17	18	19	20	21	22	23	24	25	26	27	28	29	30	31	32	33	34	35	36	36+	
England	2	0	1	2	4	5	2	4	9	1	3	0	3	0	0	1	5	0	3	0	0	0	2	1	2	4	5	1	1	2	1	0	1	15	80
Scotland	25	0	19	3	16	12	12	10	19	10	1	4	3	2	0	1	3	0	0	0	1	0	0	0	1	0	0	2	0	0	0	0	0	5	149
Wales	1	1	0	0	1	0	0	3	0	0	2	1	0	1	2	1	0	0	0	0	1	0	0	1	0	0	0	1	0	0	0	0	0	2	18
Eire	1	12	3	9	1	1	1	4	3	3	1	1	2	2	1	0	0	0	1	0	0	0	0	0	0	0	1	0	0	0	0	1	1	2	51
Ulster	0	0	1	0	1	2	0	0	1	0	0	0	0	0	3	0	1	0	0	0	0	0	0	0	0	0	0	0	0	0	0	0	0	9	18
TOTALS	29	13	24	14	23	20	15	21	32	14	7	6	8	8	3	4	8	0	4	0	2	0	2	2	3	4	6	4	1	2	1	1	2	33	316

Bibliography

The Bibliography contains all the major references to the excavations and field-studies of stone circles in the British Isles which are accessible to the general reader. These include old but invaluable works such as William Stukeley's *Stonehenge . . .* (1740), *Abury . . .* (1743), and Pennant's *Tour of Scotland* (1774).

Not included, however, but no less necessary to the serious student, are the unpublished plans of stone circles by the Rev. W. C. Lukis in the library of the Society of Antiquaries, London, or similar plans by Sir Henry Dryden in the collections of the Society of Antiquaries of Scotland, the Royal Irish Academy, Dublin, and the Central Library, Northampton. Several other local archaeological societies possess unpublished plans and notes by nineteenth-century fieldworkers.

Perhaps the greatest omission from the Bibliography is John Aubrey's MS, *Monumenta Britannica* (Bodleian MS, Top. Gen. c. 24–25), of *c.* 1665–95, in which that enthusiastic fieldworker described the condition of Stonehenge and many other stone circles in the early seventeenth century. There are many references to the *Monumenta* in the present text, and readers interested will find a section of the first part of the MS, the *Templa Druidum*, dealing with Stonehenge, published in *WAM* 16, 1876. But the whole is so disorganized that it has caused despair in better palaeographers and scholars than this writer, and in no sense can it be regarded as easily accessible. It is to be hoped that one day it will be sifted, arranged and edited in full.

ABBREVIATIONS USED IN THE BIBLIOGRAPHY

Am. Sci.	*American Scientist*
Ann. Exc. Rep.	*Annual Excavation Report* (H.M.S.O.)
Ant.	*Antiquity*
Ant. J.	*Antiquaries Journal*
Arch.	*Archaeologia*
Arch. Ael.	*Archaeologia Aeliana*
Arch. Camb.	*Archaeologia Cambrensis*
Arch. J.	*Archaeological Journal*
BBCS	*Bulletin of the Board of Celtic Studies*
CA	*Cornish Archaeology*
CBA	Council for British Archaeology
Curr. Anth.	*Current Anthropology*
Curr. Arch.	*Current Archaeology*
DAJ	*Derbyshire Archaeological Journal*
D & E	*Discovery and Excavation, Scotland*

ECA (1970)	*Early Celtic Art* (Arts Council)
GAJ	*Glasgow Archaeological Journal*
JBAA	*Journal of the British Archaeological Association*
JB Astron. Ass.	*Journal of the British Astronomical Association*
JCHAS	*Journal of the Cork Historical and Archaeological Society*
JDANHAS	*Journal of the Derbyshire Archaeological and Natural History Society*
JGAHS	*Journal of the Galway Archaeological and Historical Society*
JKAHS	*Journal of the Kerry Archaeological and Historical Society*
JHA	*Journal for the History of Astronomy*
JRIC	*Journal of the Royal Institution of Cornwall*
JRAI	*Journal of the Royal Anthropological Institute*
JRSAI	*Journal of the Royal Society of Antiquaries of Ireland*
JRSS	*Journal of the Royal Statistical Society*
Math. Gaz.	*Mathematical Gazette*
NCH	*Northumberland County History*
NMAJ	*North Munster Archaeological Journal*
NMI	National Monuments of Ireland
NSA	*New Statistical Account of Scotland* (followed by County)
ONB	*Object Name Book* (O.S. Edinburgh)
Oxon.	*Oxonensia*
PBNHPS	*Proceedings of the Belfast Natural History and Philosophical Society*
PDAS	*Proceedings of the Devon Archaeological Society*
PDAES	*Proceedings of the Devon Archaeological Exploration Society*
PDNHAS	*Proceedings of the Dorset Natural History & Archaeological Society*
PRIA	*Proceedings of the Royal Irish Academy*
PPS	*Proceedings of the Prehistoric Society*
PRS	*Proceedings of the Royal Society*
PSAL	*Proceedings of the Society of Antiquaries of London*
PSAN	*Proceedings of the Society of Antiquaries of Newcastle-upon-Tyne*
PSANHS	*Proceedings of the Somerset Archaeological and Natural History Society*
PSAS	*Proceedings of the Society of Antiquaries of Scotland*
PUBSS	*Proceedings of the University of Bristol Spelaeological Society*
PWCFC	*Proceedings of the West Cornwall Field Club*
RCAHM-E	Royal Commission for Ancient and Historical Monuments— England
RCAHM-S	Royal Commission for Ancient and Historical Monuments— Scotland
RCAHM-W	Royal Commission for Ancient and Historical Monuments—Wales
SAF	*Scottish Archaeological Forum*
Sci	*Science*
TAASFC	*Transactions of the Anglesey Antiquarian Society Field Club*
TAMS	*Transactions of the Ancient Monuments Society*
TBFC	*Transactions of the Berwick Field Club*
TCHS	*Transactions of the Cardiff Naturalists' Society*
TCWAAS	*Transactions of the Cumberland and Westmorland Antiquarian and Archaeological Society*
TDA	*Transactions of the Devon Association*
TDGNHAS	*Transactions of the Dumfries and Galloway Natural History and Antiquarian Society*

TGAS	*Transactions of the Glasgow Archaeological Society*
THAS	*Transactions of the Hunter Archaeological Society*
TISS	*Transactions of the Inverness Scientific Society*
TLCAS	*Transactions of the Lancashire and Cheshire Antiquarian Society*
TPPSNS	*Transactions and Proceedings of the Perthshire Society of Natural Science*
TSANHS	*Transactions of the Shropshire Archaeological and Natural History Society*
UJA	*Ulster Journal of Archaeology*
VA	*Vistas in Astronomy*
VCH	*Victoria County History*
WAM	*Wiltshire Archaeological Magazine*
YAJ	*Yorkshire Archaeological Journal*

Alcock, L. (1950). The Henge Monument of the Bull Ring, Dove Holes, Derbyshire, *PPS* 16, 81–6.

—(1972). '*By South Cadbury is that Camelot . . .' The Excavation of Cadbury Castle, 1966–70*. London.

Aldridge, R. B. (1970). Megalithic and Other Sites in Counties Mayo and Galway, *JGAHS* 31, 1964–5, 11–15.

Allcroft, A. H. (1927). *The Circle and the Cross*. I. London.

Anderson, J. (1886). *Scotland in Pagan Times. The Bronze and Stone Ages*. Edinburgh.

Anderson, W. D. (1915). Some Recent Observations at the Keswick Stone Circle, *TCWAAS* 15, 98–112.

—(1923). Plough-Markings on Stones, *TCWAAS* 23, 109–12.

Andrew, W. J. (1907). The Prehistoric Stone Circles, *Memorials of Old Derbyshire* (ed. Cox). Derby. 70–88.

ApSimon, A. M. (1969). The Earlier Bronze Age in the North of Ireland, *UJA* 32, 28–72.

—& Greenfield, E. (1972). The Excavation of Bronze Age and Iron Age Settlements at Trevisker Round, St. Eval, Cornwall, *PPS* 38, 302–81.

Ashbee, P. (1960). *The Bronze Age Round Barrow in Britain*. London

—(1966). The Fussell's Lodge Long Barrow Excavations, 1957, *Arch* 100, 1–80.

—(1970). *The Earthen Long Barrow in Britain*. London.

—(1972). Field Archaeology; its Origins and Development, *Archaeology and the Landscape* (ed. Fowler). London. 38–74.

—& Cornwall, I. W. (1961). An Experiment in Field Archaeology, *Ant* 35, 129–34.

Atkinson, R. J. C. (1952). Four New 'Henge' Monuments in Scotland and Northumberland, *PSAS* 84, 57–66.

—(1960). *Stonehenge* (Pelican edition). London.

—(1961). Neolithic Engineering, *Ant* 35, 292–99.

—(1962). Fishermen and Farmers, *Prehistoric Peoples of Scotland* (ed. S. Piggott). London. 1–38.

—(1965). Wayland's Smithy, *Ant* 39, 126–33.

—(1966). Moonshine on Stonehenge, *Ant* 40, 212–16.

—(1968). Old Mortality: some aspects of Burial and Population in Neolithic Europe, *Studies in Ancient Europe* (eds. J. M. Coles & D. D. A. Simpson). Leicester. 83–93.

—(1972). Burial and Population in the British Bronze Age, *Prehistoric Man in Wales and the West* (eds. F. Lynch & C. Burgess). Bath. 107–16.

—(1974). Ancient Astronomy: Unwritten Evidence, *The Place of Astronomy in the Ancient World* (ed. F. R. Hodson). London. 123–31.

—(1975). Megalithic Astronomy—a Prehistorian's Comments. *JHA* 6, 42–52.

—, Piggott, C. & Sandars, N. (1951). *Excavations at Dorchester, Oxon*. I. Oxford.

Atkinson, W. G. (1922). Report on the Further Excavations Carried out at the 'Druid's Circles' on Birkrigg, *TCWAAS* 22, 346–52.

Bailloud, G. (1974). The First Agriculturalists: 4000–1800 BC, *France Before the Romans* (eds. S. Piggott, G. Daniel, & C. McBurney). London. 102–30.

Baity, E. C. (1973). Archaeoastronomy and Ethnoastronomy so far, *Curr Anth* 14, 389–449.

Barber, J. (1972). 'The Stone circles of Cork & Kerry: a study.' Unpublished dissertation, Cork University.

—(1973). The Orientation of the Recumbent Stone Circles of the SW. of Ireland, *JKAHS* 6, 26–39.

Bateman, T. (1848). *Vestiges of the Antiquities of Derbyshire.*

—(1861). *Ten Years Diggings in Celtic and Saxon Grave Hills in the Counties of Derbyshire, Staffordshire and Yorkshire from 1848 to 1858.* London.

Beattie, J. (1966). *Other Cultures: Aims, Methods and Achievements in Social Anthropology.* London.

Beckensall, S. (1974). *The Prehistoric Carved Rocks of Northumberland.* Newcastle.

Bennett, W. (1951). Report on Excavations near Burnley, *TLCAS* 52, 204–8.

Beveridge, E. (1911). *North Uist: Its Archaeology and Topography.* Edinburgh.

Blight, J. T. (1865). Destruction of a Cornish Stone Circle, *Gent's Mag*, 31–7.

Borlase, W. (1754). *The Antiquities of Cornwall.*

Borlase, W. C. (1897). *The Dolmens of Ireland.* 3 vols. London.

Borst, L. B. (1969). The Megalithic Plan Underlying Canterbury Cathedral, *Sci* 163, 567–70.

Bowen, E. G. (1970). Britain and the British Seas, *The Irish Sea Province in Archaeology and History* (ed. D. Moore). Cardiff. 13–28.

—(1971). A Menhir in Llandysiliogogo church, Cards., *Ant* 45, 213–5.

—& Gresham, C. A. (1967). *History of Merioneth.* I. Dolgelly.

Brailsford, J. W. (1938). The Bronze Age Stone Monuments of Dartmoor, *Ant* 12, 444–63.

Brewster, T. C. M. (1968). Kemp Howe, Yorkshire E.R., *Ann Exc Rep*, 13.

Browne, B. S. (1963). Neolithic Engineering, *Ant* 37, 140–4.

Bryce, J. (1862). An Account of Excavations within the Stone Circles of Arran, *PSAS* IV, 499–524

Bryce, T. H. (1910). The Sepulchral Remains, *The Book of Arran, I. Archaeology* (ed. J. A. Balfour). Glasgow. 113–24.

Bu'lock, J. D. (1961). The Bronze Age in the North-West, *TLCAS* 71, 1–42.

Bunch, B. & Fell, C. I. (1949). A Stone Axe Factory at Pike of Stickle, Great Langdale, Westmorland, *PPS* 15, 1–20.

Burgess, C. B. (1969). Chronology and Terminology in the British Bronze Age, *Ant J* 49, 22–9.

—(1974). The Bronze Age, *British Prehistory. A New Outline* (ed. C. Renfrew). London. 165–232.

Burl, H. A. W. (1969). Henges: Internal Features and Regional Groups, *Arch J* 126, 1–28.

—(1970). 'The Stone Circles of Great Britain and Ireland, I & II.' Unpublished dissertation. University of Leicester.

—(1971). Two 'Scottish' Stone Circles in Northumberland, *Arch Ael* 49, 37–51.

—(1972). Stone Circles and Ring-Cairns, *SAF* 4, 31–47.

—(1973). Dating the British Stone Circles, *Am Sci* 61.2, 167–74.

—(1974a). The Recumbent Stone Circles of North-East Scotland, *PSAS* 102, (1969–70) 56–81.

—(1974b). Torhousekie Stone Circle, Wigtownshire, *TDGNHAS* 49, 24–34.

—& Jones, N. (1972). The Excavation of the Three Kings Stone Circle, Northumberland, *Arch Ael* 50, 1–14.

Burleigh, R., Longworth, I. H. & Wainwright, G. J. (1972). Relative and Absolute Dating of four Late Neolithic Enclosures . . ., *PPS* 38, 389–407.

Burnard, R. (1906). Stone Circles, *VCH Devon* I, 356–60.

Bushell, W. D. (1911). Amongst the Prescelly Circles, *Arch Camb* 11, 287–333.

Calder, C. S. T. (1950). Report on the Excavation of a Neolithic Temple at Stanydale . . . Shetland, *PSAS* 84, 185–205.

Calkin, B. J. (1968). The Population of Neolithic and Bronze Age Dorset and the Bournemouth Area *PDNHAS* 90, 207–29.

Camden, W. (1965). *Britannia. Newly Translated into English*. London.

Case, H. (1961). Irish Neolithic Pottery: Distribution and Sequence *PPS* 27, 174–233.

(1963). Foreign Connections in the Irish Neolithic, *UJA* 26, 3–18.

—(1967). Were Beaker Folk the First Metallurgists in Ireland? *Palaeohistoria* 12, 141–77.

—(1969). Settlement-patterns in the North Irish Neolithic, *UJA* 32, 3–27.

—(1970). in: Neolithic Comments. *Ant* 44, 105–14.

—, Bayne, N., Steele, S., Avery, G. & Sutermeister, H. (1965). Excavations at City Farm, Hanborough, Oxon, *Oxon* 29–30, 1–98.

Catherall, P. D. (1972). Henges in Perspective. *Arch J* 128, 147–53.

Chadwick, N. (1970). *The Celts*. London.

Chart, D. A. (1940). (editor) *A Preliminary Survey of the Ancient Monuments of Northern Ireland*. H.M.S.O. Belfast.

Childe, V. G. (1934). Final Report on the Excavation of the Stone Circle at Old Keig, Aberdeenshire, *PSAS* 68, 372–93.

—(1940). *Prehistoric Communities of the British Isles*. London.

Chitty, L. F. (1926). The Hoar Stone or Marsh Pool Circle, *TSANHAS* 10, 247–53.

—(1963). The Clun-Clee Ridgeway, *Culture and Environment. Essays in Honour of Sir Cyril Fox* (eds. I. L. Foster & L. Alcock). 171–92.

Christie, P. M. (1967). A Barrow-cemetery of the Second Millennium BC in Wiltshire, England, *PPS* 33, 336–66.

Clarke, J. G. D. (1936). The Timber Monument at Arminghall and its Affinities, *PPS* 2, 1–51.

Clarke, D. L. (1970). *Beaker Pottery of Great Britain and Ireland*. 2 vols. Cambridge.

—(1973). Archaeology: the Loss of Innocence, *Ant* 47, 6–18.

Cles-Reden, S. V. (1961). *The Realm of the Great Goddess*. London.

Clifford, E. M. & Daniel, G. E. (1940). The Rodmarton and Avening Portholes, *PPS* 6, 133–65.

Clough, T. H. McK. (1968). The Beaker Period in Cumbria, *TCWAAS* 68, 1–21.

Coles, F. R. (1894). The 'Stone Circle' at Holywood, Dumfriess., *PSAS* 28, 84–90.

—(1895). The Stone Circles of the Stewartry of Kirkcudbright, *PSAS* 29, 301–16.

—(1900). Stone Circles in Kincardineshire (North) and part of Aberdeenshire, *PSAS* 34, 139–98.

—(1901). Stone Circles of the N.E. of Scotland. Inverurie district, *PSAS* 35, 187–248.

—(1902). ibid. Aberdeenshire, *PSAS* 36, 488–581.

—(1903). ibid. Auchterless and Forgue *PSAS* 37, 82–142.

—(1904). ibid. The Buchan district, *PSAS* 38, 256–305.

—(1905a). Report of the Excavation of Two Stone Circles in Kincardine. (1) in Garrol Wood, Durris, (2) in Glassel Wood, Banchory-Ternan, *PSAS* 39, 190–205.

—(1905b). Stone Circles in Aberdeenshire, *PSAS* 39, 206–18.

—(1906). Stone Circles, chiefly in Banffshire, *PSAS* 40, 164–206.

—(1907). ibid, (Banffshire & Moray), *PSAS* 41, 130–72.

—(1908). Stone Circles Surveyed in Perthshire. N.E. Section, *PSAS* 42, 95–162.

—(1909). ibid. S.E. District, *PSAS* 43, 93–130.

—(1910). ibid. Aberfeldy District, *PSAS* 44, 117–68.

—(1911). ibid. Principally Strathearn, *PSAS* 45, 46–116.

Coles, J. M. (1965). Bronze Age Metalwork in Dumfriess & Galloway, *TDGNHAS* 42, 61–98.

—(1968). A Neolithic God-Dolly from Somerset, England, *Ant* 42, 275–7.

—(1971a). Scottish Early Bronze Age Metalwork, *PSAS* 101, 1968–9, 1–110.

—(1971b). Dowris and the Late Bronze Age of Ireland, *JRSAI* 101, 164–5.

—(1973). *Archaeology by Experiment*. London.

—, Orme, B., Bishop, A. C. & Woolley, A. R. (1974). A Jade Axe from the Somerset Levels, *Ant* 48, 216–20

—& Simpson, D. D. A. (1968). editors. *Studies in Ancient Europe*. Leicester.

—& Taylor, J. (1971). The Wessex Culture: a Minimal View, *Ant* 45, 6–14.

Collingwood, R. G. (1933). An Introduction to the Prehistory of Cumberland, Westmorland and Lancashire North of the Sands, *TCWAAS* 33, 163–200.

Collingwood, W. G. (1910). An Exploration of the Circle on Banniside Moor, Coniston, *TCWAAS* 10, 342–53.

—(1923). An Inventory of the Ancient Monuments of Cumberland, *TCWAAS* 23, 206–76.

Collins, A. E. P. (1956). A Stone Circle on Castle Mahon mountain, Co. Down, *UJA* 19, 1–10.

—(1957). Excavations at the Giants Ring, Ballynahatty, *UJA* 20, 44–50.

—& Waterman, D. M. (1955). *Millin Bay: a Late Neolithic cairn in Co. Down*. Belfast.

Condon, J. P. (1916). Rude Stone Monuments of the Northern Portion of Cork County. Part I, *JRSAI* 46, 58–76; 136–62.

—(1917). ibid. Part II, *JRSAI* 47, 153–64.

—(1918). ibid. Part III, *JRSAI* 48, 121–39.

Corcoran, J. X. W. P. (1969). The Cotswold-Severn Group, 1, *Megalithic Enquiries in the West of Britain* (T. G. E. Powell, J. X. W. P. Corcoran, F. Lynch & J. G. Scott). Liverpool. 13–72.

Corney, W. J. (1967). A Real Stone Row on Exmoor, *Exmoor Review* 8, 48–9.

Coutts, H. (1970). *Ancient Monuments of Tayside*. Dundee.

Cowan, T. M. (1969). Megalithic Rings: their Design Construction, *Sci* 168, 321–25.

Crampton, P. (1967). *Stonehenge of the Kings*. London.

Craw, J. H. (1930). Excavations at Dunadd and at Other Sites on the Poltalloch Estates. Argyll. No. 2. Cist and Stone Circle, Temple Wood, Ri Cruin, *PSAS* 64, 130–1.

—(1931). Further Excavations on Cairns at Poltalloch, Argyll, *PSAS* 65, 269–80.

Crawford, O. G. S. (1920). Account of the Excavations at Hengwm, Merioneth, August and September, 1919, *Arch Camb*, 99–133.

—(1957). *The Eye Goddess*. London.

Crossing, W. (1965). *Guide to Dartmoor* (1912 edition). Newton Abbot.

Cummins, W. A. (1974). The Neolithic Stone Axe Trade in Britain, *Ant* 48, 201–5.

Cunliffe, B. (1974). The Iron Age, *British Prehistory. A New Outline* (ed. C. Renfrew). London. 233–57.

Cunnington, M. E. (1929). *Woodhenge*. Devizes.

—(1931). The 'Sanctuary' on Overton Hill, near Avebury, *WAM* 45, 300–35.

Daicoviciu, H. (1960). Le Temple Calendaire des Daces à Sarmizegetusa, *Dacia* 4, 231–54.

Dalrymple, C. E. (1884). Notes of the Excavation of the Stone Circle at Crichie, Aberdeenshire, *PSAS* 18, 319–25.

Daniel, G. E. (1950). *The Prehistoric Chamber Tombs of England and Wales*. Cambridge.

—(1962). The Megalith Builders. *Prehistoric Peoples of Scotland* (ed. S. Piggott). London. 39–72.

—(1966). Editorial. *Ant* 40, 169.

—(1967). *The Origins and Growth of Archaeology*. London.

—(1968). Editorial. *Ant* 42, 167–8.

—& O'Riordain, S. P. (1964). *New Grange*. London.

Davidson, C. J. & Seabrook, R. A. G. (1973). Stone Rings on SE. Dartmoor, *PDAS* 31, 22–44.

Davies, M. (1945). Types of Megalithic Monument of the Irish Sea and North Channel Coastlands, *Ant J* 25, 125–46.

Davies, O. (1936). Excavations at Dun Ruadh, Co. Tyrone, *PBNHPS* 1, 50–75.

—(1938). Excavations at Castledamph Stone Circle, Co. Tyrone, *JRSAI* 68, 106–12.

—(1939a). Stone Circles in Northern Ireland, *UJA* 2, 2–14.

—(1939b. Excavations at Clogherny Stone Circles, *UJA* 2, 36–43.

Dawkin, W. B. (1900). On the Exploration of Prehistoric Sepulchral Remains of the Bronze Age at Bleasdale, by S. Jackson Esq., *TLCAS* 18, 114–24.

de Laet, S. J. (1958). *The Low Countries*. London.

de Valera, R. (1951). A Group of Horned Cairns near Ballycastle, Co. Mayo, *JRSAI* 81, 161–97.

Dixon, J. A. & Fell, C. l. (1948). Some Bronze Age Burial Circles at Lacra, Near Kirksanton, *TCWAAS* 48, 1–22.

Dudley, D. (1967). Tregiffian, St. Buryan, Excavation, *Ann Exc Rep*, 7.

Duke, E. (1846). *The Druidical Temples of the County of Wiltshire*. Salisbury.

Dunning, G. C. (1943). A Stone Circle and Cairn on Mynydd Epynt, Brecknockshire, *Arch Camb* 97, 169–94.

Dymond, C. W. (1877). The Megalithic Antiquities at Stanton Drew, *JBAA* 33, 297–307.

—(1878). A Group of Cumbrian Megaliths, *JBAA* 34, 31–36.

—(1879). The Hurlers. Three Stone Circles near St. Cleer, Cornwall, *JBAA* 35, 297–307.

—(1881). A Group of Cumbrian Megaliths, *TCWAAS* V. 39.

—(1902). An Exploration at the Megalithic Circle called Sunken Kirk at Swinside in the Parish of Millom, Cumberland, *TCWAAS* 2, 53–63.

Dymond, D. P. (1966). Ritual Monuments at Rudston, East Yorkshire, England, *PPS* 32, 86–95.

Edwards, I. E. S. (1947). *The Pyramids of Egypt*, London.

Elgee, F. (1930). *Early Man in North-East Yorkshire*, Gloucester.

Ellice, E. (1860). Some Pieces of Charcoal dug up in a Stone Circle near Callernish in the Lewis, *PSAS* III, 202–3.

Eogan, G. (1964). The Excavations of a Stone Alignment and Circle at Cholwichtown, Lee Moor, Devonshire, England, *PPS* 30, 25–38.

—(1967). The Knowth (Co. Meath) Excavations, *Ant* 41, 302–4.

Evans, A. J. (1895). The Rollright Stones and their Folklore, *Folklore* 6, 5–51.

Evans, E. E. (1953). *Lyles Hill, a Late Neolithic Site in Co. Antrim*. Belfast.

—(1966). *A Guide to Prehistoric and Early Christian Ireland*. London.

Evans, J. (1872). *The Ancient Stone Implements, Weapons and Ornaments of Great Britain*. London.

Evans, J. G. (1971). Habitat Change on the calcareous soils of Britain; the impact of Neolithic Man, *Economy and Settlement in Neolithic and Early Bronze Age Britain* (ed. D. D. A. Simpson). Leicester. 27–73.

Evans-Pritchard, E. E. (1965). *Theories of Primitive Religion*. London.

Evens, E. D., Grinsell, L. V., Piggott, S. & Wallis, F. S. (1962). The Fourth Report of the Sub-Committee of the SW. Group of Museums and Art Galleries on the Petrological Identification of Stone Axes, *PPS* 28, 209–66.

Evens, E. D., Smith, I. F. & Wallis, F. S. (1972). The Petrological Identification of Stone Implements from South-Western England, Fifth Report, *PPS* 38, 235–75.

Fahy, E. M. (1959). A Recumbent Stone Circle at Drombeg, Co. Cork, *JCHAS* 64, 1–27.

—(1960). A Hut and Cooking-Places at Drombeg, Co. Cork, *JCHAS* 65, 1–17.

—(1961). A Stone Circle, Hut and Dolmen at Bohonagh, Co. Cork, *JCHAS* 66, 93–104.

—(1962). A Recumbent Stone Circle at Reanascreena South, Co. Cork, *JCHAS* 67, 59–69.

Feachem, R. (1965). *The North Britons. The Prehistory of a Border People*. London.

Feather, S. W. & Manby, T. G. (1970). Prehistoric Chambered Tombs of the Pennines, *YAJ* 42, 396–7.

Fell, C. I. (1950). The Beaker period in Cumberland, Westmorland and Lancashire North of the Sands, *The Early Cultures of North-West Europe*. (eds. C. Fox & B. Dickins) Cambridge. 43–50.

—(1964a). Gamelands Stone Circle, *TCWAAS* 64, 408.

—(1964b). The Cumbrian Type of Polished Axe and its Distribution in Britain, *PPS* 30, 39–55.

—(1964c). Some Cairns in High Furness, *TCWAAS* 64, 1–5.

—(1967). Two Enlarged Food-vessels from How Hill, Thursby, *TCWAAS* 67, 17–25.

Ferguson, R. S. (1895). On a Tumulus at Old Parks, Kirkoswald, *TCWAAS* XIII, 389–99.

—(1906). Stone Circles, *VCH Cumberland* I, 245–49.

Fergusson, J. (1872). *Rude Stone Monuments in all Countries*. London.

Firth, R. (1961). *Elements of Social Organisation*. London.

Fleming, A. (1969). The Myth of the Mother Goddess, *World Archaeology* 1, 247–61.

—(1971a). Bronze Age Agriculture on the Marginal Lands of NE. Yorkshire,

Agricultural History Review 19.1, 1–24.

—(1971b). Territorial Patterns in Bronze Age Wessex, *PPS* 37, 138–66.

—(1972). Vision and Design. *Man* 7, 57–73.

—(1973a). Tombs for the Living, *Man* 8, 177–93.

—(1973b). Models for the Development of the Wessex Culture, *The Explanation of Culture Change. Models in Prehistory* (ed. C. Renfrew). London. 571–85.

—& Collis, J. (1973). A Late Bronze Age Reave System near Cholwichtown, Dartmoor, *PDAS* 31, 1–21.

Fletcher, W. (1957). Grey Croft Stone Circle, Seascale, Cumberland *TCWAAS* 57, 1–8.

Foster, I. L. & Alcock, L. (1963). editors *Culture & Environment. Essays in Honour of Sir Cyril Fox*. London.

Fowler, P. J. and Evans, J. G. (1967). Plough-marks, Lynchets and Early Fields, *Ant* 41, 289–301.

Fox, A. (1948). A Broad Down (Farway) Necropolis and the Wessex Culture in Devon, *PDAES* 4.1, 1–9.

—(1964). *South-West England*. London.

—& Britton, D. (1969). A Continental Palstave from the Ancient Field-system on Horridge Common, Dartmoor, England, *PPS* 35, 220–28.

Fox, C. (1933). *The Personality of Britain* (2nd edition). Cardiff.

—(1959). *Life and Death in the Bronze Age*. London.

Frazer, J. G. (1919). *Balder the Beautiful*, I. London.

—(1920). *Spirits of the Corn and Wild*. London.

—(1922). *The Golden Bough* (Abridged Version). London.

Freeman, P. R. (1976). A Bayesian Analysis of the Megalithic Yard, *JRSS* 139, Pt. 1.

Garden, J. (1766). A Copy of a Letter from the Rev. James Garden . . . to John Aubrey Esq, June 15, 1692, *Arch* I, 336–43.

Gelderd, C. (1912). Report on the Excavations carried out at the 'Druids Circle', on Birkrigg in the Parish of Urswick, September, 1911, *TCWAAS* 12, 262–74.

Gelling, P. & Davidson, H. E. (1969). *The Chariot of the Sun*. London.

Gilbert, M. (1962). *Pierres Megalithiques dans le Maine et Cromlechs en France*. Guernsey.

Gimbutas, M. (1953). Battle-axe or Cult Axe? *Man* 73, 51–4.

—(1974). *The Gods and Goddesses of Old Europe. 7000–3500 B.C.* London.

Giot, P. R. (1960). *Brittany*. London.

—(1971). The Impact of Radio-Carbon Dating on the Establishment of the Prehistoric Chronology of Brittany, *PPS* 37, 208–17.

Glasbergen, W. (1954). Barrow Excavations in the Eight Beatitudes, *Palaeohistoria* 2, 1–134; 3, 1–204.

Glentworth, R. & Muir, J. W. (1963). *The Soils of the Country around Aberdeen, Inverurie and Fraserburgh*. Edinburgh.

Glob, P. V. (1974). *The Mound People*. London.

Gogan, L. S. (1931). A Small Stone Circle at Mushera Beg, Cork, *JCHAS* 36, 9–19.

Graham, A. (1957). Cairnfields in Scotland, *PSAS* 90, 7–23.

Graves, R. (1961). *The White Goddess*. London.

Gray, M. (1973). Devil's Quoits, Stanton Harcourt, Oxon, *Ann Exc Rep*, 28.

—(1975). The Devil's Quoits, Stanton Harcourt, Oxon, *Oxon* 39, 96–7.

Gray, St. G. H. (1903). On the Excavations at Arbor Low, 1901–2, *Arch* 58, 461–98.

—(1907). The Stone Circle at Withypool Hill, Exmoor, *PSANHS* 52, 42–50.

—(1908). On the Stone Circles of East Cornwall, *Arch* 61, 1–60.

—(1929). The Porlock Stone Circle, Exmoor, *PSANHS* 74, 71–7.

—(1931). Rude Stone Monuments of Exmoor. Part III, *PSANHS* 77, 78–82.

—(1935). The Avebury Excavations, 1908–22, *Arch* 84, 99–162.

—(1950). Porlock Stone Circle. A note, *Arch J* 107, 87.

Green, C. P. (1973). Pleistocene River Gravels and the Stonehenge problem, *Nature* 243, 214.

Gresham, C. A. (1972). Burials in Megalithic Chambered Tombs, *Prehistoric Man in Wales and the West* (eds. F. Lynch & C. Burgess). 65–6.

Griffiths, W. E. (1960). The Excavation of Stone Circles near Penmaenmawr, North Wales, *PPS* 36, 305–18.

Grimes, W. F. (1938). Excavations at Meini Gwyr, Carmarthen, *PPS* 4, 324–5.

—(1944). Excavations at Stanton Harcourt, 1940, *Oxon* 8–9, 19–63.

—(1963). The Stone Circles and Related Monuments of Wales, *Culture and Environment. Essays in Honour of Sir Cyril Fox* (eds. I. Foster & L. Alcock). London. 93–152.

Grinsell, L. V. (1936). *The Ancient Burial-Mounds of England*. London.

—(1956). *Stanton Drew stone circles, Somerset*. London.

—(1958). *The Archaeology of Wessex*. London.

—(1959). *Dorset Barrows*. Dorchester.

—(1970). *The Archaeology of Exmoor*. Newton Abbot.

—(1971). Somerset Barrows, II. North and East *PSANHS* 115, 44–137.

Grossman, N. (1970). Megalithic Rings, *Sci* 169, 1228–9.

Gunn, G. (1915). The Standing Stones of Caithness, *TISS* 7, 337–60.

Hadingham, E. (1974). *Ancient Carvings in Britain: A Mystery*. London.

Harbison, P. (1969). The Relative Chronology of Irish Early Bronze Age Pottery, *JRSAI* 99, 63–82.

Harding, D. W. (1974). *The Iron Age in Lowland Britain*. London.

Hartnett, P. J. (1957). Excavation of a Passage-grave at Fourknocks, Co. Meath, *PRIA* 58C, 197–277.

Harvey, J. H. (1948). A Note on Long Meg, Salkeld, *Arch J* 105 (addendum).

Hawkes, C. F. C. (1974). Double Axe Testimonies, *Ant* 48, 206–11.

—& J. (1943). *Prehistoric Britain* (Pelican edition).

Hawkes, J. (1973). *A Guide to the Prehistoric and Roman Monuments in England and Wales*. London.

Hawkins, G. S. (1965). Callanish: a Scottish Stonehenge, *Sci* 147, 127–30.

—(1966a). (in collaboration with White J. B.). *Stonehenge Decoded*. London.

—(1966b). *Astro-Archaeology*. Cambridge, Mass.

Hawley, W. (1925). Report on the Excavations at Stonehenge during the Season of 1923, *Ant J* 5, 21–50.

Heathcote, J. P. (1939). Excavations at Doll Tor Stone Circle, *DAJ* 13, 116.

Heggie, D. C. (1972). Megalithic Lunar Observatories: an Astronomer's View, *Ant* 46, 43–8.

Hencken, H. O'N. (1932). *The Archaeology of Cornwall and Scilly*. London.

Henshall, A. S. (1963). *The Chambered Tombs of Scotland* I. Edinburgh.

—(1972). *The Chambered Tombs of Scotland* II. Edinburgh.

—& Stewart, M. E. C. (1954–6). Excavations at Clach na Tiompan, West Glen Almond, Perthshire, *PSAS* 88, 112–24.

Herity, M. (1970. The Prehistoric Peoples of Kerry, *JKAHS* 3, 5–14.

Hicks, R. E. (1975). Some Henges and Hengiform Earthworks in Ireland, PhD. diss. University of Pennsylvania.

Hicks, S. P. (1972). The Impact of Man on the East Moor of Derbyshire from Mesolithic Times, *Arch J* 129, 1–21.

Hoare, Sir R. C. (1812). *The Ancient History of South Wiltshire*. London.

Hodgson, K. S. (1952). Further Excavations at Broomrigg near Ainstable, *TCWAAS* 52, 1–8.

Hole, C. (1945). *Witchcraft in England*. London.

Hutchinson, G. E. (1972). Long Meg Reconsidered, I & II, *Am Sci* 60, 24–31; 210-19.

Hyslop, J. & Hyslop, R. (1912). *Langholm As It Was*. Langholm.

Innes, C. (1860). Notice of the Stone Circle of Callernish in the Lewis, and of a Chamber Tomb under the Circle, Recently Excavated, *PSAS* III, 110–12.

Ivimy, J. (1974). *The Sphinx and the Megaliths*. London.

Jackson, J. S. (1968). Bronze Age Copper Mines on Mount Gabriel, West County Cork, Ireland, *Archaeologia Austriaca* 43, 92–114.

James, E. O. (1957). *Prehistoric Religion. A Study in Prehistoric Archaeology*. London.

Jessen, J. & Helbaek, H. (1944). *Cereals in Great Britain and Ireland in Prehistoric and Early Historic Times*. London.

Jobey, G. (1968). Excavation of Cairns at Chatton Sandyford, Northumberland, *Arch Ael* 46, 5–50.

Jones, S. J. (1938). The Excavation of Gorsey Bigbury, *PUBBS* 5, 3–56.

Kavanagh, R. M. (1973). The Encrusted Urn in Ireland, *PRIA* 73 C, 507–617.

Keen, L. & Radley, J. (1971). Report on the Petrological Identification of Stone Axes from Yorkshire. *PPS* 37, 16–37.

Keillar, I. (1972). Edinkillie, Stone Circle, Moray, *D & E*, 30.

Keiller, A. (1934). *Megalithic Monuments of NE. Scotland*. Morven Institute, London.

—& Piggott, S. (1936). The West Kennet Avenue, Avebury. Excavations 1934–5, *Ant* 10, 417–27.

Kellaway, G. A. (1971). Glaciation and the Stones of Stonehenge, *Nature* 233, 30–5.

Kendall, D. G. (1971). A. Thom: Megalithic Lunar Observatories. A Review, *Ant* 45, 310–3.

—(1974). Hunting Quanta, *The Place of Astronomy in the Ancient World* (ed. F. R. Hodson). London. 231–66.

Kendrick, T. D. (1927). *The Druids. A Study in Keltic Prehistory*. London.

Kenworthy, J. B. (1972). Ring-cairns in NE. Scotland, *SAF* 4, 18–30.

Kilbride-Jones, H. E. (1934). Stone Circles: a New Theory of the Erection of the Monoliths, *PSAS* 68, 81–99.

—(1935). An Account of the Excavation of the Stone Circle at Loanhead of Daviot, and of the Standing Stones of Cullerlie, Echt . . . Aberdeenshire, *PSAS* 69, 168–222.

—(1950). The Excavation of a Composite Iron Age Monument with 'Henge' Features at Lugg, Co. Dublin, *PRIA* 53C, 311–32.

Killanin Lord & Duignan, M. V. (1962). *Shell Guide to Ireland*. London.

Kirk, W. (1953). Prehistoric Sites at the Sands of Forvie, Aberdeenshire, *Aberdeen Univ. Review* 35, 150–71.

Klindt-Jensen, O. (1957). *Denmark before the Vikings*. London.

Kühn, H. (1966). *The Rock-Pictures of Europe*. London.

LaFarge, O. (1956). *A Pictorial History of the American Indian*. London.

Lanting, J. N. & Van Der Waals, J. D. (1972). British Beakers as seen from the Continent, *Helinium* 12, 20–46.

Leask, H. G. (1945). Stone Circle, Castleruddery, Co. Wicklow, *JRSAI* 75, 266–7.

Leeds, R. T. (1939). Early Man, II, Mesolithic–Neolithic Age, *VCH Oxon* I, 238–41.

Leisner, G. & V. (1943). *Die Megalithgräber der Iberischen Halbinsel. Der Suden*. Berlin.

—(1956). *Die Megalithgräber der Iberischen Halbinsel. Der Western*. Berlin.

Le Roux, C-T. (1971). A Stone Axe Factory in Brittany, *Ant* 45, 283–8.

Le Rouzic, Z. (1930). *Les Cromlechs de Er Lannic*. Vannes.

Lethbridge, T. C. (1973). *The Legend of the Sons of God*. London.

Lewis, A. L. (1882). Notes on Two Stone Circles in Shropshire, *JRAI* 11, 3–7.

—(1883). On the Relationship of Stone Circles to Outlying Stones or Tumuli or Neighbouring Hills, with some Inferences Therefrom, *JRAI* 12, 176–91.

—(1888). Stone Circles near Aberdeen, *JRAI* 17, 44–57.

—(1896). Prehistoric Remains in Cornwall. Part 1. East Cornwall, *JRAI* 25, 2–16.

—(1898). Rude Stone Monuments on Bodmin Moor, *JRIC* 13, 107–13.

—(1899). The Stone Circles of Cornwall and Scotland, *JRIC* 14, 378–83.

—(1903). Stone Circles in Derbyshire, *Man* 3, 133–6.

—(1905). Prehistoric Remains in Cornwall. Part 2. West Cornwall, *JRAI* 35, 427–34.

—(1909). Some Stone Circles in Ireland, *JRAI* 39, 517–29.

Lewis, G. (1966). Some Radiocarbon Dates for the Peak District, *JDANHS* 86, 115–17.

Lissner, I. (1961). *Men, God and Magic*. London.

Lockyer, N. (1906a). Notes on some Cornish Circles, *Nature* 73, 366–8.

—(1906b). *Stonehenge and Other British Stone Monuments Astronomically Considered*. London.

Longworth, I. H. (1961). The Origins and Developments of the Primary Series in the Collared Urn Tradition in England and Wales, *PPS* 27, 263–306.

Love, R. (1876). The Four Stones, Beith, *PSAS* XI, 1874–6, 291–2.

Lukis, W. C. & Borlase, W. C. (1885). *Prehistoric Stone Monuments of the British Isles. I. Cornwall*. London.

Lynch, F. (1967). Barclodiad y Gawres. Comparative Notes on the Decorated Stones, *Arch Camb* 116, 1–22.

—(1969). The Megalithic Tombs of North Wales, *Megalithic Enquiries in the West of Britain* (T. G. E. Powell, J. X. W. P. Corcoran, F. Lynch & J. G. Scott). Liverpool. 107–48.

—(1970). *Prehistoric Anglesey*. Llanfegni.

—(1972). Ring-cairns and Related Monuments in Wales, *SAF* 4, 61–80.

—(& Burgess, C. (1972). editors. *Prehistoric Man in Wales and the West*. Bath.

—, Waddell, J., Allen, D., & Grealey, S. (1974). Brenig Valley excavations, 1973. Interim Report, *Denbighshire Historical Transactions* 23, 1–56.

—& Allen, D. (1975) Brenig Valley Excavations, 1974. *Denbighshire Historical Transactions* 24, 1–25.

Macalister, R. A. S. (1917). Excavations at the Stone Circle of Masonbrook, Co. Galway, *PRIA* 33, 505.

—, Armstrong, E. C. R. & Praeger, R. L. (1913). On a Bronze Age Interment with Associated Standing-stone and Earthen Ring, near Naas, Co. Kildare, *PRIA* 30, 351–60.

McCormick, D. (1968). *Murder by Witchcraft*. London.

McKerrell, H. (1971). Some Aspects of the Accuracy of Carbon-14 dating, *SAF* 3, 73–84.

—(1972). On the Origins of British Faience Beads and some Aspects of the Wessex-Mycenae Relationship, *PPS* 38, 286–301.

MacKie, E. W. (1974). Archaeological Tests on Supposed Astronomical Sites in Scotland, *The Place of Astronomy in the Ancient World* (ed. F. R. Hodson). London. 169–94.

—(1975). *Excavations at the Cultoon Stone Circle, Islay, in 1974. First Interim Report*. Hunterian Museum. Glasgow.

Maitland, W. (1757). *History and Antiquities of Scotland* I.

Manning, P. (1902). Stray Notes on Oxfordshire Folk-lore, *Folklore* 13, 288–95.

Manby, T. G. (1965). The Distribution of Rough-cut 'Cumbrian' Axes, and Related Axes of Lake District Origin in Northern England, *TCWAAS* 65, 1–37.

—(1971). The Kilham Long Barrow Excavations, 1965–9, *Ant* 45, 50–3.

Maringer, J. (1960). *The Gods of Prehistoric Man*. London.

Mason, J. R. & Valentine, H. (1925). Studfold Gate Circle, *TCWAAS* 25, 269.

Masters, L. J. (1973). The Lochhill Long Cairn, *Ant* 47, 96–100.

May, A. McL. (1947). Burial-mound, Circles and Cairn, Gortcorbies, Co. London-derry, *JRSAI* 77, 5–22.

—(1953). Neolithic Habitation Site, Stone Circles and Alignments at Beaghmore, Co. Tyrone, *JRSAI* 83, 174–97.

Megaw, J. V. S. (1968). Problems and Non-problems in Palaeo-organology: a Musical Miscellany, *Studies in Ancient Europe* (eds. J. M. Coles & D. D. A. Simpson). Leicester. 333–58.

Michell, J. (1973). *The View over Atlantis*. London.

Miles, H. (1972). *Excavation of a Barrow group on Caerloggas Downs, Stenalees, near St Austell. An Interim Report*. Exeter University.

—& T. J. (1971). Excavations on Longstone Downs, St. Stephen-in-Brannel and St. Mewan, *CA* 10, 5–28.

Mitchell, M. E. C. & Young, A. (1939). Report on Excavations at Monzie, Perthshire, *PSAS* 73, 62–71.

Mogey, J. M. (1941). The 'Druid Stone', Ballintoy, Co. Antrim, *UJA* 4, 49–56.

Moore, C. N. & Cummins, W. A. (1974). Petrological Identification of Stone Implements from Derbyshire and Leicestershire, *PPS* 40, 59–78.

Moore, D. (1970). ed. *The Irish Sea Province in Archaeology and History*. Cardiff.

Moore, P. D. (1973). Influence of Prehistoric Cultures upon the Initiation and Spread of Blanket Bog in Upland Wales, *Nature* 241, 350–3.

Morgan, C. L. (1887). The Stones of Stanton Drew: their Source and Origin, *PSANHS* 33, 37–50.

Morris, R. W. B. (1967). The Cup-and-ring Marks and Similar Early Sculptures of South-West Scotland, *TAMS* 14, 77–117.

—(1969). ibid. Part 2. South Scotland except Kintyre, *TAMS* 16, 37–76.

—(1971). The Petroglyphs at Achnabreck, Argyll, *PSAS* 103, 33–56.

Morrison, A. (1968). Cinerary Urns and Pygmy Vessels in South-West Scotland, *TDGNHAS* 45, 80–140.

Murray, M. A. (1921). *The Witch-Cult in Western Europe*. Oxford.

Musson, C. R. (1971). A Study of Possible Building Forms at Durrington Walls, Woodhenge and the Sanctuary, *Durrington Walls: Excavations, 1966–8* (eds. G. J. Wainwright with I. H. Longworth). London. 363–77.

Myatt, L. J. (1973). Survey of an Unrecorded Stone Setting near Broubster, *Bulletin of the Caithness Field Club* I, 9-10.

Neugebauer, P. V. (1929). *Tafeln sür Astronomischen Chronologie*. Leipzig.
Newham, C. A. (1966). Stonehenge—a Neolithic 'Observatory', *Nature* 211, 456–68.
—(1972). *The Astronomical Significance of Stonehenge*. Leeds.
Newton, R. G. & Renfrew, C. (1970). British Faience Beads Reconsidered, *Ant* 44, 199–206.
North, O. H. & Spence, J. E. (1936). A Stone Circle at Summerhouse Hill, Yealand Conyers, *TCWAAS* 36, 69–70.
NSA Aberdeen (1845). *New Statistical Account of Scotland, XII. Aberdeenshire.*
NSA Angus (1843). *New Statistical Account of Scotland, XI. Angus.*
NSA Dumfries (1845). *New Statistical Account of Scotland, IV, Dumfriesshire.*

O'Kelly, C. (1969). Bryn Celli Ddu, Anglesey. A Reinterpretation, *Arch Camb* 118, 17–48.
—(1971). *Illustrated Guide to New Grange* (2nd edition). Wexford.
—(1973). Passage-grave Art in the Boyne Valley, *PPS* 39, 354–82.
O'Kelly, M. J. (1952). Excavation of a Cairn at Moneen, Co. Cork, *PRIA* 54C, 121–59.
O'Nuallain, S. (1971). The Stone Circles of Kerry, *JKAHS* 4, 5–27.
O'Riordain, S. P. (1939). Excavation of a Stone Circle and Cairn at Kealkil, Co. Cork, *JCHAS* 44, 46–9.
—(1950). Excavations of Some Earthworks on the Curragh, Co. Kildare, *PRIA* 53C, 249–77.
—(1951). Lough Gur Excavations. The Great Stone Circle (B) in Grange Townland, *PRIA* 54C, 37–74.
—(1954). Lough Gur Excavations. Neolithic and Bronze Age Houses on Knockadoon. *PRIA* 56c, 297–459.
—(1964). *Antiquities of the Irish Countryside*. London.
—& L'Eochaidhe, O. (1956). Trial Excavations at New Grange, *JRSAI* 86, 52–61.

Parker, C. A. & Collingwood, W. G. (1926). *The Gosforth District: its antiquities and places of interest*. Kendal.
Partridge, J. B. (1912). Cotswold Place-lore and Customs, *Folklore* 23.
Paterson, T. G. F., Gaffikin, W. & Davies, O. (1938). An Account of Co. Cavan, UJA 1, 142–51.
Patrick, J. (1974). Midwinter Sunrise at Newgrange, *Nature* 249, 517–19.
Peach, W. A. (1961). *Stonehenge: a New Theory*. Cardiff.
Peacock, D. P. S. (1969). Neolithic Pottery Production in Cornwall, *Ant* 43, 145–9.
Pearson, W. (1970). Commondale Stone Circle. *YAJ* 42, 1969, 240.
Peltenburg, E. G. (1974). Excavation of Culcharron Cairn, Benderloch, Argyll, *PSAS* 104, 1971–2, 63–70.
Pennant, T. (1774). *A Tour in Scotland* (3rd edition). Warrington.
Pennington, W. (1970). Vegetation History in the North-West of England; a Regional Synthesis, *Studies in the Vegetational History of the British Isles* (eds. D. Walker & R. G. West). Cambridge. 41–80.
Penny, A. & Wood, J. E. (1973). The Dorset Cursus Complex: a Neolithic Astronomical Observatory. *Arch J* 130, 44–76.

Péquart, M. and St.-J., and Le Rouzic, Z. (1927). *Corpus des Signes gravés des monuments Mégalithiques du Morbihan*. Paris.

Peterson, F. (1972). Traditions of Multiple Burial in Later Neolithic and Early Bronze Age England, *Arch J* 129, 22–55.

Piggott, S. (1940). Timber Circles: a Re-examination, *Arch J* 96, 193–222.

—(1948). The Excavations at Cairnpapple Hill, West Lothian, *PSAS* 82, 68–123.

—(1950). *William Stukeley*. Oxford.

—(1954). *Neolithic Cultures of the British Isles*. Cambridge.

—(1956). Excavations in Passage-graves and Ring-cairns of the Clava group, *PSAS* 88 1954–6, 173–207.

—(1962a). Traders and Metalworkers, *The Prehistoric Peoples of Scotland* (ed. S. Piggott). London. 73–104.

—(1962b). *The West Kennet Long Barrow Excavations, 1955–6*. London.

—(1965). *Ancient Europe*. Edinburgh.

—(1968). *The Druids*. London.

—(1973). The First Agricultural Communities, *VCH Wilts* I, 2, 284–332.

—& Piggott C. M. (1939). Stone and Earth Circles in Dorset, *Ant* 13, 138–58.

—& Powell T. G. E. (1949). The Excavation of Three Neolithic Chambered Tombs in Galloway, *PSAS* 83, 103–61.

—& Simpson, D. D. A. (1971). Excavation of a Stone Circle at Croft Moraig, Perthshire, Scotland, *PPS* 37, 1–15.

Pilcher, J. R. (1969). Archaeology, Palaeoecology and C-14 Dating of the Beaghmore Stone Circle Site, Co. Tyrone, *UJA* 32, 73–91.

Plint, R. G. (1962). Stone Axe Factory Sites in the Cumbrian Fells, *TCWAAS* 62, 1–26.

Powell, A. (1948). *John Aubrey and his Friends*. London.

—(1949). editor. '*Brief Lives*' *and Other Selected Writings by John Aubrey*. London.

Powell, T. G. E. (1941). Excavation of a Megalithic Tomb at Carrigalong, Co. Waterford, *JCHAS* 46, 55–62.

—(1958). *The Celts*. London.

—(1966). *Prehistoric Art*. London.

—(1969). The Neolithic in the West of Europe. *Megalithic Enquiries in the West of Britain* (T. G. E. Powell, J. X. W. P. Corcoran, F. Lynch and J. G. Scott) Liverpool. 247–72.

—(1973). Excavation of the Megalithic Chambered Cairn at Dyffryn Ardudwy, Merioneth, Wales, *Arch* 104, 1–49.

—, Corcoran J. X. W. P., Lynch F., & Scott J. G. (1969). *Megalithic Enquiries in the West of Britain*. Liverpool.

Radford, C. A. R. (1938). The Hurlers, Cornwall. Notes on Excavations, *PPS* 4, 319.

—(1952). Prehistoric Settlements on Dartmoor and the Cornish Moors, *PPS* 18, 55–84.

Radley, J. (1966a). A Bronze Age Ringwork on Totley Moor and other Bronze Age Ringworks in the Pennines, *Arch J* 123, 1–26.

—(1966b). Glebe Low, Great Longstone, *JDANHS* 86, 54–69.

—(1969a). The Origins of the Arbor Low monument, *DAJ* 88, 100–3.

—(1969b). A Stone Circle on Kirkmoor Beck Farm, Fylingdales, *YAJ* 42, 250–1.

Raistrick, A. (1929). The Bronze Age in West Yorkshire, *YAJ* 29, 354–65.

Ravenhill, T. H. (1932). *The Rollright Stones and the Men Who Erected Them*. Birmingham.

RCAHM-E (1936). Royal Commission on Ancient & Historical Monuments. England. *Westmorland Inventory*.

RCAHM-S (1911a). Royal Commission on Ancient & Historical Monuments. Scotland. *Caithness Inventory*.

—(1911b). ibid, *Sutherland Inventory*.

—(1912). ibid, *Galloway I. Wigtownshire Inventory*.

—(1914). ibid, *Galloway II, Kirkcudbright Inventory*.

—(1915). ibid, *Berwickshire Inventory*.

—(1920). ibid, *Dumfriesshire Inventory*.

—(1924). ibid, *East Lothian Inventory*.

—(1928). ibid, *Outer Hebrides Inventory*.

—(1929). ibid, *Midlothian and West Lothian Inventory*.

—(1933). ibid, *Fife, Kinross and Clackmannan Inventory*.

—(1946). ibid, *Orkney and Shetland Inventory*.

—(1956). ibid, *Roxburghshire Inventory*.

—(1967). ibid, *Peeblesshire Inventory*.

RCAHM-W (1913). Royal Commission on Ancient & Historical Monuments. Wales. *Radnorshire Inventory*.

—(1925). ibid, *Pembrokeshire Inventory*.

—(1937). ibid, *Anglesey Inventory*.

—(1956). ibid, *Caernarvonshire Inventory*.

Renfrew, C. (1973a). Wessex as a Social Question, *Ant* 47, 221–5.

—(1973b). *Before Civilisation*. London.

—(1973c). Social Organisation in Wessex, *The Explanation of Culture Change. Models in Prehistory* (ed. C. Renfrew). London. 539–58.

—(1974). *British Prehistory. A New Outline* (ed. C. Renfrew). London.

Riley D. N. (1966). An Early Bronze Age Cairn on Harland Edge, Beeley Moor, Derbyshire. *JDANHS* 86, 31–53.

Ritchie, J. (1918). Cupmarks on the Stone Circles and Standing Stones of Aberdeenshire and Part of Banffshire, *PSAS* 52, 86–121.

—(1920). The Stone Circle at Broomend of Crichie, *PSAS* 54, 154–71.

Ritchie, J. N. G. (1967). Balnabraid Cairn, Kintyre, Argyll, *TDGNHAS* 44, 81–98.

—(1971). Excavation of a Cairn at Strontoiller, Lorn, Argyll, *GAJ* 2, 1–7.

—(1973). Orkney. Stones of Stenness, *D & E*, 68.

—(1974a). Stones of Stennes, *D & E*, 79.

—(1974b). Excavation of the Stone Circle and Cairn at Balbirnie, Fife. *Arch J*, 131, 1–32.

—& A. (1972). *Edinburgh and South-East Scotland*. London.

—& MacLaren, A. (1972). Ring-cairns and Related Monuments in Scotland, *SAF* 4, 1–17.

Ritchie, P. R. (1968). The Stone Implement Trade in 3rd Millennium Scotland, *Studies in Ancient Europe*, (eds. J. M. Coles & D. D. A. Simpson). Leicester. 117–36.

Robertson-Mackay, M. E. (1964). Basingstoke (b) bell-barrow, Hants, *Ann Exc Rep* 7.

Roe, F. E. S. (1966). The Battle-axe Series in Britain, *PPS* 32, 199–245.

—(1967). The Battle-axes, Mace-heads and Axe-hammers from South-West Scotland, *TDGNHAS* 44, 57–80.

—(1968). Stone Mace-heads and the Latest Neolithic Cultures of the British Isles, in: (eds. Coles & Simpson). 145–72.

Ross, A. (1967). *Pagan Celtic Britain*. (1974 edition). London.

—(1968). Shafts, Pits, Wells—Sanctuaries of the Belgic Britons, *Studies in Ancient Europe* (eds. J. M. Coles & D. D. A. Simpson). Leicester. 255–85.

—(1972). *Everyday Life of the Pagan Celts*. London.

Roy, A. E., McGrail, N. & Carmichael, R. (1963). A New Survey of the Tormore Circles, *TGAS* 51.2, 59–67.

Russell, V. (1959). Parochial Check-lists of Antiquities. St. Just in Penwith, *PWCFC* 2.

—& Pool, P.A.S. (1964). Excavation of a Menhir at Try, Gulval, *CA* 3, 15–26.

Rynne, E. (1969). A Stone Alignment and a Stone Circle near Rearcross, Co. Tipperary, *NMAJ* 12, 90.

—& O'h'Eailidhe, P. (1966). A Group of Prehistoric Sites at Piperstown, Co. Dublin, *PRIA* 64C, 1965–6, 61–84.

St. Leger-Gordon, R. E. (1965). *The Witchcraft and Folklore of Dartmoor*. London.

Sale, J. L. (1965). *The Secrets of Stonehenge*. (Privately printed).

Savory, H. N. (1964). Excavations at a Third Round Barrow at Pen-Dre, Letterston, (Pembrokeshire), 1961), *BBCS* 20.3, 309–25.

—(1965). The Bronze Age, *Culture and Environment. Essays in Honour of Sir Cyril Fox* (eds. I. Foster & L. Alcock). London. 71–107.

—(1970). The Later Prehistoric Migrations Across the Irish Sea, *The Irish Sea Province in Archaeology and History* (ed. D. Moore) Cardiff. 38–49.

Scott, J. G. (1969). The Clyde Cairns of Scotland, *Megalithic Enquiries in the West of Britain* (T. G. E. Powell, J. X. W. P. Corcoran, F. Lynch and J. G. Scott). Liverpool. 175–222.

—(1974). Temple Wood, Kilmartin. Stone Circle, *D & E*, 76.

Scott, Sir L. (1951). The Colonization of Scotland in the 2nd millennium BC *PPS* 17, 16–82.

Scott-Elliot, J. (1967). Whitestanes Muir. (Sites 7 and 8), *TDGNHAS* 44, 117–21.

Seaby, W. A. (1949). The Archaeology of the Birmingham Plateau and its Margins, *Archaeological News Letter* 2, 6, 85–90.

Selkirk, A. (1972). Waulud's Bank, *Curr Arch* 30, 173–77.

Simmons, I. G. (1969). Environment and Early Man on Dartmoor, Devon, England, *PPS* 35, 203–19.

Simpson, D. D. A. (1965). Food-vessels in South-West Scotland, *TDGNHAS* 42, 25–50.

—(1968). Food Vessels: Associations and Chronology, *Studies in Ancient Europe* (eds. Coles & Simpson). Leicester. 197–211.

—(1969). Excavations at Kintraw, Argyll, *PSAS* 99, 1966–7, 54–9.

—(1971). ed. *Economy and Settlement in Neolithic and Early Bronze Age Britain and Europe*. Leicester.

—(1973). Radiocarbon Dates for Northton, Outer Hebrides, *Ant* 47, 61–4.

—& Thawley, J. E. (1972). Single-grave Art in Britain, *SAF* 4, 81–104.

Skeat, W. W. (1912). 'Snakestones' and Stone Thunderbolts as Subjects for Systematic Investigation, *Folklore* 13, 45–80.

Smith, A. G. (1970). The Influence of Mesolithic and Neolithic Man on British vegetation, *Studies in the Vegetational History of the British Isles* (eds. D. Walker & R. G. West). Cambridge, 81–96.

Smith, E. E. (1974). Flint Implements from Sidmouth, *PDAES* 3, 4, 167–71.

Smith, I. F. (1965). *Windmill Hill and Avebury. Excavations by Alexander Keiller, 1925–1939*. Oxford.

—(1967). Windmill Hill and its Implications, *Palaeohistoria* 12, 469–81.

—(1971). Causewayed Enclosures, *Economy and Settlement in Neolithic and Early Bronze Age Britain and Europe* (ed. D. D. A. Simpson). Leicester. 89–112.

Smith, J. (1895). *Prehistoric Man in Ayrshire.* London.

Somerville, H. B. (1909). Notes on a Stone Circle in Co. Cork, *JCHAS* 15, 105–8.

—(1913). Astronomical Indications in the Megalithic Monument at Callanish, *JB Astron Ass* 23, 83.

—(1923). Instances of Orientations in Prehistoric Monuments of the British Isles, *Arch* 73. 193–224.

—(1930). Five Stone Circles of West Cork, *JCHAS* 35, 70–85.

Stevens, F. (1938). *Stonehenge Today and Yesterday.* London.

Stewart, M. E. C. (1959). Strathtay in the 2nd Millennium BC, *PSAS* 92, 71–84.

—(1966a). Excavation of a Circle of Standing Stones at Sandy Road, Scone, Perthshire, *TPPSNS* 11, 7–23.

—(1966b). Excavation of a Setting of Standing Stones at Lundin Farm, near Aberfeldy, Perthshire, *PSAS* 98, 1964–6, 126–49.

—(1974). Moncrieffe Stone Circle, Perthshire, *D & E*, 86.

Stone, J. F. S. & Wallis, F. S. (1951). The Third Report . . . on the Petrological Determination of Stone Axes, *PPS* 17, 99–158.

Stout, H. B. (1961). Three Stone Circles at Gretigates Sides, Cumberland, *TCWAAS* 61, 1–6.

Stuart, J. (1856). *The Sculptured Stones of Scotland* I. Aberdeen.

—(1860). Note of Incised Marks on One of a Circle of Standing Stones in the Island of Lewis, *PSAS* III, 212–4.

—(1867). *The Sculptured Stones of Scotland* II. Edinburgh.

Stukeley, W. (1740). *Stonehenge. A Temple Restored to the British Druids.* London.

—(1743). *Abury, a Temple of the Druids, with Some Others, Described.* London.

Swanton, M. J. (1974). Finglesham Man: a Documentary Postscript, *Ant* 48, 313–15.

Swire, O. F. (1966). *The Outer Hebrides and their Legends.* London.

Switsur, V. R. (1973). The Radio-carbon Calendar Recalibrated, *Ant* 47, 131–17.

Tait. J. (1965). *Beakers from Northumberland.* Newcastle.

Taylor, M. W. (1886). Prehistoric Remains on Moordivock near Ullswater, *TCWAAS* VIII, 323–47.

Thom, A. (1955). A Statistical Examination of the Megalithic Sites in Britain, *JRSS* 118, 275–95.

—(1961a). The Geometry of Megalithic Man, *Math Gaz* 45, 83–93.

—(1961b). The Egg-shaped Standing Stone Rings of Britain, *Archs.int.Hist.Sci.* 14, 291.

—(1966). Megalithic Astronomy: Indications in Standing Stones, *VA* 7 1965, 1–58.

—(1967). *Megalithic Sites in Britain.* Oxford.

—(1969). The Lunar Observatories of Megalithic man, *VA* 11, 1–29.

—(1971). *Megalithic Lunar Observatories.* Oxford.

—& A. S. (1971). The Astronomical Significance of the Large Carnac Alignments, *JHA* 2, 147–60.

—&—(1972a). The Carnac Alignments, *JHA* 3, 11–26.

—&—(1972b). The Uses of the Alignments at Le Menec, Carnac, Brittany, *JHA* 3, 151–64.

—&—(1973). A Megalithic Lunar Observatory in Orkney: the Ring of Brogar and its Cairns, *JHA* 4, 111–23.

—A. S. & A. S. (1974). Stonehenge, *JHA* 5, 71–90.

—(1975). Stonehenge as a Possible Lunar Observatory, *JHA* 6, 19–30.

—(1975). Further Work on the Brogar Lunar Observatory. *JHA* 6, 100–14.

—, A. S., Merritt, R. L. & Merritt, A. L. (1973). The Astronomical Significance of the Crucuno Stone Rectangle, *Curr Anthr* 14, 450–4.

Thomas, A. C. (1969). The Bronze Age in the South-West, *Archaeological Review*, *CBA* XII & XIII, 3–12.

—& Wailes, B. (1967). Sperris Quoit; the Excavation of a New Penwith Chambered Tomb, *CA* 6, 9–23.

Thomas, N. (1960). *A Guide to Prehistoric England*. London.

—(1964). The Neolithic Causewayed Camp at Robin Hood's Ball, Shrewton, *WAM* 59, 1–27.

—(1972). An Early Bronze Age Stone Axe Mould from the Walleybourne below Longden Common, Shropshire, *Prehistoric Man in Wales and the West* (eds. F. Lynch & C. Burgess). Bath. 161–6.

Thompson, D. (1963). *Guide to Arbor Low*. H.M.S.O. London.

Thorpe, L. (1966). *Geoffrey of Monmouth. The History of the Kings of Britain. A Translation*. London.

Tierney, J. J. (1960). The Celtic Ethnography of Posidonius, *PRIA* 60C, 189–275.

Tratman, E. K. (1958). The Lost Stone Circles of North Somerset, *PUBSS* 8, 110–18.

—(1966). Investigations at Stanton Drew Stone Circles, Somerset, *PUBSS* 11.1, 1965–6, 40–2.

—(1967). The Priddy Circles, Mendip, Somerset, Henge Monuments. *PUBSS* 11.2, 1966–7, 97–125.

Tregelles, G. F. (1906). The Stone Circles, *VCH Cornwall* I, 379–406.

Trevor-Roper, H. R. (1969). *The European Witch-Craze of the 16th and 17th Centuries*. London.

Turner, J. (1965). A Contribution to the History of Forest Clearance, *PRS* B161, 343–54.

—(1970). Post-Neolithic Disturbance of British Vegetation, *Studies in the Vegetational History of the British Isles* (eds. D. Walker & R. G. West). Cambridge. 97–116.

Tyson, N. (1972). A Bronze Age Cairn at Wind Hill, Heywood, Lancs, *Bury Arch. Group*.

Underwood, G. (1969). *The Pattern of the Past*. London.

Varley, W. J. (1938). The Bleasdale Circle, *Ant J* 18, 154–71.

—(1964). *Cheshire Before the Romans*. Chester.

Vatcher, F. de M. (1969). Two Incised Chalk Plaques near Stonehenge Bottom, *Ant* 43, 310–11.

Vatcher, L. & F. (1975). Excavation of Three Postholes in Stonehenge Car-Park, *WAM* 68, 1973, 57–63.

Waddell, J. (1970). Irish Bronze Age Cists: a survey, *JRSAI* 100, 91–139.

—(1974). Brenig 41, *Denbighshire Historical Transactions 23* (F. Lynch, J. Waddell, D. Allen & S. Grealey). 15–19.

Wainwright, G. J. (1967). The Excavation of Hampton Stone Circle, Portesham, Dorset, *PDNHAS* 88, 122–7.

—(1969). A Review of Henge Monuments in the Light of Recent Research, *PPS* 35, 112–33.

—(1970a). Excavations at Marden, Wiltshire, 1969, *Ant* 44, 56–7.

—(1970b). Ditchingham, Norfolk, *CBA Calendar of Excavations* April. 4.

—(1970c). Mount Pleasant. *Curr Arch* 23, 320–3.

—(1971). The Excavation of a Late Neolithic Enclosure at Marden, Wiltshire, *Ant J* 51, 177–239.

—(1973). Prehistoric and Romano-British Settlements at Eaton Heath, Norwich, *Arch J* 130, 1–43.

—with Longworth, I. H. (1971). *Durrington Walls: Excavations*, 1966–8. London.

Walker D. & West R. G. (1970). editors. *Studies in the Vegetational History of the British Isles*. Cambridge.

Walshe P. T. (1931). Antiquities of the Dunlavin-Donard District, *JRSAI* 61, 127–30.

Ward, J. (1905). The Stone Circles, *VCH Derbyshire*, I. 181–4.

Ward, J. C. (1876). Archaeological Remains in the Lake District, *TCWAAS* III, 243–55.

Warden A. J. (1884). *Angus or Forfarshire* I-V. Dundee.

Waterman D. M. (1964). The Stone Circle, Cairn and Alignment at Drumskinny, Co. Fermanagh, *UJA* 27, 23–30.

Watkins, A. (1925). *The Old Straight Track*. London.

Webley, D. P. (1969). Aspects of Neolithic and Bronze Age Agriculture in South Wales, *BBCS* 23, 285–90.

Webster, G. & Hobley, B. (1965). Aerial Reconnaissance over the Warwickshire Avon, *Arch J* 121, 1–22.

Welsh, T. C. (1971). Clachtoll Stone Circle, *D & E*, 45.

Westropp, T. J. (1893). Killaloe: its Palaces and Cathedral, *JRSAI* 23, 193–4.

Williams, B. (1865a). On Some Ancient Monuments in the County of Cumberland, *PSAL* III, 224.

—(1865b). Notice of an Excavation on Burnmoor, *PSAL* III, 225–6.

Williams, J. (1970). Neolithic Axes in Dumfriess and Galloway, *TDGNHAS* 47, 111–22.

Williams, W. G. (1968). Stone Age Circles 'Form Pattern of Power', *Daily Telegraph* 23.9.68.

Wilson, D. (1863). *The Archaeology and Prehistoric Annals of Scotland* I. London.

Wilson, D. R. (1975). 'Causewayed Camps' and 'Interrupted Ditch Systems', *Ant* 49, 178–86.

Wilson, J. S. & Garfitt, G. A. (1920). Stone Circle, Eyam Moor, *Man* 20, 34–6.

Windle, B. C. A. (1912). Megalithic Remains Surrounding Lough Gur, Co. Limerick, *PRIA* 30, 283–306.

Woolacott, D. (1909). Note on the Rocks of the Stone Circles at Keswick and Long Meg near Penrith, *University of Durham Philosophical Society Proc*. 3, 12–13.

Woolf, C. (1970). *An Introduction to the Archaeology of Cornwall*. Truro.

Worth, R. H. (1939). Two Stone Circles on Dartmoor, *TDA* 71, 321–8.

—(1942). A Stone Circle in the Plym Valley, *TDA* 74, 207–10.

—(1946). The Stone Rows of Dartmoor. Part 1, *TDA* 78, 285–315.

—(1947). ibid, Part 2, *TDA* 79, 175–86.

—(1953). *Dartmoor*. Newton Abbot.

Young, A. M. A., Lacaille, A. D. & Zeuner, F. E. (1943). Report on Standing Stones and Other Remains near Fowlis Wester, Perthshire, *PSAS* 77, 174–84.

Index

Stone circles that are described, however briefly, in the text are listed in the Index together with their County number from the Gazetteer.

Because major subjects such as Concentric Circles have many page references the main reference is given in **bold type**. Page numbers for illustrations, both Plates and Figures, are given in *italics*.